Your Rights

D0234022

Edited by Megan Addis and Penelope Morrow

YOUR RIGHTS
The Liberty Guide to Human Rights

Eighth Edition

LIBERTY

with

Pluto Press

LONDON • ANN ARBOR, MI

Eighth edition published 2005 by Pluto Press
345 Archway Road, London N6 5AA
and 839 Greene Street, Ann Arbor, MI 48106

www.plutobooks.com

Previous editions published 1972, 1973, 1978, 1989 by Penguin;
and 1994, 1998, 2000 by Pluto Press

British Library Cataloguing in Publication Data
A catalogue record for this book is available from the British Library.

Library of Congress Cataloging in Publication Data applied for

ISBN 0 7453 2277 8 hardback
ISBN 0 7453 2276 X paperback

10 9 8 7 6 5 4 3 2 1

Designed and produced for Pluto Press by
Chase Publishing Services, Fortescue, Sidmouth, EX10 9QG, England
Typeset from disk by Stanford DTP Services, Northampton, England
Printed and bound in Malta by Gutenberg Press Ltd

Contents

List of Contributors

Megan Addis is one of the editors of *Your Rights*. She is admitted to practise as a barrister and solicitor in New Zealand and is Liberty's Advice and Information Officer. Prior to joining Liberty she practised civil and criminal litigation in Auckland, New Zealand.

Jo Cooper contributed the chapter on peaceful protest. He is an advocate who specialises in serious criminal cases particularly those involving Human Rights issues. He edits a twice-yearly updater on public order cases for *Legal Action* each February and August.

Simon Creighton contributed the chapter on prisoners. He is a partner at Bhatt Murphy solicitors. He is the co-author of *Prisoners and the Law* (Butterworths, 2004) and contributes to *The Prisons Handbook* (ed. Mark Leech, Waterside Press, 2003).

Gareth Crossman contributed the chapter on redress. He co-edited the print version of *Your Rights* (7th edn 2000). Gareth formerly practised as a solicitor specialising in criminal law and he is now Head of Policy at Liberty.

Fiona Fairweather contributed the chapter on the rights of suspects. She is Head of the School of Law, University of East Anglia. She has written and lectured widely on police powers and is the co-author of the Legal Action Group's *Police Powers: A Practitioners Guide*, now in its third volume.

Deidre Fottrell contributed the chapter on the rights of children and young people. She is a barrister at Coram Chambers London. Her practice includes all areas of family law including public and private child law work, cohabitation disputes and Human Rights Act matters. She is also a lecturer in human rights at the University of Essex where she teaches international child law and human rights. She has acted as a consultant on human rights issues to many NGOs and the Council of Europe and has conducted human rights training of lawyers and judges. Her publications include *Revisiting Children's Rights – 10 years of the UN Convention on the Rights of the Child* (Kluwer, 2000).

Shelagh Gaskill co-contributed the chapter on the right to know. She is a Partner in Masons' I&T Group and heads up the Information Law Team. Shelagh specialises in information law that relates to the commercial exploitation of data of all types, including their acquisition, sale and exchange. She also specialises in the legal aspects of the establishment and design of databases, world-wide and group company data-flows and data protection and privacy laws in the UK, Europe and third countries. Shelagh is one of the UK's leading data protection specialists.

Tess Gill co-contributed the chapter on the rights of workers. She is a barrister specialising in sex, race and disability discrimination, equal pay and European law. She has appeared in many leading employment and discrimination cases, including representing Ms Allonby in her equal pay claim before the European Court of Justice in 2003. Prior to transferring to the bar she was a solicitor with private practice and trade union legal officer experience. She was appointed as part-time employment tribunal chair in 1995. She has published work on gender equality and is co-author of the *Discrimination Law Handbook* (Legal Action Group, 2002).

Stephanie Harrison contributed the section on sexuality discrimination. She is a barrister at 2 Garden Court chambers, specialising predominantly in public and administrative law with a strong emphasis on civil liberties and anti-discrimination.

Henrietta Hill contributed the section on race and religious discrimination. She is a barrister at Doughty Street Chambers, practising discrimination law, with a particular interest in race and criminal justice. She has published the *Blackstones' Guide to the Race Relations (Amendment) Act 2000* and in 2003 she was shortlisted for the JUSTICE/Liberty Young Human Rights Lawyer of the Year award. She spent the autumn of 2002 working on race and criminal justice issues at the Center for Constitutional Rights in New York.

Anthony Hudson contributed the chapter on free expression. He is a barrister and practises at Doughty Street Chambers. He specialises in all aspects of media and defamation law.

Chris Johnson is one of the co-contributors for the chapter on Gypsies and Travellers. He is a solicitor and partner at the Community Law Partnership, a Legal Aid firm in Birmingham, where he is the leader of the Travellers' Advice Team. He is an experienced trainer and has written many articles on the law relating to Gypsies and Travellers. He has been involved in a number of the leading cases in the area including *Drury* v *Secretary of State for the Environment*, *R (Margaret Price)* v *Carmarthenshire County Council* and *South Bucks DC* v *Porter*.

David Jones contributed the chapter on immigration. He is a barrister at 2 Garden Court Chambers, where he practises exclusively in the field of immigration, asylum and human rights law. He is a lecturer for BLS/BPP, Liberty, EIN, IAS and 2 Garden Court. He is also a contributor to *MacDonald Immigration Law and Practice* (Butterworths). David is additionally a trustee of the Electronic Immigration Network (EIN), and is co-founder of the Immigration Consortium Country Information Database (ICCID), which supplies country information to the EIN. He is also a Director of HJT Training, which specialises in immigration, asylum and human rights law training.

Catrin Lewis contributed the section on disability discrimination. She is a barrister at 2 Garden Court, specialising in all aspects of employment law. Before joining 2 Garden Court she worked for seven years at Hackney Community Law Centre. She has particular expertise in race, sex and disability discrimination cases and is regularly instructed by the Disability Rights Commission. Catrin advises on 2

Garden Court Chambers' LSC-funded 'Call Counsel' employment advice line and 'Counsel's Advice' written advice scheme. She also provides training to solicitors and voluntary sector advisers in employment law and to The Disability Rights Commission's caseworkers.

Penelope Morrow is one of the editors of *Your Rights*. She is admitted to practise as a barrister and solicitor in Victoria, Australia and is Liberty's Advice and Information Project Officer. Prior to joining Liberty she worked for the National Native Title Tribunal in Melbourne, Australia.

Angus Murdoch is one of the co-contributors of the chapter on the rights of Gypsies and Travellers. Angus is a Travellers' planning expert and has worked for the Travellers' Advice Team since 1998. He has had a number of groundbreaking cases such as *South Bucks DC* v *Porter* and *Butler* v *Bath & North East Somerset Council*. He is co-author of the Legal Action/CRE book on Gypsy and Traveller law (soon to be published) as well as the author of many articles. He is also an experienced trainer.

Catherine O'Donnell contributed the section on sex discrimination. She is a barrister at 2 Garden Court, specialising in employment law. Before coming to the bar she was Senior Researcher at the Low Pay Unit and a lecturer in European Social Policy.

Camilla Parker contributed the chapter dealing with mental health. She is an independent legal and policy consultant specialising in mental health and human rights. She is a Special Advisor on Mental Health Law to the Camden and Islington Mental Health & Social Care NHS Trust Board and was formerly a member of the Mental Health Act Commission. Camilla is also a consultant to the Mental Disability Advocacy Program, Open Society Institute, Budapest – an organisation that seeks to promote the human rights and social inclusion of people with mental health problems and learning disabilities in Central and Eastern Europe and the former Soviet Union.

Marcus Pilgerstorfer contributed the chapter on workers' rights with Tess Gill. He is a barrister and practises at Old Square Chambers, specialising in employment and discrimination law. Prior to becoming a barrister, Marcus was a caseworker for the Citizens' Advice Bureau.

Andrew Ryder contributed the conclusion for the chapter on Gypsies and Travellers. He is the Policy Development Worker at the Traveller Law Reform Coalition. As a teacher/teacher trainer he has worked with Gypsies/Travellers/Roma in the UK, Hungary, the Czech Republic and Portugal.

John Skinner contributed the chapter on the rights of defendants. He is a solicitor specialising in criminal advocacy, with rights of audience before all criminal courts. He holds a Masters degree in criminology and has lectured on the English and Welsh criminal justice system to undergraduates on US degree courses.

Paula Sparks contributed the chapter on the bereaved. She is a barrister at Doughty Street Chambers and specialises in the areas of personal injury, clinical negligence and medical law.

James Strachan contributed the chapter on privacy. He is a practising barrister at 4–5 Gray's Inn Square and specialises in public and administrative law and human rights, including privacy and the media. He has wide experience of the domestic courts and has appeared in the European Court of Human Rights. He is the co-author of 'The Law of Privacy' and 'Privacy Postponed', two recent articles on the developing law of privacy and the media. He has lectured on many aspects of the Human Rights Act 1998 and is a contributor to *Human Rights and Judicial Review: Case Studies in Context* (Butterworths) and *Commercial Law and Human Rights* (Ashgate, Bottomley & Kinley).

Louise Townsend co-contributed the chapter on the right to know. She is a solicitor in Masons' I&T Group. Louise advises on data protection issues including carrying out data protection compliance audits, advising on overseas transfers, information security, website compliance and marketing. She provides training on data protection and is co-author of a book on data protection and pensions. Louise also advises and provides training on freedom of information and speaks regularly at seminars and workshops in this area. She has been involved in producing an e-learning product for freedom of information with Video Arts and in providing comprehensive training materials for the Scottish Executive on the Scottish legislation.

James Welch contributed the chapter on the Human Rights Act 1998. He is a solicitor and Liberty's legal director. He recently represented Katharine Gun in her prosecution under the Official Secrets Act.

Marc Willers is one of the co-contributors for the chapter on Gypsies and Travellers. He is a barrister practising at 1 Pump Court. He has a human rights practice and has specialised in the representation of Gypsies and Travellers for more than 15 years. He is also a director of Friends, Families and Travellers and a member of the Travellers' Law Reform Coalition.

Foreword

Since 1934 Liberty has been working to defend civil liberties and promote human rights in England and Wales. In so doing, Liberty often finds itself in opposition to the government of the day, or up against the populist press, often seen as defending the rights of an 'undeserving' few. Liberty believes that human rights are for *everyone* and has embraced the challenge of working toward a society where the values that underpin instruments such as the European Convention on Human Rights are ingrained in the public consciousness.

Your Rights was last published at a moment of great optimism for everyone who cared about Human Rights in the United Kingdom. In the year 2000, the long-awaited Human Rights Act 1998 was finally brought into force by a young Government apparently set on making constitutional reform a defining feature. After nearly 50 years, the fundamental rights and freedoms contained in the European Convention on Human Rights (which owed so much to British drafters and values) were to be a part of British law. These values would finally be enforceable in every court and tribunal in the land but, even more importantly, they would be celebrated and understood without the need for constant legal enforcement in police stations and Parliament, in classrooms and living rooms everywhere.

Yet Human Rights do not live in a vacuum. While campaigners could be forgiven for their high hopes and personal pride, they would also have noticed some rather more worrying trends in society, policy and legislation. People's legitimate fears of crime had become a fashionable political football. Recent years had provided at least one new piece of criminal justice legislation every year – always offering new criminal offences, penalties, changes to criminal procedure or wider police powers, or all of the above. The words 'refugee' and 'asylum seeker' had once commanded compassion and respect in a Britain that has fought Hitler. Now these labels began to carry contempt, whether expressly linked with the word 'bogus' or not.

However, the greatest possible challenge to the infant Human Rights Act came as it was barely toddling to its feet. On 11 September 2001, the Human Rights Act had been in force for less than one full year. Few of us will ever forget that terrible day, where we were or the feelings we experienced. It was my second day working at Liberty. The indiscriminate killing of innocents is an abomination that offends every ounce of our humanity. No matter when or where it is perpetrated, it is right that we never accept nor excuse it. However, human beings come equipped with reason as well as emotion. We also have the benefit of history. Human Rights should be even more precious to us in difficult and dangerous times.

In the autumn and winter of 2001, there were many calls for the abandonment of our Human Rights values. Principles of equality, fairness and respect for human dignity seemed expensive luxuries to some proponents of the new War on Terror. It was easy to forget that the post-war generation who had given us these values had significant experience of the horrors and terrors of war. Equally, it was too rarely remembered that these precious ideals were supposed to distinguish us from the groups and regimes we were meant to be at war with. Crucially, insufficient thought was given to the dangers of creating injustice and thereby promoting the conditions in which lawlessness thrives.

Much has been said about the 'law-free zone' that is Guantanamo Bay, where hundreds of non-Americans (including some Britons) have been incarcerated without charge or trial since the Afghanistan War. We in Britain have been slower to notice a scandal somewhat closer to home. Since December 2001, a number of non-British nationals suspected of 'links' to international terrorism have been interned (or detained without police interview, charge or trial) at HMP Belmarsh and other high security institutions. British citizens (for the time being at least), retain our rights to be tried in a normal criminal court in the event that we are suspected of terrorism. To achieve such a policy, our Government had to derogate or opt out from Article 5 of the European Convention on Human Rights. No other European country has adopted such a course. Article 5 represents the vital right not to be subject to arbitrary or unlawful or unjustified detention and is a hallmark of all democracies. The men detained under the Anti-Terrorism, Crime and Security Act 2001 are all asylum seekers. It is believed that some are torture victims. They are held indefinitely on the basis of secret intelligence rather than evidence that could be aired in an open court. The Government (and indeed the Special Commission charged with reviewing the detentions) has refused to rule out the possibility that these men are held (at least in part), on the basis of intelligence gained by torture in other parts of the world.

Why do I mention such a development in the foreword to a book called *Your Rights?* It is very unlikely after all that any reader will personally experience this kind of detention. We at Liberty believe that everyone is less safe because of such a symbol of injustice. It also demonstrates the dangers of taking the values of equal treatment, fairness and respect for human dignity for granted.

Recent years brought many positive strides in equality protection. Gay, transgendered and minority ethnic communities enjoy more theoretical legal protection than ever before. However, continued revelations of racism in public services and the open forced destitution and vilification of asylum seekers demonstrate how far we still have to go. Terrorists come in all nationalities but (initially at least) it is so much easier to compromise the rights of foreigners.

Similarly, would internment have been so easy a policy to adopt if we all guarded the importance of fairness a little more jealously? British justice used to be the envy of the world. However, it is now all too usual to hear the presumption of innocence referred to as old-fashioned. Our Prime Minister openly says that he is more concerned about the guilty walking free than the innocent being convicted. In truth every miscarriage of justice creates more, not fewer victims of crime.

Finally, the value of respect for human dignity will remain an ideal until more is done for the very young, old and most vulnerable in our society. This book remains an important guide for non-lawyers seeking to access the law's protection. However, Human Rights are no ordinary laws. They are far too precious to be left in the hands of lawyers or politicians. Guard them well.

Shami Chakrabarti
Director of Liberty
October 2004

Introduction

Through *Your Rights* Liberty aims to provide an easily understood guide to the Human Rights Act 1998, explaining its relevance and impact in many different areas of law, ranging from rights of privacy to rights of peaceful protest. *Your Rights* is written by expert lawyers, but intended primarily for people who have no specialist legal knowledge. We have tried to present the information in an accessible way, avoiding unnecessary jargon. We hope this will assist in demystifying the Human Rights Act 1998 and give people a clearer understanding of its significance to their lives and how it can be used to improve society for all.

There have been several new developments since the last edition of *Your Rights* was published in 2000. Obviously, the Human Rights Act 1998, incorporating the European Convention on Human Rights, came into force, which allows British citizens to bring claims under the Convention in domestic courts instead of having to seek redress before the European Court of Human Rights in Strasbourg. In addition, there have been numerous changes to policing, criminal justice, immigration and discrimination, which are discussed in *Your Rights*.

Prior to the publication of the last edition three new Acts that dealt with immigration had been passed in the previous decade. Since 2000 immigration law and policy continue to change apace with the new Nationality, Immigration and Asylum Act 2002 and the Asylum and Immigration (Treatment of Claimants etc.) Bill.

Liberty has long campaigned for an independent system for dealing with complaints against the police, which culminated in the publication of Liberty's report *An Independent Police Complaints Commission* in 2000. The Independent Police Complaints Commission began operating on 1 April 2004, and our former director John Wadham has taken up the position of Deputy Chairperson of the Commission. The Criminal Justice Act 2003 also introduced several changes to the criminal justice process, which are detailed in the chapters on the rights of suspects, defendants and prisoners.

New regulations that prohibit discrimination on the grounds of sexual orientation or religion in the workplace complement both the existing anti-discrimination legislation and the rights to privacy and freedom of religion in the European Convention on Human Rights.

This edition of *Your Rights* has several new features. We have included an overview of the Human Rights Act 1998, a guide on how to find freely available legal resources in the UK and a foreword by Liberty's new Director, Shami Chakrabarti. You will also find an additional chapter dealing with the rights of the bereaved.

Given the speed with which the law changes, we had to make some difficult decisions about what should be included or excluded from the book. We had planned to include a chapter on the rights of victims and witnesses. However, we decided that the law in this area is too unsettled at present and accordingly a chapter on this issue would fast become out of date.

We would like to thank all our contributors who have so generously donated their time and expertise. Providing their services free of charge means that the income generated by this book can go to support the ongoing work of Liberty. We would also like to thank those who have contributed to *Your Rights* in the past, including Luke Clements (Travellers), Tim Eicke (Immigration), Jonathan Griffiths (Right to Know), Rachel Morris (Travellers), Ijeoma Omambala (Discrimination), Johann Wilhelmsson (Right to Know) and Nicola Wyld (Children).

We are extremely grateful to our colleagues at Liberty for their support and assistance – in particular Gareth Crossman and James Welch. Our thanks also to Liberty's volunteers Sophie Mills, Daniel Stewart and Kathryn Kenny for their hard work. Finally, our thanks to Anne Beech and the team at Pluto for their guidance and patience.

Penny Morrow
Megan Addis
October 2004

James Welch

1   The Human Rights Act 1998: An Overview

The preamble to the Human Rights Act 1998 (HRA) describes it as 'an Act to give greater effect to rights and freedoms guaranteed under the European Convention on Human Rights' (the Convention). To understand the HRA you need to know something about the history of the Convention.

1.1   THE EUROPEAN CONVENTION ON HUMAN RIGHTS

The Convention was drafted after the Second World War. British lawyers and civil servants were heavily involved in its drafting. The United Kingdom (UK) signed up to the Convention in 1953 and was one of the first countries to do so. In all, 45 countries have now signed up to the Convention including most of the East European, former communist countries and several countries that were once part of the Soviet Union. The countries that have signed up to the Convention make up the Council of Europe. The Council of Europe is quite separate from the European Union.

The Convention is divided into 'articles'. Articles 2 to 14 set out the rights that are protected by the Convention. Over the years the Convention has been supplemented by a number of protocols that have been agreed by the Council of Europe. Some of the protocols just deal with procedural issues but some guarantee rights in addition to those included in the Convention. The UK has signed up to two of the protocols that guarantee additional rights (the First and Sixth Protocols) but not to the others (the Fourth, Seventh and Twelfth Protocols).

The European Court of Human Rights (ECHR) is the international court set up to interpret and apply the Convention. It is based in Strasbourg, France and is made up of judges nominated by each of the countries that are members of the Council of Europe. Since 1966 people have had the right to bring cases against the British Government in the ECHR. Over the years there have been many cases in which the ECHR has found that the UK has breached the Convention. One reason that there have been so many findings against the British Government is that there was no way that people could get redress for breach of their rights under the Convention in the British courts. This and the fact that taking a case to the ECHR can take several years were major factors in persuading the new Labour Government to pass the HRA shortly after they came to power in 1997. Many people believe that the HRA is one of the major achievements of this government.

Because the Convention is now over 50 years old some of the language that it uses is quite outdated. However, the ECHR has often stressed that the Convention is a 'living instrument'. This means that as society and attitudes change, the ECHR will change and develop the way in which it interprets the Convention. The ECHR will still, however, tend to follow the precedents set by earlier cases – where it does

1

not it will make it clear why it is not doing so. It is therefore important to look at past decisions of the ECHR. Moreover, the HRA requires the courts in the UK to take the ECHR's past decisions into account when deciding cases under the HRA. The ECHR now posts its decisions on the internet: <http://hudoc.echr.coe.int>.

Information about the procedures followed by the ECHR and advice on how to apply to that court are set out at the end of this chapter.

The rights covered by the Human Rights Act 1998

Not all the rights set out in the Convention and its Protocols are incorporated into British law by the HRA. The HRA only incorporates the rights in Articles 2 to 12 and in Article 14 of the Convention, plus those in the First and Sixth Protocols. The incorporated rights are set out in the First Schedule to the HRA and are referred to as 'Convention rights'. We will look at these Convention rights in more detail later in this chapter.

The HRA does not incorporate Article 13 of the Convention. Article 13 provides that people whose rights under the Convention have been breached should have the right to effective redress. The Government did not include Article 13 in the HRA, as it took the view that the HRA itself would meet the requirements of the article by giving people the right to take proceedings in the British courts if they considered that their Convention rights had been breached.

1.2   HOW DOES THE HUMAN RIGHTS ACT 1998 WORK?

The HRA gives 'greater effect' to Convention Rights in two main ways:

- It makes it clear that as far as possible the courts in the UK should interpret the law in a way that is compatible with Convention rights.
- It places an obligation on public authorities to act compatibly with Convention rights.

The HRA also gives people the right to take court proceedings if they think that their Convention rights have been breached or are going to be.

Interpreting the law compatibly

Parliament makes laws but it is the courts that have to interpret them. The HRA makes it clear that when they are interpreting legislation the courts must do so in a way that does not lead to people's Convention rights being breached. Moreover, the courts are now under a duty to develop the common law – the law that has been developed through decisions of the courts themselves – in a way that is compatible with Convention rights.

What happens if the courts cannot read the law compatibly?

If the law is an Act of Parliament, the courts have no choice but to apply the law as it is, even though it breaches Convention rights. However, the higher courts (the High Court, the Court of Appeal and the House of Lords) have the power to make what is called a 'declaration of incompatibility'. This is a statement that the courts consider that a particular law breaches Convention rights. It is meant to encourage Parliament to amend the law, but the courts cannot force the Government or Parliament to amend the law if they do not want to.

A lot of law is not set out in Acts of Parliament but rather in secondary legislation. Secondary legislation is law made under the authority of an Act of Parliament. Rather than set out detailed provisions in an Act of Parliament, Parliament will frequently give the power to make detailed laws to a government minister. The Act of Parliament will give the minister the power to make law but the law itself will be set out in regulations or orders. For example, most social security law is set out in regulations rather than in Acts of Parliament.

Where the courts find that an item of secondary legislation is incompatible with Convention rights, they have the power to strike the law down or not to apply it. This applies to all courts, not just the higher ones. The only circumstance where this is not possible is where the secondary legislation merely repeats a requirement of an Act of Parliament.

Public authorities

The HRA requires public authorities to act in a way that does not breach Convention rights. The HRA does not define the term public authority, but it is clear that bodies like the police, local councils and government departments and agencies are all public authorities. Private individuals and bodies will not be public authorities for the purposes of the HRA unless they are performing a public function. So, for example, a private security company that has a contract with the Government to transport prisoners to and from court will be a public authority for the purposes of the HRA (and therefore under a duty to respect Convention rights) when it is transporting prisoners but will not be when it is guarding private property under a contract with a private organisation.

The issue of whether a person or body is a public authority for the purposes of the HRA can be very difficult to determine. As there is no definition of a public authority in the HRA this is something that the courts have to decide on.

Taking proceedings under the Human Rights Act 1998

Someone who believes that a public authority has breached their Convention rights, or is proposing to, can bring court proceedings against the public authority. A person can also raise a breach of their Convention rights as a defence in any court proceedings against them. In either case the person must be a 'victim' of the breach or potential breach, that is, someone who is directly affected by it. (This is a requirement that has its origins in ECHR case law – see section 1.4 'Taking a case to the European Court of Human Rights', p. 15 below.)

Generally, a person bringing court proceedings against a public authority under the HRA will be seeking a declaration that the public authority has breached their Convention rights or is proposing to do so. If the breach is continuing they will also want an order that the public authority should stop acting in a way that breaches their Convention rights. They may also seek compensation, although the courts have made it clear that it is not always appropriate for them to award this.

When someone brings proceedings against a public authority for breach of their Convention rights, the public authority may be able to defend itself by saying that it had no choice but to act in the way that it did because it was required to do so by an Act of Parliament. Where this happens the most the person bringing the case may hope to achieve is a declaration of incompatibility.

In most cases the appropriate court proceedings to bring against a public authority under the HRA will be an application for judicial review. Court rules require an application for judicial review to be brought 'promptly' and in any event within three months of the decision or action being challenged. Where someone does not make an application for judicial review there is a one-year time limit for starting proceedings.

Proceedings against private individuals or bodies

As private bodies and individuals are not required by the HRA to respect Convention rights, it is not possible to take proceedings under the HRA against them. This does not mean, however, that the HRA will not have an effect on court proceedings between private bodies or individuals. This is because the courts themselves are public authorities under the HRA and are also required to interpret existing laws and to develop the law in a way that is compatible with Convention rights.

1.3   THE CONVENTION RIGHTS

Below we have set out the text of each of the Convention rights incorporated by the HRA, followed by a brief commentary. In relation to each article, you will also find cross-references to chapters within *Your Rights* where the article is likely to have particular relevance.

Article 2: Right to Life

1. Everyone's right to life shall be protected by law. No one shall be deprived of his life intentionally save in the execution of a sentence of a court following his conviction of a crime for which this penalty is provided by law.
2. Deprivation of life shall not be regarded as inflicted in contravention of this Article when it results from the use of force which is no more than absolutely necessary:
(a) in defence of any person from unlawful violence;
(b) in order to effect a lawful arrest or to prevent the escape of a person lawfully detained;
(c) in action lawfully taken for the purpose of quelling a riot or insurrection.

This article provides that the Government and public authorities must protect the right to life. This may require, for example, that the police have to protect someone whose life is under immediate threat. It could also be used to argue that a patient should be able to get treatment that would save their life.

Generally, there will be a breach of Article 2 if someone is killed by a state official (usually the police, but also the army or prison officers). The only circumstances where there will not be a breach are set out in the second part of the article. However, where a death occurs in each of these three circumstances the police (or other state official responsible for the death) will have to show that they did not use any more force than was absolutely necessary. So, if someone is killed when the police are trying to arrest them, there will be breach of Article 2 if it is shown that the police used more than the minimum amount of force necessary to detain the person.

THE HUMAN RIGHTS ACT 1998: AN OVERVIEW 5

The ECHR has made it clear that Article 2 also requires that there should be a proper investigation when the police or army kill someone or when someone dies in custody. There have been several cases in the British courts where the courts have had to consider what type of investigation is necessary to meet this requirement.

The death penalty
Article 2 has been supplemented by the Sixth Protocol. The Sixth Protocol abolishes the death penalty, although it allows for exceptions in wartime. The UK has signed up to this Protocol, and the HRA completely abolished the death penalty.

Relevant chapter:

- Chapter 16: The rights of the bereaved.

Article 3: Prohibition of Torture
No one shall be subjected to torture or inhuman or degrading treatment or punishment.

The ECHR has made it clear that inhuman or degrading treatment or punishment has to be very serious to be in breach of Article 3.

People have successfully used this article to argue that they should not be deported to a country where they are likely to be tortured or where there will be inadequate protection against persecution (*Chahal v UK, Dashamir Koci v Secretary of State for the Home Department*). It could also be used to argue that someone should not be deported to a country where they are likely to be given an unfair prison sentence. The courts have also held that the seclusion of compulsorily detained mental patients might breach Article 3 (*R (Munjaz) v Mersey Care NHS Trust*). A refusal to give any financial support to asylum seekers, leaving them destitute, may also breach the article (*R (Q and others) v Secretary of State for the Home Department*).

Prisoners or people held in hospital may want to rely on the article if the conditions they are held in are particularly bad.

Relevant chapters:

- Chapter 7: The rights of prisoners
- Chapter 11: The rights of immigrants
- Chapter 12: The rights of people detained under the Mental Health Act 1983.

Article 4: Prohibition of Slavery and Forced Labour
1. No one shall be held in slavery or servitude.
2. No one shall be required to perform forced or compulsory labour.
3. For the purpose of this Article the term 'forced or compulsory labour' shall not include:
(a) any work required to be done in the ordinary course of detention imposed according to the provisions of Article 5 of the Convention or during conditional release from such detention;
(b) any service of a military character or, in case of conscientious objectors in countries where they are recognised, service exacted instead of compulsory military service;
(c) any service exacted in case of an emergency or calamity threatening the life or well-being of the community;

(d) any work or service which forms part of normal civic obligations.

This article bans slavery and limits the circumstances in which someone can be forced to work. It is unlikely to have much, if any, effect on British law.

Article 5: Right to Liberty and Security

1. Everyone has the right to liberty and security of person. No one shall be deprived of his liberty save in the following cases and in accordance with a procedure prescribed by law:
(a) the lawful detention of a person after conviction by a competent court;
(b) the lawful arrest or detention of a person for non-compliance with the lawful order of a court or in order to secure the fulfilment of any obligation prescribed by law;
(c) the lawful arrest or detention of a person effected for the purpose of bringing him before the competent legal authority on reasonable suspicion of having committed an offence or when it is reasonably considered necessary to prevent his committing an offence or fleeing after having done so;
(d) the detention of a minor by lawful order for the purpose of educational supervision or his lawful detention for the purpose of bringing him before the competent legal authority;
(e) the lawful detention of persons for the prevention of the spreading of infectious diseases, of persons of unsound mind, alcoholics or drug addicts or vagrants;
(f) the lawful arrest or detention of a person to prevent his effecting an unauthorised entry into the country or of a person against whom action is being taken with a view to deportation or extradition.
2. Everyone who is arrested shall be informed promptly, in a language which he understands, of the reason for his arrest and of any charge against him.
3. Everyone arrested or detained in accordance with the provisions of paragraph 1 (c) of this Article shall be brought promptly before a judge or other officer authorised by law to exercise judicial power and shall be entitled to trial within a reasonable time or to release pending trial. Release may be conditioned by guarantees to appear for trial.
4. Everyone who is deprived of his liberty by arrest or detention shall be entitled to take proceedings by which the lawfulness of his detention shall be decided speedily by a court and his release ordered if the detention is not lawful.
5. Everyone who has been the victim of arrest or detention in contravention of the provisions of this Article shall have an enforceable right to compensation.

Article 5 limits the circumstances in which someone can be detained. This covers detention for both long periods (for example, if you are in prison or are forced to stay as a patient in a mental hospital) and short periods (for example, if you are arrested).

For any detention to comply with Article 5 it must come within one of six sets of circumstances set out in paragraphs 5(1)(a) to 5(1)(f). The detention must also have a clear legal basis and it must be proportionate, that is, there must be an adequate reason for the detention and the detention should not be for an unreasonably long time. Where someone is detained it is up to the Government to justify the detention rather than for the person detained to show why they should be released.

Cases where the courts have found a breach of Article 5 include:

- Where the law completely removed the entitlement to bail for someone charged with a serious offence who had previously been convicted of a serious offence (*Caballero* v *United Kingdom*). The law has since been changed.
- Where a compulsorily detained mental patient was effectively required to show why he should be released, rather than the hospital having to show why he should continue to be detained (*R* v *Mental Health Review Tribunal, North and East London Region ex parte H*). Again, the law has now been changed.
- Where an elderly, chronically ill woman was held overnight for 14 hours for refusing to give her name and address to a police officer (*Vasileva* v *Denmark*).

Article 5(4) requires that someone who is detained should have the right to have their detention reviewed by a court or independent tribunal. This does not apply to prisoners who have been given a fixed-term sentence, but it does apply to life prisoners once their tariff period (the minimum amount of time that they have to spend in prison) has expired. It also applies to compulsorily detained mental patients.

Article 5 is not concerned with the conditions in which someone is detained. There cannot be a breach of Article 5 where someone who is already in detention is placed in a greater degree of detention, for example where a compulsorily detained mental patient is placed in seclusion. Such a situation may, however, raise issues under Articles 3 or 8.

Relevant chapters:

- Chapter 5: The rights of suspects
- Chapter 7: The rights of prisoners
- Chapter 12: The rights of people detained under the Mental Health Act 1983.

Article 6: Right to a Fair Trial
1. In the determination of his civil rights and obligations or of any criminal charge against him, everyone is entitled to a fair and public hearing within a reasonable time by an independent and impartial tribunal established by law. Judgment shall be pronounced publicly, but the press and public may be excluded from all or part of the trial in the interests of morals, public order or national security in a democratic society, where the interests of juveniles or the protection of the private life of the parties so require, or to the extent strictly necessary in the opinion of the court in special circumstances where publicity would prejudice the interests of justice.
2. Everyone charged with a criminal offence shall be presumed innocent until proved guilty according to law.
3. Everyone charged with a criminal offence has the following minimum rights:
(a) to be informed promptly, in a language which he or she understands and in detail, of the nature and cause of the accusation against him;
(b) to have adequate time and facilities for the preparation of his defence;
(c) to defend himself in person or through legal assistance of his own choosing or, if he has not sufficient means to pay for legal assistance, to be given it free when the interests of justice so require;

(d) to examine or have examined witnesses against him and to obtain the attendance and examination of witnesses on his behalf under the same conditions as witnesses against him;
(e) to have the free assistance of an interpreter if he cannot understand or speak the language used in court.

Article 6 guarantees the right to a fair trial in civil and criminal proceedings. It sets standards for the way that proceedings are run. Although you may feel that you have not had a fair trial if you lose your case, there will only be a breach of Article 6 if these standards have not been met.

Criminal proceedings are when someone is prosecuted for an offence. Under Article 6 criminal proceedings have a wider meaning than they usually have in English law. Under Article 6 cases against people for contempt of court or for not paying their council tax count as criminal proceedings.

Any court proceedings that are not criminal cases are civil proceedings. Article 6 covers most but not all civil proceedings. Proceedings between private people or organisations to settle a dispute between them are covered by Article 6. Proceedings between a private person or organisation and the Government or a public authority may be covered by Article 6.

Certain standards apply in both criminal and civil proceedings. These rights include:

- The right to a trial within a reasonable time.
- The right to an independent and impartial judge or tribunal.
- The right to a public hearing (although there are circumstances when the public can be excluded).
- The right to a public judgment (although this may be restricted in certain types of cases, e.g. family cases).

In civil proceedings Article 6 also protects the right to take court proceedings to settle a dispute, although this right may be restricted in some circumstances. It may also give the right to legal aid where the dispute is very complicated and you are at a disadvantage because you cannot afford a lawyer.

There are further rights in criminal proceedings. These include:

- The right to be presumed innocent until you have been proved to be guilty.
- The right to be informed at a very early stage what the accusation against you is.
- The right not to be forced to answer questions, although the court may be able to draw conclusions from your failure to answer questions.
- The right to adequate time to prepare your defence.
- The right to have legal aid for a lawyer if you cannot afford one and it is in the interests of justice for you to have one.
- The right to be present at your trial.
- The right to put your side of the case at your trial.
- The right to question the main witnesses against you and to call witnesses of your own.
- The right to an interpreter if you need one.

Relevant chapters:

- Chapter 2: How to get redress
- Chapter 6: The rights of defendants
- Chapter 7: The rights of prisoners
- Chapter 12: The rights of people detained under the Mental Health Act 1983
- Chapter 14: The rights of workers.

Article 7: No Punishment without Law

1. No one shall be held guilty of any criminal offence on account of any act or omission which did not constitute a criminal offence under national or international law at the time when it was committed. Nor shall a heavier penalty be imposed than the one that was applicable at the time the criminal offence was committed.

2. This Article shall not prejudice the trial and punishment of any person for any act or omission which, at the time it was committed, was criminal according to the general principles of law recognised by civilised nations.

This article makes it clear that no one can be found guilty of a criminal offence if what they did was not a criminal offence at the time that they did it. It prevents Parliament passing laws which make criminal offences of things done in the past. Article 7 also provides that you cannot be punished in a way that was not the law when you committed the offence. Parliament cannot backdate a law that increases the length of time you could be sent to prison for or introduces a new punishment for an offence.

It also requires that the law must be clear so that people know whether or not what they are doing is against the law.

Relevant chapter:

- Chapter 6: The rights of defendants.

Article 8: Right to Respect for Private and Family Life

1. Everyone has the right to respect for his private and family life, his home and his correspondence.

2. There shall be no interference by a public authority with the exercise of this right except such as is in accordance with the law and is necessary in a democratic society in the interests of national security, public safety or the economic well-being of the country, for the prevention of disorder or crime, for the protection of health or morals, or for the protection of the rights and freedoms of others.

Article 8 guarantees respect for four things: a person's private life, family life, home and correspondence.

Private life

Lots of issues have been held to come within the scope of a person's private life, and the ECHR has stressed that it is not possible to limit or define what comes within its scope. Things that do clearly come within the scope of a person's private life are:

- Bodily integrity – Article 8 will come into play if someone is forced to have medical treatment or if he or she is forcibly restrained.
- Personal autonomy – this means the right to make decisions about how you lead your life. People have tried to argue that the right to smoke cannabis is an issue of personal autonomy and should therefore be protected by Article 8 but the courts have not been prepared to accept this.
- Sexuality – there have been a number of cases in which the ECHR has made it clear that laws that prohibit gay men having sex breach Article 8.
- Personal identity – the ECHR decided in 2002 that British law's failure to fully recognise the new gender of transgendered people breached Article 8.
- Personal information – the holding, use or disclosure of personal information about someone is covered by Article 8. The article may also give someone the right to access personal information held about them.
- Surveillance.

Family life

This means your relationship with your close family. This includes a man and woman who are not married but who live in a stable relationship. The ECHR has not yet recognised same-sex couples as families, but this may well change and, even if it does not, it may be that the UK courts will do so.

Home

Your home is where you currently live. The right to respect for your home does not mean that you have the right to be given a home if you do not have one, or to be given a better one than you already have.

Environmental issues (noise or other pollution) may come within the scope of Article 8, because they affect both a person's private life and home.

Correspondence

This includes your phone calls and letters, as well as e-mails. People have successfully used Article 8 to challenge the police or secret services bugging their phones.

A qualified right

Article 8 is a qualified right. This means that an interference with the right can be justified. Where the interference is justified, there will be no breach of the article. The circumstances where an interference with the right can be justified are set out in the second part of the article (Article 8(2)).

For an interference to be justified it must:

- Be 'in accordance with the law' – this means that there has to be clear legal basis for the interference and that the law should be readily accessible.
- Pursue a legitimate aim – there are six legitimate aims set out in Article 8(2), e.g. 'the prevention of disorder or crime'. A public authority that intends to interfere with a person's rights under Article 8 must be able to show that what they are doing pursues one of these six legitimate aims. This is rarely a problem, as the legitimate aims are so wide.
- Be 'necessary in a democratic society' – this is usually the crucial issue. There must be a good reason for the interference with the right and the

interference must be proportionate. This means that it should be no more than is necessary.

Positive obligations

Article 8 and the other qualified articles are largely concerned with preventing the Government, the police or other state bodies interfering with people's rights. They are *negative* obligations in that they impose a duty not to do something. However, there may be circumstances where the Government is under a *positive* obligation, a duty to do something in order to protect or promote people's rights. It will always be much harder to argue that the Government is under a positive obligation than under a negative one.

Relevant chapters:

- Chapter 3: The right to privacy
- Chapter 5: The rights of suspects
- Chapter 7: The rights of prisoners
- Chapter 11: The rights of immigrants
- Chapter 13: The rights of children and young people
- Chapter 14: The rights of workers.

Article 9: Freedom of Thought, Conscience and Religion

1. Everyone has the right to freedom of thought, conscience and religion; this right includes freedom to change his religion or belief, and freedom, either alone or in community with others and in public or private, to manifest his religion or belief, in worship, teaching, practice and observance.
2. Freedom to manifest one's religion or beliefs shall be subject only to such limitations as are prescribed by law and are necessary in a democratic society in the interests of public safety, for the protection of public order, health or morals, or for the protection of the rights and freedoms of others.

Article 9 guarantees that you can think what you want and can hold any religious belief. You cannot be forced to follow a particular religion and cannot be stopped from changing your religion. You should not be indoctrinated by the state.

It also protects the right to practise your religion or beliefs. For the practice of your beliefs to be protected they must be part of a sufficiently coherent philosophical scheme. So beliefs such as veganism and pacifism are protected.

The right to practise your religion or belief is a qualified right. This means that an interference with the right can be justified. The circumstances in which an interference can be justified are similar to those which justify an interference with rights under Article 8.

Relevant chapters:

- Chapter 10: The right to receive equal treatment.

Article 10: Freedom of Expression

1. Everyone has the right of freedom of expression. This right shall include freedom to hold opinions and to receive and impart information and ideas without interference by public

authority and regardless of frontiers. This Article shall not prevent States from requiring the licensing of broadcasting, television or cinema enterprises.
2. The exercise of these freedoms, since it carries with it duties and responsibilities, may be subject to such formalities, conditions, restrictions or penalties as are prescribed by law and are necessary in a democratic society, in the interests of national security, territorial integrity or public safety, for the prevention of disorder or crime, for the protection of health or morals, for the protection of the reputation or rights of others, for preventing the disclosure of information received in confidence, or for maintaining the authority and impartiality of the judiciary.

Article 10 guarantees the right to hold and express opinions and ideas. It also guarantees the right to pass information to other people and to receive information that other people want to give to you.

Anyone can rely on Article 10 but it is clearly of particular importance to journalists and publishers of newspapers or magazines, who can use Article 10 to argue there should be no restrictions on what they write about or publish. Artists and writers can use it to defend themselves against censorship.

Article 10 is very relevant to the rights of demonstrators, as demonstrating is a means of expressing your views on an issue. (Demonstrators' rights are also protected by Article 11.) The ECHR has made it clear that it is particularly important to protect the expression of political views. In an early case under the HRA a woman who was convicted of a public order offence after she defaced an American flag in front of US service people had her conviction overturned (*Percy v DPP*).

Article 10 is a qualified right. This means that an interference with the right can be justified. The circumstances in which an interference can be justified are similar to those that justify an interference with rights under Article 8.

Relevant chapters:

- Chapter 3: The right to privacy
- Chapter 8: The right of peaceful protest
- Chapter 9: The right of free expression.

Article 11: Freedom of Assembly and Association

1. Everyone has the right to freedom of peaceful assembly and to freedom of association with others, including the right to form and to join trade unions for the protection of his interests.
2. No restrictions shall be placed on the exercise of these rights other than such as are prescribed by law and are necessary in a democratic society in the interests of national security or public safety, for the prevention of disorder or crime, for the protection of health or morals or for the protection of the rights and freedoms of others. This Article shall not prevent the imposition of lawful restrictions on the exercise of these rights by members of the armed forces, of the police or of the administration of the state.

There are two aspects to Article 11. It protects the right to protest peacefully by holding meetings and demonstrations. This may include a positive obligation to ensure that demonstrators are protected from counter-demonstrators trying to prevent their demonstration. Article 11 also protects the right to form or join a political party or other group or association, and the right to belong to a trade union. However, the right to join a trade union does not extend to police officers, soldiers and some other groups who work for the Government. Article 11 also guarantees the right not to have to join a union.

Article 11 is a qualified right. This means that an interference with the right can be justified. The circumstances in which an interference can be justified are similar to those which justify an interference with rights under Article 8. (See above, p. 10.)

Relevant chapters:

- Chapter 8: The right of peaceful protest
- Chapter 14: The rights of workers.

Article 12: Right to Marry and Found a Family
Men and women of marriageable age have the right to marry and to found a family, according to the national laws governing the exercise of this right.

At the moment the right to marry does not extend to same-sex couples. In 2002 the ECHR decided that not allowing transgender people to marry breached their rights under Article 12. The right to start a family may only apply to people who are married. If it does, people who are not married will have to rely on the right to respect for family life under Article 8 to argue for their right to have children.

Article 14: Prohibition of Discrimination
The enjoyment of the rights and freedoms set forth in this convention shall be secured without discrimination on any ground such as sex, race, colour, language, religion, political or other opinion, national or social origin, association with a national minority, property, birth or other status.

Article 14 covers discrimination on all the grounds set out in the article (sex, race, colour etc.). However, the list is open-ended. This is clear from the fact that the article refers to 'other status'. Some other grounds for discrimination are now clearly accepted as coming within the scope of Article 14, for example discrimination on the basis of someone's sexual orientation. What is not clear is how far further grounds for discrimination have to be linked to a personal characteristic or whether it is just necessary for someone to show that they have been treated differently from someone who is in a relevantly similar situation.

Article 14 is not free-standing. For there to be a breach of Article 14 the area in which a person is discriminated against has to come within the scope of one of the other Convention articles. This means that the way in which you are discriminated against has to be connected with one of the other articles. There does not, however, have to be a breach of the other article. So, a gay man who complained about the fact that he was only entitled to succeed to his deceased partner's flat on less favourable terms than a surviving heterosexual partner would have done was able to rely on Article 14 because he was discriminated against on the basis of his sexual orientation and, as the discrimination concerned his home, it was within the scope of Article 8 (*Mendoza v Ghaidan*).

Even where you can show that you have been discriminated against and that the area in which you have been discriminated against comes within the scope of another article it is still possible for the Government or public authority to argue that the discrimination is justified. They must show that there is a good reason for treating you differently and that doing so is proportionate. Where they can show this there will be no breach of Article 14.

Relevant chapters:

- Chapter 10: The right to receive equal treatment
- Chapter 11: The rights of immigrants
- Chapter 15: The rights of Gypsies and Travellers.

Article 1 of the First Protocol: Protection of Property

Every natural or legal person is entitled to the peaceful enjoyment of his possessions. No one shall be deprived of his possessions except in the public interest and subject to the conditions provided for by law and by the general principles of international law.

The proceeding provisions shall not, however, in any way impair the right of a State to enforce such laws as it deems necessary to control the use of property in accordance with the general interest or to secure the payment of taxes or other contributions or penalties.

Article 1 of the First Protocol protects people's rights to their property. Property has a very wide meaning. It can include shares, a pension and contributory welfare benefits (social security benefits that are dependent on the claimant having made national insurance contributions).

The article provides that the Government or a public authority cannot deprive a person of their property unless the law allows this and it is necessary in the public interest to do so. The Government must strike a fair balance between the interests of the property owner and the general interest of society as a whole. If your property is taken away you should be entitled to compensation.

Article 1 of the First Protocol also provides that the Government or a public authority cannot put restrictions on what someone does with their property or interfere with a person's property unless there is a law that allows them to do this and there is a good reason for doing so.

The article does not affect the right of the Government or a public authority to enforce taxes or fines.

Article 2 of the First Protocol: Right to Education

No person shall be denied the right to education. In the exercise of any functions which it assumes in relation to education and to teaching, the State shall respect the right of parents to ensure such education and teaching in conformity with their own religious and philosophical convictions.

Article 2 of the First Protocol guarantees a right of access to education. It does not require countries to provide education or to provide education of a particular type, but where there are educational facilities, people should not be denied access to them. This does not prevent schools having selection policies, though their policies may have to be justified. It is unclear whether the article applies to education at a tertiary level.

The second sentence of the article does not give parents the absolute right to have their children educated in accordance with their religious or philosophical beliefs. It merely requires schools to respect parents' beliefs.

Relevant chapter:

- Chapter 13: The rights of children and young people.

Article 3 of the First Protocol: Right to Free Elections

The High Contracting Parties undertake to hold free elections at reasonable intervals by secret ballot, under conditions which will ensure the free expression of the opinion of the people in the choice of the legislature.

Article 3 of the First Protocol says that there must be elections at reasonable intervals and that elections must be by secret ballot. It gives people the right to vote or to stand in elections, although reasonable restrictions may be put on this right. The ECHR has recently held that the law that prevents all prisoners in the UK from voting in elections breaches this article. The article does not say what method of election should be used.

Relevant chapters:

- Chapter 7: The rights of prisoners
- Chapter 12: The rights of people detained under the Mental Health Act 1983.

1.4   TAKING A CASE TO THE EUROPEAN COURT OF HUMAN RIGHTS

Even though the HRA has now come into force in the UK it is still possible to make an application to the ECHR. There are three key requirements that you must meet:

(1) You must be a *victim* of a violation of one or more of the articles of the Convention. Generally, this means you must be directly affected by a breach of the Convention. In some cases it will be enough to show you are likely to be affected by a breach or that you belong to a group of people, some of whom are likely to be affected. For example, gay men were permitted to challenge laws that criminalised gay sex even though it was unlikely that the individual applicants would ever be prosecuted because the laws were rarely enforced.

(2) Before you make an application to the ECHR you must pursue any proceedings that you could take in the UK that are capable of providing you with an adequate remedy for the breach of your Convention rights. Now that the HRA is in force this will generally mean that you will have to take proceedings in the UK under the HRA. This may not be necessary, however, where it is clear that the best you could hope to achieve from taking proceedings under the HRA is a declaration of incompatibility.

(3) You must make your application to the ECHR within six months of the conclusion of any court proceedings that you have taken in the UK that could have provided you with a remedy or, if there were no proceedings that it was reasonable to expect you to take, within six months of the event that gives rise to your application.

When you make an application to the ECHR you will be asked to complete one of the ECHR's application forms. However, it is not necessary to fill out one of these forms to meet the six-month rule. All you need to do is to get a letter to the court within the six months setting out:

1. Your details (name, address and nationality).
2. The country against which you are making your application.
3. The facts that have given rise to your application.
4. The article or articles of the Convention that you say have been breached.

You should send your letter to:

The Registrar
European Court of Human Rights
Council of Europe
F-67075 Strasbourg Cedex
France
Fax: 00 33 3 88 41 27 30

When it has received your letter the ECHR will send you one of its application forms to complete. If there is not enough space on the form you can set out your case in a longer document, which you attach to the form. It is important that you submit your completed application form within any deadline set by the ECHR or, if no deadline is set, within a few weeks of receiving it. If you do not submit the form speedily you run the risk that the ECHR will decide that you have not met the six-month deadline. If you cannot meet any deadline that is set you should contact the ECHR and try to agree an extended deadline.

Once the ECHR has acknowledged receipt of your application form it may be some time (months if not years) before you hear anything further.

At this stage the ECHR may rule your application inadmissible. The ECHR will not give reasons and there is no right of appeal. If your application is ruled inadmissible you will not be able to proceed with it.

If it is not ruled inadmissible at this stage, your application will be allocated to one of the ECHR's four sections. A panel of seven judges from that section will deal with the case. This panel will always include the judge appointed by the UK. Very significant cases may be dealt with by the ECHR's Grand Chamber. These cases are considered by a panel of 17 judges. A case could be transferred to the Grand Chamber at any stage in the proceedings.

Your application will also be communicated to the Government at this stage, that is, the Government will be informed that you have made an application and will be invited to respond. You will be given an opportunity to respond to the Government's observations and there may be further exchanges of written representations.

The ECHR will then decide whether your application is admissible. It can rule your application inadmissible if you have failed to meet one of the three requirements set out above or if the ECHR considers that it is 'manifestly ill-founded', in other words, that it is not arguable. If the ECHR finds your application inadmissible at this stage it will give reasons, but there is no right of appeal.

If the ECHR finds your application admissible it will then go on to decide whether there has been a breach of the Convention. The ECHR usually refers to this as considering the merits of the application. At this point you have the right to put in a claim for compensation. The ECHR calls this 'just satisfaction'. It should include a claim for legal expenses if you have incurred any. Your claim for just satisfaction should be sent to the ECHR within two months of the ECHR finding your application admissible. Both sides may make further representations before the ECHR decides on the merits of the application.

When the ECHR has made its decision on the merits of your application, you will be notified of the date on which its judgment will be made public. The judgment will be published on the ECHR's website on that day. If the ECHR finds that there has been a breach of your rights it may award you compensation, although it does not always do so on the basis that its finding that there has been a breach of your rights is enough.

Once a section of the ECHR has made a final decision on the merits of an application, either party, the Government or the Applicant, can ask to have the application referred to the Grand Chamber. This is the only form of appeal that the ECHR's rules allow for. The Grand Chamber only rarely agrees to a referral. There is no appeal from a final decision made by the Grand Chamber.

Hearings

The ECHR deals with most cases without holding a hearing; it reaches its decisions on the basis of written representations made by the parties. When the ECHR does decide to hold a hearing this will usually take place before the ECHR has decided on the admissibility of the application, although it may also hold a hearing after an application has been found admissible if it has not already held one.

Legal representation

Although you can make an application to the ECHR yourself, it would be wise to get a lawyer experienced in ECHR proceedings to represent you. Most cases are not communicated to the Government (i.e. they are ruled inadmissible at an early stage), and having a lawyer present your arguments for you may help you get over this hurdle.

If the ECHR decides to hold a hearing after it has found your application admissible, the ECHR rules require you to be represented by a lawyer at that hearing unless the ECHR allows otherwise.

Legal aid

The ECHR has a system of legal aid, although the payments that a lawyer receives under the scheme are very low. You can apply for legal aid once your application has been communicated to the Government. It is particularly useful to have legal aid if the ECHR holds a hearing on your case, as legal aid will pay the cost of your and your lawyer's trip to Strasbourg. Eligibility for legal aid will depend on the Legal Services Commission accepting that you would be eligible for legal aid in the UK.

If you are not eligible for legal aid, your lawyer may agree to represent you under a conditional fee agreement, that is, on the basis that they will only get paid if you win your case and get your legal costs paid by the Government. However, as very few applications to the ECHR are successful, your lawyer may be reluctant to take this risk. If you lose your case there is no possibility of you being ordered to pay the Government's legal costs.

2   How to Get Redress

This chapter deals with:

- Civil action and judicial review
- Central government
- Local government
- Health services
- Community care and benefits entitlement
- The police
- Courts and legal services
- Financial professions
- The media
- Public utilities
- Compensation for the victims of crime
- Miscellaneous complaints

2.1   CIVIL ACTION AND JUDICIAL REVIEW

Civil action

Many civil cases will concern a claim that one side has broken their contract with the other, but a civil action can also relate to the duties that are imposed by the common law without the need for there to be a contract. For example, a civil action can be brought if a person defames you or trespasses on your land. Unlike criminal proceedings – where the State almost always has the role of prosecuting individuals who are alleged to have broken the criminal law – in a civil action one party takes proceedings against another party.

Most civil cases will be brought in the County Court – although cases concerning very large sums of compensation will begin in the High Court. The usual remedy is financial – 'damages' – and sometimes a court order instructing a party either to carry out a particular course of action or to stop doing so – an injunction. You can obtain the appropriate forms to start a civil action from your local County Court, but it is advisable to seek advice from a solicitor. While taking legal action is often not cheap, you could be eligible for financial support under the Community Legal Service scheme (see below: 'Going to court').

Judicial review

If you wish to challenge the decision of a public body you may be able to do so by taking judicial review proceedings in the High Court. Judicial review can be applied for in relation to any public body, including government departments, local authorities, the police and any organisation exercising a public function. Leave to apply for judicial review is only granted to individuals who have a 'sufficient interest' in the case. The grounds for such cases will usually be that the body acted illegally (including acting in breach of human rights) or irrationally or that the decision was reached unfairly because of a defect in the procedure that led to the decision. A successful action can compel or forbid the public body from doing something. The court can also nullify a decision and make the authority reconsider it or give its view on its legality. Damages may also be available in certain circumstances. Judicial review applications must usually be initiated very quickly – within three months of the decision being challenged. It is a complicated procedure and legal advice should be sought. Public funding is available for judicial review cases (see below: 'Going to court').

An application for initial permission should be made to the High Court, which will only grant permission if there is an arguable case and the applicant has not unduly delayed in seeking permission. The opponent in the case is served with the claim form and has the opportunity to file an acknowledgement of service not more than 21 days afterwards.

The timetable laid down in court rules requires that an application for permission be made expeditiously and in any event within three months of the decision complained of. The court does have power to extend that period in some circumstances.

An application for permission is usually considered by a single judge on the basis of the papers submitted by the parties. There is no right to an oral hearing as such, although if permission is refused then the applicant may request reconsideration by way of oral hearing at that stage.

Going to court
Before taking a complaint as far as court you should always seek legal advice. You can obtain free legal advice from organisations such as Law Centres or from solicitors who offer a free initial first interview (usually 30 minutes).

If you cannot afford to pay a solicitor, you may be eligible for Public Funding (formerly Legal Aid). The Community Legal Services Fund (CLS Fund) is the scheme for providing public funding to financially eligible people with legal problems (other than criminal matters which are funded separately – see Chapter 6). The Legal Services Commission (LSC), which took over from the Legal Aid Board, administers the Fund.

Solicitors and advisers who can provide publicly funded advice will have a CLS Quality Mark that shows they have reached an approved standard. You can obtain details of all CLS advisers, including areas of specialisation, from the CLS helpline on 0845 608 1122 or by using the CLS website: <www.justask.org.uk>.

You may be entitled to public funding just to obtain advice from a solicitor and to have a solicitor write letters on your behalf. This is known as 'Legal Help'. You may also be entitled to public funding for your solicitor and/or a barrister to represent you in court. For this you will need a 'Legal Representation Certificate'. Your solicitor will need to apply for this on your behalf.

All applications for public funding are means-tested. If you are on a low income with little capital, you are probably financially eligible for public funding. In some cases, even if you are financially eligible, the LSC may decide that you should make a contribution (usually paid monthly) toward the costs of your case. The CLS website has an online calculator that will help you work out whether you are eligible or not. The value of your home can be taken into account in some situations.

Even if you qualify financially for public funding, you will also need to satisfy the merits test. In other words, the LSC needs to be satisfied that your case has good prospects of success before it will grant public funding. Sometimes your solicitor can make this assessment, or he or she may need to obtain specialist advice from a barrister to support your application.

If you are successful with a case funded by the CLS, you may be asked to pay some or all of the money back. This is called the Statutory Charge. You should make sure your solicitor has explained this to you. You may be able to come to a No Win–No Fee agreement with your solicitor. This means that you will not be charged for services unless a minimum agreed result is achieved in your case. Obviously it is important that you are both clear on what has been agreed between you. You may also be able to take out insurance to cover your legal costs in the result of an unsuccessful action.

If you have difficulty obtaining representation some organisations such as the Bar Pro Bono Unit or the Free Representation Unit do provide free representation in some cases.

Bar Pro Bono Unit
6 Gray's Inn Square
Gray's Inn
London WC1R 5AZ
Tel: 020 7831 9711
enquiries@barprobonounit.co.uk
<www.barprobono.org.uk>

You cannot approach the Free Representation Unit directly but can ask your local CAB to do this on your behalf.

2.2   CENTRAL GOVERNMENT

Complaints about the way a case has been handled by a department of central government and some non-departmental bodies such as the DVLA are dealt with by the Parliamentary Ombudsman (PO). Complaints about the devolved National Assembly for Wales and other public Welsh bodies are dealt with by the Welsh Administration Ombudsman (WAO). The following explains the procedure for submitting a complaint to the PO. Unless otherwise indicated, you can assume the same procedure will apply for the WAO.

The PO has the power to investigate complaints of injustice or loss arising from poor administration, which includes such faults as avoidable delay, bias and arbitrary decision-making. There are some matters that the PO *cannot* investigate, including government policy, the investigation of crime, national security, court proceedings, local authorities and public service personnel matters. It is entirely up to the PO to decide whether to take up a complaint and carry out an investigation. If an investigation does take place, the PO's powers include making government departments show investigators all relevant documents. There is no charge for the PO's services and any expenses you incur during the investigation can be reimbursed.

The WAO can accept complaints directly from members of the public. The PO, however, can only accept complaints submitted via an MP. Accordingly, if you feel that you lost out in some way because of central government error, you must first raise your concerns with an MP. You can approach any MP, but it is usual to approach your constituency MP first, who can be contacted locally or by writing to him or her at the House of Commons. Before approaching an MP you should ensure that you have exhausted all possible internal complaints procedures of the department or organisation you are complaining about. Also, the PO will not normally consider complaints put to an MP 12 months or more after you become aware of them.

Following an investigation, the PO may conclude that your complaint was partly or wholly justified. If this does happen, the PO may recommend that the organisation provide you with a remedy. The PO has no enforcement powers, but the government almost always accepts his or her recommendations, including recommendations of financial recompense. Regular reports are also made to Parliament, and the PO has a committee of MPs who can follow up reports.

You cannot appeal a decision of the PO. Your complaint may be reviewed, however, on the basis of fresh evidence. A member of staff who is more senior than the person who originally dealt with your complaint will review the matter in light of the fresh evidence and a reply will be sent within 18 days. Further, as a public authority, a decision of the PO can be judicially reviewed.

If you are concerned about the way in which your complaint has been dealt with or the service you have received from a member of staff, you can make use of the PO's internal complaints procedure. Your complaint will be referred to a senior member of staff who was not involved in the original investigation. The complaint will be against the PO's standards of service and you will receive a reply within 18 days. If your complaint requires a detailed review of the PO's work, it may take longer to complete a full assessment and you will be kept informed of the progress of the review. If this review shows that your complaint about the service is justified, you will be informed as to how the PO intends to resolve the problem.

Addresses for the PO are:

The Parliamentary and Health Services Ombudsman
Millbank Tower
Millbank
London SW1P 4QP
Tel: 0845 015 4033
OPCA.Enquiries@ombudsman.gsi.gov.uk
<www.ombudsman.org.uk>

The Welsh Administration Ombudsman
Fifth Floor, Capital Tower
Greyfriars Road
Cardiff CF10 3AG
Tel: 0845 601 0987
WAO.Enquiries@ombudsman.gsi.gov.uk.

2.3   LOCAL GOVERNMENT

If you have suffered an injustice as a result of maladministration by a local authority, you can complain to the Local Government Ombudsman (LGO). Maladministration can include failing to receive a service to which you are entitled, suffering financial loss or suffering distress as a consequence of something the local authority has done or has failed to do. You can complain directly to the LGO's office about maladministration by any local body, such as the local authority or police authority, but only once you have exhausted the internal complaints procedure of the body you are complaining about.

The authorities that can be complained about include district, city, borough or county councils; education appeal committees; fire authorities; police authorities (but not in relation to the investigation of crime); the Greater London Authority; Transport for London and the Environment Agency.

The LGO cannot investigate matters that have already been – or could be – appealed to a tribunal or government minister, matters concerning the community in general, court proceedings, personnel matters and the internal management of schools and colleges. The LGO will not normally investigate matters that have been known about for more than 12 months.

If the LGO decides to take up a complaint, an investigator will contact you. If the investigator makes a decision that you have suffered an injustice as a consequence of maladministration, he or she can make a recommendation to the local authority. While this is not enforceable, the local authority will almost always follow the recommendation. Possible remedies include compensation, reviewing a decision and offering an apology.

You cannot appeal the decision but it can be reviewed on the basis of new information. Also, as a public authority, decisions of the LGO can be judicially reviewed.

England

There are three LGOs in England. Each of them deals with complaints from different parts of the country.

Tony Redmond
Local Government Ombudsman
21 Queen Anne's Gate
London SW1H 9BU
Tel: 020 7915 3210
Fax: 020 7233 0396
<www.lgo.org.uk>
Areas covered: London boroughs north of the river Thames (including Richmond but not including Harrow or Tower Hamlets), Essex, Kent, Surrey, Suffolk, East and West Sussex, Berkshire, Buckinghamshire, Hertfordshire and the City of Coventry.

Patricia Thomas
Local Government Ombudsman
Beverley House
17 Shipton Road

York YO30 5FZ
Tel: 01904 663200
Fax: 01904 663269
<www.lgo.org.uk>
Areas covered: London Borough of Tower Hamlets, City of Birmingham, Cheshire, Derbyshire, Nottinghamshire, Lincolnshire and the north of England (except the Cities of York and Lancaster).

Jerry White
Local Government Ombudsman
The Oaks No 2
Westwood Way
Westwood Business Park
Coventry CV4 8JB
Tel: 024 7669 5999
Fax: 024 7669 5902
<www.lgo.org.uk>
Areas covered: London boroughs south of the river Thames (except Richmond) and Harrow; the Cities of York, Lancaster and Coventry); and the rest of England, not included in the areas of Mr Redmond and Mrs Thomas.

Wales

Derwen House
Court Road
Bridgend
Mid Glamorgan CF31 1BL
Tel: 01656 661325
<www.ombudsman-wales.org>

2.4   HEALTH SERVICES

NHS treatment and services

Anyone who is receiving or has received NHS treatment or services can complain. If you are unable to complain yourself then someone else, usually a relative or close friend, can complain for you. The procedure works the same whichever part of the NHS you wish to complain about.

It is important that you make your complaint as soon as possible after the event you wish to complain about has occurred. Usually the NHS will only investigate complaints that are made within six months of the event – or within six months of you realising that you have something to complain about, as long as this is not more than 12 months after the event itself. These time limits can be waived if there is good reason to do so.

You should tell someone close to the cause of your complaint – a doctor, nurse, receptionist or practice manager – about it. It may well be possible to sort out the problem informally. This is called Local Resolution. If you would prefer to talk to someone who is not involved in your care, you can telephone or write to the appropriate complaints manager. All NHS Trusts have complaints managers. If your complaint is about a GP, family dentist, pharmacist or optician you should contact the complaints manager at your local health authority. The telephone number is in the phone book.

You should receive a full written reply to any written complaint against a trust or health authority. The NHS tries to do this within four weeks and should inform you of progress if this is not possible.

Local family health service practitioners – GP, dentist, pharmacist, optician – have their own complaints procedure. Staff will give you details. You may wish to use this procedure before contacting the local health authority.

If you wish to avoid an adversarial situation, you can request your complaint to be dealt with by way of 'conciliation'. This procedure brings you together with the subject of your complaint along with a neutral conciliator who will try to come up with a solution that satisfies you both. The subject of the complaint must also agree to conciliation before it can take place. Conciliation is usually used with complaints about 'primary care' services (e.g. GPs), but an NHS Trust may also provide this option.

If you are not satisfied with the outcome of Local Resolution then you can ask the trust to consider taking your complaint to Independent Review. You should do this within four weeks of the result of the Local Resolution.

You will be asked to explain in writing why you are dissatisfied with the result. A specially trained member of the trust or health authority will then decide whether there should be an independent review of your complaint by a special panel. You will be informed of the decision in writing. If he decides to set up a panel, you will be told what will be investigated.

The panel has three members and will re-examine the facts, conduct interviews and take any specialist advice needed. It will then prepare a report together with its conclusions and recommendations. You will be given a copy of this and will also be informed of any action being taken.

If you are still unhappy with the result you can ask the Health Service Ombudsman (HSO) to investigate your case. The HSO will not usually look at matters that have not been through the NHS complaints procedure.

The HSO for England can be contacted at:

The Parliamentary and Health Services Ombudsman
11th Floor, Millbank Tower
Millbank
London SW1P 4QP
Tel: 0845 015 4033
Enquiries@ombudsman.gsi.gov.uk
<www.ombudsman.org.uk>

The HSO for Wales can be contacted at:

The Health Service Ombudsman
Fifth Floor, Capital Tower
Greyfriars Road
Cardiff CF10 3AG
Tel: 01222 394621

Complaints about nurses and midwives

These professions are regulated by the Nursing and Midwifery Council (NMC), which is responsible for maintaining a register of nurses, midwives and health visitors. The NMC can investigate complaints from individuals who feel a member of these professions has mistreated them. The NMC has the power to remove or caution any practitioner who is found guilty of professional misconduct.

The address for the NMC is:

Nursing and Midwifery Council
23 Portland Place
London W1N 4JT
Tel: 020 7333 6541
<www.nmc-uk.org>

Complaints about doctors

The General Medical Council (GMC) is the governing body for doctors. The GMC maintains a register of qualified doctors. The GMC can investigate complaints regarding a doctor's fitness to practise. The GMC has powers to discipline its listed doctors and can take action when:

- A doctor has been convicted of a criminal offence.
- There is an allegation of serious professional misconduct.
- A doctor's professional performance may be seriously deficient.
- A doctor with health problems continues to practise while unfit.

If your problem is of a less serious nature, you should seek to resolve it through the NHS complaints procedure (see above, p. 23, 'NHS treatment and services').

The GMC can be contacted at:

The General Medical Council
178 Great Portland Street
London W1N 6JE
Tel: 020 7580 7642
gmc@gmc-uk.org
<www.gmc-uk.org>

Complaints of medical negligence

You should initially follow the relevant complaints procedures detailed above. If this does not work, or if you are seeking compensation, you could consider going to court in a private action for negligence. Advice on this matter should be sought from a solicitor or from:

Action for the Victims of Medical Accidents
44 High Street
Croydon
Surrey CRO 1YB
Tel: 020 8686 8333
avma.uk@virgin.net

2.5   COMMUNITY CARE AND BENEFITS ENTITLEMENT

Community care

If you have a complaint concerning community care or social services, you should first contact your local authority for information on their complaints procedure. Usually you will complain to any named contact person and then, if dissatisfied, to the Director of Social Services. This may lead to informal problem-solving, registering a complaint or a formal review by a panel, which reports to the local authority. Leaflets telling you who to complain to in social services are available from Citizens' Advice Bureaux and other advice centres. If the complaint is of maladministration, it could go to the Local Government Ombudsman. As the decision is made by a public authority, judicial review may also be a possibility.

Benefits

If you do not agree with a decision made by the Department for Work and Pensions (DWP) in respect of a benefit you have claimed or are receiving, then as a first step you can ask DWP to explain the decision. If you are not satisfied with the explanation, you can ask DWP to review its decision.

Beyond internal review, it may be possible to appeal the decision to the Appeals Service who will decide your appeal at a tribunal hearing. The tribunal is made up of people who are not from DWP or Jobcentre Plus. The tribunal will only look at the evidence, the law and the circumstances *at the time* the relevant decision was made.

You can challenge a tribunal decision if you think the tribunal has made an error when applying the law. You can do this by applying to the Social Security and Child Support Commissioners. If you want to appeal to the Commissioners, you must first apply to the Appeals Service for permission. Your application will be considered at the Appeals Service by a District Chairman. The District Chairman will return your application to you, with permission granted or refused. You can then decide to send your application to the Office of the Commissioners, with the District Chairman's decision.

You will find extensive information about appealing social security decisions on the DWP's website: <www.dwp.gov.uk>.

Child support

Every Child Support Agency Centre (CSA) has a Customer Service Manager, and their phone number should be on correspondence you have received. If it is not, anyone in a CSA office will be able to give it to you. The Customer Service Manager is responsible for reviewing and acting on client complaints.

Where a complaint from a client cannot be dealt with by a Customer Service Manager, it is referred to a Senior Resolution Manager. Senior Resolution Managers are senior managers who deal specifically with clients' complaints. They have the overall responsibility for the quality of responses and take the lead in ensuring the Child Support Agency learns from complaints.

If you are not happy with the way in which the Customer Service Manager or Senior Resolution Manager has dealt with the complaint, you can write to the Area Director of your Child Support Agency Centre. The Agency has six Area Directors and each one is responsible for all the services in their area. Their names and addresses are listed at the CSA website: <www.csa.gov.uk>.

If the Area Director does not resolve the complaint to your satisfaction, you can write to the Chief Executive at:

Child Support Agency
Room BP6201
Benton Park Road
Newcastle upon Tyne NE98 1YX

Finally, an Independent Case Examiner can look at complaints about the way the Child Support Agency has handled a case, for example, if the Child Support Agency has taken a long time to deal with it or made a mistake that has not been corrected. The Independent Case Examiner cannot look at complaints about legislation.

You should also remember that you might complain to the Parliamentary Ombudsman if you wish to complain about the way your case has been dealt with.

2.6   THE POLICE

A new police complaints system

The Independent Police Complaints Commission (IPCC) commenced operation on 1 April 2004, replacing the Police Complaints Authority. The establishment of the IPCC and the overhaul of the police complaints system is the end result of calls for change from a number of quarters including Liberty, the police service and the Police Complaints Authority itself, the McPherson Inquiry into the death of Stephen Lawrence, community and complainants' groups and the Home Affairs Select Committee. During 2000/01, the Home Office conducted a public consultation and commissioned a feasibility study. Liberty also published its report on an Independent Police Complaints Commission. Finally, the Police Reform Act 2002, which established a legislative framework for the new system, was given Royal Assent. Details of the new system are explained below under relevant headings.

Complaints

Anyone can make a police complaint. You need not be a victim as such of police misconduct. You might, for example, have been a witness to an incident, which you feel should be the subject of a complaint.

If you are dissatisfied with your treatment by the police, the first thing to do is to get as many details as possible about the officer(s) who dealt with you: their names, numbers, car number and so on, as well as details of any witnesses. Such information will be important. Write down what happened as soon as you can; again this will help later.

Before making a complaint you should consider the following points:

Complaints should be made within one year of the incident. If you are worried or uncertain, always take advice first. Do not allow yourself to be pressurised by the police or anyone else into making your complaint on the spot.

Your complaint must be about a particular officer or officers, not about general police practice or policy. This is why it is important to try to identify the officer involved. If you have a general complaint concerning policing practice, you should raise the matter with your MP and the Home Office. Complaints about local policing policy can be taken up through your Police Authority, or Greater London Authority for the police in London.

Before making your complaint against the police, it is a good idea to get advice from a solicitor, Law Centre or Citizens' Advice Bureau (CAB), particularly if you are also considering a civil action against the police. If you do not have much money, you should consult a solicitor who offers Community Legal Service advice. This advice will be free, or virtually free, depending on your income and savings.

How to make a complaint

A complaint can be made verbally at a police station, but your views will be more accurately recorded if you submit your complaint in writing and retain a copy for yourself. You can also make complaints at independent organisations such as Citizens Advice Bureaux. If you make your complaint directly to the IPCC they will forward it to the relevant police force.

Complaints can be made against anyone who is a member of a force, anyone who is both employed by the police authority and under the direction and control of the Chief Constable, any special constables and any contracted staff who are designated as detention and escort officers. Give as many details as you can and be honest and accurate – the police can take legal action against you for false accusations of wrongful conduct.

All complaints *must* be recorded if they meet the criteria set out in the Police Reform Act 2002. By way of example, a complaint relating to policing policy would not meet the criteria. On the other hand, a complaint about by an individual who had been roughly handled while being arrested would meet the criteria. If the police refuse to record your complaint you can appeal against the decision to the IPCC. The police can apply to the IPCC to dispense with a complaint if, for example, it has been made maliciously. In some cases the police can close a complaint themselves. An example is when the complaint was suspended as the person complaining faced criminal charges and they do not renew their complaint after the criminal case has finished.

Local Resolution

Local Resolution was previously called Informal Resolution. It is used to settle around a third of complaints. It may take different forms, but in simple terms amounts to gaining the complainant's consent to resolve a complaint outside of an investigation and instead seek to resolve it through dialogue. It might entail a member of the police service meeting with the complainant to establish the nature of their concerns and meeting with the officer complained against. An attempt is then made to address the complainant's concerns through an explanation, some form of apology or through the use of intermediaries.

Once Local Resolution has been chosen by the complainant there is no appeal against the outcome (although you can appeal against the process used). Local Resolution is appropriate if you feel that you have been badly treated by the police but would be happy to settle for an apology or an explanation.

The Independent Police Complaints Commission

There are certain categories of complaint that must be referred to the IPCC:

- Allegations of assault.
- Allegations of 'hate' crime.
- Allegations of corruption.
- Cases involving serious injury.
- Allegations of serious offences.
- Cases involving deaths in custody.
- When police shooting is involved.

In other situations the police have discretion to refer the matter to the IPCC. The IPCC can also decide to deal with any particular case. If a case is referred to the IPCC it can be dealt with in one of three ways. In the most serious cases, the IPCC will conduct a completely independent investigation. For slightly less serious cases the IPCC will manage a police investigation ('managed' investigations). In the majority of cases the police will handle the complaint and the IPCC will supervise the investigation ('supervised' investigation) or the police alone will deal with the case ('local investigation', *not* to be confused with 'local resolution' above).

In reality, there will be some form of police involvement in all but a tiny minority of complaints. Particular areas of expertise and resources will continue to rest with the police. The mix of IPCC and police involvement in investigations will vary depending on the nature and needs of individual cases.

Once the investigation has been completed the IPCC will prepare a report or will receive a report if the police supervised the complaint. You should be kept informed of the progress of your complaint, and there is a presumption that you will be able to have access to any documents or other relevant information. Once the investigation has been concluded you will be informed of the conclusion. If the case is serious and your complaint is upheld it may result in disciplinary action or even criminal proceedings.

If you are unhappy with the manner in which a local or supervised investigation has taken place you can appeal against the decision. The appeal right does not extend to managed and investigations that the IPCC has taken on independently. However, as the IPCC is a public body you can challenge the legality of any decisions made through Judicial Review.

Taking legal action yourself – suing the police

You may bring a civil action against the police and seek damages to compensate you for your injuries and loss. The categories under which the police can be sued include the following:

- Assault and battery or the use of excessive force in arrest or detention.
- False imprisonment or restricting your liberty unlawfully – for example, detaining you without justification or for too long without charge.
- Trespass or searching property without proper authority.
- Malicious prosecution or bringing a prosecution without any good reasons that then fails.
- Negligence or failure to meet the standard of care that the police should show for the safety of people forseeably affected by their actions.

When the old Police Complaints Authority was in place, many civil cases succeeded where formal complaints failed. It remains to be seen whether the establishment of the IPCC will alter this state of affairs. You should ask a lawyer as soon as possible to advise you on your chances of success and the possible amount of damages you might receive. In February 1997 the Court of Appeal laid down guidelines on the level of damages in civil actions against the police in the case of *The Commissioner of Police for the Metropolis* v *Thompson and Hsu*. The court proposed a figure of £500 for the first hour of false imprisonment and then a downward sliding scale, with £3,000 to be awarded for 24 hours' detention. The court also proposed damages for malicious prosecution of between £2,000 and £10,000, and that exemplary damages awarded against the police should be between £5,000 and £50,000. Community Legal Service funding is available for actions against the police – subject to the merits of your case and your income and capital.

It is usual to sue the Chief Constable – who is generally responsible for the actions of police officers – of the relevant police force and so, unlike the position with police complaints, it is not essential to know the identities of the police officers involved.

If you are considering a civil action as well as making a formal complaint you should get legal advice from a solicitor or other adviser. You may be advised not to make a very detailed statement in support of your complaint because this might put you at some disadvantage in the civil action as the police will know at a very early stage the case you are going to make against them. If you have already made a complaint, refer the investigating officer to your solicitor. Be prepared for a considerable wait as civil cases can take several years to be concluded.

Prosecuting the police – criminal action
The IPCC is able to refer cases to the Crown Prosecution Service for criminal investigation. If the IPCC does not do this and you think that a crime has been committed it is possible to bring a private prosecution. You must get legal advice before bringing a private prosecution since you will need strong evidence if you are to have any chance of success. Under these circumstances there is no Community Legal Service funding available and a private prosecution can be very expensive, especially if the officer elects for trial by jury. It is important to realise that it is extremely difficult to succeed in a private prosecution and, if you do lose, you could be made liable for the legal costs incurred by the other side.

How are major incidents involving the police dealt with?
The Home Secretary can set up an independent enquiry into any matter concerning the police in England and Wales. Such enquiries are not limited to misconduct by individuals or groups of officers but can also deal with police instructions and policing policies that result in serious conflict with members of the public. Such enquiries, however, are rarely held.

Police Authorities can require chief police officers to report on any matter concerning the policing of their area; this is another way in which major incidents can be investigated.

Because the scope of public enquiries and reporting to Police Authorities is much wider than individual complaints, a campaign of public pressure is often needed before action is taken. If there has been an incident that needs to be examined in a public way, you should consider taking the matter up with relevant local organisations, your MP and elected members of the Police Authority and with the media.

Complaints about local policing practice
If you are not happy with the way the police are carrying out their responsibilities in your area, for example, if you think that their priorities are wrong or that they are unfairly treating certain sections of the community, then you should be able to talk to a community consultative group set up by your local Police Authority. Almost all Police Authorities have set up a number of consultative groups or committees in their areas. The members are appointed by the Police Authority and will usually include a combination of members from the Police Authority, the local authority and community representatives. It should be noted that the committees are merely consultative in function and have no power actually to change police practice. They function as a forum for the police to meet the public, not a mechanism for investigating or rectifying complaints.

Useful organisations

Law Centres Federation
18–19 Warren Street
London W1P 5DB
Tel: 020 7387 8570
info@lawcentres.org.uk
<www.lawcentres.org.uk>

Association of Police Authorities
Local Government House
Smith Square
London SW1P 3HZ
<www.apa.police.uk/apa_home.htm>

The Independent Police Complaints Commission
90 High Holborn
London WC1V 6BH
Tel: 0845 300 2002 (local rate)
<www.ipcc.gov.uk>

2.7   COURTS AND LEGAL SERVICES

Complaints about the courts
If you are unhappy with the service you have received from any of the court's administrative staff or with a procedural aspect of your case, such as not being given certain information by the court or because you were kept waiting for an unduly long time, you can make a complaint to the Court Service. Before making a complaint, you should make sure you have read a copy of the Court's Charter that sets out the level of service you can expect to receive when you come to court or deal with the court's administrative staff. The Charter is available free of charge at all courts.

All courts have a Customer Service Manager and a Court Manager who assist with resolving complaints. You can complain in person and the staff will attempt to resolve the matter on the spot. Alternatively, you can submit a complaint in writing to the Court Manager at the court you have been dealing with. The Court Manager will confirm receipt of your complaint and carry out an investigation. At the end of the investigation you will receive a reply. If the Court Manager upholds your complaint, you will receive an apology and an explanation of how the Court Manager intends to avoid a repeat of the problem.

If you are not satisfied with the Court Manager's reply, you can write to the Group Manager, who will review your complaint and the Court Manager's decision. If after receiving a reply from the Group Manager you are still not satisfied, you can write to the Court Service Customer Service Unit. You will need to explain that you have already complained to the Court Manager and the Group Manager.

You can contact the Customer Service Unit at:

Court Services Headquarters
Southside
105 Victoria Street
London SW1E 6QT
Tel: 020 7210 8500
cust.ser.cs@gtnet.gov.uk
<www.lcd.gov.uk>

Please note that this procedure does not cover complaints about individual lawyers, case decisions or court policy.

Complaints about judges

If you are dissatisfied with the way in which a judge has decided your case, your only option is to appeal against the decision. However, if you wish to complain about a judge's *personal* behaviour towards you, you can write to the Department of Constitutional Affairs at:

The Department of Constitutional Affairs
Selborne House
54–60 Victoria Street
London SW1E 6QW

Your letter should include your name and address, the details of the relevant court and judge, the case/application number, the date of the hearing and the reason for your complaint.

Complaints against solicitors

There are three sorts of complaints you might have against a solicitor: a complaint about charges being too high, a general complaint about the way you have been dealt with by your solicitor, or a complaint involving negligence by your solicitor. In all cases you should complain in the first instance to the firm itself so that, if possible, your grievance can be settled without taking the matter further. If the solicitor who has acted for you will not address your complaint, you should refer the matter to the senior partner in the firm, or the partner who has specific responsibility for dealing with complaints. If your complaint is not resolved in this way, the action you take next will depend on the nature of your complaint.

Complaints about overcharging

Once you have tried to resolve this informally, for matters that have not involved court proceedings, you can ask your solicitor to apply to the Law Society for a

Remuneration Certificate. There are two ways you may be able to have your bill checked to see if it is fair and reasonable.

The remuneration certificate procedure is a free service provided by the Law Society's Consumer Complaints Service. This scheme is only available to you if your solicitor's bill is for work that has not involved court proceedings. If you think your solicitor's bill is too high, you should contact them as soon as possible. It's important to note that strict time limits apply for challenging your solicitor's bill. If you cannot come to an agreement about the fee, write to your solicitor asking him or her to apply to the Consumer Complaints Service (CCS) for a remuneration certificate. Again, please bear in mind that strict time limits apply.

Your solicitor will have to fill in an application form and send it to you for your comments. Once the solicitor receives your comments, they will send the application form, your comments and the original file of papers to the CCS remuneration certificate department. Please remember that you must ask your solicitor to apply for a certificate because you cannot apply yourself.

Assessment is the way of having your bill assessed by the courts. (In other words, the court will check that your bill is fair.) Although assessment is the only method for checking bills that involves court proceedings, you can also use it for all other types of work. You may have to pay the court costs.

For more information about assessment, you can phone the Supreme Court Costs Office on 020 7947 6000 and ask for a copy of their information sheet.

Complaints about professional conduct or negligence
If your complaint is about the way your lawyer has handled your case or if you feel he or she may have been negligent, the Consumer Complaints Service (CCS) (formerly the Office for the Supervision of Solicitors) may be able to help. They investigate complaints of poor service and/or misconduct made against any solicitor in England or Wales. The CCS can order compensation up to £5,000, require a solicitor to correct a mistake, or discipline a solicitor for misconduct. The CCS runs a helpline that gives information on all aspect of complaints. The number is 0845 608 6565.

If you are dissatisfied with a decision of the CCS, or the way your complaint was handled by them, you have three months from the date of their decision to refer the matter to the Legal Services Ombudsman (LSO). The LSO is appointed by the Lord Chancellor to ensure that the system for handling complaints about the legal profession is well regulated.

If you've suffered a loss or hardship as a result of your solicitor's dishonesty, you can apply for a grant from the Compensation Fund. The CCS runs this on behalf of the Law Society. This fund can be used to replace money that a solicitor has stolen or which he or she has failed to pay over to you. However, the fund will only normally compensate you if you have no other way of getting your money back.

Consumer Complaints Service
Victoria Court
8 Dormer Place
Leamington Spa
Warwickshire CV32 5AE
Tel: 01926 820 082/3
Fax: 01926 431 435

The Office of the Legal Services Ombudsman
22 Oxford Street
Manchester M2 3WQ
Tel: 0161 236 9532
Fax: 0161 832 5446
lso@olso.gsi.gov.uk
<www.olso.org>

Complaints about other peoples' solicitors

If your complaint is about someone else's solicitor, the CCS can only help if it involves professional misconduct. They cannot investigate your complaint about the poor service given by someone else's solicitor.

If you complain about the way someone else's solicitor has behaved, they can only help you if the solicitor has breached the rules of professional conduct that all solicitors must follow. Often, a solicitor will just be doing what's best for their client and not what's best for any other person who may be involved.

If you complain about the conduct of someone else's solicitor, the CCS does not have the power to pay you any compensation even if they approve your complaint.

Complaints against barristers

The General Council of the Bar (GCB) is the governing body for barristers and is responsible for dealing with complaints about the conduct of barristers. If you are dissatisfied with the conduct of your barrister or the service you have received, as a first step it is worthwhile raising your concerns with your solicitor (if you have one). If you cannot resolve the matter this way, you should then consider submitting a complaint to the GCB. Your complaint should be submitted within six months. The GCB has the power to award up to £5,000 compensation to a complainant and in cases of serious misconduct can actually disbar the barrister.

For two hundred years barristers enjoyed an immunity that prevented disgruntled clients from suing them for damages for loss incurred as a result of the barrister's negligence in representing the client in court. The House of Lords removed the immunity in 2000. The decision removed immunity with respect to all proceedings, both civil and criminal, and also affects solicitors who act as advocates in court.

The General Council of the Bar
3 Bedford Row
London WC1R 4DB
Tel: 020 7242 0082
<www.barcouncil.org.uk>

2.8   FINANCIAL PROFESSIONS

There are many professions that deal with financial affairs, such as accountants, banks, mortgage brokers and insurance companies. Many of these professions have established bodies that perform a regulatory function. If you have a problem with the service you have received from a provider of financial services you should complain to the company involved first and then to the appropriate regulator. The Financial

Services Ombudsman incorporates the work of a number of former regulators and deals with complaints relating to most financial services including banks, building societies and insurance providers.

Contact details for regulators:

The Financial Ombudsman Service
South Quay Plaza
183 Marsh Wall
London E14 9S
Tel: 0845 080 1800
enquiries@financial-ombudsman.org.uk
<www.financial-ombudsman.org.uk>

Estate Agents Ombudsman
Beckett House
4 Bridge Street
Salisbury SP1 1YO
Tel: 01722 333 306
<www.oea.co.uk>

Pensions Ombudsman
11 Belgrave Road
London SW1V 1RB
Tel: 020 7834 9144
enquiries@pensions-ombudsman.org.uk
<www.pensions-ombudsman.org.uk>

2.9   THE MEDIA

If you are upset by something shown on television or in the press or covered on radio, or feel that you personally have been misquoted or wrongly represented, you can complain directly to the organisation involved and/or to the regulatory bodies.

Press
For the press, the Press Complaints Commission (PCC) is the current official watchdog. Initially, it operates a telephone helpline that can give you the name and address of the relevant editor so you can complain directly. Beyond this, the PCC upholds a code of practice that penalises inaccuracy and intrusiveness. Written complaints should be sent to:

The Press Complaints Commission
1 Salisbury Square
London EC4Y 8JB
Tel: 020 7353 3732
<www.pcc.org.uk>

Radio and television
For radio and television, you should first complain to the programme's producer. You may address complaints about the BBC to the appropriate senior manager or directly to:

The Director-General
BBC Broadcasting House
London W1A 1AA
Tel: 020 7580 4468
<www.bbc.co.uk>

In the case of a commercial station, complaints should be sent to the Programme Controller.

At the end of December 2003 the responsibilities of the Broadcasting Standards Commission were assumed by the Office of Communications (Ofcom). Ofcom also replaced the Independent Television Commission, Oftel, the Radio Authority and the Radio Communications Agency.

Ofcom is now responsible for considering complaints of unjust or unfair treatment and unwarranted infringements of privacy, as well as the portrayal of violence and sex and standards of taste and decency. Complaints to Ofcom should be made within a reasonable time after the relevant broadcast (usually three months). Ofcom has the power to require the broadcaster to publish a summary of a complaint and of Ofcom's findings.

If your complaint is not satisfactorily dealt with by the broadcaster, you should write to Ofcom at:

The Office of Communications
Ofcom Contact Centre
Riverside House
2a Southwark Bridge Road
London SE1 9HA
Tel: 0845 456 3000 or 020 7981 3040
<www.ofcom.org.uk>

See also Chapter 9.

Advertisements
If your complaint is directed at the content or tone of an advertisement in any medium, you should complain to:

The Advertising Standards Authority
2 Torrington Place
London WC1E 7HN
Tel: 020 7580 5555
inquiries@asa.org.uk
<www.asa.org.uk>

If you feel that the media has personally defamed you, you may wish to bring a civil action for defamation.

See also Chapter 9.

2.10   PUBLIC UTILITIES

Since the privatisation of the gas, electricity, water and telephone companies, the Government has created watchdog bodies for each industry. If a complaint to the company itself at a local or regional level – addresses will be in the phone book – does not lead to a solution, you should complain to the regulator. Such complaints may be about standards of service or matters relating to billing. Below are the relevant general addresses.

Electricity & gas

Ofgem is the regulator for the gas and electricity industries. Its stated role is to promote choice and value for all customers. Contact details are:

Ofgem
9 Millbank
London SW1P 3GE
Tel: 020 7901 7000
<www.ofgem.gov.uk>

Energywatch is an independent consumer organisation representing the interests of all gas and electricity consumers. Energywatch can investigate customer complaints, assist in resolving disputes and can refer matters to Ofgem for possible enforcement action. Energywatch can only assist if you have first attempted to resolve the problem yourself directly with the energy supplier. If you have a complaint you can contact Energywatch by telephone or e-mail as follows:

Tel: 0845 906 0708 for gas complaints
0845 601 3131 for electricity complaints
0800 88 77 77 for general enquiries
enquiry@energywatch.org.uk
<www.energywatch.org.uk>

Water

Office for Water Services (Ofwat) is the regulator for the water industry. Contact details are:

Ofwat
Centre City Tower
7 Hill Street
Birmingham B5 4UA
Tel: 0121 625 1300
enquiries@ofwat.gsi.gov.uk
<www.ofwat.gov.uk>

Watervoice operates through nine regional committees in England and a committee for Wales, representing the interests of customers in respect of price, service and value for money. It also investigates complaints from customers about their water company. If you have a complaint about your water company that you have not been able to resolve with the company itself, you can contact Watervoice and ask them to investigate your complaint for you.

Watervoice work closely with Ofwat, and full details of how to submit complaints to Watervoice are available on the Ofwat website: <www.ofwat.gov.uk>.

Telecommunications

Ofcom is the regulator for the UK communications industries, with responsibilities across television, radio, telecommunications and wireless communications services. Contact details for Ofcom are:

Ofcom Contact Centre
Riverside House
2a Southwark Bridge Road
London SE1 9HA
Tel: 0845 456 3000
contact@ofcom.org.uk
<www.ofcom.gov.uk>

Post

The Postal Services Commission (Postcomm) is the regulator for postal services in the UK. Postwatch can provide advice and information on postal services and will deal with complaints where customers have been unable to resolve problems with their postal services provider.

The Postal Services Commission
Hercules House
Hercules Road
London SE1 7DB
Tel: 020 7593 2100
info@psc.gov.uk

2.11   COMPENSATION FOR THE VICTIMS OF CRIME

If you are the victim of a criminal act, there are three ways in which you could obtain compensation from the offender:

- A compensation order made by the court as part of a guilty verdict. This is not an award you can directly apply for yourself, and it is important that the prosecution at the trial knows as much information as possible that might persuade the judge to make such an order.
- A civil action suing for damages. Seek advice from a solicitor or a Citizens' Advice Bureau before attempting this.
- An application to the Criminal Injuries Compensation Scheme, set up to assist those injured by crimes of violence. You may apply for an award even if the offender has not been arrested, as long as you have not been awarded any compensation by either of the first two methods above.

Information on the latter scheme is available from:

Criminal Injuries Compensation Authority
Tay House
300 Bath Street
Glasgow G2 4LN
Tel: 0141 331 2726

The website enables you to make an online assessment of whether you may be eligible for compensation.

If your claim arises from a road traffic offence, unless it was a deliberate attempt to run you over, you should claim from the offender's insurance company. If the offender is uninsured, payments can be made by the Motor Insurers' Bureau, an organisation funded by the insurance companies. Their address is:

Motor Insurers' Bureau
6–12 Capital Drive
Linford Wood
Milton Keynes MK14 6XT
Tel: 01908 830001
<www.mib.org.uk>

2.12   MISCELLANEOUS COMPLAINTS

Complaints about many consumer issues should be taken to the appropriate section of your local authority or county council, such as environmental health and trading standards. They may also be able to advise on housing complaints against private landlords, but specialist advisers in this field exist at Citizens' Advice Bureaux, law centres and similar organisations.

National Association of Citizens' Advice Bureaux
Myddleton House
115–123 Pentonville Road
London N1 9LZ

3   The Right to Privacy

This chapter deals with:

- Article 8 – the right to respect for private and family life, home and correspondence
- Confidential information
- Spent convictions and the rehabilitation of offenders
- Telephone tapping and interception of communications
- Surveillance and undercover human intelligence sources
- Other types of surveillance
- Investigation of electronic data protected by encryption
- Use of photographs, fingerprints, DNA samples and other samples taken at police stations
- Harassment, unwanted letters and telephone calls
- Power of officials to enter your home
- Searches by Customs and Excise officials
- Gender identity and sexuality
- Privacy and the media
- Further information

3.1   ARTICLE 8 – THE RIGHT TO RESPECT FOR PRIVATE AND FAMILY LIFE, HOME AND CORRESPONDENCE

In essence, the incorporation of Article 8 of the European Convention on Human Rights (the Convention) into UK law by the Human Rights Act 1998 (HRA) creates a general right to respect for privacy where none previously existed. Article 8 offers general protection for a person's private and family life, home and correspondence from arbitrary interference by the State. This right affects a large number of areas of life ranging from surveillance to sexual identity – it is framed extremely broadly. However, the right to respect for these aspects of privacy under Article 8 is qualified. This means that interferences by the State can be permissible, but such interferences must be justified and satisfy certain conditions. Any interference with your right must be:

- In accordance with law; and
- In the interests of the legitimate objectives identified in Article 8(2); and
- Necessary in a democratic society.

In accordance with law
In many cases decided by the European Court of Human Rights (ECHR), interferences with privacy have been in breach of Article 8 because they have not satisfied this

first condition. In order for an interference to be in accordance with law, the interference must have a proper legal basis, such as a piece of legislation or rules of a professional body. The law or rule must be understandable, detailed and clear enough to allow a person to regulate his or her behaviour – a secret, unpublished memo in a government department will not suffice, for example. Some well-known scenarios involving interference that could not be justified under Article 8(2) have been the telephone tapping, or bugging, of individuals by the police using procedures and systems not authorised expressly by statute.

The legitimate objectives

The second condition that the interference must satisfy is that it must pursue an identified legitimate aim. The legitimate objectives set out in Article 8(2) are:

- Acting in the interests of national security, public safety or the economic well-being of the country.
- Acting for the prevention of disorder or crime.
- Acting for the protection of health or morals.
- Acting for the protection of the rights and freedoms of others.

These objectives are widely drawn, and it will often be possible for an interference to be categorised as in pursuit of one of these legitimate objectives, for example, telephone tapping for the purposes of investigation or prevention of crime. More difficult questions arise where there are competing interests at issue, such as balancing privacy rights against the right of freedom of expression in cases of publication of photographs or materials about a person's private life. In some cases it will be important to distinguish between a lawful interference in someone's private life *in the public interest*, as opposed to an unlawful one that has occurred merely because it is something in which *the public might be interested*.

Necessary in a democratic society

Even if the infringement of privacy is in accordance with the law, and it is for one of the legitimate objectives, it must still be 'necessary' in order for it to be justified under Article 8. This is the third and most stringent condition that any infringement must satisfy, bringing in a requirement that the act must be 'proportionate'.

The requirement of proportionality is often colloquially described as 'not using a sledgehammer to crack a nut'. In essence, this means that the nature and extent of each interference must be judged against the end it is meant to achieve, and any interference with your rights under Article 8 that goes further than is necessary may well be unlawful. For example, a blanket policy of excluding prisoners during examinations of their legally privileged correspondence was considered a disproportionate interference with their rights to privacy and correspondence under Article 8.

The more severe the infringement of privacy, the more important the legitimate objective in each case will need to be. In most cases, the interference will be judged against whether it meets a pressing social need, and the extent to which an alternative, less intrusive interference would achieve the same result.

The nature of privacy rights

The right to respect for private and family life, home and correspondence in Article 8 brings wider protection than might be thought at first glance. Respect for private life includes a right to develop one's own personality, as well as to create relationships with others. For example, Article 8 has been critical in providing basic protection for the rights of homosexual and transsexual people. It has also been used to extend protection to a person's office space as well as his or her domestic home. More recently, in the English and Welsh courts, it has been recognised that a right of privacy may be enjoyed by a company as well as an individual.

Protection of private life and the home may also be relevant to decisions made in planning and environmental contexts. Permitting the carrying out of an unpleasant development nearby your home, for example a nuclear plant or waste site, which will affect your enjoyment of your property, may be an interference with your rights under Article 8, which will need to be justified in the ways set out above. Similarly, your rights to refuse medical treatment and to maintain your personal autonomy will usually involve your rights protected by Article 8.

The Convention is often described as a 'living instrument'. This means that the nature of Convention rights and the extent to which they should be protected will depend upon society's values at any one time. With regard to Article 8, a very good illustration of this is the rights of transsexual people. Previously, the ECHR had decided that the UK's failure to allow someone who had had gender reassignment surgery to obtain a new birth certificate altering their legal sex did not amount to a breach of Article 8 rights. However, the ECHR stressed that this would need to be reassessed in the light of any material changes in attitudes towards and scientific knowledge and insight into transsexualism. In July 2002, the ECHR decided that the time had come where such rights had to be recognised and found that the UK was in breach of its obligations under the Convention. This has resulted in new legislation from the Government, which will allow persons with gender dysphoria to apply for a gender recognition certificate. A person in receipt of such a certificate will be entitled to be treated as of their new acquired gender for all purposes and will not generally have to reveal their biological sex at birth.

The duty of public authorities
The requirement on public authorities to act compatibly with Article 8 of the Convention is contained in section 6 of the HRA. Section 6 provides that central government, local government and other public bodies such as the police and the courts must all act compatibly with your rights.

Strangely, there still seems to be no general right to protection from invasion of privacy by other individuals in society. However, the right to respect for privacy under Article 8, along with existing protections in a number of different areas of common law, and the new obligation on courts to interpret statutory law compatibly with Convention rights wherever possible, should go some way to protecting against invasion of privacy in practice.

Because of the reluctance to recognise a freestanding principle of protection from invasion of privacy, it is still necessary to pay close attention to the piecemeal protection that currently exists in general common law and different statutes in order to have a full understanding of the privacy rights you enjoy. Further, any interference with the right to respect for private and family life, the home and correspondence by public authorities must now also be justifiable in accordance with the tests in Article 8.

It is also now clear that a public authority may be liable for *any* breaches of your right to respect for private and family life, home and correspondence, even where, for example, it unlawfully obtains information in breach of your rights that is subsequently used and admitted as evidence against you in civil or criminal proceedings.

3.2   CONFIDENTIAL INFORMATION

The law protecting confidential information is an important part of your right to privacy. The law of confidence has its origins in the commercial world of protecting trade secrets and confidential lists of business contacts. It has now grown far beyond this, and has recently been used in cases involving celebrities objecting to media intrusion of their private lives. Rather than speak in terms of a right to privacy, the courts have preferred to recognise such a right through actions based on breaches of confidence. Now photographs taken of people in both private and public places, or information obtained about a person's activities from another person, may be treated as confidential. A person may be able to sue where such confidential information is published or used in breach of the implied obligations of confidence.

The protection available to you must inevitably be balanced against the important right of freedom of expression and disclosure of information in the public interest. For example, celebrities often seek public interest in their lives and may sometimes hold themselves up as a role model in a particular area. For this reason, they may sometimes find it harder to persuade the court to protect information about their personal life when a newspaper wishes to publish it. For example, a Premiership footballer lost his case to try and prevent a newspaper publishing articles about his adulterous love affairs and visits to lap-dancing clubs where the other parties to the affair wished to publish their story, and a television presenter lost his attempt to prevent publication of details about his visit to a brothel. However, the fact that an individual has achieved prominence in the public eye (be it as a celebrity or an MP) does not entitle the media to publish anything at all they wish about their private life, and the courts will still protect against the invasion of their privacy. Those who do not seek public interest at all will inevitably have a stronger case for seeking protection against disclosures of information relating to their personal lives by other people.

Historically, protection of confidential information depended on three main elements:

- The information itself would have to be confidential in nature – for example, health records or personal diaries.
- The person with the information must be under a duty to keep it confidential.
- The proposed use of the information must be incompatible with that duty.

The requirement of a duty of confidentiality can often be created by a contract. Members of the Royal households, for instance, have to promise never to reveal what they learn in the course of their employment, and some general contracts of employment may be subject to such duties. But people who never think in terms of contracts share many secrets. There are many relationships that are by their nature confidential: for example, between a lawyer and a client, and between a doctor and a patient. The courts have been also willing to recognise that duties of confidence can be owed between spouses and even friends.

The courts no longer need to construct an artificial relationship between people in order to recognise that a duty of confidentiality has arisen. If a third party obtains information and knows or learns of its confidential character, he or she can be required to respect the confidence. This means that a newspaper to whom a secret is sold or given can be ordered not to publish it. Secret documents, accidentally sent to third parties, may need to be returned. The language of 'duty of confidence' can even apply to a thief who steals private papers or documents. For the duty to arise, it may simply be sufficient for any reasonable person, standing in the shoes of the person who has obtained the information, to have realised that the information is confidential.

The requirement that the information has to be confidential in nature is now less strictly applied. While the information must have the basic attribute of inaccessibility to others, the court will not refuse an injunction because the information has leaked out to a limited extent or is available by any person with some degree of background knowledge (for example, information contained on a website is in principle available to any member of the public, but may in practice require knowledge for it to be accessed). However, there will come a point – as in the *Spycatcher* saga where a book containing confidential information was being widely published abroad – when it is plainly pointless to pretend that there is any secret left to be preserved.

There is obviously potential for a clash of interests here: between the rights of the person wanting the information to be kept secret, and the rights of the person who wants to disclose it or the public interest in that disclosure. For example, an employee may learn secret information about his or her employer during the course of his or her employment. The employer may expect this to be kept secret. But where this information reveals serious wrongdoing, it may be in the public interest for the employee to reveal it to the relevant authorities, and the media may have a legitimate interest in notifying the public. These latter rights involve considering the principle of freedom of expression and the public interest in disclosure of confidential information. In many cases, a balance of the competing interests is often very difficult to strike.

Injunctions

Many breach of confidence cases take the form of applications for injunctions. An injunction is a type of court order that either prohibits or compels a particular action. By way of example, where a celebrity becomes aware that a newspaper is going to publish a story about his or her private life, the celebrity may seek an injunction stopping the story being published in the first place. If the story has already come out, the celebrity may seek an injunction preventing any further publication. Important guidelines to courts deciding whether to issue injunctions in these cases were laid down by the Court of Appeal in the case of the adulterous footballer mentioned above, Gary Flitcroft. In accordance with these guidelines, the court must balance, on the one hand, the important right to private life and the confidentiality of the information, as against the important right of freedom of expression, which supports the newspapers' rights to publish stories. Anyone who wants to prevent publication of material by the media must pay very careful regard to the guidelines set out by the Court of Appeal and the particular factors that are considered relevant, including the status of the individual seeking the protection, the nature of the information that is to be disclosed and any relevant privacy codes that might apply to the media in question (considered further below).

If a person wishes to stop publication pending a full trial of the case, he or she is usually expected to give an undertaking to pay the defendant compensation if the action eventually fails. Since most people are unlikely to have the means to be able to give this kind of undertaking, such injunctions tend to be available only to the rich. If publication takes place before the plaintiff can act, the courts can still award damages or order the defendant to account for any profits made as a result of the disclosure.

It is hoped that actions for breach of confidence will result in the development of a coherent right to privacy that can offer protection to all people and not just those with deep pockets. Recent cases have demonstrated that if someone with a telephoto lens takes a picture of another person engaged in a private act (even from some distance), without their consent, the subsequent disclosure of the photograph may amount to a breach of confidence – in the same way as if that person had found or stolen a diary in which the act was recounted and proceeded to publish it.

3.3   SPENT CONVICTIONS AND REHABILITATION OF OFFENDERS

One particular kind of information that a person may understandably want to keep confidential is that relating to a past criminal conviction. On the other hand, some people may have a legitimate need to know about previous convictions. The Rehabilitation of Offenders Act 1974 (ROA) generally allows people to start with a clean slate after they have paid their debt to society, subject to a number of important exceptions.

How a conviction becomes spent

The way in which a conviction can become 'spent' under the ROA will depend upon the sentence received for the offence and the rehabilitation period that applies to that sentence. The principles apply to convictions in a criminal court, findings in a juvenile court, certain offences in service disciplinary proceedings and hospital orders under the Mental Health Act 1983.

The time required before the conviction is spent – the rehabilitation period – will be different depending upon the nature and length of the sentence, be it a term of imprisonment, a fine, probation, or an absolute or conditional discharge. Relevant rehabilitation periods are set out below.

The rehabilitation period always runs from the date of the conviction and will generally depend upon compliance with the sentence. When the sentence has been served and the applicable rehabilitation period has expired, that conviction will be 'spent' and usually will not need to be disclosed in the future, for example, when you are applying for a job, completing an insurance proposal form, or applying for credit facilities or a tenancy of property.

Relevant rehabilitation periods

Sentence	Rehabilitation period
Prison for more than 2½ years	Never
Prison for more than 6 months but less than 2½ years	10 years[*]

Dismissal with disgrace from Her Majesty's service	10 years[*]
A sentence of Borstal training	7 years
Prison for 6 months or less	7 years[*]
Dismissal from Her Majesty's service	7 years[*]
Imprisonment or detention in YOI or youth custody for 6 months or less	7 years[*]
Detention in respect of conviction in service disciplinary proceedings	5 years[*]
Fine	5 years[*]
Young offender detention for over 6 months but less than 2½ years	5 years
Probation order or community order	5 years
Hospital order under Mental Health Act 1983	5 years or 2 years after order ceases to have effect, whichever is the longer
Young offender detention for 6 months or less	3 years
Absolute discharge	6 months
Conditional discharge, binding over, care order, supervision order, reception order	1 year after making of order or 1 year after the order ends, whichever is the longer
Disqualification	The period of disqualification

[*]Note: These periods are reduced by half if the offender was under 18 at the date of conviction.

Excluded sentences

Convictions resulting in the following sentences can never become spent:

- A sentence of imprisonment, youth custody detention in a young offender institution or corrective training, for a term of more than two and a half years.
- A sentence of imprisonment for life.
- A sentence of preventive detention.
- Detention during Her Majesty's pleasure or for life or a sentence of custody for life.

New convictions and other principles affecting rehabilitation period

If you are convicted during the rehabilitation period of an offence that can only be tried by a Magistrates' Court, the new sentence will carry its own rehabilitation period and will not affect the earlier one. If the second offence is more serious and you receive a sentence covered by the ROA, the earlier conviction will become spent only when the later one becomes spent. If a person is given a sentence that can never become spent, this also prevents an earlier unspent conviction from becoming spent.

It is important to note that it is the *length of the sentence imposed by the court* that is relevant and not, for example, the length of time actually served in prison. A sentence counts in the same way whether you are actually sent to prison or the sentence is suspended.

Where a person receives two or more prison sentences in the course of the same court case, the rehabilitation period depends on whether the sentences are ordered to take effect concurrently – at the same time – or consecutively – one after another. As an example of what is meant by this, if two six-month sentences are concurrent, the offences are treated separately, giving each conviction a rehabilitation period of seven years. However, if the sentence is consecutive, they are treated as a single term of 12 months, with a rehabilitation period of ten years.

The effect of rehabilitation

Once the rehabilitation period has expired, not only do you not generally have to reveal the previous conviction, but it also cannot be revealed by anyone else without your permission. The objective is to put you in the position you would have been in if you had not committed the offence at all.

If someone maliciously and without lawful authority publishes or reveals to another person that you have a spent conviction, you may be able to recover damages for defamation.

Evidence in legal proceedings

A spent conviction cannot be used in evidence in a civil court, tribunal, arbitration or disciplinary or similar hearing. You should not be asked questions about spent convictions and, if you are, you need not answer them unless you wish to do so.

This does not apply in:

- Service disciplinary proceedings.
- Applications for adoption, custody, wardship or guardianship or in care proceedings.
- Where the court or tribunal is satisfied that justice cannot be done except by hearing evidence about the spent conviction.
- Criminal proceedings – however, the Lord Chief Justice has issued a practice direction requiring that no one should refer in open court to a spent conviction without the authority of the judge, whose authority should not be given unless 'the interests of justice so require'.

Provision of services

Some contracts, such as insurance policies, are governed by the legal principle that all relevant information must be disclosed by the person seeking insurance, whether or not it is asked for – otherwise the contract could be treated as invalid. Clearly, the existence of a driving offence or an offence of dishonesty could be relevant to an insurance company's assessment of the risk and the appropriate level of the premium. However, the ROA clearly states that your duty to disclose all relevant information does *not* extend to disclosing convictions that are spent.

Going abroad

The ROA applies only to the UK and has no effect so far as the laws of other countries are concerned. This means, for example, that applicants for immigration and work permits or for visas to countries such as the USA will be under a duty to disclose spent convictions – unless the law of the relevant country has an Act similar to the ROA, in which case the extent of your duty will often be made clear on the application form. If in doubt about the law of the country concerned, ask the relevant embassy or high commission in the UK.

Exceptions to the ROA

The ROA is often criticised for its many and wide exceptions to the general principle. If you fall within any of the exceptions, you will be treated as if the ROA had never been passed and you will not be entitled to rehabilitation for an otherwise spent conviction. These exceptions are listed in the Orders made by a relevant government minister and relate in particular to matters of national security, the care of those who are considered to be vulnerable and to the administration of justice.

Excepted professions, occupations and offices

There are exceptions to the general rule in the ROA that a person does not have to disclose a spent conviction. If you apply to join particular professions, or take up certain occupations or offices, you will normally be asked to disclose all previous convictions including spent ones – although you must be told why. Furthermore, a spent conviction, or the failure to disclose it, may be a good ground to exclude or dismiss you.

The following is a list of excepted professions, occupations and offices:

Accountant	Medical practitioner
Chiropractor	Nurse and midwife
Dealer in securities	Optician
Dentist, dental hygienist or dental auxiliary	Osteopath
Director, controller, etc.	Pharmaceutical chemist
of insurance company or building society	Police constable
Firearms dealer	Prison board of visitors
Judicial appointment	Prison officer
Justices' Chief Executive, Justices' Clerk	Probation officer
and assistants	Teacher
Lawyer	Traffic warden
Manager or trustee of unit trust	Veterinary surgeon

Other excepted occupations include:

- Any office or employment where the question about spent convictions is asked for the purpose of safeguarding national security – for example, if you wish to be employed by the UK Atomic Energy Authority, the Civil Aviation Authority or as an officer of the Crown.
- Certain types of work in health and social services where the work involves access to people over 65, people suffering from serious illness or mental disorder, alcoholics or drug addicts, blind, deaf or dumb people, persons who are substantially and permanently handicapped by illness, injury or congenital deformity, or where the work is concerned with the provision of care, recreation or leisure facilities, schooling, social services, supervision or training, to people under 18.
- Applications for certain certificates or licences – for example, those for firearms, explosives or gaming – require that your spent convictions must be disclosed and allow the licensing authority to take them into account. Failure to disclose a spent conviction could lead to the refusal or loss of the certificate or licence and even to prosecution.

Employment

Employers often wish to ask questions about a potential employee's previous convictions. The general rule under the ROA is that you can treat such questions as *not* relating to spent convictions (provided you are not concerned with the ROA's excepted professions, occupations or offices). If you decide not to disclose a spent conviction you cannot be denied employment or subsequently dismissed on the ground that you failed to disclose it. Likewise, failing to disclose a spent conviction is not generally a lawful ground for excluding you from any non-excepted office or profession. Nor can a spent conviction be a lawful ground for prejudicing you in the way you are treated in an occupation or employment.

If, therefore, you are excluded or dismissed from employment on the ground of a spent conviction, you may be able to take the matter to a court or to an industrial tribunal. However, you should first seek legal advice.

It has also been shown that a significant number of employers have been adopting a practice of asking prospective or existing employees to obtain a copy of their criminal record pursuant to rights under the Data Protection Act 1998 (DPA), which allows people to see records about themselves. There was concern that this type of indirect access of employers to personal information – known as 'enforced subject access' – circumvented the safeguards intended by the DPA and resulted in persons disclosing information to potential employers about spent convictions in circumstances where such information need not have been disclosed. See also Chapter 4.

Access to criminal records for employment purposes is now formalised in a statutory framework set up by the Police Act 1997 (PA). The new system involves a centralised procedure for criminal record checks for employment-related and voluntary appointment purposes. All checks are now carried out by the Criminal Records Bureau (CRB). A check can only be applied for with the knowledge and consent of the person who is the subject of the check. Each application will require payment of a fee. If you are required to make such an application, you should also find out who will be responsible for payment of this fee, that is, yourself or the potential employer. The CRB will then carry out the check by examining various databases and then issue one of three types of certificates, depending upon the nature of the check required. This in turn will depend upon the nature of the employment or voluntary appointment for which the person is applying.

(1) Basic-Level Check and Criminal Conviction Certificate

This check will be available upon request of the applicant for any type of employment or voluntary appointment. The Criminal Conviction Certificate should show only details of convictions – if any – that are unspent under the ROA. A copy of the certificate should only be provided to the person who is the subject of the check. It will then be up to that person to decide whether or not to show it to his or her potential employer. These types of certificate will not be job-specific and may be used more than once.

(2) Intermediate-Level Check and Criminal Record Certificate

This type of check will be available for any person seeking a position involving regular contact with persons under 18 years of age or with persons who may otherwise be vulnerable or for occupations that are excepted from the ROA, including nurses, lawyers, accountants, police officers and traffic wardens.

This check requires a joint application from both the relevant person and the potential employer or organisation seeking the check. The potential employer or organisation must be a registered person in order to be able to make such a joint application.

This type of check will result in the issue of a Criminal Record Certificate, which will provide information about both spent and unspent convictions and also police cautions, reprimands or warnings.

Where the position being sought involves close contact with children or other vulnerable individuals, the certificate will also contain details of whether the applicant is named on lists of those considered unsuitable to work with children held by the Department for Education and Skills and the Department of Health under the Protection of Children Act 1999 and Education Reform Act 1988.

If your name appears on these lists then you should have been informed at the time by the relevant Department that your name had come to its attention and why. You should also have been given the opportunity to make representations about the incident in question. There are rights of appeal to the Care Standards Tribunal – formerly known as the Protection of Children Act Tribunal – in respect of inclusion on these lists.

A copy of the resulting Criminal Record Certificate will be sent to both the applicant and to the registered potential employer or organisation who countersigned the application.

(3) High-Level Check and Enhanced Criminal Record Certificate

This type of check will be available for all those who are applying for work that regularly involves caring for, training, supervision or being in sole charge of those aged under 18 or vulnerable adults. The check will also be available for any person seeking registration as a child minder or day carer, or approval as a foster carer or parent, or seeking gaming or lottery licences or judicial appointments. Like an Intermediate-Level Check, it will require a joint application from the relevant person and the potential employer/organisation, which must itself be registered.

The check will result in the issue of an Enhanced Criminal Record Certificate, which will show all of the details contained on a Criminal Record Certificate – this will include unspent and spent convictions, cautions, reprimands and warnings and appearances on the Department of Education and Skills, and Department of Health lists. It may also show additional information held by the police that is not about convictions, but which the chief officer of the relevant police force considers relevant to the job or voluntary work sought.

This 'other relevant information' may include criminal intelligence information, records of acquittals and results of inconclusive police investigations as well as uncorroborated allegations from informants. Again, any such certificate will be provided to both the applicant and the potential employer/organisation. If the chief officer of the relevant police force considers that including the information on the certificate may prejudice interests of the detection or prevention of crime, it can be revealed *separately* to the potential employer/organisation and will not appear on the Enhanced Criminal Record Certificate at all. In such cases, the applicant for a certificate will be unaware that such relevant information has been provided, or of its content, and the potential employer/organisation will not be entitled to disclose that information to the applicant.

If you apply for any of these certificates and upon receipt discover that the main information contained in it is inaccurate, you have a statutory right to apply for a new certificate. Your application must be in writing. The CRB will then have to consider your application, and if it agrees that the certificate is inaccurate, it will be obliged to issue a new certificate. The CRB will not generally, however, be able to exercise editorial functions in respect of 'other relevant information' supplied by other bodies such as the police and included on an Enhanced Criminal Record Certificate. Where you consider that information is inaccurate or not relevant, you may wish to take up the matter with the relevant chief officer of the police force that disclosed the information.

If you have applied for an Enhanced Criminal Record Certificate and are concerned that the police may hold other relevant information that might be disclosed but which is not accurate or relevant, you may need to take legal advice on your ability to make representations or take action to prevent its disclosure in the future.

Consideration of disclosed information by prospective employers

It is for the prospective employer or particular organisation to decide upon your suitability for the position, taking into account only those offences and information that may be relevant to the particular job in question. They should consider such matters as the nature of the offence, when it occurred and its frequency. The fact that you have a criminal record does not automatically mean that you are unfit for particular employment or unfit to work with children or vulnerable adults.

All those registered bodies entitled to make joint applications for either an Intermediate- or High-Level Check will be required to adhere to a Code of Practice designed to ensure that the information released by the CRB is used sensibly and fairly. The registered body will be expected to have written policies on the recruitment of ex-offenders and to store certificates securely and dispose of them once used. They will also be expected to have proper procedures to ensure that the relevance of any conviction to the particular position is carefully assessed so that persons are not unfairly excluded from employment opportunities. Unfortunately, this Code of Practice will not apply to potential employers who require you to provide a Criminal Conviction Certificate.

If you are concerned that a prospective employer may take into account a conviction or entry upon a certificate that you consider to be irrelevant to the job applied for, you may wish to make representations to that employer in writing explaining the circumstances surrounding the entry and why you consider it to be irrelevant. If you are denied employment on the basis of that entry, you should seek legal advice: in limited circumstances, it may be possible to challenge the decision. In the case of a registered body relying upon a Criminal Record Certificate or Enhanced Criminal Record Certificate, a failure to adhere to the Code of Practice will clearly be relevant.

It is a criminal offence to make a false certificate, to alter an existing certificate, to use someone else's certificate as your own or to allow someone else to use your certificate as his or her own, with intent to deceive. It is also a criminal offence for a person to disclose information provided for the purpose of a Criminal Record

Certificate or Enhanced Criminal Record Certificate in an unauthorised manner and without the consent of the person to whom the certificate relates or other statutory authorisation.

The disclosure of information under these procedures and use of that information by prospective employers is subject to your rights to respect for privacy under Article 8. It is clear that disclosure and use of information about you will generally constitute an interference of your right to respect for privacy that will only be permissible if justified under Article 8(2). In many cases such interference may be for a legitimate aim since it will be directed at the prevention of crime, the protection of morals and the protection of the rights of others. Such interference must still, however, be necessary and proportionate to that legitimate aim. Blanket policies of disclosure, or disclosure of material that is plainly irrelevant to your particular circumstances, could well amount to a breach of Article 8 of the Convention.

Furthermore, disclosure of information that is untested and has not resulted in any criminal conviction – such as uncorroborated allegations from informants or criminal investigations – has the potential to amount to breaches of other basic rights such as the presumption of innocence contained in Article 6(2) of the Convention. This will invariably depend upon your particular circumstances and the method and purpose of the disclosure.

In January 2004 the High Court considered a Chief Constable's use of the powers of disclosure on an Enhanced Criminal Record Certificate. The court emphasised that the Chief Constable was required to exercise those powers carefully and carry out an assessment of the likely impact on the applicant of releasing any such information. Information released must be reliable, when viewed objectively. Significantly, where a Chief Constable has provisionally decided to release other relevant information, fairness will often require that the person affected should have an opportunity to make representations to the Chief Constable before that disclosure takes place. Where these principles of fairness are not observed, you may be able to challenge the issue of the certificate and the disclosure of the information and obtain a new certificate.

The adequacy of current vetting procedures for employees in jobs that bring them into contact with children and other vulnerable groups are currently under review. Following the trial and conviction of Ian Huntley in December 2003 for the murders of Jessica Chapman and Holly Wells, the Home Secretary announced an urgent public inquiry into these issues. Sir Michael Bichard was appointed as Chairman. The Bichard Inquiry took evidence from over 60 witnesses between December 2003 and March 2004. At the time of writing, its report is not concluded but is expected to take into account the public concern over the so-called Soham case, and to make far-reaching recommendations to 'significantly improve the ways in which children and other vulnerable people are protected from potential abusers'. Sir Michael will take the unusual step of reconvening the Inquiry six months after publication of this report to review progress made on implementing his recommendations.

For further information on the CRB:

Criminal Records Bureau
PO Box 91
Liverpool L69 2UH

Police disclosure of information

In addition to police disclosure of information for the purposes of certificates under the Police Act 1997 (dealt with above), the police may also be able to disclose information about you in certain circumstances whether or not information has been requested.

The fundamental rule is that police information – including information on convictions – should not be disclosed without the consent of the relevant person unless there are important considerations of public interest to justify departure from the general rule of confidentiality. This means that there must be a pressing social need and that the disclosure must be proportionate. Comments made in police interviews, for example, are in principle confidential and remain so even if not used in criminal proceedings. The police are not entitled to punish people and cannot do so by 'naming and shaming' people about whom they have information such as previous convictions.

Exceptions to the general principle of non-disclosure may arise where there is a need to:

- Protect vulnerable members of society.
- Ensure good and honest administration of the law.
- Protect national security.

In such circumstances, the police may be able to disclose information about you to other persons without your consent, including information on a person's past convictions, cases pending and other such background information as would be admissible in court.

The circumstances where the police will generally report convictions to particular types of employer or professional bodies (and also cautions where the job involves substantial access to children) are set out in paragraphs 11 and 12 and Schedule 2 of Home Office Circular 45/86: 'Police Reports of Convictions and Related Information'. Under this guidance, the police are asked to report convictions and cautions in cases of substantial access to children as and when they occur to the specified employers or supervising authorities on the basis that they may affect a person's suitability to continue in a profession or occupation, particularly where the offences involve violence, dishonesty, drink or drugs. The groups of persons affected include: British Telecom staff, Civil Aviation Authority staff, civil servants, dentists, lawyers, magistrates, medical practitioners, pharmaceutical chemists' staff (and various professions supplementary to medicine), post office staff, probation officers, social workers, teachers (including student teachers) and ancillary staff, UK Atomic Energy Authority staff, British Nuclear Fuels staff, and youth workers.

In accordance with the requirements of fairness and respect for Article 8 rights, disclosure of this type of information should generally be on notice to the person affected, who should be given a proper opportunity to make an application to the court before disclosure takes place if he or she believes the disclosure is unjustified. Moreover, the disclosure will need to be for a pressing social need and proportionate, and the police must consider each case on its own facts.

All the other parts of Circular 45/86 have been cancelled, and the Home Office has issued new guidance dealing with disclosure of information by the police in other circumstances, Circular 047/2003: 'Revised Arrangements for Police Checks'. This guidance provides that police checks for employment purposes should generally follow the procedures for disclosure of information through the CRB. It suggests that very exceptionally the police should be prepared to carry out emergency police checks where someone is likely to have substantial unsupervised access to the vulnerable and the CRB is unable to process the application within the time available.

Circular 047/2003 also identifies circumstances where the CRB procedures are not appropriate, including checks for jury service or other cases where disclosure to the individual person may not be appropriate. The circular emphasises that the governing principle in these cases is that the police must safeguard sensitive personal information, and must not disclose it to a third party unless there is good justification. Even if a case has been tried in open court and the subject of media reports, disclosure by the police for operational purposes will not be justified, whether it be conviction data or other intelligence. While the police have common law powers to disclose such information, disclosure is the exception. Any decision to disclose must be taken having regard to the ROA, the Data Protection Act 1998 and the HRA, and disclosure will constitute an interference with your Article 8 rights, which the police must be able to justify.

Annex B, Part 1 of Circular 047/2003 identifies those persons who will continue to be checked by the police *outside* the provisions of the CRB including motor salvage operators, parties to divorce and cohabitees or future marital partners at the request of a court welfare officer enquiring into child welfare issues, nuisance neighbours and parents to whom a local authority proposes to return a child in care.

Again, this area of the law is currently under review following the Soham case. As many of the concerns raised regarding Ian Huntley related not to his past convictions, but to *suspicions* about his previous behaviour, the Bichard Inquiry is reviewing the effectiveness of intelligence-based record-keeping and information-sharing between the police and other agencies.

Sharing information

Under section 115 of the Crime and Disorder Act 1998, as amended by the Police Reform Act 2002 (CDA), principles of information-sharing have been formalised. This section gives power to any person to disclose information to police authorities and chief constables, local authorities, probation committees, health authorities or persons acting on their behalf so long as such disclosure is necessary for the purposes of any provision of the CDA. These purposes include a range of measures, such as: local crime audits, anti-social behaviour orders, sex offender orders and local child-curfew schemes. In addition, the CDA requires local authorities to exercise their own functions with due regard to the need to do all that it reasonably can to prevent crime and disorder in its area.

The power to share information, however, does not override existing safeguards for disclosure of personal information contained in other legislation or the common law, such as defamation, data protection principles set out in the DPA and duties of confidentiality. If the information is covered by the DPA, information will need to be processed fairly and lawfully, only be disclosed in appropriate circumstances, be accurate and relevant, not be held longer than necessary and be kept securely. See also Chapter 4.

Where duties of confidentiality apply, the disclosure will only be justified if there is an overriding justification for breaching confidentiality. The principle of information-sharing only ensures that all persons have the *power* to disclose material, but does not impose any duty to do so. Decisions as to whether or not material should be disclosed will be subject to the principles discussed above and, in the cases of disclosures by a public authority, directly subject to the right to respect for private life contained in Article 8 of the Convention.

Many public authorities have issued protocols setting out the ways in which information is to be shared between organisations or bodies. An example is that of the Metropolitan Special Police Notice, 'The exchange of information under the Crime and Disorder Act'. If personal information about you has been, or is intended to be shared between public bodies, you should find out if there is any relevant protocol affecting the way in which such information is to be provided.

The Home Office has issued guidance on this information-sharing power, which can be found in chapter 5 of the Home Office Circular 9/1999: 'Guidance on Statutory Crime and Disorder Partnerships'.

Although theoretically the presumption should be in favour of the privacy of your information, and data sharing should only occur when in accordance with law, for legitimate reasons, and when necessary and proportionate, the political tide appears to be turning. In April 2002 the Prime Minister praised a report from the Performance Innovation Unit of the Cabinet Office that suggested a reversal of the current position – a new presumption *in favour* of data sharing unless good reason is shown not to do so. Similarly, the Children's Bill making its way through Parliament at the time of writing is based on an assumption that data should be shared, with little consideration given to differing levels of access to various public bodies. The Bill provides for the creation of databases that will hold information about all children in England and Wales and track their interaction with social workers, the police, the NHS and other public bodies. It is worth noting that these provisions of the Children's Bill have received heavy criticism from many organisations, including Liberty. It remains to be seen what form the final Act will take.

Unauthorised disclosure of convictions or other information
The ROA makes it an offence if:

- An official unlawfully discloses someone else's spent conviction, in the course of his or her official duties. The penalty is a maximum fine up to level 4 on the standard scale (currently £2,500).
- Any person who obtains details of a spent conviction from any official record by means of fraud, dishonesty or a bribe. The penalty is up to six months' imprisonment and/or a maximum fine up to level 5 on the standard scale (currently £5,000).

If someone wrongfully reveals that you have a spent conviction, you can:

- Report the matter to the police and ask that the incident be investigated with a view to prosecution of the person responsible.
- Consider suing the person concerned for defamation.
- Make a formal police complaint.
- Consider a claim for breach of confidence or infringement of your rights under Article 8.

You should seek legal advice about formal court action and note that public funding is not available for defamation actions.

Furthermore, the police and other bodies who hold confidential information are likely to owe duties to the provider of such information, for example, a police informer, to take reasonable care to prevent such confidential information being disclosed to the public unintentionally. If the police are negligent in the handling of such confidential information, you may be able to sue them for negligence and claim damages.

Sex Offenders Register

The Sex Offenders Act 1997, as amended by the Criminal Justice and Courts Services Act 2000 (SOA 1997), imposed a requirement on people convicted or cautioned in respect of sex offences, or found not guilty by reason of insanity, to notify the police of their name and address, date of birth, national insurance number, any change of address and qualifying periods of a stay away from home. This requirement was re-enacted with amendments in Part II of the Sexual Offences Act 2003 (SOA 2003), which came into force in mid-2004. The obligations dealt with below are those that arise under the SOA 2003 unless otherwise indicated.

Although the requirement has often been regarded as creating a 'paedophiles register', the definition of sex offences in Schedule 3 to the SOA 2003 (formerly Schedule 1 of the SOA 1997) is very wide and is not confined to offences against children or to non-consensual sex offences. However, for many of the offences listed, the requirement to notify is dependent on the sentence received. The requirement to notify the police of relevant details lasts for the time of the 'notification period', which runs from the date of conviction, order or caution and, again, the length of the notification period depends upon the sentence received. These are set as follows:

Sentence	Notification period
Imprisonment for life or for more than 30 months or admission to hospital under restriction order	Indefinitely
Imprisonment for more than 6 but less than 30 months	10 years
Imprisonment for 6 months or less, or admission to hospital without restriction order	7 years
Caution	2 years
Conditional discharge	Period of conditional discharge
Any other	5 years

Finite notification periods are halved if the person is under 18 when convicted or cautioned.

A person subject to a notification requirement must generally notify the police with the relevant information within three days of the date of conviction, order or caution. It will be an offence to fail to comply with the notification requirement, punishable on conviction by indictment to imprisonment for a term not exceeding five years or a fine or both, or on summary conviction, to a fine or a maximum of six months' imprisonment or both.

The notification requirement has been found not to amount to a retrospective penalty in contravention of rights under Article 7(1) of the Convention. The requirement also arises in respect of sexual offences committed outside the UK where the offence constituted an offence under the law in force in the country in question, and would have constituted a specified sexual offence if it had been committed in England and Wales.

Disclosure and use of information contained on this register will be governed by the same principles set out above and, in particular, the right to respect for privacy contained in Article 8 of the Convention.

The SOA 2003 abolishes offences of consensual sexual activity between men of consenting age and makes provision to abolish notification requirements for those previously convicted or cautioned in relation to sexual activity with a man who was aged 16 at the time. A person who was subject to a notification requirement for one of these offences in the past may apply to the Home Secretary for a decision to be taken as to whether or not the notification requirements should continue to apply. In making the decision, the Home Secretary must consider any representations included in the application and any available record of the investigation of the offence and of any proceedings relating to it that appear to him to be relevant. He is not, however, to seek evidence from any witness. Further guidance on this procedure can be obtained from looking at Home Office Circular 19/2004: 'The Removal of Offenders Convicted of Buggery and Indecency Between Men from The "Sex Offender Register" (Schedule 4, Sexual Offences Act 2003)'.

3.4   TELEPHONE TAPPING AND INTERCEPTION OF COMMUNICATIONS

Telephone tapping

It is an offence for any person intentionally, and without lawful authority, to intercept any communication in the course of its transmission through a public telecommunication system and – except in specified circumstances – through a private telecommunication system. This offence is established under the Regulation of Investigatory Powers Act 2000 (RIPA). This offence does not apply to stored communications, however, such as automatically recorded calls or messages on answering machines.

RIPA allows for the interception of telephone calls by appropriate authorities – for example, Security Service, Secret Intelligence Service, NCIS, GCHQ, Police or Customs – under authorisation of the Home Secretary. Such authorisation is provided by way of an interception warrant, which must name or describe either one person as the interception subject, or a single set of premises where the interception is to take place. In limited circumstances the Home Secretary may issue a 'certified' interception warrant, which can disapply some of the requirements of a normal warrant and, in particular, the requirement to specify a person or premises. These certified warrants should only normally be issued in relation to 'external communications' sent or received outside the UK. This could cover interception of communications channelled through a foreign Internet Service Provider (ISP).

The procedure to be followed and the information to be provided when seeking an interception warrant from the Home Secretary are set out in 'The Interception of Communications Code of Practice'. An interception warrant can only be issued if the Home Secretary believes that it is necessary for a reason relating to national security, serious crime or the economic well-being of the UK (the 'stated reasons') and it is proportionate in the circumstances. As well as balancing the intrusiveness of the interception against the operational need for it, the Home Secretary must consider whether the information sought could reasonably be obtained by other means. The Code of Practice also includes special rules regarding 'collateral infringement of privacy'. Tapping a telephone does not only infringe the privacy of the person who owns the telephone – the interception subject – it also affects anyone who calls or is called by that person. If communications relating to medical, religious, journalistic or legally privileged material are likely to be involved, the application for an interception warrant should draw attention to this as it will give rise to an unusual degree of collateral infringement of privacy. This is to be taken into account by the Home Secretary when considering the application.

An interception warrant is usually only valid for three months. A warrant may be renewed during this three-month period for a further six months if considered necessary for one of the 'stated reasons' above. These reasons are wide, and the scope for investigating the propriety of an official tap or intercept authorised by the Home Secretary is extremely limited. The Interception of Communications Commissioner (IOC Commissioner) is responsible for reviewing the way in which the Home Secretary exercises his powers to issue interception warrants, and publishes a report each year. However, the IOC Commissioner has no powers beyond this reporting function. RIPA establishes the Investigatory Powers Tribunal (IPT) which can investigate whether there was a warrant and, if so, whether it was properly issued. However, the complainant is not given access to the government's reasons and therefore is unlikely to have a proper chance to test whether the issue of the warrant was justified or not.

Where it is found that an interception warrant has been improperly issued, the IPT has power to order compensation and the destruction of the recorded material. If the interception took place without a warrant the only sanction is a criminal prosecution – to which the Director of Public Prosecutions must consent.

At present, interception warrants are intelligence-gathering tools only. RIPA prohibits material derived from interception warrants being adduced as evidence in court. This, however, is currently under review.

Duties on communication service providers

RIPA imposes duties on communication service providers to provide assistance to effect an interception authorised by an interception warrant. A statutory duty of confidentiality is imposed on the police, civil servants, postal and telecommunication workers to keep secret the contents of any interception warrant, the details of its issue and implementation, and everything in the intercepted material. It is an offence to give disclosure of any of this secret material, subject to specific defences including disclosure to legal advisers.

Other forms of acceptable interception

Apart from interception authorised by an interception warrant, interception will not be an offence under RIPA if the interception is carried out with 'other lawful authority' as defined by RIPA. This includes situations where the consent of both parties is obtained to a telephone conversation being recorded, or where there are reasonable grounds for believing that both parties have consented. It also includes situations where one party consents, and surveillance has been authorised under Part II of RIPA – a system known as 'participant monitoring'. This covers directed and intrusive surveillance and covert human intelligence techniques that might be used by the Police or the Intelligence services.

There are also other specified forms of lawful authority that may apply, such as interception pursuant to regulations made by the Secretary of State in relation to business communications or where the interception is carried out pursuant to other specific statutory powers such as under the Prison Act 1952 or the National Health Services Act 1977.

Stored communications may be accessed by means other than a warrant. They may be obtained with lawful authority through a search warrant or a production order (under the Police and Criminal Evidence Act 1984).

So far as private telephone systems are concerned, there will also be no criminal offence if the interception is conducted by the person who has the right to control the operation or use of the private telephone system, or another person who has the express or implied consent of such a person. While not an offence, this type of interception can give rise to civil liability under RIPA. Either party to an intercepted call on a private telephone system may bring a civil claim against the person who has intercepted the call, if there was no consent or no reasonable grounds for believing that there was consent to the interception. If you discover that your telephone calls on a private phone system have been intercepted without your consent or without notification that such interception might take place, then you may be able to claim against the person who intercepted them.

RIPA applies to calls made from cordless telephones and mobile telephones. It is also wide enough to cover e-mail, internet messages, text and pager messages as communications through a telecommunications system.

Interception of post
Under section 1 of RIPA, it is an offence to carry out intentional interception without lawful authority of any communication in the course of its transmission through any postal service. A person commits an offence if, without authorisation, he or she intentionally intercepts letters or packages sent to you through the mail.

Interceptions of this type are subject to the same system of authorisation that applies to interception of telecommunications, including interception warrants issued by the Home Secretary.

The term 'postal system' is defined in RIPA as a system that is offered, or provided to, a substantial section of the public in any one or more parts of the UK. It will probably therefore cover systems such as Document Exchange (DX), but it is unlikely to cover interception of purely internal mail at an office by an employer.

Obtaining and disclosing communications data
'Communications data' is a statutory term that covers a variety of information likely to be held by, or be available to, a 'communications service provider' such as a telephone company, postal company or ISP. Communications data is 'content-neutral data', which can include a customer's details such as name and address, and the types of communication that he or she has received or made but will not include the substance of those communications. For a telephone company, this will

include numbers called and how long calls lasted; for a postal company, it will include details of the type of post received so far as it can be ascertained from the outside of the item delivered; for an ISP it will include details of the websites visited. While access to this information will not involve intercepting a communication, it can still involve a substantial interference with your right to privacy. Such information will often reveal significant detail about your life, your interests and your activities.

Chapter II of Part I of RIPA is intended to regulate the ways in which such information can be obtained and disclosed by public authorities. The framework establishes a system for authorities such as the police to obtain authorisation to issue notices to a communications service provider requiring disclosure of certain information. In September 2003 the list of public bodies entitled to access types of communications data was greatly expanded, and now includes bodies such as the Food Standards Agency, the Charities Commission and the Gaming Board for Great Britain.

In order for an authorisation to be granted, it must be necessary and proportionate. In order to be 'necessary' one of the specified reasons must apply: national security; prevention or detection of crime; prevention of disorder; economic well-being of the UK; public safety; protection of public health; assessment or collection of tax or duty or other governmental charge; preventing, in an emergency, death or injury or damage to a person's health; or any other purpose specified by the Secretary of State by order. An authorisation may be granted by a 'designated person'. For each public authority entitled to access communications data, specific offices and ranks of people are designated as sufficiently senior to grant authorisations. The ranks and offices differ depending on the public authority: for example, a Regional Control Manager may grant an authorisation for the Welsh Ambulance Services, but at the United Kingdom Atomic Energy Authority Constabulary a Superintendent is needed.

It remains to be seen whether the broader grounds that appear to permit disclosure of potentially private information, and the absence of any real regulation of these authorisations and notices for disclosure of these data by an independent person or body, will prove to be compatible with the right to respect for privacy under Article 8. The authorisation process is subject to the monitoring of the IOC Commissioner, and complaints about such authorisation may be brought before the IPT in the same way that applies to interceptions. This system of accountability is subject to the same weaknesses identified in respect of interception.

Under Part 11 of the Anti-Terrorism, Crime and Security Act 2001, the Home Secretary has issued a Code of Practice relating to the *retention* of communications data held by communications providers. The Code of Practice is voluntary and advocates retention of information. The Home Secretary has power to make an order *requiring* such retention if, in his opinion, the voluntary code proves ineffective; he has already stated his intention to convert the voluntary code to a mandatory one so it is likely this power will be exercised.

3.5   SURVEILLANCE AND UNDERCOVER HUMAN INTELLIGENCE SOURCES

Bugging by the police was for many years subject only to Home Office guidelines published in 1984 – 'Guidelines on the Use of Equipment in Police Surveillance Operations'. However, the Police Act 1997 (PA) put police bugging on a statutory footing for the first time. Under the PA, the use of bugs by the police in relation to homes, offices and hotel bedrooms requires prior authorisation by a Commissioner – a serving or retired High Court judge – unless the need for surveillance is urgent in which case a Commissioner must be informed as soon as practicable.

Under the PA the police still did not need prior authority from a judge if the surveillance could be carried out without the need to go onto, or interfere with, private property. The use of such intrusive surveillance was subject only to a Code of Practice issued under section 101(3) of the PA. However, Part II of RIPA now regulates those areas of surveillance not covered by the PA and, in particular, surveillance and use of undercover human intelligence sources that do not involve physical interference, or entry onto property.

It is important to note that unlike the position for interception of communications, surveillance that is unauthorised under RIPA will not automatically be an offence or amount to a civil wrong. Accordingly, unless a civil wrong takes place within an established cause of action – such as where trespass to property has occurred – then the only action available for unauthorised surveillance will be a claim under the HRA that the public authority in question had failed to act compatibly with your rights under Article 8 of the Convention in carrying out the surveillance. In other words, no crime is necessarily committed if a listening device is placed in a bedroom without authorisation.

Part II of RIPA divides surveillance techniques requiring authorisation into three categories: directed surveillance; intrusive surveillance; and the use and conduct of covert human intelligence sources (CHIS). In all categories, the term 'covert' refers to behaviour calculated to ensure people subject to surveillance are unaware that it is or may be taking place. All three types of surveillance require different types of authorisation. Directed surveillance and use of covert human intelligence sources can be authorised on grounds wider than those for authorising interception of communications.

Directed surveillance

This is covert, but not intrusive, surveillance that is likely to reveal private information about a person (even though that person may not be specifically identified in relation to the operation) and that is not an immediate response to circumstances or events. It requires only internal authorisation by a designated person who believes it is proportionate to what is sought to be achieved. The necessary grounds are far broader than the Article 8(2) ECHR grounds: national security; prevention and detection of crime; prevention of disorder; economic well-being of the UK; public safety; protection of public health; assessment or collection of any tax, duty or other governmental charge; any other purpose specified by the Secretary of State by order.

Directed surveillance could include the bugging of a public place, the taking of photographs of someone in a public place, or even the use of listening devices or photographic equipment in respect of activities in a house, provided the equipment is kept outside the house and the equipment gives information of less quality and detail than devices that could have been placed in the house itself.

Intrusive surveillance

This is covert surveillance carried out by an individual or a surveillance device in relation to anything taking place on residential premises or in any private vehicle.

It also covers use of any device outside the premises or vehicle where it can give information of the same quality and detail as if the device were in the premises or vehicle. It does not cover location devices for vehicles (trackers).

Intrusive surveillance may be authorised only by the Home Secretary or one of a limited number of others, such as the Chief Constable of a police force. The grounds are narrower than for directed surveillance: first, it must be necessary for national security, prevention or detection of serious crime, or the economic well-being of the UK; secondly, its use must be proportionate to the end to be achieved, and the person considering authorisation must consider whether the information could reasonably be obtained using other means. All authorisations for intrusive surveillance are also subject to scrutiny by a Surveillance Commissioner, who must be notified as soon as reasonably practicable after the grant or cancellation of any authorisation. The authorisation will not take effect until the Surveillance Commissioner grants prior approval unless the case is urgent. The Surveillance Commissioner has power to quash any authorisation if the statutory requirements have not been met.

Surveillance for detecting use of televisions is not considered to be either directed or intrusive.

Covert human intelligence sources (CHIS)

This applies to information obtained by a person who establishes or maintains a personal or other relationship with a person for the covert purpose of using it to obtain or provide access to any information. This type of surveillance covers use of informants and undercover officers. Again, CHIS may be authorised by a range of designated persons, depending on the public authority carrying out the surveillance. The grounds are identical to those for directed surveillance, and the designated person must consider the use of CHIS proportionate. CHIS authorisations are subject to one additional requirement: there must be arrangements in place to ensure that: the source is subject to day-to-day responsibility by an appropriate officer; there is general oversight by another appropriate officer; there is an officer responsible for maintaining a record of the use made of the source; and there are restrictions on access to the records that disclose the identity of the source. The CHIS authorisation process is covered by Codes of Practice issued by the Home Office: the Code of Practice on Covert Surveillance and the Code of Practice on Covert Human Intelligence Sources.

Where CHIS use surveillance devices when acting undercover – that is, wires or hidden cameras – these devices are not considered 'intrusive' unless they are to be left on residential premises after the informant or undercover officer has left. Accordingly, authorisation for use of such devices where carried by a CHIS is not subject to the more stringent controls that should normally apply to this type of intrusive surveillance.

It remains to be seen whether the distinctions drawn between these different types of surveillance, and the different applicable safeguards, provide sufficient respect for private life. There may be occasions where surveillance falls into the category of directed surveillance – because, for example, the device used is not put onto residential premises and produces less clear results – but it is equally as intrusive as surveillance that might have been carried out by using devices placed in the residential premises themselves. 'Residential premises' is also a far more limited category than the broad definition of 'home' in the ECHR. In terms of the adequacy of the safeguards, while the publication of procedures such as the CHIS Codes of Practice may satisfy one of the requirements under Article 8 that such surveillance be in accordance with law, it remains to be seen whether the application of the procedures to particular cases will always meet the requirements of the Convention rights and be justified. For example, if the police carry out surveillance without prior authorisation on the grounds that it was urgent or because they have obtained the consent of a landowner but not the occupant – for example, a hotel owner but not the room occupant – then it is possible that this will be an unacceptable interference for the purposes of Article 8.

The Security Service and GCHQ

The Security Service Act 1989 gave the security service (MI5) legal recognition. Burglary and other interferences with property by the security service can only be authorised by the Home Secretary personally. The intrusion must be necessary to obtain information for one of MI5's functions. These are broadly defined as the protection of national security and safeguarding the economic well-being of the UK against threats posed by persons outside the country.

There is a complaints procedure in respect of authorisations by MI5 for intrusions onto property. Complaints may be made to a senior judge who is appointed to act as the Intelligence Services Commissioner – formerly the Security Service Commissioner. The IPT is the appropriate forum for challenging any other activity of the MI5. The Commissioner and IPT's powers are limited and the process denies the complainant a proper opportunity to hear the case against him or her.

The Intelligence Services Act 1994 – as amended by the Security Service Act 1996 and RIPA – sets up a similar complaints and tribunal procedure for the Security Intelligence Service (MI6), responsible for the foreign secret services and the Government Communications Head Quarters (GCHQ), the government's listening centre. It also set up a parliamentary committee to supervise the work of all three security services. Unfortunately, none of these is likely to provide any significant level of accountability for the activities of these bodies.

2.6   OTHER TYPES OF SURVEILLANCE

CCTV surveillance

Closed circuit television (CCTV) systems have been set up in many towns and cities, usually by local authorities and often in partnership with the police. Despite its prevalence CCTV is still not regulated expressly by statute. A decision of the ECHR concerning use of CCTV footage of a public street demonstrates that you nevertheless still have certain rights in respect of such information and that a public authority may act incompatibly with your rights if it misuses CCTV footage.

Use of CCTV systems by private or public bodies may also be subject to the requirements of the Data Protection Act 1998 (DPA). The DPA covers information that relates to an individual. Until recently, the DPA was thought to cover most CCTV use as it related to individuals who were captured on camera. However, a recent Court of Appeal case has shown that the scope of the DPA is far narrower than was previously thought. It is now clear that only certain CCTV activities are covered. The court decided that for information to relate to an individual, it had to affect their privacy. To help judge this, the court decided that two matters were important: (1) a person had to be the focus of the information and (2) the information must tell you something significant about them. Whether or not the DPA covers a CCTV system thus depends on how it is used. If a particular person is intended to be the focus of CCTV and the information from the CCTV tells one something significant about that person, the data from the CCTV are likely to be covered by the DPA and the operator's use of CCTV must comply with the provisions of the DPA.

Basic CCTV systems, such as those in a shop for security purposes, are now unlikely to be covered provided that the operator is not using the images for checking on staff. If, however, the CCTV is used remotely to zoom in on people, or for monitoring particular individuals, or the film recorded is used for anything other than for providing to law enforcement bodies, then the CCTV is likely to be covered by the DPA. The Information Commissioner has issued additional CCTV guidance in light of the Court of Appeal case.

Recording

It is not an offence for one party to a telephone call to make a recording of it, even if the other party is unaware of what is being done. Indeed, this can often be a useful way of proving that someone has been making malicious or nuisance calls. However, the evolving doctrine of breach of confidence that is wide enough to cover concepts of privacy may well mean that a person can be stopped from revealing what was said and recorded in such a situation, if it was apparent that the conversation was confidential, and if there is no public interest in such disclosure or the invasion of the person's privacy is otherwise unjustified.

Similarly, use of recorded information, as with use of photographs containing confidential information, may well be subject to the requirements of the DPA.

Claims in respect of other surveillance

In respect of all these types of potential interferences with your private life by the State or state agencies (public authorities) there will be a requirement that they must satisfy the requirements of Article 8, namely, that any interference is in accordance with the law, for a legitimate objective, and proportionate.

In respect of interference with your private life by private individuals of the types mentioned above, the developing law of breach of confidence could well provide further protection. You may be able to stop distribution of recordings of conversations or events in a public place if it is apparent that the conversation was confidential. The publication of photographs of private acts, obtained for example by a telephoto lens, may be restrained through the breach of confidence doctrine or through claims under the DPA. Even filming of a person or a company's operations in a public place where the public has free access may amount to an interference with privacy, which could be restrained under the law using Article 8 of the Convention. If you think you have been the subject of intrusive surveillance of any type, then you should take further advice in the light of the latest developments.

3.7   INVESTIGATION OF ELECTRONIC DATA PROTECTED BY ENCRYPTION

Encryption protects electronic messages from unauthorised access and use, which is particularly important for secure internet and e-mail use. Increased use of encryption technologies has prompted the Government to enact controversial legislation allowing access to electronic data protected by encryption.

In order to open an encrypted message, an electronic 'key' is needed. Under Part III of RIPA, there is power for authorised persons to serve a 'Section 49 Notice' on a person. The notice can be used to require a person to provide information, which may be protected by a key where such disclosure is necessary in the interests of national security, for the prevention or detection of crime or in the interests of the economic well-being of the UK, or for securing the effective exercise by any public authority of any statutory power or duty. No notice should be issued unless it is proportionate and it is not reasonably practicable to obtain the information without giving notice.

The notice must be in writing and must specify the nature of the protected information sought. The person who receives the notice will then be entitled to use the key in his or her possession to obtain access to the encrypted information, and then to disclose that information in intelligible form. This process will not require disclosure of the key itself. Disclosure of the key itself may be required, but only where there are special circumstances where to direct otherwise would defeat the object of the disclosure, and the requirement for disclosing the key is proportionate.

Authorisation for the issue of such notices must be obtained in accordance with the requirements of Schedule 2 of RIPA.

The ability to obtain access to encrypted messages represents a significant interference with the right to private life, as well as potentially undermining the effective development of e-commerce. It remains to be seen how the courts will look at the use of such powers to obtain disclosure of sensitive material in light of Article 8 of the Convention.

3.8   USE OF PHOTOGRAPHS, FINGERPRINTS, DNA SAMPLES AND OTHER SAMPLES TAKEN AT POLICE STATIONS

Under the Police and Criminal Evidence Act 1984 (PACE), the police have wide powers to take photographs, fingerprints and body samples of persons without their consent where they had been charged with, or convicted of, a recordable offence. These powers have been considerably extended by amendments contained in the Criminal Justice Act 2003. Under the new powers, the police may also take fingerprints and body samples without consent where a person has been detained in consequence of an arrest for a recordable offence (before charge).

Previously, fingerprints and DNA samples taken would have to be destroyed in the event of the person being acquitted, or if the charges were dropped or not pursued. Following amendments to PACE by the Criminal Justice and Police Act 2001, the police now have powers to retain fingerprints and DNA samples lawfully taken from any person – regardless of whether or not they are subsequently convicted of an offence. These records will then be held on databases, but should be used for subsequent detection of crime only.

There was significant concern that this power was incompatible with the right to respect for private life under Article 8 of the Convention, but the Court of Appeal has recently upheld this power in its application to retained fingerprints and samples taken from persons charged with recordable offences. This decision is being appealed to the House of Lords, who will hear the appeal in July 2004. It appears that it will be normal policy for most police forces in the UK to retain fingerprints and DNA samples.

The power to take photographs of suspects and thereafter to retain these photographs for the prevention or detection of crime has recently been extended by amendments to PACE brought about by the Anti-Terrorism, Crime and Security Act 2001. Under a new section, section 64A of PACE, the police have wider powers to take photographs, and to retain these photographs even where the suspect is subsequently released, not charged or acquitted of an offence. It remains to be seen whether this power, involving a more direct interference with Article 8 through the visual identification of individuals, would be found to be similarly compatible with the rights under Article 8 as in the case of fingerprints and DNA samples.

See also Chapter 5.

3.9   HARASSMENT, UNWANTED LETTERS AND TELEPHONE CALLS

Under the Telecommunications Act 1984, it is a criminal offence to leave grossly offensive messages over the telephone or make indecent or obscene or menacing telephone calls or calls that cause annoyance, inconvenience or needless anxiety. The criminal courts may in certain circumstances treat such harassment as grievous bodily harm if psychological damage results. If the perpetrator is known and is persistent in making calls the courts are increasingly willing to grant injunctions to prevent this type of harassment. It is also established that the making of numerous obscene telephone calls to a considerable number of people may be conduct capable of constituting a public nuisance.

It was previously hoped that the courts would be willing to develop the law of nuisance – the legal category into which many of these claims fall – so as to grant rights of protection to people in respect of property that they do not own. This would have enabled the law to move towards openly protecting domestic privacy. However, this advance was halted by a decision of the House of Lords. The Protection from Harassment Act 1997 (PHA) attempted to remedy this gap in the law. The PHA makes it a criminal offence to pursue a course of conduct that amounts to harassment of a person. The PHA also creates a civil statutory tort of harassment, which enables a person to obtain a civil court injunction to stop harassment occurring and to claim damages where appropriate. This is a very important piece of legislation, which can potentially provide protection in neighbourhood disputes, cases of racial harassment, bullying at work, confrontation with the media or stalking, as well as hate mail and persistent unwanted telephone calls.

Harassment is not defined in the PHA, and so it will be a matter for assessment based on the facts in each case. It is important to note that there must be a 'course of conduct' in order to bring a claim. This means that there must be at least two incidents representing harassment – more than one telephone call – and the person who is carrying out the harassment must know or ought to know that it would amount to harassment. It has been established that a publication of a series of newspaper articles by a newspaper can constitute a course of conduct amounting to harassment.

The PHA was amended by the Criminal Justice and Police Act 2001 with effect from 1 August 2001 to make it clear that the PHA protects an individual from *collective* harassment by two or more people. This amendment remedied a potential loophole where two or more people each carried out only one act of harassment.

The Home Office has issued guidance to the police on the PHA explaining its importance in protecting people from harassment. The guidance is contained in Home Office Circular 28/2001: 'Protection from Harassment Act'.

Hate mail is usually anonymous, but if it can be traced the sender can also be prosecuted under the Malicious Communications Act 1988, which makes it an offence to send a letter or other article that conveys an indecent or grossly offensive message or a threat, or which contains information known to be false and the purpose of the letter is to cause distress or anxiety. The category of communications covered by the Malicious Communications Act 1988 has been expanded by the Criminal Justice and Police Act 2001 to include electronic communications or articles of any description. This new definition will cover hate telephone calls, e-mails or text messages. The defence to such an offence has also been amended so that it will be necessary to show that a demand made in such a communication was made on reasonable grounds, and the person making it held an honest and reasonable belief that the threat made was a proper means of reinforcing that demand.

Prior to the Unsolicited Goods and Services Act 1971, 'inertia selling' was common. The technique was to send goods to customers who were then charged for them if they did not go to the trouble of returning them. Regulation of inertia selling is now covered by the Consumer Protection (Distance Selling) Regulations 2000, which came into force on 31 October 2000. Under these regulations, a recipient of unsolicited goods may keep them as free gifts. The regulations also make it an offence for a sender to try and obtain payment for such goods. The Unsolicited Goods and Services Act 1971 continues to make it an offence to send obscene or indecent books, magazines, leaflets or advertising material describing or illustrating human sexual acts.

Relatively new forms of harassment of a similar type include faxing, e-mailing and text messaging. These types of persistent harassment can be annoying and distressing. If you are subject to this form of harassment, you should consider reporting the matter to the police for the purposes of a criminal prosecution under the Malicious Communications Act 1988 or the PHA, as well as considering bringing your own action under the PHA. In the case of faxes or text messages, you can also contact your telephone service provider and request them to assist in tracing the source of the unwanted faxes and texts. In the case of e-mails, you can also contact your ISP for a similar purpose. If the irritating e-mails are marketing 'spam', and sent from Europe, they may be covered by the Privacy and Electronic Communications (EC Directive) Regulations 2003. They came into force in the UK on 11 December 2003. The Regulations make e-mail marketing 'opt-in' in many cases (the recipient must have given prior consent) and provide greater privacy protection in cyberspace. The Information Commissioner is in charge of enforcing these Regulations.

Intrusion or harassment by neighbours and others

In many respects the laws that protect you from the harassment of neighbours and others in respect of property you own or occupy is based on the principle that every person's home is their castle. The right to keep others out of your property is one of the defining characteristics of property ownership or occupation. Those who are fortunate enough to own or rent their home are entitled to injunctions to prevent intrusion and damages to compensate for trespass. Harassment of tenants by their landlords for the purpose of encouraging the tenants to leave can be particularly expensive for landlords. Under the Housing Act 1988 the tenants can claim the additional value that the house or flat has for the landlord with vacant possession. Harassment of this kind, calculated to cause an interference with a tenant's peaceful enjoyment and comfort within the property, can also be a criminal offence under the Protection from Eviction Act 1977.

Neighbours who do not physically intrude on your property may nonetheless make life intolerable in a variety of ways. Unreasonable use of their neighbouring land can amount to an actionable wrong in the tort of private nuisance. This might be anything from the growing of plants and shrubs that adversely affect your property to the keeping of noisy animals. Again an injunction or a claim in damages can be used to restrain such behaviour. It could also be the subject of a claim under the PHA as indicated above.

People who come to your door to sell goods, ask you to give to a charity, persuade you to support a particular religion or political party or ask questions for a market research survey have no right to enter your home. You can refuse to talk to them and they must leave when you ask them to.

Harassment that occurs outside the confines of your own home or in places that you yourself do not own can form the basis of a claim under the PHA, provided the harassment concerned amounts to a course of conduct. There are many possible instances of such harassment, such as confrontation by a person in a public place or persistently following someone. In such cases, you may wish to consider reporting the matter to the police for the purposes of bringing criminal proceedings as well as considering bringing your own civil action in order to obtain an injunction to prevent that person from continuing with their behaviour.

Where harassment occurs through offensive behaviour at work, the same remedies under the PHA are potentially available. If you find yourself subject to this form of harassment, you should normally follow any procedures of reporting suggested by your employer – reporting to an appropriate senior manager or union representative. You may also have a claim against your employer in the Employment Tribunal. You should take legal advice in these circumstances.

3.10   POWER OF OFFICIALS TO ENTER YOUR HOME

Officials are subject to different rules of procedure because each is governed by a different statutory source, and there is no general code that covers their conduct. Normally any official must produce evidence of identity and authority before entering and may not insist on entering without first giving you at least 24 hours' notice. If, after such notice, you refuse to let him or her in, the Magistrates' Court may give authority to enter without your consent, by force if necessary. In general, if someone asks to come into your home, claiming to be an official, you should:

- Ask to see the caller's identity card.
- Ask the caller what authority he or she has to enter your home.
- If in doubt, refuse entry and contact the office from which the official claims to come, in order to check his or her credentials.

If you have a complaint to make about the way an official behaves, you should approach the appropriate authority. For example, in the case of a local authority official, you should complain to your local councillor, in the case of a gas or electricity official, the gas or electricity company. In the case of a VAT inspector, the collector in charge of VAT at the local office or, in the case of a tax inspector, the Commissioners for the Inland Revenue. There may also be the possibility of a complaint to an official regulator or an ombudsman. See also Chapter 2.

It is also important to remember that all public authorities seeking to exercise powers of entry under various Acts will still be required to act compatibly with Article 8 rights as incorporated by the HRA. This means that whenever a decision is made that will result in an intrusion of your privacy – a decision to enter into your home without your consent – then the public authority must do so in accordance with the law and for one of the legitimate objectives. Also the nature of the entry must be proportionate to the need for such entry. It may well be possible to challenge a decision to enter your home if the public authority concerned does not observe these principles.

Fire Brigade

A member of a local authority fire brigade who is on duty – or a police officer – may enter any premises where a fire has broken out, or where there is reason to believe a fire has broken out. Other premises, such as neighbouring houses, may also be entered if this is necessary for fire-fighting purposes. The fire officer can force entry if necessary. The permission of the owner or occupier does not have to be obtained. Under the Fire Services Act 1947, it is an offence to obstruct or interfere with any member of a fire brigade who is involved in fighting a fire and the maximum penalty is a fine of level 3 (currently £1,000).

Gas and Electricity Boards

An official of a gas or electricity company may enter your home if:

- You agree to let the official enter.
- A magistrate has given the official a warrant authorising the official to enter.
- There is an emergency and the official has reason to believe that there is danger to life or property.

A gas or electricity board official is entitled to ask to enter your home, or to apply to a magistrate for a warrant, in order to:

- Inspect the meter or any other fittings.
- Disconnect the supply in certain circumstances.

In order to obtain a warrant, the official must show that:

- You have been given at least 24 hours' notice; and
- He or she has asked to be admitted and you have refused; or
- The premises are unoccupied.

Entry must be at a reasonable time and the official must leave the house as secure against trespassers as it was when he or she arrived, and make good any damage caused.

It is a criminal offence to obstruct a person who has a warrant or who asks to be admitted in an emergency; the maximum penalty is a fine on level 3 (currently £1,000). It is not an offence to refuse to let the official enter if there is no emergency and the official does not have a warrant – Rights of Entry (Gas and Electricity Boards) Act 1954; Electricity Act 1989 and Gas Act 1995.

Water companies
An authorised official of a water company may enter any premises at a reasonable hour in order to:

- Inspect water meters.
- Ascertain whether there has been any contravention of the law relating to water supplies.
- Detect waste or misuse of water.

In the first two cases (but not the last) 24 hours' notice must be given. Entry can be obtained in an emergency or under a warrant.

Housing
An official authorised by the local authority may enter any house in the area at any reasonable time in order to:

- Make a valuation or survey, where a compulsory purchase order is being considered or has been issued.
- Examine the premises and make a survey where a notice requiring repairs, a demolition order, a closing order or a clearance order has been issued.
- Measure the rooms, etc., to determine whether there is or has been overcrowding.
- Ascertain whether there is or has been a contravention of the Housing Act regulations.

The official must have a written document of authority and must give at least 24 hours' notice. Under the Housing Act 1985, it is an offence to obstruct the official, providing the official is authorised and has given notice; the maximum penalty is a fine at level 2 (currently £500).

Planning
An authorised local authority official may enter premises at any reasonable time for various planning purposes, including:

- Preparing or approving development plans.
- Dealing with applications for planning permission.
- Making a valuation in connection with compensation.
- Making a survey in connection with a compulsory purchase order.
- Investigating whether development has occurred without planning permission.

The official must give 24 hours' notice. The local authority must also pay compensation for any damage caused. Under the Town and Country Planning Act 1990, it is an offence to obstruct the official, provided that proper notice has been given; the maximum penalty is a fine at level 2 (currently £500).

Rating

A local assessor may enter any property in the area in order to carry out a survey or make a valuation for the purposes of drawing up rating valuation lists. The official must give three days' notice. Under the Local Government Finance Act 1992 it is an offence to obstruct the official provided that proper notice has been given; the maximum penalty is a fine at level 2 (currently £250).

Social Security

An inspector may enter business premises at any reasonable time in order to interview employers, employees and self-employed people about their contributions record. It is an offence not to produce National Insurance Certificates or other relevant documents. It is also an offence to refuse to answer the inspector's questions, except that you are not obliged to give information that will incriminate yourself or your spouse – this does not include a so-called common law husband or wife. The maximum penalty for either offence is a fine at level 3 and a further limited fine for each day that the offence continues.

An investigator – such as an official trying to find out if a person is cohabiting – does not have a right to enter your home. If the official forces entry, or refuses to leave after you ask him or her to do so, he or she is committing a trespass and you may be able to take legal action.

Tax

A tax inspector can obtain a warrant from a circuit judge if he or she reasonably suspects that an offence involving serious fraud in relation to tax has been committed. The warrant authorises the inspector to enter and search private premises and remove documents. Under the Taxes Management Act 1970, any application for a warrant must be made with the approval of a Commissioner for the Inland Revenue.

VAT

A VAT official may enter any premises at a reasonable time for any purposes connected with administering value added tax. The official may enter without a warrant, and may also inspect goods, which are liable to tax. If the official has reasonable grounds for suspecting you of an offence related to VAT, he or she may apply to a magistrate for a warrant authorising him or her to:

- Enter, by force if necessary, at any reasonable time within 14 days of the warrant being issued.
- Seize any documents relating to the investigation.
- Search any people on the premises – women can only be searched by women.

Under the Value Added Tax Act 1984, obstructing a VAT official could amount to an assault for which you could be prosecuted.

Mental health

Under the Mental Health Act 1983 an approved social worker may at all reasonable times enter and inspect any premises in which a mentally disordered person is living if there is reasonable cause to believe that he or she is not being properly cared for. The social worker must produce identity if requested.

Magistrates have the power to issue a warrant authorising a police officer to enter premises – by force, if necessary – if they have reasonable cause to suppose that a mentally disordered person is being ill-treated there, or is unable to look after himself or herself. A social worker and a doctor must accompany the police officer.

Infectious diseases and illness

In the case of notifiable diseases – e.g. plague and cholera – a magistrate may make an order for the compulsory medical examination of suspected sufferers and carriers, and for the removal to and detention in hospital of anyone suffering from such a disease where it appears that proper precautions are not being taken to prevent the spread of the disease – Public Health (Control of Diseases) Act 1984. AIDS is dealt with similarly to notifiable diseases, but slightly less stringently; there is no provision for compulsory examination provided the suspected sufferer or carrier is already receiving treatment from a doctor.

On a certificate from the appointed local authority officer, the local authority may serve notice on an occupier to disinfect or destroy articles likely to retain infection within a fixed period, if doing so would tend to prevent the spread of any infectious disease. The occupier has 24 hours to inform the local authority that he or she will comply, failing which the local authority has the right to enter and to do the necessary work. The occupier can be forced to reimburse the local authority, and the provision for compensation for the destroyed articles is not very satisfactory. Where an infectious disease occurs in a house, the local authority may also, at its own cost, remove persons from the premises, acting with a magistrates' warrant if there is no consent. This is not limited to the notifiable diseases mentioned above.

Magistrates also have the power to issue a warrant authorising an officer of a local authority to enter premises to remove to hospital persons who are so chronically ill or old as to be unable to look after themselves, and who are not being properly looked after by others. Seven days' notice to the person of such an application must be given – National Assistance Act 1948.

The Civil Contingencies Bill, being considered by Parliament at the time of writing, enables the Queen through Order in Council (or a Government Minister if this is not practicable) to make regulations to deal with an 'emergency' that has occurred or is about to occur. The term 'emergency' is defined very broadly and includes a situation that threatens serious damage to public welfare in the UK – an epidemic could fall within this definition. The Bill specifies a non-exhaustive list of provisions that may be included in the emergency regulations, including, among other things, forced movement to or from a particular place or forcing/prohibiting travel at particular times.

Pests and vermin

The occupier of land is under an obligation to notify the local authority if rats or mice in substantial numbers live on or resort to the land. The local authority may serve notice on the owner or occupier (or both) of land, including buildings, requiring them to take specified steps within a specified time to keep the land free of mice or rats.

Where premises are so filthy or unwholesome as to be prejudicial to health, or are verminous, the local authority may require corrective measures, including, for example, disinfecting or the removal of wallpaper. If necessary, the notice may require the occupiers of infested premises, and neighbouring premises that might be affected, to vacate the premises while gas is employed to destroy vermin. In such a case, the local authority must provide temporary alternative accommodation at its own expense.

It is an offence to disobey the notice – maximum penalty a fine at level 1 (currently £200), or level 3 (currently £1,000) in the case of a mice or rat notice. In the event of disobedience, the local authority also has the power to enter the land to do the work itself – Public Health Act 1936, Prevention of Damage by Pests Act 1949.

Foster homes

A local authority can authorise someone, for example a social worker, to inspect any home where a child is being fostered. The inspector must produce an official document, showing that he or she has the right to enter. It is an offence to refuse to allow the inspector to enter; the maximum penalty is a fine at level 3 (currently £1,000) – Children Act 1989.

Search orders

The courts have the power to issue a form of civil search warrant called a Search Order. This type of order was previously developed by the courts and known as an Anton Piller order – based on the title of a case of the same name. Authority to grant a Search Order is now contained in section 7 of the Civil Procedure Act 1997.

A Search Order is a form of injunction that requires a party to permit entry for certain persons to property in order to conduct a search for, and if necessary to seize, evidence. Such orders are often made in cases involving pirate goods, such as unauthorised video copies of popular films. These are usually applied for and obtained from the court without notice to the person who is intended to be the subject of the order in order to ensure that there is no prospect of evidence being removed or destroyed before the search can take place. However, a Search Order can be issued in any case where the court is persuaded that the defendant is the sort of person who might destroy relevant evidence in his or her possession if the order is not made.

Strictly speaking, a Search Order is not a search warrant because it does not directly empower the holder to enter or search premises. Instead, it requires the person in charge of the premises to let the holder in. The order has much the same effect as a search warrant, however, since it is a contempt of court to refuse to let the holder in.

A Search Order must be served by a supervising solicitor, but it will usually allow him or her to be accompanied by others. Those persons specified in the Search Order may only accompany the supervising solicitor. The supervising solicitor should be experienced in the area, and should not be a member or employee of the firm acting for the person who obtains the Search Order.

If you are served with a Search Order, ask the supervising solicitor for an explanation of what is going on: he or she has a duty to offer to explain the effect of the order to you fairly and in everyday language. Take a good look at the terms and conditions attached to the order, many of which explain your rights in the situation. For example, you will normally be entitled to refuse entry before 9.30 a.m. or after 5.30 p.m. or at all on Saturday and Sunday, unless the Search Order expressly states otherwise. The supervising solicitor must give you an opportunity to take legal advice. In view of the seriousness of the matter, it would be sensible to do so.

It is likely to be a very rare case in which your lawyer would advise you not to comply with the order, but you are entitled to apply to the court to ask for it to be varied or set aside, provided you do so immediately. You will, however, be required to allow the supervising solicitor to enter your premises and remain there while you make such an application.

Nearly all Search Orders will contain a provision forbidding you to tip off others – apart from your lawyer – about their existence. Often the person who has obtained the Search Order will have put in place means of telling whether others have been tipped off. He or she may have persons watching for such activity and, if you were caught arranging for others to dispose of inconvenient evidence, you would risk prison for contempt of court.

If you are an unaccompanied female and the supervising solicitor is male, then at least one other person named in the Search Order must be female and accompany the supervising solicitor on his search. Only materials covered by the terms of the Search Order may be removed from your property. If, however, such materials include items that exist only in computer-readable form, then you will be required to give access to the computers with all necessary passwords to enable them to be searched. The search may only be conducted in your presence or someone who is your responsible employee.

The supervising solicitor is under a strict duty to behave responsibly. In one case where it was held that the solicitor acted oppressively, he was ordered to pay substantial compensation.

Bailiffs
Bailiffs are officers of the court, although private companies may employ them, and their job is to seize property. Courts can make a variety of orders, which are enforced by bailiffs. Their rights to enter your home are complex and will depend on the order made by the court. In virtually all cases they are entitled to enter your home, but only in a few cases, such as eviction orders, are they entitled to break down external doors or force their way in. They can, however, climb through unlocked windows and break down internal doors and may put pressure on you to invite them in.

If they are employed by the court following a judgment debt they can seize any goods or possessions belonging to the debtor but cannot seize anything needed personally for his or her job – for instance, tools, books and vehicles – or used for basic needs – clothing, bedding, furniture, household equipment and food. Thus they can take stereo equipment, televisions, video recorders etc. Bailiffs cannot seize property belonging to people other than the debtor. The goods are then usually impounded for a short period – five days – before being sold by auction. Often the goods are left on the premises until sold. This is known as taking walking possession. If walking possession has been taken, then baliffs may subsequently break locks to gain access to the house to take full possession of the goods.

3.11   SEARCHES BY CUSTOMS AND EXCISE OFFICIALS

Approximately 40,000 travellers each year are stopped and bodily searched at customs points throughout the UK under powers conferred by the Customs and Excise Management Act 1979. The nature of the search may take a number of forms, from a pocket search to a full strip or intimate body search. Most people find such searches distressing and humiliating, and frequently ask the question 'Why me?'

When may you be searched?

A customs officer may ask to search you or anything you have with you if he or she reasonably suspects that you are carrying:

- Any item that is liable to excise duty or tax that has not been paid; for example, perfume, alcohol, cigarettes, in excess of the duty-free allowance.
- Any item that is prohibited or restricted from being imported or exported; for example, illegal drugs.

A request to search you does not mean that you are under arrest; it means that you are to be detained while a search is carried out. If you are placed under arrest, you must be told.

Length of detention

How long you may be detained for will depend on the circumstances, but in all circumstances the length of detention must be reasonable and not exceed the time taken for the actual search, which is usually completed in under ten minutes. If you decide to leave before being searched, the customs officer may let you go or you may be arrested. You may also be charged with the offence of obstructing or impeding a customs officer.

What amounts to reasonable suspicion?

A customs officer does not have to be certain that you are carrying an unlawful item in order to justify a search. But there must be some concrete basis for the officer's suspicion that relates to you. The mere fact that you have arrived from a particular destination, that you are dressed in a certain way or that you are carrying particular items such as condoms, cigarette papers or petroleum jelly, which could be associated with drug use or drug trafficking, is not in itself sufficient justification. However, a combination of these or other facts, such as suspicious behaviour, an unusual quantity of luggage, unexplained journeys abroad, etc., may give rise to enough reasonable suspicion to justify you being searched.

What must you be told?

The customs officer must tell you what you are suspected of: for example, 'I have reasonable grounds to suspect that you are carrying illegal drugs.' Although you should ask why you are suspected of a particular offence, the customs officer does not, in fact, have to tell you.

If you are asked to submit to a rub-down search, you must be told that you have the right to go before a senior customs officer if you do not agree with the search. In the case of a strip or intimate search, you must be told that you have the right to be taken before either a senior customs officer or a magistrate who will then decide whether or not the search should take place.

Going before a senior customs officer or magistrate

If you decide to exercise your right to go before a senior customs officer or a magistrate, you are entitled to be present to hear the reasons why you should submit to a body search and have the opportunity to say why you disagree. If you wish someone to speak on your behalf, you should say so.

If you decide that you wish to go before a magistrate there may be some delay, but arrangements should be made to ensure that a magistrate is available at all times. It would not be reasonable to expect you to wait more than a couple of hours. If you are told or if it appears that the delay will be any longer than this, you should ask to see the most senior officer in attendance at the airport or port so that you may make an official complaint. If you decide to leave because of the unreasonable delay, you should ensure that the customs officer knows that this is the reason. Otherwise, you do run the risk of being arrested if you decide to leave prior to the search taking place.

After hearing the evidence from both the customs officer requesting the search and yourself, the senior officer or magistrate – depending on whom you request to be taken before – will then direct whether or not the search is to take place and the form that the search may take.

What form may the search take?

The nature and extent of the search depends on what you are suspected of carrying and where you are suspected of concealing it. It may take any of the following forms:

- A 'pocket search' – i.e. removal of all items from pockets.
- A 'rub-down' – i.e. the body is frisked.
- A search of outer clothing – i.e. removal of outer coat, jacket, hat or gloves.
- A strip search.
- An intimate search.

Customs officers are instructed to ensure that any person searched is treated courteously and considerately. Only a person of the same sex as the person being searched can carry out all 'rub-down' and strip searches.

Strip search

A strip search is essentially a visual search of your body. You will be accompanied by two customs officers of the same sex as yourself to a private room and asked to remove your clothing. Customs officers are under a duty to make every reasonable effort to reduce to the minimum the embarrassment that you may experience. For example:

- You need not be completely naked at any time. It will usually be possible for the top and bottom halves of the body to be unclothed and reclothed separately. If this is not suggested to you, you should ask that you be allowed to undress in this way.
- If you are required to be naked, a blanket or other suitable covering should be provided. Again, if this is not offered to you, you should request it.

An intimate search

An intimate search consists of the physical examination of one or more of your body orifices – i.e. mouth, nose, ears, anus and genitalia – and may only be done if an officer of at least the rank of senior executive officer authorises it. The reason why it is thought necessary must be explained to you. Only a doctor or a nurse may carry out the examination. No person of the opposite sex who is not a doctor or nurse should be present, nor should anyone whose presence is unnecessary. An intimate search of a juvenile (an individual under 18 years old) or of a person who is mentally ill or mentally handicapped may only take place in the presence of an appropriate adult, who is of the same sex as the person being searched, unless the juvenile requests otherwise and the adult agrees.

If you do not consent to an intimate search, it is most unlikely that the doctor or nurse will agree to carry it out. However, you must remember that you run the risk of being arrested if you do not consent, particularly if the search has been authorised by a magistrate.

It is unclear what type of redress is available if a strip search or intimate search is carried out in a manner that interferes with your rights under Article 8 of the Convention. The House of Lords recently upheld a decision that a woman who had been strip searched in breach of prison rules should receive no damages. The incident took place before the HRA came into force, so the courts could make a different decision in a similar case in future.

If you are arrested

A customs officer may arrest you if he or she has reasonable grounds to suspect that you are committing, or have committed, an offence as described above. You must be informed of why you are being arrested. The customs officer has the same powers to search you as described above if you are not under arrest, and you have the same rights to be taken before a senior officer or a magistrate. In addition, if you are under arrest, customs officers have the power to request that you submit to an intimate search if they believe you have an article on you that may cause a physical injury to yourself or others while in detention.

A customs officer of the same sex as yourself may carry out this search but only where a senior officer has authorised that it is not practicable for a doctor or nurse to do so. If you are under arrest, you may be detained for longer: up to 24 hours, or if it is alleged that you have committed an arrestable offence, up to 36 hours and to a maximum of 96 hours if a magistrate authorises further detention.

During detention you have the right:

- To inform someone of your arrest.
- To consult a solicitor in private.

However, exercising these rights may be delayed by 36 hours if you have been arrested for an arrestable offence. You are entitled to a copy of your custody record. An intimate body sample such as urine or blood can only be taken with your consent in writing.

If you wish to make a complaint

If you feel that you have been unreasonably subjected to a body search or have any objections to the way in which it was carried out, you may complain in writing to the Collector – the person in overall charge of the airport or port – at the address of the airport or port at which the search took place. You may also take up the matter with your MP and request that your complaint be referred to the Paymaster General at the Treasury, the minister responsible for Customs and Excise.

Other searches

There may be other circumstances when a person is subject to a personal search by officials other than the police. In the case of prisoners, or persons visiting prisoners, there are powers granted to prison officials to conduct searches in certain specified circumstances under the Prison Rules. In every case, there are likely to be detailed provisions regulating the circumstances for such searches and the conduct of such searches.

If you are subjected to such a search, which is carried out without proper authority, or in breach of regulations affecting such a search, then you may have a claim for assault or battery. You should take legal advice if you wish to take action for such a claim.

3.12   GENDER IDENTITY AND SEXUALITY

The incorporation of Article 8 into domestic law via the HRA brings with it the requirement upon the State to respect aspects of private life including gender identity and sexuality and corresponding rights to develop relationships with whom one chooses.

So far as gender identity is concerned, in July 2002 the ECHR found the UK's refusal to allow those who had undergone gender reassignment the ability to alter the gender registered on their birth certificate to be in breach of Convention rights. The UK is introducing legislation which seeks to remedy this position. The form of legislation currently proposed under the Gender Recognition Bill provides a procedure whereby a person with medically diagnosed gender dysphoria will be able to apply for a Gender Recognition Certificate. A full Gender Recognition Certificate is intended to allow a person to achieve recognition in their acquired gender for all purposes. In order to be eligible, an applicant must (among other things) have or have had gender dysphoria, must have lived in their acquired gender for a period of two years ending with the date of the application, and must intend to continue to live in the acquired gender until death. The proposed legislation does not require you to have undertaken gender reassignment surgery.

A person is not entitled to a full Gender Recognition Certificate if he or she is still married in accordance with his or her previous gender. An applicant for a certificate must provide a statutory declaration as to whether or not they are married. If married, but otherwise meeting the requirements for a certificate, you will only be entitled to receive an interim gender recognition certificate. This certificate will become a ground upon which an existing marriage is voidable if a decree of nullity is sought within six months of the grant of the interim certificate. If the marriage is annulled, then a full Gender Recognition Certificate can then be obtained.

A full Gender Recognition Certificate entitles you to obtain issue of a new birth certificate showing your new gender. However, there are some areas where historical gender will continue to be relevant, including parenthood, earlier commission of gender-specific offences and sporting competitions.

A person with gender dysphoria who has not obtained a certificate still enjoys rights to respect for private life and statutory protection does exist, including specific protection in relation to protection from discrimination for employment purposes.

As to sexuality, where a public authority seeks to discriminate against homosexuals, be it a ban on entering into forms of employment such as the armed forces, or something akin to differential treatment, such as a different age of consent, then it will almost certainly be acting contrary to Article 8, as recent decisions of the ECHR have shown.

3.13   PRIVACY AND THE MEDIA

One area where the rights under Article 8 of the Convention have had a significant effect is in relation to the media. The laws of breach of confidence, trespass, nuisance, surveillance, harassment etc., apply equally to the media, and you may be able to bring actions against the media where they have infringed those laws. Libel may restrict some intrusions on private life but only if the words are defamatory in that they discredit the individual or lower him or her in the estimation of others. In reality, however, actions for libel are of limited use as a means of protecting against intrusions of privacy. If the words relate to a private matter but are substantially true, then an action for libel is likely to be successfully defended. Moreover, public funding is not available for libel actions so they are less useful to an individual of limited means.

In practice, it has often been very difficult to control the worst excesses of the media, and flagrant breaches of the rights of privacy of individuals have been allowed to go on without redress. This does not simply apply to celebrities or royalty. In many cases, the media have significantly intruded upon the rights of unknown individuals who have become famous or, more usually, infamous as a result.

In the absence of any right to privacy as such, lawyers have had to resort to strange suits to try and prevent invasions of privacy. In this respect, actions for malicious falsehood were on the rise. In theory, public funding for actions of this type is available. Malicious falsehood was notoriously used as a cause of action against a newspaper that photographed and interviewed a famous actor who was recovering in hospital from brain surgery at a time when he was not in a fit state to consent to such an interview. The court dealing with the claim recognised that the remarks that the patient had made were wrongly portrayed as part of a voluntary and exclusive interview.

However, the newspaper got round this problem by publishing a statement that the interview was not voluntary or exclusive. This did not enable the real mischief, the invasion of the actor's privacy at a time when he was most vulnerable and sensitive, to be dealt with, and the courts have been criticised for failing to develop the law so as to protect people in positions such as this. The ingredients for an action in malicious falsehood are also difficult to establish. The victim must show that the words are false, that they were published maliciously and that they have either caused financial loss or, in some cases, were likely to cause such loss.

Copyright can also be used as a way of preventing publication of private papers or pictures, but working out who owns copyright – and who is therefore the right person to bring an action – can be a complicated matter. Additional protection is given to a person who commissions photographs for private or domestic purposes. Even if the photographer owns copyright, that person can prevent their publication.

It is these inadequacies that may be resolved by the incorporation of Article 8. It is clear from the recent cases involving press intrusion that the courts are prepared to give effect to the rights under Article 8 by expanding the existing cause of action of breach of confidence.

The courts are also themselves under an obligation to act compatibly with Article 8. Although there is no requirement on private individuals or companies – such as journalists and newspapers – to act compatibly with Article 8, the courts may be increasingly willing to develop the common law so as to provide proper protection for privacy. A recent decision from the House of Lords suggests that there is continued reluctance to recognise a new right to privacy, and the Government has rejected a recent Select Committee proposal urging the introduction of such a right. However, the development of existing causes of action will give much wider protection than was previously the case.

If you find yourself subject to unwanted press intrusion of this nature, then you should take legal advice in light of the latest developments of the law. This is a rapidly changing area. You may have a potential action for harassment under the PHA. You may have an action for breach of confidence. You may have an action for breach of the DPA. You will also have the right to complain to either Ofcom, the Office of Communications, which regulates UK television and radio services, or the Press Complaints Commission. It is worth noting that the Press Complaints Commission is more likely to be responsive to privacy complaints involving 'intrusion into grief or shock', such as the publication of photographs taken at a funeral.

However, in every case, there will be a requirement to protect the right to freedom of expression and the right of the media to publish material of public interest. Each case will need to be carefully examined to see if the interests of freedom of expression outweigh your rights to private life. As a general rule, the courts will not intervene to protect you merely because the media is intending to publish material in a particularly lurid way. The courts are not there to judge the taste of an article. They will be concerned with whether or not the material itself should be disclosed or published at all. Where you are seeking to prevent the media from publishing an article or putting out a programme, then the courts will apply the principles relating to injunctions that have been set out in the case involving the footballer Gary Flitcroft.

The court guidelines have been developed in consequence of the express provisions in the HRA dealing with claims for injunctions that concern freedom of expression. Freedom of expression is, of course, a right that is also incorporated by the HRA through Article 10. In the context of the media, there will always be a tension on the one hand between protecting the right to freedom of expression and a free press with respect to rights of privacy on the other. Section 12 of the HRA deals expressly with this tension and makes it clear that any person seeking to restrain publication of material that might affect the exercise of freedom of expression will:

(1)   Take all practical steps to notify the intended publisher or show that there are compelling reasons why that person should not be notified.
(2)   Need to satisfy the court that the underlying claim is likely to succeed at trial.
(3)   Need to deal with the court's obligation to have particular regard to the Convention right to freedom of expression; and

(4) Where such material is journalistic, literary or artistic, will need to deal with the court's obligation to have particular regard to:

    (a) the extent to which the material is, or is about to become, available to the public and it would be in the interest of the public for it to be published;

    (b) any relevant privacy code.

This provision is designed to ensure that freedom of expression is not stifled by well-timed injunctions sought by persons at a time when the publisher of the material will not be able to deal with the application properly. However, it does not prevent you from seeking to obtain an injunction in circumstances where there has been an unjustifiable breach of your privacy and you have a good case of succeeding in litigation against the person responsible.

See also Chapter 9.

3.14   FURTHER INFORMATION

Bibliography

Home Office Circular 28/2001: 'Protection from Harassment Act'
Home Office Circular 19/2004: 'The Removal of Offenders Convicted of Buggery and Indecency Between Men from The "Sex Offender Register" (Schedule 4, Sexual Offences Act 2003)'

Shelagh Gaskill and Louise Townsend

4   The Right to Know

This chapter deals with:

- Subject access under the Data Protection Act
- DPA exemptions
- Health records
- Social work records
- Education records
- Housing records
- Credit reference agency records
- Other data protection rights
- Enforcing the DPA
- Government and public sector information
- Environmental information
- Further information

This chapter mainly describes the rights you have under the Data Protection Act 1998 (DPA) and related legislation to access and correct personal information held about you. Many organisations, both public and private, hold files on the people they deal with. This chapter covers the right of access to personal files from health and housing departments, schools and governments, as well as credit reference agencies. It also covers exemptions such as information that is held for national security purposes, references or information that is likely to cause recipients serious harm.

Also discussed is your right to access government and public sector information under the Freedom of Information Act 2000 (FOIA).

4.1   SUBJECT ACCESS UNDER THE DATA PROTECTION ACT

Personal data

Your main rights to see personal data about yourself, held on computer and on paper, come from the DPA. The DPA provides a right of access to personal information about you held by public authorities and private bodies, regardless of the form in which it is held. It also requires those holding personal data about you to explain why they are holding that data and to give you a brief description of the other people or organisations they intend to give your information to and their purposes for using it.

Following a Court of Appeal decision in 2003 (*Durant* v *Financial Services Authority*), the Information Commissioner issued more detailed guidance on the meaning of personal data. The Information Commissioner has provided the following examples of information that would be considered personal data:

- Information about the medical history of an individual.
- An individual's salary information.
- Information concerning an individual's tax liabilities.
- Information comprising an individual's bank statements.
- Information about an individual's spending preferences.

The Information Commissioner has provided the following examples of information that would not be considered personal data:

- Mere reference to a person's name where the name is not associated with any other personal information.
- Incidental mention in the minutes of a business meeting of an individual's attendance at that meeting in an official capacity.
- Where an individual's name appears on a document or e-mail indicating only that it has been sent or copied to that particular individual, the content of that document or e-mail does not amount to personal data about the individual unless there is other information about the individual within it.

In practice, this will mean that not all information that can be retrieved from a computer search against an individual's name or unique identifier is personal data.

Structured files

Under the DPA, the right of access to non-computerised records is in most cases limited to information held in structured files. These are collections of files or papers organised in a way that makes it easy to find information about a particular individual. This includes files that are indexed or arranged by reference to the name of the person concerned, or to some other identifying feature such as their household, street name, postcode, car number plate, national insurance or other reference number.

The DPA does not, in general, allow you to see personal data held on paper that is not organised in this way. A set of files containing correspondence from many people arranged in date order, and not by the name of the person sending the letter, would probably not be covered – unless it was separately indexed by name. Occasional references to you in other kinds of files or papers would usually not be covered either.

In brief, the position is:

- You can see personal data held on computers about you by anyone – or in other forms where data can be processed automatically.
- You can see personal data held about you manually where it is held in structured files.
- You can see health, social work, housing and school records held on paper. This applies to all information, not just that held in structured files.
- When the FOIA is fully in force, all information held by any public authority about you, even unstructured information, will become accessible under the DPA. This right of access will be available from January 2005.

Applying under the DPA

The person holding information – data – about you is called the data controller. To apply for access to any personal data about yourself, write to the data controller, saying that you are applying under section 7 of the DPA. Sending your request by recorded delivery will help avoid any later dispute about whether it was received. If the data controller has different offices or branches and you are not sure which to write to, telephone first and ask. Alternatively, contact the Information Commissioner's office or look at the data controller's register entry, which can be found on the internet at: <www.informationcommissioner.gov.uk>.

Organisations must register under the DPA and provide an address for subject access requests in their register entry. The register entry must also specify the purposes for which information is held. A data controller must not hold or use the information for purposes incompatible with those stated in the register entry.

Before supplying information, the data controller is entitled to ask you for proof of your identity and for any further details needed to locate data held about you. It may help if you say what your relationship to the organisation is (e.g. customer, employee, student, patient), give any relevant dates or reference numbers and say which of its offices or branches you have dealt with – but don't volunteer any information you regard as confidential or private. You do not need to say why you want the information. The data controller cannot refuse access because you might use the data to criticise the controller, complain or take legal action.

You may have to pay a fee. At the time of writing the maximum fee is £10, although some organisations charge less or nothing. If information is held about you in both computer form and in structured paper files, a single £10 fee covers both. Different rules apply to educational records and manual health records, where you could be charged up to £50 – including the cost of all photocopies – and credit reference agency records where the maximum fee is £2.

The data controller must normally give access within 40 days of receiving your request and any supplementary details needed. It must supply the information in permanent form. This normally means a printout or a photocopy, but could also include copies of microfiches, X-rays, or audio/video cassettes. Any unintelligible terms, such as computer codes, must be explained.

The data controller can refuse to supply a permanent copy of the data if this is not possible or would involve disproportionate effort. You are still entitled to inspect the information at the data controller's premises.

Parents and children
The DPA has no minimum age requirement for applicants. Children can apply for their own records provided they are capable of understanding the nature of the request. A parent or guardian can apply on the child's behalf only if (a) the child has given consent, or (b) the child is too young to have the understanding to make an application or is incapable of such understanding. A parent concerned about a young child's health probably would be able to see his or her medical record. But a parent wishing to defend him or herself against allegations of child abuse, or looking for evidence to support a custody claim, probably would not.

Inaccurate information
The DPA gives you the right to have inaccurate data about yourself corrected. This applies if the data are incorrect or misleading about any matter of fact or contain an opinion based on data that are factually incorrect or misleading. In such cases you are entitled to require the data controller to correct, erase, destroy or block the use of the information. Opinions cannot be challenged unless they are based on

wrong facts – but if you disagree with an opinion, it is worth asking for your own views about the disputed data to be added to the record. There is, however, no explicit right to have this done.

You should send a written notice to the data controller asking for a correction, saying why you think the information is incorrect. If the data controller refuses to comply with your notice, you can complain to the Information Commissioner or apply directly to the court. It will usually be to your advantage to go to the Commissioner first, since this costs nothing and does not prevent you going to the court later.

4.2   DPA EXEMPTIONS

The data controller can withhold certain kinds of exempt information from you. The main exemptions apply to:

Personal information about someone else
This will not normally be released to you without that person's consent. However, the DPA does allow such information to be disclosed without consent if this is reasonable in all the circumstances. In deciding whether it is reasonable, the controller must consider in particular whether a duty of confidentiality is owed to the other person, what efforts have been made to obtain the person's consent, and whether the person is capable of giving consent or has expressly refused it.

If the information can be disclosed to you in a way that does not identify the individual – for example, by deleting the name of the individual or other identifying features – then you are entitled to it.

Information identifying someone who has supplied information about you
It is not enough for the data controller to suspect that you might be able to identify the individual concerned. The information must itself be enough to identify the person. The information someone else supplies about you is not exempt – unless its disclosure would in itself identify who had supplied it.

Only identifiable individuals, not organisations, are protected. Thus information that would reveal that a former employer had supplied information about you would not be exempt unless you would be able to identify the particular individual – for example, a particular manager. This exemption does not protect the identity of a health professional, social worker or teacher who has provided information that is recorded on your health, social work or educational record. This is discussed further below.

Law enforcement
Personal data held for the purpose of preventing or detecting crime, apprehending or prosecuting offenders, or assessing and collecting any tax or duty are exempt if disclosure would prejudice one of those purposes.

The exemption is not restricted to bodies such as the police or Inland Revenue. So, information about suspected fraud held by a bank or a social security officer could also be covered.

Not all law enforcement information is necessarily exempt. If you are the victim of a crime you may be able to see what is held about you without much risk of prejudicing the purpose for which the record is held. But if you are the suspect, the chance of the information being withheld will be much greater.

Information revealing how anyone is classified under a system for assessing potential tax evasion or benefit fraud is exempt where the exemption is required in the interests of the operation of the system.

National security

Information can be withheld from you on national security grounds. You can challenge a refusal to disclose by going to the Information Commissioner in the normal way unless a Cabinet minister has issued a certificate stating that the exemption is required in order to safeguard national security. In this case, you could apply to the Information Tribunal, which could overturn the certificate, but only on the very limited grounds that the minister had no reasonable grounds for issuing it, or it may be able to declare that the certificate does not apply to the personal data in question. Alternatively, you could apply to the Investigatory Powers Tribunal or IPT (which deals with issues relating to national security) on the basis that the refusal to disclose was not justified on national security grounds and therefore not protected by the certificate. The IPT may then look 'behind the scenes' to check whether the refusal was acceptable.

References

References are exempt in many, but not all, cases. You will have no right to obtain a confidential reference from the person or body that gave it, even if it could be disclosed without identifying the individual concerned. But you would be entitled to see a reference held by the person to whom it was supplied (e.g. an employer who has turned down your job application), except where this would identify the individual who gave it. The fact that it may identify the organisation that gave it is not relevant. Even information identifying the individual who gave the reference might have to be disclosed if it was reasonable to do so in all the circumstances.

Negotiations

Information is exempt if it would reveal the data controller's intentions in relation to any negotiations with you and if disclosure would prejudice those negotiations. General opinions and intentions towards you are, however, not exempt.

Examination marks and examiners' comments

These are exempt – but only for a time. You are entitled to see these 40 days after the examination results have been announced or five months after your request has been received, whichever is shorter.

Adoption records and reports

These are exempt. See also Chapter 13.

Other exemptions

The DPA contains many other exemptions. For example, for data used solely in connection with an individual's personal or family affairs; for data kept solely for statistical, historical or research purposes and published anonymously; for data processed for the publication of journalistic, literary or artistic material; and for lawyer–client communications.

Will you know what has been withheld?

One of the weaknesses of the DPA is that you need not be told whether exempt information has been withheld. You have no right to be told whether you have been given access to the full file or only an edited version. You may even get a deliberately ambiguous reply to your request, such as 'We hold no data on you, which we are required to disclose to you.' This could mean that no information is held on you, or that there is a file, but everything in it is regarded as exempt.

Nevertheless, it is worth asking if anything has been held back: it may be difficult for the person involved to evade a direct question. If you suspect you have been refused access to information that is not genuinely exempt you can ask the Information Commissioner to investigate.

4.3   HEALTH RECORDS

You have additional rights of access to your own health records. Under the DPA you are entitled to see all information relating to your physical or mental health that has been recorded by or on behalf of a health professional in connection with your care. This applies not just to computerised data and structured files but to unstructured data as well. The right of access covers both NHS and private medical records, and information of any age, however long ago it was recorded.

The health professionals whose records can be seen are doctors, dentists, opticians, pharmacists, nurses, midwives, health visitors, clinical psychologists, child psychotherapists, osteopaths, chiropractors, chiropodists, dieticians, occupational therapists, physiotherapists, radiographers, speech therapists, music and art therapists, orthopaedists, prostheticists, medical laboratory technicians and scientists who head health service departments.

Your access rights are more limited if:

- Information about your health is held by someone who does not fall within the DPA's definition of a health professional, such as records held by various kinds of psychotherapists or alternative practitioners.
- Information is held by a health professional who is not and never has been responsible for your care, such as a DSS doctor responsible for deciding whether you are entitled to disability benefit.

In these cases, you are entitled to see computerised data and structured files, but not unstructured information. However, you have additional rights to see medical reports supplied for insurance or employment purposes.

Charges

If you just want to inspect your health records, and not have copies, access must be given without charge, so long as any information has been added to your record in the last 40 days. This should allow free inspection by anyone who has recently been seen by a health professional.

If you ask for copies, you can be charged up to a maximum of £10 for all copies supplied to you where the information is held on computer and a maximum of £50 for manual records or a mixture of manual and computer records, including copies of non-paper records such as X-rays. You cannot be charged more than this however many copies are involved.

Other people's health records

You will not normally be able to see confidential information about another person, such as another member of your family, which has been recorded in your own health record unless that person consents or it is reasonable in the circumstances to disclose this to you. The same applies to information identifying an individual who has supplied information about you, other than health professionals.

A health professional does not need another health professional's permission to show you information recorded by that person. So your GP cannot withhold a letter from a hospital consultant on the grounds that he or she needs the consultant's permission for disclosure.

Parents

Parents normally require their child's consent before they can see the child's health records. If the child is too young to give an informed consent, the parent may be given access except where the child gave information in the expectation that it would not be revealed to the parent or expressly asked for it not to be disclosed. The same rule applies to a situation where the data subject is an adult incapable of managing his or her own affairs and the person seeking access is someone who has been appointed by a court to manage those affairs.

Relatives of someone who has died

There is no right to the deceased's records. The only exception is if the death may have been caused by negligence. In this case, a provision in the Access to Health Records Act 1990 allows someone who might be entitled to compensation – usually a dependant – to get records relating to the cause of death. All other provisions of this Act have been repealed.

Serious harm

In addition to the other exemptions in the DPA, information likely to cause serious harm to the physical or mental health or condition of the applicant or someone else is exempt. This decision can be taken only after consulting a health professional, normally the doctor treating the patient for the condition concerned. If the health professional's opinion was given more than six months ago, a new opinion must be obtained.

This provision might allow information to be withheld from, for example, someone with a mental illness whose condition could be seriously aggravated by seeing the record. It is not, however, a blanket exemption for psychiatric or any other class of patients. Studies have shown that most psychiatric patients benefit from seeing their medical records provided they have been written in the knowledge that they might be seen and someone is available to help explain them.

This exemption refers to serious harm – not to harm or distress. It should not permit doctors to withhold upsetting news from patients who want the truth, particularly if they could be helped to come to terms with it by support and counselling.

Medical reports for employers or insurers

If your doctor writes a report on your health for an insurance company or an employer, you have the right to see it before it is sent, under the Access to Medical Reports Act 1988. Only reports by doctors who are or have been involved in your medical care are covered. A report by an independent doctor, who has never treated you and acts solely for the insurer or employer, is not subject to this Act, and will only be accessible under the DPA.

An employer or insurer cannot contact your doctor unless they have your written consent and have informed you of your rights under the DPA. You must be invited to say whether you want to see the report before it is sent. If you say yes, the doctor should wait 21 days before sending it, to allow you to arrange to see it. Get in touch with your doctor straight away and ask to be contacted as soon as the report is ready.

No charge can be made if you inspect the report only; if you want a copy you can be charged a reasonable fee. If information has been withheld under an exemption, for example, for serious harm, you are entitled to be told.

If you see the report and are unhappy with it – for example, if you feel it involves an unacceptable breach of your privacy or misrepresents the position – you have the right to stop it being sent. But if you do, the employer or insurer may not be willing to offer you the job or insurance policy, so do not take this step lightly.

The doctor is required to keep a copy of the report for six months after sending it and to let you see it if you ask. This may be valuable if you are unexpectedly refused insurance or employment.

If you believe that a doctor, employer or insurance company has breached the DPA, you can apply to a court for an order requiring compliance. If a doctor has sent a report without your consent, this may be a breach of medical confidentiality. You may have grounds for a complaint to the General Medical Council.

4.4   SOCIAL WORK RECORDS

You are entitled under the DPA to see all information held about you by a local authority social services department, including unstructured information. In addition to the normal DPA exemptions, information can be withheld if disclosure would be likely to cause serious harm to your or any other person's physical or mental health.

A parent would not normally be entitled to see a child's records without the child's consent. If the child is too young to consent, the parent can apply on the child's behalf. Any information that a child has provided in the expectation that it would not be shown to the parents is exempt.

These exemptions mean that a parent who is accused of child abuse is unlikely to be given access to the child's records, or to information provided by the child but recorded on the parent's file. But the parent should be able to see other information recorded about him or herself, such as the notes of an interview or home visit, so long as disclosure would not expose the child to risk or prejudice law enforcement.

A family member caring for a mentally handicapped adult who cannot give an informed consent to their application has no explicit right of access to that person's file, unless they are acting under a power of attorney or an order of the Court of Protection.

Information about someone else that is recorded on your file, and anything that would identify an individual who has provided information about you, will normally be exempt, unless disclosure to you is reasonable in the circumstances.

The Department of Health has issued a guidance paper, 'Data Protection Act 1998 Guidance to Social Services', on access to social records. It is available on the internet at <www.dh.gov.uk> or by writing to:

Department of Health Publications
PO Box 777
London SE1 6XH

4.5   EDUCATION RECORDS

Parents, and pupils who are 16 or over, have had the right to see local education authority (LEA) school records for a number of years. The DPA has now extended this right to younger pupils. There is no minimum age: any pupil who makes a written request to see their school records is entitled to do so, unless the pupil does not have the ability to understand what they are asking for. The right applies to any information produced by a teacher, an education welfare officer or an employee of the LEA. Access must be given within 15 school days.

In addition to the general exemptions in the DPA:

• Information likely to cause serious harm to the pupil or someone else's physical or mental health is exempt.
• Information about a possible risk of child abuse can be withheld from a parent if disclosure would not be in the child's best interests.

Education records can be inspected free of charge. Photocopying charges are limited to a maximum of £1 for the first 20 pages, plus a further £1 for every subsequent ten pages, up to a maximum of £50. This maximum applies regardless of how many pages are supplied.

4.6   HOUSING RECORDS

If you are or have been a local authority tenant, have applied to be one, or have bought your council home, you have the right to see the council's housing records on you, including unstructured information. Housing records often contain information about a whole family. Under the DPA, you have no automatic right to information about other family members without their consent, unless disclosure is reasonable in the circumstances. It will normally be regarded as reasonable to reveal information about other family members held in connection with a tenancy. However, if other members of your family have no objection, it may be safest to include signed statements from them saying that they agree to the release of any personal information held about them.

4.7   CREDIT REFERENCE AGENCY RECORDS

When you apply for a loan, credit card, bank account or mortgage, the chances are that the company involved will run a check on you with a credit reference agency. These agencies check the electoral register to confirm that people live where they say they do, and report on bad debts, bankruptcies and perhaps on how well people keep up repayments of existing loans. If any of the information about you is wrong, it could be extremely damaging. The DPA allows you to see this information.

If you are about to apply for a mortgage or other major loan it may be worth checking in advance to see what information credit reference agencies hold on you. Correcting any errors in advance could help you avoid problems at a later stage, when you may not be able to get things put right in time.

When you apply, you should state that your request is limited to personal information relating to your financial standing. The data controller then has to reply within seven working days. The maximum fee it can charge you is £2 and you should enclose this with your application.

Under the Consumer Credit Act 1974 you are entitled to have incorrect information corrected. If the file contains mistakes, the agency must correct them and tell you what it has done within 28 days. If it refuses, or you are not satisfied with the amendment, you can send it a note of correction of up to 200 words, which it must add to your file and send out whenever information about you is supplied in the future.

If you are having problems obtaining credit as a result of the credit records of, for example, other family members living at the same address as you, you can apply to have your credit records 'disassociated' from theirs. You need only make such an application to one of the main credit reference agencies. That agency will also notify the others.

If you have problems obtaining credit, it may be useful for you to read 'No Credit' published by the Information Commissioner.

The three main credit reference agencies in the UK are:

Call Credit plc
One Park Lane
Leeds LS3 1EP
Tel: 0113 244 1555
Fax: 0113 234 0050
Info@callcredit.plc.uk
<www.callcredit.plc.uk>

Equifax plc
Credit File Advice Service
PO Box 3001
Glasgow G81 2DT
commercialuk@equifax.com

Experian Ltd
Talbot House
Talbot Street
Nottingham NG1 5HF
Tel: 0115 941 0888
Fax: 0115 934 4905
<www.uk.experian.com>

4.8   OTHER DATA PROTECTION RIGHTS

In addition to providing you with a right of access to personal data, the DPA also places other obligations upon data controllers. A data controller must only use information about you in accordance with the data protection principles. Among other things, these require that the information must be collected and used fairly and lawfully, that the information must be accurate and adequate and not held longer than necessary for the purposes for which it is held. These purposes must be specified in the data controller's data protection register entry. The information must not be used in a manner incompatible with those purposes. The data protection principles also require that information must not be transferred to countries outside Europe if those countries cannot guarantee the same level of protection of the rights and freedoms afforded under the DPA.

Some structured manual files will not be fully covered by these further obligations until 24 October 2007.

The data controller's register entry must state in general terms the kinds of organisations to whom it may want to disclose data, but need not give the names of the specific organisations. For example, it may tell you that disclosures will be made to local authorities, but not which ones.

You cannot be required, under the terms of a contract, to obtain your health records and pass them on to an employer or anyone else. When the DPA is fully in force it will also prohibit an employer or service supplier from requiring you to obtain and pass on to it information from your criminal or police records. However, Part V of the Police Act 1997, which governs access to criminal records for employment purposes, allows employers to require prospective employees to obtain a certificate of convictions from the Criminal Records Bureau.

4.9   ENFORCING THE DPA

If a data controller fails to comply with any of the DPA's requirements – for example, if it withholds information that is not exempt, fails to respond to your request within 40 days, or refuses to correct demonstrably inaccurate information – you can complain either to a court or to the Information Commissioner. The Commissioner is usually preferable, as this costs you nothing.

Also, if you have suffered damage because a data controller has contravened the DPA, you are entitled to compensation under section 13. The Information Commissioner, however, has no power to award compensation – you will need to take the organisation to court. In proceedings brought under this section it is a defence for the data controller to prove that he had taken such care as in all the circumstances was reasonably required to comply with the requirement concerned.

4.10   GOVERNMENT AND PUBLIC SECTOR INFORMATION

The Freedom of Information Act (FOIA) comes fully into force on 1 January 2005. This will provide a legal right of access to information held by public authorities and will require public authorities proactively to make information available. Public authorities include government departments and agencies, local authorities, NHS bodies, schools and universities, publicly owned corporations and quangos.

Until January 2005 you may be able to obtain information under the non-statutory 'Code of Practice on Access to Government Information' – also known as the 'Open Government' code.

Even when the FOIA comes into force, other access rights may continue to exist. For example, the Local Government (Access to Information) Act 1985 allows the public to attend meetings of local authorities and their committees and sub-committees and to see agendas, reports, minutes and background papers before those meetings – subject to a series of exemptions.

Changes to the DPA for public sector information

When the FOIA comes fully into force in January 2005, the DPA will be amended to create a right of access to all personal information held by public authorities, even unstructured information.

If you request unstructured information from a public authority about yourself, you will be required to describe what this information is and you may be required to pay a fee of up to £60 depending on how long it takes the public authority to find this information. If the cost to the public authority exceeds a certain limit then it may not have to provide the information, but it will contact you to let you know.

This means that from January 2005 you may obtain access to all information that a public authority holds about you, but from private sector companies you will still only be able to access the computerised and structured information described above.

Publication schemes

The FOIA requires public authorities to disclose information without specific request under 'publication schemes'. Each public authority will be required to have a publication scheme, which must explain the types of information made available by that authority, the methods by which access to that information can be obtained and whether there is a charge.

If you are interested in obtaining information from a public authority (other than personal information about yourself), you should start by looking at the authority's publication scheme to see whether the information you require is listed. Publication schemes may be available from an authority's website or by contacting the authority. Examples of information you may find available are policies and procedures, statistics and financial information.

Access requests

In addition, the FOIA will create a new legal right to non-personal information held by all public authorities. The right will be enforced by the Information Commissioner and will be subject to a number of exemptions, but the starting point is that you can ask for any information from a public authority.

Exemptions

The FOIA exempts various kinds of information from disclosure. Some exemptions apply absolutely – for example, information obtained by the authority in confidence from a third party and information that is prohibited from disclosure by a court. If an authority gets a request for this sort of information, it does not have to disclose it.

Other exemptions do not apply absolutely. They only apply once a public interest test has been applied. This means that information falling within the exemption should only be withheld where the public interest in withholding the information outweighs the public interest in making it available. Authorities should always favour disclosing information. Examples of non-absolute exemptions are where disclosure would prejudice the commercial interests of the authority or a third party or the formulation of government policy. It may be difficult to argue that a request you are making that concerns you alone is a matter of public interest. But if the information you are seeking has wider implications (e.g. if it shows that a department is routinely ignoring its own rules or that people are not receiving a benefit to which they are entitled) you may want to argue that there is a public interest in disclosure.

Fees

Public authorities are entitled to charge a fee for dealing with access requests. The fee will be calculated depending on how much it costs the authority to deal with the request, for example, how long it takes to find the information. At the time of writing it is likely that the most you will be required to pay is £60 plus any associated costs such as copying, but, if the cost to the authority exceeds a certain limit, it may not have to provide the information. If this is the case it should write to you and let you know and may tell you what information it could provide within the cost limit.

Applying for information

You should make your application in writing to the body that holds the information you want. Your letter should say that you are asking for the information under the FOIA and ask for a reply to be sent to you within 20 working days – the response time required by the FOIA. Make your request as specific as possible: this will reduce your chances of being charged a fee, or having your request turned down altogether. You are entitled to say whether you would prefer a copy of the information, a digest or summary, or the chance to come and inspect it, and the authority will have to take account of this. If it cannot comply with your preferred choice it will let you know and provide the information in another way.

Authorities have a duty to provide advice and assistance to those wishing to make requests. Therefore, if you are not sure what to ask for or how to make a request, an authority should always help you as much as possible to do this.

Complaints and enforcement

If you are refused information, you should usually be told which exemption has been relied on. If you think information is not in fact exempt, you should ask the authority concerned to review its decision. The review will normally be carried out at a more senior level within the authority. If, after this, you are still dissatisfied, you can complain to the Information Commissioner, but you must normally have asked the authority to reconsider its own decision first. The FOIA does not provide a right for individuals to sue public authorities for its breach.

4.11   ENVIRONMENTAL INFORMATION

The Environmental Information Regulations 1992, which implement a European directive, provide a general right of access to information about the environment held by public bodies, again subject to broad exemptions. Government departments, local authorities and other bodies with 'public responsibilities for the environment' must make available information about the state of the air, water, land, and animal and plant life; about activities that adversely affect any of these; and about measures designed to protect them from damage. The UK has also signed the 1998 Aarhus Convention on Access to Environmental Information, and future regulations to comply with it are likely to strengthen public rights to such information by providing a right of appeal and reducing the number of exceptions to the duty to disclose information.

4.12   FURTHER INFORMATION

Useful organisations

Information Commissioner
Wycliffe House
Water Lane
Wilmslow
Cheshire SK9 5AF
Info line: 01625 545 700
Fax: 01625 524 510
Mail@ico.gsi.gov.uk
<www.informationcommissioner.gov.uk>

Open Government Unit
Home Office
50 Queens Ann's Gate
London SW1H 9AT
Tel: 0870 000 1585
Text phone: 020 7273 3476
Fax: 020 7273 2965
Public.enquiries@homeoffice.gsi.gov.uk
<www.homeoffice.gov.uk>

Office of Parliamentary Ombudsmen
Parliamentary Commissioner for
Administration
Milbank Tower
Milbank
London SW1P 4QP
Tel: 0845 015 4033
Fax: 020 7217 4160
OPCA.Enquiries@ombudsman.gsi.gov.uk
<www.ombudsman.org.uk>

Campaign for Freedom of Information
Suite 102, 16 Baldwin Gardens
London EC1N 7KJ
Tel: 020 7831 7477
Fax: 020 7831 7461
admin@cfoi.demon.co.uk

5   The Rights of Suspects

This chapter deals with:

- Overview of police powers and the rights of suspects
- Police powers to stop and search persons and vehicles (without arrest)
- Police powers to search premises
- Police powers of arrest
- The rights of suspects in the police station
- Anti-terrorism powers
- Further information

5.1   OVERVIEW OF POLICE POWERS AND RIGHTS OF SUPSECTS

Most police powers and corresponding rights for suspects are to be found in the Police and Criminal Evidence Act 1984 (PACE) and in the accompanying Codes of Practice. PACE was the product of years of discussion about police powers. It was based on the recommendations in the Report of the Royal Commission on Criminal Procedure – published in 1981 – HMSO Cmnd 8092. The terms of reference for this body were to strike a balance between the interests of the community on the one hand, and the rights and liberties of the individual suspect on the other. PACE has been amended many times since then, most recently by the Criminal Justice Act 2003 (CJA 2003). Legislation since 1984 has not always protected the rights of suspects, particularly anti-terrorism legislation. Some provisions have been and will be open to challenge under the Human Rights Act 1998 (HRA), with particular reference to Articles 6 and 8 of the European Convention of Human Rights (the Convention). Many challenges so far, however, have been unsuccessful.

If any police powers are abused:

- The evidence obtained by the police may be inadmissible in court.
- You may make an official police complaint.
- You may be able to bring a civil action against the police.
- You may be able to bring judicial review proceedings or an action under the HRA against the police.

Civilians performing police duties

The Police Reform Act 2002 gives chief police officers the power to delegate some duties to civilians, and therefore you might find that you are dealing with such a person.

They must wear a uniform with an approved badge and carry their authorisation with them when performing these duties. The badge must be produced to you if you ask for it. A difficulty that might arise is that the authorisation does not usually state exactly what powers the civilian has, and these vary considerably.

With the exception of forcing entry to premises, where their right to use reasonable force is restricted to entry to save life or limb or preventing serious damage to property, they can use reasonable force to carry out their duties in the same way that the police can.

Obstructing, resisting or assaulting them in the execution of their duty is a summary offence.

They are bound like the police to follow the Codes of Practice as well as legislation. Complaints about them will be dealt with by the Independent Police Complaints Commission (IPCC), and, as in the case of illegal action by police officers, you could consider bringing a civil action. Any evidence that has been obtained as a result of such activity could be inadmissible in a trial.

5.2 POLICE POWERS TO STOP AND SEARCH PERSONS AND VEHICLES (WITHOUT ARREST)

Part 1 of PACE empowers any constable acting with reasonable grounds for suspicion to stop, detain and search you or your vehicle, or anything in or on your vehicle for certain items. Any items found may be seized. The provisions of PACE are supplemented by a Code of Practice on stop and search, Code A. The contents of Code A must be observed by the police, although the remedy for failure to observe is usually to make a police complaint – or if prosecuted to raise an objection in court – rather than to take legal proceedings against the police.

PACE also provides some safeguards for other well-used police powers of search. These might relate, for instance, to searches for drugs under the Misuse of Drugs Act 1971 or for firearms under the Firearms Act 1968. The safeguards also apply in a limited way to controversial powers of stop and search introduced by the Criminal Justice and Public Order Act 1994, which can be used when it is feared that an incident involving serious violence may take place.

The police do not have general powers, apart from those specified in a statute, to stop and search you. You should always ask a police officer to explain on what basis they are searching you. If no search power exists you should not be searched unless you are entering sports grounds or other premises and your consent to the search is a condition of entry.

What the police can search for

The power to stop and search in PACE enables a constable to search for stolen or 'prohibited articles' or knives – with the exclusion of short-bladed penknives. PACE defines two categories of prohibited article:

- An offensive weapon.
- An article made or adapted for use in connection with one of a list of offences including burglary, theft, taking a conveyance without authority (or being carried in one), obtaining property by deception and criminal damage.

Virtually any article could come within this second definition, but there would have to be some evidence of the use of the article or the intention of the person making, adapting or carrying it, otherwise a constable would not have reasonable grounds to search.

The police also have power to stop and search for specific items under a number of other statutes. Most particularly, the Misuse of Drugs Act 1971 enables a constable to stop and search you or your vehicle for 'controlled drugs'.

Where the search may take place
The PACE power of stop and search may be used by the police in most public and some private places as follows:

- A place to which, at the time of the proposed stop and search, the public – or any section of the public – has access as a matter of legal right or because there is permission.
- Any place – other than a dwelling – to which people have ready access at the time of the proposed stop and search.

These categories are obviously very wide and can include private property, for example, front gardens and car parks. Whether you have 'ready access' might depend on whether a gate or door is locked, or whether a plot of land is fenced.

However, a constable may not search you or your vehicle if you are on land that is used for the purpose of a dwelling, without having reasonable grounds for believing that you do not reside in the dwelling and are not in the place with the express or implied permission of a person who does reside in the dwelling. There is clearly a heavy responsibility on the constable in such cases, since the reasonable grounds must be justified objectively. These provisions are intended to protect such people as window cleaners, post and milk deliverers and casual visitors.

Reasonable grounds for suspicion
Most stop and search powers can only be exercised where the constable is acting on 'reasonable suspicion'. This includes the power to search a person for illegal drugs under the Misuse of Drugs Act 1971 and the power to search for stolen or prohibited items under PACE. The meaning of 'reasonable suspicion' is found in Code A.

There must be some basis for the officer's belief, related to you personally, which can be considered and evaluated by an objective third person. Mere suspicion based on hunch or instinct might justify observation but cannot justify a search.

However, reasonable suspicion can sometimes exist without specific information or intelligence and on the basis of some level of generalisation stemming from the behaviour of a person. For example, if an officer encounters someone on the street at night obviously trying to hide something, this clearly constitutes conduct that might reasonably lead the officer to suspect that stolen or prohibited articles are being carried.

The power must be used fairly, responsibly, with respect for people being searched and without unlawful discrimination. This would include discrimination on grounds of race, colour, ethnic origin, nationality or national origin. Accordingly, reasonable grounds for suspicion cannot be based solely on attitudes or prejudices towards certain types of people, such as membership of a group within which offenders of a certain kind are relatively common – for example, young football fans. Nor can it be based solely on your skin colour, age, hairstyle, mode of dress or previous convictions.

Stopping and detaining

A police officer who has reasonable grounds for suspicion can stop and detain you in order to conduct the search. Before doing the search they can ask you questions to confirm or eliminate that suspicion. If their suspicion is eliminated by the questioning or any other circumstances, you are free to leave and you must be told this. The police have no powers to stop you in order to find grounds that would justify a search.

Any police officer, whether or not in uniform, may search you personally, but usually only a constable in uniform may stop a vehicle. A police officer may detain you or your vehicle for a search, but the police officer must inform you as soon as the detention begins.

The detention may only last for as long as is reasonably required to permit a search to be carried out at the place of detention or nearby. You cannot be compelled to remain with your vehicle while the vehicle is searched, but you may wish to do so. Police officers have other powers to stop a vehicle, for example, to check whether it is roadworthy or stolen, but not to search it.

If you are lawfully detained for a search, but no search in fact takes place (for instance, because the grounds for suspicion are eliminated), the detention in the first place is not unlawful.

Searching

In carrying out a search the police may request, but cannot force, you to remove any clothing in public other than an outer coat, jacket or gloves. This is so even if the street is empty. Code A permits the police to put their hands in the pockets of outer clothing and feel around inside collars, socks and shoes if this is reasonably necessary in the circumstances. Similarly, subject to the restriction on removal of headgear, they can search your hair in public. A more thorough search, for instance, involving the removal of a hat or shoes, or a strip search, may take place in private, but it must be near to where you were stopped. Thus it could take place, for example, in a police van. No search involving exposure of intimate parts of the body may take place in a police van. Code A states that such searches must be by a police officer of your sex and must be in the absence of anyone of the opposite sex, unless you specifically request otherwise.

The power to search a vehicle includes a power to search anything in or on it. If an unattended vehicle is searched, a notice to this effect must be left behind, inside the vehicle if reasonably practicable. The notice must state the police station to which the constable is attached, that any claims for compensation should be made to that police station, and that you are entitled to a copy of the search record if requested within 12 months of the search.

A constable may use reasonable force, if necessary, in the detention and conduct of the search, but force can only be necessary if you are first given the opportunity to co-operate and refuse.

Seizure

The police may seize anything for which they have a power to search, for example, under PACE, stolen or prohibited items. However, they may also seize any other item if it is not practicable to determine what it is at the time of search or if it is attached to an item that they do have power to seize.

Information to be given before search

Prior to conducting a search under any power to search before or without arrest, a constable must take reasonable steps to bring the following to your attention:

- If the constable is not in uniform, proof that he or she is a constable, which Code A says must be by showing a warrant card.
- Information on police powers to stop and search and the individual's rights in these circumstances.
- The constable's name and police station.
- The object of the proposed search.
- The constable's grounds for proposing to search.
- The availability of a search record and how to obtain one if one is not made at the time of the search.

The search may not be commenced until the constable gives you such information, and the information must be given even if not requested.

Search records

A constable who has carried out a search under any power to search without or before making an arrest must make a written record on the spot, unless there are exceptional circumstances that make this wholly impracticable. If a record cannot be made at the time it must be made as soon as practicable afterwards, unless there are very good reasons for not being able to do so, for example, an inability to obtain information owing to large numbers involved.

Code A requires the search record to include your name, or if the police do not know your name, a description of you and a note of your ethnic origin. The record must identify the person making it and state the object of the search, the grounds for making it, the date, time and place, whether anything – and if so what – was found, and whether any – and if so what – injury or damage resulted from the search.

You should be given a copy of the record immediately. If this is not possible you can obtain a copy of the record for a period of up to 12 months (unless a record was exceptionally not made in the circumstances described above).

You are entitled to a record even if the police only detain you in order to do a search but do not perform a search because the grounds for the search are eliminated. Similarly, you can have a record where the police request you, in a public place, to account for yourself. This does not apply to general conversations or in the exceptional circumstances described above.

Roadblocks

Police powers to set up roadblocks – referred to in section 4 of PACE as road checks – do not derive from PACE but from other sources: road traffic legislation – Section 163 of the Road Traffic Act 1988 – and case law. If a roadblock is for certain purposes, PACE provides that the police must follow certain procedures.

Incidents involving serious violence

Under section 60 of the Criminal Justice and Public Order Act 1994, a police officer of the rank of inspector or above may issue a written authorisation for additional search powers on the basis of a reasonable belief that incidents involving serious violence may take place or that people are carrying dangerous instruments or offensive weapons in the area without good reason. The powers relate to pedestrians and vehicles in a specified locality, for a specified period, not exceeding 48 hours at a time.

Where an authorisation has been issued, any constable in uniform may stop and search any pedestrian or anything carried by the pedestrian, or any vehicle or anyone in it, for offensive weapons and dangerous instruments and may seize any such items that are found. In addition, the police may require you to remove any item that they reasonably believe you are wearing wholly or mainly for the purpose of concealing your identity. They can seize such items and any you were intending to wear wholly or mainly for that purpose. This clearly includes removal of head and face coverings. Where the covering is worn for religious reasons the police have to be sensitive about the removal, and it should not be removed in public and, if possible, not in the presence of anyone of the opposite sex.

Very importantly, under these powers, the police do not need to have any suspicion that they will find the items for which they may search. Code A applies, except for the provisions on reasonable suspicion, where searches may take place and on the minimisation of embarrassment. It is unclear whether these powers to stop and search may be exercised on private premises. The stops and searches are subject to the same safeguards concerning provision of information, the nature of the search and record-keeping as the powers under PACE. In addition, a pedestrian or driver of a vehicle who has been stopped is entitled to a written statement to that effect within 12 months of the search.

Failure to stop or to remove an item worn by you when required to do so under these new powers is a summary offence, with a maximum sentence of imprisonment of 51 weeks. In addition, it will also amount to an offence of obstructing a police officer in the exercise of his or her duty.

It was thought that powers to search anyone in a particular locality without any reasonable suspicion might be in breach of Article 8 or Article 5 of the Convention. A recent ruling by the High Court suggests that unless it can be shown the power has been exercised arbitrarily, no breach of the Convention will be found – see *R (on the application of Gillan and another)* v *Metropolitan Police Commissioner and another*.

'Statutory undertakers' – other police forces
'Statutory undertakers' are bodies authorised by statute to run a railway, transport, dock or harbour undertaking, the larger of which employ their own police forces. One example is the British Transport Police, whose members have the powers of constables within a geographically limited area. Members of these forces have many of the same powers as members of regular police forces, subject to certain limitations. These are not the same as private security organisations that enjoy no special 'policing' powers.

A constable employed by a statutory undertaker may stop, detain and search any vehicle – but not a person – before it leaves a goods area on the premises of the statutory body. Such stops are carried out routinely and need not be justified by any suspicion nor recorded. There is no statutory limitation on what may be searched for, and Code A does not apply to these searches.

The Ministry of Defence has its own police force, which has the same powers as civilian police officers.

5.3   POLICE POWERS TO SEARCH PREMISES

The police have powers to enter, or to enter and search, your premises for many reasons. Some of these powers are set out in PACE, but the police also have power to enter and search under other statutes, for instance the Theft Act 1968. It should be noted that the police do not always need to have a search warrant, although they must always have a reason for the search. There is a Code of Practice, Code B, setting out how the police should conduct searches. The relevant articles of the Convention here are Article 8 (right to privacy and family life) and Article 10 (right to freedom of expression).

Code B applies generally to all searches of premises, including those with the consent of the occupier except in the following circumstances:

- Routine scene of crime searches.
- Calls to a fire or burglary made by or on behalf of an occupier.
- Bomb threat calls.
- Where it would cause disproportionate inconvenience to the person concerned.

Powers of entry and search must be fully justified before use, and the police should always consider whether their objectives could be met by other less obtrusive means. In all cases the police should exercise their powers courteously and with respect for all persons and property, and only use reasonable force when necessary.

If the police exceed their powers any evidence obtained as a result may not be admissible as evidence in a trial.

Search with your consent

The police may search your premises if you consent, as well as where they have legal powers to do so. They can assume consent to a routine scene of crime search. However, Code B provides that before seeking your consent the officer in charge should state the purpose of the proposed search, inform you that you are not obliged to consent and that anything seized may be used in evidence. For the search to be lawful you must consent in writing. If you live in rented accommodation the police should not search the premises solely on the basis of your landlord's consent unless you are unavailable and the matter is urgent.

Search of premises under a magistrate's warrant

Magistrates have the power to issue search warrants under many Acts of Parliament – for example, to search for stolen goods under the Theft Act 1968, Misuse of Drugs Act 1971 and for racially inflammatory material under the Public Order Act 1986. More importantly, they have a power under PACE to issue a warrant authorising the police to enter and search premises for evidence of a serious arrestable offence. Magistrates should only issue warrants under this section if there are reasonable grounds for believing that the police will not be able to obtain access to the evidence without a warrant, for example, if consent will not be forthcoming. In addition, magistrates should be satisfied that there are reasonable grounds for believing:

- The material is likely to be of substantial value – whether by itself or together with other material – to the investigation of the offence.

- That it is likely to be 'relevant evidence', that is, anything that would be admissible as evidence at a trial.
- That it does not consist of or include items subject to legal privilege, 'excluded material' or 'special procedure material'.

This power clearly applies to premises owned or occupied by someone who is not implicated in the alleged offence.

The Police Act 1997 gives statutory authority for police 'bugging' and allows the police, with the prior authority of a Commissioner – a serving or retired High Court judge – to go on to private property to plant surveillance devices and also to search and seize evidence. In order to use such powers the police will have to be satisfied that the action is necessary because it is likely to be of substantial value in the prevention or detection of serious crime, and that what the action seeks to achieve cannot reasonably be achieved by other means. The prior authority of a Commissioner is not required where the authorising officer believes the search is urgent. This belief does not need to be on reasonable grounds. These powers are extremely invasive of privacy, and the police action will be assessed very carefully against the right to privacy in Article 8 of the Convention. The protections afforded by the Police Act itself may be inadequate under Article 8 of the Convention, as the authorisation is only from a Commissioner.

Material that has special safeguards
PACE gives special protection from search – but not necessarily from seizure – to some types of material felt to be sensitive. These categories are 'excluded material', 'special procedure material' and 'legally privileged material'.

Excluded material
There are three kinds of excluded material:

- Personal records – examples of material that should normally be excluded are medical and psychiatric records, records kept by priests, the Samaritans, possibly school and college records, records of advice given by law centres and Citizens' Advice Bureaux.
- Human tissue or tissue fluid.
- Journalistic material – that is, material acquired or created for the purposes of journalism. There is no need for the holder of such material to be a professional journalist.

In order to qualify as excluded material the items must have been held in confidence. This is a concept that can be legally complex.

The police cannot easily obtain a warrant to search for this material. They must follow a set procedure, which will normally involve a hearing before a judge who decides, among other things, whether it would be appropriate to allow the police access to the material. Only the person in possession of the material, who will not necessarily be the suspect, and the police have a right to make representations at the hearing. If the judge decides to permit access, however, the suspect may make representations at that stage. If the judge considers it appropriate, he or she will make an order compelling production of the material to the police. If the person in possession fails to produce the material, he or she may be in contempt of court and the judge may issue a warrant to the police to search his or her premises.

In some circumstances, if the police can convince the judge that the situation is urgent, they may be able to obtain a warrant from the judge without the party in possession of the material knowing.

Special procedure material
There are two categories of special procedure material:

- Material that is not excluded material but is held in confidence by certain persons.
- Journalistic material that is not excluded material, either because it is not held in confidence or does not consist of documents.

Examples of special procedure material are company accounts or stock records held on behalf of a client by a bank, solicitor or accountant. The procedure enabling the police to obtain this material is broadly the same as for excluded material. The police have additional powers to apply for the production of this material where it is considered to be evidence of a 'serious arrestable offence'. The judge will have to decide, among other things, whether it would be in the public interest to allow the police access to the material. For instance, if the police were to make an application for newspaper photographs, the judge may need to consider the rights of the press to freedom of expression under Article 10 of the Convention. The material must also be of 'substantial value' to the investigation, and not merely be of benefit or useful.

Legally privileged material
The definition of items subject to legal privilege is crucial, since these items are exempt from most powers of search and should not be seized. There are three categories of legally privileged material:

- Communications to do with giving legal advice.
- Communications to do with legal proceedings.
- Items connected with either of the above communications.

In each category the definition hinges on the term 'professional legal adviser', which clearly includes barristers, solicitors and solicitors' clerks. There is no requirement that the adviser should work for a firm of solicitors and, therefore, the adviser may come from a law or advice centre. Although the advice of an unqualified person will not be privileged unless acting as an agent for a solicitor or barrister, it will in most cases be excluded material.

Items held with the intention of furthering a criminal purpose are not legally privileged. However, a letter from a solicitor advising a client of potential criminal liability if a particular course of conduct were pursued would be privileged.

Entry and search without a search warrant
The police are given powers to enter premises without a warrant by many Acts of Parliament. For example, under the Gaming Act 1968 they have power to enter licensed premises to carry out inspections. Other powers include searches for drugs under the Misuse of Drugs Act 1971, and for firearms under the Firearms Act 1968.

In addition, they may have the right to enter premises without a warrant to deal with or prevent a breach of the peace. PACE provides them with several other powers:

- To execute a warrant of arrest or commitment.
- To arrest someone for an arrestable offence.
- To arrest someone for various offences under the Public Order Acts 1936 and 1986 – such as riot, violent disorder, affray, threatening behaviour and disorderly conduct; the Criminal Law Act 1977 – offences relating to trespass; and the Criminal Justice and Public Order Act 1994 – failure to comply with an interim possession order.
- To recapture a person who has escaped from lawful custody.
- To arrest a child or young person who has been remanded or committed to local authority accommodation.
- To save life or limb or prevent serious damage to property.

The police officer need not be in uniform unless entering under a power set out in the Public Order Acts or the Criminal Law Act. The police officer may search the premises, but the power of search is only a power to search to the extent that is reasonably required for the purpose for which the power of entry is exercised. Any further search may be unlawful and may be the subject of a complaint or civil action.

It was held by the European Commission of Humans Rights that the police violated Article 8 of the Convention (the right to privacy) in connection with an entry to premises to prevent a breach of the peace. There would have been no need for the police to enter as they had if they had considered the situation appropriately. Their entry was disproportionate to the legitimate aim pursued.

Search of premises on arrest
PACE provides the police with clear authority to enter and search premises after an arrest. If you have been arrested for an arrestable offence, the police may search premises occupied or controlled by you for evidence of that offence or of some other arrestable offence connected with or similar to that offence. The police do not, however, have power to enter and search after executing an arrest warrant in extradition proceedings. The police officer conducting this search should normally have with him or her written authorisation on the Notice of Powers and Rights for the search by an officer of at least the rank of inspector.

If you have been arrested for any offence, not just an arrestable offence, the police may enter and search any premises you were in at the time of the arrest or immediately before it for evidence of the offence for which you were arrested. Again, in both cases the police are only permitted to search to the extent reasonably required to find the evidence sought, and if the search is excessive, you may have the remedy of a police complaint or a civil action against the police.

Conduct of searches of premises
The conduct of searches is governed by PACE and Code B. A search warrant may authorise anyone to accompany the constable who is executing it. Such persons have the same powers as the police, but they can only exercise them in the company, and under the supervision, of the police. Entry and search must be within one month from the date of the warrant's issue. You have a right to see the warrant and to be

supplied with a copy. You also have a right, unless it is impracticable, to Notice of Rights and Powers, setting out police powers and occupiers' rights.

You are also entitled to see the police officer's warrant card as a means of identification if he or she is not in uniform and, in any case, the police officer should identify him or herself. If you are not present but someone else who appears to the police to be in charge of the premises is available, then they have the same rights as you.

A warrant authorises entry on one occasion only. The search should only be to the extent necessary to achieve its objective and should end as soon as the objects being searched for have been found. Similarly, once the officer in charge of the search is satisfied that whatever is being sought is not on the premises, the search should end.

The police have a right to use force if necessary to affect an entry or search, but only such force as is reasonable. All searches should take place at a reasonable hour, unless the constable conducting the search believes that waiting until such time would frustrate the purpose of the search. You are entitled to have a friend or neighbour witness a search unless the officer in charge has reasonable grounds for feeling this would seriously hinder the investigation. You do not have a right to delay a search unreasonably while you find a witness.

The warrant must be endorsed afterwards by the police to show the following:

- Whether articles or persons specified in the warrant were found.
- Whether any other articles were seized.
- The date and time of the search's execution.
- The names of the officers who executed it, except where the investigations are linked to terrorism in which case warrant numbers and duty stations should be shown.
- Whether a copy of the warrant, together with a Notice of Powers and Rights, was handed to the occupier or left at the premises.

The occupier of the premises that have been searched has a right to inspect the search warrant, which should be returned to the Magistrates' Court within 12 months.

Seizure of property

When the police have authority to search premises they normally have a corresponding right to seize whatever the search is meant to yield.

'Premises' has a very wide meaning and includes tents and caravans, for instance. It might be necessary to seize the whole 'premises' and the police have power to do this.

When the police are lawfully on any premises, including when they are there with your consent, they have wide powers to seize anything on the premises, including a vehicle, if they have reasonable grounds for believing that:

- It has been obtained as a consequence of the commission of an offence.
- It is evidence in relation to any offence; and
- It is necessary to seize it in order to prevent it being concealed, lost or damaged, altered or destroyed.

'Anything' includes fingerprints.

If the police find something which they have reasonable grounds for thinking is something they are authorised to seize and it is not possible at the time to determine whether it is actually such a thing, they can seize as much of it as is necessary to make that determination. However, they must be very careful not to remove more than is strictly necessary.

The police can also seize material they have no power to seize if it is attached to something that they do have power to seize and they are not able to separate the two.

The police may require computerised information coming within these categories to be produced in a form that allows them to remove it. Excluded material and special procedure material are not protected from seizure once the police are lawfully on the premises. No power, however, authorises the seizure of material reasonably believed by a constable to be legally privileged unless it is attached to an object they have a power to seize and it is not possible to separate them.

The police have limited rights to photograph or copy any document or other article they have the power to seize.

If you request it, the police must provide a record of seized items within a reasonable time. Lawfully seized articles may be retained so long as is necessary, for example, for production in court, but the articles cannot be kept for use as evidence in a trial or for forensic examination if a photograph or copy would suffice.

Under the Criminal Justice and Police Act 2001 there are special provisions that relate to the retention of items seized where their status cannot be determined or where they are attached to items that can lawfully be seized.

5.4   POLICE POWERS OF ARREST

The police may arrest with or without a warrant. There are many powers of arrest under a warrant issued by a justice of the peace or judge, and the rules governing each of them is set out in the statute creating the power. This section deals with police powers of arrest without a warrant. Article 5 (the right to liberty and security of the person) of the Convention is the article most likely to be violated here. Article 5 permits arrest on several grounds, the most relevant here being to prevent the commission of offences. This will be closely scrutinised by the court, as it does not for instance authorise any general powers of arrest to maintain order.

Powers of arrest without a warrant are mostly governed by PACE and can be grouped into the following categories:

- Arrest at common law for breach of the peace.
- Summary arrest for an 'arrestable offence'.
- Arrest subject to conditions.
- Arrest under specific powers.
- Arrest for the purpose of fingerprinting.
- Arrest for failure to answer police bail.
- Arrest for breach of a police bail condition.
- Arrest to have a sample taken.
- Arrest of a young person for breaching conditions of remand.

Most powers of arrest without warrant contained in other statutes enacted prior to PACE were repealed by section 26 of PACE. The powers that have been specifically preserved are listed in Schedule 2 of PACE and include power under the Bail Act 1976 to arrest without warrant someone who has been bailed in criminal proceedings if a constable has reasonable grounds for suspecting the person will not surrender in to the custody of the court or is likely to breach a condition of bail.

Arrest at common law for breach of the peace

A breach of the peace is not in itself a criminal offence, but the police and any other person have a power of arrest where there are reasonable grounds for believing a breach of the peace is taking place or is imminent. The Court of Appeal defined a breach of the peace as being 'an act done or threatened to be done which either actually harms a person, or in his presence, his property, or is likely to cause such harm being done' – see *R* v *Howell*. This power of arrest will, of course, be closely scrutinised in connection with Article 5 (the right to liberty and security), Article 10 (the right to freedom of expression) and Article 11 (the right to freedom of assembly and association).

Summary arrest for arrestable offences

PACE uses the phrase 'summary arrest' to mean arrest without a warrant and lists the arrestable offences for which the police can arrest without a warrant. The following are arrestable offences:

- Offences for which the sentence is fixed by law, including murder – life imprisonment.
- Offences carrying a maximum sentence of imprisonment for five years or more – these include serious offences of violence and dishonesty, but also some relatively minor offences such as shoplifting.
- Offences listed in Schedule 1A of PACE, which carry sentences that are, or can be (e.g. if tried summarily), less than five years' imprisonment. The list is added to from time to time and was most recently expanded by the Criminal Justice Act 2003. Examples include:
    - offences under section 12(1) Theft Act 1968 (taking a motor vehicle without consent)
    - offences under section 3 Theft Act 1968 (making off without payment)
    - offences under section 1 of the Protection of Children Act 1978 (indecent photographs of children)
    - the offence of possession of cannabis or cannabis resin under the Misuse of Drugs Act 1971.

This power of arrest may be carried out by either a police officer or any other person performing a citizen's arrest against:

- Anyone actually committing, or whom he or she reasonably suspects to be committing, an arrestable offence.
- Where an arrestable offence has been committed, anyone who is guilty or whom he or she reasonably suspects to be guilty of the offence.

A police officer may arrest in the same circumstances as any person, and may also arrest:

- Anyone whom he or she reasonably suspects to be about to commit an arrestable offence.
- Where he or she reasonably suspects an arrestable offence has been committed.

'Reasonable suspicion' means that the person making the arrest must actually have suspicion and also that the suspicion is on reasonable grounds. If the arresting person is acting on instructions, he or she must have enough information to believe there are reasonable grounds for suspicion. This will always be a question of fact in the particular circumstances. It could be, for instance, that knowledge that the arrested person had an opportunity to commit the offence is reasonable grounds for suspicion.

Serious arrestable offences

There is a further concept in PACE described as the 'serious arrestable offence'. The definition of a serious arrestable offence does not affect the powers of arrest. However, where the offence is a serious arrestable offence, the more draconian powers under PACE relating to the detention of a subject can be invoked, such as detention without charge for up to 96 hours, denial of access to a solicitor and delaying notification of detention to a friend for up to 36 hours, the authorisation of road checks, and so on.

The following are included in the list of serious arrestable offences:

- Treason, murder, manslaughter, rape, kidnapping, incest or intercourse with a girl under 13, buggery with a boy under 16, indecent assault constituting gross indecency, causing an explosion likely to endanger life or property, certain offences under the Firearms Act 1968, causing death by dangerous driving, hostage taking, torture and many drug-related offences, ship hijacking and Channel Tunnel train hijacking, taking indecent photographs of children, publication of obscene matter.
- Any other arrestable offence if its commission has led or is intended to, is likely or threatened to lead to any of the following consequences: serious harm to the security of the State or to public order, serious interference with the administration of justice or with the investigation of offences, the death or serious injury – including disease and impairment – of any person, or a substantial financial gain or serious financial loss to any person.

Arrest subject to conditions

Often in a minor case an arrest is unnecessary. The alleged offender can be summonsed by post to attend court on a particular date and there is no need to go to a police station at all. However, PACE also gives the police powers of arrest for all offences, no matter how trivial, petty or minor, which do not automatically carry a power of arrest. The power of arrest can only be used where:

- A constable has reasonable grounds for suspecting that you have committed or attempted, or are committing or attempting to commit, an offence – but not where it is suspected that an offence will be committed in the future.
- It appears to the constable that service of a summons is impracticable or inappropriate because any of the general arrest conditions are satisfied.

Thus, the assumption is that the police should proceed by way of summons for minor offences and the power of arrest ought to be used only if this is impracticable or inappropriate. The impracticability or inappropriateness of the summons must arise from one of the general arrest conditions, which are as follows:

Name and address

- If your name is unknown to, and cannot be readily ascertained by the police. You cannot be made to wait while your name is ascertained or confirmed, but might agree to do so to avoid being arrested.
- If the police have reasonable grounds for doubting that you have given your real name.
- If you have failed to furnish a satisfactory address for the service of a summons – that is, one at which, it appears to the constable, you will be for a sufficiently long period to be served or at which some other specified persons will accept service of a summons.
- If the police have reasonable grounds for doubting whether an address furnished is satisfactory.

Prevention
If the police have reasonable grounds for believing that an arrest is necessary to prevent you causing physical injury to yourself or to somebody else, or suffering physical injury, or causing loss of or damage to property, including your own, or committing an offence against public decency, or causing an unlawful obstruction of the highway.

Protection
If the police have reasonable grounds for believing that arrest is necessary to protect a child or other vulnerable person (undefined) from you.

If you have been arrested under this power and are on the way to the police station, you must be released if a constable is satisfied that there are no longer any grounds for keeping you under arrest, for example, if you suddenly find some kind of identification or if there is no longer any risk of damage or injury.

Arrest under specific powers
The specific statutory powers are listed in PACE and some subsequent legislation and relate mainly to the armed forces, animals, absconders, children and offences under legislation concerning immigration, road traffic, public order and so on. Many of these powers have conditions attached, for instance that the officer should be in uniform.

Arrest for the purpose of fingerprinting
This power of arrest is designed to apply to somebody who appears at court after receiving a summons and who has not been taken to a police station under arrest.

A constable may make an arrest without a warrant in order to have fingerprints taken at a police station. The following conditions must apply:

- You must have been convicted of a recordable offence – that is, most offences other than trivial or traffic offences.
- You must not have been fingerprinted in the course of the police investigation – or in connection with any matter since conviction – or if you were fingerprinted the set is incomplete or of insufficient quality to allow satisfactory analysis, comparison or matching.
- A 'conviction' here includes being cautioned in respect of a recordable offence that at the time of the caution you have admitted and also includes a warning or reprimand under the Crime and Disorder Act 1998.
- You must have failed to comply, within seven days, with the requirement made within one month of the date of conviction to attend a police station for fingerprinting.

Arrest for failure to answer police bail
Under a power inserted into PACE by the Criminal Justice and Public Order Act 1994, the police can arrest you without warrant if you are released on bail from police detention, subject to a duty to attend at a police station and you fail to attend at the appointed time. You must be taken as soon as possible after the arrest to the police station to which you should have reported.

Arrest for breach of bail condition
Under a power inserted into PACE by the Criminal Justice Act 2003, the police can arrest you without warrant if you are released on bail from police detention and a constable has reasonable grounds for suspecting you have breached any of the conditions of bail. You must be taken as soon as possible after the arrest to the police station to which you are required to report.

Arrest to have a sample taken
Under a power inserted into PACE by the Criminal Justice and Public Order Act 1994, the police may arrest you in order to take samples that could have been taken while you were in detention for a recordable offence. The following conditions must apply:

- You must either have been charged or convicted of the offence and either not have had a sample taken or the sample was unsuitable or insufficient.
- You must have failed to comply with a request to attend a police station in order to have a sample taken.

This power is likely to be used where the police need to conduct a DNA analysis.

Arrest of a young person for breaking conditions of remand
The Criminal Justice and Public Order Act 1994 inserted a provision into the Children and Young Persons Act 1969 whereby the police may arrest you in the following circumstances: where you are a person who has been remanded or committed to local authority care and conditions under this legislation have been imposed and the police have reasonable grounds for believing you have broken any of the conditions.

You must be taken as soon as practicable before a magistrate and in any event within 24 hours. The magistrate must decide whether a condition has been broken. If it has, then the magistrate must remand you. The Children and Young Persons Act 1969 applies as though you were charged with or convicted of the offence for which the original remand or committal had been made. If a condition has not been broken, then the remand or committal continues subject to the same conditions as previously.

Information to be given on arrest
An arrest is unlawful unless you are told that you are under arrest and the grounds for the arrest at the time. Such an unlawful arrest will become lawful when the police tell you the reason for the arrest. This information must be given at the time of the arrest or as soon as possible afterwards. The information need not be given if it was not reasonably practicable to do so because, for example, you escaped from arrest before it could be given. You must also be cautioned if you attend voluntarily at a police station, or any other place with a constable without having been arrested, that you are entitled to leave at will unless placed under arrest.

Arrest other than at a police station
After arrest, a constable must take you to a police station as soon as is practicable – subject to certain exceptions and the power to release you en route. A constable may, however, delay taking you to a police station if your presence elsewhere is necessary in order to carry out such investigations as it is reasonable to carry out immediately, such as a search of premises. If there are no grounds for keeping you under arrest the police should release you either with or without bail. If you are released in these circumstances the only condition of bail can be that you are required to attend at a police station. Once you have been released on bail there is nothing preventing you being rearrested if new evidence justifying a further arrest comes to light after your arrest.

Use of force
Under PACE the police are allowed to use reasonable force when exercising their powers. Use of excessive force that causes injury or death to a person detained in police custody may certainly raise issues under Article 2 (right to life) or Article 3 (right not to be subjected to inhuman or degrading treatment). In particular, an obligation arises to conduct an investigation and provide an explanation as to how the injury or death occurred.

Search of a person on arrest – other than at a police station
A police officer may search you (including your mouth) where there are reasonable grounds for believing that:

- You may present a danger to yourself or to somebody else.
- You may have concealed on you anything that might be used to assist an escape from lawful custody or which might be evidence relating to any offence.

You cannot be required to remove any of your clothing in public other than an outer coat, jacket or gloves.

Police detention

The circumstances in which an arrested person may be kept in police detention are set out in PACE. The detention is unlawful unless the provisions of PACE are complied with. A key figure in the scheme is the custody officer, a police officer of at least the rank of sergeant.

Normally, the period of detention without charge should not exceed 24 hours, although in some cases the maximum period, with extensions, is as long as 96 hours. There are a number of stages at which continuation of custody must be authorised, in the early stages by police officers and in the later stages by magistrates. Provision is made for the appointment of custody officers and the performance by them and any other constable in charge of the prisoner of important duties. The custody officer is responsible for ordering your immediate release if he or she becomes aware at any time, perhaps after representations from a solicitor, that the grounds for the detention have ceased to apply and that there are no other grounds for continued detention. Conversely, you may not be released except on the authority of a custody officer at the police station where detention was last authorised. The custody officer is also responsible for keeping a custody record in which all information required to be logged by PACE and the Codes of Practice is recorded. Your solicitor or 'appropriate adult' (see later) must be permitted to consult your custody record as soon as practicable after their arrival at the station and at any other time during your detention. You or your legal representative is entitled to a copy of this very important document on leaving police detention or appearing before the court. This entitlement lasts for 12 months after release.

On arrival at or after arrest at the police station

As soon as is practicable after your arrival at the police station or answering to bail, or after arrest at the police station, the custody officer must determine whether there is sufficient evidence to charge you with the offence for which the arrest was made. The custody officer may detain you for as long as is necessary to make such a determination, which includes waiting for others arrested with you to be interviewed. If the custody officer decides that there is sufficient evidence to charge you, then you should be charged and must be released unless one of the post-charge detention conditions applies.

Detention without charge

If the custody officer decides that there is insufficient evidence to charge you, then you must be released. If the custody officer has reasonable grounds for believing that detention without charge is necessary to secure or preserve evidence relating to an offence for which you are under arrest, or to obtain such evidence by questioning you, he or she may order further police detention. The grounds for the detention must be recorded in writing on the custody record. You must be told what these grounds are.

Detention without charge cannot be authorised in your own interest, or to prevent the repetition or continuation of an offence, or to authorise police 'fishing trips' as the evidence must relate to an offence for which you are under arrest. If the custody officer has reasonable grounds to believe that you will not answer questions – for example, because your solicitor has said so – detention cannot be extended to obtain evidence by questioning. Detention for questioning in such circumstances may well be unlawful.

Review of detention

Periodic reviews of detention must be carried out for all persons in police custody pending the investigation of an offence. If you have been charged the review is carried out by the custody officer. If you have not been charged it is carried out by an officer of at least the rank of inspector who has not at any stage been directly involved with the investigation. The general rule is that the first review must be not later than six hours after the detention was first authorised, and subsequent reviews must take place at intervals of not more than nine hours.

Before deciding whether to authorise your detention, the review officer must give you (unless you are asleep) and your solicitor or the duty solicitor an opportunity to make oral or written representations. Representations by a solicitor may be made over the telephone. The representations might relate, for example, to the amount of evidence already obtained or to your refusal to answer questions.

An inspector may in certain circumstances, carry out these reviews by telephone or using video-conferencing facilities. You or your representative can make representations, in the appropriate way and records must still be kept.

The detention clock

PACE limits the length of time for which you can remain in police detention. Such limitations are based on the passage of time from a particular point.

The general rule is that the time starts on your arrival at the first police station to which you are taken after arrest. If arrest takes place at the police station the time starts when you are arrested. There may be some delay between arrest and arrival caused by necessary investigation, but there is a general provision that an arrested person must be taken to a police station as soon as is practicable after arrest.

There are special rules if the arrest takes place outside England and Wales or in a different police area from the one in which you are questioned. You should not be interviewed except at a police station, unless there are special circumstances, for instance, that a delay may lead to interference with evidence or harm to other people.

Detention limits and police extensions

The general rule is that you may not be kept in police detention for more than 24 hours without being charged. This period can be extended by a maximum of 12 hours on the authority of an officer of the rank of superintendent or above after giving opportunity for representations to be made. The extension can only be authorised where:

- The officer has reasonable grounds for believing that the offence is an arrestable offence.
- The investigation is being conducted diligently and expeditiously.
- Detention without charge is necessary to secure or preserve evidence of an offence for which you are under arrest or to obtain evidence by questioning.

The authorisation cannot last beyond 36 hours from when the detention clock began.

Detention limits and magistrates' extensions

You must be released by the end of 36 hours from the starting point, unless an application is made to a Magistrates' Court sitting in private. The application is made on oath by a police officer and supported by written information, which must state the nature of the offence; the general nature of the evidence for the arrest; what enquiries have been made and are proposed; and the reason for believing the continued detention is necessary.

You are entitled to a copy of the information and to be legally represented – you can have an adjournment to obtain legal representation. The police officer will be at court to be cross-examined and representations may be made to the magistrate(s). These might be directed, for example, towards any delay in the investigation or in making the application, whether there is a serious arrestable offence involved, whether detention is necessary, and whether there is sufficient evidence for you to be charged.

The court may only authorise further detention if:

- The offence is a serious arrestable offence.
- The investigation is being conducted diligently and expeditiously.
- Further detention is necessary to secure or preserve evidence relating to the offence or to obtain such evidence by questioning you.

The court may authorise further detention for up to 36 hours from the time that the application is granted. A further extension of up to 36 hours may be granted if the same procedure is followed. The total maximum period of detention is 96 hours from the original starting point – except under the Terrorism Act 2000 where the maximum is currently seven days.

Detention after charge

After you have been charged, the custody officer must order your release unless one of the following post-charge detention conditions applies:

- Your name or address is unknown or doubted.
- Detention is necessary to prevent your committing an offence – if you were arrested for an imprisonable offence – or from causing physical injury to any other person or damaging property – if you were not arrested for an imprisonable offence.
- Detention is necessary to prevent your failing to appear in court to answer bail.
- Detention is necessary to prevent your interfering with the administration of justice or with the investigation of offences.
- You are over 14 and detention is necessary to take a sample of urine or a non-intimate sample (see later) in order to find out whether you have specified Class A drugs in your body.
- Detention is necessary for your own protection.
- A juvenile needs to be detained in his or her own interest – this is additional to the other grounds that may apply equally to juveniles.

A person who has been detained after charge must be taken to court as soon as practicable and not later than the first sitting after charge. The police are also able to impose bail conditions.

5.5   THE RIGHTS OF SUSPECTS IN THE POLICE STATION

The rights of suspects after arrest are contained principally in PACE and in the Code of Practice on the Detention, Treatment and Questioning of Persons and the Code of Practice on Identification of Persons by the Police – Codes C and D.

Any breaches of these codes by the police may result in disciplinary action against them and, if the breaches are sufficiently serious, any confession you make may not be admitted as evidence in a trial. Codes C and D contain detailed provisions governing the conditions of detention, for instance, on the right to legal advice and the right not to be held incommunicado, as well as on searches, exercise and medical treatment. These codes also provide that if you are classed as a vulnerable person, for example, if you are mentally disordered, mentally vulnerable or a juvenile, an appropriate adult, not a police officer, should be present to look after your interests. Anyone who has a disability, for instance, if they are blind or deaf, is also entitled to special treatment under the codes. Annex E of Code C contains a summary of provisions relating to mentally disordered and otherwise mentally vulnerable people.

If you are arrested and taken to a police station or if you are arrested at a police station, the custody officer must, among other things, determine whether you are, or might be, in need of medical treatment, require an appropriate adult and/or an interpreter to help check documentation. The custody officer has to make a formal risk assessment defining the categories of risk relevant to your custody and must make sure any response to any specific risk assessment, for example, ensuring a reduction in opportunities for self-harm. This risk assessment must be kept under review.

So far as your questioning and treatment by the police in custody are concerned, Article 3 (prohibition of torture, inhuman or degrading treatment), Article 6 (the right to a fair trial) and Article 8 (the right to privacy) have been and will continue to be very important. They are particularly important when applying to the court to have evidence, usually confessions, excluded from your trial.

Personal searches at the police station

The custody officer is under a duty to ascertain all property that you have with you on arrest. The custody officer may make a record of all or any of the items he or she finds, and this may be in the custody records. The Criminal Justice Act 2003 has changed the law on this point very recently, and the current version of Code C is not quite accurate. The Criminal Justice Act 2003 will presumably prevail, pending an update to Code C. A police officer of the same sex may search you, using reasonable force if necessary if you refuse to co-operate. The same issues as apply to the use of reasonable force when making an arrest apply here. You should be told the reasons for the search. Under Code C, if a list of property has been made, you are allowed to check it. You should only sign the list if you are sure it is correct.

Clothes and personal effects, not including cash, may be seized only if the custody officer believes you may use them to cause physical injury to yourself or to somebody else, to damage property, to interfere with evidence, to assist an escape, or if he or she has reasonable grounds for believing that they may be evidence relating to an offence. You should be given the reasons for the seizure.

If you refuse to identify yourself, or an officer has reasonable grounds for suspecting that you are not who you say you are, an officer of the rank of inspector or above may authorise that you are searched or examined, or both, for any mark, including features and injuries that would identify you as a person involved in the commission of an offence. The mark can be photographed and used for any purpose related to the prevention or detection of crime, the investigation of crime or the conduct of a prosecution and afterwards it can be retained. This relates to offences in the UK or abroad.

No searches under these provisions should be made by anyone of the opposite sex to you, and intimate searches are prohibited.

Strip searches

A strip search is a search involving the removal of more than outer clothing. A strip search may only take place if the custody officer considers it necessary to remove an article that you would not be allowed to keep. They should not be authorised routinely. The courts have recognised that strip searches may be deeply humiliating and that the removal of a brassière, for instance, would require considerable justification. No person of the opposite sex except for an appropriate adult who has been specifically requested by the person being searched may be present at such a search, nor anyone whose presence is unnecessary. Except in cases of urgency there must be two people present other than the person being searched, when the search involves exposure of intimate parts of the body. One of these may be the appropriate adult, if relevant. Reasons for a strip search and the results of the search must be recorded on the custody record.

Intimate body searches

An intimate body search consists of the physical examination of any one or more of a person's bodily orifices, including the anus, vagina, ears and nose but not the mouth. The police can only carry out an intimate body search in limited circumstances. They can search you if a police officer of at least the rank of inspector has reasonable grounds for believing that:

- You may have concealed on you something that you could use to cause physical injury to yourself or to others, and that you might use it while you are in police detention or in the custody of a court.
- You have concealed Class A drugs – such as heroin and cocaine, but not cannabis or amphetamines – on yourself and that you are in possession of the drugs either with intent to supply them to somebody else or with a view to committing a customs offence.
- You must have the reasons explained to you before the search is carried out and every reasonable effort must be made to persuade you to hand over the article(s) rather than be searched.

A search for drugs – Class A drugs only – may only be carried out by a registered medical practitioner or a registered nurse. It should only be carried out at a hospital, at a registered medical practitioner's surgery or at some other place used for medical purposes. An intimate search for potentially harmful items should also be carried out by a doctor or nurse, but may be conducted by a police officer if an officer of at least the rank of inspector believes that it is not practicable for it to be carried out by a doctor or nurse. The search may be carried out at a police station. Code C stresses that the performance of this search by a police officer is a last resort and should only take place when the authorising officer is satisfied that the risks associated with allowing items to remain with you outweigh the risks associated with removing them.

In the case of all the above searches, Article 3 and Article 8 must be considered. Anything that goes further than that which is necessary for the prevention of disorder or crime would be in violation of these articles.

The right to decent conditions

Code C says that there should only be one person in each cell, but only 'so far as is practicable'. Police cells must be adequately heated, cleaned, ventilated and lit. Bedding should be clean. Access to toilet and washing facilities must be provided.

The police should check on persons in cells once an hour, or every half-hour on those who are drunk. At least two light meals and one main meal should be offered in any period of 24 hours. Brief outdoor exercise should be offered daily if practicable. If restraints have to be used the reasons for doing so have to be recorded. Article 3 of the Convention is of course relevant here. The more vulnerable the suspect, for example, a juvenile or someone who is mentally disordered, the more stringent the safeguards will have to be.

The right to medical treatment

A detained person is entitled to a medical examination by an appropriate healthcare professional. He or she may also be examined by a GP of his or her own choice at his or her own expense. He or she is entitled to have medication where appropriate.

The custody officer must also call the police surgeon if a detained person is injured, or appears to be suffering from physical illness or mental disorder, or otherwise appears to need medical attention.

Most of the information in connection with requests, examinations, medication and so on must be recorded in the custody record. There are some exceptions where this information would appear capable of providing evidence of an offence, but then the record must show where the information is recorded.

The right to legal advice

If you are arrested and held at a police station or other premises you have a statutory right to consult a solicitor in private and free of charge at any time. A duty solicitor scheme is in operation at every police station in England and Wales, so that free telephone advice or a free visit from a solicitor is available. On arrest the custody officer should inform you, orally and in writing, of this right, as well as the right to have someone informed of the arrest. You should also be informed of your right to consult the Codes of Practice, and that these are continuing rights – if you do not take advantage of them when offered you can do so at any time you are in the police station. The police must remind you of your right to see a solicitor at many points during your detention: for instance, before the beginning or recommencement of any interview or before a review.

Access to legal advice may be delayed by the police for up to 36 hours from the relevant time if you are detained for a serious arrestable offence, a drug-trafficking offence or certain other specified offences where the police are attempting to recover property and you have not yet been charged with an offence. Delay may be authorised only by an officer of at least the rank of superintendent if he or she has reasonable grounds, which must be recorded in writing, for believing that the exercise of the right to legal advice would lead to any of the following:

- Interference with evidence of a serious arrestable offence.
- Harm to others.
- The alerting of accomplices.
- Hindering the recovery of property.

Once the reason for authorising the delay ceases to exist, there may be no further delay in permitting access. Delays are rare and even then they often will not be justified.

Code C provides that if you ask for legal advice you should not be interviewed until you have received it, unless:

- Delay is authorised; or
- An officer of at least the rank of superintendent reasonably believes that delay caused by waiting for a solicitor involves risk or harm to persons or property; or
- This would unreasonably delay the investigation; or
- The solicitor cannot or will not attend and you do not want to use the duty solicitor scheme or the duty solicitor is not available; or
- You consent in writing or on tape to the interview going ahead.

You may consult your solicitor in person, on the telephone or in writing. If you are not allowed to see a solicitor, you should think very carefully indeed before answering any questions or making a statement. If you are denied access to legal advice, as opposed to choosing not to take advantage of it, no adverse inferences may be drawn from you exercising your right to silence while that situation persists.

It should be noted that the right to have a solicitor present when being interviewed and also to communicate privately with a solicitor is viewed extremely seriously by the courts, and any unnecessary deprivation may be viewed as a violation of Article 6 of the Convention (the right to a fair trial). Evidence obtained as a result may be excluded from any subsequent trial.

The right not to be kept incommunicado

If you are detained in a police station or other premises, you are entitled to have one friend, relative or person who is known to you or likely to take an interest in your welfare notified of your whereabouts as soon as possible and at public expense. The right is subject to the same delay as consultation with a solicitor except that it can be authorised by an officer of the rank of inspector or above. You may exercise this right each time you are transferred to another police station. If the person cannot be contacted, you may try two others, and after that the police have discretion as to whether you can try to contact any others.

The police should caution you that what is said in any letter, call or message may be given in evidence, except that the police should not listen to a call or read a letter to a solicitor.

With juveniles, the police have an additional duty to inform the person responsible for their welfare as soon as possible and to request their attendance at the police station. There are no provisions permitting delay.

The conduct of interviews

The conduct of interviews is covered by Code C. The overriding principle is that all persons in custody must be dealt with expeditiously and released as soon as the need for detention has ceased to apply. Except in very limited circumstances interviews should only take place in a police station. You should always be cautioned before an interview and be reminded that you have a right to legal advice (unless the circumstances as described in that section apply). Before a detainee is interviewed the custody officer, in consultation with others, shall assess whether the detainee is fit enough to be interviewed. You should be told why you are being interviewed and the nature of the offence or further offence. At the beginning of an interview at a police station, the interviewing officer, after cautioning you, should put to you any significant statement or silence that occurred before your arrival at the police station, and you should be asked to confirm, deny or add to it. A significant statement or silence is one that is capable of being used in evidence against the suspect or of giving rise to an inference under the Criminal Justice and Public Order Act 1994.

An accurate written record should be made of each interview – whether or not it takes place at a police station – unless the interview is tape- or video-recorded. You have a right to see the interview record and you should sign it only if it records exactly what you have said.

Virtually all interviews are now tape-recorded and procedures must follow the Code of Practice for tape-recording, Code E. In many cases the interview must be video-recorded, in which case the police should follow the Code of Practice for videotaping interviews, Code F. Less formal interviews, which are subsequently written up by police officers in their notebooks, are still quite common and you usually have no chance to check the accuracy of their notes.

There are special provisions to protect juveniles, mentally disordered and otherwise mentally vulnerable suspects during interview. The use of prolonged or oppressive questioning, or the denial of access to a solicitor, or other breaches of the codes or PACE, which are not merely technical, may render confessions inadmissible in evidence at court. There may, in addition, be a breach of Article 3 of the Convention, which can be used as part of the argument to have the confession excluded.

The point at which questioning must cease (except in very limited circumstances) has recently been extended in the latest version of Code C. Questioning can continue until the officer in charge of the investigation:

- Is satisfied that all questions they consider relevant to obtaining accurate and reliable information about the offence have been put to the suspect (including those which would permit an innocent explanation);
- Has taken account of all other available evidence; and
- Reasonably believes there is sufficient evidence to provide a realistic prospect of conviction.

In any period of 24 hours a detainee must be allowed a continuous period of at least eight hours' rest. This period should normally be at night.

Also there should be regular breaks in interviewing for meals and light refreshments as described in Code C.

Questioning should cease as soon as the interrogating officer believes that there is sufficient evidence for a prosecution to be brought successfully. You should then be taken before the custody officer and charged or informed that you may be prosecuted.

Curtailment of the right of silence

The right of silence, long considered the most fundamental right of a suspect, was curtailed by the Criminal Justice and Public Order Act 1994. This permits the court hearing the charge against you to draw such inferences as appear proper from the fact of your silence in the following circumstances:

- Failure to mention a fact when questioned under caution before charge that is relied on in your defence.
- Failure on being charged with an offence or informed of likely prosecution to mention a fact that it would have been reasonable for you to mention at the time.
- Failure or refusal to account for objects, substances or marks found on your person, in or on your clothing or otherwise in your possession, in the place where you were arrested.
- Failure or refusal after your arrest to account for your presence at a place at or about the time the offence is alleged to have been committed.

No inferences may be drawn, however, if you were not given an opportunity to consult a solicitor prior to being questioned, charged, informed of a prosecution, or requested to explain the matters referred to above. The caution in these cases is differently worded from that stated below. It is simply 'you do not have to say anything, but anything you do say may be given in evidence'.

Before inferences can be drawn in the last two cases the officer should first have explained in ordinary language, among other things, the nature of the offence, the possibility of adverse inferences being drawn and that a record is being made of the interview that could be used in the trial. This is in addition to the caution that is now worded as follows:

'You do not have to say anything. But it may harm your defence if you do not mention when questioned something which you later rely on in court. Anything you do say may be given in evidence.'

This caution must be given before any questioning of someone who is suspected of committing an offence about his or her involvement in the offence. You should normally be cautioned on arrest and before any interviewing or continuation of an interview. If you are charged, you should be cautioned in the same way, but if you are questioned after charge, the caution is simply that anything you say may be used in evidence but that you do not have to say anything (as above). This is because there is no provision in the Criminal Justice and Public Order Act 1994 for inferences to be drawn from silence after charge.

The restrictions introduced by the Criminal Justice and Public Order Act 1994 have been reviewed many times by the courts. The European Court of Human Rights regards any inroads into the right of silence very seriously under Article 6 of the Convention (the right to a fair trial), and there have been many challenges to the provisions of the Criminal Justice and Public Order Act 1994.

You cannot be convicted of an offence solely on the basis of your failure or refusal to answer questions or furnish information.

Fingerprints

Fingerprints, which include palm prints, may be taken from anyone over the age of ten without consent and without a court order in any of the following circumstances:

- If you have been detained after an arrest for, or been charged with, or informed you will be prosecuted for a recordable offence, and your fingerprints have not already been taken in the course of the investigation.
- In any of the above circumstances where the fingerprints have been taken before but did not constitute a complete set or were not of sufficient quality.
- If you have been convicted of a recordable offence or cautioned in respect of a recordable offence you have admitted or been warned or reprimanded under the Crime and Disorder Act 1998 for a recordable offence.
- If you answer to bail at a court or police station, if the court or an officer of at least the rank of inspector believes on reasonable grounds that you are not the same person whose fingerprints were taken on a previous occasion or where you actually claim to be a different person.

Recordable offences are specified in regulations and include all but the most trivial offences.

Where fingerprints are taken without your consent, reasons must be given before they are taken, and those reasons must be recorded. Reasonable force may be used. If the police obtain your consent to fingerprinting, it must be in writing if given at a police station. Consent in the case of a child – aged ten to 14 – is the consent of his or her parents alone and in the case of a young adult – aged 14 to 17 – of the parents and him or herself.

Before your fingerprints are taken, with or without your consent, you should be told that they might be the subject of a speculative search. This means that they can be checked against other fingerprints held in records by or on behalf of the police.

Fingerprints taken in connection with immigration cases are subject to separate rules.

Photographs

If you are detained at a police station you can be photographed without your consent and the photographs can be used by, or disclosed to, any person for any purpose related to the prevention or detection of crime, the investigation of an offence or the conduct of a prosecution. This relates to offences in the UK or abroad. Any item or substance worn on or over your head or face can be removed and reasonable force can be used, if necessary, to take the photographs.

Intimate and non-intimate samples

An intimate sample is a sample of blood, semen or any other tissue, fluid, urine, saliva, pubic hair or a swab taken from a bodily orifice other than the mouth. An intimate sample – other than urine – may only be taken by a doctor, registered nurse or registered healthcare professional and dental impressions by a registered dentist, and only if an officer of at least the rank of inspector authorises it and you consent to it in writing. Consent for juveniles is the same as for fingerprinting. The authorisation may only be given if the officer has reasonable grounds for believing that the sample will confirm or disprove your involvement in a recordable offence.

If you refuse to consent without reasonable cause the court or jury may – in committal proceedings or at a trial – draw such inferences from the refusal as appear proper, and the refusal may be treated as corroboration of any evidence against you to which the refusal is material. You must be warned of this before being asked to provide such a sample. This provision was inserted with rape suspects in mind.

Also, even if you are not in police detention, if in the course of investigating an offence the police previously took at least two non-intimate samples from you for the same means of analysis, often DNA, which prove to be insufficient, they can take an intimate sample from you with your written consent.

The provisions for breath tests and blood or urine samples in cases of drunk drivers are quite separate.

A non-intimate sample is a sample of hair other than pubic hair, a sample taken from a nail or from under a nail, a swab taken from any part of a person's body other than an orifice, and a skin impression (except dental impressions). Non-intimate samples may be taken with your written consent (consent for juveniles is the same as for fingerprinting) or without consent if:

- You are in police detention after an arrest for a recordable offence and have either not had a sample taken already in the course of the investigation or you have but it was insufficient.
- You are in police detention or being held in custody on the authority of a court and an officer of at least the rank of inspector authorises it. He or she may do this if there are reasonable grounds for believing the sample will confirm or disprove your involvement in a serious arrestable offence. Reasons for taking the sample must be provided to you and recorded.
- You have been charged with or informed you will be reported with a view to summons for a recordable offence and have either not had a non-intimate sample taken in the course of investigation of the offence or such a sample was taken but it was not suitable or was insufficient for the same means of analysis – often DNA.
- You have been convicted of a recordable offence.

Speculative searches

The police have powers to take fingerprints and samples to compare with any on their databases. Before such fingerprints and samples are taken, you should be informed that they might be used for such a speculative search.

Destruction of fingerprints and samples

Any fingerprints and samples that are taken from you in the course of an investigation into an offence, other than where you are not a suspect, for instance, where you were the victim of a burglary, may be retained by the police for further use in preventing, detecting, investigation and prosecuting offences, whether in the UK or abroad. This applies even if you were acquitted of the criminal offence. The House of Lords has held that this does not contravene either Article 8 or Article 14 of the Convention. If you were not a suspect then they can be retained if you consent in writing. If you do not consent they must be destroyed.

Identification by witnesses

Procedures for identification parades or other group identifications, video identifications with others, confrontation by witnesses and the showing of photographs to witnesses are set out in detail in the Code of Practice dealing with the identification of witnesses, Code D, and you should consult these and where possible have a solicitor present.

Making notes

If you have been involved in any incident with the police or you have witnessed an incident, it is advisable to make and keep full notes as soon as possible after the events in question. The police are allowed to refer to notes in court. This happens not because police officers have some special status as witnesses – they do not – but because the notes are contemporaneous, that is, notes that are made at the time or as soon as reasonably practicable thereafter. Contemporaneous notes are not in themselves evidence, but they can be used to refresh the witness's memory.

You have the same right to use notes. A delay in writing the notes of several hours or even a day or so may not prevent you from using the notes. Even if you cannot use them at court they will be a helpful record of the events.

If you are detained at a police station, Code C provides that you should be supplied on request with writing materials. This may be delayed in certain circumstances. When making notes:

- Write out a full and legible note of everything that happened in the correct sequence of events.
- Write down everything that was said, word for word if possible, particularly any conversation you had with police officers.
- Record the names and numbers, if you know them, of the police officers involved.
- Sign the notes at the bottom and put the time and date.
- If you see a solicitor, hand over the notes and make sure you get a copy to keep for yourself.
- If you are going to court, take the notes with you.
- If there are witnesses to the incident, take their names and addresses if possible and ask them to make notes.

If you have been injured, for example, by the use of excessive force by the police during your arrest, you must:

- Have photographs taken if there are any visible injuries.
- See a doctor so that your injuries are recorded.

The photographs and medical evidence may be of great value to you if you are charged with a criminal offence or if you wish to make a police complaint or sue the police.

5.6   ANTI-TERRORISM POWERS

The Terrorism Act 2000 (TA 2000) and the Anti-Terrorism Crime and Security Act 2001 (ATSA 2001) have widened police powers in recent years with respect to terrorism. There are three published codes of practice under the legislation and the Codes of Practice accompanying PACE have been amended to deal with some of the legislative effects.

The most useful and possibly the only up-to-date source of information on these is to be found on the Home Office website <www.homeoffice.gov.uk>.

The powers described below are in addition to all the general powers the police have under other legislation, that is, PACE and the common law. They have extra powers at ports and airports that are not included below. This section outlines powers in relation to individuals rather than organisations.

These additional powers apply in the investigation of 'terrorism'. Terrorism is defined by the TA 2000 as:

- The use or threat of action where the action:
  - involves serious violence against a person;
  - involves serious damage to property;
  - endangers a person's life, other than that of the person committing the action;
  - creates a serious risk to the health or safety of the public or a section of the public; or
  - is designed to seriously interfere with or seriously disrupt an electronic system; and
  - the use or threat of this action is designed to influence the government or to intimidate the public or a section of the public; and
  - the use or threat is made for the purpose of advancing a political, religious or ideological cause.

The use or threat of action as above that is not intended to influence the government or to intimidate the public or a section of the public will still be terrorism if it involves the use of firearms or explosives.

The term 'action' includes action outside the UK. 'Public' includes the public of any country other than the UK and 'Government' means the government of the UK or part of the UK or anywhere else.

Proscribed organisations
The Secretary of State has discretion to designate an organisation as a proscribed one, just as he can deproscribe one. You can find a list of proscribed organisations in Schedule 2 to the TA 2000. The list is updated as necessary. Currently it includes Northern Ireland-related organisations and many others of which the following are just examples:

Al Qu'ada
Egyptian Islamic Jihad
Al Gama'at al-Islamiya
International Sikh Youth Foundation
Hisballah External Security Organisation
Kurdistan Workers' Party
Palestinian Islamic Jihad-Shaqaqi

Terrorism offences
Most actions that are usually described as terrorism such as murder, arson, bombings etc. are offences under the general criminal law. However, there are some offences created specifically by the TA 2000. These include:

- Membership of a proscribed organisation or supporting a proscribed organisation.
- Possession of money with intent to use it for terrorism.
- Failure to stop a vehicle in accordance with police requirements under the terrorism legislation.
- Providing instruction or training for the purposes of committing terrorist offences.

Stop and search
These refer to persons and vehicles, and it is an offence to fail to stop a vehicle.

When a police officer reasonably suspects you are a terrorist you can be stopped and searched to discover whether you have anything in your possession that could constitute evidence that you are a terrorist. Since being a terrorist is not in itself an offence, unless you are a member of a proscribed group, this power means that the police do not have to suspect you of committing an offence or of carrying prohibited articles.

In addition, the police can designate specific areas to be places where they have special powers in relation to terrorism. This means that within these localities people and vehicles can be stopped and searched by the police if they consider it expedient to do so to prevent acts of terrorism. There is no need for any reasonable suspicion.

They should be looking for articles that could be used in connection with terrorism, but the powers can be used whether or not the police have grounds for suspecting the presence of articles of that kind.

Failure to stop a vehicle or obstructing a police officer in the exercise of these powers is an offence punishable with a fine, a prison sentence of six months or both.

Authorisations to designate areas as subject to these powers last for 28 days but they can be renewed. The Secretary of State has powers to intervene in such authorisations.

Powers of arrest
Offences under the terrorism legislation are all arrestable offences and there are also specific powers of arrest in the terrorism legislation. You can be arrested without warrant if you are reasonably suspected of being a terrorist. Because of the wide definition of terrorism it may be possible that you could be arrested under the terrorism legislation or other legislation – or even common law – but if you are arrested under the terrorism legislation the other provisions in relation to investigating terrorism come into operation. This arrest power may well be incompatible with Article 5 of the Convention.

Search of premises
Police powers to enter and search premises without a warrant generally are wide enough to cover most terrorist situations. Nevertheless there are special powers in the terrorism legislation. A senior police officer can authorise a search of your premises

if there are reasonable grounds for believing the case is one of great emergency and that in the interests of the State immediate action is necessary.

There are also powers for the police to cordon off certain areas so that they can enter and search premises within the cordon for material that would be of substantial value to the investigation.

The police may also obtain a warrant from a magistrate to search for material likely to be of substantial value to the investigation, provided that there are reasonable grounds for believing it is on particular premises.

Detention

The legislation permits terrorist suspects to be detained for longer than other suspects and for them to have fewer or more constrained rights. The maximum period of detention without charge for someone arrested under terrorism legislation is 14 days, but this is subject to judicial authorisation. Access to a solicitor, although the latter can be consulted privately, can be delayed for 48 hours, with additional grounds for delay to those that apply to other suspects. The same applies to the right to have someone notified of arrest.

5.7   FURTHER INFORMATION

Useful organisations

British Transport Police
15 Tavistock Place
London WC1H 9SJ
Tel: 020 7830 8800
Free phone: 0800 405 040
<www.btp.police.uk>

Ministry of Defence
The Ministerial Correspondence Unit
Room 222, Old War Office
Whitehall
London SW1A 2EU
Tel: 0870 607 4455
public@ministers.mod.uk
<www.mod.uk>

Independent Police Complaints Commission (IPCC)
90 High Holborn
London WC1V 6BH
Tel: 0845 300 2002
Fax: 020 7404 0430

6   The Rights of Defendants

This chapter deals with:

- Prosecution
- Bail
- Representation and funding
- Venue
- Trial
- Sentence
- Appeals
- The Criminal Cases Review Commission
- The European Convention on Human Rights
- Further information

The 'defendant' is the term used in the criminal courts for a person who is accused of an offence.

This area of law has been changing rapidly as recent governments have sought to reduce crime and cut the costs of delivering justice, sometimes at the expense of defendants' rights. The present Home Secretary shows every intention of continuing this rate of change. The recent McPherson Report into the Stephen Lawrence case, and the incorporation of the European Convention on Human Rights (the Convention) into English and Welsh law, have brought opposing pressures for change in the criminal justice system.

6.1   PROSECUTION

The initial decision whether or not to prosecute you is normally taken by the police, although they may consult the Crown Prosecution Service (CPS) lawyers in more complex cases. Prosecutions can be commenced by charge or by summons. Once a prosecution has been started, the responsibility passes to the CPS, who will then decide whether to proceed with, to alter or to drop the charges. They also have the power to take over private prosecutions and can then discontinue them.

The police can only charge you if you are under arrest. They may charge you with one or more offences, and then release you on bail to attend court in a few days, or keep you in custody, when they must produce you at the next sitting of the local Magistrates' Court. Alternatively, for less serious offences you should normally be released without charge and sent a summons by post a few weeks later. The same summons procedure will be used for offences for which you have not been arrested, for example, if the police stop you but do not arrest you for a driving offence. You cannot be prosecuted for most driving offences unless you have either been warned verbally by the police at the time that you may be prosecuted or the police have sent you a notice of intended prosecution within 14 days of the offence.

Both summons and charge sheet will set out the details of the offence or offences and the place, time and date that you must attend court. The sworn information on which a less serious offence is charged must be laid before the court within six months of the incident.

6.2 BAIL

From the police station

Once you have been charged with an offence, the police must release you on bail unless the custody officer reasonably believes that:

- There is doubt about your name or address;
- Detention is necessary to protect you or somebody else; or
- You will fail to attend court or interfere with witnesses or the administration of justice.

The police can attach conditions to your bail, such as living at a fixed address, reporting to a local police station, a curfew, avoiding named people or places, or providing a financial guarantee for your attendance at court.

If you fail to attend court without reasonable excuse, you commit a separate offence under the Bail Act 1976. If you break any of the conditions of your bail, you can be arrested and brought in custody to the next sitting of the local Magistrates' Court, who may then take away your bail.

From the court

If you are on police bail with conditions, you can apply to the Magistrates' Court to vary the conditions. If the police have kept you in custody, they must produce you at the next sitting of the local Magistrates' Court, which then takes any decisions about bail if your case continues after the first hearing. The court can grant bail with or without conditions, or remand you in custody.

Before conviction, you have a right to be granted bail unless certain exceptions apply. The most significant of these are where the court finds that there are substantial grounds for believing you may do one or more of the following:

- Fail to attend at court.
- Commit further offences.
- Interfere with witnesses.

The factors the court will consider in deciding this include the charge, the evidence, your own background (including your job and family), any previous convictions you have and whether you have previously absconded when on bail.

If the court has concerns on these grounds, it can attach conditions to your bail, including those already mentioned; residence at a bail hostel; payment of a cash security into court; or providing a surety.

A surety is someone who knows you personally and offers the court a sum of money to guarantee you will attend court when required. He or she does not have to pay the money into court, but has to show that it is available. If you then do not turn up at court on time, the surety may have to pay the money or even go to prison if unable to do so. Your surety will have to attend the court or police station in person to sign as surety. You will not be released from custody yourself until he or she has done so. The surety should not have a criminal record, and should provide proof that the necessary funds are available, for example, a bank statement or building society book. It is an offence to lend someone money to enable him or her to stand surety.

If you are charged with an offence that does not carry a possible sentence of imprisonment, the court can normally only refuse bail if you have failed to attend in the past and it believes you would do so again.

Where conditions are attached to your bail, or bail is refused, the court must state its reasons for doing so. In cases of rape or homicide, the court must also state reasons if it decides to grant bail.

If you are refused bail at your first hearing, you can apply again at the second hearing of your case, or if there is a change in your circumstances relating to bail.

If the Magistrates' Court refuses your application for bail or imposes conditions that you are unhappy with or cannot meet, you can appeal to a Crown Court judge even if your case can only be heard in the Magistrates' Court.

In serious cases, the prosecution can appeal to the Crown Court judge against the granting of bail by the magistrates, although this is unusual.

If you are under 17 when bail is refused, you will not be remanded straight to custody, but will be accommodated by the local authority, which may place you with your family, in a children's home, or apply to the court to place you in secure accommodation. See also Chapter 13.

If you are refused bail and are remanded in custody, custody time limits will apply to your case. Once the custody time limit has expired the court must release you on bail unless the prosecution has obtained an extension from the court beforehand. The limits are 56 days for Magistrates' Court trial, 70 days for committal to the Crown Court, and 112 days from committal to Crown Court trial. To extend these limits, the prosecution has to justify the time they are taking to bring your case to trial.

6.3   REPRESENTATION AND FUNDING

Criminal lawyers fall into two categories:

- Solicitors, who will be your first point of contact, see clients, take instructions, prepare cases and appear in the Magistrates' Court. Some solicitors with a higher qualification also appear in the Crown Court.
- Barristers specialise in advocacy, mainly in the higher courts, and will be instructed by your solicitor on your behalf, if necessary. Barristers work from chambers in central locations, while solicitors have offices that may be local to your home or to the court where you appear.

If you have not already seen a solicitor at the police station, it is a good idea to consult one before your first court appearance, although you may have little time in which to do so.

Legal services are not cheap, and most defendants in the criminal courts rely on public funding (legal aid) to provide representation. Sadly, the Government has recently cut back on the availability of legal aid.

At your first appearance in the Magistrates' Court you can seek the help of the court duty solicitor, free of charge. This service is provided by a rota of independent local solicitors, and is often the best way of obtaining advice and, if necessary, representation on a straightforward or minor case. However, you cannot get help from the duty solicitor if you are not in custody and have not been charged with an offence for which you could be sent to prison.

If your case is at all serious or complex and you cannot afford a solicitor, you will need to apply to the court for a Representation Order. In doing so, you may nominate a solicitor of your own choice to represent you, and you should seek his or her assistance in completing the application forms. You should try and see a solicitor as soon as possible after you have been charged. Some solicitors may want to charge you for seeing you to complete the application forms, but many will be prepared to see you without charge if they are reasonably confident that you will be granted a Representation Order.

In deciding whether to grant you a Representation Order, the court applies a merits test to determine whether it is in the 'interests of justice' for you to be represented at public expense. This means whether your case is serious enough or sufficiently complex. The basic threshold of seriousness is whether there is any risk of imprisonment. In the case of young people, the criteria are more relaxed.

If a Representation Order is refused, you can renew your application to the court in writing or orally in court.

If you are granted a Representation Order, there will be no charge to you for your defence costs in the Magistrates' Court. However, if you plead guilty, or are found guilty, you will normally be ordered to pay a contribution to the prosecution costs. Should your case proceed to the Crown Court, you will be required to complete a statement of means, and may be ordered to pay a contribution to your defence costs as well as the prosecution costs at the end of the case. However, this is unlikely to happen if you are found not guilty.

At the time of writing the Government has announced plans to extend the power to claim a contribution to defence costs to defendants dealt with in the Magistrates' Court as well as the Crown Court.

You may of course choose to pay privately for a lawyer to represent you, whether or not public funding is available.

If you are not represented, you are still entitled to have a friend or adviser to sit with you in court to give you advice and help take notes. This person is referred to as a 'Mackenzie' friend, and cannot speak for you in court.

6.4   VENUE

This term is used by lawyers to refer to the court in which your case will be heard. All cases begin in the Magistrates' Court or, if you are under 18, in the Youth Court. Over 90 per cent of cases are concluded in the Magistrates' Court. They are heard by a bench of two or three lay Justices of the Peace, who are trained volunteers, or a single legally qualified District Judge, formerly known as a Stipendiary Magistrate.

There are three categories of offences:

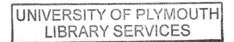

Summary offences

Most offences are 'summary', which means they can only be heard in the Magistrates' Court. These include common assault, threatening behaviour and nearly all motoring offences. They may not be imprisonable at all, or may carry a maximum sentence of no more than six months.

Magistrates decide whether you are guilty or not guilty. Where there is a dispute about whether certain evidence is admissible or not (i.e. whether one side or the other can rely on it), they will decide that issue. This means that they sometimes hear things that they then have to disregard. There is no jury.

Indictable-only offences

At the other end of the scale, a small number of the most serious offences, such as murder, rape or robbery, are tried on indictment only. This means they must be tried in the Crown Court before a judge, who rules on the law and passes sentence, and a jury of 12 members of the public, chosen at random, who hear the evidence and decide on the facts whether you are 'guilty' or 'not guilty' of the charge.

The judge's maximum sentencing powers extend up to life imprisonment, but in all cases the sentence is limited by the maximum sentence fixed by Parliament for the offence charged.

These cases pass through the Magistrates' Court speedily, with the magistrates deciding on preliminary issues such as bail and representation only, and are usually sent to the Crown Court after one or two hearings.

Either-way offences

In between are a number of offences, such as assaults resulting in injury, theft and other offences of dishonesty, and burglary, which may be tried in either the Magistrates' Court or the Crown Court.

In either-way offences, a somewhat complex procedure, known as 'plea before venue', takes place in the Magistrates' Court. First, you indicate how you intend to plead to each of the charges. If you enter a guilty plea, then the Magistrates' Court goes on to consider sentence, but may still decide to commit you to the Crown Court for a heavier sentence than it has power to impose. The magistrates cannot pass a sentence of more than six months' imprisonment for any one offence, but, where you are convicted of two or more either-way offences, they can impose a total of up to one year in prison.

If you indicate a not guilty plea to an either-way charge, and the prosecution is proceeding against you on that charge, then the Magistrates' Court first considers whether its powers of sentence are sufficient in principle to deal with the case. If not, for example, for most dwelling-house burglaries, the magistrates send the case to the Crown Court.

If the magistrates decide that they can hear the case, that is, that their powers of sentence are sufficient, you still have the right to elect trial by jury in the Crown Court. However, the present Government has already attempted legislation to remove this right and give the courts the last say.

When given this decision, you need to weigh carefully the advantages and disadvantages of each court. Rates of acquittal on not-guilty pleas are significantly higher in jury trials, and many defendants feel they receive a fairer hearing before a jury than before magistrates, who may have become 'case-hardened'. This is especially so where challenging police officers' evidence or arguing for the exclusion of evidence that may be inadmissible, as the magistrates will hear this anyway.

Jury trial involves significant delays and greater prosecution and defence costs, which you may be ordered to pay if you are convicted. You are also opting for a court with greater sentencing powers in the event of your conviction.

The choice may not be straightforward, and again it is best to obtain legal advice before making it. You are entitled to a summary of the prosecution evidence, or copies of their witness statements, before deciding. This is known as 'Advance Information'.

In the Youth Court, the process is simpler. All charges are heard there, unless, on certain 'grave' charges carrying very long maximum sentences, the Youth Court sends the case to the Crown Court for trial. Youths have no right to elect jury trial. The Youth Court now has increased powers of sentence up to a maximum of two years in custody. If you are under 15, these powers are only available if the Youth Court decides you are already a 'persistent' offender. See also Chapter 13.

6.5   TRIAL

If you plead not guilty, the court will fix a date for your trial, or may, in the Crown Court, put it in a warned period of one or two weeks, when it could be heard on any day. You will need to arrange for any witnesses you wish to call in your defence to attend court on the trial date. When they do so, they will have to wait outside court and not discuss the case until after they have given their evidence.

Before trial, the prosecution must disclose to you details of any 'unused material', that is, evidence in its possession that it will not be using at trial, which may be relevant to your case. You must have the chance to examine it. In the Crown Court, you must then provide to the court and the prosecution a brief statement of your defence in outline. In the Magistrates' Court, this is optional, but you can use it to seek further disclosure from the prosecution, who must again review all material in its possession, when it receives it, and disclose anything relevant to your defence.

When the trial begins, the prosecution will open its case with a brief speech setting out what it intends to prove against you. They call witnesses in turn, and play any tape or video evidence.

The basic rule is that evidence must be given orally in court on oath. You will have the opportunity to question each witness in turn. This is called cross-examination, and when you do so you must state which part of the witness's evidence you dispute, and give them the chance to respond.

Written statements cannot be read out in court unless you or your lawyer have been given a copy and have not objected to this. There are certain limited areas in which written evidence can be read without your agreement, for instance, where the court allows it because a witness is abroad, or is absent having been put in fear, or a statement is compiled from details of transactions a witness could not be expected to remember. Objects or documents produced by a witness as evidence can be made 'exhibits' in the case.

At the end of the prosecution case, if it has failed to provide any evidence of a vital ingredient of the charge against you, you can make a submission to the court that there is no case for you to answer. Otherwise, you then have the choice of whether or not to go into the witness box and give evidence yourself. If you do so, you will be cross-examined by the prosecutor. If you do not, you risk the court concluding that you have no answer to the charge, or none that will stand up to cross-examination.

If you do give evidence, the prosecution will not normally be able to ask you about any previous convictions you may have. However, if you give or call evidence of your own good character (i.e. suggest that you do not have any previous convictions when you do), or attack the character of any prosecution witnesses (as opposed to disputing their evidence), the court may allow them to do so.

Afterwards you may then call any witnesses in your defence. The prosecution will be able to cross-examine your witnesses. You or your lawyer can then make a concluding speech, arguing your case. In the Crown Court, the judge sums up the case to the jury. The jury or the magistrates then retire to consider their verdict.

The 'burden' of proof is on the prosecution. It brings the case and it must prove, by admissible evidence, each element of the charge against you. Another way of describing this is the 'presumption of innocence': you do not have to prove your innocence, it is presumed unless and until the prosecution proves the contrary. There are certain limitations to this basic proposition. For instance, where you argue self-defence on an assault charge, you will have to raise some evidence that you felt yourself to be at risk of attack, which the prosecution then has to disprove.

The 'standard' of proof is that the jury, or magistrates, must be sure of your guilt. Another way of expressing this is that they must be satisfied 'beyond reasonable doubt' that you committed the offence charged. If, for example, the jury think you probably committed the offence, but cannot be certain that you did, you should be found not guilty.

The verdict of the court is one of guilty or not guilty. A not-guilty verdict is not a finding of innocence, but means that the prosecution has failed to prove by admissible evidence that you committed the offence. In practice, it means that in normal circumstances you cannot be tried again for the same offence. Jury verdicts must be unanimous unless, after two or three hours, the judge allows a majority verdict of ten jurors. The magistrates' verdicts are by majority.

If you are acquitted, you can apply to the court for your personal expenses and your legal costs to be reimbursed, but not for any loss of earnings. Your witnesses can claim their expenses and also loss of earnings from the court. You may also wish to consider a civil claim against the police where, for instance, there is evidence of malicious prosecution. See also Chapter 2.

6.6   SENTENCE

If you are found guilty, or have pleaded guilty, the court will then go on to consider how to sentence you. At this point, the court will be told of any previous convictions you may have.

The sentences available to the court range from discharges (conditional or absolute) and fines, through community penalties such as community rehabilitation and punishment orders, up to custody. Variations of these are available in the Youth Court.

If a compensation order is asked for, the court should make one or state their reasons for not doing so. They must take account of your ability to pay compensation or a fine, and will normally fix a weekly or monthly rate of payment that you can afford. If the court later finds you have deliberately avoided paying, you can be sent to prison.

If considering a community penalty, the court will normally adjourn for a pre-sentence report to be prepared by the Probation Service. They must do so if considering custody, unless, when dealing with an adult, the court deems it unnecessary. Reports are usually prepared in two to four weeks and, although the right to bail no longer applies, there is a presumption that, if you are already on bail, this will be continued. Where the court has a specific sentence in mind, reports can be provided on the spot.

Imprisonment can be imposed only where the court considers the offence and associated offences so serious that only a prison sentence is appropriate. Where sentencing for more than one offence, the court must not simply add up the sentences passed for the individual offences, but review the totality of the sentence. Credit is normally given for pleas of guilty in the form of a reduction of a sentence, up to a maximum of one-third, depending on how soon the guilty plea was notified to the prosecution.

Before you are sentenced, you can tell the court of any mitigating factors relating to yourself or the offence, and call character witnesses or submit written character references to the court. The court may also require medical or psychiatric reports before passing sentence. The court should not pass a sentence of imprisonment on you without giving you the opportunity to be legally represented.

See also Chapter 7.

6.7   APPEALS

If you feel the court has made the wrong decision in your case, there are several routes of appeal open to you.

Appeals from the Magistrates' Court
You have a right of appeal from the Magistrates' or Youth Court to the Crown Court. If you have pleaded guilty, you can only appeal against your sentence; if you pleaded not guilty, you can appeal against conviction and sentence.

Notice of appeal must be given to the court and to the prosecutor within 21 days of the conclusion of your case. You can apply for representation for the appeal.

These appeals are complete rehearings of your case in the Crown Court, but before a judge and two magistrates. There is no jury. If your appeal is against conviction, the evidence will be heard afresh, and the court will reach its own conclusion, by a majority if divided.

If your appeal against conviction fails, or if your appeal is against sentence only, the court will then review the sentence passed, and can substitute any sentence the original court could have passed, up to the maximum sentence available to that court. This means there is a possibility that your sentence could be increased. An additional risk is that you might be ordered to pay the costs of an unsuccessful appeal.

The decision of the Crown Court on appeal is final, and there is only one, relatively unusual, situation in which you can pursue your case further.

Appeals to the High Court

Where you consider that either the Magistrates' Court or Youth Court, or the Crown Court when hearing your appeal, have made an error of law or acted in excess of their jurisdiction (i.e. power), you can appeal on a point of law to the Divisional Court, a section of the High Court. This is done by way of asking the lower court to 'state a case' for the Divisional Court's consideration. You have 21 days in which to ask the court to 'state a case'.

These proceedings are available to both the prosecution and the defence. The procedure is complex, and you will need the help of a lawyer. Criminal Representation Orders are now available. You cannot challenge decisions of fact in this way, but only raise questions of law.

Should you succeed in the Divisional Court, your case is likely to be sent back to the lower court with directions for its reconsideration.

A similar procedure, but one that is available before your case has been concluded, is to apply for judicial review of the lower court's decision in the High Court. For example, a decision by the Youth Court to refuse jurisdiction and send a case to the Crown Court can only be challenged in this way. However, no Criminal Representation Order is available, and you will have to apply to the Community Legal Service for means-tested funding.

See also Chapter 2.

Appeals from the Crown Court

Where your case has been heard in the Crown Court, other than on appeal, you can give notice of appeal to the Court of Appeal (Criminal Division) within 28 days of the decision to be appealed. Thus, if you appeal against conviction after your trial, you may have to give notice to the court before you are actually sentenced. The notice must state your grounds of appeal.

Your original Crown Court Representation order includes advice on appeal from your advocate, and the drafting of grounds, if appropriate. These appeals are not a rehearing. The Court of Appeal will consider written and oral arguments, but rarely hears fresh evidence and will only intervene in an appeal against conviction if the conviction is shown to be 'unsafe'. Where the appeal is against sentence only, the Court of Appeal does not have the power to increase the sentence, but will only reduce it where it is shown to be 'wrong in principle' or 'manifestly excessive'.

The prosecution can also refer serious cases to the Court of Appeal where it considers the Crown Court sentence passed was 'unduly lenient', in which case your sentence may be increased.

Your application will first be considered by a single judge, who can grant or refuse leave to appeal. If leave is refused, the single judge has power to direct that time spent in prison already does not count towards your sentence, thus effectively lengthening it. This power is rarely used at this stage, but, if you are refused leave to appeal and go on to pursue your appeal in the full court, the court has the same power and is more likely to use it. If leave is granted, a Representation Order is likely to be granted for you to be represented by an advocate at your appeal.

Lastly, there is always the risk of being ordered to pay the costs of an unsuccessful appeal, but, again, this is unlikely if leave has been granted.

Appeal from the Court of Appeal

There is a limited right of appeal to the House of Lords, but only where a point of law of 'general public importance' is certified. The procedure is arcane and you will certainly need the help of a lawyer in these circumstances.

Bail pending appeal

In each of these situations, if you are in custody, it is possible to apply for bail to be granted until your appeal is heard, either to the lower court whose decision you are appealing, or to the court where your appeal is to be heard. In practice, this is very rarely granted, but making the application may speed up the hearing of your case.

6.8   THE CRIMINAL CASES REVIEW COMMISSION

Set up in 1995 in response to public concern after a series of well-publicised miscarriages of justice had come to light, the Criminal Cases Review Commission (CCRC) is the last resort for a dissatisfied defendant.

You can ask the CCRC to review your case. They have the power to investigate and to refer Crown Court cases back to the Court of Appeal, or Magistrates' Court cases back to the Crown Court on appeal. They should not normally do so unless they are satisfied that there is 'a real possibility' that the verdict or sentence passed would not be upheld.

However, the CCRC is restricted in that referrals can only be based on arguments or evidence not raised in the original hearing or appeal, unless there are 'exceptional circumstances'. As a result, you cannot simply regard the CCRC as a court of final appeal, but rather as a means of bringing possible miscarriages of justice back into the court system where further information comes to light, or there is continuing public concern.

6.9   THE EUROPEAN CONVENTION ON HUMAN RIGHTS

In the criminal justice context the most important articles of the European Convention on Human Rights (the Convention) are Articles 5, 6 and 7.

Article 6 guarantees the right to a fair trial. This includes the right to a public trial within a reasonable time. Additionally, specific rights given to people being prosecuted for a criminal charge include:

- The right to be presumed innocent.
- The right to be informed of the case against you in a language you understand.
- Enough time and facilities to prepare your defence.
- The right to defend yourself and to be legally represented, free of charge, when this is in the 'interests of justice'.

- Ensure that prosecution witnesses attend and can be cross-examined, and to call defence witnesses on the same terms.
- Have an interpreter, if necessary, free of charge.

Article 5 guarantees that you cannot be deprived of your liberty, except where the correct legal procedure has been followed and in specified circumstances. This includes where someone has been convicted of an offence and given a prison sentence and where someone is detained in order to bring them before a court once they have been charged. If you are arrested, you must be informed promptly of the reason for your arrest. If you are charged and held in custody you must be brought before a court promptly. If you are remanded in custody pending trial, you must be tried within a reasonable time. Where you are not detained for the purposes of punishment (e.g. if you are a life prisoner who has served their tariff or a psychiatric patient detained under the Mental Health Act 1983) you are entitled to have your detention reviewed periodically by an independent tribunal.

Article 7 guarantees that you cannot be punished for something that was not an offence at the time you did it or given a sentence that is more than the maximum that applied at the time you committed the offence.

In theory, the English and Welsh criminal justice system should comply with all the requirements of the Convention. In practice, it has been found wanting on a number of occasions. For instance, the European Court of Human Rights has ruled that the children convicted of James Bulger's murder were too young to receive a fair trial in the adult court. It has also ruled that persons accused of a second rape or homicide should not be denied the possibility of applying for bail in the English and Welsh courts. These cases may seem unworthy examples, but often the best test of a system of justice is its ability to uphold the rights of unpopular defendants. If these are eroded, then all of us are potentially at risk in the future.

6.10   FURTHER INFORMATION

Useful organisations

Criminal Cases Review Commission
Alpha Tower
Suffolk Street
Queensway
Birmingham B1 1TT
Tel: 0121 633 1800
Fax: 0121 633 1804/1823
Info@ccrc.gov.uk

Simon Creighton

7   The Rights of Prisoners

This chapter deals with:

- The basic rights of prisoners
- Reception
- Complaints and requests to the Prisons Ombudsman
- Legal proceedings in court
- Access to lawyers
- Visits, letters and telephones
- Marriage and family
- Access to prison records
- Classification, categorisation and allocation
- Discipline, adjudication and punishment
- Medical treatment
- Work, exercise and education
- Parole
- Tariff or minimum term
- Further information

7.1   THE BASIC RIGHTS OF PRISONERS

Prisoners retain certain basic rights, which survive despite imprisonment. The rights of access to the courts and of respect for one's bodily integrity – that is, not to be assaulted – are such fundamental rights. Others may be recognised as the law develops. Prisoners lose only those civil rights that are taken away either expressly by an Act of Parliament or by necessary implication. For example, one right taken away by statute is that prisoners detained following conviction do not have a right to vote. The test in every case is whether the right is fundamental and whether there is anything in the Prison Act 1952, the Prison Rules 1999 or elsewhere that authorises the prison authorities to limit such a right.

The test now applied is that the State can only place limits on prisoners' rights if they are necessary for the prevention of crime or for prison security. Any limitations placed upon such rights must also be proportionate to the aim that the authorities are seeking to achieve. There are a large number of cases that have been heard by the European Court of Human Rights (ECHR) that help clarify the extent to which limitations can be imposed.

National Offender Management Service
As of June 2004, the Prison Service and Probation Service merged into a single body – the National Offender Management Service (NOMS). NOMS is responsible for all

offenders, whether serving their sentences in prison, the community or both, and its objectives are to punish offenders and reduce reoffending. Within the service, there should be a single person responsible for offenders, but this is distinct from the day-to-day responsibility for prisons and probation. At this early stage, the full effect of establishing NOMS is not yet clear.

Prison Rules

In law, the Prison Rules have legal force only insofar as the Prison Act 1952 gives authority for the Rule: legal challenges to the Rules have been successful in cases where the courts have held that the Prison Act 1952 does not authorise the scope of a particular Rule. The Prison Rules provide a structure and framework for the regulation of prison life. Breach of the Rules by the prison authorities does not of itself give you the right to sue in the courts for damages.

More detailed instructions are given in the Standing Orders and Prison Service Orders and Instructions. These are internal directives, which govern the conduct of prison life, issued to prison governors and prison officers. They do not have any direct legal force in that they can be challenged if they breach the scope of the Prison Act or Prison Rules. They are, however, a vital source of information about prisoners' rights and entitlements, and can provide important evidence as to the proper practice that should be adopted by the prison authorities. A failure to follow the guidance contained in these documents cannot amount to a denial of a prisoner's legitimate expectation.

7.2   RECEPTION

On reception into prison, you will be searched and may be photographed. The prison authorities will keep any property that you are not allowed to have with you in prison. A list will be made on arrival of all property, and you must be given the opportunity to check it is correct before signing it. All cash must be paid into an account, which is under the governor's control. All prisoners should be issued on arrival with a copy of the Prisoners' Information Handbook. A copy of the Prison Rules must be made available to any prisoner who requests it.

7.3   COMPLAINTS AND REQUESTS TO THE PRISONS OMBUDSMAN

How to make a complaint

Within prison, complaints and/or requests may be made in person, or in writing to a governor or to the Independent Monitoring Board (IMB). A governor must be available each day to hear complaints or requests. You need not give the reason for your application to see the governor, and an application may be made direct in writing and in confidence to the governor or chair of IMB. You will have to give a reason if you wish the complaint to be dealt with in confidence, and it may be that the person complained about will be told of the complaint anyway – which rather discourages complaints of this nature. If a complaint is made to the governor, you should normally receive a written reply within seven days.

Some issues – called reserved subjects – may only be dealt with by NOMS. These include parole, transfer to or removal from mother and baby units, Category A status, life sentence prisoners' transfers and deportation. Complaints on these issues will be dealt with by the relevant department and should also be replied to within six weeks. The booklet *How to Make a Request or Complaint: Information for Prisoners*, which details the procedures, should be available in prison libraries.

The Ombudsman

The Ombudsman can investigate complaints only when the internal complaints system has been exhausted. You must complain within one month of the final decision made by NOMS. The complaint should normally be made personally by you, or with your signed authority, but the Ombudsman will usually accept complaints made by solicitors on behalf of their clients.

The Ombudsman will normally take around 12 weeks to investigate the matter and will then issue a report either upholding or rejecting the complaint. If it is upheld, recommendations will be made to NOMS about the individual case and any general issues that it raises. The Ombudsman cannot investigate decisions made by the Parole Board, decisions made personally by ministers or clinical judgements made by medical staff.

You may also raise complaints with any outside organisation or person, for example, your MP, the Parliamentary Commissioner for Administration, the European Parliament, the ECHR, the police. Petitions may also be made to the Queen and Parliament.

7.4   LEGAL PROCEEDINGS IN COURT

Prisoners have the absolute right to commence legal proceedings in the courts either in person or through a solicitor. Prisoners can conduct:

- Normal civil proceedings such as divorce or breach of contract.
- Cases where the prisoner is suing the prison authorities, for example, for assault or medical negligence.
- Judicial review in the High Court of an administrative or disciplinary decision that affects him or her.

The High Court has reviewed a wide range of decisions by the prison authorities, including parole and parole revocation, security categorisation, transfer, censorship, segregation and the separation of a mother from her baby. The Race Relations (Amendment) Act 2000 applies to prisons, and discrimination – for example, in the allocation of jobs – would be actionable in the courts. The High Court will intervene by way of judicial review only when it can be shown that a decision has been taken that is wrong in law – for example, where the prison authorities had no power to do what they did – or the decision was flawed by procedural unfairness. A breach of the Prison Rules does not automatically give a prisoner grounds to sue the prison authorities to obtain compensation for their failure to comply with the Rules. In such cases, the prisoner will need to establish some form of compensable loss or damage resulting from the breach of the Rules.

Right to be present at court

At present, if you are a prisoner acting without a solicitor and wish to be produced at court to present your case in person you must apply to the prison governor by completing the relevant request form. This includes a requirement that you undertake to pay the costs of your production. These costs should be limited to production from the prison nearest to the court, and the level at which they are set should have regard to what you can actually afford to pay. The courts have recognised that there may be an appearance of bias if the Home Office refused to produce at court a prisoner who was unable or who had refused to give an undertaking as to costs in an action when the Home Office is the defendant to the action. If you are faced with this difficulty you should apply to the court that is to hear your action for guidance. Any refusal to produce a prisoner, particularly when the action is against the Home Office, may be in breach of Article 6 of the Convention, the right to a fair trial.

7.5   ACCESS TO LAWYERS

As a prisoner you have an absolute right to have visits from and to correspond with your solicitor. You do not have to tell the prison authorities why you wish to contact your solicitor, nor make any complaint about prison treatment to the authorities before contacting a solicitor for legal advice. This right was first recognised by the ECHR, and any attempts to interfere with such access are closely scrutinised by the courts. This right also includes preserving the confidentiality of any legally privileged material held by prisoners in their possession in prison.

7.6   VISITS, LETTERS AND TELEPHONES

There are detailed regulations on communications, set out in Standing Order 5, which is publicly available from Her Majesty's Stationery Office and which should also be available in the prison library.

Visits

Convicted prisoners are entitled to a visit on reception to prison and then a minimum of two visits every four weeks. Governors should allow more visits if facilities and staffing make this possible, and many prisons do so for prisoners on the standard and enhanced regimes. You will be issued with visiting orders (VOs), which must be sent out, with the visitors' names on them. Visitors then present the order on arrival at prison. Up to three adults and four children are normally allowed at once. Most prisons now require visitors to telephone in advance of their visit to ensure that there is sufficient space for it to take place.

Unconvicted prisoners may have daily visits. These should total at least one and a half hours a week, though in practice such visits are likely to be limited to short daily visits.

NOMS has issued instructions to prevent prisoners who are convicted of violent or sexual offences from receiving visits from children in certain circumstances. If you are in this group, you can only receive visits from your biological children or from children with whom you lived before you were imprisoned. Exceptions will only be made to this rule on an individual basis.

Visits from legal advisers and probation officers do not count against your visit entitlements. Nor is there a restriction on the number of visits allowed from a legal adviser.

The Assisted Prison Visits Scheme exists to help close relatives with the costs of travel. All prisoners, convicted and unconvicted, are eligible for assisted visits if the relative(s) qualify because of their low income.

The prison governor or IMB may grant extra visits if they are considered necessary for the welfare of you or your family. If you are located far from home, you may save up to 26 visits a year and then be transferred temporarily to a prison near your family to have these accumulated visits. You must have served at least six months since being allocated to a prison to be eligible for accumulated visits.

Restrictions

It is a criminal offence to pass items to a prisoner during a visit, for which the visitor can be fined or imprisoned. Most prisons only allow property to be handed in through official channels and not on a visit.

The governor has power to refuse or restrict visits on the grounds of security, good order and discipline, or if he or she believes doing so will prevent or discourage crime. The governor can:

- Refuse visits from certain people.
- Order supervised visits, that is, in a small room with a prison officer present.
- Order closed visits where there is a glass partition between prisoner and visitor.

There is power to search and strip search visitors entering or leaving prisons. This is providing that no more than reasonable force is used, that the decision to search is not perverse and that the search is conducted in a seemly and decent manner and only by members of the same sex as the visitor.

The right to receive visits falls within Article 8 of the Convention, which protects the right to a private and family life. However, Article 8 does allow restrictions to be placed on these rights where the governor believes it necessary to prevent crime or to preserve prison security and good order and discipline. It is this proviso that allows the governor to restrict visits or to ban visitors, but in each case, the prison governor will be required to explain why the restriction is necessary.

Police interviews

Police officers may interview you in prison, but only if you are willing. The provisions of the Police and Criminal Evidence Act 1984 (PACE) and the Codes of Practice do not generally apply to interviews in prison, but instructions to the prison authorities say that the spirit of the provisions must be observed as though the interview were at the police station. Copies of the Codes of Practice must be made available in the prison library. You also, of course, have the right to consult a legal adviser before any interview takes place.

Letters

As a convicted prisoner, you may send one letter a week on which the postage will be paid – the 'statutory letter' – and at least one privilege letter, the postage for which must be paid for out of your private cash allowance. The statutory letter must not be withdrawn or withheld as part of punishment for a disciplinary offence. In addition, prisoners may be granted special letters, which do not count against the statutory or privilege letters allowance. A special letter should be granted, for example, after conviction to allow you to settle your business affairs, when transferred to a different prison or to make arrangements regarding employment and accommodation on release.

In practice, prisoners in many prisons may send and receive more letters than this minimum allowance. Prisoners in open prisons have no restriction on the volume of their correspondence.

As an unconvicted prisoner, you may send as many letters as you wish at your own expense and will be allowed two second-class letters a week on which the postage will be paid by the prison authorities.

Censorship

Mail is censored in high security prisons and for all Category A prisoners, but otherwise letters will not routinely be read. Additional powers exist to vet letters sent by prisoners convicted of sexual offences against children. There is power for the governor to return an 'excessive' number of letters from a correspondent, and if they are 'overlong' the governor may request letters be limited to four sides of A5 paper. Letters may be returned to the sender if these requests are ignored. Complaints about prison treatment are no longer prohibited and letters – whether to family, to MPs, the ECHR or to other reputable organisations – may not be stopped on this ground.

Letters between you and your adviser are protected from interference and may not be read or stopped, whether or not legal proceedings have been issued. There may be examination of such correspondence only to the minimum extent necessary to check that it is bona fide legal correspondence. If a letter is to be inspected it must be done in your presence.

Telephones

Card-operated telephones for the use of prisoners are being installed in all prisons so that those in prison can maintain closer links with family and friends. For security reasons all calls will be recorded and all calls may be monitored and recorded, except those to legal advisers, the Samaritans and other reputable organisations. Use of the telephone may be limited by the governor, but should not be restricted as part of a disciplinary punishment unless the offence was directly related to the misuse of the cardphone or phone card. The Prison Rules do not provide any absolute right to use telephones, and pilot schemes have been introduced in some prisons to impose restrictions on the use of telephones by having pre-recorded messages informing the recipient of the call that the person calling is in prison. Although these types of restrictions are not prohibited by the Prison Rules, they may, in some circumstances, breach Article 8 of the Convention.

Contacting the media

Prisoners are not generally allowed to telephone the media from cardphones and must make an application for permission to do so to the governor. The High Court has held that, in exceptional cases, it would be wrong for such a request to be refused but that in most cases a written letter from the prisoner to the press would be sufficient. Letters sent to the media can be stopped if they contain information about your past criminal offences or of others, identify members of staff or are sent in return for payment. Serious comment on the criminal justice system is allowed. It used to be policy for journalists visiting prisons to be asked to sign an undertaking stating that any material obtained would not be used for publication or professional purposes. The House of Lords ruled in 1999 that it was unlawful for this to be applied as a blanket policy. Visits from journalists can now be permitted on application to the prison governor. The visits will normally be allowed if the prisoner wishes to discuss a matter relating to their conviction or sentence, but may be more difficult to obtain in other circumstances. A refusal to allow a journalist to visit may potentially breach Article 10 of the Convention and, if the visit is concerned with a miscarriage of justice, Article 6.

7.7   MARRIAGE AND FAMILY

High-risk prisoners who wish to get married must make arrangements with the prison authorities for a service to take place within the prison. Low-risk prisoners may be given escorted leave or temporary release to marry outside prison.

As a prisoner, especially if you are serving a long sentence, you may wish to start a family with your partner by use of artificial insemination. Prison Department policy is that this should only be allowed where there are exceptionally strong reasons, and where the applicant couple are legally married. Article 12 of the Convention guarantees the right to marry and found a family: a refusal by the Prison Department to allow you to marry or to start a family by artificial insemination could be challenged under this article. In one case involving a lifer, the courts upheld a decision made by the prison authorities not to allow artificial insemination to take place, but this decision is currently being considered by the ECHR.

Women prisoners with children

There are a limited number of mother and baby units within the prison system. You can keep a baby up to the age of nine months in Holloway, 18 months at Styal – both closed prisons – and 18 months at Askham Grange. If the baby has reached these age limits before you have served your sentence, you may be forced to give up looking after your baby, either then or at an earlier stage. However, the Court of Appeal has held that this policy must not be applied rigidly and that each case must be looked at on its own merits. This means that there may be circumstances where it is appropriate for a child to remain with his/her mother beyond 18 months.

7.8   ACCESS TO PRISON RECORDS

The Data Protection Act 1998 (DPA) allows prisoners to have copies of their prison records. Applications should be made in writing to the Discipline/Custody Office, Personnel Department or Library. A fee of £10 is payable to obtain these. The prison must normally give access within 40 days of receiving your request and any supplementary details needed.

Disclosure can be refused on a number of grounds, including that the information identifies third parties or that disclosure may prejudice the detection or prevention of crime. A weakness of the DPA is that you need not be told whether exempt information has been withheld. You have no right to be told whether you have been given access to the full file or only an edited version.

The DPA also gives you the right to have inaccurate data about yourself corrected. This applies if the data is incorrect or misleading about any matter of fact or contains an opinion based on data that is factually incorrect or misleading. In such cases you are entitled to require the prison to correct, erase, destroy or block the use of the information. Opinions cannot be challenged unless they are based on wrong facts – but if you disagree with an opinion, it is worth asking for your own views about the disputed data to be added to the record. There is, though, no explicit right to have this done.

If you feel that NOMS has contravened its obligations under the DPA, you can complain to the Information Commissioner.

See also Chapter 4.

7.9   CLASSIFICATION, CATEGORISATION AND ALLOCATION

Differentiated regimes

All prisoners, including unconvicted and civil prisoners, are required to be classified to one of three regimes: basic, standard or enhanced. The prison governor, based on your performance in custody – for example, your disciplinary record – takes this decision.

Each regime offers a different level of incentives and privileges. Commonly, prisoners on the basic regime will receive the bare legal minimum in terms of visits or access to private cash and wages. Those on the standard and enhanced regimes will receive progressively more favourable facilities, although the precise nature of these will vary according to each prison's security category. These regulations also require a number of key items such as phone cards, cigarettes and stamps to be purchased from the private cash allowance.

Prison categories

There are broadly five categories of prison:

- Local prisons for unconvicted and short-term prisoners.
- Dispersal prisons for high security prisoners.
- Training prisons for long-term prisoners who do not need the highest security.
- Category C prisons, which are closed but have less internal security.
- Open prisons for prisoners not believed to be a risk to the public or in danger of escaping.

Male and female prisoners will be held completely separately from each other, although this may be in the same prison. Immediately after conviction, a male prisoner will be held at a local prison while his security categorisation and allocation are decided. Because there are fewer young offenders institutions and women's prisons, the arrangements are not exactly the same. Women's prisons and young offenders' institutions are simply divided into open and closed establishments.

Categorisation

There are four security categories:

Category A: prisoners whose escape would be highly dangerous to the public, police or security of the State and for whom the aim must be to make escape impossible.

Category B: prisoners who do not need the highest conditions of security but for whom escape must be made very difficult.

Category C: prisoners who cannot be trusted in open conditions but who do not have the ability or resources to make a determined escape attempt.

Category D: prisoners who can reasonably be trusted to serve their sentences in open conditions.

Category A prisoners also have an escape risk classification based upon their ability and willingness to escape. The classifications are exceptional, high and standard escape risk.

Women prisoners and young offenders may be made Category A, but normally they will either be allocated to open or closed conditions.

Category A prisoners have greater restrictions upon them for security reasons, and their visitors will be vetted by the police on behalf of the prison authorities. These prisoners are entitled to a formal, annual review of their security categorisation during which the reports prepared on them will be disclosed and the prisoner invited to make written representations to the decision-making committee. Legal advice and assistance can be sought in making these written representations.

The governor makes categorisation decisions (other than for category A prisoners and lifers), and the prisoner casework unit through the complaints or requests procedure can review these. A prisoner can then either make a complaint to the Ombudsman if the decision is considered to be unfair. Alternatively, he or she could apply to the High Court for judicial review of his or her categorisation if there were evidence that it had been arrived at unlawfully, for example, by taking account of irrelevant information or applying the wrong criteria.

Allocation

You may be allocated to any prison in England and Wales according to the offence, sentence, security category and individual circumstances of the prisoner. There is no right to be located close to home, but you can apply for transfer – as can your family, who might wish to put in evidence, for example, from a GP about the difficulties illness causes in travelling long distances. The Ombudsman can intervene in an allocation decision if it can be shown to be unfair. An application can be made to the High Court if the decision is, for example, wrongly motivated, especially if it deprives an unconvicted prisoner of access to his or her lawyers and family.

7.10   DISCIPLINE, ADJUDICATION AND PUNISHMENT

Offences

The Prison Rules create a number of offences against discipline that can be punished by the governor. If the alleged offence is very serious, it should be referred to the police for prosecution in the criminal courts. If there is to be a referral to the police, a disciplinary charge should still be laid against you and, if the governor is satisfied that there is a case to answer, he or she should adjourn the hearing pending the outcome of the police investigation. If the police decide not to proceed in the outside courts, the governor may continue the proceedings. However, you cannot be tried for the same offence in both the criminal courts and before the governor. There is an offence of prison mutiny, which can be punished with imprisonment for up to ten years, a fine or both. It is committed if two or more prisoners engage in conduct intended to further a common purpose of overthrowing lawful authority in a prison. You may be regarded as taking part in a mutiny if you fail to leave when there is a reasonable opportunity to do so.

Offences under the Prison Rules range from the more serious, which are also criminal offences, such as assault, to more minor offences, for example, refusing to work or disobeying a rule or regulation. The Prison Rules allow for additional days to be awarded to your sentence following a finding of guilt for a more serious offence. Such an award can only be made by an independent adjudicator and not a prison governor (see below). In privately run prisons, the controller of the prison and not the director conducts internal disciplinary hearings.

Discipline procedure

The procedures for prison discipline are set out in the Discipline Manual – a copy of this should be available to you on request or can be purchased from the Home Office at a price of £2.50. The essential points are:

- A charge must be laid as soon as possible and, save in exceptional circumstances, within 48 hours of the discovery of the offence.
- Pending enquiry by the governor, a prisoner who is to be charged may be segregated. After the governor's first enquiry, segregation is only permissible under Rule 45.
- The charge must be in sufficient detail for the prisoner to know exactly what is alleged against him or her.
- If the governor considers that an award of additional days would be appropriate if the charge is proven, the case should be referred to an independent adjudicator. In such cases, the independent adjudicator must conduct a first hearing within 28 days of the referral. Independent adjudicators are district judges (magistrates) who will sit in the prison to hear such charges.
- Where cases are referred to an independent adjudicator, there is a right to be legally represented at the hearing and the legal aid scheme makes provision for such representation.
- In cases where the charge is not serious and is to be dealt with by a governor, the governor must ask if the prisoner understands the procedure and if he or she wishes to be legally represented or assisted, but is not obliged to grant a request for legal representation; as an alternative, the prisoner can ask for the assistance of a 'Mackenzie friend'.
- If legal representation is refused, the prisoner may still request an adjournment in order to get legal advice from a solicitor.
- In all cases, the prisoner may request copies of statements or other written material that is to be used in evidence.

- At the hearing the prisoner must be allowed to put questions to witnesses who give evidence against him or her and to call witnesses who are relevant to his or her defence.
- The case must be proved to the criminal standard of proof, that is, beyond a reasonable doubt.

The maximum number of additional days that an independent adjudicator may order to be served as punishment for an offence is 42. If found guilty of more than one offence arising from the same incident, punishment may be ordered to run consecutively, but the total period may not exceed 42 days.

Other punishments that are available at both internal and independent adjudications include forfeiture of facilities – maximum 42 days; stoppage of earnings – maximum 42 days; cellular confinement – maximum 14 days; or exclusion from work – maximum 21 days. These punishments are available to both independent adjudicators and prison governors.

Review of punishment

You may ask the prisoner casework unit to review a finding of guilt or the punishment imposed. This procedure applies to both internal and independent adjudications. Before doing so, you should always request a copy of the record of the disciplinary hearing, which must be provided free of charge. The Ombudsman or the High Court can review governor's disciplinary hearings if the adjudicator made a mistake in law or adopted a procedure that was unfair.

You can apply to the governor for cancellation of additional day awards if a period of six months has passed without further awards being made. Neither the seriousness of the original disciplinary offence nor the criminal offence for which you are serving your sentence is relevant to the question of whether an award of additional days should be reduced in whole or part. The question is whether your behaviour and attitude have shown an improvement. The guidelines state that normally no more than half of additional days awarded should be returned on any one application.

Mandatory drugs tests

All prisoners can be required to undertake a mandatory drug test; either on a random selection or if the governor has reasonable suspicion that an individual is using or supplying controlled drugs. It is a disciplinary offence to refuse a test or to test positive for a controlled drug. There are statutory defences that the prisoner had lawful excuse to take the drug – for example, as prescribed medicine – or that it was administered to the prisoner without his/her knowledge or consent. In cases where the prisoner disputes the scientific finding, it is possible to instruct an independent expert to conduct a test on the sample. The ECHR has held that mandatory drug testing in prisons is lawful.

Many prisons also have drug-free wings where prisoners undertake voluntary drugs tests. If you test positive for the use of a controlled drug, this test should not be used to commence disciplinary proceedings.

Segregation

You can be segregated either as punishment following adjudication – maximum 14 days, for the maintenance of good order and discipline, or at your request for your own protection. Prisoners segregated as a punishment must first be certified fit for such punishment by the medical officer, who should also see the prisoner daily during segregation and may order a return to normal location on medical grounds.

If you are segregated in the interests of good order or discipline (GOOD) you may not be segregated for more than three days without the authorisation of either a member of the IMB or the Home Secretary. This authorisation may be for a maximum of one month, but may be renewed from month to month. Reasons for the segregation must be given as soon as possible and as far as practicable in writing if you request it.

Transfer

Prisoners considered to be seriously disruptive or subversive may be transferred on a temporary basis to another prison for a period of up to one month for a cooling-off period. You must be told of the reason for transfer in writing within 24 hours of the action being taken. If you are transferred under this provision, you must not be automatically segregated at the new prison. This will happen only if the governor of the new prison considers it necessary and the same rules concerning segregation as detailed above will apply.

As a last resort, you can be selected for a place in the Close Supervision Centres (CSCs). These are special units at Woodhill and Durham prisons where the most dangerous and disruptive prisoners are held. The decision to place a prisoner in a CSC is made by a committee on behalf of the Secretary of State and will be reviewed monthly by that committee. Conditions in the CSCs are very severe, although they have been modified somewhat as a result of legal action taken by prisoners. Prisoners subjected to a prolonged stay in a CSC have argued that there has been a breach of the prohibition against inhuman and degrading treatment under Article 3 of the Convention, but modifications to the system have made such challenges much harder.

Temporary confinement

Prison officers are instructed not to use force unless absolutely necessary, and when necessary to use no more force than is absolutely necessary to achieve the required objective. As a violent or unmanageable prisoner, you may be placed temporarily in a special or strip cell, but not as punishment. Nor may you be held in such a cell after you have ceased to be violent. The cell will be stripped of furniture except for a mattress or have cardboard furniture that cannot cause injury. This can only be done on the authority of the governor.

Restraints

The governor may order prisoners to be put in physical restraints where necessary to prevent injury to themselves, others, damaging property or creating a disturbance. Body belts, which are made of a leather belt around the waist with handcuffs attached to restrain movement, may be used for this purpose.

Physical restraints should only be used in rare and extreme cases. If restraints are used, the medical officer and a member of the IMB must be informed without delay. If the medical officer disagrees with the order to put the prisoner under restraint the governor must comply with his or her recommendation.

Observation

If you are put into a special cell or mechanical restraint, you must be observed every 15 minutes and be visited by the governor and medical officer twice every 24 hours. You may not be held for longer than 24 hours in mechanical restraints without the written authorisation of a member of the IMB or an officer of the Home Office – who is not an officer of the prison. If you are held wrongly – either unnecessarily or for too long – in a body belt or other restraint, you will be entitled to claim damages in the court for assault.

7.11   MEDICAL TREATMENT

As of April 2003, responsibility for funding prison health services shifted from the Home Office to the Department of Health. This was the first step in a five-year process that will see prison health become part of the National Health Service (NHS). Primary Care Trusts will then become responsible for the commissioning and provision of health services to prisoners in their areas.

For the time being, however, convicted prisoners remain in the care of the Prison Medical Service, which is not part of the NHS. You do not, therefore, have the right to consult the doctor or dentist of your choice for treatment. However, the Prison Medical Service has accepted that prisoners are entitled to the same standard of medical care as under the NHS, and in some prisons medical care is provided by outside GPs who visit the prison on a daily basis. If you are party to legal proceedings, an independent doctor may visit you where examination is relevant to those proceedings. If you are an unconvicted prisoner and willing to pay any expenses involved, you may be visited and treated by the doctor or dentist of your choice.

Access to medical records

The DPA allows you to have copies of your medical records. A fee of £10 is payable to obtain these. Disclosure can be refused on the basis that it would cause serious harm to the physical or mental health of the patient or any other individual.

See also section 7.8, Access to prison records, p. 145 and Chapter 4.

Confidentiality

All medical information about you should be treated in confidence and is not to be disclosed except for specifically defined purposes. The same confidentiality applies to prisoners who are HIV positive. The prison guidelines say that if it seems desirable in the inmate's interest to inform a third party that he or she is HIV positive, a member of staff must consult the prisoner and must obtain the prisoner's consent before disclosing the information. The prison authorities may be liable in damages if they negligently reveal confidential information – for example, that a prisoner has committed sexual offences – as a result of which he is assaulted.

7.12   WORK, EXERCISE AND EDUCATION

Work

All convicted prisoners may be required to work unless the medical officer has certified the prisoner unfit for all or a specific type of work. It is a disciplinary offence to refuse to work or intentionally to fail to work properly. Account should be taken of your religion so that you are not required to work on recognised days of religious observance. This forced labour for convicted prisoners is permitted by the Convention.

The Prison Rules give the maximum working day as ten hours, but do not give a minimum working day. Prison workshops are exempt from the provisions of the Factories Act: if injured at work you must rely upon a civil claim of negligence in order to claim damages for your injury. In practice, governors are required to observe the requirements of the Factories Act and the Health and Safety at Work Act 1974; governors are also instructed to give Health and Safety Executive inspectors access to all areas of the prison.

If found guilty of a disciplinary offence you may be excluded from working with other prisoners as part of your punishment for a maximum of 21 days and/or have your earnings stopped or reduced. Wages can only be stopped to their full value for a period of 42 days, but the length of this punishment can be spread out over 84 days – that is, the loss of half of one's earnings over this period of time.

Exercise
Convicted prisoners no longer have a statutory right to one hour's exercise each day. There is a right to one hour's physical exercise a week, and it is aimed to allow one hour's exercise in the open air a day if circumstances permit. Healthcare advice is that this period should not normally be reduced to less than half an hour a day.

Education
NOMS is under a general duty to provide evening classes at every prison and to encourage prisoners to profit from the educational facilities provided. This does not mean that you have the right to the educational course of your choice, and the prison authorities have a wide discretion as to what educational facilities they provide and who is to benefit from them.

Local education authorities provide a programme of evening classes in all prisons, but classroom space is often limited. Facilities for daytime study and remedial teaching vary. The governor is responsible for assessing a prisoner's needs and suitability for further study. He or she can release individuals from work duty for study. Permission from the prison authorities can be obtained to take a correspondence course, and long-term prisoners often study Open University courses leading to a degree. All prisons have at least one library.

Prisoners of compulsory school age
Governors are instructed that prisoners of compulsory school age should have educational and vocational training for at least 15 hours a week and should be denied education only as a last resort. If there were inadequate educational facilities offered to young offenders of statutory school age, this would potentially be in breach of Article 2 of the Second Protocol of the Convention.

The governor may suspend or end attendance at educational classes if he or she believes it necessary to prevent disruption or for security reasons, or if a disciplinary punishment – for example, segregation – prevents it. However, removal from education may not in itself be ordered as a punishment.

Reading and writing materials

You are entitled to have supplied to you, at your own expense, books, newspapers, writing materials and other means of occupation, except those that appear objectionable. Generally, material should only be denied if it includes matter that incites or involves criminal or disciplinary offences. While it may be permissible to withhold a particular issue of a publication, a blanket ban may be subject to challenge in the courts.

7.13   PAROLE

Various Criminal Justice Acts have regularly updated the parole system and, as a result, different systems apply depending on when the sentence was passed. For example, prisoners sentenced before October 1992 are liable to a slightly different set of release and licence dates than those sentenced after that date. It is always advisable to seek specialist advice on parole and licence dates given the many changes that have been made to the system. The broad outline of the system below is that contained in the Criminal Justice Act 1991 and the Crime and Disorder Act 1998, and is followed by an explanation of the new system introduced by the Criminal Justice Act 2003 (CJA 2003).

Current system

Under the current system, if you are serving less than four years you will automatically be released halfway through your sentence. If you are serving 12 months or less release is unconditional. Those serving over 12 months will be released on licence until the three-quarters point of your sentence and will be subject to compulsory supervision by NOMS. Conditions may be attached to the licence, for example, to attend medical or psychiatric treatment, not to undertake certain types of work, not to communicate with named people. If you breach your licence you can be recalled to prison until the three-quarters point of your sentence.

Once released, if you commit any offence punishable by imprisonment between the time of your release and the date when your original sentence runs out, then you will be liable to serve the balance of the original sentence that is outstanding at the time of the fresh offence.

For those serving four years or more, the system of parole is as follows: you will be eligible for release on parole once half of the sentence has been served; at the two-thirds stage of the sentence you will be released automatically on a non-parole licence. Recommendations by the Parole Board to release prisoners serving 15 years or more must be approved by the Secretary of State.

Between the two-thirds automatic release point and the three-quarters point in the overall sentence, the 'at risk provisions' with regard to further offences that are imprisonable apply as they do for short-term prisoners. If a further prison sentence is imposed for committing an offence while on licence, this stands as a sentence in its own right and will normally be ordered to be served consecutively with any further sentences imposed.

Long-term prisoners who are in breach of parole licence conditions may be recalled to prison and, if recalled, you may remain in prison until the three-quarters point of the original sentence. If recalled, you must be told of the reasons for recall and can appeal against the decision in writing to the Parole Board. In those circumstances, your licence will run until the very end of your sentence, and if you breach this licence again, then you can be held until your sentence expiry date.

The Criminal Justice Act 2003

The CJA 2003 contains radical changes to the current sentencing and parole system which are being introduced gradually throughout 2004. It has introduced a new range of sentences such as intermittent custody where people spend part of the week in prison and part in the community. It is also intended to introduce a system where prisoners convicted of offences that are neither violent nor sexual will receive parole automatically at the halfway point of their sentence.

The CJA 2003 creates two new kinds of determinate sentences, one for under 12 months and one for 12 months and over, both of which include periods on licence. 'Custody Plus' will replace the current custodial sentence of less than 12 months. The court will decide the total length of the sentence, which must be no longer than 51 weeks and then apportion it between a custodial period and a licence period. The custodial period must be at least two weeks and cannot be more than 13 weeks. The licence period must be at least six months and is subject to conditions. The sentencing court sets the licence conditions to be included. If the offender breaches the licence conditions, he or she will be recalled to custody for part or all of the remaining supervision period.

In relation to determinate sentences of 12 months or longer, offenders will be released automatically at the halfway point, irrespective of the length of the sentence. Offenders will remain on licence until the end of their sentence, subject to recall. The Parole Board will no longer be involved in decisions about the release of such prisoners, except where the offender has been assessed as dangerous by the court.

The parole process

The parole process for all prisoners begins six months before you are first eligible for release on parole. A dossier will be compiled of all the material to go before the Parole Board, and you will be shown all such reports – unless it is considered some material should not be shown: any proposal to withhold material must be referred to the chair of the Parole Board – and his or her comments and representations will go before the Parole Board when the case is considered. An interview is then arranged with a member of the Parole Board and the record of this interview is disclosed to you and then placed with the other papers. You should be told whether parole has been granted three weeks before you are eligible for release, and reasons for the decision will be given. The release dates of long- and short-term prisoners will be subject to postponement if additional day awards have been made as punishment for disciplinary offences.

The Home Secretary has power to release any prisoner on compassionate grounds in exceptional circumstances. This power is normally reserved for prisoners who are in the advanced stages of a terminal illness. If you are so released, you will be subject to supervision up to the three-quarters point in your sentence – or, for those serving less than 12 months, the halfway point.

Home Detention Curfew – 'tagging'

Early release for short-term prisoners – those serving less than four years – on Home Detention Curfew (HDC), commonly referred to as 'tagging', was introduced on

1 January 1999. The scheme requires prison governors to consider all prisoners serving more than three months but less than four years for release on HDC. From July 2003, the scheme was extended to include young offenders.

Certain prisoners are excluded from the scheme: prisoners subject to a hospital order; violent and sexual offenders serving extended sentences; prisoners facing deportation; prisoners who have been released early under an HDC and have been returned to custody; people serving sentences for fine default and contempt of court; and prisoners who have breached an early release licence and have received a further prison sentence. In addition, as of July 2003, prisoners with a history of sexual offending (regardless of current offence) and those serving sentences for certain other offences, including racially aggravated offences will be 'presumed unsuitable' for release unless there are *exceptional* circumstances. The Home Office has indicated that they expect very few prisoners subject to a presumption of unsuitability to be released early on exceptional grounds.

The length of the sentence being served determines the length of time that can be spent out of prison on HDC. The accompanying table shows how HDC will apply depending on the length of your sentence.

If you are eligible to apply, you must satisfy a risk assessment before being approved for HDC. Prison Service Order 6700 contains detailed guidance on how risk must be assessed. Although there is a presumption in favour of release, the overriding issue for the governor is to ensure that there is no risk to the public. Decisions made by the governor can be appealed both internally at the prison and then to the Area Manager.

Sentence length	Period to be served before HDC available	Curfew period
3 months or more but less than 4 months	30 days	Between 2 weeks and 1 month
4 months or more but less than 12 months	One quarter of the sentence	Between 1 month and 3 months
Between 12 months and under 18 months	One quarter of the sentence	Between 3 months and 4½ months
Between 18 months and under 4 years	135 days less than half the sentence	135 days

A further change to the scheme has been recently introduced and is aimed at dealing with 'notorious' prisoners eligible for HDC and likely to pass the risk assessment. The Home Office believes early release of such prisoners will undermine public confidence in the scheme and on this basis has removed the right of a prison governor to determine whether such prisoners are fit for release under HDC. The final decision in such cases will now rest with the Chief Executive of NOMS.

Extended sentences

A type of sentence introduced in 1998 is likely to become much more common in the future. This sentence is known as an 'extended sentence' and is imposed on people convicted of sexual and violent offences who are considered to pose an ongoing danger to the public but whose offences do not justify a life sentence or exceptionally long custodial periods. The sentence is comprised of two parts: a fixed term in prison and then a further term on licence that is much longer than the usual licence period. You will be released from the fixed term in the usual manner, but will be subject to supervision for the entire licence period. If you breach the licence, you can be recalled to prison for the entire licence period. The only safeguard is that the recall must be confirmed by the Parole Board, and you are entitled to an oral hearing in front of the Parole Board. If the recall is confirmed, you are entitled to further annual oral hearings. The procedure for those hearings is almost identical to the procedure outlined below for life sentence prisoners.

Life sentence prisoners

Life sentences can be imposed on the following:

- Any adult convicted of murder – this is known as the mandatory life sentence.
- Anyone convicted of murder when under the age of 18 receives a sentence of detention at Her Majesty's Pleasure (HMP).
- People convicted of a second serious violent or sexual offence will normally receive an automatic life sentence.
- For a range of offences where the maximum penalty is life imprisonment – for example, rape, grievous bodily harm – the court may impose a life sentence if it is considered that the person poses a danger to the public. This is referred to as a discretionary life sentence.

There used to be a difference in the provisions for setting the tariff and releasing mandatory lifers from all other lifers, but the CJA 2003 has now removed those differences. There are, however, some transitional provisions for mandatory lifers sentenced prior to December 2003, which are explained below.

7.14   TARIFF OR MINIMUM TERM

When sentencing, the trial judge will usually fix the punishment period – the tariff – to be served before release can be considered. The length of this tariff may be appealed as with a determinate prison sentence. For prisoners convicted of murder, the CJA 2003 contains mandatory guidance to judges as to how long the tariff should be including, in some cases, whole life.

Existing mandatory lifers

If serving a sentence for murder imposed before 2004, you should have had a tariff set by the Home Secretary following recommendations by the trial judge and the Lord Chief Justice. Providing the tariff period has not already expired, you are entitled to apply to the High Court to have your tariff reset by a High Court judge. This will be done purely on the judge reading the papers – representations from the prisoner and materials concerning the offence submitted by the Home Office. The tariff cannot be increased over the level previously set. There is some debate as to whether Article 6 should allow for oral hearings to be allowed for this process.

A group of around 700 mandatory lifers had not had a tariff set when the new law was passed. Their cases will be automatically referred to a High Court judge for the tariff to be set.

Reviews

Three years before the end of the tariff period, the Parole Board will review your case to see if you are suitable to be moved to an open prison to prepare for release. Most lifers are expected to go to an open prison to prepare for eventual release. The review is conducted by the Parole Board reading the case papers and your written representations but without a hearing. Although the Parole Board can recommend a move to an open prison, this is not binding on the Secretary of State who has the final decision. The exception to this process are those lifers with very short tariffs who may not have time for such a review and who can, in theory, be released from a closed prison.

At the end of the tariff period there will be a parole review to determine suitability for release. This has usually been held as an oral hearing before a panel of the Parole Board who make the final decision on release. The panel will meet at the prison where you are located to consider the case. You are entitled to legal representation – and Legal Aid is available to prepare and conduct the case. You are entitled to see all reports that go before the panel except those that would adversely affect the health or welfare of you or others. In such a case the reports must still normally be shown to the legal representative, although the Parole Board has recently argued that in extreme cases where witness protection is an issue, part of the proceedings can be conducted in private with representation by a Special Advocate who will see the material in question. Although this process has been upheld by the High Court, it remains the subject of a challenge in the Court of Appeal.

If the Panel is satisfied that it is no longer necessary for the protection of the public that you be detained, then you will be released. If the panel does not direct release, you are entitled to have your case considered again by the panel at intervals of not more than two years.

A pilot scheme has been in operation for mandatory lifers to see if the oral hearing can be dispensed with in cases where it is not needed. Under this scheme, there is first an opportunity for the Parole Board to consider the case having read the papers and your representations. An oral hearing is then only convened if either you or the Secretary of State is not happy with the outcome of the review on the papers. It seems likely that this scheme will be extended to all lifers in the future.

Release

Release will only be authorised if it is felt that you no longer pose a risk of committing further offences and if there is a satisfactory release plan. Life-sentenced prisoners can be detained on this risk factor after the tariff has expired. If you are released, you will remain on life licence and can be recalled to prison by the Home Secretary or the Parole Board if the terms of the licence are breached or if your behaviour causes concern. If a prisoner in this position is recalled, a further review will be conducted by the Parole Board to decide on the fairness of the recall.

Compassionate release

All prisoners are entitled to apply for permanent compassionate release from prison at any time in their sentence. The power to grant compassionate release rests with the Secretary of State and is a wholly discretionary power. The guidelines issued state that it will be considered in cases where a prisoner is terminally ill or in tragic family circumstances where there is an urgent and immediate need for the presence of the prisoner in the family home. In both cases, the facts giving rise to the application must be new – that is, they were not known at the time sentence was passed – and the Secretary of State needs to be satisfied that there is no risk of further crimes being committed. In order for an application to be made, the governor of the prison must forward the case to the Sentence Enforcement Unit of NOMS who will then consider whether the case should be referred to the Parole Board for advice. Only a tiny number of these applications are granted each year, and the power is most often used in cases where a prisoner is terminally ill to enable the prisoner to be released to a hospice or hospital. Applications based on tragic family circumstances are very rarely granted.

Temporary release

Prisoners may be released for a set period – usually between two and five days – on the authority of the prison governor. This can be for compassionate reasons, such as attendance at a funeral or for medical treatment, or on resettlement licence. Before temporary release can be granted, you must pass a risk assessment carried out in the prison. Compassionate temporary release can be granted at any point in your sentence, but is not available if you are a Category A prisoner. A resettlement licence can be granted after you have reached your parole eligibility date, but if parole is refused, the application will be suspended for a period of six months. For those serving less than four years, an application can be made after you have served one-third of your sentence. Certain groups are ineligible for any form of temporary release, such as high-risk prisoners, or those who are to be deported at the end of their sentence.

Lifers are not eligible for temporary release until moved to open prison. However, you can apply for escorted town visits once you are in a Category C prison.

Discharge

On release, personal clothing and belongings are returned. Suitable clothing will be provided if the prisoner's clothing is inadequate. Money received on reception will be returned and most prisoners will be eligible for a discharge grant. Those serving less than 14 days are not entitled to the discharge grant, though the prison authorities may give a subsistence allowance to enable you to get to the local DSS office. A travel warrant to an address in the UK will also be given.

7.15   FURTHER INFORMATION

Useful organisations

Advice for Prisoners' Families
Riverbank House
1 Putney Bridge Approach
London SW6 3JD
Prisoners' Families Helpline: 0808 808 2003
Tel: 020 7405 8090
Fax: 020 7405 8045
<www.prisonersfamilieshelp.org.uk>

Inquest (Deaths in Custody)
89–93 Fonthill Road
London N4 3JH
Tel: 020 7263 1111
Fax: 020 7561 0799
inquest@inquest.org.uk

Justice
59 Carter Lane
London EC4V 5AQ
Tel: 020 7329 5100
Fax: 020 7329 5055
admin@justice.org.uk
<www.justice.org.uk>

Miscarriages of Justice UK
52 Outmore Road
Sheldon
Birmingham B33 0XL
Tel: 0121 789 8443
mojonational@aol.com
www.mojo.freehosting.net

NACRO
169 Clapham Road
London SW9 0PU
Tel: 020 7582 6500
Fax: 020 7735 4666
communications@nacro.org.uk
<www.nacro.org.uk>

**Partners of Prisoners and Families
Support Group (POPS)**
Valentine House
1079 Rochdale Road
Blackley
Manchester M9 8AJ
Tel/Fax: 0161 702 1000
mail@partnersofprisoners.co.uk
<www.partnersofprisoners.co.uk>

Prison Reform Trust
15 Northburgh St
London EC1V 0JR
Tel: 020 7251 5070
Fax: 020 7251 5076
prt@prisonreformtrust.org.uk
<www.prisonreformtrust.org.uk>

Prisoner's Advice Service
Unit 210, Hatton Square
16–16a Baldwin Gardens
London EC1N 7RJ
Tel: 020 7405 8090
Fax: 020 7405 8045
admin@prisonersadvice.org.uk
<www.prisonersadvice.demon.co.uk>

Women in Prison
36 Aberdeen Studios
22 Highbury Grove
London N5 2EA
Tel: 020 7226 5879
Fax: 020 7354 8005
info@womeninprison.org.uk
<www.womeninprison.org.uk>

Bibliography

Creighton, S. and King, V., *Prisoners and the Law* (London: Butterworths, 2000) (new edition due 2004)
Leech, M., ed., *The Prisons Handbook* (London: MLP, 2003)
Livingstone, S., Owen, T. and MacDonald, A., *Prison Law* (Oxford: Oxford University Press, 2003)

Jo Cooper

8 The Right of Peaceful Protest

This chapter deals with:

- The historic right of peaceful protest
- Where to find the law
- Marches
- Static demonstrations, rallies and assemblies
- Meetings
- Picketing
- Using the highway
- Street collections, leafleting, petitions, posters and newspapers
- Bye-laws
- Other police powers to restrict protest
- In practice – organising a protest action
- Dealing with the police
- Challenging police decisions
- Supporting people arrested at the protest
- Public order offences
- Serious offences of violence
- Less serious offences
- Further information

8.1 THE HISTORIC RIGHT OF PEACEFUL PROTEST

To speak of rights at all in this context is to recognise the constitutional shift which is now in progress.

Mr Justice Stephen Sedley, November 1999

Public protest is deeply rooted in our political culture. There have been countless times in the past – even in the recent past – when public demonstrations of support for a cause, or opposition to a policy or government, have changed the course of history. 'People power' can be a potent political force, whether at a national or a local level; whether to do with political causes or single issues; whether in support of striking workers or bereaved families, or in opposition to globalisation, or the waging of unjustified wars. When people have nothing else to fight with, it is often their solidarity with each other – to stand together and be counted across communities and even across continents – that proves to be their most powerful weapon.

For as long as there have been governments there have been rules to restrict protest and dissent. Over the centuries the law in this area has developed piecemeal, adapting to the prevailing attitudes and concerns of the governments and courts of the day. This dynamic process reflects the struggle that lies at the heart of public order law – the natural tension between the amount of freedom we demand as demonstrators and the amount of restriction we as electors permit our Parliament to impose.

For centuries, legislators have resisted the notion of positive rights in the field of public protest and political expression. While it might have been said that we were free to do anything that was not otherwise proscribed by law, to say that we had a positive right to assemble, to march together, to chant and to campaign – rights that might be weighed against the undoubted rights of property owners, road users or business people – was to swim against a strong current of judicial thinking and an ever-rising tide of repressive legislation, which appeared to tolerate protest only if it did not challenge or cause inconvenience to anyone. The constitutional shift that fundamentally altered this position was the incorporation into domestic law, in October 2000, of the European Convention on Human Rights (the Convention). In the field of political protest the Convention has effect in four key areas:

- Right to peaceful assembly – Article 11
- Right to freedom of expression – Article 10
- Right to freedom of thought, conscience and religion – Article 9
- Right to respect for private and family life – Article 8

It forbids any public body, such as the police and local government, from acting in ways that conflict with the principles set out in the Convention.

It enables demonstrators to use the courts, in principle, to challenge decisions that would restrict protest; and might enable them to mount defences to non-violent criminal offences connected with political protest.

It is important to remember that the Convention does not give a trump card to political protest – especially at a time when concerns over safety and security are a prime concern of Government. The rights of individuals to assemble together and express themselves freely are only two of a series of rights set out in the Convention that deserve to be considered and weighed against each other.

There are particular reasons to review the state of public order law today. Despite the positive promise of the Human Rights Act 1998 (HRA) the courts have been slow in practice to increase the scope of rights available to protestors. Parliament, on the other hand, has been quick to hand out new statutory powers – under the Terrorism Act 2000, the Criminal Justice and Police Act 2001, the Anti-Terrorism, Crime and Security Act 2001 and the Criminal Justice Act 2003 – which all increase the scope of police to prevent the free movement of protestors and other members of the public, and the free expression of political protest.

There are always concerns that such wide discretionary powers tend to be exercised by the police in an unaccountable and discriminatory way. Choosing which powers to exercise, which protests to control and how to control them will often involve very delicate policy and security considerations. In the past, sensitive to criticism on political and human rights grounds, the police tended to use their considerable powers against *protest* less often than the frequent use of criminal charges against *protesters themselves*. However, following the events of 11 September 2001 and the Iraq War, police forces are now able to respond ever more boldly with modes of policing that are frankly and unapologetically repressive.

However, public protest should not be driven underground at a time of international political upheaval. On the contrary, maintaining proper structures to ensure that legitimate political protest can find a voice is a positive duty of government. Maintaining the freedom to express dissent remains a powerful indicator of the political health of a nation.

In the middle years of this decade the challenges facing all those engaged in the public expression of political opinion are immense. It is possible, however, to rise to, confront and often overcome such challenges. Knowing your rights and having a good understanding of the scope of laws aimed at curtailing protest and restricting the expression of political opinion, and in particular how they intersect with Convention rights, are powerful tools. This is especially so if you find yourself negotiating with the police when planning a protest, or with a local authority over permission to distribute political literature. It is also wise to seek the advice of organisations, such as Liberty, that can provide advice and guidance on protest rights and public order issues.

In the remainder of this chapter we set out:

- The formal regime for regulating public protest.
- The practical consequences for organisers.
- The principal public order offences directed at demonstrators.

8.2   WHERE TO FIND THE LAW

The most important statutory provision is the Public Order Act 1986 (POA), extended by the Criminal Justice and Public Order Act 1994 and the Crime and Disorder Act 1998, and recently amended by the Anti-Social Behaviour Act 2003. These statutes set out the powers of the police to impose conditions on marches and on static demonstrations such as rallies, pickets and vigils. The POA also sets out the main public order offences, such as riot, affray and threatening behaviour, which are directed at people on demonstrations.

Not all public protest takes the form of organised marches through town centres by people carrying placards and chanting slogans. Although the POA introduced extensive controls on such traditional forms of political expression, there has been a movement away from formal protest in favour of a proliferation of imaginative and diverse actions, some on private land. These new types of action have enabled political messages to be sent and damaging practices to be frustrated away from the restrictive controls of the police.

Inevitably, one of the stated reasons given in later years for extensions of the provisions of the POA was that the police needed additional powers to regulate new and varied methods of mass action, including raves, festivals, roads protests and hunt sabotage. The result is a statutory regime that is broader than ever before, with extensive powers that can be used not just against these and other 'targeted' groups, but also against all manifestations of political protest, both formal and informal.

Another significant statute is the Police and Criminal Evidence Act 1984, as amended by the rash of new measures post 2000, which give the police powers to arrest and detain people suspected of committing criminal offences.

Even after these major pieces of recent legislation, public order law is far from unified. This is because, as well as their powers under these statutes, the police retain some historic 'common law' powers, such as the power to take action to prevent a breach of the peace. There are also numerous bye-laws, passed by local authorities, which are specific to particular areas and often restrict our rights or impose obligations on us. Other legislation sometimes regulates the right to demonstrate, for instance, picketing during industrial disputes is regulated by employment laws.

Another important source for today's law is reported cases, showing how the courts have approached particular situations in the past. All laws have to be interpreted – the courts have to decide exactly what counts as a 'public place', for example – and the precedents from previous court decisions are a useful indication of how they might react if the same situation were to occur again. Many of these cases are reported regularly in publications such as *Legal Action* (see section 8.18, 'Further information', p. 190), which has a comprehensive round-up of public order cases every February and August.

All the above – our domestic statute law, common law and all the cases that interpret them – are now considered in the light of the Convention. The most important provisions in the field of public protest include Article 5, the right to liberty; Article 6, the right to fair trial; Article 8, respect for private and family life; Article 9, freedom of thought, conscience and religion; Article 10, freedom of expression; and Article 11, the right of peaceful assembly. In addition, Article 14 of the Convention outlaws discrimination over the exercise of those rights on the basis of race, sex, religion, colour and political opinion or other status.

Our courts also have to consider the many cases in which the European Court of Human Rights (ECHR) has given guidance on the meaning of the Convention. The ECHR has been operating for decades, and Convention law is already highly developed. Unlike our approach to interpreting domestic law, the ECHR has been creative, applying the spirit of the Convention to new situations that arise rather than insisting on applying the letter of an outdated law. As a result, the Convention Articles themselves are only a starting point. Important additional rights – particularly in the context of the criminal law – have been read in to the Convention by the ECHR.

See also Chapter 5.

8.3   MARCHES

The POA refers to marches as 'processions' and to all other static demonstrations as 'assemblies'. A 'procession' is simply defined as people moving together along a route; the law does not provide a minimum number to constitute a procession, so even a handful of people going to a town hall to hand in a petition will constitute a procession. The POA gives the police extensive controls over processions. Organisers of most processions must give advance notice to the police. The police may impose conditions on processions and, in limited circumstances, have them banned. Failure to comply with these provisions is a criminal offence.

Who is the organiser?
There is no legal definition. For a big procession an official organiser will probably have been selected well in advance of the date. For an informal event the organiser could be anyone who takes the lead. Some spontaneous events will have no organiser.

Advance notice

The rules are designed to ensure that the police are told, in advance, about the vast majority of political marches. Specifically, they say that notice should be given of any procession if it is intended to:

- Demonstrate support for or opposition to the views or actions of any group.
- Publicise a cause or campaign.
- Mark or commemorate an event.

Notice need not be given if it is not reasonably practicable to do so in advance. This is intended to allow for a completely spontaneous procession, for example, when a meeting turns itself into a march or, as Christian CND put it, when it is necessary 'to call acts of witness or protest at short notice'. If a prosecution is brought, it will be for the Magistrates' Court to decide whether notice of any kind could have been given. A last-minute telephone call to the police is advisable to show you are prepared to follow the spirit of the law. A record should be kept of the call.

Notice is also not required if it is a funeral procession or a procession commonly or customarily held. This will include the Lord Mayor's Show in the City of London, the Notting Hill Carnival and other annual local parades, including those organised by religious groups. If a protest march occurs regularly (weekly, annually) at the same time along the same route, then no notice should be required.

Where notice is required it must be in writing and must include:

- The date of the procession.
- The time it will start.
- The proposed route.
- The name and the address of the organiser.

The written notice must be delivered to a police station in the area where the procession is planned to start (or the first police area in England), either by hand or by recorded delivery six clear days in advance. 'Six clear days' means, effectively, a full week in advance, for example, on Saturday for a procession the following Saturday.

If a procession is planned at short notice (less than one week), then the organiser is required to deliver written notice by hand as soon as reasonably practicable.

Offences connected with notice

The organiser commits an offence (maximum penalty is a fine up to level 3 – currently £1,000) if:

- Notice was not given as required.
- The date, starting time or route differs from that given on the notice.

There is no power of arrest, but the police could rely on their general power of arrest (see section 5.4, 'Police powers of arrest', p. 107). In practice, in the handful of prosecutions brought under this section of the POA since 1987, it has proved very difficult for the police to prove that a particular person was the organiser of a march. Unless the police can do so, their powers to prosecute are greatly curtailed. Even if they can, it is a defence if you can prove either:

- You were not aware that notice had not been given or not given in time; or

- The different date, starting time or route was due to circumstances beyond your control or was changed with the agreement of the police or by direction of the police.

Police conditions on marches

There is no guarantee that the police will allow your proposed procession to take place as you want it. The police have extensive powers to impose conditions on marches, and even to ban them. In advance, the Chief Constable (or the Metropolitan Police Commissioner in London) can impose conditions relating to the route, number of marchers, types of banners or duration, or restrict entry to a public place. These conditions must be in writing. After the procession has begun the most senior officer on the spot can impose similar conditions, which do not have to be in writing. The POA says that conditions can be imposed only if the senior officer reasonably believes that the procession may result in:

- Serious public disorder; or
- Serious damage to property; or
- Serious disruption to the life of the community.

The senior officer may also impose conditions if he or she reasonably believes that the purpose of the organisers is to intimidate others 'with a view to compelling them not to do an act they have a right to do, or to do an act they have a right not to do'. The conditions must be ones that the officer believes are necessary to prevent disorder, damage, disruption or intimidation.

Where organisers have sufficient notice of proposed conditions, they can be challenged in the courts (see section 8.13, 'Challenging police decisions', p. 177). In particular, with the incorporation of the Convention, the police are under a positive duty not to act incompatibly with the Convention, and conditions may be challenged on the grounds that they are excessive or unreasonable, or do not respect Convention rights such as Article 10 and Article 11.

Failure to comply with a valid condition, properly imposed, is a criminal offence with different penalties for organisers and other participants.

Banning marches

The POA gives police power to ban all or a 'class' of processions in a local area for up to three months, by way of a banning order. If a Chief Constable (or the Commissioner in London) is satisfied that the powers to impose conditions will not be sufficient to prevent serious public disorder if the procession takes place, then he must apply for a banning order.

Outside London, the Chief Constable applies to the district council for a banning order. The district council is not obliged to make the order, and it must have the Home Secretary's consent to any banning order it does make. In London, the Commissioner makes the order with the Home Secretary's consent.

A banning order can cover all or part of a district (or all or part of the Metropolitan Police area or the City of London) and can ban all processions or just those within a certain class (for example, processions marking the death of a political terrorist). A blanket ban on all processions is often imposed, even though it is designed to prevent one march only. The standard formula is to ban 'all public processions other than those of a traditional or ceremonial character'. Once again, banning orders can be challenged in advance by reference to the Convention, but failure to comply with a valid banning order, properly imposed, is a criminal offence.

8.4   STATIC DEMONSTRATIONS, RALLIES AND ASSEMBLIES

The POA gives the police specific powers to control static demonstrations that are similar to those for processions. The POA previously defined a 'public assembly' as being 20 or more people gathered together in a public place that is at least partly in the open air. In relation to England and Wales, the Anti-Social Behaviour Act 2003 has amended this provision. With effect from 20 January 2004 two people can now constitute a public assembly. A public place is any highway (including the pavement) and any other place to which the public or a section of the public can have access, and therefore includes parks and gardens, shopping precincts, shops and offices, restaurants and pubs, cinemas, football stadia, rights of way, and so on. An attempt to regulate a very small group of individuals under the POA may be open to challenge as a breach of Article 11, the right of peaceful assembly. Note also that although the police have power to impose conditions, there is no power to ban a public assembly altogether, and no advance notice need be given of any public assembly.

Police conditions on rallies and assemblies
Conditions may be imposed on a public assembly that restrict:

- The place – for example, by forcing pickets to move from embassy gates.
- The duration – for example, by reducing a 24-hour vigil to four hours.
- The numbers – for example, by reducing a mass picket from thousands to 20.

Similar to the powers concerning processions, the Chief Constable (Commissioner in London) can impose conditions in advance (in writing) or the most senior officer on the spot can impose conditions as soon as two people have assembled. The grounds for doing so – such as fear of serious public disorder – are also the same as for processions. Whenever the police impose conditions they must consider the Convention rights of those who may be affected and be prepared to justify them in court if challenged.

Police powers to ban 'trespassory assemblies'
A 'trespassory assembly' is 20 or more people on land in the open air without the permission, or in excess of the permission, of the occupier. A group of 30 celebrators at Stonehenge without permission would constitute a trespassory assembly because the land there is privately owned.

Unlike a simple assembly, the police have power to ban any trespassory assembly where there is a risk of serious disruption to the life of the local community, or where there is a risk to an important site or building. The police can impose a ban over an area up to five miles around the site, prevent people travelling to the assembly, and can arrest those who organise or take part in the assembly itself.

This is a widely drawn provision, which puts a great deal of power in the hands of occupiers of land. Liberty was involved in a test case in 1999 to challenge the legality of a ban on a group of people who were holding a small demonstration on a public roadway. It was a peaceful, non-obstructive gathering on a road that was open to the general public, but the police said that because the group were not 'passing and re-passing' – that is, doing what the road was traditionally intended for – they were legally classified as trespassers. The House of Lords agreed with Liberty that the highway was there to be used for peaceful political protest and that the public therefore had a right of peaceful assembly on the highway.

Offences connected with conditions on marches and rallies

If you know that a POA condition has been imposed on either a procession or a public assembly, it is an offence if you do not comply, either as an organiser or as an ordinary participant. It is also an offence to incite others not to comply. If you know that a procession or trespassory assembly has been banned, it is an offence for you to organise, to take part in it or to incite others to take part in it.

In principle the police can arrest organisers or demonstrators, which in a large gathering gives them extremely wide discretionary powers as to whom they choose to remove from the scene. The maximum penalty for organisers or those who incite is 51 weeks' imprisonment or a fine at level 4 (currently £2,500) and for participants a fine at level 3 (currently £1,000). It is a defence to prove that any failure to comply with a condition was beyond your control.

8.5   MEETINGS

Public meetings

A public meeting is one that is open to the public to attend, with or without payment, and is held in a public place (a place to which the public have access on payment or otherwise). Many private premises, including town halls and council buildings, church halls, football stadia and pubs, become 'public places' when public meetings are held there. A meeting could be any number of people, and there is no duty to advertise it or to offer tickets widely. Local council meetings are public (except for confidential parts of the agenda).

If you are the organiser of a public meeting on private premises, you must ensure that you comply with the terms and conditions for the use of the premises, including all fire and safety regulations, and that the meeting is conducted in an orderly manner. Stewards should be easily identifiable, but they should not wear a uniform to promote a political objective or signify membership of a political organisation. They must not try to take over the functions of the police or use force to promote a political objective (these acts would be illegal). They can assist in the admission and seating of members of the public and in the control of disorder or to remove members of the public who go too far in their heckling.

It is an offence under the Public Meeting Act 1908 to try to break up a lawful public meeting by acting in a disorderly manner or to incite others to do so. The maximum penalty is six months' imprisonment and/or a fine up to £1,000. If a police officer is present and reasonably suspects you of trying to disrupt the meeting, then, at the chairperson's request, he or she can ask you for your name and address. It is an offence if you fail to give these details or give a false name or address (maximum penalty is a fine at level 1 – currently £200). These offences do not carry a power of arrest, although the police could rely on their general powers of arrest. See also section 5.4, 'Police powers of arrest', p. 107.

If there is serious disruption or aggression, and if the police believe that you are involved, then, relying on their common law powers to prevent a breach of the peace, the police could ask you to leave the meeting, threatening you with arrest if you refused, or they could arrest you for an offence under section 4 or section 5 of the POA.

Any meeting of two or more people that is wholly or partly in the open air is a 'public assembly' and subject to conditions imposed by the police under the POA. If such a meeting is attended by 20 or more people *and* held on land without the owner's permission, it may be a trespassory assembly and could be subject to a banning order. Organisers should be aware that plain clothes police officers might attend political meetings without authority for the purpose of collecting information.

Election meetings

The Representation of the People Act 1983 makes special provision for public meetings held at the time of local or national elections. All candidates are entitled to use rooms in local schools and other publicly owned meeting halls, free of charge, for election meetings provided that the meetings are open to the public and are intended to further the candidates' prospects by discussion of election issues. Some local authorities have refused permission to the National Front to use their premises for election meetings on the grounds that the National Front did not intend their meetings to be genuinely open to the public or because damage was likely to be caused to the premises. In 1986, the Court of Appeal upheld the right of a British National Party candidate to be allowed to use a schoolroom for an election meeting and ruled that a candidate who was refused such access could sue the local authority to enforce his or her rights under the election law. The Representation of the People Act 1983 makes it an offence, punishable with a fine up to level 5 (currently £5,000), to disrupt, or to incite others to disrupt, an election meeting. If a police officer reasonably suspects you of trying to disrupt the meeting, then, at the chairperson's request, he or she can ask you for your name and address. It is an offence if you fail to give these details or falsify them (maximum penalty is a fine at level 1 – currently £200). Police powers for public meetings also apply to election meetings.

Private meetings

A meeting is private if members of the public are not free to attend, in payment or otherwise (for example, the meeting of a trade union branch or a political party). A private meeting remains private even though it is held in a public building such as a town hall. Organisers can refuse entry or require someone to leave. Private meetings are governed by the rules of the organisation involved, or by conditions specified by the organisers together with any requirements, for example, as to maximum numbers, which apply to the premises where the meeting takes place. Unless the organisers invite the police, they have no right to enter a private meeting and can be asked to leave unless they are present to prevent crime or an imminent breach of the peace.

8.6   PICKETING

For more than a century, trade unions and organised groups of workers have used picketing as a powerful means of protecting their employment rights and improving the conditions in which they are expected to work. In recent years, picketing has been used by campaigning and protest groups as an effective way of bringing their views to public attention, for example, by picketing premises where politicians are due to attend, demonstrating outside head offices of organisations and 'blockading' ports and airports supporting live animal exports. The law gives special status to picketing when it is related to an industrial dispute, but no special exemption under the criminal law. However, most picketing is lawful unless it causes an obstruction of the highway or is designed to intimidate.

You are protected under the civil law if you picket in connection with an industrial dispute at or near your workplace for the purpose of peacefully obtaining or communicating information or peacefully persuading any person to work or abstain from working (Trade Union and Labour Relations (Consolidation) Act 1992). Employers have increasingly used the civil courts to get injunctions in order to limit the effectiveness of picketing. Injunctions have been granted on the basis that it was not the workplace of some or all of the pickets, or that the picketing was not peaceful. Unions that continue to picket in breach of an injunction are in contempt of court and liable to pay very heavy fines. By injunction the court can limit the location and number of pickets and impose conditions on their conduct.

No legal case has been decided that specifies that a particular number of pickets at the location of an industrial dispute will always be lawful. But a government Code of Practice, which the courts can refer to, suggests that the number of pickets at any entrance to a workplace should not generally exceed six. In applications for injunctions, the civil courts have tended to set the upper limit of the number of pickets that must be allowed at six. Other cases have given the police very wide discretion to limit the number of pickets if they believe it to be necessary to prevent a breach of the peace or an obstruction of the highway.

Secondary picketing – picketing at a workplace or premises where you do not work – does not have the same civil law protection, but is not a criminal offence. It is worth remembering that the police do not have any enhanced powers over secondary pickets and it is not their job to enforce the civil law on picketing, even if an injunction is in force. Their general powers in this area are dealt with below.

Police powers and picketing

Giving the police greater power to control and restrict picketing was a primary purpose of the POA. Any picket of two or more people is a 'public assembly' and therefore subject to police conditions under the POA. In addition to the power to impose conditions, the police possess a wide range of public order powers to restrict and control picketing and to arrest pickets for various offences. These include:

- Obstruction of the highway on the basis of too many pickets, even if they are moving, or a single picket trying to compel a driver to stop and listen.
- Obstruction of the police – for example, refusing to comply with lawful directions when the police are acting to prevent a breach of the peace.
- Using threatening, abusive or insulting words or behaviour (section 4, POA).
- Disorderly conduct likely to cause harassment, alarm or distress (section 5, POA).

- Aggravated trespass (section 68, Criminal Justice and Public Order Act 1994).

See below, section 8.15, 'Public order offences', p. 182.

8.7   USING THE HIGHWAY

The law provides a specific right to use a public highway: the right to pass and repass along the highway (including the pavement), and the right to make ordinary and reasonable use of the highway. Reasonable use includes orderly processions and peaceful non-obstructive public assemblies on the highway.

Any unreasonable obstruction of the highway is a criminal offence (see below, 'Highway obstruction', p. 187). There may also be bye-laws – laws relating to a particular area – that restrict activities that are incidental to the right to use the highway (see below, next section, and section 8.9, 'Bye-laws', p. 171). Since access to the public highway is often, in practice, central to the exercise of powers to demonstrate, the courts should be slow to countenance any improper restriction by police.

8.8   STREET COLLECTIONS, LEAFLETING, PETITIONS, POSTERS AND NEWSPAPERS

Generally speaking, the law allows wider latitude for collecting money for charitable operations than for commercial or political ones, both of which are more closely regulated by licensing. 'Charitable purposes' means any charitable, benevolent or philanthropic purpose. It includes the relief of poverty and the advancement of religion or education at home or abroad, but it does not include collections to raise funds for a political party or for a political campaign, such as CND or animal liberation. However, the law relating to these subjects is confused and inconsistently applied by the police. If in doubt, check bye-laws with the local authority and the police beforehand.

There is no need to obtain a licence or certificate for handing out leaflets or collecting signatures for a petition. A leaflet must have on it the name and address of the printer. Some bye-laws contain restrictions on the places where leafleting may take place; check the bye-laws at the town hall. The police may also move leafleters if they appear to be causing an obstruction. It is an offence to hand out leaflets that are threatening, abusive or insulting or those that are intended to stir up racial hatred.

A petition to Parliament is governed by special rules and must conform to special wording. Copies of the rules can be obtained from the House of Commons.

Sticking up posters in public places is quite legal, so long as:

- You have the consent of the owner of the hoarding, fence or wall in question.
- The poster is no more than six feet square.
- It advertises a non-commercial event, including political, educational or social meetings.

- There is no bye-law to prevent it.

Persons over 18 may sell newspapers in the street or from door to door, as long as the sale is for campaigning purposes. If the sale is for profit, it becomes street trading or peddling (if door to door), both of which are illegal without a licence. Sometimes difficulty is caused because the police believe that the newspaper or magazine is less of a campaigning document and more a device to raise money for a political organisation. Also, the sale of newspapers may obstruct the highway, which is a criminal offence (see below, 'Highway obstruction', p. 187).

8.9   BYE-LAWS

Many activities on the highway and in other public places such as parks and gardens and on common land are restricted by local bye-laws. Bye-laws for parks may, for example, prohibit public meetings, bill-posting, the erection of notices, stalls and booths, and the sale or distribution of pamphlets and leaflets. They will usually give the police and local authority officials the power to remove anybody who breaches the bye-laws.

Ministry of Defence bye-laws are used, for example, to keep trespassers out of US Air Force bases. The RAF Greenham Common bye-laws listed 12 prohibited activities, beginning with entering the protected area except by way of an authorised entrance, and including affixing posters to perimeter fences.

A copy of local bye-laws should be on sale at the local town hall and also available for inspection. Bye-laws for land owned by an authority such as Network Rail, or by a government department, will be available directly from that authority. Often, bye-laws have to be prominently displayed near entrances to private land, and they should show the address from which to obtain copies.

It is an offence to breach a bye-law, and the penalty is usually set out in the particular bye-law. Recent cases supported by Liberty have shown that when a charge is brought, bye-laws can be challenged on the basis that they are *ultra vires*, that is, beyond the scope of the Act of Parliament that created them, or that they are obviously unreasonable or inconsistent with or repugnant to the general law. Further, the courts would not enforce bye-laws that would operate to defeat a person's Convention rights.

8.10   OTHER POLICE POWERS TO RESTRICT PROTEST

In addition to the powers that the police are given by the POA, they have traditional powers, such as those relating to breach of the peace and obstruction of the highway, and those conferred by local bye-laws, which can be used to move or disperse a crowd that has assembled for a common purpose.

There are several nineteenth-century statutes (Metropolitan Police Act 1839, City of London Police Act 1839, and Town Police Clauses Act 1847) that enable the Commissioners of Police in London and the City or local councils outside London to make regulations and give directions to prevent obstruction and to keep order. Directions are given to constables and are not required to be made public. There are no conditions that must be satisfied before directions can be given, and, therefore, little scope to challenge them as excessive or unjustified. When lawful directions have been issued (for example, not to continue down a particular street), and you have been 'acquainted' with them, you commit an offence if you do not comply. You could also be charged with obstructing the police (see below, 'Police obstruction', p. 186).

At the beginning of each Parliamentary session, the Metropolitan Police Commissioner is instructed by Parliament to give directions under the Metropolitan Police Act 1839 to police officers 'to disperse all assemblies or processions of persons causing or likely to cause an obstruction, disorder or annoyance' within a specified area around Westminster whenever Parliament is sitting.

The police must rely on their general powers of arrest or powers to prevent a breach of the peace (see below, 'Breach of the peace', p. 188). You commit an offence (maximum sentence, a fine up to level 2 – currently £500) if you fail to disperse after you are made aware of the Commissioner's Directions, which normally means that the police must read them to you, or at least summarise their effect, before they can arrest you. It is a defence to show that the free passage of MPs would not have been obstructed. The directions do not affect processions or meetings on a day when Parliament is not sitting.

Police directions are often used to restrict protest events, but over the last decade police forces in different parts of the country seem to have been more ready to turn to these discretionary powers to regulate not just political demonstrations, but also raves and festivals, and the movement around the country of groups of people such as pickets, football supporters, new age travellers or road protesters. When directions are made, the police can be given very wide powers indeed, as the following examples – all from the last decade – show:

- During the News International dispute at Wapping the Metropolitan Commissioner's directions, which were renewed monthly during the dispute, gave the police authority to close streets – even to residents – and to stop any person walking or driving in any street in Tower Hamlets.
- When a 'Stop the City' demonstration was planned, the City of London Commissioner issued directions under which the police arrested people who distributed leaflets or gathered in groups of three or more.
- In Salisbury, the district council made an order banning 'hippies' from the town centre for two days and restricted them to a designated route.

In the City of London, the 'Ring of Steel' anti-terrorist roadblocks were originally set up under police powers to stop and search suspected offenders, but after protests the police conceded in practice that they had no special grounds to think that the people caught up in the roadblocks were terrorist suspects. The roadblocks continued, but were then justified by reference to directions issued by the City of London Police Commissioner. In due course, the Government brought in specific statutory powers, but the episode highlighted the use of 'Commissioner's Directions' in anticipation of powers not yet granted under statute.

New police powers of stop and search
Historically, the exercise of powers of stop and search depended on the individual police officer concerned having reasonable suspicion that the individual to be searched was carrying a prohibited article. This is no longer always the case.

Police are now able to designate an area in which individuals may be searched for knives or other weapons whether or not officers have any grounds to suspect the individual of having any. Police have recently been given additional new powers, within a designated area, to require the removal of facial coverings that they believe are being worn to avoid identification. In practice these powers are hugely significant in a public order context since they permit generalised and unaccountable stops and searches of any or all of the protesters at a given location.

The Terrorism Act 2000 takes this a stage further. Areas may be designated in which officers can stop vehicles and search the driver or anyone else inside. The power also covers pedestrians. Once again, this is a general power to search for evidence of terrorism (defined very broadly in section 1) regardless of any particular suspicion against the individual to be searched.

Liberty has been at the forefront of challenges to police actions of this type that appear to be designed to stifle free expression. Liberty believes that the concept of 'terrorist' employed in the Terrorism Act 2000 is far too wide and should be restricted by the courts to those situations that are clearly outside the realm of legitimate public protest.

8.11   IN PRACTICE – ORGANISING A PROTEST ACTION

It is easy to be intimidated by all the laws that exist to regulate the expression of public protest. Liberty has long argued that the drift towards ever more repressive public order laws is counter-productive – that the more regulation Parliament provides, the more likely it is that campaigners and organisers of demonstrations will simply refuse to co-operate with the police in advance of an event. Instead, they will leave the police to cope with unexpected numbers of people who assemble at a location with no clear idea of what to do, where to go or who to turn to for direction. Recent demonstrations in major cities in relation to global capitalism and the cancelling of Third World debt were characterised by large numbers of people assembling at short notice with highly diverse political interests and demonstrating styles. Following the 'J18' demonstration in the City of London in 1999, police leaders accepted that their own responses were often inappropriate and heavy-handed, with problems of communication, insufficient numbers and lack of mobility a recurring theme.

Political demonstrations come in all shapes and sizes, however, and organisers must decide for themselves what they want from a particular action, and whether co-operation with the police in advance of the event is likely to support or defeat those aims. Some of the most successful protest groups of the last decade have seen the restrictive legal framework as one of the necessary challenges that their own good organisation can overcome, or at least accommodate.

Although the police have been given very wide powers to regulate public protest under the POA, the actual exercise of these powers has been remarkably rare since the POA came into force. Conditions are not routinely imposed on demonstrations, and banning orders have not been used as extensively as opponents of the legislation first feared. In fact, only a handful of the hundreds of thousands of prosecutions brought under the POA since 1987 have been for offences connected with organising marches or assemblies, defying banning orders or even breaching conditions imposed by police. The vast majority have been for the public order offences, ranging from riot to disorderly conduct, each of which involved allegations of specific offensive conduct by the person concerned, usually at the demonstration itself.

The following sections show how complying with the law and negotiating with the police might be accommodated in the practical arrangements that organisers will be making, in any event, in preparation for a protest of significant size; and how structures developed to support the action itself can be adapted to support protesters who are arrested.

What sort of action?

Whether you are planning a simple picket or vigil, or a set-piece march and rally, you will have started by asking what sort of action will best achieve the results you are seeking. Are you seeking to persuade an identifiable group of people about a particular decision – councillors, perhaps, about a local planning issue – or are you seeking to demonstrate or mobilise support in the wider community for a long-running cause or campaign? As organisers, you will match the public support and other resources available to you with the sort of impact you want to create. Are you seeking favourable publicity? Many groups, big and small, have secured a place in the public eye by the careful use of media opportunities and attractive or eye-catching stunts, as well as by more traditional shows of mass political support.

Stewards and legal observers

Whatever the nature of the action, an efficient stewarding operation avoids many of the interactions between protesters and police that have the potential for conflict. Protesters are usually quite happy to follow sensible instructions so long as they know that they are part of the organisers' plan rather than some arbitrary decision made on the spot by an officious police officer. Stewarding, therefore, gives confidence to your protesters, while also enabling information about particular difficulties to reach the organisation room, or chief stewards at the protest, very quickly.

It is important to appreciate, however, that the police and organisers may have very different views of what 'efficient stewarding' means. From the organisers' point of view the real job of the stewards is to make sure that the event takes the course that the organisers want, not necessarily to solve problems for the police or to smooth things over where real conflicts exist. What the stewards are told to do might differ quite substantially from what the police want them to do. The police sometimes put conditions on demonstrations and assemblies that need to be challenged as unreasonable. Stewards can then play a very important role in that challenge (see below, section 8.13 'Challenging police decisions', p. 177).

Stewards should be briefed prior to the protest on what exactly they should be doing, and whom they should report to in the event of difficulty. They are part of the organisation of the event and should be identifiable as such both to police and protesters by bibs, armbands, special T-shirts or badges (but obviously not a quasi-military uniform). At a march, for example, they should have a map of the proposed route and the telephone number of an organisation room, if you have one (see below, 'Organisation room', p. 175).

Some organisations have ad hoc groups of legal observers who are prepared to attend demonstrations of any size and make an independent note of numbers and movements of police and protesters. In the event of arrests, they will make immediate notes of witnesses's names and addresses. Observers can be a great help if events turn sour, but in any case their presence at a demonstration can be reassuring to protesters and police alike. It is important that they perceive themselves to be independent of the protest itself and its organisation. They may, therefore, wish to be identified in a way that distinguishes them from other people on the march, including stewards, for example, by special badges, armbands or bibs. Often law students or lecturers from local colleges are prepared to provide this service if given enough notice. Inexperienced legal observers should be briefed by a solicitor, preferably in good time before the protest (see below, 'Legal cover', p. 175).

Stewards and legal observers should know where to meet immediately after the event for a debriefing when any feedback or information they have – for example, notes from legal observers – can be retrieved. They should also be available to come to a defendants' meeting if one becomes necessary (see below, 'Defendants' meeting', p 179). Whether you predict there might be trouble or not, it can do no harm to pencil in such a meeting to take place two or three days after the event. Arranging such a meeting provides a safety net that will enable you to begin to draw all your resources together should there ever be a defendants' group that needs to rely on them.

Advance publicity and press liaison
Prior to the event itself, advance publicity for demonstrators should include a clear statement of the venue for assembly, the time of departure (for a march) and the time and place of the eventual rally. Any venues you advertise ought – as a matter of good practice – to have been agreed with the owners/local authority/police in advance. Otherwise, if you are forced to change any of these arrangements, your supporters may never get to the protest.

Protest actions are designed to be widely seen and their intended message understood. You might prepare a press statement to be sent out to the media in advance setting out the message you want them to grasp – and, hopefully, to broadcast on your behalf – about why the event is taking place. Ideally, this should include contact telephone numbers of one or two people who are prepared to be quoted speaking on your behalf and a reference point at the protest itself so that journalists know where to go if they want to get an official statement or reaction to something that has happened.

The advantage of preparing a press release in advance is that local journalists will put the event in their news diary, which may ensure fuller coverage. Also, they may be more interested in difficulties you have with the police in the run-up to the event, especially if you decide to tell the press that you are preparing to challenge proposed conditions.

Organisation room
On the day of the event itself there ought to be a reference point away from the demonstration – a union office, for example – with a telephone number, fixed or mobile, which might be circulated widely on a leaflet that arrested people will be likely to have with them when in the police station. This will also be the number used by stewards or legal observers if they want to contact the organisation room during the event itself. Other available phones can be used for outgoing calls – to the police station, to the standby lawyer or perhaps to the press.

Legal cover

Ideally, you will have arranged a standby lawyer well in advance of the action who is prepared to be contacted during the demonstration itself and to follow through with representation for arrested demonstrators if they require it. The standby lawyer should be a criminal solicitor with particular experience of dealing with demonstrations. If you do not know of such a lawyer, organisations such as Liberty will help you find one in your area. If you experience difficulties negotiating with the police in advance, the standby lawyer may be prepared to help you.

Debriefing

Taking time to listen to feedback from those who have helped you organise the event is more than just good practice – where there have been arrests such an exercise is essential. It is also an opportunity to recognise the job done by stewards and legal observers, to thank them and to make sure you have their contact numbers for the next time you need them.

8.12   DEALING WITH THE POLICE

Deciding whether to make contact

Whenever it is anticipated there may be police interest in a proposed action, as part of your preparations it will be worth weighing the benefits and costs of speaking to the police well in advance. Sometimes it will be a legal obligation to do so (see above, 'Advance notice', p. 164). The benefits of establishing contact with the police are likely to include, if not always good will, at least some co-operation. With some or all of the above measures in place you will be in a strong position to satisfy the police that you will be able to regulate your own event without outside help. Confident organisers who impress with their thoroughness and practicality are more likely to be able to convince sceptical police that a proposed event should proceed exactly as planned. Where they are able to do so, the worry that the event might be hijacked by police interference will be eased, and organisers will then be able to concentrate on getting their political message across to the public.

The costs of contacting the police might include the fact that they may use your information to trigger the use of their powers to restrict a protest or, exceptionally, to ban it altogether. It is worth remembering that communications to police – especially those in writing – could be used in court if the police wanted to show that a particular person was an organiser of an illegal demonstration.

Despite their substantial human resources and weaponry, the police are very often intimidated by the idea of large numbers of people taking to the streets to make their protest heard. Where police react in a hostile way, it is often through fear of the unknown. In practice, many police forces respond positively to constructive engagement – they like to know that someone who is organising a demonstration has anticipated the likely numbers and thought about the route, stewarding and safety. They also like to know that there will be someone at the protest whom they can talk sensibly to in an emergency. In a protest that continues over days or weeks, maintaining clear channels of communication with a senior officer, even if you consider police tactics to be unhelpful, can have positive benefits for protesters.

Meeting the police in advance

When you tell the police you are holding a demonstration they will often ask you to a meeting with them. There is no requirement that you attend, but it is quite sensible that you do. You will have to prepare for the meeting quite carefully, with details of arrangements for stewarding and crowd control, first aid and access by emergency vehicles, maps and plans, a detailed timetable and an estimate of numbers. Relying on your knowledge of the community and any other events likely to take place on the same date, try to anticipate police objections.

For the police, this meeting can be an information-gathering exercise. The Metropolitan Police, for instance, have an official-looking form, which asks you for the information you must give in advance by law, but also a lot of other information – names of speakers, for example. It is important to be aware of the information you must provide and to decide in advance how much you wish to say to the police beyond that. If in doubt at the meeting on how to respond, you can always say that you want to consult your committee or co-organisers. You don't have to agree to everything the police propose. You can tell the police directly that you do not agree to a certain condition, or that you will consider whether to or not.

If the demonstration is likely to be big in size or impact, especially if it is in the centre of a major city, there may be a large number of police present at this meeting – traffic police, public order police, local area police and note-takers, and so on. It is always worth taking another person with you (or maybe one or two more) – a fellow committee member, a friend or even a friendly solicitor. It is best to agree in advance on how you will handle this, so that everyone is clear who is there to speak to police, to make decisions or to take notes. Since police forces probably differ quite a lot, it may be worth talking to other groups who have organised demonstrations in your area before going to a meeting with the police.

Who to put forward

Choose as your own representative(s) for such a meeting the person on your team who is likely, for whatever reason, to get the most constructive and sympathetic response from the police side. This person need not be a 'spokesperson' in a formal sense, or have any position of responsibility for your organisation or even for the direction of the protest itself. Indeed, it is often better that the person's only role is to facilitate communication between the parties rather than to be a decision-maker in her/his own right. This ensures the person has a good reason to report back to others to consider police proposals, and it may lessen the personal pressure that can be brought to bear on the negotiator by police.

8.13 CHALLENGING POLICE DECISIONS

Even when the police threaten to impose conditions, organisers have a great deal of discretion about whether and when to challenge the police decision. Sometimes organisers are prepared to agree to police alterations to their original proposals – a minor alteration to the proposed route, perhaps – knowing that this means in practice that the police are unlikely to interfere further with a route they have themselves adopted. Organisers may even prefer to adapt their protest to what they consider to be unreasonable police requests simply to ensure the event goes ahead without its political message being blunted by unnecessary conflict with the police. But where organisers decide to challenge unacceptable police conditions it is possible for them to do so very effectively. This section suggests some starting points.

Mobilising political support

Although the police regard their own decisions as 'operational', in practice they involve setting priorities between the interests of different groups in society. Ultimately, where the right balance lies is really a political matter and the police are sensitive to criticism from MPs and councillors, local interest groups or trades councils. Members of the police committee may be concerned by 'operational' policing decisions they consider to be oppressive.

Mounting a legal challenge in advance

With the help of legal advisers, organisers could test the legality of police conditions through a court case in advance of the action itself. In order to seek a judicial review of a police decision you would need to argue that either:

- The decision was improperly reached (for example, because the proper procedure was not followed or improper considerations were taken into account); or
- The decision is unlawful because it would involve the police acting incompatibly with the Convention; or
- The decision was so unreasonable or arbitrary that no reasonable chief officer could have reached that conclusion.

Cases brought to challenge banning orders prior to the incorporation of the Convention by the Human Rights Act 1998 showed that the courts have been very unwilling to interfere with police decisions, especially if to do so would involve substituting their own assessment of the facts, and the possible prospects of disorder, damage, disruption or intimidation, for the assessment made by senior police officers. Now that the positive rights of protesters must be made an express part of the decision-making process, the courts are more willing to engage in the balancing exercise themselves – after all, they, like the police, are under an obligation to give effect to the principles in the Convention.

Applications for judicial review must be made to the High Court in London. Urgent applications can be heard quickly. In many instances, however, you will be informed of conditions to restrict processions or assemblies too late to apply to the High Court. There is no one with immediate power to overrule the senior officer on the spot if he decides to impose conditions.

Where protesters themselves defy police conditions it will be for the police to decide whether to make arrests and seek prosecutions. If in a subsequent trial it turns out that the conditions were indeed invalid, the prosecutions would fail and arrested persons may be entitled to damages.

Help from Liberty

Liberty has been able to advise protest groups, unions and political groups about the best way to challenge police operations that threaten to defeat civil liberties. In the past the organisation has supported lawyers and lay people who have challenged such decisions, and has itself been prepared to take test cases when important issues of principle have been at stake. Liberty will either be able to help you or will refer you to a specialist solicitor or campaigning group who have dealt with similar problems in the past.

8.14   SUPPORTING PEOPLE ARRESTED AT THE PROTEST

Where people have been arrested at a protest event and charged with offences, they become defendants in the criminal process and face the possibility of a criminal record and sometimes the threat of prison. It is often very frightening for protesters to be torn from the solidarity of a demonstration to find themselves facing the music on their own. An important part of what organisers can do for defendants, as their cases progress over the months that may elapse before a trial, is to provide support.

Defendants may be helped by support and reassurance in many different ways – it will often be a question of adapting your resources to the calls that are made on them – but one of the most straightforward and practical measures is to ensure that there is always someone from your organisation at court with defendants for each appearance.

In the immediate aftermath of the event, however, there are some standard procedures to be performed, starting with the defendants' meeting. It is best to plan this two or three days after the event just in case it may be needed. Too soon, and defendants may still be in custody. Too late, and a lot of your resources, especially witnesses, will have dispersed, perhaps forever.

Defendants' meeting

A defendants' meeting puts people who have been charged with offences in touch with the people who organised the event, sometimes for the first time. Defendants may need immediate help to get lawyers or Legal Aid, for example, or even just floors to sleep on if they have to remain away from home for a court hearing. The meeting is an opportunity to give defendants reassurance if they need it, and to tell them what support they can expect from your organisation. There may be questions about bail conditions, Legal Aid or bind-overs, for example, or how their cases are likely to develop. The standby lawyer may be prepared to attend such a meeting, but will not give specific legal advice to defendants about their individual cases.

The defendants' meeting is a very important practical opportunity to match defendants to the witnesses who saw them being arrested. It is useful to do this quickly while memories are fresh. Often witnesses will not have met the defendants before and will not know them by name. Unless they come to a meeting and see the defendant, the only method of matching them to the right arrest is by their description of the arrested person, or by the time and location of the arrest. Where there have been many arrests, particularly at a mobile protest like a march, there is often great confusion about location, order and times of arrests. Sometimes the only way to sort out which witnesses saw which arrests is to have everyone in the same room at the same time.

Defendants might want to provide passport photographs of themselves or, if you have a camera at the meeting, might want you to take photos of them, to help with identification. This is often an enormous help to you, witnesses and lawyers where there are more than a handful of arrests. Make sure that defendants are happy for you to circulate their photos and other information about them that they give you.

Legal help and self-help

Defendants charged with 'less serious' criminal offences may find it difficult – in some cases impossible – to get Legal Aid (or 'funded representation' as it is now known). The first priority will be to complete the application form as fully as possible, pointing out, for example, that a particular defendant may have a special need for representation because of the complexity of the case or the consequences of conviction, which might include the loss of a job or the loss of previous good character. Completing the application is a skilled job – lawyers will help defendants to apply for funded representation if necessary. If it is refused, lawyers will usually offer to represent the client at their normal hourly charging rate, which is often out of the reach of all but well-off defendants. Occasionally, lawyers will represent defendants for a lower fee, or even free of charge. It is always worth asking, especially if a particular lawyer is already representing other defendants from the same demonstration.

Defendants who are unable to obtain, or afford, legal representation will have to rely on self-help – and your help – to conduct their defence. Some organisations have proved that they can be very effective in supporting defendants who defend themselves, often by establishing a legal team within the organisation that pools knowledge and experience, and provides a clear reference point for defendants. It is worth remembering that even if a defendant is denied funded representation, he or she may still seek free advice from a solicitor's firm. Self-representing defendants are entitled to the assistance of a 'Mackenzie friend' to advise and support them in court.

Michael Randle represented himself successfully at the Old Bailey in 1991 when he stood trial for assisting the escape from prison of George Blake. Randle's book, *How to Defend Yourself in Court*, draws on his experience and is a very useful resource and inspiration for defendants and their supporters, whether legally represented or not. The book is now out of print, but may be available second hand or from some libraries.

See also Chapter 6.

Supporting the legal team

Once a person arrested for a criminal offence instructs a lawyer, the relationship is a personal one between the client and the lawyer, and is therefore subject to professional confidentiality. Although the lawyer will not be prepared to speak about the details of the client's case to anyone else, most sympathetic lawyers will wish to retain close contact with any organisation that has their client's best interests at heart. Moreover, they may wish to rely on you to get things done that they do not have the knowledge or resources to do themselves.

Sometimes several solicitors will be acting for different defendants. Unless you are able to help them with an overview of what happened when and where during the course of the whole event, individual solicitors may never get the full picture. It is very important, for example, for them to know which arrests may be linked with each other. Accurate information about the time and location of arrests will be very helpful when defence lawyers seek film or photographs of the event from journalists who covered it. It is best to get this overview completed when events are fresh in everyone's mind and you have willing supporters to help.

Preparing material for defendants and their solicitors
At the earliest opportunity – within a few days of the defendants' meeting – organisers should marshal all the material they have at their disposal and make it available to defendants and their lawyers. This will include brief accounts of the following matters:

- Facts about the event itself – who you are; how you prepared for the event; negotiations with the police before and at the event; who spoke for the organisation; who represented the police; what conditions were imposed/ agreed; what steps were taken by police/organisers to publicise conditions; whether any conditions were broken. Include a map of the route showing, if possible, location and time of arrests. Also reports – in the form of brief statements – where stewards and legal observers have made observations about the event that might be relevant. Include telephone numbers to enable lawyers to contact individuals directly if their evidence may be helpful.
- A full list of defendants' names, addresses and telephone numbers, including, if possible, time and location of arrest, police station taken to, offence they are charged with, and the date and venue of first court appearance. If defendants are happy to supply passport-sized photographs of themselves (or wanted you to take photographs at the defendants' meeting), you can include a photocopied sheet with them all on.
- A full list of witnesses' names, addresses and telephone numbers, marked (if known) with the names of the defendants whose arrest they saw.
- A list of media representatives – especially photographers and television news teams – who you think were at the event. A useful source is the bylines on media coverage – this can be followed up on the internet or in the local library without having to buy all the newspapers. Wherever a news story might be helpful it should be circulated. You might also include the list of organisations to which you sent your press release. Lawyers may then be able to follow up whether they had anyone at the event.
- A list of defence solicitors, so you know whom to circulate information to. It will also help solicitors to communicate with each other if they know who else is being represented by whom.

Where more is needed later, defendants will know exactly whom to ask.

Dealing with the media
In the run-up to the trials of defendants who plead not guilty – sometimes a delay of many months – you may want to look closely at the media coverage of the event and respond constructively by telephone or e-mail to journalists, by 'letters to the editor' or by press release to anything that is said that you know is not true.

The police are adept at public relations and will invariably have their own publicists, who are experienced journalists, handling press enquiries about the event and its aftermath. The media will often take this version as gospel, presuming the guilt of anyone unfortunate enough to have been arrested. While there are no doubt other factors at play, this may sometimes be due to their perception that there is no other reliable source to challenge what the police say.

As well as supplying information from your organisation, you may be able to put the media in touch with ordinary protesters who had a very different impression of the way the event took place. If you know that celebrities at the event (such as local politicians) are likely to be supportive, you can ask them if they, too, are prepared to be interviewed.

It will give confidence to defendants to see that you are active about putting media coverage right. It also advertises the work that you are doing in case defendants or potential witnesses did not know how to get in touch.

Practical help

It is often useful to talk to people who are experienced at organising protest events to get ideas on ways to get the most impact from the available resources and, in the event of unexpected arrests, on ways of supporting defendants and their legal teams. Up-to-date information can be obtained via the internet if you search for links to 'politics', 'protest' and 'action'.

8.15   PUBLIC ORDER OFFENCES

The right of protest may only be exercised peacefully. Otherwise, a wide variety of offences may be committed. The POA contains many of the more common public order offences such as riot, affray and threatening behaviour. But there are many offences elsewhere in the law that may be used against activities in public, such as assault, criminal damage and having an offensive weapon. Some specific offences connected with marches, assemblies and meetings were set out earlier in the chapter.

8.16   SERIOUS OFFENCES OF VIOLENCE

The three main offences in the POA for group violence are riot, violent disorder and affray.

Riot

It is an offence of riot if you use violence where at least 12 people are together using or threatening violence for a common purpose and in such a way that 'a person of reasonable firmness' witnessing the events would fear for his or her safety. This is the most serious of public order offences. The offence can only be tried in the Crown Court, and the Director of Public Prosecutions must consent to the case being brought. The maximum penalty is ten years' imprisonment and/or a fine.

Violent disorder

You are guilty of violent disorder if you use or threaten violence where at least three people are together using or threatening violence and in such a way that a person 'of reasonable firmness' would fear for his or her personal safety.

This offence is used especially for group violence, such as disturbances commonly associated with football hooliganism, or where weapons are used. It can be tried in the Crown Court with a maximum penalty of five years' imprisonment and/or a fine, or the Magistrates' Court with a maximum penalty of six months' imprisonment and/or a fine up to level 5 – currently £5,000.

Affray

It is an affray if you use or threaten violence to somebody else in such a way that an onlooker, a person 'of reasonable firmness' would fear for his or her personal safety (*effrayer* is the French word meaning 'to frighten'). No such person need actually be present. The offence refers to the reaction of a notional bystander to underline the fact that it is a public order offence rather than another type of assault offence. It follows that the test for guilt is whether the bystander, as opposed to the actual object of the threats, is made to fear for her/his own safety. Street fighting, with or without weapons or missiles, is an affray. It can be tried in the Crown Court with a maximum penalty of three years' imprisonment and/or a fine, or the Magistrates' Court with a maximum penalty of six months' imprisonment and/or a fine up to level 5 – currently £5,000.

Grievous bodily harm and actual bodily harm

Serious assaults on individuals include the offences of inflicting grievous bodily harm and assault occasioning actual bodily harm. These offences are set out in the Offences Against the Person Act 1861. If you cause or inflict grievous bodily harm on somebody or wound them (that is, cut the skin), the maximum penalty is life imprisonment. If the person dies, the charge may be murder or manslaughter. If the injury is less serious, such as bruising or grazes, the charge may be assault occasioning actual bodily harm, with a maximum penalty of five years' imprisonment.

Knives and other offensive weapons

You are guilty under the Prevention of Crime Act 1953 if you have an offensive weapon in a public place without lawful authority or reasonable excuse. There are three types of weapon: first, those designed for causing injury such as a knuckle-duster, dagger or flick-knife; second, those adapted for causing injury such as a broken bottle; third, anything intended for use to cause injury (whether or not it falls into the first two categories), such as a brick or baseball bat.

Under the Criminal Justice Act 1988 it is an offence to have a knife in a public place without reasonable excuse. The section does not apply to a normal pen-knife with a blade of less than three inches, but mere possession of any other article that has a blade or is sharply pointed is an offence unless you can prove you had a good reason for carrying it – for example, for use at work or for a hobby.

This is a very widely drawn offence that in principle would include possession of innocent household implements such as knitting needles, hat pins or even plastic picnic cutlery. The unusual form of the offence puts the burden on the defendant to satisfy the court that she or he had a reasonable excuse for possession of the item in a public place. In practice, this gives the police and prosecuting authorities enormous discretion to choose which type of people to stop and search, arrest and prosecute.

Offensive weapon and bladed article charges can be tried in the Crown Court with a maximum penalty of four years' imprisonment and/or a fine, or in the Magistrates'

Court with a maximum penalty six months' imprisonment and/or a fine of up to £5,000.

The Knives Act 1997 gives police additional powers, on the authority of a police inspector, to stop and search at random for knives or offensive weapons without needing specific suspicion of an offence being committed by the particular person concerned. This power has been further extended to permit officers to require the removal of masks, and to seize items that might be used to conceal identities. This has been used at mass demonstrations to give the police, in effect, a pretext for a general power of stop and search.

8.17   LESS SERIOUS OFFENCES

Assault
You are guilty of common assault (under the common law) if you engage in an act that intentionally or recklessly causes another person to expect immediate personal violence, anything from a punch or a kick to throwing something at somebody. If injury is caused, a more serious charge of assault may be brought. Common assault can only be tried in the Magistrates' Court. The maximum penalty is six months' imprisonment.

You commit a separate offence with a similar penalty if you assault a police officer in the execution of his or her duty. At a trial the prosecution would have to show that the police officer was acting lawfully. In practice, especially in a confused demonstration situation, proving beyond doubt that police action was lawful is often difficult. This offence is the highest-level 'summary only' offence (that is, an offence that can only be tried in a Magistrates' Court) and a custodial sentence, even for a first offender, is a real possibility.

Threatening, abusive or insulting words or behaviour
It is an offence under section 4 of the POA if you use threatening, abusive or insulting words or actions towards somebody else, and:

- You intend the other person to fear that violence is going to be used; or
- The other person is likely to expect violence; or
- Violence may well be provoked.

This offence is normally used where threats, abuse or insults are likely to cause a breach of the peace: rival football supporters hurling abuse, threats at the picket line, abusive language by rival demonstrators. The charge is often used against protesters who, in the view of the police, go beyond the bounds of ordinary protest, but in all cases the behaviour must be directed towards another person. It is also an offence if threatening words are on a banner or placard or even a T-shirt or badge.

This offence can only be tried in the Magistrates' Court; there is no right to trial by jury. The maximum penalty is six months' imprisonment and/or a fine up to level 5 (currently £5,000).

Intentional harassment
It is an offence under section 4A of the POA if you use threatening behaviour with intent to cause a person harassment, alarm and distress. Introduced to deal with

cases of racial harassment, this section has been used more frequently to prosecute 'stalkers'. The penalties are as for section 4.

Disorderly conduct
It is an offence under section 5 of the POA if you use threatening, abusive or insulting words or behaviour or disorderly behaviour within the hearing or sight of a person likely to be caused harassment, alarm or distress (unless your conduct was reasonable, see below). There must be a victim present at the scene of the crime. That person must be identified, but need not be brought to court. Police officers are unlikely to be victims of this offence.

This is the lowest-level public order offence. It is intended to cover minor acts of hooliganism, especially behaviour directed at the elderly and other vulnerable groups. It was much criticised when it was introduced in the POA because it covered behaviour that was hitherto not considered to be criminal. In particular, it covers behaviour that falls short of any violence or the threat or fear of any violence.

Perhaps because this offence broke new ground, a new form of defence was included in the Act. It is a defence if you prove that your conduct (even if it was otherwise disorderly) was reasonable, perhaps because of the circumstances in which the behaviour occurred. An example might be where distressed relatives at a funeral speak out about a person they believe to be responsible. Although the conduct might objectively be disorderly, and might also cause distress, it might yet be perfectly reasonable in the circumstances. Cases since the incorporation of the Convention show that in assessing reasonableness, the court has to consider whether prosecuting you (and thereby denying you the right under Article 10, to freedom of expression) is a proportionate response in all the circumstances of the case.

The offence carries a unique two-stage power of arrest, allowing police to arrest only if the person has been warned to stop the disorderly conduct and has then gone on to repeat it. The offence can be tried in the Magistrates' Court only. The maximum penalty is a fine up to level 3 (currently £1,000); there is no power to send a person convicted of this offence to prison.

Harassment
The Protection from Harassment Act 1997 (PHA) contains further provisions designed for stalkers. Under section 1 it is an offence for a person to pursue a course of conduct that harasses, and that the person knows or ought to know amounts to harassment. The offence is punishable by imprisonment of up to six months and/or a fine up to level 5 (currently £5,000). It is an offence of aggravated harassment under section 4 where a complainant is also put in fear of violence (with a sentence of up to five years' imprisonment and an unlimited fine). The PHA creates a statutory tort of harassment and makes it a criminal offence to breach a civil injunction restraining any conduct of harassment.

Once again there is a 'reasonableness' defence, which invites the court to consider whether it is appropriate for the behaviour to be restricted (and the defendant criminalised) given the circumstances of the case.

The PHA may have been targeted at stalkers, but one of the first cases in which it was used was an attempt by an animal research laboratory to prevent a group carrying out a vigil and related actions outside its premises. The defendants, supported by Liberty, argued that the PHA should not be used to restrict rights to public protest. The court agreed, saying that it would resist any attempt to interpret the statute widely. Later cases, however, have seen the courts taking a more relaxed approach to interpretation, and successful prosecutions have been brought against pickets, hunt saboteurs and other political protesters.

Aggravated trespass
The offence of aggravated trespass is committed when a person:

- Trespasses on land; and
- When a lawful activity is taking place on that land or land nearby; and
- He or she does anything intending to intimidate, obstruct or disrupt that activity.

The offence, under section 68 of the Criminal Justice and Public Order Act 1994, goes hand-in-hand with powers to prevent protesters joining an aggravated trespass. The powers are similar to the exclusion zone powers for trespassory assemblies. Once protesters are within a five-mile radius exclusion zone they can be turned back, and can be arrested and charged with an offence if they refuse to comply. The offence of aggravated trespass carries imprisonment of up to 51 weeks and/or a fine up to level 4 (currently £2,500).

Criminal damage
It is an offence under the Criminal Damage Act 1971 if you damage or destroy property or threaten to do so intentionally or recklessly and without lawful excuse. There is a full range of offences from arson with intent to endanger life (maximum penalty life imprisonment) to damage of property under £5,000 in value (Magistrates' Court only, with a maximum penalty of 51 weeks and/or a fine at level 4 – currently £2,500). The damage need not be permanent. Even graffiti designed to wash away in the rain may be criminal damage.

Police obstruction
It is an offence if you wilfully obstruct a police officer in the execution of his or her duty. This is widely used by the police at demonstrations and in other public order contexts. Obstruction of a police officer means simply doing any act that makes it more difficult for the police to carry out their lawful duty (Magistrates' Court only, maximum penalty one month's imprisonment and/or a fine up to level 3 – currently £1,000). It is used against those who refuse to move on or to keep back, or against those who interfere with police work, for example, by objecting to a lawful arrest or search. In practice, proving officers were acting 'in the execution of their duty' can be very difficult for the prosecution, especially in complicated situations involving multiple arrests. There is no specific power of arrest for this offence, and so the police have to rely on their 'general arrest powers' where the circumstances permit (see section 5.4, 'Police powers of arrest', p. 107). Where an arrest can be justified, no warning need be given in advance.

'Watching and besetting'
It is an offence under the Trade Union and Labour Relations (Consolidation) Act 1992 (maximum penalty six months' imprisonment and/or a fine up to level 5 – currently £5,000) to intimidate others, if, for example, you:

- Use violence to intimidate someone or his or her family or damage property.
- Persistently follow someone.
- Hide someone's tools or clothes.
- 'Watch and beset' or picket someone's home or place of work. (NB: it is not unlawful to picket peacefully at your own place of work.)
- Follow someone in the street, with two others, in a disorderly manner.

This applies only if you do any of these acts with the intention of compelling the person not to do something he or she has a legal right to do (for example, the right to use the highway to go to work) or to do something he or she has a legal right not to do (for example, the right not to join the picket). Persuasion, even vigorous persuasion, will not amount to an offence unless it crosses into the realm of compulsion. Although designed for employment disputes, this offence has recently been used against a group of road protesters.

Highway obstruction

You commit an offence if, without lawful authority or excuse, you wilfully obstruct the free passage of the highway.

This is a widely drawn offence. It is often seen in practice as a police licensing power over public gatherings. The police use it to remove sit-down demonstrators, to keep marchers from leaving the agreed police route, to control pickets and in every conceivable public order context on the highway. Often the police will give a warning to move before making an arrest, although there is no legal requirement to do so. Nevertheless, a failure to give a warning may be relevant to the reasonableness or otherwise of the use of the highway.

The offence is obstructing the highway, not other highway users. So it is not necessary to prove that any other person was actually obstructed – the 'obstruction' can be made out if you simply occupy a section of highway. In practice the offence turns on whether a particular obstruction was reasonable rather than whether there was, in fact, an obstruction. The test of reasonableness is always objective. Was there an actual obstruction? If there was, how long did it last? Where was it? What was its purpose?

There is an established right to peaceful, non-obstructive protest on the highway, and so if the court concludes that you were simply exercising this right, you would not be found guilty of the offence.

The test of reasonableness can very often be argued successfully in demonstration cases, particularly where the police have taken no action in the past, or where the place of protest is a regular post or where the actual obstruction was trivial. In practice, it is often very helpful to have photographs to show just how extensive – or limited – a particular obstruction was.

Since the incorporation of the Convention any court considering the question of reasonableness would also have to consider the impact of their decision on the exercise of your Convention rights. So, for example, a demonstrator who is prosecuted for obstruction of the highway may be able to invoke the right to peaceful assembly in Article 11 as a defence in the Magistrates' Court.

The offence can be tried in the Magistrates' Court only. The maximum penalty is a fine up to level 3 (currently £1,000). There is no power to send a person convicted of highway obstruction to prison.

Drunk and disorderly

It is an offence under the Criminal Justice Act 1967, to be guilty, while drunk, of disorderly behaviour. The maximum penalty is a fine up to level 3 – currently £1,000.

Wearing uniforms

You may commit an offence under the Terrorism Act 2000 if you wear a uniform in public signifying membership or support of a 'proscribed organisation', such as Al-Qu'ada, the IRA and the Ulster Freedom Fighters. The maximum penalty is six months' imprisonment and/or a fine up to level 5 (currently £5,000).

Sentences

In deciding an appropriate sentence, the courts will always consider the gravity of the offence, the circumstances of its commission and the previous character of the defendant. Defendants who plead guilty are entitled to credit because a guilty plea indicates remorse for their behaviour.

There are powers to sentence to imprisonment in all serious cases. Prison has to be considered a real possibility in offences such as threatening behaviour and assault, especially where the police are involved. However, the majority of public order cases dealt with in the Magistrates' Court are disposed of by way of community penalty (such as a community punishment order) or a fine. Wherever there is a real risk of imprisonment, defendants are entitled to Legal Aid (now known as funded representation), subject to their means.

Two common offences – highway obstruction and disorderly conduct – are not imprisonable under any circumstances, and a third offence – obstructing police – is technically imprisonable, but this power is used very rarely indeed.

Fine levels

In fixing the amount of a fine the court must take into account the means of the offender. The court may give the offender time to pay, for example, within three months, or at so much a week. If the court imposes a sentence of imprisonment in default and the fine is not paid, the court may send the offender to prison, but only after a careful review of the offender's means.

Breach of the peace

There is no offence of breach of the peace. But if a police officer sees a breach of the peace or reasonably believes that a breach of the peace is about to start, he or she may arrest, disperse or detain those causing the problem and, if necessary, take them before a Magistrates' Court to be bound over.

There is a breach of the peace whenever a person causes harm or appears likely to cause harm to persons or property or acts in a manner the natural consequence of which is to provoke others to violence.

If a breach of the peace occurs, one or more of the public order offences of threatening behaviour, disorderly conduct, assault or criminal damage is likely to have been committed. In such a case, the police can choose whether to charge an offence or go before the magistrates for a bind-over order.

Bind-overs

The Magistrates' Court may bind you over to keep the peace for a specified period in a number of different circumstances:

- You may be brought before the court for committing a breach of the peace (under the Justices of the Peace Act 1361).
- You may be brought before the court on a complaint made by any person at the court.
- In proceedings for a criminal offence, a witness or a defendant (even if acquitted) may be bound over.

A bind-over order is not a conviction or a penalty. It is an undertaking as to future conduct. Its purpose is to prevent offences being committed in the future. The order will bind you over to keep the peace for a period of time for a specified sum, say £200 for 12 months. If you breach the order and are brought back to court, you will have to pay up to the whole amount. Sometimes a surety is taken, which in effect is a promise made by another person to pay money into court if you should breach the terms of the bind-over order. If you refuse to be bound over in the first place, you can be sent to prison for up to six months. You should always be given the opportunity to say in court why you should not be bound over, if you wish to, or why you are not in breach of an order.

Bind-over orders are often used against demonstrators and protesters. Sometimes the prosecution drops a charge, such as obstruction of the highway, if the defendant agrees to be bound over and the court also agrees. In some cases, unions will advise their members who have been picketing not to accept bind-overs if they wish to return to the picket line. A bind-over cannot of itself prevent someone returning to an otherwise lawful protest but it is an inhibiting factor.

Liberty believes that the bind-over order is an outdated form of justice and that it is wrong to give the courts the power to send somebody to prison for refusing to be bound over, particularly when no offence has been committed. A test case brought by Liberty in the ECHR in 1998 clarified the law by restricting the circumstances in which bind-overs might be ordered and also by limiting the terms of bind-over orders to restrict future conduct that broke the law rather than future conduct that merely amounted to bad behaviour.

Anti-social behaviour orders

Under the Crime and Disorder Act 1998, a 'relevant authority', which includes the police, can apply for an anti-social behaviour order (ASBO) against any individual who it is proved has acted in an anti-social manner, that is acting in a manner likely to cause harassment, alarm or distress, and likely to do so again. The ASBO itself will prohibit further anti-social acts. Breach of an ASBO is an offence, with a maximum penalty of six months' imprisonment and/or a fine at level 5 (currently £5,000) if tried summarily or five years' imprisonment and/or unlimited fine if tried on indictment.

So far, anti-social behaviour orders have been used as a means of dealing with unruly youths, rather than demonstrators and protesters. It is certainly conceivable, however, that ASBOs might be used as a means of curbing long-term protest actions, such as those staged outside animal laboratories. The terms of any such order will need to comply with the Convention, and in particular Article 10, freedom of expression and Article 11, freedom of assembly.

8.18   FURTHER INFORMATION

Bibliography
Blackstone's Criminal Practice (Oxford: Oxford University Press, 2004)
Cooper, J., 'Public Order Review', *Legal Action* (regular round-up of recent public order decisions each February and August)
Randle, M., *How to Defend Yourself in Court* (Civil Liberties Trust, 1995)
Wilson, D., *Campaigning ... the A-Z of Public Advocacy* (Hawksmere Press, 1995)

Anthony Hudson

9   The Right of Free Expression

This chapter deals with:

- The European Convention on Human Rights
- Defamation
- Copyright and allied property rights
- Criminal law restrictions on freedom of expression
- Contempt of court
- Controls on broadcasting, films, videos and cable
- Further information

Freedom of expression is one of the essential foundations of a democratic society and one of the basic conditions for its progress and for each individual's self-fulfilment. It is applicable not only to information or ideas that are favourable, received or regarded as inoffensive or as a matter of indifference, but also to those that offend, shock or disturb. Freedom of expression is of particular importance as far as the press is concerned because it is incumbent on the press to impart information and ideas on political issues and other areas of public interest.

9.1   THE EUROPEAN CONVENTION ON HUMAN RIGHTS

Article 10 of the European Convention on Human Rights (the Convention) protects the right to freedom of expression. Prior to the coming into force of the Human Rights Act 1998 (HRA), the right to freedom of expression was a negative one: you were free to express yourself, unless the law otherwise prevented you from doing so. The European Court of Human Rights (ECHR) found English and Welsh domestic law wanting on numerous occasions. With the incorporation of the Convention into English and Welsh domestic law, the right to freedom of expression is now expressly guaranteed.

However, the right to freedom of expression in Article 10 is not absolute. Interferences with the right to freedom of expression may be permitted if they are prescribed by law, pursue a legitimate aim and are necessary in a democratic society, that is, satisfy a pressing social need. The legitimate purposes for which freedom of expression can be limited are:

- National security, territorial integrity or public safety.
- The prevention of disorder or crime.
- The protection of health or morals.
- The protection of the reputation or rights of others.
- The prevention of the disclosure of information received in confidence.
- For maintaining the authority and impartiality of the judiciary.

See also Chapter 1.

9.2   DEFAMATION

Under Article 10(2) of the Convention, the protection of the reputation of others is a legitimate ground for restricting the right to freedom of expression. Libel and slander are legal claims that protect an individual's reputation against defamation. An individual is defamed when a person publishes to a third party words or matter containing an untrue imputation against his or her reputation.

Libel and slander

If the publication is in a permanent form (for example in a book, magazine or film), then the defamation is libel. It is slander if the publication is in a transient form (speech). Signs, gestures, photographs, pictures, statues, cartoons etc. can also give rise to a claim for defamation, but the most obvious types of defamatory statements are written or spoken words.

The principal practical difference between claims for libel and claims for slander is what a claimant must prove to succeed in his or her claim. In libel claims, the claimant does not have to prove that he or she has suffered loss or damage as a result of the publication. In contrast, in claims for slander, the claimant must prove actual damage. There are, however, several exceptions to the rule that actual damage must be proved in claims for slander. For example, if the spoken words accuse the claimant of committing a crime; of having a contagious disease; of being unfit for his or her office, business or profession; or if the communication is an attack on the credit of trades people; or an accusation of being unchaste or adulterous against a woman or girl. In these cases damage is presumed and need not be proved.

Meaning and defamation

There is no single comprehensive definition of what is defamatory. Various suggestions have been made before the courts, including any material that:

- Is to a person's discredit.
- Tends to lower him or her in the estimation of others.
- Causes him or her to be shunned or avoided.
- Causes him or her to be exposed to hatred, ridicule or contempt.

For a statement to be defamatory the imputation must tend to lower the claimant in the estimation of right-thinking members of society generally. Even if the words damage a person in the eyes of a section of society or the community, they are not defamatory unless they amount to a disparagement of the reputation in the eyes of right-thinking people generally.

A statement that amounts to an insult or is mere vulgar abuse is not defamatory. This is because the words do not convey a defamatory meaning to those who heard them (simple abuse is unlikely to cause real damage to a reputation). It is arguable that the defence of vulgar abuse is not available if the statement is a libel. The reason for this distinction is that it is more likely that written words will be taken seriously and understood to have a defamatory meaning.

In contrast to most civil cases, juries usually hear defamation claims. Once the judge has decided that the words – or other material – could possibly have a meaning that is damaging to the claimant's reputation, the jury's role is twofold. First, it must determine what the words mean in their natural and ordinary sense. Second, the jury must decide whether that meaning is defamatory. When deciding what the words mean the intention and knowledge of the person who published the words are irrelevant.

The law of defamation recognises two types of meanings. The first type of meaning is the natural and ordinary meaning of the words. This is not limited to the obvious and literal meaning, but includes any inference that the ordinary, reasonable reader would draw from the words. The second type of meaning is the innuendo meaning:

False innuendo
An alternative meaning that the ordinary, reasonable person who can read between the lines would infer from the words is known as the 'false innuendo' meaning.

True innuendo
True innuendo arises when words that appear to be innocent to some people appear as defamatory to others because they possess special knowledge or extra information (e.g. reading about someone getting married wouldn't seem damaging to their reputation – unless you knew that they were already married!).

A claimant can ask that the court consider a statement's false or true innuendo meaning.

Publication
The words complained of must have been published by the person sued to a third party. Publication includes any means of communication even if only to one other person. Owing to the breadth of the term publication, many individuals with only a slight connection to the work can find themselves ensnared in defamation proceedings. However, the Defamation Act 1996 provides a defence to persons who are not authors, editors or commercial publishers of the statement if they took reasonable care in relation to its publication and they did not know and had no reason to believe that what they did caused or contributed to the publication of a defamatory statement. This is intended to cover printers, distributors, online service providers and live broadcasters.

The High Court has held for the purposes of the Defamation Act 1996 that an Internet Service Provider (ISP) that transmits a posting from its news server to subscribers who want to use it is not the publisher of the posting, although at common law it would be considered to be. However, the court held that because the ISP had not removed the offending material as soon as it was notified of its existence, it had not acted reasonably and the defence under the Defamation Act 1996 was not available.

Identification
A claimant must prove that the defamatory statement refers to him or her. In most cases this can be done without difficulty, as the claimant will be named. However, a claimant who has not been referred to by name must prove that the words complained of were understood by some readers as referring to him or her. The claimant can rely on the fact that he or she was referred to by a nickname or initials or that he or she was a member of a class or group of people included in the defamatory statement.

The fact that a publisher did not intend to refer to the claimant is irrelevant to the question of whether or not that person has been defamed. A person whose name is the same or similar to that of a fictitious character can sue for defamation if the words complained of would be understood to refer to the claimant by reasonable people who knew him or her. Similarly, a member of a group or class of people can sue in relation to a defamatory allegation referring to the group as a whole, if the group is sufficiently small that the allegation would be understood to refer to him or her personally.

Right to sue

As well as individuals, any trading corporation can bring defamation proceedings where the statement damages its business or trading reputation. Non-trading corporations can sue in respect of defamatory statements damaging their property or financial interests. It has been held that trade unions cannot sue, although the correctness of the decision has been doubted. In any event, individual trade union officers may bring an action if referred to. Bankrupts can sue for defamation and keep any damages recovered.

Groups without a legal identity cannot complain of libel. Therefore, victims of racism cannot get redress under defamation law where there is no pointer in the statement to an individual. Similarly, an unincorporated club cannot sue for libel, whatever the damage to its reputation, although individual members, if referred to, may. This will depend on whether the statement would be reasonably understood as referring to the claimant.

In 1993 the House of Lords ruled that government bodies cannot sue for defamation. This covers organs of local and central government including the Crown and government departments that have corporate status. They considered it was of the 'highest public importance that a democratically elected body or any governmental body, should be open to uninhibited public criticism'. The decision expressly does not preclude an individual member of a governmental body from suing if the words complained of are capable of being understood to refer to that individual. The decision was, however, used to prevent a political party (James Goldsmith's Referendum Party) from pursuing a defamation claim.

Only the living can sue for defamation. If a claimant dies after bringing a claim for defamation but before a verdict has been reached, the claim comes to an end and does not continue for the benefit of his or her estate.

Funding

Public funding is generally unavailable either to bring or defend defamation proceedings. Some lawyers may be willing to act on a 'no win, no fee' basis.

Time limits

A claim for libel or slander must be brought within one year of the date of publication. The court does, however, have the discretion to allow a claim to proceed outside this time limit if it considers it to be 'equitable'. In exercising its discretion the court will take into account the length of and the reasons for the delay and the extent to which relevant evidence is likely to be unavailable or less cogent.

Defences

Justification (truth)

It is a complete defence to an action for defamation to prove that the defamatory imputation is substantially true. It is not necessary for a defendant to show that there was a public interest in publication, nor does it matter whether he or she acted maliciously. If relying on the defence of justification the burden of proof is on the defendant to prove that the allegations made are true. The defendant must prove it on the balance of probabilities, that is, the allegation is more likely than not to be true.

A defendant is not required to prove that every allegation is true. The Defamation Act 1952 provides that where the words complained of contain two or more distinct allegations a defence of justification can still succeed if the words not proved to be true do not materially injure the claimant's reputation having regard to the imputations that are proved true.

A defendant cannot rely on the defence of justification in relation to the publication of the details of spent convictions, as defined by the Rehabilitation of Offenders Act 1974, if the claimant can show that the publisher acted 'maliciously'.

An allegation published by repeating a rumour cannot be justified by proving that there was such a rumour. A defendant is required to prove the substance of the allegation.

Since the burden of proving the truth of an allegation is on the defendant, claimants enjoy a distinct advantage in defamation claims. Justification has to be used with great care. It can often be difficult to obtain sufficient admissible evidence to persuade a jury that the statement is true. This will sometimes result in the media being unable to publish allegations that are generally believed to be true, but which they may not be able to prove to the standard required in court. Further, an unsuccessful defence of justification is likely to increase the level of any damages awarded.

Fair comment

If a defendant can prove that the defamatory statement is an expression of opinion on a matter of public interest and not a statement of fact, he or she can rely on the defence of fair comment.

The courts have said that whenever a matter is such as to affect people at large, so that they may be legitimately interested in, or concerned at, what is going on or what may happen to them or to others, then it is a matter of public interest on which everyone is entitled to make fair comment.

The comment must be based on true facts that are either contained in the publication or are sufficiently referred to. It is for the defendant to prove that the underlying facts are true. If he or she is unable to do so, then the defence will fail. As with justification, the defendant does not to have to prove the truth of every fact provided the comment was fair in relation to those facts that are proved.

Fair does not mean reasonable, but signifies the absence of malice. The views expressed can be exaggerated, obstinate or prejudiced, provided they are honestly held. If the claimant can show that the publication was made maliciously, the defence of fair comment will not succeed.

The ECHR has repeatedly emphasised the distinction between facts and value judgments, and has held that a defendant cannot be required to prove the truth of a value judgment.

Privilege
If untrue defamatory allegations are published on an occasion of privilege, they will be protected from a claim for defamation. Although the law of defamation exists to protect reputations, it is recognised that in particular situations it is to the benefit of society generally for people to be able to communicate without the fear of being sued for defamation. This is so despite the risk that a person's reputation will be damaged and they will not be able to restore it by bringing a claim for defamation.

Absolute privilege
Absolute privilege provides a complete defence regardless of how malicious or untrue the allegation is. It is confined to proceedings in Parliament or courts in England and Wales. The Defamation Act 1996 provides a statutory absolute privilege for contemporary or court-postponed fair and accurate reports of court proceedings in England and Wales, the European Court of Justice, the ECHR and any international criminal tribunal established by the United Nations Security Council, or by an international agreement to which the UK is a party.

Qualified privilege under the Defamation Act 1996
Qualified privilege provides a conditional defence. If a statement published on an occasion of qualified privilege is published maliciously, then the defence will fail.

The Defamation Act 1996 provides a statutory qualified privilege for material that is of public concern and for the public benefit. The Act distinguishes between statements that attract qualified privilege without explanation or contradiction and those that are privileged subject to explanation or contradiction.

Statements that qualify for qualified privilege without explanation or contradiction are as follows:

- Fair and accurate reports of public proceedings of legislatures, courts, government-appointed public inquiries, international organisations/ conferences anywhere in the world.
- A fair and accurate copy of or extract from any register or other document required by law to be open to public inspection.
- A notice or advertisement published by or on the authority of a court, or of a judge or officer of a court, anywhere in the world.
- A fair and accurate copy of or extract from matter published by or on the authority of a government or legislature or by an international organisation or an international conference anywhere in the world.

The defence of qualified privilege will be lost if the claimant shows that he or she requested the defendant to publish a reasonable letter or statement by way of explanation or contradiction, and the defendant refused or neglected to do so in relation to the following reports and statements:

- A fair and accurate copy of or extract from a notice or other matter issued for the information of the public by or on behalf of:
  - a legislature in any Member State or the European Parliament;

- the Government (or any authority performing governmental functions) of any Member State or the European Commission;
- an international organisation or international conference.
- A fair and accurate copy of or extract from a document made available by a court in any Member State or the European Court of Justice, or by a judge or officer of any such court.
- A fair and accurate report of proceedings at any public meeting or sitting in the United Kingdom of:
  - a local authority or local authority committee;
  - justices of the peace acting otherwise than as a court exercising judicial authority;
  - a commission, tribunal, committee or person appointed for the purposes of any inquiry by any statutory provision, by Her Majesty or by a Minister of the Crown or a Northern Ireland department;
  - a person appointed by a local authority to hold a local inquiry in pursuance of any statutory provision;
  - any other tribunal, board, committee or body constituted by or under, and exercising functions under, any statutory provision;
  - a fair and accurate report of proceedings at any public meeting held in a Member State.

A meeting is public if those who organise it open it to the public or, by issuing a general invitation to the press, manifest an intention or desire that the proceedings of the meeting should be communicated to a wider public. This would usually include most press conferences.

Qualified privilege at common law

Complaints or information passed under a public or private legal, social or moral duty to another individual with a duty to receive (including the relevant authorities) are protected by common law qualified privilege. Examples include replying to an enquiry for an employment reference, or to enquiries about a crime, and statements volunteered about crime or about the conduct of candidates for public office.

The courts have been reluctant to extend the defence of qualified privilege to provide the media with a 'public interest' defence. However, in *Reynolds* v *Times Newspapers Ltd*, the House of Lords recognised the 'high importance of freedom to impart and receive information and ideas' and observed that the 'press discharges vital functions as a bloodhound as well as a watchdog'. Their Lordships declined to develop political information as a new subject-matter category of qualified privilege. They did, however, state that 'the court should be slow to conclude that a publication was not in the public interest, and therefore, the public had no right to know' especially when the information was in the field of political discussion. The court was to take into account the following ten, non-exhaustive, matters:

- The seriousness of the allegation.
- The nature of the information, and the extent to which the subject-matter is a matter of public concern.
- The source of the information.
- The steps taken to verify the information.
- The status of the information.

- The urgency of the matter.
- Whether comment was sought from the claimant.
- Whether the article contained the gist of the claimant's side of the story.
- The tone of the article.
- The circumstances of the publication, including the timing.

Malice

The defences of fair comment and qualified privilege will fail if the claimant can prove that the defendant was motivated by malice when publishing the allegations. Express malice has been defined as a dominant desire to injure the person who is defamed. Absence of an honest belief in the defamatory allegations is generally conclusive evidence of express malice.

Offer of amends

Under the Defamation Act 1996, a publisher can make an offer of amends. This is an offer to publish a suitable correction and a sufficient apology and to pay the claimant compensation and costs. If the offer to make amends is not accepted by the claimant, then it will be a defence to defamation proceedings unless the claimant can prove that the defendant knew or had reason to believe that the statement complained of:

- Referred to the claimant or was likely to be understood as referring to him or her; and
- Was both false and defamatory.

Remedies

Interim injunctions

The courts exercise exceptional caution when considering an application for a pre-trial – or interim – injunction. Interim injunctions will not be granted unless the words complained of are unarguably defamatory; there are no grounds for concluding that the statement may be true; there is no other defence that may succeed; and there is evidence that the defendant will repeat the defamatory allegations.

Injunctions to prevent defamatory statements being made where the exact words to be published are not known with reasonable certainty cannot be obtained.

Section 12 of the Human Rights Act 1998, which takes into account the British tradition of a strong free press and provides an extra safeguard for the Convention right to freedom of expression, applies when a court is considering whether to grant an interim injunction. Relief is not to be granted in the absence of the respondent unless the applicant has taken all practicable steps to notify the respondent, or there are compelling reasons why the respondent should not be notified. Further, interim injunctions are not to be granted unless the court is satisfied that the applicant is likely to establish that publication should not be allowed. A claimant must convincingly establish a real prospect of success.

Damages

The claimant's reputation is vindicated by the amount of damages (or financial compensation) he or she is awarded. A successful claimant cannot force the defendant to publish a correction or an apology. A jury usually decides the award of damages in defamation cases. Special damages compensate the claimant for actual financial loss. General damages compensate the claimant for the damage to his or her reputation.

General damages can take the form of compensatory, aggravated and exemplary damages. Exemplary (or punitive) damages can be awarded where the defendant publishes the defamatory matter because the prospects of material advantage to him or her outweigh the prospects of material loss.

The role played by juries in determining the level of damages awarded has, in the past, meant that libel awards were highly unpredictable and have been criticised as excessive. In 1995 the ECHR held that an award of £1.5 million in 1989 breached Article 10 of the Convention, as the amount of damages could not be considered necessary for the protection, reputation or rights of others.

Since then the Court of Appeal has held that judges, and counsel, should be free to draw the attention of juries to awards made in personal injury cases. The appropriate range of award can also be indicated to the jury. Damages for even the most seriously defamatory allegation are unlikely to exceed about £200,000.

Other claims

Malicious falsehood
To be successful in a claim for malicious falsehood the claimant must prove that:

- The defendant published words about the claimant which were false;
- They were published maliciously; and
- The publication has caused special damage.

The Defamation Act 1952 provides that it is not necessary to allege or prove special damage:

- If the words are likely to cause pecuniary damage to the claimant and are published in writing or another permanent form.
- If the words are likely to cause pecuniary damage to the claimant in respect of any office, profession, calling, trade or business held or carried on by him at the time of the publication.

The Protection from Harassment Act 1997
A person must not pursue a course of conduct that amounts to harassment of another and which he or she knows or ought to know amounts to harassment of the other. The Act states that 'harassing' someone includes alarming them or causing them distress. It also defines a 'course of conduct' as having to involve conduct on at least two occasions, and states that such conduct can include speech.

A person who pursues such a course of conduct is guilty of an offence punishable by up to six months' imprisonment and/or a fine of £5,000. A court may also impose a restraining order for the purpose of protecting the victim of the offence.

A civil claim can also be brought against a person who pursues such a course of conduct. It is a defence to civil or criminal proceedings to show that the course of conduct was:

- Pursued for the purpose of preventing or detecting crime.
- Pursued under any enactment or rule of law or to comply with any condition or requirement imposed by any person under any enactment.
- Was reasonable in the particular circumstances.

In 2001 the Court of Appeal held that the Protection from Harassment Act 1997 could apply to articles published in a newspaper.

Negligence
Where a claimant can show that (a) the defendant owed him or her a duty of care; (b) the defendant breached that duty by failing to exercise reasonable care; and (c) the claimant has suffered loss, he or she can recover compensation in respect of statements made to third parties that have adversely affected his or her relationship with that third party. For example, a former employee can bring a claim in negligence where his or her former employer provides an inaccurate and damaging reference to a prospective employer.

Press Complaints Commission
Complaints about the unethical behaviour of newspapers and magazines can be made to the Press Complaints Commission (PCC). The PCC cannot award damages. If a complaint is upheld, the newspapers concerned will be obliged to publish any critical adjudication in full and with due prominence.

9.3   COPYRIGHT AND ALLIED PROPERTY RIGHTS

Meaning of copyright
Copyright is a statutory right to stop others copying or exploiting authors' works in various other ways without permission. Copyright typically lasts for the duration of the author's life plus another 70 years. The Copyright, Designs and Patents Act 1988 (CDPA) creates several different categories of 'work' in which copyright can exist, and different owners or authors of works. The principal categories of protected work are:

- Original literary, dramatic, musical or artistic works, including photographs.
- Sound recordings, such as tapes, CDs and digital files such as MP3s; films, television and sound broadcasts, and cable programmes.
- The typographical arrangements of published editions.

Copyright does not exist in a literary, dramatic, musical or artistic work unless it is original. This simply means that some limited work or effort must have gone into the work by its creator and that it was not copied from another work. Even street directories or television programme schedules can attract copyright as literary works.

Owning the copyright in a work gives the owner the exclusive right to:

- Copy the work.
- Issue copies to the public.
- Perform, show or play the work in public.
- Broadcast the work or include it in a cable programme service.
- Make adaptation of the work or do any of the above in relation to an adaptation.

Anyone who, without the consent of the copyright owner, does any of the above acts, infringes the owner's copyright.

Copyright does not exist in a work until it is recorded in some written or other form. For example, a musical work is not protected until recorded on a digital audio tape or the like. It is generally the reproduction of that form that is restricted. Ideas themselves are not protected, and recourse in such cases is made to the developing law of confidence.

The ownership of copyright is distinct from the ownership of the physical record of the work. For instance, a photographer may own the copyright of the artistic work he or she creates, but not the film on which it is recorded. Separate ownership of the physical property can restrict the use of the work. The owner or author of the copyright is normally the creator or creators of it in the case of a literary, dramatic, musical or artistic work. However, special rules apply in relation to copyright of other works and all works created in the course of employment.

Defences to infringement of copyright
The owner of the copyright can bring an action against someone who infringes that copyright. A claim for copyright infringement can be defended on various grounds, including:

- Copyright does not exist in the work.
- The act complained of is not a restricted act.
- The act did not involve a substantial part of the work.
- The copyright owner consented to the act.
- The infringement was in the public interest.
- It was a 'permitted act'.

It is worth noting that there is no defence of 'personal use'. So, for example, recording a CD that you own onto a tape just for your own use is still against the law.

While it has long been the case that such seemingly minor breaches of copyright have not been pursued by the owners, the current popularity of downloading music tracks (and other media) from unsanctioned websites has led the music industry to declare that legal action may be brought against individual 'downloaders' even if they are downloading for personal use.

Consent
Copyright is not infringed if the owner consents to the copying or other exploitation of the work. The first difficulty is identifying who is the owner of the various copyrights. In some works (e.g. a television play) it is possible for different people to own the copyright in the script, the photographs, the sound track, the dramatic screenplay, the film recording, the play and the broadcast. Even if the owners can be identified, there is generally no obligation on them to sell reproduction rights.

Some websites only offer access to music tracks etc. with the approval of the recording artists and record labels. Downloading from these sites will be lawful because the owners of the copyright have given their consent.

Public interest
Public interest does not appear in the statute. However, the courts have said that, just as they will not stop publication of confidential information that is in the public interest, they would not prohibit the infringement of another's copyright where the

public interest in publication outweighed the private right of property. The defence
is based on the idea that the public's need to know should sometimes override the
copyright owner's right to restrict or prevent publication (and takes into account
the right to freedom of expression explained above).

Permitted acts under the Copyright, Designs and Patents Act 1988
Permitted acts include use of a work for:

- Research or private study.
- Criticism, review or reporting of current events provided it is fair dealing.
- Incidental inclusion.
- Things done for the purposes of instruction or examination.
- Anthologies for educational use.
- Copying by libraries and archives.
- Anything done for the purposes of parliamentary or judicial proceedings.
- Copying of material open to public inspection or on an official register.

Fair dealing
The fair use of another's work for the purpose of criticism or review, or the reporting
of current events, does not amount to an infringement of copyright. The originator of
the work must be acknowledged in a criticism or review and in the print media's news
reporting, but not in the broadcast media. Fair dealing does not apply to photographs.
In an important case concerning a critical book about Scientology, which made
use of unpublished internal Scientology documents, the courts confirmed that the
defence of fair dealing could apply, even though the work had not previously been
published and even though the criticism was directed at the contents of the work
rather than its style.

'Moral rights'
The concept of the 'moral right' was introduced by the Copyright, Designs and
Patents Act 1988. Authors of copyright works have the right to be identified as such
and the right not to have their works subjected to derogatory treatment, although
this is subject to complex limitations and qualifications. A new right of privacy was
introduced to limit the ways in which photographs commissioned for private and
domestic purposes, for example, wedding photographs, can be used.

Copyright and passing off
The law will prevent one trader passing off its goods as those of another. Passing off
is primarily concerned with commercial disputes. It has five elements:

- A misrepresentation.
- Made by a trader in the course of trade.
- To prospective customers of his or her or ultimate consumers of goods or
  services supplied by him or her.
- Which is likely to damage the business or goodwill of another trader.
- Which causes actual damage to the business or goodwill of another trader.

Passing off has been used to prevent one newspaper using a name and layout that is confusingly similar to another newspaper, and by authors to prevent their name being used on a work that is not their own.

Criminal sanctions for breach of copyright

There are criminal sanctions for making or dealing with articles that infringe copyright. The criminal provisions and penalties for commercial copyright piracy have been made more severe as a result of the growth in national and international piracy of copyright material (bootleg videos and the like). Penalties range from imprisonment for up to two years to fines and forfeiture of infringing material and equipment for making infringing material.

The civil courts, in response to growing copyright piracy, have also been prepared to grant to copyright owners what in practice are private search warrants to track down the sources for bootleg operations.

9.4   CRIMINAL LAW RESTRICTIONS ON FREEDOM OF EXPRESSION

Blasphemy

At common law, blasphemy and blasphemous libel are indictable offences. These offences are rarely prosecuted, although in 1977 Mary Whitehouse brought a successful private prosecution against *Gay News* magazine for the publication of a poem on the homoerotic musings of the centurion guarding the body of Christ. The intentions of the publisher are irrelevant and there is no defence of public good, namely, that the material was published in the interests of science, literature or art.

The offences apply only to attacks on the Church of England and by extension to attacks on Christianity. Consequently, opponents of Salman Rushdie's novel *The Satanic Verses* were unable to bring a blasphemy prosecution as the courts declined to extend the offence to protect Islam.

Under the Law of Libel Amendment Act 1888, a prosecution cannot be brought against the proprietor, publisher, editor or any person responsible for the publication of a newspaper – this does not include a journalist – in respect of any libel published without the order of a High Court judge. The accused must be given notice of the application and be given an opportunity to be heard.

In 1996 the ECHR considered that blasphemy laws must be a matter for individual countries to decide. The British Board of Film Classification (BBFC) had refused to classify a video film entitled *Visions of Ecstasy* on the grounds that it would infringe the criminal law of blasphemy. The video concerned the erotic fantasies of a sixteenth-century Carmelite nun who experienced powerful ecstatic visions of Jesus Christ. The ECHR considered that the refusal to classify the video did not infringe the Article 10 right to freedom of expression.

Obscenity

Obscenity is concerned with the harmful effect of the article on its reader or audience. The law governing obscene publications is to be found principally in the Obscene Publications Act 1959. Commercial dealings in obscene items, or possession of them for these purposes, are an offence. With or without a prosecution, the items can be seized under a magistrate's warrant and, after a hearing to determine whether they contravene the statute, can be forfeited.

The test of obscenity – to 'deprave or corrupt'

The Obscene Publications Act 1959 adopted as the core of its test of obscenity the famous phrase of Lord Chief Justice Cockburn in 1868: does the article have a tendency to deprave or corrupt the persons who are likely to read, see or hear it? Courts have since interpreted 'deprave or corrupt' as implying a powerful and corrosive effect. There must be more than an immoral suggestion or persuasion or depiction; it must constitute a serious menace.

The courts must have regard to the effect of the item taken as a whole. What matters is the likely audience, and a publisher is entitled to rely on circumstances of distribution that will restrict those into whose hands the article might fall. It is necessary to show that it would have the tendency to deprave or corrupt a significant proportion of the likely audience.

Defence of merit

The most important change introduced by the Obscene Publications Act 1959 was a new defence that publication – in the case of magazines and books – is in the interests of science, literature, art or learning, or of other matters of general concern. A similar but rather narrower defence – the interests of drama, opera, ballet or any other art, or of literature or learning – applies to plays and films. The use of this defence was demonstrated in the first major case under the Act when the publishers of D.H. Lawrence's novel *Lady Chatterley's Lover* were acquitted at the Old Bailey in 1960.

Drugs and violence

Obscenity cases do not necessarily involve sex. There have been occasional prosecutions and forfeitures of books that advocated the taking of prohibited drugs. In 1968, while allowing the appeal of the publishers of *Last Exit to Brooklyn*, the Court of Appeal said that the encouragement of brutal violence could come within the test of obscenity. In recent years, 'video nasties' have also been dealt with under the Act.

Indecency offences

In contrast to obscenity, indecency is concerned with material that is offensive to public susceptibilities and a nuisance rather than harmful. No easy definition of indecency exists. The courts have said that this is something that 'offends against the modesty of the average man, offending against recognised standards of propriety at the lower end of the scale'. It depends on the circumstances and current – and in some cases local – standards. This vagueness is problematic. Posters for causes such as animal rights, which are deliberately intended to shock their audience, have sometimes had to contend with indecency prosecutions. Indecency is easier to prove than obscenity because there is no defence of public good, there is no need to consider the article as a whole and there is no need to satisfy the 'deprave and corrupt' test.

There is no general crime of trading in indecent articles – as there is with obscene ones – but a number of specific offences incorporate the indecency test. Thus, it is a crime to send indecent matter through the post, or to put it on public display unless entry is restricted to persons over 18 and payment is required, or the display is in a special part of a shop with an appropriate warning notice. The indecency offences do not apply to:

- Television broadcasts, although the BBC and private television companies operate under internal prohibitions on indecent matter.
- Exhibitions inside art galleries or museums.
- Exhibitions arranged by or in premises occupied by the Crown or local authorities.
- Performances of a play or films in licensed cinemas.

Telephone calls of an obscene nature can also be caught by the indecency laws as a public nuisance. In 1996, the Court of Appeal ruled that a telephone call or calls that cause psychiatric injury can amount to an assault or grievous bodily harm.

In addition to these offences, local councils can now adopt powers to regulate sex shops and sex cinemas in their areas. Council licences always prohibit the public display of indecent material, and licences can be revoked if breaches of these conditions occur. Similarly, the music and entertainment licences granted by local authorities will often be conditional on the licensee ensuring that no indecent display takes place. Breach of this condition is both an offence and a ground for withdrawing the licence.

Importation of indecent articles

Customs regulations prohibit the importation of indecent articles. The bookshop 'Gay's the Word' was prosecuted under these provisions for importing books concerned with homosexuality. However, the European Union (EU) provisions on free trade have substantially undermined these restrictions. A cardinal principle of the EU is that one Member State should not set up trade barriers to goods from another Member State if there is a legitimate internal market in the same goods. In the case of the UK, there is a legitimate market in indecent – but not obscene – articles as long as the traders observe the restrictions noted above. Consequently, Britain cannot discriminate against the importation of the same indecent books from other EU countries. European law prevails over the British customs regulations. For these reasons the prosecution of 'Gay's the Word' was dropped.

Racial hatred

Public Order Act 1986

The offences of inciting or stirring up racial hatred have been progressively expanded since they were first introduced in 1965. They are currently contained in the Public Order Act 1986 (POA). In brief, they prohibit the use of threatening, abusive or insulting words or behaviour, or displaying any written material that is threatening, abusive or insulting with the intention of stirring up racial hatred or where racial hatred is likely to be stirred up.

Racial hatred is defined by the POA as hatred against a group of persons in the UK defined by reference to colour, race, nationality – including citizenship – or ethnic or national origins.

An offence may be committed in a public or a private place. No offence is committed, however, where the words or behaviour are used, or the written material is displayed, by a person inside a dwelling and are not heard or seen except by other persons in that or another dwelling. The inadvertent use of words that are threatening, abusive or insulting is not an offence. A police officer may arrest without a warrant anyone he or she reasonably suspects is committing the offence.

There are other offences of publishing or distributing material; presenting or directing a play; distributing, showing or playing visual images or sounds; broadcasting a television programme, except programmes transmitted by the BBC or IBA; or distributing a cable programme with the same characteristics – that is, being threatening, abusive or insulting – and which is either intended to stir up racial hatred or likely to have this effect. In addition, it is an offence to possess racially inflammatory material unless ignorant of its contents. The police can obtain a search warrant for such material and magistrates can order its forfeiture.

The Crime and Disorder Act 1998

The Crime and Disorder Act 1998 gave statutory force to the idea of 'racially aggravated offences', and in 2001 this Act was amended to include religiously aggravated offences. Racially or religiously aggravated offences include assault, criminal damage, public order offences and harassment. An offence is racially or religiously aggravated if:

- At the time of committing the offence, or immediately before or after doing so, the offender demonstrates towards the victim of the offence hostility based on the victim's membership – or presumed membership – of a racial or religious group.
- The offence is motivated wholly or partly by hostility towards members of a racial or religious group based on their membership of that group.

If a person is convicted of the racially or religiously aggravated form of assault, criminal damage, public order offence or harassment, then the court has increased sentencing powers. In relation to other offences, if the offence is racially or religiously aggravated the court is required to treat it as an aggravating factor, that is, a factor that increases the seriousness of the offence.

The Official Secrets Acts

The protection of government secrets is governed by the Official Secrets Acts of 1911 and 1989.

The Official Secrets Act 1911 (the 1911 Act) provides that it is an offence for any person for any purpose prejudicial to the safety or interests of the State to:

- Approach, inspect, pass over, be in the neighbourhood of or enter any prohibited place.
- Make any sketch, plan, model or note that is calculated to be or might be or intended to be directly or indirectly useful to an enemy.
- Obtain, collect, record, or publish, or communicate to any other person any secret official code word, or pass word, or any sketch, plan, model, article or note, or other document or information that is calculated to be or might be or is intended to be directly or indirectly useful to an enemy.

A prohibited place is defined, extensively, in the 1911 Act, and effectively includes any place, property or establishment that either belongs to or is used by the Crown.

If convicted of an offence under the 1911 Act a person can be sentenced to up to 14 years' imprisonment.

The Official Secrets Act 1989 (the 1989 Act) provides for a series of offences prohibiting disclosure of information relating to the following six categories:

- Security and intelligence.
- Defence.
- International relations.
- Assisting criminals.
- Information resulting from unauthorised disclosures or entrusted in confidence.
- Information entrusted in confidence to other states or international organisations.

Members of the security and intelligence services
A person who is or has been a member of the security and intelligence services, or a person notified that he or she is subject to the provisions of the 1989 Act, is guilty of an offence if, without lawful authority, he or she discloses any information, document or other article relating to security or intelligence that has been in his or her possession by virtue of his or her position as a member of the security and intelligence services or in the course of his or her work. There is no requirement that the disclosure should be damaging or has harmed the State.

A person who is or has been a Crown servant or government contractor is guilty of an offence if, without lawful authority, he or she makes a 'damaging disclosure' of any information, document or other article relating to:

- Security or intelligence – section 1.
- Defence.
- International relations.

'Damaging disclosure' is defined differently under each section. For information relating to security or intelligence, a disclosure is damaging if it causes damage to the work of, or any part of, the security and intelligence services; or is of information or a document or other article that is such that its unauthorised disclosure would be likely to cause such damage, or which falls within a class or description of information, documents or articles the unauthorised disclosure of which would be likely to have that effect.

Under the 1989 Act, a person who is or has been a Crown servant or government contractor is guilty of an offence if, without lawful authority, he or she discloses any information, document or other article, the disclosure of which:

- Results in the commission of an offence.
- Facilitates an escape from legal custody or the doing of any other act prejudicial to the safekeeping of persons in legal custody.
- Impedes the prevention or detection of offences or the apprehension or prosecution of suspected offenders.

It is also an offence to disclose any information obtained from a telephone tap.

The 1989 Act also restricts the activities of Crown servants or government contractors, but it also extends to others including journalists. It is an offence to disclose without lawful authority any information, document or other article protected by disclosure under the 1989 Act that has been disclosed to him or her by a Crown servant or government contractor without lawful authority, or entrusted to him or her by a Crown servant or government contractor in confidence.

It must also be proved that the disclosure was damaging, the defendant disclosed the information knowing, or having reasonable cause to believe, that it would be damaging, and he or she disclosed the information knowing, or having reasonable cause to believe, that it was protected against disclosure by the 1989 Act and that it had come into his or her possession as a result of an unauthorised disclosure.

None of these offences provides for a defence of public interest or moral duty.

In 2001, during the trial of the ex-MI5 agent David Shayler, the Court of Appeal held that the defence of duress or necessity was available under the 1989 Act when a defendant committed an otherwise criminal act to avoid an imminent peril of danger to life or serious injury. In 2002 the House of Lords held that a defendant prosecuted under the 1989 Act was not entitled to be acquitted if he or she showed that it was, or that he or she believed that it was, in the public or national interest to the make the disclosure in question.

More recently, charges brought under section 1 of the 1989 Act against former GCHQ employee Katharine Gun were dropped after the Crown Prosecution Service (CPS) offered no evidence against her. Ms Gun had been charged after she had disclosed to the *Observer* newspaper that the United States had asked the United Kingdom to spy on other members of the United Nations Security Council prior to the Iraq war in 2003. She admitted that she had made the disclosure, but offered the defence of necessity on the basis that she had been obliged to act in order to prevent an illegal war in which many soldiers and civilians would die. While the defence was never tried in court, the CPS said that the case against Ms Gun was dropped owing to insufficient evidence, suggesting that her claim of necessity was taken seriously by those prosecuting.

Other secrecy offences
Apart from the Official Secrets Acts, there are dozens of specific statutory offences of disclosing information in the hands of the government. Frequently, they are imposed where a government department has powers to acquire information under compulsion. These 'mini' Official Secrets Acts also lack a public interest defence.

'Whistle-blowing'
Employment law provides specific protection for disclosures made by workers in the public interest. The Employment Rights Act 1996 protects 'whistleblowers' by providing a cause of action for any worker who is victimised or dismissed after they have made a 'qualifying disclosure' that is also a 'protected disclosure'. A qualifying disclosure is the revealing of any information that the worker reasonably believes tends to show that:

- A criminal offence has been or will be committed.
- A legal obligation will not be or has not been complied with.

- A miscarriage of justice has occurred or will occur.
- An individual's health and safety has been or will be endangered.
- The environment has been or will be damaged.
- Any of these matters are being concealed.

However, a qualifying disclosure will only be protected in limited circumstances. Generally the disclosure must be made to a legal adviser or an employer or other person responsible, but protection also applies to public disclosures if the worker is acting in good faith and not for personal gain and he or she reasonably believes that they will be victimised if they make the disclosure (or if the disclosure relates to a particularly serious example of one of the matters listed above).

See also Chapter 14.

9.5   CONTEMPT OF COURT

Article 10(2) of the Convention expressly provides that the right to freedom of expression can be limited in order to maintain the authority and impartiality of the judiciary.

The scope of contempt law
Contempt of court serves the primary function of protecting the integrity of court proceedings. The law relating to contempt of court is found in the Contempt of Court Act 1981 and in the common law.

Contempt of Court Act 1981
The Contempt of Court Act 1981 (CCA) was enacted following a decision of ECHR that English contempt law contravened Article 10 of the Convention. It was intended to give greater protection to freedom of speech. The CCA introduces a strict liability rule. The strict liability rule indicates that conduct tending to interfere with the course of justice – particularly legal proceedings – may be treated as a contempt of court regardless of whether there was any intent to so interfere.

The strict liability rule applies only to publications. These are defined so as to include any speech, writing, broadcast or other communication in whatever form that is addressed to the public at large or any section of the public.

Two important limitations on the impact of the strict liability rule are:

- It applies only to a publication that creates a substantial risk that the course of justice in the proceedings will be seriously impeded or prejudiced.
- It applies to a publication only if the proceedings are active.

When contempt can be used
The CCA sets out when proceedings become active. Different tests apply for criminal and civil cases. In criminal cases, proceedings become active for the purposes of the strict liability rule with:

- An arrest without warrant.
- The issue of a warrant.
- The service of a summons.

- The service of an indictment.
- Oral charge.

Criminal proceedings cease to be active:

- Upon acquittal or sentence.
- Upon any other verdict, finding or decision that puts an end to the proceedings.
- By discontinuance or by operation of law.

In civil cases the proceedings become active when arrangements for a hearing are made. They cease to be active when the case is disposed of, discontinued or withdrawn.

What amounts to contempt of court

A publication must create a substantial risk of serious prejudice to the course of justice for it to amount to contempt. In determining whether a publication has created a substantial risk of serious prejudice, the courts will consider all the circumstances surrounding the publication and the proceedings in question. It is clear that for a publication to be contempt a slight or trivial risk of serious prejudice is not enough, and nor is a substantial risk of slight prejudice.

In making an assessment of whether the publication does create a substantial risk of serious prejudice the court will consider:

- The likelihood of the publication coming to the attention of a potential juror.
- The likely impact of the publication on an ordinary reader at the time of publication.
- The residual impact of the publication on a notional juror at the time of trial.

In assessing the likelihood of a publication coming to the attention of a potential juror, the court will consider whether the publication is distributed in the area from which jurors are likely to be drawn and the number of copies circulated.

In assessing the likely impact of the publication on an ordinary reader, the court will consider the prominence of the article in the publication and the novelty of the content of the article in the context of likely readers.

The court will also take into account the length of time between publication and the likely date of trial, the focusing effect of listening over a prolonged period to evidence in a case, and the likely effect of the judge's directions to a jury.

In 2002 the *Sunday Mirror* was found guilty of contempt in relation to its publication of an article during the 2001 trial of the Leeds United footballers Lee Bowyer and Jonathan Woodgate. The article, released while the jury were deliberating, strongly suggested that the assault with which the two men were charged had been racially motivated, despite the judge stressing in his summing-up that the prosecution was not alleging a racist motive. It was found by the court that the article created an atmosphere in which justice could not be done, and a retrial had to be ordered. Despite there being no suggestion that the newspaper had intended to prejudice the trial, the High Court found it guilty of contempt under the strict liability rule.

It should be noted that even irreverent comment about defendants in a forthcoming criminal trial may constitute contempt of court. In 1996 the Court of Appeal found that the makers of the television programme *Have I Got News For You* were in contempt of court when jokes were made that the Maxwell brothers (who were to be tried for the Mirror Group pension fraud) were obviously guilty of fraudulent conduct, even though the programme was broadcast six months before the trial.

The above factors apply primarily to cases that will be heard by a jury – criminal cases in the Crown Court and some civil cases, for example, defamation claims. In contrast, where cases are heard on appeal or by judges alone, it is much less likely that the court would find that there was a substantial risk of serious prejudice, as professional judges are, as a result of their training, expected not to be influenced by the media in reaching a decision.

Defences

The CCA expressly provides that a person is not guilty of contempt of court under the strict liability rule if at the time of publication – having taken all reasonable care – he or she does not know and has no reason to suspect that the proceedings are active.

It is also a defence for a distributor of a publication to show that, having taken all reasonable care, he or she did not know and had no reason to suspect that the publication contained matter that created a substantial risk of serious prejudice.

As well as these two fairly limited defences, the CCA permits the publication of material that would otherwise amount to contempt if:

- It is a contemporaneous report of legal proceedings.
- It involves the discussion of public affairs.

The protection afforded by this defence is subject to the power of the court to make a postponement order under the CCA. Postponement orders can be made where the court considers it necessary to avoid a substantial risk of prejudice in the proceedings before the court and in any other proceedings pending or imminent. Reporting can be postponed for as long as the court considers necessary.

The media can challenge postponement orders by way of judicial review, under section 159 of the Criminal Justice Act 1988, which states that any aggrieved person may appeal to the Court of Appeal against an order made by a Crown Court judge or by an application to the court that made the original order. The courts have repeatedly stated that the media ought to be given an opportunity to make representations about the propriety of an order restricting reporting.

A publication made as part of a discussion in good faith of public affairs or other matters of general public interest does not breach the strict liability rule if the risk of impediment or prejudice was merely incidental to the discussion. Thus Malcolm Muggeridge was free to write about the issues of terminating medical support to deformed babies even though a doctor was on trial for the murder of a child with Down's Syndrome. Muggeridge focused on a by-election in which the issues of principle had been raised and did not mention the trial. The House of Lords held that the newspaper could rely on the public interest defence.

Common law contempt of court

The CCA expressly provides that it does not restrict liability for contempt of court in respect of conduct intended to impede or prejudice the administration of justice.

Common law contempt is therefore preserved. A publisher is liable in contempt for an intentionally prejudicial publication made when proceedings are pending or imminent. Proceedings can be pending or imminent even prior to the arrest of a suspect.

Publication of a confidential document in defiance of an injunction prohibiting its disclosure would also amount to common law contempt. This principle was extended in the *Spycatcher* litigation in which the Court of Appeal held that other publishers not directly subject to the injunction, acting on their own behalf, could be in contempt of court by publishing the same material where this would frustrate the court's intention to keep the material secret.

Other restrictions on court reporting

Article 6 of the Convention protects the right to a fair and public hearing in the determination of civil rights and criminal charges. This article states that judgment is to be given publicly, but it allows for the press and the public to be excluded from court proceedings in the interest of 'morals, public order or national security in a democratic society, where the interests of juveniles or the protection of the private life of the parties so require, or to the extent strictly necessary in the opinion of the court in special circumstances where publicity would prejudice the interests of justice'.

It is very unusual for courts to depart from the principle of open justice. There is a statutory power to do so in particular cases – for example, official secrets prosecutions – and a general power where the public's presence would defeat the ends of justice. The courts have repeatedly stressed that it is only exceptional circumstances that will justify excluding the public or restricting reporting. The public may be present in court, but photography is prohibited.

These powers are in addition to restrictions on reporting that apply without the need for a specific order. Only very brief reports can be carried, for instance, of proceedings in a Magistrates' Court of a case, which might eventually be sent to trial by a judge and jury at a Crown Court. Newspapers can name the parties, their lawyers and whether bail was granted, but very little else until the trial is over. A defendant has the right to have these restrictions lifted, but if the co-accused differs in his or her attitude to publicity, the court decides.

In sex offence cases the complainant must remain anonymous, even if the defendant is acquitted, unless the court orders otherwise or the complainant waives his or her right to anonymity. Unlike the rest of the public, the press have a right to attend Youth Court hearings, but they are prohibited from identifying defendants or witnesses, or from publishing their photographs. Young people do not have automatic anonymity in other courts, but the courts can make orders in specific cases.

The Administration of Justice Act 1960 provides that the publication of information relating to proceedings before any court sitting in private shall not of itself be contempt of court except where:

- The proceedings relate to the exercise of the inherent jurisdiction of the High Court with respect to minors, are brought under the Children Act 1989 or otherwise relate wholly or mainly to the maintenance or upbringing of a minor.
- The proceedings are brought under the Mental Health Act 1969.
- The court sits in private for reasons of national security.

- The information relates to a secret process that is in issue in the proceedings.
- The court has expressly prohibited the publication of such information.

It is important to note, however, that publication of such information will not be contempt unless it would have been contempt at common law.

The Court of Appeal has recently stated that hearings in chambers (a judge's private rooms) are not confidential or secret, and information about what occurs in chambers should be made available to the public when requested. To disclose what occurs in chambers does not constitute a breach of confidence or amount to contempt as long as any comment that is made does not substantially prejudice the administration of justice. This is subject to the situations listed in the Administration of Justice Act 1960, and where the court orders otherwise.

In 1981, Parliament permitted the limited use of tape recorders in court with the judge's leave. There are administrative directions that applications should be treated sympathetically. Taping can be used only as an aid in compiling an accurate record of what was said. Public reproduction is banned.

Reporting the proceedings of tribunals

In addition to the regular criminal and civil courts, there is a bewildering array of courts, tribunals and inquiries. It is impossible to generalise about when the public have a right of access. If they do, there will usually be a qualified privilege to protect the publisher of a fair and accurate report from libel actions. The strict liability contempt provisions will apply only if the body is exercising the judicial power of the State. By way of example, licensing authorities act administratively and therefore their proceedings are never 'active' for the purpose of the strict liability provisions. Employment tribunals and mental health review tribunals, on the other hand, do exercise a statutory judicial jurisdiction. Their proceedings will be active from the time a hearing date is set, but of course there will be no contempt unless the publication poses a serious threat to the integrity of the proceedings.

Enforcement

Prosecutions under the strict liability rule can be brought only with the Attorney General's consent. This was intended to ensure that some consideration was given to the public interest before prosecutions were brought. If the Attorney General refuses to prosecute, there is no right to challenge such a decision. In 1995 the Taylor sisters, whose convictions for murder were quashed by the Court of Appeal after a trial by media, failed in their attempt to get the court to review the refusal of the Attorney General to prosecute the press for contempt. In recent years, Crown Court judges have been more prepared to discharge defendants in criminal trials who have been the subject of media coverage commenting on their guilt or innocence.

While private parties cannot prosecute for contempt, they can, if they would suffer particularly from a publication that offended against the rule, seek an injunction to stop publication.

9.6   CONTROLS ON BROADCASTING, FILMS, VIDEOS AND CABLE

Article 10(1) of the Convention specifically states that the article does not prevent states from requiring the licensing of broadcasting, television or cinema enterprises.

By its charter the British Broadcasting Corporation (BBC) is intended and expected to censor the programmes it transmits. However, the BBC is regulated in part by the Office of Communications (Ofcom).

Ofcom is the regulator for the UK communications industries, replacing the Broadcasting Standards Commission (BSC), the Independent Television Commission (ITC), Office of Telecommunications (Oftel), the Radio Authority and the Radiocommunications Agency. It has responsibilities across television, radio, telecommunications and wireless communications services. Ofcom's principal duties are to further the interests of citizens in relation to communications matters and the interests of consumers in relevant markets where appropriate by promoting competition. Ofcom's specific duties include applying adequate protection for audiences against offensive or harmful material and unfair treatment or the infringement of privacy. From December 2003 Ofcom assumed the regulatory role of the BSC, ITC, Oftel and the Radio Authority (collectively termed the 'legacy regulators').

Ofcom can impose the following sanctions: it can direct a broadcaster not to repeat a programme or advertisement; direct a broadcaster to publish a correction or adjudication ('lesser sanctions'); or it can fine a broadcaster; and shorten or revoke a licence (excluding the BBC, Channel 4 or S4C) ('greater sanctions'). These powers to penalise licensees and ultimately to revoke licences mean that Ofcom wields considerable influence.

Until it completes its process of consultation, Ofcom has adopted the Code of Practice published by the ITC. The ITC Programme Code sets out the editorial standards that audiences are entitled to expect from commercial television services in the UK. This requires that commercial television programmes do not offend against good taste or decency and are not likely to encourage crime or lead to disorder; that news is presented with due accuracy and impartiality, and that due impartiality is preserved with regard to matters of political or industrial controversy or related to current public policy. The BSC fairness and privacy code of guidance and the BSC standards code of guidance also represent Ofcom's current policy.

It is a criminal offence to broadcast without a licence, and the prosecution does not need to prove an intent to do so. Therefore, pirate radio stations have to keep one step ahead of the Department of Trade Inspectors, who can forfeit equipment as well as prosecute for infringements.

The Government has a power to direct that certain matters should not be broadcast on both commercial television and on the BBC. It used this power in 1988 to ban spoken comment by or in support of Sinn Fein, the Ulster UDA or any of the organisations proscribed under earlier anti-terrorism laws. A challenge to the gagging order by the National Union of Journalists (NUJ), on the basis that it infringed the right of freedom of expression in Article 10 of the Convention, failed in the House of Lords and the application was rejected by the European Commission of Human Rights.

In 1993 the Government exercised its power to control what is broadcast by proscribing the Red Hot satellite channel, a carrier of pornographic material. This was upheld after an initial legal challenge, although there may have been an infringement of EU broadcasting law. The Government even retains the power to send in troops to take control of the BBC in the name of the Crown in extreme circumstances.

Unlike newspapers that can openly propagate their own views, the television companies cannot editorialise on matters – other than broadcasting issues – that are politically or industrially controversial or relate to current public policy. Subliminal messages are prohibited, and religious broadcasting is specifically controlled.

In a 2003 case before the House of Lords, the ProLife Alliance (a political party opposed to abortion and euthanasia) challenged the BBC's decision not to show its party political broadcast, which featured disturbing images of aborted foetuses. Both the BBC and independent broadcasters are subject to a duty not to show programmes that are likely to offend public feeling, but the Alliance argued that its rights under Article 10 of the Convention should outweigh such concerns. However, the House of Lords upheld the BBC's judgement of what would be offensive to the public, holding that Parliament had made it clear that a correct application of this standard should outweigh the right to free expression.

Ofcom also regulates political advertising. Current Ofcom policy is contained in the Advertising Standards Code originally published by the ITC. In effect, advertising on behalf of an organisation whose objects are mainly or wholly political, or advertising that is directed towards a political end, is banned. This covers radio advertising about atrocities in Rwanda and Burundi by Amnesty International. The *Index on Censorship* magazine has suffered a similar ban, which was held not to breach Article 10 of the Convention.

There are limits to Ofcom's duties. The Court of Appeal has accepted that in judging whether all the constituent parts of a programme satisfy the good taste canon, the ITC could take account of the purpose and character of the programme as a whole. The duties set out above had also to be reconciled with ITC's other duties, for instance, to secure a wide showing of programmes of merit. Channel 4 was deliberately created to provide programmes calculated to appeal to tastes and interests not generally catered for by ITV, and to encourage innovation and experimentation in the form and content of programmes. Inevitably, this can only be done in some cases at the risk of causing offence to those with mainline tastes. The requirement of impartiality in non-news programmes can be satisfied over a series of programmes, and a tradition has developed of allowing more latitude to personal view programmes that are balanced by others.

The courts have discouraged legal challenges to the ITC and its predecessor, the IBA, for vetting programmes, and their decisions on individual programmes generally can only be quashed if they are so perverse as to be unreasonable. This will undoubtedly also apply to Ofcom. The BBC is now regulated, in part, by Ofcom. BBC compliance with the programme codes is regulated by Ofcom. Issues concerning accuracy and impartiality remain the responsibility of the BBC Governors.

Radio or television programmes broadcast by the independent broadcasters or the BBC can be reviewed by Ofcom. Complaints of unjust or unfair treatment or unwarranted infringements of privacy in, or in connection with, the obtaining of material included in sound or television broadcasts, may be made by a person affected. They are known as 'fairness complaints'. Complaints cannot be made in connection with someone who has died more than five years previously, but within this period a member of the family, a personal representative or someone closely connected can make a fairness complaint to Ofcom. Written complaints can be made by anyone about the portrayal of violence or sexual conduct or about alleged failures of programmes to attain standards of taste and decency – a 'standards complaint' – within two months of a television programme and three weeks of a radio programme.

Ofcom cannot order the payment of any money to the complainant, but can insist on the responsible body publishing Ofcom's findings and, more significantly, can insist on an approved summary being broadcast within a stipulated time.

The Obscene Publications Act applies to television and radio broadcasts, although since 1990 no prosecutions have been brought.

The British Board of Film Classification

The British Board of Film Classification (BBFC) is a hybrid system. There is no general requirement that a film must have a BBFC certificate before being shown, but this position is achieved indirectly by the power of local councils to license cinemas. Most licences have a condition attached that only films with a BBFC certificate will be shown. Like television and radio programmes, films can be prosecuted under the Obscene Publications Act, although feature films (not less than 16 millimetres) can be prosecuted or forfeited only with the approval of the Director of Public Prosecutions.

The BBFC has been given an enlarged role in relation to videos and DVDs. Here it is a censor in law as well as in practice, and it is an offence to supply an unclassified video or DVD or to breach any restrictions that have been imposed by the BBFC (as to minimum age, type of supplier, and so on). Videos and DVDs concerned with sport, religion, music and education are exempt, but not if they show or are designed to encourage human sexual activity (or force or restraint associated with it), or mutilation, torture or other gross acts of violence towards humans or animals. Videos are also not exempt, if they show human genitalia or human urinary or excretory functions. The BBFC has to consider whether videos or DVDs are suitable for viewing in the home. There is an appeal structure for those who submit videos or DVDs to the BBFC, but the sizeable fees charged by the Board and the delays that the process necessarily entails can cause grave difficulties for producers.

Operators' licensing

Ofcom has the power to license operators. The Broadcasting Act 1990 lays down a number of restrictions on who may hold Ofcom's broadcasting licences, including restrictions on political or religious bodies. All programmes included in the licensed services and all advertising must comply with a number of general standards and specific advertising and sponsorship standards, and comply with Ofcom's Fairness and Standards Codes. Such standards include the requirement that persons under the age of 18 are protected, that no material likely to encourage or to incite the commission of crime or lead to disorder is included, that news is presented with due impartiality and reported with due accuracy and that adequate protection for members of the public from offensive and harmful material is provided. Licensees must also ensure that the inclusion of advertising that may be misleading, harmful or offensive is prevented. Ofcom has the ultimate sanction of withdrawing an operator's licence if these or the other conditions are broken.

Television licensing

A TV Licence is needed if a television is used to view or record television programmes. Under the Wireless Telegraphy Act 1949 it is an offence to install or use a television without a licence, which is triable summarily and subject to a maximum fine of £1,000. There are different rules for students, businesses, those aged over 74 years, hotels, residential care homes and second homes.

The Department for Culture, Media and Sport sets the amount of the TV Licence and decides who needs to have a licence. The Broadcasting Act 1990 made the BBC responsible for the administration of the licence. TV Licensing is the trading name used by BBC's agents.

TV Licensing have to apply to a magistrate for a search warrant in order to enter a property to be able to check whether there is an unlicensed TV there. Such a search warrant can only be granted if the magistrate is satisfied that there are reasonable grounds for suspecting that an offence under the Wireless Telegraphy Act 1949 is being committed. Article 8 – the right to respect for your private and family life – may be infringed if an Enquiry Officer enters a home without a warrant and without the occupier's consent.

9.7   FURTHER INFORMATION

Useful organisations

The British Board of Film Classification
3 Soho Square
London W1D 3HD
Tel: 020 7440 0299
Fax: 020 7287 0141
<www.bbfc.co.uk>

British Broadcasting Corporation
Controller
Fair Trading
BBC, Broadcasting House
London W1A 1AA
<www.bbc.co.uk>

Campaign for Freedom of Information
Suite 102
16 Baldwin Gardens
London EC1N 7KJ
Tel: 020 7831 7477
Fax: 020 7831 7461
admin@cfoi.demon.co.uk
<www.cfoi.org.uk>

Campaign for Press and Broadcasting Freedom
2nd Floor, Vi & Garner Smith House
23 Oxford Road
Walthamstow
London E17 9NL
Tel: 020 8521 5932
Freepress@NOSPAM.cpbf.org.uk
<www.cpbf.org.uk>

Department for Culture, Media and Sport
2–4 Cockspur Street
London SW1Y 5DH
Tel: 020 7211 6200
enquiries@culture.gov.uk
<www.culture.gov.uk>

National Union of Journalists
Headland House
308–312 Gray's Inn Road
London WC1X 8DP
Tel: 020 7278 7916
Fax: 020 7837 8143
Info@nuj.org.uk
<www.nuj.org.uk>

Newspaper Society
Bloomsbury House
Bloomsbury Square
74–77 Great Russell Street
London WC1B 3DA
Tel: 020 7636 7014
Fax: 020 7631 5119
ns@newspapersoc.org.uk
<www.newspapersoc.org.uk>

Ofcom Contact Centre (regulating body for the Radio Authority and the ITC)
Riverside House
2a Southwark Bridge Road
London SE1 9HA
Tel: 0845 456 3000 / 020 7981 3040
Fax: 0845 456 3333
Contact@ofcom.org.uk

Press Complaints Commission
1 Salisbury Square
London EC4Y 8JB
Helpline: 020 7353 3732
Fax: 020 7353 8355
Complaints@pcc.org.uk
<www.pcc.org.uk>

TV Licensing
Bristol BS98 1TL
0870 241 6468

Race and religious discrimination, *Henrietta Hill*
Sex discrimination, *Catherine O'Donnell*
Sexual orientation discrimination, *Stephanie Harrison*
Disability discrimination, *Catrin Lewis*

10   The Right to Receive Equal Treatment

This chapter deals with:

- UK law on equality and discrimination
- Race discrimination
- Religious discrimination
- Sex discrimination
- Sexual orientation and transgender discrimination
- Disability discrimination
- Further information

10.1   UK LAW ON EQUALITY AND DISCRIMINATION

The UK has specific legislation on equality that outlaws discrimination and provides a mechanism for individuals to lodge complaints when they experience unlawful discrimination. Currently, there is direct legislation dealing with discrimination on the grounds of sex, race and disability that applies in a number of fields, including employment, education, housing and the provision of goods and services. The operation of each Act is dealt with in detail below.

Currently, there is no direct legislation dealing with discrimination on the grounds of age, religion or sexual orientation. However, with effect from December 2003, new regulations came into force that make specific provision outlawing discrimination on grounds of religion and sexual orientation in the employment and education fields. Draft regulations on age discrimination were introduced in 2003. The regulations will be presented to Parliament in 2004 and are expected to come into force on 1 October 2006.

The Human Rights Act 1998 (HRA), which incorporates the rights contained in the European Convention of Human Rights (the Convention) into UK law, is also relevant in challenging discrimination. However, unlike UK equality legislation, the HRA can only be enforced directly against public bodies, such as the police or a local authority and private bodies exercising public functions. Courts and tribunals are themselves public bodies and must interpret and apply legislation in a way that is compatible with the Convention. Moreover, it is possible to rely on the Convention in any court or tribunal proceedings, including, for example, proceedings in an Employment Tribunal.

Article 14 of the Convention prohibits discrimination on many grounds including sex, race, religion, political opinion as well as 'any other status'. 'Other status' has been interpreted broadly to cover, for example, marital status, sexuality and prisoners, and would more than likely cover disability.

Article 14 is not a free-standing guarantee of equal treatment or a prohibition on discrimination more generally. Rather, it prohibits discrimination in respect of access to other Convention rights and is intended to guarantee equality before the law of the Convention. Article 14 must be used in combination with one or more of the other Articles in the Convention. The other right need not have been breached, but the facts complained of must at least come within the ambit of the substantive right. By way of example, men who have been widowed have used Article 14, together with Protocol 1, Article 1 (protection of property rights) to argue that benefits that were paid to women when their husbands died should also be paid to men when their wives died. They were able to use Article 1 Protocol 1 because benefits can sometimes count as property for the purposes of this Article.

It is only differences in treatment of people in *analogous* situations that fall within Article 14, and thus far the European Court of Human Rights (ECHR) has interpreted this condition quite strictly. However, there is no requirement that the difference in treatment has caused a detriment to the complainant.

Discrimination can be justified with reference to the aims and effects of the measure complained of, and whether there is a reasonable relationship of proportionality between the means used and the aims to be achieved. There are a number of areas where the ECHR has recognised that it will take very weighty reasons to justify discriminatory measures. These areas include sex and race, but not sexual orientation or disability as yet.

See also treatment of Article 14 in Chapter 1.

Equality bodies

Under each of the existing discrimination Acts separate equality commissions have been established:

- Commission for Racial Equality.
- Disability Rights Commission.
- Equal Opportunities Commission.

In October 2003, the Government announced plans for a single equality body for Britain. The proposed body has a working title of the Commission for Equality and Human Rights (CEHR).

It is envisaged that the CEHR will be responsible for tackling all forms of discrimination and ensuring all equality laws are enforced, including new laws dealing with discrimination on the grounds of age, religion and belief, and sexual orientation. Promotion of human rights will also be included within the CEHR's remit.

A Government taskforce has been formed to determine how the body should function. At this stage, there is no clear timeframe for when the CEHR will become operational. It is expected, however, that the existing equality commissions will continue until at least 2006.

10.2   RACE DISCRIMINATION

The Race Relations Act 1976 (RRA) covers race discrimination in employment and training; education; housing; the provision of goods, facilities and services, and advertising. In 2001 it was amended by the Race Relations (Amendment) Act 2000 (RRA 2000) to include discrimination by all public bodies.

The RRA applies to England, Wales and Scotland, but not to Northern Ireland, which now has its own legislation. If you believe you have been discriminated against, you must make a complaint either to the Employment Tribunal (for employment-related matters) or to the County Court (for other forms of discrimination).

What is race discrimination?

The RRA sets out the circumstances in which discrimination on the grounds of race is unlawful. It defines four types of discrimination: direct discrimination, indirect discrimination, victimisation and harassment. The RRA defines 'racial grounds' as being on the grounds of colour, race, nationality or ethnic or national origin. Most people think of race discrimination as being less favourable treatment on the grounds of colour or race. However, discrimination on the grounds of nationality, ethnic or national origin is equally unlawful. Thus if a workplace contains Afro-Caribbean and African employees and the employer treats the African employees less favourably by allocating them the menial or less interesting work, that could amount to less favourable treatment on racial grounds. Similarly, if a Japanese bank offered its services to Korean customers on less favourable terms than those offered to other customers, the bank's actions could constitute less favourable treatment on racial grounds.

It is equally unlawful to treat someone less favourably on the grounds of another person's race, so that it is discrimination to treat a white employee less favourably because he or she has a black partner. Note though that, for technical reasons, harassment is only unlawful if it is on grounds of race or ethnic or national origin.

Direct race discrimination

Direct discrimination occurs when a person treats you less favourably on racial grounds than he or she would treat, or treats, some other person. Sometimes direct discrimination is very obvious, but it can be more subtle. The following are all examples of direct discrimination:

- Refusing entry to a person – 'no blacks here'.
- A pub or club operating quotas to prevent black members or customers from exceeding a specific number or proportion.
- Refusing a person a job or promotion on the grounds that customers will not like being served by a person of that race.

The RRA will also protect you if you have suffered less favourable treatment because of the race of a third party. For example, if a white employee is dismissed for refusing to obey his or her employer's instructions to refuse to serve Asian customers, he or she would have a direct discrimination claim under the RRA.

Generally, you need to point to someone compared to whom you have been treated less favourably, called a 'comparator'. However, if you cannot do this, the court or tribunal considering your case may construct a hypothetical comparator for you. Sometimes when abusive language is used and it is obvious that it is race-specific, there is no need to try and find a comparator as it is apparent that this is less favourable treatment than another person not of that ethnic group would receive.

The intention and motive of the discriminator are irrelevant to the question of whether a person has been subject to unlawful direct discrimination on the grounds of race. Once a race discrimination claim has been found to be proven, a court must consider the intention and motive of the discriminator when looking at the question of compensation and other remedies.

Segregation

Segregation on racial grounds is defined by the RRA as direct discrimination. Providing separate washing facilities for white and Asian employees, even if the facilities are of the same standard, might be an example of segregation on racial grounds. Similarly, only employing ethnic minorities in 'back room' roles where they have no contact with the public but allowing others a full range of roles and duties might be an example of segregation on racial grounds.

Indirect race discrimination

Indirect discrimination occurs when a racial group is unjustifiably at a disadvantage in its ability to comply with a specific provision, criterion or practice. You can only bring a complaint if you suffer the disadvantage yourself. The following are examples of indirect discrimination:

- A job that requires the employee to be clean-shaven would put Sikhs in general at a disadvantage.
- Excluding job applicants who live in a certain area of a city, where that area is occupied by a higher proportion of ethnic minority people, would put ethnic minority candidates at a disadvantage.

If such a requirement cannot be objectively justified with reference to criteria other than race, a claim for indirect discrimination would lie.

The concept of indirect discrimination has never been user-friendly. The legal definition used to refer to a 'condition or requirement' rather than a 'provision, criterion or practice,' and the case law this generated was complex and not very accessible. People hope that this part of the new definition will be easier to understand and to apply.

Although the new definition applies to claims of discrimination in employment, education, services and certain public functions such as healthcare, the old definition will continue to apply to other sorts of discrimination, which adds to the complexity. Perhaps because the law in this area is so tricky this provision of the RRA has been underused. Therefore, if you consider that you have been indirectly discriminated against you should consider seeking specialist help.

Intention is a relevant question in a claim based on indirect discrimination. The motive of the alleged discrimination is not considered when the tribunal or court is deciding whether, in fact, you have been discriminated against. However, once a finding of indirect discrimination has been made, a tribunal or court can decide not to make an award of compensation to you because it is satisfied that the discrimination was unintentional.

Victimisation

Victimisation occurs when one person treats you less favourably than he or she treats, or would treat, someone else in those particular circumstances because you have done any of the following:

- Brought proceedings against the discriminator or any other person under the RRA.
- Given evidence or information in connection with proceedings brought by any person against the discriminator or any other person under the RRA.
- Otherwise done anything under or by reference to the RRA in relation to the discriminator or any other person.
- Alleged that the discriminator or any other person has committed an act that (whether or not the allegation so states) would amount to a contravention of the RRA.
- The discriminator knows that you intend to do any of those things or suspects that you have done, or intend to do, any of them.

If bringing a claim, it is not necessary for you to show that the alleged discriminator was consciously motivated by the fact that you had done a protected act.

Allegations of discrimination must be made in good faith in order to be protected by the victimisation provisions of the RRA. An example of a situation in which a claim of victimisation might arise is where an employee accuses his or her boss of discriminating against him or her on the grounds of race and as a result of the complaint is demoted or disciplined. Or, if a white colleague suggests that a manager has treated a black employee unfairly and then finds him or herself ostracised or subject to unwarranted criticism from that manager or his or her employer, this too might amount to unlawful victimisation.

Racial harassment
Regulations introduced in 2003 make it unlawful for an individual to harass you at work, in education, services and some other areas such as healthcare. Harassment is defined as unwanted conduct that has the purpose or effect of violating your dignity, or creating an intimidating, hostile, degrading, humiliating or offensive environment for you, on grounds of race or ethnic or national origins. This should be a useful tool for those who have been subjected to repeated bullying at work, as it is a more straightforward definition than that of direct discrimination.

Responsibility for acts of discrimination
The RRA makes discrimination unlawful in various contexts. These are considered below. It also makes it unlawful to instruct someone to carry out an unlawful act of discrimination or to induce or attempt to induce, directly or indirectly, such an act. Only the Commission for Racial Equality (CRE) may bring proceedings in respect of such unlawful instructions and/or inducements.

Employment and training
Part II of the RRA deals with race discrimination in employment and training. Employers are made responsible for the unlawful acts of their employees, which are acts done during the course of employment. The employer can avoid liability for the unlawful acts of employees if it can be shown that the acts complained of fell outside the scope of employment. Courts and tribunals must take a commonsense view as to what is meant by 'in the course of employment' in accordance with the layperson's understanding of those words.

Employers can also avoid liability for their employees' acts of discrimination if they can show that they took such steps as were reasonably practicable to prevent their employees from doing such unlawful discriminatory acts. Such steps might include the provision of equal opportunity training, ethnic monitoring of the workforce, the distribution of an equal opportunities policy statement and its implementation.

It is also unlawful for a person, including an employee, to aid another to do an unlawful act of discrimination. Thus, where an employee devises a plan to send a racially offensive card to an employee who is a member of a racial group and enlists the help of a colleague to carry out that plan, both the originator of the plan and the colleague may be guilty of unlawful discrimination on the grounds of race.

It is unlawful for an employer to discriminate against you on grounds of race in any of the following ways:

- Refusing to hire you or consider you for a job.
- Offering you a job on less favourable terms than other people.
- Refusing to promote you or transfer you to another job.
- Refusing to make provision for you to be trained.
- Giving you less favourable fringe benefits.
- Putting you on short-time work, dismissing you or making you redundant.

The RRA covers both permanent and temporary jobs, whatever the size of the firm. It covers apprentices and trainees as well as other employees; partners in a firm of six or more partners (such as a solicitors' firm); the police (who are not technically employees); subcontracted workers (such as the 'lump' building workers or night cleaners); and employment agencies.

It is unlawful for the Government to discriminate on race grounds in appointing people to serve on public bodies. These provisions have also been extended by the RRA 2000. It is also unlawful for trade unions and professional associations to discriminate in any of the following ways:

- Deciding whom to admit to membership.
- Refusing to let you join.
- Only allowing you to join on less favourable terms.
- By giving you fewer benefits, facilities or services or refusing to let you have any of these benefits (for example, legal services, representation in a dispute).
- Expelling you or subjecting you to any other disadvantage.

Similarly, it is unlawful for any licensing body (for example, the Law Society, which licenses solicitors; the Director General of Fair Trading, who licenses credit and hire businesses; or the police, who license taxi-drivers) to discriminate on racial grounds in deciding who can have a licence. Furthermore, whenever one of these bodies has to consider an applicant's 'good character' before giving a licence, they will be able to take into account any evidence about previous unlawful race discrimination. So, for instance, magistrates who are renewing a publican's licence should take account of any evidence that the publican or his or her employees had previously refused to serve ethnic minority groups.

The Courts and Legal Services Act 1990 extends the non-discrimination provisions of the RRA to the legal profession.

Genuine occupational requirements

It has already been noted that not all race discrimination is made unlawful by the RRA. Racial discrimination is still lawful where being a member of a particular racial group is a 'genuine occupational requirement'. This might apply where someone of a particular racial group is needed for reasons of 'authenticity' such as in restaurants, dramatic performances, or for artists' or photographic modelling, or if the case involves employment of someone to provide personal services to a particular racial group, where someone of the same racial group can do the job most effectively.

The CRE has published a Code of Practice for the elimination of racial discrimination and the promotion of equality of opportunity in employment, which can be obtained from the CRE. The Code of Practice sets out guidelines of good race relations, practice and although it is not enforceable in law, Employment Tribunals need to take its provisions into account.

Training

It is unlawful for any of the following training organisations to discriminate on race grounds:

- Industrial training boards.
- Employment Services Agency.
- Training Services Agency.
- Employers' organisations that provide training.
- Any other organisation designated by the Home Secretary.

These organisations are, however, allowed to practise 'positive discrimination', where there have been no people of a particular racial group, or very few, doing a particular kind of work, either in the whole of Britain or in a region, in the previous 12 months. In this case they will be allowed to run training courses or provide facilities for that racial group only, or to encourage people from that group to take up a particular kind of work.

Employers will also be allowed to run training courses for a particular racial group only, or to encourage them to take up a particular kind of work, where there have been no people of that racial group, or very few, doing that kind of work in the firm during the previous 12 months.

Trade unions and professional organisations are also allowed to organise special training courses to encourage people from a particular racial group to hold posts within the organisation (for example, as shop stewards or officials) where there have been very few or no people from that group holding such posts in the previous 12 months.

Education

Discrimination in the field of education is dealt with by Part III of the RRA. The RRA applies to schools or colleges maintained by a local education authority (LEA), independent ('public' or fee-paying) schools or colleges, special schools, grant-maintained 'opted-out' schools and universities. The Home Secretary can also designate other establishments to be covered by the law.

It is unlawful for any educational body (including the governors of a school or college and an LEA) to discriminate on race grounds in any of the following ways:

- The terms on which they admit you.
- Refusing to admit you.
- Providing more facilities or better facilities for particular racial groups.
- Expelling you or in any other way putting you at a disadvantage.
- Acting in any other way that involves race discrimination.

It is lawful for LEAs and other bodies to provide special facilities to meet the particular needs of a racial group (for example, for language classes).

Overseas students

There is only one exception to the education sections of the RRA and this concerns overseas students. It is lawful for any organisation or individual providing education or training to discriminate on racial grounds against people who are not ordinarily resident in Great Britain and who do not intend to remain in Great Britain after their period of education or training. This means, for instance, that it is lawful for colleges or halls of residence to charge higher fees to overseas students.

Housing

Housing and premises, such as business premises, are also covered by Part III of the RRA. In general, it is unlawful for someone to discriminate on race grounds, when selling, letting, subletting or managing property, in any of the following ways:

- In the terms on which you are offered the premises.
- By refusing to let you buy or rent the premises.
- By treating you differently from other people on a list of people wanting to buy or rent the premises.
- By refusing to agree to the transfer of a lease to you.
- By refusing you access to any benefits or facilities in the premises you occupy.
- By evicting you or subjecting you to any other disadvantage.

The law covers private landlords and owner-occupiers as well as local authorities.

Exceptions in housing

There are three main exceptions:

(1)   Owner-occupiers selling or letting their property are excluded, provided that they do not advertise or use an estate agent.
(2)   Small residential premises (for example, small boarding houses or shared flats) are excluded. To qualify as 'small residential premises', the owner or occupier (or a near relative) has to live permanently in the house or flat; part of the house or flat, other than stairs or storage space, has to be shared with other people; and there must be only two households (other than the owner's or occupier's household) or not more than six people (other than the owner's or occupier's household) in the house or flat. A boarding house containing more than six lodgers, in addition to the landlord/lady's family, would not be allowed to discriminate, but a boarding house with fewer lodgers would be allowed to.
(3)   Charities and membership bodies whose main purpose is to provide benefits for a particular racial group are allowed to provide housing for that group only. But

these organisations will not be allowed to discriminate on grounds of colour, only on grounds of race, nationality or national or ethnic origin.

Goods, facilities and services

Part III of the RRA also covers any 'goods, facilities or services' that are offered to the public or a section of the public. This means, for instance, the services and facilities offered by hotels, boarding houses, pubs and restaurants, banks, insurance companies, credit houses and hire purchase firms, transport authorities and local authorities. A recent case has also held that it might cover the investigation of crime too. Direct or indirect discrimination by any such organisation will be unlawful.

Any contract (for example, to buy goods or supply services) that includes a term that discriminates on racial grounds is void and can be amended by applying to the County Court to strike out that term formally.

Exceptions in provision of goods, facilities and services

There are a number of situations where race discrimination remains lawful:

- Any arrangement where someone takes a child, elderly person or someone needing special care and attention into his or her home to be looked after (for example, fostering children).
- Goods, facilities or services provided outside Britain, or insurance arrangements to cover a situation outside Britain. (But the services of, for instance, a travel agent in Britain, even though it arranges foreign travel, will still be covered.)
- Charities and voluntary organisations whose main purpose is to provide benefits for a particular racial group (but these organisations will not be allowed to discriminate on grounds of colour, only on grounds of race, nationality or national or ethnic origin).
- Special arrangements can be made for members of a particular racial group who have particular needs for education, training, welfare, and so on (for example, language classes).
- Discrimination on grounds of nationality, place of birth or length of residence is permitted in:
  (a)   selecting people to represent a particular place or country in a sport or game;
  (b)   deciding who is eligible to compete in any sport or game, according to the rules of the competition.

Prisons

The provisions prohibiting unlawful discrimination in housing and in relation to goods, facilities and services have been held to prevent the unlawful discrimination by prison officers in the allocation of work to prisoners. They also probably make unlawful other discrimination occurring in the prison regime (for example, more unfavourable withdrawal of privileges from, and more frequent strip searches of, black prisoners).

Clubs

Before the RRA 2000, private clubs, such as political and working-men's clubs, were allowed to discriminate on race grounds. It is now unlawful for any club or society with 25 or more members to discriminate on race grounds in any of the following ways:

- Refusing to allow you to join.
- Offering you less favourable terms of membership.
- Giving you fewer benefits, facilities or services or refusing to let you use or have any of these benefits (for example, social facilities).
- Expelling you from the club or changing the terms of your membership.
- Putting you at a disadvantage in any other way.

But a club or society whose main purpose is to provide benefits for people of a particular racial group, whatever its size, will continue to be allowed to discriminate on race grounds (although not on grounds of colour).

Advertisements
It is unlawful to insert, publish or cause to be published an advertisement that indicates that an employer, a company or anyone else intends to discriminate unlawfully. The absence of an intention to discriminate is no defence.

Only the CRE is able to take legal action against discriminatory advertisements. If you see an advertisement that you believe breaks the law you should bring it to the CRE's attention. You can also make a complaint yourself about the advertisement to the person displaying it.

Discrimination is allowed where exceptions in the law exist, for example, advertisements for jobs to which the genuine occupational qualification applies, for employment outside the UK and for posts and training where positive action is permitted. But an advertisement for employment in a private household must not be racially discriminatory.

Public authorities
In April 2001 the RRA was amended to put in place a key recommendation of the McPherson Report, which looked into the death of Stephen Lawrence, namely, that the prohibition on race discrimination in the RRA should extend to the police. The RRA 2000 went further and extended the RRA to all public bodies. This gives people new rights to challenge race discrimination by bodies such as the police, local government, mental hospitals and the prisons in the courts. The prohibition on discrimination by public authorities can now be found in section 19B of the RRA. These provisions do not apply to some immigration decisions, and to decisions not to prosecute someone.

General and specific duties on public authorities
As a result of the RRA 2000, public authorities have a general duty. Each listed authority is required '... in carrying out its functions ... to have due regard to the need – (a) to eliminate unlawful racial discrimination; and (b) to promote equality of opportunity and good relations between persons of different racial groups'. This means that the authority needs to look carefully at its policies and consider how they need to be changed to ensure they meet these aims.

Certain public authorities can also be subjected to 'specific duties' set out by the Home Secretary. So far this has been a requirement to produce a Race Equality Scheme, and to have in place arrangements for monitoring the ethnicity of staff.

Commission for Racial Equality

The CRE was set up by the RRA with the duties of:

- Working towards the elimination of discrimination.
- Promoting equality of opportunity and good relations between persons of different racial groups generally.
- Keeping under review the working of the RRA and, when required by the Home Secretary or when it otherwise thinks it necessary, to draw up and submit to the Home Secretary proposals for amending it.

In carrying out its duties, the CRE has the following powers:

- To undertake formal investigations into discriminatory practices that are unsuitable to be dealt with on an individual basis.
- To support, including financially, individuals taking up complaints of discrimination.
- To issue Codes of Practice on employment. The first code was approved by Parliament in 1984. It is not legally binding, but can be used in evidence at an Employment Tribunal.
- To examine areas of policy outside the scope of the RRA.
- To issue non-discrimination notices. This happens if the CRE decides, as a result of a formal investigation, that the law has been broken.
- To fund research and other projects.
- To apply for an injunction if it believes someone has broken the law and is likely to go on doing so. In the following circumstances, it is the CRE alone that can take action, such as applying for an injunction, if discrimination has taken place:
  (a) if an advertisement demonstrates an intention to discriminate unlawfully.
  (b) if someone instructs an employee or agent to discriminate unlawfully.
  (c) if someone puts pressure on anyone else to discriminate unlawfully.
- To enforce the specific duties introduced by the RRA 2000.

CRE investigations

The CRE can conduct 'formal investigations' into any subject it chooses – for instance, employment patterns in a region, the recruitment policies of a firm, housing allocation policies in local authorities, and so on.

The CRE must give notice of its intention to hold a formal investigation and draw up terms of reference. If it is investigating a particular organisation or person, and states in the terms of reference that it believes they are discriminating unlawfully, then it will be able to require them to give evidence or produce information. The power to take evidence and summon witnesses will also apply in other investigations with the consent of the Home Secretary, or if the aim of the investigation is to see whether a non-discrimination notice is being obeyed.

Either during or at the end of an investigation, the CRE can make recommendations for changes that would promote equality of opportunity. These recommendations will not be legally binding, but could be used to bring pressure on the organisation or person, or as evidence in an individual case against them.

Non-discrimination notices

The CRE will be able to issue a non-discrimination notice if it decides, during a formal investigation, that an organisation or individual has discriminated unlawfully. The non-discrimination notice requires the organisation or person named in it to stop discriminating unlawfully and, if necessary, to let the people concerned know what changes have been made in their procedures or arrangements in order to obey the non-discrimination notice. Before issuing the notice, the CRE must warn the organisation or person concerned that it is thinking of doing so, and give it or them 28 days to make representations. Once the notice is issued, the organisation or person named can appeal to the Employment Tribunal (in an employment case) or the County Court. The appeal must be made within six weeks of the issue of the notice.

If the appeal fails, or no appeal is made, the non-discrimination notice becomes final; in other words, it can be enforced. The CRE keeps a register of notices that have become final, and anyone is entitled to inspect this register and take a copy of any notice in it.

Injunctions

A non-discrimination notice can only be enforced if the CRE goes to court and gets an injunction. It can do this at any time within five years of when the notice becomes final if it thinks that the organisation or person named in the notice will continue to discriminate unlawfully. An injunction is an order by a County Court or the High Court ordering someone to stop acting in a particular way. If the organisation or person does not obey the injunction, they will be in contempt of court and the CRE can apply to the court to have the people involved fined or imprisoned.

The CRE may also apply to the County Court for an injunction without issuing a non-discrimination notice in the following circumstances:

- If someone has successfully brought a complaint against an individual or organisation and the CRE considers that the individual or organisation will go on discriminating unlawfully.
- If the CRE considers that someone has discriminated unlawfully and is likely to go on doing so; in this case, the CRE must itself apply to the Employment Tribunal or County Court to get a finding that the person concerned has in fact discriminated unlawfully.
- If the CRE considers that someone has published an unlawful advertisement, instructed an employee or agent to discriminate unlawfully, or put pressure on anybody else to discriminate unlawfully. Only the CRE can take action on these kinds of unlawful acts.

Commencing proceedings and time limits for race discrimination claims

A complaint about race discrimination in employment must be brought to an Employment Tribunal within three months of the act or failure to act being complained of. A complaint about race discrimination under Part III of the RRA (goods, facilities and services, public functions etc.) must be brought to a County Court or Sheriff's Court, within six months of the act complained of.

The tribunal or court has discretion to extend the time for bringing a complaint of race discrimination if, in all the circumstances of the case, it considers it just and equitable to do so. A tribunal might be persuaded to extend the time for presentation of your claim or allow a late claim to proceed if you can provide a good explanation for your delay in making a claim. Explanations that might be accepted are that you were not aware of your right to make a complaint under the RRA; that you have been ill and that prevented you lodging your complaint in time; or that you were trying to resolve matters within the organisation by pursuing an internal grievance or appeal. In all these cases a tribunal or court would expect to have evidence from the complainant put before them before they allowed a late claim to proceed.

The burden of proof and questionnaires

In order to win a case of race discrimination, you must show that you were being treated less favourably than someone of different racial or national origins would be treated and that the treatment you received was because of or on the grounds of your race. It is also necessary to show that you suffered some detriment or disadvantage as a result of this differential treatment. The courts have recognised the difficulties of proving a discrimination claim and have given guidance, now set down in the RRA, that in direct discrimination and victimisation claims it may be permissible to infer that unlawful discrimination has occurred from the primary facts. Therefore, if you are able to show a difference in treatment between you and another person and a difference in race, then a tribunal is entitled, but not required, to draw the inference that the reason for the difference in treatment is on racial grounds. There is also a very useful procedure under section 65 whereby you can serve a questionnaire on the alleged discriminator and ask them to explain why they treated you as they did.

Remedies

If a complaint of race discrimination is successful, a court or Employment Tribunal has the power to make a declaration and to consider the grant of a number of remedies. A court or tribunal can award compensation if it thinks it is just and equitable to do so. Provided that you can prove that you have suffered the losses alleged, there is no limit on the compensation that a tribunal or court can award. Injury to feelings is a detriment or disadvantage recognised by Employment Tribunals and the courts for which compensation may be awarded. A court or tribunal can also make an order for the payment of compensation for past or future loss of earnings if you have suffered financial loss as a result of the discrimination you are complaining about. If you have suffered injury to your health as a result of the unlawful discrimination, you can also receive compensation for this injury. It is important to remember that the burden of proof is on you. This means that you must provide the Employment Tribunal or court with enough evidence to prove your claim.

Criminal liability for acts that stir up racial hatred

The Public Order Act 1986 (POA) prohibits certain acts intended or likely to stir up racial hatred. No prosecution for these offences may be brought without the Attorney General's permission. The POA covers:

- The use of words or behaviour or displays of written material that are threatening, abusive or insulting and intended to stir up racial hatred. The acts do not have to be committed in public; however, such acts, if committed in a private dwelling, are outside the POA.

- Publishing or distributing to the public written material that is threatening, abusive or insulting and intended to stir up racial hatred or which, in the circumstances, is likely to stir up racial hatred. This will include racist graffiti as well as newspaper articles and other similarly offensive racist material that is threatening, abusive or insulting.
- The public performance of a play that involves the use of threatening, abusive or insulting words or behaviour intended to stir up racial hatred or that, in the circumstances, are likely to stir up racial hatred. There are defences to this offence that apply in very limited circumstances. The offence is primarily aimed at the presenter and director, but actors who alter their lines will be within the prohibition.
- Distributing, showing or playing a recording of visual images (including video recordings) or sound that is threatening, abusive or insulting and which is intended to stir up racial hatred or which, in the circumstances, is likely to stir up racial hatred.
- Broadcasting (including a programme in a cable programme service) that is threatening, abusive or insulting and which is intended to stir up racial hatred or which, in the circumstances, is likely to stir up racial hatred.

See also section 8.15, 'Public order offences', p. 182.

Inflammatory material

The POA also makes it an offence to have possession of written material that is threatening, abusive or insulting, or a recording of visual images or sound that is threatening, abusive or insulting with a view to use it, and with the intention that racial hatred will be stirred up or in circumstances in which it is likely to be stirred up. Powers of entry, search and forfeiture are given in respect of such material. Again, prosecutions may only be brought with the Attorney General's consent.

In the POA, 'racial hatred' is defined as hatred against a group of persons in Great Britain defined by reference to colour, race, nationality (including citizenship) or ethnic or national origins. This definition does not include religion. It may also exclude Gypsies and Travellers. See also Chapter 15.

The Criminal Justice and Public Order Act 1994

The Criminal Justice and Public Order Act 1994 renders racial, sexual and other forms of harassment in the street and at work a criminal offence punishable by imprisonment. It creates a new offence of causing intentional harassment, alarm or distress by the use of threatening, abusive or insulting words, behaviour, writing, sign or other visible representation. It also makes the publication of racially inflammatory material an arrestable offence.

The Protection from Harassment Act 1997

The Protection from Harassment Act 1997 is designed to protect individuals from harassment and similar conduct. It was passed for the purpose of dealing with 'stalking', but there is no reason why in appropriate circumstances it should not be used to protect victims of racial harassment. It does not define harassment, although it makes clear that alarming a person or causing a person distress may constitute harassment. It creates an offence of putting people in fear of violence being used against them. There is a racially aggravated form of this offence. It creates a criminal offence of harassment with a maximum term of imprisonment of six months and/or a fine. It also provides a civil remedy to victims and permits the grant of an injunction and an award of damages.

The Crime and Disorder Act 1998

Section 29 of the Crime and Disorder Act 1998 creates a category of racially aggravated offences. These are: malicious wounding or grievous bodily harm and actual bodily harm. On summary conviction both carry liability to a term of imprisonment not exceeding six months or to a fine. On conviction the maximum term of imprisonment is a term not exceeding seven years, or a fine, or both. There is also an offence of racially aggravated common assault, which carries a maximum term of six months on summary conviction or a fine or both; and on conviction on indictment to imprisonment for a maximum of two years or a fine or both.

10.3   RELIGIOUS DISCRIMINATION

There is often an overlap between race and religion and so certain religious groups, such as Sikhs and Jews, have been held to be covered by the RRA. As explained above, the HRA can also be used to enforce the right to religious freedom. However, with effect from December 2003, new regulations came into force that make specific provision outlawing discrimination on grounds of religion in the employment and education fields – the Employment Equality (Religion or Belief) Regulations 2003 (EERBR).

The EERBR follow a similar structure to the RRA and include many of the same concepts. Under the EERBR it is unlawful to subject someone to direct or indirect discrimination, victimisation or harassment on grounds of their religion, religious belief, or similar philosophical belief. The sorts of discrimination that are prohibited in employment and education under the EERBR are virtually identical to those in the RRA.

If you have been the victim of religious discrimination at work you must take your claim under the EERBR to the Employment Tribunal, or if your complaint is of religious discrimination in education your remedy would be to go to the County Court. There are similar provisions relating to vicarious liability, questionnaires and remedies as in the RRA.

10.4   SEX DISCRIMINATION

This section deals with sex discrimination in education; housing; the provision of goods, facilities and services; advertising, and social security. The duties and powers of the Equal Opportunities Commission are also explained here.

Sex discrimination in pay and terms and conditions of work is dealt with in Chapter 14 dealing with the rights of workers, as is information on maternity rights for working women.

The law relating to sex discrimination is heavily influenced by European Union law. Article 141 of the Treaty of Rome provides that 'Each Member State shall ensure that the principle of equal pay for male and female workers for work of equal value is applied.' Article 141 is extended by additional Directives, the most relevant being the Equal Pay Directive (Directive 75/117) and the Equal Treatment Directive (Directive 76/207) (ETD).

The Sex Discrimination Act 1975, as amended (SDA), covers discrimination in the following areas:

- Employment.
- Education.
- Goods, facilities and services.
- Housing.

The SDA covers discrimination against men and women. The SDA has been amended to bring within its scope discrimination against transsexual people in employment and vocational training. There is now a statutory definition of 'gender reassignment' in the SDA. Discrimination on the grounds of sexual orientation is dealt with by new regulations which came into force in December 2003 (see below, section 10.5, 'Sexual orientation and transgender discrimination', p. 240).

The SDA also makes it unlawful to discriminate against married people in the fields of employment and vocational training. Otherwise, discrimination against people because of their marital status is currently lawful, although it may be that this is challenged on human rights grounds in due course.

There are other exceptions within the areas that are covered by SDA. These are mentioned below, under the relevant headings.

Discrimination in some of the areas not covered by the SDA continues to be addressed through European Union law. For example, an EC directive on equal treatment in social security has led to some changes in Britain's social security benefits in recent years. For example, men and women now have equal treatment in short-term, contributory benefits, such as unemployment benefit. Women may also claim income support on behalf of their partners and dependants, although in practice this is rare. Discrimination against married women claiming the invalid care allowance (ICA) has now been outlawed following a successful test case under the European directive. Married and cohabiting women claiming ICA may also put in for back payments to December 1984, if applicable to their case.

What is sex discrimination?
The SDA defines discrimination in two ways: direct and indirect.

Direct discrimination
Direct discrimination is when you are treated less favourably than someone of the opposite sex in the same circumstances as you because of your sex. For example, admitting only boys to a GCSE course in electronics at a mixed school would be direct discrimination; so would offering hire-purchase facilities only to men, or half-price entry to a disco only to women.

Indirect discrimination
There are now two definitions of indirect discrimination.

In employment or vocational training indirect discrimination occurs when an employer applies a provision, criterion or practice that, although it appears neutral, is to the detriment of a considerably larger proportion of women than of men, and cannot be shown by the employer to be justifiable irrespective of the sex of the person to whom it is applied. It must also actually be to the detriment of the person in question.

In the other areas of the SDA, indirect discrimination occurs when a condition or requirement is applied that disproportionately disadvantages one sex more than another and which cannot be objectively justified. The proportion of one sex who can comply must be considerably smaller than the proportion of the other sex who can comply, and the individual who complains must suffer because he or she cannot comply.

For example, an after-school computer club open only to pupils taking an examination course in computer science could be against the law if hardly any girls took the examination course. Similarly, a housing association that excluded single parents from membership could be indirectly discriminating because the vast majority of single parents are women.

Proving discrimination
Once you have shown that your treatment was, on the face of it, discriminatory, the employer then has to prove that the reason for it was not, in fact, your sex.

Victimisation
The SDA also protects you against victimisation for taking action under either the SDA or the Equal Pay Act 1970. This provision makes it unlawful to treat you less favourably than anyone else because you have done any of the following:

- Made a complaint under either of the Acts.
- Helped someone else to make a complaint.
- Given evidence in a court or tribunal in a case under either of the Acts.
- Accused someone of breaking either of the Acts.
- Taken any other action in connection with either of the Acts.

So, for example, it would be an act of unlawful victimisation for a former employer to refuse to provide an ex-employee with a reference because that ex-employee has brought proceedings against him or her.

You do not need to show that the discriminator was consciously motivated by the fact that you carried out one of the above protected acts. Allegations of discrimination must be made in good faith in order to be protected by the victimisation provisions of the SDA.

See also Chapter 14.

Sexual harassment
Unlike the Race Relations Act 1976 (RRA), the SDA does not contain any express provisions in relation to harassment. However, sexual harassment is a form of direct discrimination. It is recognised as a serious issue and the source of much misery and distress for victims and their families. Sexual harassment can take a variety of forms. The term suggests a degree of repetition in the conduct or behaviour complained of, but this is not always necessary. A single incident can in some circumstances be properly described as sexual harassment. The 'European Commission Code of Practice on Measures to Combat Sexual Harassment' provides a helpful outline definition.

It states that sexual harassment includes unwanted conduct of a sexual nature, or other conduct based on sex, affecting the dignity of women and men at work. It can include unwelcome physical, verbal or non-verbal conduct. Sexual harassment may include ridicule, unwelcome comments about appearance, demands or requests for sexual favours and even actual physical assault. Men may also be subject to sexual harassment, as some recent Employment Tribunal decisions have acknowledged.

In order to succeed in a claim founded on sexual harassment, you must show that the behaviour complained of is less favourable treatment on the grounds of sex and that you have suffered a detriment as a result.

Public hearings and publicity

The fact that Employment Tribunal hearings, in particular, are public hearings and are often attended by the press has on occasion deterred individuals who have been subjected to harassment from pursuing their case to tribunal. Where cases involve allegations of sexual misconduct, Employment Tribunals are able to make an order prohibiting publication of any matter likely to enable members of the public to identify an individual affected by or making the complaint. The tribunal is able to make such an order either on the application of the parties or of its own motion.

In cases where sexual offences are alleged, the tribunal's written decisions must also exclude matters likely to assist in the identification of individuals involved in the proceedings.

Protection from Harassment Act 1997

The Protection from Harassment Act 1997 (PHA) is designed to protect individuals from harassment and similar conduct. It was passed for the purpose of dealing with 'stalking'. In appropriate circumstances it can be used to protect victims of serious sexual harassment. The PHA does not define harassment, although it makes clear that alarming a person or causing a person distress may constitute harassment. It creates an offence of putting people in fear of violence being used against them. It creates a criminal offence of engaging in a course of conduct that amounts to harassment with a maximum term of imprisonment of six months and/or a fine. A course of conduct must involve conduct on at least two occasions. The PHA also provides a civil remedy to victims and permits the granting of an injunction restraining the harasser from pursuing the course of conduct as well as an award of damages. A court can award an injunction even if the harasser has not actually been convicted of harassment.

Education

With regard to education, the SDA makes it unlawful to discriminate on grounds of sex, directly or indirectly, in any of the following areas:

- Admissions policies.
- Access to classes, courses or other benefits, facilities or services provided by the school or college.
- Any other unfavourable treatment.

The SDA permits the continuation of single-sex schools, but also places a general duty on local education authorities to provide education without sex discrimination. This might mean, for example, that although a single-sex girls' school may not offer a design and technology course through its own curriculum, the LEA has to ensure that if boys in the same area have the opportunity to study this subject, arrangements are made to enable girls to take it, perhaps by attending a nearby mixed school for those lessons.

The following bodies can be held responsible for discrimination under the SDA:

- All schools, colleges and other educational establishments maintained by LEAs. Depending on the circumstances of the case, the LEA itself and/or the governors of the institution can be held responsible. Governors can be held responsible individually or collectively.
- Independent or private schools. The proprietors would be responsible.
- Universities and other higher education institutes. The governing body would be responsible.
- Other establishments designated by the Secretary of State for Education. These include other establishments in receipt of grants (such as grant-maintained schools) from central government or the local authority. The governing body in each case is responsible for any discrimination.

Educational trusts

The SDA allows educational trusts to change their terms, with consent from the Secretary of State for Education, in order to apply their benefits to both sexes.

Exceptions in education

- Single-sex schools and colleges. A single-sex institution planning to turn co-educational can apply for permission to discriminate by admitting more members of one sex for a limited period.
- Co-educational schools that provide boarding accommodation for one sex only may continue to do so. If provided for both sexes, accommodation must be equal though it may be separate.
- Education provided by charities set up to benefit one sex only.
- Higher and further education courses in physical training.
- In sport, single-sex competitive sport is allowed 'where the physical strength, stamina or physique of the average woman puts her at a disadvantage to the average man'. In practice, this has often been used to exclude girls from certain sports at school.

See also Chapter 13.

Housing

The SDA makes it unlawful to discriminate in renting, managing, sub-letting or selling accommodation. Owner-occupied properties, small boarding houses and flat-sharing, however, are excluded from the SDA. Single-sex housing associations are also exempt.

Mortgages

Building societies, local authorities or any other body that grants mortgages are breaking the law if they treat women applicants any less favourably than they would treat a man in the same circumstances. For example, they may not apply different rules regarding earnings levels, age, dependants, and so on.

Goods, facilities and services

This covers a wide range of public and private services, including pubs, cafés, restaurants, hotels, transport, banking, insurance, hire purchase, recreation and entertainment. The list of exceptions to this part of the SDA, however, is just about as long as the list of situations it does cover. The exceptions are:

- Private clubs, such as working men's clubs and sports clubs. (Note: this is unlawful under the RRA.)
- Political parties. Women's sections and conferences are still lawful.
- Religious bodies may continue to discriminate if necessary because of their doctrine or because not to do so would offend 'a significant number' of its members.
- Hospitals, prisons, hostels, old people's homes and any other places for people needing 'special care'.
- Competitive sport, if an average woman would be at a disadvantage because of her physical capacity compared to the average man.
- Charities and non-profit-making organisations set up to provide facilities or services for one sex only. This does not mean such organisations may discriminate across the board – for example, by restricting their office workers to one sex only – but they may discriminate in the provision of services, including who is employed in actually providing those services.
- Insurance companies and similar bodies. These may discriminate if it is on the basis of actuarial or other data on which it is reasonable to rely. For example, women can be offered cheaper car insurance than men because statistics show they are safer drivers.
- Facilities and services that need to be restricted to one sex only in order to preserve 'decency and privacy'. This covers toilets, saunas, changing rooms and so on.
- Certain provisions in relation to death or retirement are also excluded.
- Occupational pension schemes and redundancy payment schemes are outside of the SDA.

Discriminatory contractual terms

Contractual terms that conflict with the SDA are void. This applies to any term of a collective agreement or rule made by employers, organisations of workers, professional organisations or regulatory bodies. Individuals affected by such terms or rules have the right to apply to the Employment Tribunal to have the term or rule declared invalid.

Advertisements

If an advertisement for a job covered by the SDA states or implies an intention to discriminate against men or women applicants, a complaint could be made to an Employment Tribunal under the employment sections of the SDA, as the advertisement would count as part of the arrangements made by the employer to fill a vacancy.

Advertising in other areas, for example, for accommodation, entertainment or services, is also covered by the SDA, but complaints about discriminatory advertising may only be taken up by the Equal Opportunities Commission (EOC). If you see a discriminatory advertisement, you can report it to the EOC.

Sexism in advertising, through offensive images of women used to sell products, for example, is not outlawed by the SDA. But complaints of sexism or anything else you consider to be illegal, indecent, dishonest or untruthful can be made to the Advertising Standards Authority.

Public bodies
Unlike the RRA, the SDA does not impose a statutory duty on all public bodies to carry out its functions with regard to eliminating unlawful sex discrimination and to promoting equal opportunity.

The Equal Opportunities Commission
The EOC was set up under the SDA with the following duties:

- To work towards the elimination of sex discrimination.
- To promote equality of opportunity between men and women generally.
- To keep the SDA and the Equal Pay Act under review and propose amendments to the Secretary of State.

In carrying out its duties, the EOC has the following powers:

- To undertake formal investigations into discriminatory practices that are unsuitable to be dealt with on an individual basis.
- To support, including financially, individuals taking up complaints of discrimination.
- To issue Codes of Practice on employment. The first code was approved by Parliament in April 1985. It is not legally binding but can be used in evidence at an Employment Tribunal.
- To examine areas of policy outside the scope of the SDA, for example, social security, taxation, maternity rights.
- To issue non-discrimination notices. This happens if the EOC decides as a result of a formal investigation that the law has been broken.
- To fund research and educational activities.
- To apply for an injunction if it believes someone has broken the law and is likely to go on doing so. In the following circumstances, it is the EOC alone that can take action, such as applying for an injunction, if discrimination has taken place:
  - (a) if an advertisement demonstrates an intention to discriminate unlawfully;
  - (b) if someone instructs an employee or agent to discriminate unlawfully; or
  - (c) if someone puts pressure on anyone else to discriminate unlawfully.

How to complain about sex discrimination
A complaint under the SDA must be taken to an Employment Tribunal if it concerns employment, including cases of victimisation concerned with employment. Your

complaint of discrimination must be lodged within three months of the discrimination complained of.

Complaints of discrimination in education, housing and the provision of goods, facilities or services must be made to the County Court. Complaints concerning education must first be made to the Secretary of State for Education. If the matter has not been resolved to your satisfaction within two months, you may then proceed with action in the County Court. Complaints about housing, goods, facilities and services must be made within six months of the discrimination taking place.

There is a discretion to extend the time for the presentation of a complaint brought in either the court or the Employment Tribunal provided that the court or tribunal is satisfied that it would be just and equitable to do so having regard to all the relevant circumstances and the reasons for the late presentation of the claim.

10.5   SEXUAL ORIENTATION AND TRANSGENDER DISCRIMINATION

Recent legal developments

In recent times, significant developments have taken place in the recognition of the rights of sexual minorities, and great strides have been made in securing equal treatment for gay men, lesbians, bisexuals and transgendered people. A summary of these changes is set out below, with more detailed information provided in the remainder of this section.

A number of reforms to the criminal law introduced since 2000 have removed most of the remaining discriminatory sexual offences. Many of these reforms have been prompted by successful challenges in the ECHR.

The Employment Equality (Sexual Orientation) Regulations 2003 came into force in December 2003, giving effect to a European Union Council Directive extending the right of equal treatment in employment to sexual minorities by prohibiting discrimination on the grounds of sexual orientation.

The Civil Partnerships Bill, being considered by Parliament at the time of writing, will give legal recognition to same-sex relationships registered as a civil partnership and place same-sex partners who have registered their partnership on the same footing as married couples in respect of matters relating to family relations, pensions, social security and property rights.

The Gender Recognition Bill, also making its way through Parliament at the time of writing, provides for legal recognition of a change of sex for those diagnosed as suffering from gender dysphoria and will have the effect of eliminating much of the discriminatory impact of the previous law, which denied a current sex identity to transgendered people.

See also Chapter 3.

Sexual orientation discrimination

There have never been laws criminalising sexual relations between women, though there have been some prosecutions for 'insulting behaviour' (see below) and 'indecent assault'.

Laws pertaining specifically to sex between gay men have been around since 1885. Over the years thousands of men have been prosecuted, imprisoned and disgraced through the enforcement of these laws. The first wave of reforms came in the 1950s when consensual sex between men aged 21 and over was decriminalised (except in the armed forces), providing the act was carried out in private. The definition of privacy meant that an act would not be legal if it took place where a third person was, or was likely to be present. In 2000, the gay rights organisation Stonewall successfully challenged these privacy restrictions in the ECHR as a breach of the right to privacy in Article 8 of the Convention (*ADT* v *UK*). The age of consent for gay men was reduced from 21 to 18 in 1994, and was finally equalised in 2001.

On 12 January 2000, the ban on homosexuals serving in the armed forces was lifted with immediate effect. Once again, this followed a successful challenge in the ECHR (*Smith and Grady* v *UK*) which ruled that the ban and its application breached Article 8 of the Convention. The British Government has introduced a code of conduct governing personal relationships in the armed forces under which sexual orientation is essentially a private matter for the individual. The code applies to all personnel without regard to gender, sexual orientation, ethnicity or religious background. The code sets out circumstances in which the service has a duty to intervene in the personal lives of its personnel. The test to be applied is whether the actions or behaviour of an individual have, or are likely to have an impact on the efficiency or operational effectiveness of the service.

The Sexual Offences Act 2003 (SOA 2003), which came into force in May 2004, repeals most of the remaining discriminatory sexual offences targeting gay men, including buggery, gross indecency and soliciting. There are some concerns about a new offence created by the SOA 2003 of 'sexual activity in a public lavatory'. Gay men in particular are concerned that although the offence is phrased in a neutral way, in reality it will be used by police primarily against gay men. The Home Office has provided assurances that this is not the case and that the law will be enforced in a balanced way. The term 'public lavatory' is defined quite broadly and includes a public lavatory to which the public or a section of the public has access to whether for payment or otherwise. Accordingly, having sex in a locked cubicle in a night club, for example, would be an unlawful act. It remains to be seen, however, whether prosecution for such an act would withstand a challenge as a breach of Article 8 of the Convention.

There were a number of gay men who were convicted of gross indecency or buggery in relation to sexual acts with 16 or 17 year old men before the age of consent for gay men was lowered to 16. The Sex Offenders Act 1997 included these as offences that lead to automatic placement on the sex offenders register. With the age of consent already lowered to 16 and the offences of gross indecency and buggery now abolished, the SOA 2003 sets out a procedure whereby such offenders can apply to the Home Secretary for removal from the sex offenders register. The Home Office has issued guidance on how this procedure is to be administered: 'The Removal Of Offenders Convicted Of Buggery And Indecency Between Men From The "Sex Offender Register"' (Home Office Circular 019/2004).

Remaining discriminatory offences

Despite recent reform of the criminal law, some offences that have been historically used to target gay men, and in some cases lesbians as well, remain in place. Prosecutions of these offences are rare and, it is thought, would be open to challenge under Article 8 of the Convention. The offences are set out below:

Displaying affection in public

Lesbians, gay men or bisexuals who hold hands or kiss or fondle each other in public in the same way as heterosexuals may be committing an offence of 'insulting behaviour' under the Public Order Act 1986. Much will depend on the particular facts of the case and, as it is an offence that can only be tried in the Magistrates' Court, it will usually depend on the moral and political views of the magistrates as to whether the behaviour is regarded as insulting. The term 'insulting' is not defined by the law; it has to be given its ordinary meaning, but the higher courts have upheld a conviction under similar (though not identical) legislation where two men were fondling each other's genitals and buttocks over their clothes in the course of saying goodnight in a public place.

Conspiracy to corrupt public morals

This is a rarely used but powerful criminal offence, invented by the judiciary rather than passed by Parliament. It has been used in particular to prohibit gay men advertising in the 'contact' pages of magazines. Essentially, it is an offence to conspire or agree to do some act which, in the opinion of a jury, is calculated to corrupt or debauch public morals. In 1973, the House of Lords upheld, by a majority, the conviction of a magazine containing explicit gay contact ads on the ground that encouraging homosexuality is the sort of thing a jury might properly consider to be a 'corrupt practice'. However, the people placing the advertisements were not prosecuted. Since 1973, there have been no further prosecutions of this kind and explicit advertisements are now commonplace. The law, however, has not been repealed so there is always the possibility of a prosecution in the future.

Sado-masochism

In 1993, the House of Lords, in the case of *R v Brown* ruled that certain sado-masochistic sex involving the infliction of injury that is more than merely 'transient and trifling' is a criminal offence. This is so even where there is express consent to the act or acts. Although the defendants in that case were gay men, it applies equally to the activities of heterosexuals and lesbians. Nevertheless, the Court of Appeal in a later case involving a married couple (*R v Wilson*) distinguished that case from the *Brown* decision. The ECHR has held that the UK was not in breach of the Convention in prosecuting the defendants in the *Brown* case. However, with the HRA now in force, it is thought a domestic challenge may have good prospects of success.

See also Chapter 3.

Recognition of 'hate crimes'

A hate crime is generally recognised as a crime motivated by the prejudice of the offender toward a particular group of people. Hate crimes against gay men, lesbians, bisexuals and transgendered people are very common. In 1995, Stonewall carried out a study into the incidence of homophobic hate crime in Britain. The study revealed that one in three gay men and one in four lesbians had experienced at least one violent attack during 1990–95. The statistics for young gay men and lesbians were even higher.

Offences aimed at dealing with hate crime motivated by race or religion were introduced in 1998. Further offences relating to incitement to racial hatred were introduced in 2002. There are no comparable offences relating to homophobic hate crime. However, the Criminal Justice Act 2003 provides for increased sentences for offences motivated by hostility based on sexual orientation. In accordance with this provision, when sentencing the court is required to treat any such hostility as a aggravating factor and state so in open court. At the time of writing it had not come into force, so its full effect on sentencing practice is not yet clear.

Legal recognition of same-sex partnerships

The Civil Partnership Bill (CPB) allows a same-sex couple to obtain legal recognition of their relationship by forming a civil partnership, registered in the same way as a civil marriage at a registry office. The establishment of a civil partnership will have wide-ranging legal implications with civil partners assuming practically the same legal rights and obligations as a married couple in family law matters, in respect of financial relationships, property, pensions and social security.

Eligibility

In accordance with the CPB in its current form, in order to qualify for registration as civil partners, the couple must be:

- Of the same sex.
- Not already a civil partner or married.
- Not under 16 years of age.
- If over 16 but under 18, have the consent of the relevant persons or bodies.
- Not in prohibited degrees of relationship (e.g. siblings, parent/child).

The partnership can be ended by dissolution on application of either partner if it has irretrievably broken down or is a nullity or the other partner is presumed dead. A separation order can also be granted before dissolution.

The CPB also allows for the recognition of same-sex relationships registered under the law of other countries.

Effect of registration

The effect of registering a civil partnership is that the civil partners will be treated on the same or equivalent basis as a married couple for the purposes of the law. The effect of registration, therefore, extends to property and financial arrangements so that, for example, a civil partner can acquire beneficial interest in property if they make a substantial contribution to any improvements. Registration also ensures that the civil partner is treated as the next of kin for inheritance purposes and where consent for medical intervention is required, or as a dependant under the Fatal Accidents Act. These aspects of the CPB are considered in further detail in the relevant sections below.

Sexual orientation discrimination in employment

Many employees suffer discriminatory treatment at work because they are known or believed to be lesbian, gay or bisexual. There have also been cases of discriminatory treatment of gay men by colleagues and employers on the grounds that they may be HIV positive. Discrimination against a lesbian, gay or bisexual worker can take many forms including refusing to employ the worker, denying the worker promotion or dismissing the worker or by responding to hostile pressure from other employees to, for example, move the worker concerned to different duties or a different location, or by failing to protect the worker from harassment or abuse. Up until December 2003 a lesbian, gay or bisexual worker was not protected from such treatment by existing UK discrimination legislation.

This position was confirmed by the House of Lords in two cases that considered whether discrimination on the grounds of sex within the Sex Discrimination Act 1975 (SDA) included discrimination relating to a person's sexual orientation (*Macdonald* v *Ministry of Defence* and *Pearce* v *Governing Body of Mayfield Secondary School*). Macdonald's case involved dismissal from the armed forces on the grounds of sexual orientation and Pearce's case involved the failure of a school to take effective measures to protect a teacher from being subjected to persistent abuse and harassment relating to her sexual orientation by pupils.

The House of Lords held that since the SDA did not expressly cover sexual orientation there was no basis for interpreting the expression 'on the ground of her sex' expansively so as to include cases of discrimination solely on the ground of sexual orientation. In the context of the SDA, 'sex' meant gender and did not include sexual orientation.

In both cases the House of Lords concluded that because lesbian and gay men would be treated the same – that is, both dismissed or subject to homophobic abuse – there was no sex discrimination. The relevant comparator for a gay man was not a person of the opposite sex but rather a person of the opposite sexual orientation, rejecting the argument that the correct comparator was a woman sexually attracted to men.

This means that for sexual orientation discrimination cases taking place before December 2003 there is no protection under the SDA unless the applicant can demonstrate on the facts that a person of the opposite sexual orientation would not have been treated unfavourably.

An example of this is the Dan Air case. The company, an airline, adopted a policy of only employing women cabin staff and refusing even to consider male applicants. The underlying rationale for this discrimination was sexual orientation on the grounds that if a gay man was employed passengers might be exposed to the risk of becoming HIV positive. The EOC investigated Dan Air's policy and found that there were no medical grounds for implementing it, with the result that the company was in breach of the SDA. The EOC issued a non-discrimination notice and Dan Air subsequently changed its policy. The company was discriminating against all men in their desire to exclude gay men, and so was breaking the law.

Another strategy for those with over one year's service was (and is) to claim unfair dismissal under the Employment Rights Act 1996 (ERA). Employees who are dismissed, or forced out of their job (through what is called 'constructive dismissal'), in circumstances that involve sexual orientation discrimination can argue that following the HRA, the ERA should be interpreted to give effect to their right to private life under Article 8 and non-discrimination under Article 14 of the Convention. See also Chapter 14.

The position now is transformed, in any case, with the introduction of the Employment Equality (Sexual Orientation) Regulations 2003 (EESOR). The EESOR give effect to a European Union Directive extending the Equality Provisions to sexual minorities not previously protected by Community law. The EESOR make it unlawful to discriminate on grounds of sexual orientation in employment and vocational training.

What is sexual orientation discrimination?

The EESOR prohibits discrimination on the grounds of 'sexual orientation' in the fields of employment and vocational training. Sexual orientation is defined as meaning a 'sexual orientation toward persons of the same sex, persons of the opposite sex or persons of the same sex and the opposite sex'. Accordingly the EESOR prohibit discrimination against not just lesbians and gay men, but heterosexual and bisexual people as well.

The EESOR covers four types of discrimination: direct discrimination, indirect discrimination, victimisation and harassment.

Direct sexual orientation discrimination

Direct discrimination occurs when, on the ground of your sexual orientation, a person treats you less favourably than he or she treats or would treat other persons. The obvious example is where a person is dismissed because of his or her sexuality. However, the EESOR also cover cases of *perceived* sexual orientation. For example, if someone is dismissed because she is thought to be a lesbian, she can claim sexual orientation discrimination. This provision enables gay applicants not to have to 'come out' in order to bring a claim, and also protects those heterosexual applicants that become the subject of stereotypical homophobic assumptions about appearance or manner.

Protection is not limited to circumstances where the less favourable treatment is due to sexual orientation of the victim, but includes the sexual orientation of others. For example, where someone is told to discriminate against customers on the grounds of their sexual orientation but refuses and is dismissed, they can claim under the EESOR.

Indirect discrimination

The definition of indirect discrimination on the grounds of sexual orientation mirrors the new definition in the Race Relations Act 1976 (RRA). Indirect discrimination occurs when a group of people of the same sexual orientation is unjustifiably at a disadvantage in its ability to comply with a specific provision, criterion or practice. You can only bring a complaint if you suffer the disadvantage yourself. It has been argued in a recent case, for example, that allocation of employment-related benefits by reference to marital status is indirect discrimination against employees with same-sex partners, because such couples cannot marry. However, please bear in mind that the law on employment benefits and same-sex couples is currently uncertain. You should check with a solicitor if you are in any doubt as to your eligibility for such benefits.

The definition in the EESOR is different from the indirect discrimination provision in the SDA, which provides that the person discriminated against must show that the provision criterion or practice is to the detriment of a considerably larger proportion of women than men, is not justifiable, and is to her detriment. The definition of indirect discrimination in the EESOR should be more easily established.

Victimisation

Victimisation occurs when one person treats you less favourably than he or she treats, or would treat, someone else in those particular circumstances because you have done any of the following:

- Brought proceedings against the discriminator or any other person under the EESOR.
- Given evidence or information in connection with proceedings brought by any person against the discriminator or any other person under the EESOR.
- Otherwise done anything under or by reference to the EESOR in relation to the discriminator or any other person.
- Alleged that the discriminator or any other person has committed an act which (whether or not the allegation so states) would amount to a contravention of the EESOR.
- The discriminator knows that you intend to do any of those things or suspects that you have done, or intends to do, any of them.

Allegations of discrimination must be made in good faith in order to be protected by the victimisation provisions of the EESOR.

Harassment

Harassment on the grounds of sexual orientation is a separate unlawful act. The EESOR makes it unlawful for a person to subject you to harassment on the grounds of your sexual orientation. Harassment is defined as unwanted conduct that has the purpose or effect of violating your dignity, or creating an intimidating, hostile, degrading, humiliating or offensive workplace environment for you.

In considering claims of harassment, the Employment Tribunal must consider whether the conduct would *reasonably* be considered as having that effect in all the circumstances, as well as the particular perception of the person bringing the claim. The requirement of reasonableness introduces an objective element to the consideration of harassment, rather than just relying on whether the employee genuinely felt harassed. As harassment is a separate unlawful act, it is not necessary to point to a comparator.

Unlawful acts by an employer

It is unlawful for an employer to discriminate against you on the grounds of your sexual orientation in any of the following ways:

- Refusing to consider you for employment.
- Refusing to offer you employment.
- Offering you employment on terms less favourable than for other people.
- Refusing to make provision for you to be trained.
- Refusing to promote you or transfer you to another job.
- Giving you less favourable employment benefits.
- Dismissing you or causing you any other detriment.

Employment is defined in similar terms to the provisions in the RRA and the SDA, that is, work under a contract of service or apprenticeship, or a contract personally to do any work. The EESOR also outlaws discrimination by trade organisations, bodies conferring professional and trade qualifications, training providers, employment agencies and educational institutions.

Again, as with the RRA and the SDA, there is protection for contract workers and those who work for employment agencies. There are also special provisions in relation to office-holders, police officers, barristers and advocates, partnerships, those undergoing vocational training, and a range of other situations.

Protection extends to post-employment discrimination if such discrimination, which includes subjecting the person to a detriment or to harassment, 'arises out of and is closely connected to the relationship'. One example of this type of discrimination is where an employer refuses to give a reference to a former employee.

Defences and exceptions

Genuine occupational requirements have been used in other discrimination legislation to proscribe circumstances in which discrimination in employment is not prohibited. Likewise, it is a defence to a discrimination claim under the EESOR if the employer can show that being a person of a particular sexual orientation is a 'genuine occupational requirement' (GOQ). The defence allows the employer to refuse to offer employment to someone of a particular sexual orientation, to fail to promote them or to dismiss them. Further exemptions apply specifically to employment for the purposes of an organised religion (the 'religion exemption'), and to employment benefits allocated by reference to marital status (the 'marital status' exemption).

The general GOQ defence arises where it can be established that the nature of the employment or the context of it means that being of a particular sexual orientation is a genuine and determining occupational requirement and it is proportionate to apply the requirement. It is difficult to envisage a context in which this defence could be established, given the need to show an objective and proportionate reason for excluding a person from employment or training because of their sexual orientation. Individual prejudice, whether based on moral, religious or other cultural factors, should not be a basis for establishing a GOQ.

The 'religion exemption' provides that an employer can decide to terminate someone's employment (or not to appoint them, etc.) on the basis of their sexual orientation where the employment is 'for purposes of an organised religion' and the employer takes such action in order to comply with the doctrines of the religion or 'to avoid conflicting with the strongly held views of a significant number of the religion's followers'.

The effect of the marital status exemption is that benefits awarded on the basis of marital status cannot be challenged as being discriminatory on the ground of sexual orientation.

The religion and marital status exemptions have caused a great degree of concern on the part of unions and gay rights activists. Six unions challenged both exemptions by way of judicial review, arguing that they did not correctly implement EU law and that they contravened Articles 8 and 14 of the Convention (*R (on the application of Amicus – MSF section and others) v Secretary of State for Trade and Industry*). The challenge was unsuccessful in the High Court. At the time of writing it was not clear whether any or all of the unions would appeal the decision.

There are also exceptions for differences in treatment related to the following:

- National security; and
- Positive discrimination.

Commencing proceedings and time limits for sexual orientation discrimination claims

A complaint about sexual orientation discrimination in employment must be brought to an Employment Tribunal within three months of the act or failure to act being complained of. This means that you should count forward three months from the date of the last discriminatory act, subtract one day, and submit your claim before midnight on that day. The tribunal has a discretion to allow claims to be submitted late in certain circumstances. A complaint about sexual orientation discrimination by an educational establishment must be brought to a County Court or Sheriff's Court, within six months of the act complained of. The tribunal or court has discretion to extend the time for bringing a complaint of sexual orientation discrimination if, in all the circumstances of the case, it considers it just and equitable to do so.

The burden of proof and questionnaires

The burden of proof, as in other discrimination cases is transferred to the respondent (alleged discriminator) once you have established a prima facie case of discrimination and there is no adequate explanation for the difference in treatment between persons of your sexual orientation and persons of another.

You can also make use of the very useful 'questionnaire' procedure as a means of gathering information relevant to your claim. This procedure allows a person who believes he or she has been unlawfully discriminated against to serve a questionnaire on the alleged discriminator asking for an explanation as to the way he or she was treated. If it is served within three months of the act complained of or within 21 days of the day a complaint is made to the tribunal, or later with the tribunal's permission, you can use the questions and replies as evidence in the tribunal.

The employer is under no legal obligation to reply to the questionnaire, but if they do not, the tribunal can take this into consideration when making their decision about the discrimination.

Remedies

If a complaint of sexual orientation discrimination is successful, a court or Employment Tribunal has the power to make a declaration and to consider the grant of a number of remedies. A court or tribunal can award compensation if it thinks it is just and equitable to do so.

Discrimination in housing

Historically lesbian and gay relationships involving cohabitation have not been treated as equal to heterosexual relationships involving cohabitation. However, the law has significantly developed in this area. In a 1999 case decided by the House of Lords (*Fitzpatrick* v *Sterling Housing Association*), it was decided that a same-sex partner can be treated as a 'family member' and therefore entitled to succeed to a council house tenancy. With the HRA in force, the Court of Appeal has gone further, interpreting the term 'spouse' so as to include a same-sex partner (*Mendoza* v *Ghadian*) and thereby entitling the same-sex partner to succeed under a tenancy in the same circumstances as a husband or wife would. This case has been appealed and is before the House of Lords at the time of writing.

Many of these issues will be resolved once the CPB becomes law. Same-sex partners who choose to register as civil partners will be treated in the same way as married partners and will have the equivalent rights to enter and occupy the family home, to succeed in a tenancy upon the death of a partner, and be treated as a partner for housing and other housing-related benefits.

In this area, UK domestic law has applied a more liberal, progressive and egalitarian approach than Strasbourg, with the European Commission of Human Rights (predecessor of the ECHR) consistently refusing to treat same-sex relationships as capable of constituting family life and entitled to be treated as equivalent to marriage or heterosexual relationships.

Welfare benefits

In accordance with the CPB, same-sex partners who register as civil partners will be treated the same as a married couple for the purposes of social security benefits, child support and tax credits. Those who have not registered their partnership but have lived together as if they were civil partners are to be treated as heterosexual unmarried couples living together as husband and wife.

Under the CPB, amendments can be made to pensions legislation to allow for surviving civil partners or dependants of deceased civil partners to benefit as any reference to spouse or marriage will be read to include civil partners or civil partnerships.

Immigration

In recent times there have been substantial positive developments in the field of immigration law, with the Home Office introducing rules providing for the admission of same-sex partners on the same basis as unmarried heterosexual partners – although the favourable distinctions based upon marriage remain. The CPB makes provision for the recognition of same-sex relationships registered overseas. This should facilitate entry of non-national same-sex partners.

Foreign nationals are also entitled to apply for asylum if they can demonstrate that there is a real risk of persecution, on the grounds of their sexuality, in the country that they would be returned to. In cases where a same-sex partner faces expulsion and an indefinite or permanent separation from his or her partner some protection is also provided by Article 8 of the Convention, which protects the right to private and family life.

Under European Union law non-EU national spouses and family members of EU nationals are entitled to admission to the UK with EU nationals exercising Community law rights. 'Spouse' has been held by the European Court of Justice not to extend to non-married couples, but there is no authorative definition of family member. This is an area where Member States have considerable discretion, and in principle the UK can apply its more liberal approach reflected in cases in other areas of law, such as housing law (*Mendoza* and *Fitzpatrick*) when construing the free movement provisions of Community law. The CPB contains a power to make provision for civil partners to be treated as married couples for the purpose of Community law, so express provision may be made in the near future.

See also Chapter 11.

Parental rights

There is no law against lesbians, gay men or bisexuals being parents. Many lesbians and gay men marry or live in heterosexual relationships before coming out and thus already have children. An increasing number of couples and individuals have children by way of artificial insemination, or by surrogacy or adoption.

Lesbians, gay men or bisexuals who seek custody of or access to their children following a break-up may discover that the law treats them less favourably than heterosexuals in the same circumstances, although attitudes among the judiciary are liberalising. A parent can apply to the courts for a residence order (custody) or for an access order (contact). Granting such orders is a matter of discretion for the judge hearing the application. Judges have often been biased against lesbian or gay parents. For example, mothers who have had primary care of the children are usually given a residence order in disputes between parents, but if the court knows she is a lesbian her task of obtaining the order may be more difficult and the chances for the father increased. However, there are examples of the courts granting custody to both lesbians and gay men.

Local authorities allow applications to foster and adopt from both lesbians and gay men, whether single or in a couple. Provisions were introduced in the Adoption and Children Act 2002 to allow non-married couples, which includes same-sex couples, to become the legal parents of adopted children. This did not mean that in the past non-married partners could not adopt; rather it meant that only one partner would automatically obtain legal rights and the other had to apply to the court for a parental rights order, which is usually a matter of formality.

If the CPB becomes law, it will be a watershed in this area. Same sex couples registered as a civil partnership are to be treated in exactly the same way as married couples as far as family law is concerned. Accordingly the CPB defines a couple as including two people who are the civil partners of each other and two people, whether of different sexes or the same sex, living as partners in an enduring family relationship. It provides for amendments to the Children Act 1989 to include a civil partner as a parent to any child of the family. Express provision is made for civil partners to obtain parental responsibility orders in respect of their civil partner's child or other child of the family, for a civil partner to be appointed as guardian of a child, to apply for a residence or contact order, to adopt and to be responsible for financial provision for a child.

See also Chapter 13.

Ban on promoting homosexuality
The most significant piece of legislation affecting gay men, bisexuals and lesbians since the reforming 1967 Act was section 28 of the Local Government Act 1988, which barred the 'intentional promotion of homosexuality' by local authorities. This provision also prohibited the publishing of material with the intention of promoting homosexuality and the promotion of teaching in any maintained school of 'the acceptability of homosexuality as a pretended family relationship'. It became increasingly controversial and unsustainable, and in November 2003 the Government finally repealed it.

This should end practices adopted by some local authorities under the auspices of complying with section 28, such as banning:

- The publication of a list of advice agencies for young people because a couple of the hundreds of entries were lesbian and/or gay organisations.
- The performance of a play by a 'theatre in education' group because it contained a scene involving a gay man.
- The publication of a cartoon in a Women's Unit newsletter because it was a lesbian parody of heterosexual attitudes.

- The confirmation by a gay teacher of his sexuality when asked about it by children in his class.
- The stocking in public libraries of the gay and lesbian weekly newspaper *The Pink Paper*.

See also Chapter 13.

Transgender discrimination

Transvestites
There is nothing in the law to stop anyone dressing in clothes traditionally worn by members of the opposite sex. Sometimes, however, transvestites have been arrested for 'insulting behaviour', and in theory they could in some circumstances be convicted of this offence, but such situations are very rare. In 1996 the Employment Appeal Tribunal rejected an appeal from a local authority employee who claimed unlawful sex discrimination after he had been threatened with disciplinary proceedings for wearing at work what was conventionally regarded as female wear (*Kara v London Borough of Hackney*).

Transsexuals and transgendered people
It is lawful to undergo gender reassignment (sex change) surgery. Treatment is generally funded by the National Health Service, although the practice varies depending upon the policies of the particular Health Authority. Litigation successfully challenged the approach of several authorities that treated the funding of this treatment as of low priority and essentially equivalent to cosmetic surgery.

The right to gender reassignment treatment has been held to constitute an aspect of private life, with the ECHR finding a violation of Article 8 where a German health insurance company refused to reimburse the applicant for the expense of gender reassignment surgery (*Van Kuck v Germany*).

Up until 2002, the law in the UK was that having undergone gender reassignment treatment, a transgendered person had no consequent right in law to be regarded as a member of the opposite sex from that into which he or she was born. Transsexuals were able to obtain most official documents (except birth certificates) such as passports, medical cards, driving licences and income tax forms in the new identity, but for the purposes of the law the person remained the biological sex at birth.

The position changed in 2002 when the ECHR departed from its previous case law and ruled that the UK's refusal to recognise the reassigned sex of a transsexual person and the denial of the right to marry was a breach of both Articles 8 and 12 of the Convention (*Goodwin v UK*).

The House of Lords consequently ruled that UK marriage laws were now incompatible with the Convention, and the Government introduced legislation to give effect to this judgment and the ECHR's ruling in the form of the Gender Recognition Bill (GRB). At the time of writing the GRB is being considered by Parliament and has passed though committee stage in the House of Commons.

The Gender Recognition Bill
The purpose of the GRB is to provide transgendered people with legal recognition in their acquired gender. Legal recognition will be achieved when a gender recognition certificate is issued by a Gender Recognition Panel made up of at least one legally

and one medically qualified member. The GRB does not require that the person has undergone gender reassignment treatment to qualify. Indeed, the GRB properly recognises that a person's gender identity, and not surgery, is the defining factor. The effect of obtaining a gender recognition certificate will be significant. For example, a male to female transsexual person will be recognised as a woman in English and Welsh law for all purposes including the criminal law, entitlement to state benefits and occupational pension schemes. Importantly, she will also be entitled to be issued with a new birth certificate reflecting the changed gender and will be able to marry someone of the opposite sex or enter into a civil partnership with someone of the same sex.

Applying for a Gender Recognition Certificate

The GRB sets out a procedure for application to a Gender Recognition Panel for a gender recognition certificate. A person can apply if they are:

- At least 18 years of age; and
- Living in the other gender; or
- Have changed gender under the law of a country or territory outside of the UK.

For a certificate to be granted the applicant must establish that he or she:

- Has or has had gender dysphoria; and
- Has lived in the acquired gender for a period of two years at the date of the application; and
- Intends to continue to live in the acquired gender until death.

The applicant must provide the necessary medical evidence from specified qualified medical practitioners confirming the diagnosis of gender dysphoria, and, where relevant, giving details of any treatment undergone or planned for the applicant. If the applicant has changed gender outside of the UK appropriate evidence of that change must be provided.

The applicant must also provide a statutory declaration stating that he or she:

- Meets the two-year qualifying period.
- Is or is not married.
- Any other information as required by the Secretary of State or the panel.

The panel must issue a full recognition certificate if these criteria are met. If the applicant is married, an interim certificate will be granted until the marriage is annulled or dissolved. If the panel refuses the application, there is a right of appeal on points of law.

Discrimination in employment

As has been stated earlier, there is statutory protection against discrimination for those who have undergone, plan to undergo or are undergoing gender reassignment. The relevant provisions are to be found in the SDA, which was amended in 1999. The provisions provide protection from discrimination in the fields of employment, discrimination in relation to barristers and advocates and in other fields insofar as they relate to the provision of vocational training.

The statutory definition of gender reassignment for the purposes of the SDA is as follows: 'a process undertaken under medical supervision for the purpose of reassigning a person's sex by changing physiological or other characteristics of sex, and includes any part of that process'.

It is unlawful for an employer to discriminate against a person undergoing, intending to undergo or who has undergone such a process in any of the following ways:

- Refusing to consider the person for employment.
- Refusing to offer the person employment.
- Offering the person employment on terms less favourable than for other people.
- Refusing to make provision for the person to be trained.
- Refusing to promote the person or transfer the person to another job.
- Giving the person less favourable employment benefits.
- Dismissing the person or causing the person any other detriment.

Where somebody is subjected to a detriment because of absence from work (for medical treatment), the test to be applied is whether a person is treated less favourably than he or she would have been if the absence were due to sickness or injury; or if the absence was owing to some other cause. Courts and tribunals must have regard to the circumstances of the case and consider whether it is reasonable for the person to have been treated less favourably.

Pre-operative transsexuals are in a weaker legal position, generally speaking, than post-operative transsexuals. Although there is no question that employers and others must not discriminate against those intending to undergo gender reassignment, in considering what amounts to less favourable treatment it does not follow that all such persons are entitled immediately to be treated as members of the sex to which they aspire. The status of transsexual does not automatically entitle the employee to be treated as a woman, with respect to toilet and other personal facilities. Thus, a formerly male employee cannot, by presenting as female, necessarily and immediately assert the right to use female toilets. On the other hand, a permanent refusal of the choice of toilets to someone presenting as a woman could be an act of discrimination even if the person has not undergone the final surgical intervention. A judgment has to be made by an employer – and a tribunal – as to when a male-to-female transsexual becomes a woman and is entitled to the same facilities as other women. This is said to depend 'on all the circumstances', including the stage reached in treatment, how the employee presents, and the views of other employees.

Once the GRB becomes law, for those whose change of gender has been recognised and a certificate issued there will be no question as to how they are to be treated, but there will be many persons in transition who do not qualify for the certificate. This should not prevent employers, in the interim, from making the necessary adjustments to preserve the privacy and dignity of the transsexual employee.

Genuine occupational requirements and exceptions

The exceptions relating to genuine occupational requirements also apply to transsexuals. Transsexuals may be lawfully denied jobs that involve intimate physical searches made pursuant to statutory powers, but only where there is a real and not theoretical possibility of having to carry out such searches. The Employment Appeals

Tribunal, for example, has held that this provision does not exclude transsexuals from serving as police constables, where the carrying out of intimate physical searches is mostly carried out in practice by doctors, although technically is part of a police officer's job.

Work done in private homes for specific purposes may also form a basis for refusing to employ transsexual people. In either case, however, the employer would have to establish the general occupational requirement and also that there were not reasonable alternative arrangements short of complete exclusion from the employment that could be taken.

Where the person is undergoing or intends to undergo gender reassignment, they can be excluded from work that involves living in premises provided by the employer where accommodation and facilities have to be shared, and where it is not reasonable for alternative arrangements to be made. Also excluded are claims in relation to jobs where the holder provides vulnerable individuals with personal services promoting their welfare, and where in the reasonable view of the employer, these services cannot be provided by a person undergoing gender reassignment.

These exceptions will have limited impact following the decision in *Goodwin* and the requirement to recognise the transgendered person in their current sexual identity. The GRB amends the SDA so that in the future these exceptions will not be available once the person has been recognised in the acquired gender and a certificate issued.

Marriage and family
Once the GRB becomes law, amendments to the marriage laws will mean that a transsexual person can marry according to their acquired gender, although it will remain a ground for annulment if one party married without knowledge of the previous gender. There is, however, no obligation on the Church of England or Wales to solemnise such marriages. Any previous marriage will have to be annulled or dissolved before full recognition is given so that there will be no retrospective recognition of past marriages.

It is somewhat of an anomaly that recognition of the changed gender does not affect the status of the person as the father or mother of a child, and parental rights and responsibilities remain the same. No provision has been made to allow for the children of transsexual fathers conceived through IVF to be registered on the child's birth certificate, continuing the position held not to be a violation of Articles 8 and 12 by the ECHR in 1996 (*XYZ* v *UK*).

Pensions and state benefits
Even before the GRB, it was held contrary to the Equal Pay provisions for the partners of a transsexual worker or a worker with a transsexual partner to be denied any work-related benefits including pension rights where the entitlement is dependent upon marriage. The European Court of Justice ruled in 2004 that following *Goodwin* UK domestic law denying transsexuals the right to change of a birth certificate and to marry should be disapplied where it had the discriminatory effect of excluding transsexual partners from receiving benefits under a pension because of their inability to marry (*KB* v *UK*).

These matters should be resolved once the GRB comes into force as it provides for transsexual people to be treated according to their acquired gender insofar as certain survivor's benefits are concerned including Widowed Mother's Allowance,

Widow's Pension, Widowed Parent's Allowance, incapacity benefit and retirement pensions. Because a number of these benefits are gender-specific and benefit women only, female-to-male transsexuals can also lose these entitlements after recognition has been granted.

Likewise a male-to-female transsexual will be entitled to a retirement pension at 60 while a female-to-male transsexual will not qualify until 65 and will lose entitlement if receiving the pension when the recognition certificate is issued.

10.6   DISABILITY DISCRIMINATION

The Disability Discrimination Act 1995 (DDA) is the first legislative attempt to address comprehensively the issue of discrimination against disabled people. The DDA is divided into six parts. Part 1 defines the meaning of 'disability' and 'disabled persons'. Part 2 deals with discrimination in employment. Part 3 deals with discrimination in other areas, namely, the provision of goods, facilities and services. Part 4 deals with education. Part 5 deals with public transport. Part 6 established the National Disability Council, which has now been superseded by the Disability Rights Commission.

The DDA has been brought into force in stages. The provisions relating to employment and the provision of goods and services came into force in November 1996. New duties on schools and other education bodies took effect in September 2002, and the requirement that service providers must look at making reasonable adjustments to physical barriers is effective as of 1 October 2004.

The framework of the DDA differs significantly from that of both the Sex Discrimination Act 1975 (SDA) and the Race Relations Act 1976 (RRA), as the DDA contains no general principle of equal treatment. Instead, under the DDA as from 1 October 2004 there are now five separate definitions of what constitutes discrimination: direct discrimination; disability-related discrimination, which may be justified; failure to make a reasonable adjustment; and victimisation; in addition there is also now specific protection against harassment. The notion of justification is incorporated into the definition of disability-related discrimination. This means that disability-related discrimination is only unlawful when a person is treated less favourably for a reason related to their disability, and when that reason cannot be justified under the DDA. As a result of this approach there are differing definitions of discrimination for the purposes of Part 2 and Part 3 of the DDA. A further difference from the SDA and RRA framework is that DDA does not recognise the concept of indirect discrimination as such.

The scope of the DDA is also more limited than that of the SDA and the RRA, and although the police, prison service, office holders, practical work experience, partners in firms, and barristers are all now covered, along with employees of firms employing fewer than 15 people, some exceptions will remain.

Meaning of disability
Section 1 of the DDA sets out the definition of 'disabled person'. To benefit from the DDA's protection, you must either be a person who has a disability or be a person who has had such a disability. In deciding whether you are a disabled person within the meaning of the DDA four questions fall to be considered:

1. Do you have a physical or mental impairment?
The terms physical or mental impairment are to be interpreted in their broadest sense. Frequently, medical evidence will be required in order to show whether or not there is a mental or physical impairment. Mental impairment is further defined in Schedule 1 paragraph 1(1) of the DDA as 'suffering from a mental illness which is clinically well recognised'.

2. Does the impairment affect your ability to carry out normal day-to-day activities in respect of at least one of the following?
Mobility, manual dexterity, physical co-ordination; continence; ability to lift, carry or otherwise move everyday objects; speech, hearing or eyesight; memory or ability to concentrate, learn or understand; or perception of risk or danger and does it have an adverse effect. The effect of medical treatment must be discounted. This means that the court or tribunal must try to determine the effect that the impairment would have without the treatment.

3. Is the adverse effect substantial?
Substantial means more than minor or trivial. There may be a cumulative effect.

4. Is the adverse condition long-term? Has it lasted or is it likely to last for one year or more?
Progressive conditions such as cancer and HIV are currently dealt with on the basis that a person with the condition is disabled as soon as the condition is symptomatic, provided that it is likely to result in a substantial adverse effect on their activities in the future. The Government's draft Disability Discrimination Bill 2003, however, proposes to change this so that progressive conditions constitute disability from diagnosis. If the Bill becomes law, this would provide protection under the DDA to more people from an earlier stage.

As with the SDA and RRA, the DDA requires a person who believes they have been discriminated against to make comparisons between the treatment they have received and the treatment received by a person who has not been discriminated against. The DDA is accompanied by, and must be read in conjunction with, a variety of Regulations and other materials. The latter includes 'Guidance on Matters to be Taken into Account in Determining Questions Relating to the Definition of Disability' and the new 'Code of Practice – Employment and Occupation' laid before Parliament on 20 May 2004, which replaces 'The Code of Practice for the Elimination of Discrimination in the Field of Employment Against Disabled Persons' as from 1 October 2004; neither of these are legally binding, but both should be taken into account when deciding cases under the DDA.

Employment
Discrimination in employment is dealt with in Part 2 of the DDA. Job applicants and contract workers, as well as employees, are among those protected by the DDA. Less favourable treatment, namely discrimination, is unlawful:

- In the arrangements made for appointing you as an employee;
- In the terms on which employment are offered to you;
- By refusing to offer you employment;
- In the terms of your employment;
- In the opportunities offered to you for training, promotion, transfer or any other benefit of employment;

- By refusing to offer you such opportunities; and
- By dismissing you or subjecting you to any other detriment.

From October 2004 'Direct discrimination' is defined as treating a disabled person less favourably, on grounds of a disabled person's disability, than a person not having that particular disability, whose relevant circumstances including his or her abilities, are the same as, or not materially different from, those of the disabled person.

'Disability-related discrimination', or less favourable treatment, is when an employer discriminates against you if, for a reason that relates to your disability, he or she treats you less favourably than they would treat a person to whom the reason does not apply and they cannot show that the treatment is justified.

The concept of 'disability-related' less favourable treatment under the DDA is different from that used in the RRA and the SDA, in that there is no requirement to compare 'like with like'. In both the RRA and SDA it is necessary to compare the treatment of the person alleging discrimination with the treatment of someone with their same characteristics, save for race or gender. Under the DDA, however, if you are alleging 'disability-related' discrimination against your employer you do not need to find such a comparator. All that is required is that you have been treated less favourably than others, where the reason for the treatment is related to your disability. For example, where an employee is injured at work, is off sick for five months and is then dismissed because his or her doctor cannot give a definite date for a return to work, providing the employee is found to be a disabled person within the meaning of the DDA, the dismissal is less favourable treatment under the DDA because it is for a reason relating to his or her disability. The employer will then have to show that the treatment/dismissal was justified, taking into account the duty to make reasonable adjustments. It would be irrelevant that the employer would also have dismissed a non-disabled person who had been off sick for five months, as the true comparator is a non-disabled person who has not been off sick. This is because the reason for the disabled person's sickness, and thus absence, is related to their disability, whereas this would not be the case for a non-disabled person who was off sick.

An employer also discriminates against you if he or she fails to provide such reasonable adjustments to the working environment as are required by the DDA. Examples of what a reasonable adjustment might be include physical alterations to the workplace as well as changes in work practices.

The duty to make reasonable adjustments arises where a feature of the workplace or working arrangements places you at a disadvantage compared to a person without the disability. If the reason for the less favourable treatment could be resolved by a reasonable adjustment to the working environment, then the employer's less favourable treatment is unlawful where the employer has failed to make the adjustment. It is not necessary that any adjustment is guaranteed to work, only that there is a substantial possibility that it will. As from 1 October 2004 the DDA no longer permits an employer to justify a failure to comply with the duty to make reasonable adjustments.

Victimisation occurs when a worker is punished or treated differently as a result of complaining about discrimination or raising the issue or doing any other 'protected act', and is the same as the victimisation provisions existing under the SDA and RRA.

There is a further category of discrimination, which is harassment. Harassment occurs where, for a reason related to the disabled person's disability a person engages in unwanted conduct which has the purpose or effect of:

- Violating the person's dignity, or
- Creating an intimidating, hostile, degrading, humiliating or offensive environment for him.

It is not necessary for an employer to know you are disabled before he or she can be guilty of unlawful discrimination; although the fact that an employer does not know and could not reasonably be expected to know, will be relevant in looking at whether they can justify their potential discrimination, for example, their failure to make reasonable adjustments.

Reasonable adjustments

Where any provision, criterion or practice applied by or on behalf of an employer, or any physical features of premises occupied by an employer, place you at a substantial disadvantage in comparison with persons who are not disabled, and the employer knows or could reasonably be expected to know that you have a disability and are likely to be adversely affected by the working arrangements or premises, then the employer must take such steps as are reasonable in all the circumstances to prevent the disadvantageous effect.

The duty to make reasonable adjustments is not limited to employers, but is also relevant to trade unions and employers' associations as well as users of contract workers. The duty is not a general one, however: it is owed to individual disabled persons when the relevant circumstances arise. If the employer does not know or could not reasonably be expected to know that an applicant or employee has a disability and is likely to be disadvantaged, then the duty is not imposed. However, the Code of Practice suggests a degree of positive enquiry is required from the employer. Thus an employer must do all he or she could reasonably be expected to do to inform him or herself of the position.

The DDA provides some illustrations of what steps might be taken by way of a reasonable adjustment. These include allocating some of your duties to another person; transferring you to fill an existing vacancy; altering your working hours and permitting absences from work for rehabilitation, assessment or treatment. Further, an employer is not obliged to take steps to make adjustments, he or she is only being required to take such steps as are reasonable in all the circumstances. The DDA provides a list of factors that will be taken into account in assessing whether an employer has acted reasonably in refusing to make an adjustment. These are:

- The extent to which the step would prevent the effect in question.
- The extent to which it is practicable for the employer to take the step.
- The financial and other costs which would be incurred by the employer in taking the step and the extent to which it would disrupt any of the employer's activities.
- The extent of the employer's financial and other resources.
- The availability to the employer of financial or other assistance with respect to taking such a step.

This list is not exhaustive and there may be additional factors that should be considered in determining reasonableness.

Justification

Most conduct which is potentially unlawful under Part 2 of the DDA cannot be justified as from 1 October 2004. 'Disability-related' less favourable treatment can only be justified if the reason for it is both 'material' to the circumstances of the particular case and 'substantial'. The Code of Practice explains that justification means that the reason has to relate to the individual circumstances in question and carry real weight and be of substance. Prior to the changes introduced in October 2004 the courts had decided that the employer has a wide margin of discretion in relation to justification, and tribunals should only interfere where the employer has acted outside that wide range.

However, from 1 October 2004, where an employer fails to comply with a duty to make a reasonable adjustment, then if that reasonable adjustment would have made a difference to the reason being used to justify the less favourable treatment, the treatment cannot be justified.

It is worth noting that while the cost of an adjustment may make it an unreasonable one to have to make, the average cost of an adjustment since the DDA has been in operation is £200. Many adjustments cost nothing at all. Advice and funding for adjustments is also available to employers through the 'Access to Work' scheme run by the Department for Work and Pensions (DWP) and accessible via job centres.

From October 2004 justification will only apply to 'disability-related' less favourable treatment; it will no longer be possible to justify a failure to make reasonable adjustments – either an adjustment will be reasonable or it will not.

Liability of employers and principals

An employer is responsible for acts of discrimination carried out by his or her employees in the course of their employment whether or not it was done with the employer's knowledge or approval. This is so unless the employer can show that he or she has taken such steps as were reasonably practicable to prevent the employees from committing the acts of discrimination complained of. The DDA also applies to contract workers and their principals.

Advertisements

Currently the DDA only provides that where a discriminatory advertisement has appeared and you have applied, and been rejected, for employment and you have made a complaint against that employer to the Employment Tribunal, the tribunal will assume that the decision is related to your disability unless shown otherwise. However, under the draft Disability Discrimination Bill 2003, it is intended that it will become unlawful to publish or cause to be published discriminatory advertisements.

Aiding unlawful acts

A person who knowingly aids another person to do an act made unlawful by the DDA is treated as if he or she had committed the acts of discrimination themselves. Such a person will have a defence if he or she has been told that the action is not discriminatory and it was reasonable for him or her to rely on such a statement.

Trades unions and trade associations

The DDA makes unlawful discrimination by trade organisations, which includes trade unions, organisations of employees, and organisations whose members carry out a particular trade or profession. The DDA prohibits discrimination in the terms upon which such an organisation is prepared to admit you to membership, and the refusal to accept an application for membership from you. The DDA prohibits discrimination in the case of a disabled person who is already a member of the organisation concerned in:

- The way in which the organisation affords you access to any benefit, or by refusing or deliberately omitting to afford you access to the benefit;
- By depriving you of membership, or varying the terms on which you are a member; and
- By subjecting you to any other detriment.

The provision of goods, facilities and services

Part 3 of the DDA prohibits discrimination against a disabled person in the provision of goods, services or facilities. The provisions include services provided by public authorities as well as those provided by private agencies or individuals, irrespective of whether or not there is a charge for the services concerned. Examples of the types of activities covered by the provisions of this part of the DDA include: communications, information services, hotels and boarding houses, financial and insurance services, entertainment facilities, training, employment agencies and the use of any public place. Education and transport services are dealt with separately under the DDA. Public authorities undertaking enforcement duties such as the police or prison service may also be excluded. Private clubs are also excluded, except on occasions where the club provides services to the public. However, there are proposals under the draft Disability Discrimination Bill 2003 to extend the scope of the DDA to cover private clubs acting in a private capacity.

Discrimination in respect of goods and services occurs when a service provider treats you less favourably for a reason that relates to your disability, and the treatment cannot be justified under the provisions of the DDA. The service provider also discriminates if he or she fails to provide you with a reasonable adjustment when required to do so under the DDA, and that failure cannot be justified. As such the DDA imposes a proactive and not a reactive duty.

Under the DDA the following discrimination is unlawful:

- Refusing to provide a service which is provided to, or which the organisation is prepared to provide to, members of the public without justification; or
- Treating you less favourably in the standard of service or in the manner in which the service is provided without justification; or
- Providing the service on less favourable terms without justification.

It is also unlawful for a person to fail to comply with the duty to make reasonable adjustments, so that the effect is to make it impossible or unreasonably difficult for you to make use of the goods, facilities or services. From 1 October 2004 it will also be unlawful discrimination if a service provider fails to make reasonable adjustments in the physical features of premises or to overcome physical barriers to access.

Justification

Justifications for otherwise discriminatory treatment are included in Part 3 of the DDA, and they are capable of excusing both a failure to provide a reasonable adjustment and 'disability-related' but not 'direct' discrimination. They are as follows:

- If the less favourable treatment is necessary in order not to endanger the health and safety of any person, including you.
- If you are incapable of giving informed consent or of entering into an enforceable agreement and for that reason the treatment is reasonable in that case.
- Where you have been refused service, this must be necessary because the provider of services would otherwise be unable to provide the service to members of the public.
- Where the less favourable treatment relates to the standard, manner or terms of which a service is provided, this must be necessary in order to provide the service either to you or to other members of the public.
- Where there is a difference in the terms on which the service is provided to you, this must reflect the greater cost to the provider of providing the service to you.

In order to be able to rely on the defence of justification, the service provider must be able to show that, in his or her opinion, one or more of the above conditions are satisfied and that, in all the circumstances of the case, it is reasonable for him or her to hold that opinion.

Reasonable adjustments

The duty on the service provider to make reasonable adjustments is quite different from the similar duty that applies to an employer or prospective employer. Service providers are required to take such steps as are reasonable in the circumstances to amend policies, procedures and practices; and to remove or alter physical features, or provide a reasonable means of avoiding them, or provide a reasonable alternative means of delivering the service where a disabled person would otherwise find it impossible or unreasonably difficult to use the service. The service provider is also under a duty to provide auxiliary aids or services wherever these would facilitate the use by disabled persons of such a service.

Where there are physical barriers to access, the service provider can respond in three specified ways:

- By removing or altering the physical feature concerned.
- By providing a reasonable means of avoiding the physical barrier.
- By providing a reasonable alternative means of delivering a service.

There are no provisions in this part of the DDA that set out the factors to be taken into account when determining the reasonableness of making adjustments. However, the Disability Rights Commission (DRC) has produced a new Code of Practice to accompany the new responsibilities under the DDA coming into force on 1 October 2004, which service providers will need to be aware of and implement. In relation to the reasonableness of making adjustments it is suggested that the following factors may be relevant:

- Whether taking particular steps would be effective in overcoming the difficulty that you face in getting access.
- The extent to which it is practicable for the service provider to take the steps.
- Financial and other costs of making the adjustment.
- The amount of disruption caused by taking the steps.
- Money already spent on making adjustments.
- The availability of financial or other assistance.

The Secretary of State has power to establish a financial ceiling on the extent of costs that it is reasonable for a service provider to incur in making adjustments. It is worth noting that nothing in the provisions of the DDA requires a service provider to take any steps that would fundamentally alter the nature of the service, facility or business provided or conducted.

Purchase or rental of premises

Under the DDA discrimination in the sale, letting, assignment, sub-letting or management of premises is unlawful. The definition of premises extends to land, business and residential properties. The behaviour prohibited is:

- Refusing to dispose of premises to you; or
- Offering the premises on less favourable terms to you; or
- The less favourable treatment of you in relation to any list of persons in need of premises of that description.

Discrimination against you is also prohibited:

- In the way in which you are permitted to make use of any benefits or facilities;
- By refusing to allow you the use of such benefits or facilities; or
- By evicting you or subjecting you to a detriment.

The provisions for the justification of the less favourable treatment outlined above are very similar to those permitted in relation to the general provision of goods, facilities or services. Private sale and small dwellings are excluded from these provisions, although the draft Disability Discrimination Bill 2003 proposes new powers to modify or abolish the small dwellings exemption. Currently there is no duty to make reasonable adjustments in this area, although again the draft Bill proposes changes that would require reasonable steps to be taken to provide auxiliary aids where these would allow or facilitate disabled persons' use of the premises or of any facility. Examples of what this could mean in practice would be the addition of items such as handrails and/or ramps, rather than making structural alterations to buildings.

Education

Education is covered in Part 4 of the DDA. As from September 2002 new duties have been introduced to provide greater support to disabled pupils in schools. The Special Educational Needs and Disability Act 2001 (SEN) amended the DDA to prevent discrimination against disabled people in their access to education. This introduces new duties in three main areas:

- The duty not to discriminate;
- The planning duties upon educational establishments;
- The Special Educational Needs (SEN) framework.

Disability discrimination duties
These are imposed on schools and bodies responsible for the provision of further or higher education. The duties are not to treat disabled pupils or students less favourably for disability related reasons, which is similar in scope to the duty placed on employers, trade unions or suppliers of goods and services; and to make reasonable adjustments to avoid putting disabled pupils at a substantial disadvantage, although this last duty is much more limited in scope. The DDA provides that disabled students may not be discriminated against in:

- The arrangements it makes for determining admission to the school, or further or higher education establishment;
- The terms on which it offers admission or by refusing an application for admission;
- The education or associated services provided for or offered to pupils at the school, or further or higher education establishment.

Planning duties
There are now requirements on Local Education Authorities (LEAs) and schools to improve access to education over time. LEAs must draw up accessibility strategies and schools must prepare accessibility plans, which have to address three areas of planned improvements in access for disabled students:

- Improvements in access to the curriculum;
- Physical improvements to increase access to education and associated services;
- Improvements in the provision of information in a range of formats for disabled students.

The governing body of a maintained school must explain in its annual report to parents the admission arrangements for disabled pupils, how the governing body helps disabled pupils gain access and what it will do to make sure they are treated fairly as well as information about the school's accessibility plan.

The SEN framework
The SEN framework is meant to make provision to meet the special educational needs of individual children. A child has special educational needs if he or she has a learning difficulty that calls for special educational provision. Children with a disability have special educational needs if they have any difficulty in accessing education and if they need any special educational provision to be made for them. Anything additional to or different from that which is normally available in schools in the area will count. The framework encourages children with special educational needs to be educated in mainstream schools so long as that is compatible with the efficient education of other children.

These amendments to the DDA increase parental access to information from the school, and extend the jurisdiction of the SEN Tribunal to deciding whether schools or colleges have discriminated under the DDA. It has been renamed the SEN and Disability Tribunal. If parents do not agree with the decisions made by the local education authority about the nature of their child's needs or about how their child's needs should be met they can appeal to the Tribunal.

See also Chapter 13.

Transport
Part 5 of the DDA is concerned with access to certain public transport vehicles and to the infrastructure of transport.

Licensed cabs
The Secretary of State has the power to define by regulations standards of access that new taxis will be required to meet. It will be an offence for a taxi driver to fail to comply with any such requirement or to drive a vehicle that fails to conform to the said Regulations. The equivalent requirements can be imposed on vehicles used under a contract to provide hire car services at designated transport facilities. Once the Regulations are in force, the licensing authority will not be able to grant licences to taxis unless vehicles comply with the accessibility provisions. The Secretary of State can grant licensing authority exemptions from the above licensing restrictions provided specified criteria are met. These are that, having regard to the circumstances in its area, it would be inappropriate to apply the access requirements and that the application of such standards would result in an unacceptable reduction in the number of taxis in the area.

The DDA itself requires taxi drivers to carry the disabled passenger while he remains in his wheelchair; not to make any additional charges for doing so; if the passenger chooses to sit in a passenger seat, to carry the wheelchair; to take such steps as are necessary to ensure that the disabled passenger is carried in safety and reasonable comfort, and to give such assistance as may be reasonably required. The DDA also imposes comparable requirements on taxi drivers in relation to the treatment of disabled persons with guide dogs and hearing dogs.

Buses, coaches and other public service vehicles
Under the DDA the Secretary of State has the power to make regulations covering access to public service vehicles for disabled persons to ensure that disabled persons can get on and off buses and coaches in safety and without unreasonable difficulties, and to be carried in such vehicles in safety and reasonable comfort.

The Public Service Vehicles Accessibility Regulations 2000 were brought into force on 30 August 2000. They apply to public service vehicles used to provide local or scheduled services with a capacity exceeding 22 passengers. Small buses and minibuses are therefore excluded, as are vehicles used for holiday tours, day trips or private hire and vehicles that are operated on a commercial basis for hire and reward rather than for 'public service'. However, the draft Disability Discrimination Bill 2003 proposes to end this exemption and require all providers of transport services to comply with the provisions of the DDA.

Rail
Rail Transport Regulations mirror those relating to public service vehicles. The Rail Vehicle Accessibility Regulations 1998 came into force on 1 November 1998.

They apply to new rail vehicles used on railways, tramways, monorail systems or magnetic levitation systems. The DDA does not provide for an end date to be set by which time all rail vehicles would have to comply with the regulations so practical implementation of disabled facilities may take many years.

Disability Rights Commission

The Disability Rights Commission (DRC) was formally launched on 25 April 2000. It has two sites based in London and Manchester. It consists of 15 commissioners, two-thirds of whom are disabled. The DRC had a budget of £11 million in its first year. The DRC operates in a similar way to the CRE and EOC. It has a statutory duty to work towards the elimination of discrimination against disabled persons and to promote the equalisation of opportunities for disabled persons in all fields of activity. In addition, the DRC is required to review the working of the DDA. It has the power to conduct formal investigations and to issue non-discrimination notices. It also has the power to enter into legally binding agreements in writing with a person believed to have committed or be committing an unlawful act.

One of the priorities of the DRC has been to establish an information and advice service for individuals and organisations. It has also established a conciliation service for claimants under the DDA. The DRC is empowered to provide assistance to individuals in bringing cases where the case raises a question of principle; where it is unreasonable to expect the individual complainant to deal with the case unaided; or where there is some other special circumstance that makes it appropriate to provide assistance.

The DRC has produced a number of Codes of Practice designed to enable individuals and businesses and other organisations to understand the provisions of the DDA and their rights and responsibilities under it.

Enforcing the DDA

A complaint of unlawful discrimination in relation to employment must be brought in the Employment Tribunal. Proceedings should be started within three months of the act of discrimination complained of, or of the last act if it is a continuing act of discrimination, such as an ongoing failure to make reasonable adjustments. The tribunal does have discretion to hear a case presented outside the time limits if it considers it just and equitable to do so. In deciding whether or not to allow a complaint presented out of time to proceed, the tribunal can take into account any relevant factors including the strength of the case, the reasons for the delay and the extent to which a person's disability has impeded the ability to bring a case within the prescribed time limits.

Claims in relation to unlawful discrimination in the provision of goods, facilities or services must be brought by civil proceedings in the County Courts. Claims must be brought within six months of the act of discrimination complained of. The courts have discretion to extend the time for bringing a complaint if they consider it just and equitable to do so. Also, where a disabled person has consulted the network of assistance agencies established under the DDA before the end of the six-month period, the time limit will be extended by a further two months.

Remedies

The Employment Tribunal can make such orders as it considers just and equitable including a declaration of the rights of the parties; compensation for foreseeable damages arising directly from the unlawful act of discrimination; damages for injury to feelings; and a recommendation that within a specified period of time the respondent takes reasonable action to remove or reduce the adverse effects on the complainant of any matter to which the complaint relates. In the County Court, injunctive relief is also available.

The DDA provides for limits to be prescribed as to the maximum amount of damages that can be awarded as compensation for injury to feelings under Part 3 (non-employment cases).

10.7   FURTHER INFORMATION

Race discrimination: Useful organisations

Commission for Racial Equality
St Dunstan's House
201–211 Borough High Street
London SE1 1GZ
Tel: 020 7939 0000
Fax: 020 7939 0001
info@cre.gov.uk
<www.crc.gov.uk>

Society of Black Lawyers
11 Cranmer Road
Kennington Park
London SW9 6EJ
Tel: 020 7735 6592

Runnymede Trust
Suite 106,
The London Fruit and Wool Exchange
Brushfield Street
London E1 6EP
Tel: 020 7377 9222
Fax: 020 7377 6622
Info@runnymedetrust.org.uk
<www.runnymedetrust.org>

Sex discrimination: Useful organisations

Advertising Standards Authority
2 Torrington Place
London WC1E 7HW
Tel: 020 7580 5555
Fax: 020 7631 3051
enquiries@asa.org.uk
<www.asa.org.uk>

Equal Opportunities Commission
Arndale House
Arndale Centre
Manchester M4 3EQ
Tel: 0845 601 5901
Fax: 0161 838 1733
info@eoc.org.uk
<www.eoc.org.uk>

Child Poverty Action Group
94 White Lion Street
London N1 9PF
Tel: 020 7837 7979
Fax: 020 7837 6414
staff@cpag.org.uk
<www.cpag.org.uk>

Rights of Women
52–54 Featherstone Street
London EC1Y 8RT
Tel: 020 7251 6577
Fax: 020 7490 5377
Text phone: 020 7490 2562
info@row.org.uk

Sexual orientation

Campaign for Homosexual Equality (CHE)
PO Box 342
London WC1X ODU
Tel: 077 023 2615
Fax: 020 8743 6252
Secretary@c-h-e.fsnet.co.uk
<www.c-h-e.org.uk>

GALOP (Gay Policing project)
PO Box 32810
London N1 3ZD
Tel: 020 7704 6767
Shout line: 020 7704 2040
Minicom: 020 7704 3111
Fax: 020 7704 6707
Info@Galop.org.uk
<www.galop.org.uk>

Lesbian and Gay Youth Alliance
<www.queeryouth.org.uk>
London switchboard: 020 7837 7324

London Friend
86 Caledonian Road
London N1 9DN
Office: 020 7833 1674
Tel: 020 7837 3337 (gay help line)
Tel: 020 7837 2782 (lesbian help line)

Outrage!
PO Box 17816
London SW14 8WT
Tel: 020 8240 022
Outrage@blueyonder.co.uk
<www.outrage.org.uk>

Stonewall Group
46 Grosvenor Gardens
London SW1W 0EB
Tel: 020 7881 9440
Fax: 020 7881 9444
Minicom: 020 7881 9996
Info@stonewall.org.uk
<www.stonewall.org.uk>

Terrence Higgins Trust
52–54 Gray's Inn Road
London WC1X 8JU
Tel: 020 7831 0330
Fax: 020 7242 0121
Info@tht.org,uk
<www.tht.org.uk>

Transgender discrimination: Useful organisations

Beaumont Society
(For Transvestites and Transsexuals)
27 Old Gloucester Street
London WC1N 3XX
Tel: 01582 412 220
<www.beaumontsociety.org.uk>

Disability discrimination: Useful organisations

The British Council of Organisations for Disabled People
Litchurch Plaza
Litchurch Lane
Derby DE24 8AA
Tel: 01332 295 551
Fax: 01332 295 580
Minicom: 01332 295 581
General@bcodp.org.uk
<www.bsodp.org.uk>

The Disability Alliance
1st Floor, East Universal House
88–94 Wentworth Street
London E1 7SA

Tel: 020 7247 8776
Fax: 020 7247 8765
<www.disabilityalliance.org>

Disability Rights Commission
DRC Contact Centre
Freepost
MID02164
Stratford-upon-Avon CV37 9BR
Tel: 0845 762 2633
Fax: 0845 777 8878
Text phone: 0845 762 2644
<www.drc-gb.org>

David Jones

11   The Rights of Immigrants

This chapter deals with:

- The framework of immigration control
- Persons who are subject to immigration control
- European Union Nationals and European Union Association Agreements
- Persons subject to domestic immigration control
- Refugees
- The European Convention on Human Rights
- British nationality
- Future developments
- Further information

11.1   THE FRAMEWORK OF IMMIGRATION CONTROL

United Kingdom law

The basic framework of UK immigration law – that is, the laws controlling the entry into, residence in and departure from the UK – is still provided by the Immigration Act 1971. This Act has been substantially amended and supplemented by several Acts including the Immigration Act 1988, the Asylum and Immigration Appeals Act 1993 and the Asylum and Immigration Act 1996, the Human Rights Act 1998 (HRA), the Immigration and Asylum Act 1999, and the Nationality, Immigration and Asylum Act 2002. Additionally, at the time of writing, the Asylum and Immigration (Treatment of Claimants etc.) Bill 2003 is being debated in Parliament. The Bill, if implemented in its current form, will effect further significant changes to the UK immigration and asylum system, particularly with regard to the range of remedies available to those subject to adverse immigration decisions.

There are also several other statutes that affect immigration control: these statutes range from nationality laws, which extend or restrict rights of abode (to the Falkland Islands and Hong Kong respectively), to the Immigration and Asylum Act 1999, which imposes fines on carriers who bring passengers without the required documents into the UK.

While the various Immigration Acts provide the statutory basis for the control of immigration, the powers granted under the Acts are very general. How those powers are to be exercised is set out in much more detail in the Immigration Rules. These Rules attempt to be wide-ranging and fairly precise, and try to cover every conceivable type of application and state the requirements for each. The Immigration Rules are not in the form of legislation or secondary legislation, but they are set out in House of Commons Papers and come into force unless disapproved of by Parliament. They are not, therefore, exposed to detailed, parliamentary scrutiny. The Immigration Rules currently in force are included in House of Commons Paper No. 395.

Situations and applications not covered by the Immigration Rules are dealt with 'outside the rules' and are at the discretion of the immigration authorities. In some cases, the immigration authorities have formulated policies to deal with certain categories of applications outside the Immigration Rules. The Home Office issues detailed instructions to immigration officers (including the Immigration Directorate Instructions, Asylum Policy Instructions, and the Operational Guidance Manual) on how they should operate the Immigration Rules. A disclosable version of these Instructions is published on the internet, as are some of the concessionary policies 'outside the rules'.

Not all of these policies are published. In some instances they come to public attention only because they have been referred to in Parliament, for example, when a Home Office minister explains the Government's approach or attitude to an issue. Alternatively, the existence of a policy may be referred to in a court or tribunal in individual cases. Some policies have been set out in letters from the Home Office to certain organisations. Other policies have been leaked. Consequently, in order to have a complete picture of the immigration law as it applies at any time, it is not only necessary to know the current legislative framework and the Immigration Rules, but also to know about the practice of the Home Office.

Since the end of 1996, the use of standard forms in making certain applications to the Home Office has been compulsory (this does not apply to applications governed by European Union (EU) law). The Home Office insists on the completion of all sections of the forms, the provision of answers to all questions and the supply of all original documents or a reasonable explanation offered. An incomplete or improperly completed application will be rejected, and this may lead to any complete application being received after the original leave has expired and the applicant becoming an overstayer without a right of appeal. With the exception of those applying for a residence permit under EU law, if the applicant seeks the return of his or her documents, for example, in order to be able to travel, the Home Office will consider the application to have been withdrawn.

European Union law

The law of the EU has an increasingly significant impact on domestic immigration law. This is not only due to the direct effect of EU laws on the free movement of persons, but also due to the co-ordination and harmonisation of matters of immigration and asylum that takes place at the political and policy level of the EU. Following the amendment to the European Community Treaty (the EC Treaty) by the Treaty of Amsterdam in May 1999, the EC Treaty now also contains a chapter expressly dealing with immigration and asylum matters, which includes the Schengen arrangements between the continental Member States of the EU. This does not, however, apply to the UK, which has opted out of the application of that part of the EC Treaty. The UK has reserved the right to opt into all or any measure adopted under that part of the EC Treaty.

11.2   PERSONS WHO ARE SUBJECT TO IMMIGRATION CONTROL

British citizens

British citizens are not subject to immigration control. This may seem obvious, but for the purposes of UK immigration law, not every person holding a British passport is also a British citizen. There are several other categories of people entitled to hold British passports, such as British Overseas Citizens, British Dependent Territories Citizens and British Protected Persons. These individuals are subject to immigration control and have to comply with the immigration rules on entry and residence. They are also not British nationals for the purpose of exercising EU free movement rights in other EU Member States.

Commonwealth and Irish citizens

Commonwealth citizens with the right of abode and Irish citizens travelling from Ireland are not subject to immigration control. Permission to enter is not required from an immigration officer and passports will not be stamped.

Commonwealth citizens retain the right of abode if they had that right under the Immigration Act 1971 immediately before 1 January 1983 and have not ceased to be Commonwealth citizens. Before 1 January 1983 the requirements for the right of abode for Commonwealth citizens were that:

- One of their parents was born in the UK.
- They were women who were married to a man who was a British citizen or a Commonwealth citizen with the right of abode.

European Union nationals

There are special regulations for EU nationals who are subject to only a limited form of immigration control. This exception also applies to other designated States with whom the EU has negotiated free movement agreements.

Others

Everybody else is subject to full immigration control and can only come to the UK with the permission of an immigration officer and if they come, must qualify under the immigration rules for a specific purpose.

11.3   EUROPEAN UNION NATIONALS AND EUROPEAN UNION ASSOCIATION AGREEMENTS

Member States

The EU comprises 15 Member States: Austria, Belgium, Denmark, Finland, France, Germany, Greece, Ireland, Italy, Luxembourg, the Netherlands, Portugal, Spain, Sweden and the UK.

The European Economic Area

The European Economic Area (EEA) took effect from 1 January 1994. It comprises the EU and two of the remaining countries from the European Free Trade Association (EFTA), Iceland and Norway. Switzerland and Liechtenstein, which are both in EFTA, are not yet part of the EEA.

Accession States

A further ten States gained accession to the EU on 1 May 2004. The new Accession States are: Cyprus, the Czech Republic, Estonia, Hungary, Latvia, Lithuania, Malta, Poland, Slovakia and Slovenia.

The terms of accession permit existing Member States to impose restrictions on free movement rights for nationals of accession countries. Consequently, only nationals of Cyprus and Malta will obtain unfettered rights of free movement on the date of accession. Nationals of the remaining States are subject to a number of severe restrictions – including either the suspension of rights for two years or the imposition of work permit requirements, or both – by all existing members of the Union including the UK.

At the time of writing the UK Government has indicated that it does not intend to limit the rights of accession nationals beyond requiring registration on entry, and engagement in continuous work for two years before benefits such as job seekers' allowance and income support can be claimed (the benefits threshold is currently six months for nationals of existing Member States).

Rights of free movement
Nationals of the Member States of the EU and of the EEA enjoy the right of free movement under EU law, and are only subject to limited immigration control. The right of free movement is primarily governed by the EC Treaty, regulations and directives adopted under it, and the European Economic Area Agreement.

Although immigration authorities are entitled to continue to check the passports or identity cards of those seeking to enter in order to ascertain identity and nationality, they are not entitled to ask any further questions about intention, availability of funds, sponsors or the like. The rights of residence of nationals of a Member State are dependent upon their qualification within one of the following categories:

- *Workers*: These include part-time workers and work-seekers, though the latter may be required to leave a Member State if they have not found employment and have no prospect of doing so within a certain period, usually six months.
- *The self-employed*: Those seeking to provide services in a Member State or those who travel to a Member State in order to receive services. The latter category includes tourists and 'window-shoppers'. The right of residence is, however, tied in its duration to the time required to provide or seek the services in question.
- *Students*: As long as they provide assurance, in the form of a declaration or otherwise, that they have sufficient funds not to become reliant on state benefits. In the case of students only spouses and children of a student also enjoy a (derived) right of entry and/or residence.
- *Retired persons*: Those who have retired after working and/or living in the UK for more than three years, or who have to stop work after more than two years in the UK due to permanent incapacity, or who, irrespective of length of residence or work in the UK, have to retire because of an accident at work or an occupational disease are entitled to remain permanently, as are their dependants. Those who seek to retire to the UK, not having worked here, enjoy a right of residence only so long as they can demonstrate that they have health insurance and sufficient funds not to have to rely on benefits.
- *All others*: As long as they can show that they have sufficient funds not to become dependent on benefits and that they have health insurance.

EU law and British nationals
Although the EU right of free movement is now an integral part of UK law (through the operation of the European Communities Act 1972, the Immigration Act 1988

and the Immigration (European Economic Area) Order 1994), UK immigration authorities and the courts have always maintained that domestic immigration law is completely independent from it and the two systems enjoy no point of contact.

Consequently British nationals can only invoke EU law in the UK on their return after exercising their right of free movement in another Member State. With this EU law dimension a UK national can, for example, invoke EU law in order to enable the admission of a foreign spouse to the UK without the need to obtain entry clearance.

British nationals who can invoke free movement rights are generally required to elect which system they wish to rely upon. This choice should be carefully considered as it can have short- and long-term consequences. For example, while opting for the EU route may ensure swifter entry than seeking to obtain entry clearance to the UK for the foreign spouse of a British national, the applicant may then find that choosing the European route means that they will not have a right to be considered for Indefinite Leave to Remain (ILR), which would have been considered after one year's residence as a spouse under domestic immigration rules but will only be considered after four years as the spouse of an EEA national.

Dependants
Spouses, children under 21 or those still financially dependent upon their parents, and dependant relatives (of the EEA national or the spouse) in the ascending line, such as parents and grandparents, all enjoy a right of free movement, which entails a right of entry and a right of residence (subject to certain conditions) as a matter of EU law.

This derived right of entry and residence is enjoyed irrespective of the nationality of the family member. However, Member States are entitled to, and the UK does, impose visa requirements upon family members of certain nationalities. However, unlike national visas, these visas (known as EEA family permits) are free of charge.

As a rule, the rights of residence of family members who are not EEA nationals or who do not otherwise have their own right to reside either under EU law or domestic law end as soon as the Member State national ceases to be resident in the UK. The children of an EEA national in education in the UK enjoy an independent right of residence to complete their education even if the parents leave.

When the family relationship with the EEA national is terminated by divorce, the dependant's entitlement survives during periods of separation and the decree nisi and only ceases with the decree absolute. The only exception to this rule applies to family members of those who have retired in the UK after having worked here for the requisite time.

The right of residence of family members may survive beyond the death of the EEA national where the spouse dies during his or her working life, for example, after continuous residence of two years, or as a result of an accident at work.

Residence documents
Individuals exercising their right of residence under EU law are entitled to apply for a residence permit (for EEA nationals) or a residence document (for dependant family members). These are not compulsory and cannot be a prerequisite for the exercise of the right of residence but there are significant practical advantages in obtaining one, as it provides convenient proof of one's status in the UK. Residence permits and

residence documents must be valid for at least five years and should be issued free of charge. They will be issued upon provision of evidence of nationality, family status or economic activity (or health insurance and sufficient funds).

EU law requires that a decision on the issue or refusal of a residence permit must be made as soon as possible and in any event within six months. Lengthy delays are unacceptable, and the European Commission has suggested that the appropriate time scale should be equivalent to the time it takes to issue British nationals with a passport.

Settlement

As a matter of domestic law, EEA nationals and their family members who have been resident in the UK for four years can apply for ILR, which is a prerequisite for naturalisation as a British citizen. However, under current practice of the Nationality Directorate of the Home Office, EEA nationals and those exercising EU free movement rights are presumed to be settled even without having applied for and been granted ILR. As a result, children born to those exercising EC free movement rights may be entitled to British nationality and a British passport.

Exclusion and enforcement

EEA nationals and their families can be prevented from entering the UK or be removed from the UK only if it is justified on grounds of public policy. The immigration authorities have to show that the individual is a present and sufficiently serious threat to a fundamental interest of UK society to warrant exclusion or removal. Such steps can only be justified on the basis of the individual's conduct itself and may not be taken for general preventative purposes.

In relation to any decision concerning entry to or residence in the UK, as well as the issue of or refusal of a residence permit or passport, the applicant is entitled either to appeal (where the decision is a decision to withdraw or not renew a residence permit) or to apply for judicial review. Here EU law itself requires certain procedural safeguards to be in place and limits the cases in which the right of appeal may only be exercised from outside the country.

European Union Association Agreements

Nationals of states of Central and Eastern Europe under Association Agreements with the European Union
Since the collapse of the Soviet bloc, the EU has concluded Association Agreements (so-called Europe Agreements) with the majority of Central and Eastern European States, including Bulgaria, the Czech Republic, Estonia, Hungary, Latvia, Lithuania, Poland, Romania, Slovakia and Slovenia.

The aim of these agreements was to prepare the named States for accession to full membership of the EU. This has now been achieved by ten of the 15 Accession States, who were admitted to the EU on 1 May 2004.

For those States such as Bulgaria and Romania who are in the second wave for accession, the EU Association Agreements continue to provide their nationals with a right of establishment in the UK on an exclusively self-employed basis. Though the rights are expressed in terms virtually identical to those granted to EEA nationals, they are expressed so as to exclude any employment.

Turkish nationals and their families

In addition to EEA nationals and their families, EU law provides for limited rights of free movement under a number of Association Agreements and Co-operation Agreements with non-EEA countries.

The oldest such Association Agreement is that with Turkey, dating back to 1963, with an Additional Protocol of 1970. The rights granted to Turkish nationals are not reflected either in the Immigration Rules or in the Immigration (European Economic Area) Order, and anybody seeking to benefit from them will therefore have to refer directly to EU law.

The Additional Protocol includes a 'stand-still' provision that has the effect of requiring Member States, including the UK, not to introduce any new restrictions on the rights of Turkish nationals to set up in business as self-employed persons after the Agreement gained effect in 1973. Only Turkish nationals who initially have been admitted to the UK and been allowed to take up economic activity can benefit from this right. Although it does not provide the Turkish national with a directly effective right of establishment (as is enjoyed by EEA nationals), the Additional Protocol means that the Immigration Rules that should be applied to them are not those in force now but the Immigration Rules in force in 1973, which imposed much less stringent requirements on being allowed to set up in business.

The rights of Turkish workers are laid down in a Decision of the Association Council, Decision 1/80 (unpublished). This provides Turkish workers, who have been in 'legal employment' in a Member State for a certain period of time, with a right to have their permission to work renewed and to have their right of residence renewed in line with the right to work. The requirement for 'legal employment' means that, again, in order to benefit, a Turkish national has to have been admitted to and must have been allowed to work under UK domestic law. This could, however, go well beyond those who have obtained a work permit and include au pairs and others allowed to work incidental to their primary activity. The scheme operates in these terms:

- One year's legal employment gives the Turkish worker a right to have his or her right to work renewed for the same employer and to have his or her leave to remain renewed in line. A Turkish national can only benefit from this right if he or she has been employed with the same employer for the whole year.
- Three years' legal employment with the same employer entitles a Turkish worker to a further renewal. At this stage the employer may be altered, although the occupation pursued must remain the same. Again, there is an entitlement to have the right of residence renewed in line with the right to work. In order to benefit from this right the Turkish national must have been employed with the same employer for three continuous years. If the Turkish worker has changed employment within the three years, she or he will either have to rely on the 'one year' rule, if one year has been achieved. If not, he or she will fall outside the benefit provided by Decision 1/80.
- After four years' legal employment, a Turkish worker is entitled to free access to the labour market, which includes a right to give up his or her job and to be a job seeker for a reasonable period of time, probably similar to that allowed for job seeking EEA nationals.

When calculating the period of time that has been spent in 'legal employment', time 'clocked up' solely as a result of a pending appeal will not be counted unless and until the appeal has been successful.

Nationals of the Maghreb states and others benefiting from European Union Law
In addition to the above Association Agreements, the EU has concluded a series of Association Agreements and Co-operation Agreements with countries including Algeria, Morocco and Tunisia. The significance of these agreements in immigration terms is extremely limited because they merely provide for non-discrimination clauses akin to those included for workers in the Europe Agreements. The provisions do not create either a right of entry or residence, nor do they create a right for nationals of these countries to have their leave to remain extended until the expiry of their employment contract.

11.4   PERSONS SUBJECT TO DOMESTIC IMMIGRATION CONTROL

Applicants falling into this category may be divided into two classes, visa and non-visa nationals.

Visa nationals normally require entry clearance whatever the purpose of their travel to the UK. Entry clearance can be obtained from a British Embassy or High Commission abroad and must be sought before travelling. The list of current visa countries is set out in Appendix 1 to the current Immigration Rules. The list is regularly amended, and care should be taken to ensure no changes have been made before travelling.

Entry clearance now has effect as leave to enter, substantially reducing the powers of immigration officers at the port of entry to refuse admission.

There are exceptions to the normal rule that visa nationals must seek entry clearance prior to travel. No visa is required for those seeking to re-enter during the currency of an original leave provided it was granted for a period in excess of six months or for those in possession of a visit visa who re-enter the UK within the validity of the original visa.

Non-visa nationals require entry clearance prior to arrival only if they intend to stay permanently in the UK or are coming for the purposes of work. This does not mean that admission is automatic, merely that a decision on an applicant's entitlement to enter under the immigration rules is performed at the point of entry to the UK rather than prior to their travel.

Non-visa nationals can apply for an 'entry certificate' prior to travelling, which is equivalent to an entry clearance, and possession of which substantially reduces the prospect of being refused admission on arrival in the UK.

Coming to settle
Normally, only the close relatives of people already settled in the UK (that is, people allowed to stay permanently) will be allowed to settle with them. Applicants must get entry clearance and satisfy other conditions before travelling. There are still long delays in processing these applications, particularly those submitted in India. Most people will be allowed to come only if their relatives can show that the person joining them can be supported and accommodated 'without recourse to public

funds'. Public funds for immigration purposes are exhaustively defined by the Immigration Rules.

Once an individual has been granted ILR or settlement there are no further immigration restrictions on what they can do in the UK. They are able to work or set up in business without needing any extra permission. If they leave the UK, they will be allowed in again without requiring entry clearance provided they have not been away for more than two years and that they confirm they are returning to stay. People who were settled and have been away for more than two years may still be allowed to settle again in certain circumstances, for example, if they have lived in the UK for the majority of their life.

ILR can now be revoked, however, where it is determined that status was acquired by deception, or where the holder's continued presence in the UK is considered a threat to national security. An in-country right of appeal exists in such cases.

Spouses

To gain admission as a spouse capacity it must be proved to an entry clearance officer that:

- You are the husband or wife of a person present and settled in the UK.
- You intend to live together permanently with your settled spouse.
- You have met; and
- There is adequate support and accommodation for yourselves and your dependants without reliance on public funds.

When an application is successful, the applicant will be allowed in for two years. Before the end of the second year, an application to the Home Office for settlement or ILR should be made. To qualify the Home Office must be persuaded that the couple still intend to stay together and can support and accommodate themselves without relying on public funds before this is granted.

English and Welsh law and the Immigration Rules do not recognise polygamous marriages for the purposes of seeking entry to the UK as a spouse.

Unmarried couples

The immigration rules now facilitate admission to the UK for unmarried couples. The conditions for admission, while comparable to those applicable to spouses in some respects, are more demanding. The principal requirements are that:

- You are the unmarried partner of a person present and settled in the UK and you have lived together in a relationship akin to marriage for two years.
- Your partner has a right of abode or ILR and you have lived together in a relationship akin to marriage for four years; and
- Any previous marriages or similar relationships have permanently broken down.
- You are not related by blood.
- You intend to live together permanently with your partner.
- There is adequate support and accommodation for yourselves and your dependants without reliance on public funds.

A period of two years' leave to enter will generally be granted following a successful application. As with spouses, an application for ILR may be submitted at the end of the two-year period, which will be granted provided the Home Office is persuaded that the relationship is subsisting, the couple intend to remain together permanently and there will be no recourse to public funds.

Domestic violence

Persons admitted to the UK as a spouse or unmarried couple whose relationships permanently break down as a result of domestic violence may still be able to secure ILR even where they have failed to complete the initial period of probationary leave. This is because of a 'domestic violence concession' announced by the Home Office in July 1998, which may help women who have been the victims of domestic violence. Applicants must provide evidence, the nature of which is specified by the Home Office, which establishes that the violence complained of caused the breakdown of the relationship. Qualification in this category is not easy as the evidential requirements are strictly imposed, and may include the production of police reports, exclusion orders and medical records of injuries.

Fiancés and fiancées

In order to come to the UK to get married an applicant has to meet similar criteria to spouses, and in addition show that he or she intends to get married soon after arrival in the UK. If granted entry clearance, the applicant will be allowed entry for six months, during which time he or she is expected to get married. Those admitted in this category will not be allowed to work until they get permission from the Home Office to stay. If successful, they will be granted permission to stay for two years, after which they will be granted settlement if they continue to satisfy the requirements.

Children

Children under 18 may be allowed to join parents in the UK (or to join one parent if the other parent is dead) if:

- They obtain entry clearance.
- Both their parents (if living) are settled in the UK.
- The parent(s) can adequately support and accommodate the child without reliance on public funds.

If children are coming to join one parent and the other parent is still alive but not coming to live in the UK, or coming to join a relative other than a parent, it must be proved either that:

- The parent living in the UK has had sole responsibility for the child's upbringing.
- There are serious and compelling family or other considerations making the child's exclusion from the UK undesirable.

The rules are difficult to satisfy. In practice, however, they are not interpreted so strictly for children under 12 coming to join their mothers.

The term 'sole responsibility' is not interpreted literally. It is acknowledged that to some degree a delegation of responsibility must occur as a result of physical separation. To determine whether the rule is satisfied it is necessary to look at what is done in the child's life, by whom and whether it has been done at the direction of the UK-settled parent. Evidence of protracted financial support, genuine interest and affection and regular consultation between the settled parent and the overseas carer as to matters of schooling, upbringing and activities may fulfil the requirement.

The 'serious and compelling considerations' criteria is stricter still. Factors include: evidence of the incapacity and/or unwillingness of the carer overseas to continue to look after the child, the child's living conditions, the particular vulnerability of younger children and the importance of maintaining family unity.

Adoption
It has long been possible for adopted children under the age of 18 to enter the UK where it can be demonstrated that the adoption has occurred in accordance with the decision of a competent administrative authority or court in the country where the child is resident, and where the other elements of the Immigration Rules are met (see below).

Since 1 April 2003 'de facto' adoption has been formally permitted by the Immigration Rules, which allow the admission of adopted children from countries where no legal adoption procedure exists, or where the system operating is not recognised by the UK. A de facto adoption will be regarded as having taken placed where the adoptive parent(s) can show that:

- They have lived together abroad for a period of 18 months.
- They have cared for the child for the 12 months immediately before the application for entry; and
- They have assumed the role of the child's parents and there has been a genuine transfer of parental responsibility.

Regardless of which of the adoption categories into which the child falls all parents seeking leave to enter must also demonstrate that:

- The adoption took place because the natural parents were unable to care for the child.
- The child has lost or broken ties with the natural family.
- That the reason for the adoption was not simply to bring the child to the UK.
- That the child can be adequately maintained and accommodated without recourse to public funds.

If a child in any of the above categories is deemed to be leading an independent life, is married or has formed an independent family unit before reaching the age of 18, he or she will not be eligible to be admitted under the Immigration Rules concerning 'children'.

Parents and grandparents
Parents and grandparents over 65 years can join children or grandchildren settled in the UK if it can be demonstrated that:

- They are a widow or widower (separated parents are equated with widow), or a couple one of whom is over 65; or
- They have remarried but cannot look to the spouse or children of your second marriage for financial support; and
- They are wholly or mainly financially dependent on children in the UK.
- There are no other close relatives in the country of origin to turn to for care and support.

- They and their spouse can be supported and accommodated by their children in the UK without reliance on public funds.

Home Office guidance establishes that elderly parents and grandparents in this category should be granted ILR without detailed enquiry where a reliable undertaking of support has been given by the settled child.

Admission for dependant parents and grandparents aged less than 65 years in this category is more problematic. Persons falling into this category must demonstrate that they are 'living alone in the most exceptional compassionate circumstances' in order to qualify for entry. Isolation and social stigma as a result of separation from family, high crime rates in the home area, poor living conditions and the distress caused by separation from UK settled family are among factors that may cumulatively meet the test. Physical isolation is not a prerequisite.

Children over 18 and other relatives

Other relatives wanting to join family in the UK have to get entry clearance, and have to show that they are related as claimed to someone settled in the UK. It must also be shown that they have been financially dependent on this relative, that they can be supported and accommodated without recourse to public funds, and that they were living alone in the most exceptional compassionate circumstances without other close relatives to turn to.

These criteria apply only to sons and daughters over the age of 18, and to the sisters, brothers, uncles and aunts of people settled in the UK who generally qualify only when they are over 65. It is very rare for anyone to qualify under this rule.

Appeal rights

Refusal of entry clearance
A refusal of entry clearance in any of the above categories will attract a right of appeal exercisable from overseas.

Refusal of leave to enter
An applicant arriving at a port of entry in the UK with entry clearance who is then declined leave to enter also possesses a right of appeal and may remain in the country while pursuing the remedy. However, should an applicant requiring entry clearance arrive at a UK port of entry without the required leave, he or she will be refused leave to enter automatically and will have no right of appeal against the decision. Should a human rights ground be asserted, however, and the right to family life could likely be invoked in all of the above categories, then an in-country right of appeal will be generated if the refusal of leave to enter is nonetheless maintained. The prospects of successfully prosecuting such a case are minimal, however, unless it can be shown that there are compelling reasons why entry clearance could not be obtained prior to travel, the UK courts being committed to maintaining the integrity of the immigration system and what they would perceive to be merely queue-jumping.

Refusal of extension or variation of leave
For persons in the above categories seeking to extend an initial grant of limited leave, or persons admitted to the UK in a different capacity who are endeavouring to vary their status, provided that the respective application is submitted during the

currency of the original leave, any refusal will be able to be appealed. Additionally, should the existing leave expire while a decision is outstanding, the applicant can remain in the UK lawfully and the conditions applicable to the original admission continue to apply. If an adverse decision is reached and should the applicant appeal, leave is again effectively extended on identical conditions until the appeal process is concluded and will include time spent in the UK exercising appeal rights.

Coming to work

The categories of entry clearance for the purposes of work have been radically extended in recent times as the Home Office seeks to achieve its dual objectives of facilitating managed migration while deterring asylum seekers and those asserting protection needs under the European Convention on Human Rights (the Convention).

Work permit

Work permits must be obtained before travel from Work Permits UK (WPUK), although there is now facility to switch into this category by persons with leave to enter in other employed capacities. It is the employer's responsibility to obtain the permit and demonstrate that the UK labour market will not be adversely affected. The employer must be an active trading entity in the UK, and both the position and the employee must meet specific skills standards:

- A degree-level qualification.
- A Higher National Diploma-level occupational qualification entitling a person to do a specific job.
- A general HND-level qualification plus one year's work experience.
- A high level of skill or specialist skills acquired through doing the type of job for which the permit is sought for at least three years (National Vocational Qualification Level 3 or above).

A work permit is issued for one individual and for one post, and is valid for up to five years. It is specific to the employer and position in respect of which the application was made.

Certain professions are regarded as Shortage Occupations. Admission for people in these categories is simplified. WPUK publish a list that is updated and amended regularly.

The spouse and the children under 18 of a work permit holder may be allowed to come to the UK to join him or her as long as both parents are living or coming to live in the UK and they can be supported and accommodated without recourse to public funds. They must get entry clearance before coming and will be allowed to stay for the same length of time as the work permit holder.

Where a permit is refused there is a right to a review by a senior officer but no right of appeal.

Some work does not require a work permit. Ministers of religion, missionaries, journalists working for overseas newspapers, servants of diplomats, people working for overseas governments and international organisations, among others, do not need a work permit, but still have to get permission before they come.

Leave to enter may be granted to writers or artists if they can show that they can support and accommodate themselves from the proceeds of their art or writing and any savings without having to take any other work or to claim benefits.

Highly Skilled Migrants Programme

The Highly Skilled Migrants Programme (HSMP) was introduced as an inducement to attract the best-qualified foreign talent to the UK. The programme is based on a point-scoring system. Applicants must accrue a total of 65 points, with marks being allocated for age, higher education qualifications, previous work experience, prior earnings, and significant or exceptional achievement. Points can also be gained through the qualifications possessed by the applicant's partner.

Those that achieve the required number of points must also:

- Demonstrate an ability to pursue a career.
- Possess an offer of employment, have registered with recruitment consultants, or have surveyed the UK labour market to show available positions in their profession through the production of appropriate job advertisements.
- Produce a business plan if seeking to establish themselves in business.
- Be able to maintain and accommodate themselves without recourse to public funds.
- Demonstrate a competence in English.

Applications are processed in the UK and where successful will attract an initial grant of 12 months' leave to enter or remain. Leave is not particular to any one employer.

If the application is made for entry clearance under the HSMP while outside the UK, there is no right of appeal against a refusal, only a right to a maximum of two reviews. For those persons legally present in the UK seeking to change to HSMP a right of appeal may result from a negative decision depending on the category of their initial entry.

Working holidaymakers

Commonwealth citizens between the ages of 17 and 30 who wish to enter the UK for the purposes of employment and vacation may seek entry clearance as Working Holidaymakers (WHM). To qualify applicants must:

- Be unmarried, or married and entering with a person who also meets the requirements.
- Have the means to pay for an onward journey.
- Be able to maintain and accommodate themselves without recourse to public funds.
- Intend to take employment incidental to the holiday.
- Not have dependant children who will reach five years of age before the leave.
- Have no commitments that will require them to earn a regular income.
- Intend to leave the UK at the end of the working holiday.

Leave to enter will be granted for a maximum of two years. WHM can vary to work permit employment after 12 months and to HSMP before 12 months. Those who are refused entry clearance or leave to enter in this capacity have a right of appeal.

Business persons, innovators and investors

The factor common to the following categories is their objective, namely to attract inward investment into the UK to the benefit of the UK economy.

Business persons: Applicants who have £200,000 to invest in a UK venture may be admitted in this capacity provided they can show that:

- There is a genuine need for the investment.
- It will create two jobs for UK residents.
- That they will be actively involved in management and will be an equal or majority shareholder.
- That they can maintain and accommodate themselves without public funds for the duration of their stay.

Innovators: This category is directed at the 'e-economy' and emerging sciences. There is no minimum investment level and so it is more attractive to young, talented entrepreneurs. Qualification is assessed on a points-based system with a 100-point threshold. Points are scored on the basis of the applicant's personal characteristics, business plan, and the potential economic benefit of the project to the UK.

Investors: Individuals with a personal wealth of £1,000,000 who are prepared to make a minimum investment of £750,000 in the UK can seek to enter as investors. They cannot take employment if admitted in this category but do have the freedom to establish themselves in business if they have further funds.

Applications under these categories are referred to the Home Office business casework team. If successful an initial period of 12 months' leave will be granted, which can subsequently be extended for a further three years and will eventually lead to settlement.

Coming for a short stay

Visitors

Applicants wanting to visit Britain must satisfy an immigration officer that they are seeking entry for a period of less than six months, that they intend to leave at the end of that period, and that they have enough money to support and accommodate themselves for the length of the visit without needing to work or to claim benefits. It is acceptable to be supported and accommodated by someone who lives in the UK, but an applicant may be asked detailed questions about the relationship, what they do in the UK and how they can support and accommodate the applicant. Immigration officers may also look at the applicant's personal circumstances, such as education, employment and family ties, and form a view about the 'incentive to return' to the applicant's country at the end of the stay.

If the applicant is a visa national, they need to get a visa in advance; if not, they can arrive at a port or airport and seek admission there. Six months is the longest time allowed to a visitor. Applications for extensions as a visitor will be refused, except in special circumstances such as illness, and may jeopardise future visits.

Business visitors

The requirements for entry are generally the same as for regular visitors. People admitted on this basis cannot engage in employment or 'productive work' in the UK, and there is no distinction between paid and unpaid. Entry is designed to facilitate attendance at meetings, trade fairs, to negotiate and complete contracts with UK businesses, or to undertake fact-finding missions, checking detail or examining goods, and receive training. Leave is granted for a maximum of six months and is subject to the usual maintenance and accommodation requirements.

Study
Those who want to study may be allowed to come to the UK if they can show that they have been accepted for a full-time course of study at a recognised college or independent (fee-paying) school, that they have the money to pay the fees and to live in the UK without needing to work or to claim benefits, and that they intend to leave the UK at the end of their studies. 'Full-time' normally means at least 15 hours of daytime classes per week, studying one subject or related subjects.

Overseas students have to pay fees that cover the full cost of their courses and are not usually eligible for local authority grants.

A student will normally be allowed entry for one year or the duration of the course, whichever is shorter, and can apply to the Home Office to extend this time to continue a course. If a student has not yet been accepted by a college he or she may be allowed in for a short time in order to enrol and can then apply to the Home Office for an extension.

A student wanting a short period of post-qualification training or on-the-job experience may be allowed to stay on as a trainee on the understanding that this is temporary and that a transfer to ordinary employment will not be allowed. If a student has spent more than four years on short courses of under two years, or appears to be chopping and changing courses with no end in sight, or has not been attending studies regularly, an extension will be refused.

Students are permitted to take part-time or holiday jobs provided their college does not object and provided permission is first obtained from the Department of Employment.

The spouse of a student and children under 18 may be permitted to live here for the period of study, as long as they can be supported and accommodated without recourse to public funds. The family of a student does not have a right to stay independently of the student. Where the student is to be in the UK for more than a year, permission may be obtained for the spouse to take up employment.

Control after entry, appeals and enforcement action

Registration with the police
Aliens who are over 16 and who are 'relevant foreign nationals' normally will be required to register with the local police where they are admitted for purposes of employment for longer than six months, or for longer than six months as an au pair, a student, a business person or self-employed, an investor or person of independent means or a creative artist or the spouse or child of such a person. A 'relevant foreign national' includes the citizens of countries listed in Annex 2 to the Immigration Rules, stateless persons and those holding non-national travel documents. This requirement may also be imposed on any other foreign national aged 16 or over who has been given limited leave to remain, where exceptionally it is thought necessary to ensure compliance with the conditions imposed on the leave. The police have to be informed of the individual's name, date of birth, nationality, marital status, address, occupation and immigration status. They must be informed of any future changes. This requirement will only be lifted if the individual is later allowed to stay permanently.

Powers of arrest

Police constables and immigration officers have the power to arrest, without warrant, anyone who has or whom they suspect has committed an immigration offence. The Asylum and Immigration Act 1996 increases the number of immigration offences, the powers of search and arrest in relation and the penalties for immigration offences, while the Immigration and Asylum Act 1999 has increased the powers of arrest, search and fingerprinting.

It is a criminal offence not to give information to an immigration officer, or to give false information or documents. There is effectively no right of silence as the responsibility is on the individual to show that he or she qualifies for the status being claimed under the law. The very wide power under the immigration laws allows for the investigation and detention of suspects under these administrative provisions who do not benefit from the same level of rights as others. This leads to frequent questioning of black people about their immigration status when they come into contact with the police for any other reason, often when there is no other cause for suspicion.

The Codes of Practice under the Police and Criminal Evidence Act 1984 do not apply to immigration officers, although they have agreed to follow them voluntarily. See also Chapter 5.

Those who knowingly remain longer than they have been allowed by immigration officers or the Home Office without asking permission become 'overstayers' and commit a criminal offence. It makes no difference whether they have overstayed for many years or for a few days. They can be arrested and appear before a Magistrates' Court, which can impose a fine, a sentence of imprisonment or recommend that the person be deported.

Those who are not British citizens, or Commonwealth citizens with the right of abode, or Commonwealth or Irish citizens who settled in the UK before 1 January 1973 and who have lived in the UK ever since, can be recommended for deportation by a court if convicted of any crime for which the penalty could be imprisonment, even if they have previously been allowed to stay permanently. Special conditions apply where the individual recommended for deportation is an EEA national or the family member of such a national. There is a right of appeal against this as part of the sentence. The recommendation is not binding, and it is up to the Home Office whether to carry out the recommendation. Unless the court specifically directs release from detention, the individual will be detained while the Home Office makes its decision.

Administrative removal

The Home Office can instigate the removal of people subject to immigration control for: entering illegally, overstaying, for breaking other conditions of stay, or for obtaining leave to enter by deception. There is no discrete, merits-based right of appeal on this basis unless human rights issues are raised in the course of the initial application.

Deportation

The Home Office can also decide to deport someone on the grounds that his or her presence is 'not conducive to the public good'. This is a very vague term that can include people who have been convicted of a criminal offence but whom the court did not recommend for deportation, or people who are alleged to have made a marriage of convenience. There is a right to an immigration appeal, but if the Home Secretary decides that your presence is non-conducive on the grounds of national security, that appeal is to the Special Immigration Appeals Commission (SIAC) rather than to the adjudicator and the Immigration Appeal Tribunal (IAT).

Once any appeal has been exhausted, the Home Secretary can sign a deportation order and the individual can be sent out of the country. While the order is in force, they cannot return to the UK. They can apply for the order to be revoked, either to the UK Embassy or High Commission in their own country or to the Home Office, but the order is not normally revoked until it has been in force for at least three years. If the order is revoked, the applicant is not entitled to return, but only to apply to return if he or she can satisfy the immigration rules.

Persons can be treated as illegal entrants either because they entered the country without being questioned by immigration officers or because it is alleged that they, or even another person, misled immigration officers or did not disclose information that was relevant and, therefore, they should not have been allowed entry.

Voluntary departure
There are also provisions for fares to be paid for people settled in the UK who want to return to their countries of origin if it is 'in that person's interest to leave the UK'. People receiving in-patient treatment in mental hospitals may be sent back, under section 90 of the Mental Health Act 1983, to receive treatment in their country of origin, again if it is 'in the interests of the patient to remove him'. No definition of this is given, and there are no legal safeguards against these powers.

11.5   REFUGEES

Government policy
Hostility towards refugees is now pervasive, with popular misconceptions about refugees being reinforced by politicians, who demand tough action against 'bogus refugees and economic migrants'. Deterrence and disbelief are as a result the watchwords of the present asylum system. The plain object of the Immigration and Asylum Act 1999, the Nationality, Immigration and Asylum Act 2002 and the Asylum and Immigration (Treatment of Claimants etc.) Bill being debated by Parliament at the time of writing, together with the mass of rules and policy statements that give them effect, is unquestionably the construction of a system that actively seeks to deter those seeking refuge from persecution from choosing the UK, and dehumanises any who do. These dual objectives are achieved through the combination of a variety of mechanisms including: the imposition of restrictive visa controls, criminal sanctions on those assisting entry, ever more stringent sanctions on carriers found to have conveyed asylum seekers, the operation of an escalating detention estate, a stigmatising and demoralising assistance programme, and increasingly restrictive access to independent review of adverse decisions.

Qualification
A refugee is defined by the Convention Relating to the Status of Refugees 1951 (CSR) as someone who, being outside his or her own country, has a 'well-founded fear of being persecuted for reasons of race, religion, nationality, membership of a particular

social group or political opinion'. The CSR is not part of domestic law but the Asylum and Immigration Appeals Act 1993 states that nothing in the immigration rules and practice should contravene the CSR.

The burden is on the applicant to demonstrate that he or she qualifies for protection under the CSR. The threshold is not high. In principle the applicant needs only to establish that there is a reasonable likelihood that he or she will encounter persecution if he or she is returned to his or her home country.

Article 3 of the Convention provides an absolute prohibition on torture, inhuman and degrading treatment. Qualification under Article 3 of the Convention is also ordinarily contemplated by the Home Office pursuant to an application for asylum. The protection afforded by Article 3 and the tests and standards of proof required to be satisfied in order to secure qualification are considered to be identical to qualification under the CSR, except that Article 3 does not require an applicant demonstrate that a risk exists for a particular reason.

Application procedure

In-country applicants for asylum must now attend Immigration Nationality Department offices in either Croydon or Liverpool in person in order to have their applications recorded. Those claiming asylum while still in the transit area at a port, will be processed there.

Bio-data is taken at the point of application and initial screening interviews are performed to determine the mode of entry in order to decide whether the UK is the State responsible for processing the asylum application, and whether the applicant is entitled to support and accommodation. Asylum seekers can also have their finger-prints taken. Most applicants are then granted temporary admission to the UK having been screened, with conditions attached requiring residence at a specified address and signing on.

Particular categories of applicant are detained and a substantial number of these are transferred to the Oakington Reception Centre in Cambridgeshire, where their cases are subject to fast track processing. They will be detained at the reception centre throughout the initial assessment period, which usually lasts for seven to ten days. The House of Lords has held that this procedure has been deemed to comply with Article 5 of the Convention, which prohibits arbitrary detention.

All applicants are now required to complete a statement of evidence form (SEF). This statement will be issued at the point of application and must be returned complete within 14 days of receipt. Failure to return the form in time may lead to an application being refused for non-compliance. An interview with an Immigration Officer should follow, at which enquiry is generally limited to requests for elaboration and/or clarification of matters referenced in the SEF statement. Attendance is mandatory. Processing time has been substantially reduced with applications in mid-2004 not uncommonly being determined at first instance within five to six weeks.

Assuming the Home Office do decide to refuse, the applicant will have ten working days in which to submit grounds of appeal.

Third country removal

Where it is established in the course of the Home Office's enquiry into the claim that the applicant travelled over the territory of another EU Member State (or designated territory) and had an opportunity to claim asylum there, then the UK may make enquiries of the authorities in that State to determine whether the applicant can be removed there.

Support and accommodation

The Home Office now administers benefits and accommodation for asylum seekers through the National Asylum Support Service (NASS). With few exceptions those seeking asylum are excluded absolutely from obtaining support from the welfare state. To qualify asylum seekers have to show that they are without adequate accommodation and unable to support themselves to the extent that they are destitute.

The support is based on providing the equivalent of 70 per cent of the value of income support and dispersing them out of London and the South East to areas where there is a ready supply of empty properties. Initially it was possible to opt for maintenance only, allowing applicants to remain with friends and family settled in the south of the country. Recent reforms prevent this opt-out and applicants either take the package of funding and accommodation or nothing at all.

Under section 55 of the Nationality, Immigration and Asylum Act 2002, to ensure access to NASS assistance it is imperative that claims for asylum are made 'as soon as reasonably practicable' after arrival in the UK (currently defined by the Home Office as within 72 hours of entry) as a failure to do so may lead to a refusal of all forms of support and accommodation for the duration of the claim. Where this refusal occurs, assistance will only be reinstated if it can be established, on an application for judicial review, that the decision was unlawful, or the applicant's physical and emotional condition deteriorates to a point at which a breach of Article 3 of the Convention can be established. It should be noted that it became clear early on that the Home Office practice was to interpret section 55 very strictly, and many asylum seekers found themselves without food or shelter. As a result there have been a number of higher court challenges concerning whether someone has claimed asylum quickly enough, as well as which point the Article 3 'inhuman and degrading treatment' threshold is met once someone has been refused support and becomes destitute. There is no right of appeal against a refusal to provide support, and the only way of challenging such a decision is by using judicial review. In some circumstances, if there is a real danger of a vulnerable person becoming destitute imminently, which may breach his or her rights under Article 3, the court may grant emergency injunctive relief compelling the Home Office to accommodate him or her.

Where support is granted the applicant will remain eligible for assistance until the exhaustion of the application and appeal process, and for 21 days afterwards.

Legislation now allows the Home Office to fulfil its obligation to support and accommodate asylum seekers by placing applicants in what are euphemistically known as 'accommodation centres', but are in reality little better than open detention facilities. No centres are currently in operation.

Appeal rights

In most cases, asylum seekers have an in-country right of appeal against a refusal to grant refugee status, although the time limits for appeal in certain cases are so short that it may be practically impossible to get legal advice and to prepare a case thoroughly. Under the recently introduced 'fast track procedure', for instance – which at the time of writing applied only to those held in Harmondsworth Detention Centre

– an appeal can be finally disposed by the appeal authority within approximately ten days of the initial refusal by the Home Office.

Following the implementation of the Nationality, Immigration and Asylum Act 2002, however, asylum applicants from designated, or 'white list', countries, defined as those the Home Office regard as 'generally safe', possess a right of appeal exercisable only from the country in which they have expressed a fear of persecution, if their claims are certified to be 'clearly unfounded'. At present there are 24 countries on the list though the Secretary of State retains a power to add more at his or her discretion:

> Cyprus; the Czech Republic; Estonia; Hungary; Latvia; Lithuania; Malta; Poland; Slovakia; Slovenia; Albania; Bulgaria; Serbia and Montenegro; Jamaica; Macedonia; Moldova; Romania; Bangladesh; Bolivia; Brazil; Ecuador; Sri Lanka; South Africa; Ukraine.

Those who are subject to certification on this basis have no redress except by way of judicial review.

For those who can access it, the appeal system currently has two tiers. An applicant's appeal is initially placed before an Adjudicator, from whose decision the unsuccessful party is entitled to seek permission to appeal to the IAT. If permission is granted, the case will proceed to a full hearing before a Tribunal panel. If refused, the appellant's only redress is an application for 'statutory review' before the High Court. Statutory review, which applies in respect of all Adjudicator decisions handed down after 9 June 2003, is a reduced form of judicial review, which allows an appraisal of merits on the papers only and precludes a subsequent oral renewal if permission is declined.

For those refused asylum by the Home Office after 2 October 2000 who have exhausted their appeal rights, the prospects of mounting a successful fresh application are limited following the introduction of the 'one-stop appeal system', particularly where the renewed claim is based on events or evidence predating disposal of their initial application. The one-stop system obliges applicants, and their dependants, to present all of the matters upon which they wish to rely in support of their applications for leave to remain at the earliest opportunity, and at least prior to the final determination of initial appeal proceedings, and imposes penalties on those failing to do so, which enables the Home Office to refuse to entertain the late application or refuse a right of appeal, regardless of the merits of the claim.

The rules and processes relating to asylum seekers place additional hurdles in the way of a successful application. If applicants arrive in the UK without being stopped or having to transit in another country considered to be safe, they are required to apply for asylum on arrival (not least to be able to claim benefits insofar as they are still available), to tell their story in a consistent way, not to damage or destroy any relevant document and not to undertake activities that are inconsistent with previous beliefs or said to be calculated to enhance his or her claim. The asylum seeker can also be penalised for the actions of anyone acting on his or her behalf.

Rights on recognition

If the applicant is recognised as a refugee, the applicant and his or her family will be granted ILR immediately.

Refugees who were not accompanied to the UK by their families can apply under the Immigration Rules for family reunion once they are recognised. Admission is usually granted for spouses where the marriage predated the application for asylum, and for dependant children. Exceptionally, extended family members may be considered. Maintenance and accommodation requirements are generally waived.

Once recognised as a refugee, an individual is protected against discrimination by the CSR. They are then free to work, change jobs or engage in economic activity without needing any further permission from the Home Office. If they want to study, they will be treated as a home student for the purposes of fees and eligibility for grants. Refugees are also entitled to a CSR Travel Document.

Alternative status

If the Home Office does not believe that an applicant is a 'refugee' within the narrowest meaning of the CSR, but thinks that in the circumstances he or she should not have to return at the present time, 'humanitarian status' (which replaces 'Exceptional Leave to Enter or Remain') may be granted.

For those who are granted humanitarian status, family reunion cannot ordinarily be achieved for four years, and even then all aspects of the Immigration Rules must be satisfied.

Those with humanitarian status can work, but must fulfil other criteria to be entitled to educational grants. They are also generally required to travel on their own national passports unless they can show that this facility has been denied them.

11.6   THE EUROPEAN CONVENTION ON HUMAN RIGHTS

It became unlawful for any public authority to act in a way that is incompatible with an individual's rights under the Convention. 'Public authority' in this context includes not only the Home Office and Immigration Officers, but may also include private companies fulfilling a 'public' function. The most obvious example in the context of immigration and asylum law are private companies charged with the running of immigration detention centres or privately contracted interpreters employed in asylum interviews.

The protection provided by the Convention applies to every person within the jurisdiction of the UK authorities, irrespective of whether they have leave to enter or remain in the UK. Most importantly, it includes those who have been granted temporary admission, which means that even though they are physically present in the UK, in law they are not deemed to have actually ever been given permission to enter the UK.

Consequently all immigration decisions taken by the Secretary of State, Immigration Officers or entry clearance officers after 2 October 2000 are subject to a separate right of appeal and/or cause of action for breach of the Convention. Case law makes it clear that nobody is to be deported or removed if such action would be contrary to the UK's obligations under Article 3 of the Convention.

Further under the Nationality, Immigration and Asylum Act 2002, although there is no freestanding appeal, human rights can be introduced as a discrete ground of appeal when challenging any immigration decision, and where such a decision is held to be incompatible with the UK's convention obligations, humanitarian protection or discretionary leave to enter or remain will ordinarily be extended, although the Immigration Rules do not provide for it.

The principal rights

Article 3 of the Convention prohibits torture or inhuman or degrading treatment or punishment. This provision not only protects against torture, inhuman or degrading treatment or punishment inflicted by British public authorities but also protects against the removal of any individual to a country where there is a real risk of that individual suffering treatment that would amount to torture or inhuman or degrading treatment or punishment. Unlike the CSR, the protection offered by Article 3 is absolute and applies regardless of the individual's immigration history or criminal record.

When seeking to determine the legality of a decision by the Home Office to detain a person subject to immigration control, Article 5 of the Convention, which protects the right to liberty and security of the person, may be invoked. The courts have found the UK's Immigration Detention procedures, as set down in the Home Office's 'Operational Guidance Manual', to be generally compatible with Article 5, and can properly be regarded as representing the Secretary of State's view of what is proportionate. However, by necessary inference detention in contravention of that policy must be regarded as a breach of Article 5 on the grounds that it is disproportionate.

Article 8 provides the right to respect for private and family life. The concept of 'family' in the context of Article 8 is wide and includes spouses, children (whether legitimate or illegitimate), and relatives in the ascending line, such as grandparents, aunts and uncles and even foster parents, provided the emotional ties between family members can be shown to be very strong. In relation to children, even natural fathers who have had little or no contact with their children since their birth can enjoy a right to family life with those children. Although Article 8 is particularly important in the case of removal or refusal of admission of a spouse or parents (or other family member) of an individual who has a right of residence in the UK, there are two important notes of caution:

Even though there is a right to respect for family life this, in principle, does not extend to a right to respect for the choice of marital or family home. Where there is an alternative country in which the spouses/family can reside and there are no 'insurmountable obstacles' to relocation and settlement there, or where a person subject to immigration control could return to the country of origin and obtain entry clearance as a family member in the ordinary way without risk or excessive delay, declining residence in the UK may not amount to an interference with the right to respect for family life.

Unlike Article 3, the protection of the right to respect for private and family life is not absolute. Interferences can be justified in law provided that the interference is prescribed by law, in the pursuit of a legitimate aim and proportionate. Any decision involving Article 8 therefore includes a sometimes difficult balancing act between the different interests involved.

11.7   BRITISH NATIONALITY

The British Nationality Act 1981 came into force on 1 January 1983. It defines who is British by birth and how people may become British through naturalisation or registration.

Birth in the UK

People who were born in the UK before 1983 were automatically British citizens by birth. The only exception to this was children whose parents were working in the UK as diplomats at the time they were born.

Anybody born in the UK after 1 January 1983 is automatically British if at the time of the birth:

- One of their parents was a British citizen.
- One of their parents was allowed to stay permanently in the UK.

The legitimacy of the child is no longer relevant. Previously where children were born outside of marriage British nationality could only be passed through the mother. The Nationality, Immigration and Asylum Act 2002 now allows nationality to be inherited from the father provided that paternity can be established to the satisfaction of the Home Office.

Where neither parent is British at the time of the child's birth, but they later become settled, they can then apply for their child to naturalise.

If children are not able to inherit a nationality from either of their parents and are born stateless, and if they live in the UK for the first seven years of their life without gaining any nationality, their parents can apply for them to settle and then become British. The Nationality, Immigration and Asylum Act 2002 provides that stateless children can acquire nationality after five years of continual residence, but this provision is not yet in force.

Naturalisation

People who are settled in the UK may be eligible to apply for British citizenship by naturalisation. If an applicant is married to a British citizen, acquiring citizenship is relatively straightforward. Applicants must show that:

- They are settled in the UK.
- They have lived legally in the UK for at least three years and have not been out of the UK for more than 270 days in that period, nor more than 90 days in the year before the application.
- They are of good character.

If the applicant is not married to a British citizen qualification is more onerous. People in this class must show that:

- They have been settled in the UK for at least a year.
- They have lived legally in the UK for at least five years and have not been out of the UK for more than 450 days in those years, nor more than 90 days in the year before the application.
- They are of good character.
- They intend to continue to live in the UK.

Standard application forms must be completed. Acceptance is at the discretion of the Home Office. Applicants must also demonstrate a sufficient knowledge of the English, Welsh or Scottish Gaelic language as a prerequisite for naturalisation. Recent legislation has added to pre-existing language requirements, and applicants must demonstrate they possess 'sufficient knowledge about life in the UK' and must take a citizenship pledge at a formal ceremony.

Duty to give reasons
In all cases of naturalisation, the Home Office claimed that it did not have to give any reasons for refusing an application. However, the courts have held that where the Home Office is intending to refuse British nationality for particular reasons, the applicant must be afforded the chance to comment before a final decision is made. If the reason for refusal is technical, such as having been abroad longer than allowed, the Home Office will generally inform the applicant. There is no right of appeal against refusal although it is possible to reapply. Since the Al Fayed brothers challenged the Home Office refusals to give any reasons for refusing them a passport, the Home Secretary announced in December 1997 that in future, 'in principle', reasons for refusal of citizenship would be given.

Deprivation of citizenship
The Home Office now has the power to deprive a person of citizenship where it is satisfied that that person has done something seriously prejudicial to the vital interests of the UK or a British Overseas Territory. The power has been introduced as another mechanism for combating those perceived to be connected with terrorist activities.

This facility adds to the previous power to revoke citizenship, which existed where naturalisation or registration was demonstrably achieved pursuant to fraud, false representations or the concealment of material facts.

These powers cannot be exercised, however, if the subject would be rendered stateless as a result, and a right of appeal exists.

11.8   FUTURE DEVELOPMENTS

At the time of writing, the Asylum and Immigration (Treatment of Claimants etc.) Bill 2003 (the Bill) was progressing through Parliament. Under the proposed regime, the chances of winning a right to stay in the UK are drastically reduced, while the prospect of being detained and criminalised is once again substantially increased.

Reform of systems of appeal and review
The Bill proposes the introduction of a single tier of appeal to the Asylum and Immigration Tribunal (AIT). The AIT will not be accountable to any other court.

If the first instance adjudicator makes an error in deciding the appeal there will be the limited opportunity to apply to the AIT for a review of that decision. The review is only by reference to written submissions, with no opportunity for an oral hearing.

The grounds of review at present are described as 'erroneous construction of or application of a provision of the Act'. These are extraordinarily narrow and would exclude the ability to challenge a decision, for example, on the basis that it was not in accordance with the Immigration Rules.

Clause 10 of the Bill initially proposed that the AIT would not be accountable to any other court, so that there would be no judicial scrutiny of decisions made by the AIT. As a result there will be no case law. Given the current relatively inconsistent decisions produced by adjudicators and, on occasion the AIT, this situation can only get worse. In addition, Clause 10 also sought to exclude the higher courts' jurisdiction in relation to virtually any immigration decision taken in connection with a person's removal or deportation from the UK.

The Government's proposals made it clear that it was no longer concerned with upholding its treaty obligations or according due respect to the centuries-old legal tradition of separation of powers but merely with the speed with which it can process a claim. In many cases this will cause injustice and the return of people to countries where they risk persecution, torture and inhuman and degrading treatment.

Only a threatened rebellion in the House of Lords prompted the Government to reconsider its proposals and withdraw the threat of absolute exclusion from access to the High Courts. Its seems probable now that we will see a retention of the system of statutory review (a limited form of judicial review, which allows for a decision on the papers but no oral review of a refusal) in respect of AIT decisions and an extension of this system to the classes of immigration decision referred to above.

Punishing the undocumented

Clause 2 will make it an offence, punishable by imprisonment, for any non-British or EEA national arriving at a UK port not to have a passport. There will be a defence of reasonable excuse, however. It is assumed that travel to seek asylum will be such a defence. The clause ushers in a more draconian punitive response in respect of those persons who are deemed to have deliberately destroyed a travel document on the instructions of an agent. In this class of cases there will be no defence of 'reasonable excuse'.

In the same vein Clause 3 will also penalise asylum seekers seeking entry under cover of forged documents. Concern exists as to whether there are any available defences in forgery and counterfeiting legislation to protect persons fleeing persecution.

The undoubted effect of Clause 2 and 3 will be the further criminalising of asylum seekers. These provisions contravene both Article 31 of the CSR, which dictates that asylum seekers should not be punished owing to the method of their entry, and similar decisions from the High Court. However, this is not evidently regarded as a significant obstacle, with the Government's underlying agenda of legislating to deter asylum seekers from pursuing protection in the UK clearly being regarded as of greater import.

Extending powers of arrest

Clause 8 extends enforcement powers and will afford an Immigration Officer the power of arrest without warrant where in the course of exercising a function under the Immigration Acts he or she forms a 'reasonable suspicion' that a person has committed or attempted an offence of conspiracy to defraud at common law.

Electronic tagging

Clause 15 seeks to introduce a system of electronic monitoring applicable to any person who is currently subject to a residence restriction. Of concern is the fact that no criteria are furnished to identify how the system should be administered and to whom it would apply. Coupled with the restrictions on residence, reporting, employment and curfew, Clause 15 empowers the Secretary of State to use tagging well beyond genuine alternatives to detention and to use the device simply as an expedient tracking and control mechanism.

While such tagging may be regarded as preferential to detention by some clients, it serves only to reinforce negative stereotypes, strengthening the association between asylum seekers and criminality given that currently tagging is utilised only in respect of convicted criminals. The efficacy and appropriateness of tagging in the asylum context is further thrown into doubt by research that shows that the effects of tagging on the wearer revealed severe levels of humiliation, which could in some circumstances lead to the breakdown of family life.

Coerced co-operation with enforcement action

Clause 14 also proposes the prosecution and sentencing on conviction of up to two years of persons subject to enforcement action who fail to co-operate with the process of removal or deportation. An offence will be committed in circumstances where the Secretary of State requires a person to take specified action that it is believed will or may enable a travel document to be obtained, the possession of which will facilitate the person's deportation or removal, and the individual declines to co-operate. The requirements that the Secretary of State may impose include the provision of information or documents, fingerprints, photographs, co-operation with the presentation of an application to an agent of a foreign government, completion of forms accurately, attendance at interviews and making of appointments. Failure to comply with a requirement 'without reasonable excuse' will be punishable. The Bill offers no indication of what factors may be deigned capable of founding the defence.

Further removal of support from asylum seekers

Clause 26 creates a fifth class of person – namely a failed asylum seeker family – who will no longer be entitled to NASS support. This highly controversial clause could mean that families who inevitably become destitute may have their children taken into care and accommodated by local authorities. These could be subject to challenge by parents under Article 8 of the Convention – the right to respect for private and family life – if this practice is actually adopted.

11.9   FURTHER INFORMATION

Useful organisations

The AIRE Centre
17 Red Lion Square
London WC1R 4QH
Tel: 020 7831 4276
<www.airecentre.org>

Bail for Immigration Detainees (BID)
Main office:
London
Tel: 020 7247 3590
info@biduk.org
<www.biduk.org>
Regional offices in Oxford and Portsmouth

Immigration Advisory Service
County House
190 Dover Street
London SE1 4YB
Tel: 020 7976 1200
Fax: 020 7403 5875
<www.iasuk.org>

**The Immigration Law Practitioners'
Association**
Lindsey House
40–42 Charterhouse Street
London EC1M 6JH
Tel: 020 7251 8383
Fax: 020 7251 8384
Info@ilpa.org.uk
<www.ilpa.org.uk>

Joint Council for Welfare of Immigrants
115 Old Street
London EC1V 9RT
Tel: 020 7251 8708
Fax: 020 7251 8707
Info@jcwi.org.uk
<www.jcwi.org.uk>

Refugee Council
240–250 Ferndale Road
London SW9 8BB
Tel: 020 7346 6700
Fax: 020 7346 6778
Info@refugeecouncil.org.uk
<www.refugeecouncil.org.uk>

Refugee Legal Centre
153–157 Commercial Road
London E1 2DA
Tel: 020 7780 3200
Fax: 020 7780 3201
RLC@Refugee-Legal-Centre.org.uk
<www.refugee-legal-centre.org.uk>
Regional offices in Dover, Leeds and Oakington

**United Kingdom Council for Overseas
Students' Affairs (UKCOSA)**
9–17 St Albans Place
London N1 ONX
Tel: 020 7288 4330
Fax: 020 7780 3201
<www.ukcosa.org.uk>

**United Nations High Commission for
Refugees**
Millbank Tower
21–24 Millbank
London SW1P 4QP
Tel: 020 7828 9191
Fax: 020 7630 5349
Info@unhcr.org.uk

12 The Rights of People Detained Under the Mental Health Act 1983

The Mental Health Act 1983 (the MHA) provides for the circumstances in which individuals, who are considered to have a 'mental disorder', may be detained and compulsorily treated for their mental disorder in hospital. This chapter considers your rights under this legislation, covering the following areas:

- The definition of 'mental disorder'
- Informal admission to hospital
- Compulsory admission to hospital
- The Nearest Relative
- Compulsory treatment
- Discharge from hospital
- Rights in hospital
- Powers in the community
- Review of the Mental Health Act 1983
- Further information

The Code of Practice to the Mental Health Act 1982 (the Code of Practice) provides guidance on the implementation of the MHA. In 2003 the Court of Appeal pointed out that the Code of Practice had a very important role in protecting the human rights of detained patients and stressed that the Code of Practice should be observed unless there are very good reasons for not doing so.

12.1 THE DEFINITION OF 'MENTAL DISORDER'

'Mental disorder' is defined as:

mental illness, arrested or incomplete development of mind, psychopathic disorder and any other disorder or disability of the mind.

Mental illness is not defined in the MHA, and the courts have considered a definition unnecessary, suggesting that the test should be what the ordinary sensible person would decide on a case-by-case basis. The conditions that are generally accepted as falling under the category of 'mental illness' include schizophrenia and mood disorders. Most admissions under the MHA requiring the category of mental disorder to be specified are admissions of individuals with a diagnosis of a mental illness.

The MHA defines three other forms of mental disorder:

- *Severe mental impairment*: 'a state of arrested or incomplete development of mind which includes severe impairment of intelligence and social functioning and is associated with abnormally aggressive or seriously irresponsible conduct on the part of the person concerned'.
- *Mental impairment*: 'a state of arrested or incomplete development of mind (not amounting to a severe mental impairment) which includes significant impairment of intelligence and social functioning and is associated with abnormally aggressive or seriously irresponsible conduct on the part of the person concerned'.
- *Psychopathic disorder*: 'a persistent disorder or disability of mind (whether or not including significant impairment of intelligence) which results in abnormally aggressive or seriously irresponsible conduct on the part of the person concerned'.

The European Court of Human Rights (ECHR) in the case of *Hutchison Reid* v *United Kingdom* recently established that detention could be lawful even where the patient is suffering from a psychopathic disorder that cannot be treated in hospital.

The MHA states that a person cannot be treated as mentally disordered solely on the grounds of 'promiscuity or other immoral conduct, sexual deviancy or dependence on alcohol or drugs'.

The terms used in the MHA are legal, not medical, categories. While recognising these terms have no legal meaning in the context of the MHA, many people, in particular people who use mental health services, prefer terms such as 'mental health problems' and 'mental distress' when describing their experience.

12.2   INFORMAL ADMISSION TO HOSPITAL

Individuals who are willing to be admitted into hospital and receive treatment for their mental disorder can be admitted 'informally', that is, without the need to be compulsorily admitted under the MHA.

In 1998, the House of Lords ruled that people who lack the capacity to agree, but do not object, to their admission to hospital for treatment for their mental disorder may also be admitted informally (*R* v *Bournewood Community and Mental Health Trust*). This means that none of the safeguards available to patients detained under the MHA are available to such individuals. For example, there is no independent review of the decision to admit them to hospital nor do they fall under the remit of the Mental Health Act Commission (MHAC), which oversees the implementation of the MHA and visits detained patients.

Following the House of Lords' decision a complaint was made to the European Court of Human Rights on the grounds that the informal admission breached Article 5 of the European Convention on Human Rights (the Convention), which protects against unjustified detention, and Article 14, which prohibits discrimination (it was argued that it is discriminatory to offer those patients admitted informally fewer protections than those admitted compulsorily). While the judgment in *H.L. v United Kingdom* has not yet been released, the arguments based on Articles 5 and 14 were considered serious enough at the preliminary stage to merit a full hearing of the Court.

12.3 COMPULSORY ADMISSION TO HOSPITAL

Part II of the MHA sets out the civil admission process, commonly known as 'sectioning'. Part III of the MHA sets out the circumstances in which the criminal courts can order individuals to be detained in hospital and the Home Secretary can order the transfer of prisoners to hospital.

Civil admission

Usually an application for a person's compulsory admission to hospital is made by an Approved Social Worker (ASW), that is, a social worker who has specialist training and experience in dealing with people with mental disorder. The person's Nearest Relative also has the power to make the application but this power is used rarely.

The application must be supported by two medical recommendations. At least one of the doctors must be approved under section 12 of the MHA as having special experience in the diagnosis or treatment of mental disorder. One of the recommendations should, if practicable, be given by a doctor who has a previous acquaintance with the patient. In emergencies, where it is of urgent necessity for the person to be admitted and obtaining a second medical recommendation would cause undesirable delay, an application may be made on the basis of one medical recommendation (see below).

Before applying for a person to be detained in hospital under the MHA, the approved social worker must assess whether detention in hospital is the most appropriate way of providing for the individual's needs. An application for compulsory admission may be made in respect of an individual who is already in hospital on an informal basis.

Admission for assessment

Section 2 of the MHA provides that a person may be detained in hospital for a period of up to 28 days if:

- His or her mental disorder is of 'a nature or degree' that warrants detention in hospital for assessment or assessment followed by medical treatment; and
- It is considered that he or she ought to be detained in the interests of his or her own health or safety or with a view to the protection of others.

The power to detain under section 2 cannot be renewed.

Admission for treatment

Under section 3 of the MHA a person with a specific form of mental disorder, namely, mental illness, mental impairment, severe mental impairment or psychopathic disorder, may be detained for an initial period of up to six months if certain conditions are met:

- The mental disorder must be of a 'nature or degree' that makes it appropriate for the person to receive treatment in hospital; and
- It must be necessary for the health or safety of the person or for the protection of others that he or she receives such treatment, which cannot be provided unless the person is detained under this section.

- In the case of a person who has a psychopathic disorder or mental impairment, such treatment must be likely to alleviate or prevent a deterioration of the person's condition. This is known as the 'treatability test'.

Provided the conditions for further detention are met, detention under section 3 can be renewed for a further six months and then subsequently renewed on a yearly basis.

Emergency powers of detention

Emergency applications for admission
Under section 4 of the MHA an 'emergency application' for admission to hospital may be made on the recommendation of just one doctor where the grounds for detention under section 2 are met, but the person needs to be admitted urgently and there is insufficient time to obtain a second medical recommendation. The power lasts for a maximum of 72 hours.

Holding powers
Patients who are in hospital may be detained in hospital for short periods to allow time for the admission procedure to be completed. The doctor in charge of the patient's treatment, or the doctor's nominated deputy, may authorise the patient's detention for up to 72 hours ('the doctor's holding power'). A qualified nurse may detain a patient *receiving treatment for a mental disorder* for up to six hours where the nurse considers that the person should be immediately restrained from leaving hospital ('the nurse's holding power').

Police powers to remove a person to a place of safety
The MHA provides the circumstances in which the police can remove a person to a place of safety, which in most cases will be a police station or hospital, for up to 72 hours, in order to make arrangements for the person's treatment and care.

From premises
A magistrate may issue a warrant on hearing from an ASW that there is reasonable cause to suspect that a person believed to be suffering from mental disorder is not being cared for properly. The warrant will authorise a police officer, accompanied by an ASW, to enter the premises (by force if need be) and, if thought fit, remove the person to a place of safety.

From a public place
The police may, in the interests of the person or for the protection of others, remove to a place of safety a person found in a public place who appears to be suffering from a mental disorder and to be in immediate need of care and control. The MHA states that the person should be examined by a doctor and interviewed by an ASW. The Code of Practice states that if having examined the person, the doctor concludes that the person is not mentally disordered within the meaning of the MHA, the person should be immediately discharged. This advice takes into account that Article 5 of the Convention requires certain conditions to be met in order for the detention to be lawful, including that the mental disorder must be established by objective medical expertise (*Winterwerp* v *The Netherlands*). Thus if the doctor considers that the person does not have a mental disorder, the detention is no longer justified.

Admission via the courts

Individuals who are accused or convicted of an offence may be ordered by the courts to be detained in hospital to be assessed and/or treated for their mental disorder.

For example, under section 37 of the MHA, the court may make a hospital order where a person has been convicted of an offence for which he or she could be imprisoned, other than cases where the court is required to give a life sentence, such as murder. The court needs to be satisfied, on the basis of the evidence of two doctors, that:

- The person is suffering from mental illness, severe mental impairment, mental impairment or psychopathic disorder; and
- The mental disorder is of a nature or degree that makes it appropriate for the person to be detained in hospital for medical treatment.
- In the case of psychopathic disorder and mental impairment, such treatment must be likely to alleviate or prevent a deterioration of the person's condition.

Furthermore, the court must be of the opinion, taking into account such matters as the nature of the offence and the character of the offender, that a hospital order is the most suitable method of disposing of the case.

In certain cases the Crown Court may add a restriction order to a hospital order. Such an order would be made if, having regard to issues such as the nature of the offence and the risk of the offender committing further offences if discharged, the court considers that such an order is necessary for the protection of the public from serious harm. The restriction order may be made without limit of time or for a period decided by the court, but it is more usual for the order to be made without limit of time.

The consent of the Home Secretary is required before a patient who is subject to a restriction order (often referred to as a 'restricted patient') can be granted leave from hospital, transferred to another hospital or discharged from hospital.

The Crime (Sentences) Act 1997 provides the Crown Court with further powers including the power to specify the level of security in which the patient should be detained by ordering that a restricted patient is detained in a particular hospital unit. This would mean that the patient couldn't be transferred to another unit, even if it is in the same hospital, unless the Home Secretary authorises such a move.

Duty to give information to detained patients

The MHA requires steps to be taken to ensure that patients understand their rights as soon as possible after their detention has begun. The information that must be given, both orally and in writing, includes the section under which the patient is detained, the effect of this section and the patient's right to apply to a Mental Health Review Tribunal.

12.4   THE NEAREST RELATIVE

The Nearest Relative has certain powers and rights in connection with the patient's compulsory admission to hospital under the civil admission provisions. The MHA sets out a list of people who are eligible to be the Nearest Relative, and it will be necessary to consider the list in the light of the patient's current personal circumstances to identify who the Nearest Relative is at that time. For example, individuals who have been living together as 'husband and wife' for six months or more will be each other's Nearest Relative (unless one of them is married and has not permanently separated from their spouse). A recent court ruling has established that, in the light of the Human Rights Act 1998, the MHA should be interpreted so that the term 'husband or wife' should include same-sex partners. Prior to this decision same-sex partners were only considered to be each other's Nearest Relative if they had lived together for five years or more.

The MHA includes the following provisions that refer to the Nearest Relative:

- Before an application under section 2 or within a reasonable time after the application the Approved Social Worker (ASW) must take steps to inform the Nearest Relative of the patient's detention and Nearest Relative's power to discharge the patient.
- The ASW must consult the Nearest Relative before making an application under section 3 unless such consultation is not reasonably practicable or would involve unreasonable delay. If the Nearest Relative objects to the application being made, it cannot go ahead unless the County Court displaces the Nearest Relative.
- The Nearest Relative can apply for the patient to be detained under section 2, 3 or 4 of the MHA.
- The Nearest Relative can require the local social services authority to carry out an assessment of the need to make an application for the patient's admission to hospital.
- The Nearest Relative can seek to have the patient discharged from hospital – although this can be prevented by the doctor in charge of the patient's care.

In *JT* v *United Kingdom* the European Commission of Human Rights upheld JT's complaint that the absence of any means to change the identity of her Nearest Relative under the MHA violated her right to private and family life under Article 8 of the Convention. This case was settled, with the UK Government proposing to amend the relevant part of the MHA so that patients are able to apply to a court for their Nearest Relative to be replaced where they reasonably object to a certain person acting in that capacity. However, this proposed amendment has not been made to the MHA. Added pressure was put on the Government by the case of *R (on the application of M)* v *Secretary of State for Health* in which the Administrative Court held that the provisions of the MHA preventing removal or change of the Nearest Relative were incompatible with Article 8. Nevertheless, amendment of the Act is still pending.

12.5   COMPULSORY TREATMENT

The MHA provides for circumstances in which medical treatment for mental disorders may be given where the patient either refuses to give, or is incapable of giving, consent. The provisions for such compulsory treatment are set out in Part IV of the MHA. These powers do not apply to everyone who is detained under the MHA. Patients detained under section 2 or 3 or under a hospital order are subject to the compulsory treatment provisions, but these provisions will not apply to those who are detained under the emergency powers of the MHA, such as a doctor's holding power.

Capacity to consent to treatment

Every adult is presumed to have the capacity to decide whether or not to accept treatment even if the reasons for refusing are irrational or non-existent. The fact that a person suffers from mental disorder does not necessarily mean that he or she is incapable of giving or refusing consent to the treatment proposed.

Treatment requiring consent or authorisation

Save for emergencies, medication administered for a period exceeding three months and electro-convulsive therapy (ECT) may only be given with the patient's consent or if a Second Opinion Appointed Doctor (SOAD) has authorised such treatment.

The SOAD must consider whether, having regard to the likelihood of the treatment alleviating or preventing a deterioration of the patient's condition, the treatment should be given.

Before deciding whether to authorise the treatment the SOAD must interview the patient, discuss the treatment with the doctor in charge of the patient's treatment and consult two other people who are professionally concerned with the patient's medical treatment. If the SOAD authorises the treatment, written reasons for this decision should be given to the patient unless such information is considered likely to cause serious harm to the physical or mental health of the patient or another person.

Treatment requiring consent and authorisation of a second doctor

Invasive treatment such as psychosurgery may only be given with the patient's consent and the authorisation of a doctor appointed by the MHAC. The doctor and two appointees of the MHAC who are not doctors must be satisfied that the patient has consented to the treatment.

Urgent treatment

In limited circumstances, for instance, where the treatment is immediately necessary to alleviate serious suffering by the patient, such treatment may be given without the procedures set out above. However, irreversible or hazardous treatment can only take place without these procedures if immediately necessary to save the life of the patient.

Treatment without consent or authorisation

Other treatments for mental disorder, which when the provisions of the MHA were being considered by Parliament were described as 'general nursing and other general care', can be provided without the person's consent or the involvement of a second independent doctor.

Given that these treatments were considered to be non-controversial, no special safeguards were thought necessary. However, the courts have held that this provision of the MHA authorises treatment, such as feeding by naso-gastric tube, on the basis that such treatment was for the patient's mental disorder. In the case of force feeding this was considered to be treatment ancillary to the treatment for the patient's anorexia. The MHAC has recommended that naso-gastric feeding should only be given with the patient's consent or, in the absence of consent, if authorised by a SOAD.

Treatment and the European Convention on Human Rights

The ECHR made clear in *Winterwerp* v *Netherlands* that Article 5(1)(e) does not provide a right to treatment appropriate to the detained person's mental health needs. However, the Court has stressed that the detention of a person 'as a mental health patient' will only be lawful under Article 5(1)(e) if the person is detained in a hospital or other appropriate setting. In a more recent case *Aerts* v *Belgium* the ECHR found a violation of Article 5(1)(e) because that Mr Aerts received no treatment required by the condition that gave rise to his detention.

In the light of the Human Rights Act 1998 (HRA) the courts have confirmed that compulsory treatment may engage articles under the Convention, in particular, Article 3 (prohibition on torture, inhuman or degrading treatment or punishment) and Article 8 (right to private and family life). Accordingly, consideration of the particular circumstances of each case is required to ensure that the treatment is justified. Treatment should only be given in the absence of consent if the proposed treatment is in the patient's best interests and has been convincingly shown to be medically necessary.

See also Chapter 1.

12.6   DISCHARGE FROM HOSPITAL

Temporary leave

The doctor in charge of the patient's care and treatment (referred to in the MHA as the Responsible Medical Officer (RMO)) may grant leave to the detained patient, subject to any conditions that the RMO considers necessary in the interests of the patient or the protection of other persons. Leave for restricted patients is subject to the Home Secretary's consent. The RMO may revoke the leave and recall the patient if it is necessary to do so in the interests of the patient's health or safety or the protection of others, but the patient cannot be recalled if the period of detention has expired.

The MHA includes powers to return a patient who is absent without leave. For example, patients who are detained under section 3 of the MHA may be returned to hospital, by an ASW, the police or anyone authorised by the hospital, within six months of absconding from hospital or until their period of detention expires, whichever is the later. Restricted patients may be returned at any time.

Discharge and patients detained under the civil admission procedures

Patients who are detained under the civil admission procedures can be discharged from hospital by the RMO, the Hospital Managers, the Mental Health Review Tribunal (MHRT) or the patient's Nearest Relative.

The Responsible Medical Officer

The RMO can discharge patients detained under the civil admission procedures of the MHA at any time. However, as discussed above, under the Convention a person's continued detention on the ground of mental disorder is only justified if the mental disorder persists. There is no duty on the RMO to discharge a patient as soon as the criteria for detention no longer apply. However, the Code of Practice states that patients should be discharged from compulsion as soon as it is clear that the application of the powers under the MHA is no longer justified.

Nearest Relative

The Nearest Relative has the power to discharge a patient detained under section 2 or 3 of the MHA. However, the patient's RMO can prevent this discharge by issuing a report to the hospital managers stating that if discharged the patient is likely to act in a manner dangerous to other persons or to him or herself. This is known as a barring certificate. If a barring certificate is issued, the Nearest Relative is not permitted to apply again for the patient to be discharged for a period of six months.

Mental Health Review Tribunals (MHRT)

MHRTs provide an independent review of the need for the patient's continued detention under the MHA and have the power to discharge the patient from detention.

The MHRT consists of three people: a lawyer, a doctor and a 'lay person', who may be, for instance, a social worker. In 2001, the Court of Appeal held that the MHA was incompatible with the Convention because it placed the burden of proof on the patient to show that the conditions for detention were no longer met in order for the MHRT to be required to discharge the person from detention. Following this decision, the MHA was amended so that MHRTs are required to discharge patients from detention if they are not satisfied that the conditions for detention continue to be met.

Patients detained under section 2 may apply to a MHRT in the first 14 days of detention. Patients detained under section 3 may apply to a MHRT in the first six months of detention and in each subsequent period of detention, if renewed. Patients are entitled to legal representation, and staff on the ward should be able to provide details of solicitors who undertake this work. Once appointed, the solicitor can apply to the Community Legal Service for funding to cover the legal costs of representing the person at the MHRT, which is non-means tested.

If an RMO issues a barring certificate in respect of a patient detained under section 3 the Nearest Relative may apply to a MHRT within 28 days.

MHRTs are considered to be a 'court' for the purpose of Article 5(4) of the Convention, which requires that the determination of the lawfulness of detention be carried out 'speedily'. Following the introduction of the HRA, seven detained patients issued legal proceedings, claiming that their rights under Article 5(4) had been breached because the review of their detention by the MHRTs had been unreasonably delayed by repeated cancellation of hearings. Their claims were successful, with the court blaming central government and awarding damages for the excessive length of time the claimants were detained before their cases were heard.

Hospital Managers

The Hospital Managers have the power under the MHA to discharge patients from hospital. Where the person is detained by an NHS Trust the Hospital Managers will usually be a committee of individuals living in the local community, with an interest in mental health, who have been appointed to exercise the powers of discharge on behalf of the NHS Trust. Unlike MHRTs, the Hospital Managers have no statutory criteria to consider when deciding whether to discharge the patient. However, the Code of Practice provides guidance on the practice and procedures to be adopted by Hospital Managers in exercising this power. Furthermore, in the light of the HRA, the Hospital Managers are required to discharge the person if they are not satisfied that the conditions for detention continue to apply.

The Hospital Managers are under a duty to refer cases to an MHRT if the patient has not made an application within a certain period. For instance, if a patient has been detained under section 3 for six months or more and no application has been made to the MHRT, the Hospital Managers must refer the case to the MHRT.

Patients detained under a hospital order
Patients detained under a hospital order can be discharged by the RMO and the Hospital Managers but not by their Nearest Relative and can only apply to an MHRT after the first six months of detention.

Patients detained under a hospital order with restrictions
Restricted patients cannot be discharged by their Nearest Relative and can only be discharged by the RMO or the Hospital Managers with the consent of the Home Secretary. Restricted patients can only apply to an MHRT after the first six months of detention.

Where an MHRT decides that a restricted patient can leave hospital, the MHRT can order that the patient be conditionally discharged. This means that the Home Secretary may recall the patient to hospital at any time. In most cases the MHRT will attach conditions to the conditional discharge, such as requiring the patient to live wherever specified by the professionals appointed to supervise the patient in the community. Failure to comply with such conditions is likely to lead to the patient being recalled to hospital.

A recent House of Lords' decision considered the position of a patient whose conditional discharge has been ordered, but who remains in detention because the conditions of the discharge cannot be met. It was held that this continued detention did not breach Article 5 of the Convention as long as the legality of the detention could be periodically reconsidered.

12.7   RIGHTS IN HOSPITAL

Property and finance
Under existing law, all adults are presumed to have the capacity to manage their own affairs unless the contrary is shown. The fact that a person is detained in hospital under the MHA does not mean that he or she is incapable of managing his or her personal or financial matters. If a person is considered to be incapable of managing his or her own financial affairs, an application can be made to the Court of Protection to appoint a receiver to do so.

The right to receive visitors
Detained patients have the right to be visited by their friends and family. The Code of Practice makes it clear that visitors should only be excluded in limited, and clearly documented, circumstances. Such circumstances could include cases where the

visit is likely to cause a deterioration of the patient's mental health or where there are concerns that the visitor may bring illicit drugs into the hospital.

Where such visits are refused, this must be justified under Article 8 of the Convention on the ground that the refusal is in the interests of public safety, preventing crime and disorder and protecting the health, rights and freedoms of others.

Correspondence
The MHA provides that if there has been a written request by the recipient, postal packets sent by a detained patient may be withheld.

For patients detained in the high security hospitals (Broadmoor, Rampton and Ashworth) the MHA provides for further potential restrictions on correspondence. Postal packets sent by such patients may be withheld from the addressee if the managers of the hospital consider that the postal packet is likely to cause distress to the addressee or others (not including members of staff of the hospital) or danger to any person. The MHA also states that post sent to such patients may be withheld from them if it is necessary to do so in the interests of the safety of the patient or the protection of other persons. These restrictions do not apply to correspondence between the patient and certain recipients, such as a Member of Parliament, the patient's legal adviser and the MHRT.

Voting
The Representation of the People Act 2000 removed the bar on the use of a psychiatric hospital address for registration purposes and thus the bar on detained mental patients voting. The removal of this restriction enables both voluntary and detained civil patients to register to vote either at that address or another address with which they have a local connection. However, this Act also introduced a ban on voting for those detained in hospital via the criminal courts.

Complaints
Detained patients who are not happy with their care and treatment can make a complaint under the National Health Service (NHS) complaints procedure. If they are not happy with the hospital's response they can ask the MHAC to investigate their complaint.

12.8   POWERS IN THE COMMUNITY

Supervised discharge
The Mental Health (Patients in the Community) Act 1995 introduced into the MHA the new power of aftercare under supervision, which is more commonly known as supervised discharge. Under this power, patients who have been detained in hospital for treatment for their mental disorder can be required to comply with certain conditions on their discharge from hospital such as residing at a particular place and attending an outpatients' clinic for medical treatment.

Conditions for supervised discharge
The patient's RMO may apply for a patient to be made subject to supervised discharge upon his or her discharge from hospital, where the patient is 16 years or over

and the patient is liable to be detained in hospital for medical treatment on the following grounds:

- The patient is suffering from mental illness, severe mental impairment, mental impairment or psychopathic disorder; and
- There would be a substantial risk of serious harm to the health or safety of the patient or the safety of other persons, or of the patient being seriously exploited, if he or she were not to receive the aftercare services to be provided to the patient under section 117; and
- Being subject to supervised discharge is 'likely to help secure' that the patient receives the aftercare services to be provided.

Application for discharge
The application must be supported by written recommendations of an ASW and a doctor. The application must include details of the person who has agreed to supervise the patient's care in the community. The supervisor will have the power to take and convey the patient to any place where the patient is required to reside or to attend for the purpose of medical treatment, occupation, education or training, or authorise another person to do so.

The doctor in charge of the patient's aftercare may direct at any time that the supervised discharge should end, but before doing so would need to consult the patient and others involved in the patient's care. Supervised discharge will cease if the patient is detained in hospital for treatment for mental disorder or made subject to guardianship. The patient may apply to an MHRT to be released from supervised discharge.

Supervised discharge applies for six months, at which point it can be renewed for a further six months. The power can be then renewed annually.

Guardianship
Under the MHA a person can be made subject to guardianship. The guardian, who could be a local authority or an individual, has similar powers to the supervisor in supervised discharge, such as the power to require the patient to reside at a specified place; they do not, however, have the power to take and convey the patient.

A person who is 16 years or over may be made subject to guardianship if he or she suffers from mental disorder – mental illness, severe mental impairment, psychopathic disorder or mental impairment – and the mental disorder is of a nature or degree that warrants the person's reception into guardianship. The use of guardianship must be considered necessary in the interests of the welfare of the patient or for the protection of other persons.

The application is made by an approved social worker or the person's Nearest Relative and must be based upon two medical recommendations. The medical recommendations must state that the grounds for detention are met and include an explanation as to why the patient cannot be appropriately cared for without the powers of guardianship.

Guardianship lasts for six months and can be renewed for a further six months, then subsequently renewed on a yearly basis. The Nearest Relative can object to the guardianship taking place and can discharge the patient from guardianship

The provision of services in the community

People living in the community who have mental health problems will need access to services whether or not they have formerly been detained under the MHA.

NHS and Community Care Act 1990

Under the NHS and Community Care Act 1990 local social services authorities are responsible for assessing an individual's needs for community care services and arranging the provision of any such services. If it appears to the local authority that the person has health or housing needs the local authority is required to invite the relevant health or housing authority to assist in the assessment. 'Community care services' include accommodation, home help and social support as well as aftercare under section 117 of this Act.

Care Programme Approach

Under the Care Programme Approach individuals who are receiving specialist mental health services should have an assessment of their health and social care needs. A care plan, which sets out what services and support that person should receive to meet such needs, should then be prepared. The Code of Practice states that before a decision is taken to discharge or grant leave to a patient, the RMO should ensure, in consultation with the other professionals concerned, that the patient's needs for health and social care are fully assessed and that the care plan addresses them.

Aftercare services

Section 117 of the MHA places a joint duty on health authorities and local authorities to provide aftercare services, in co-operation with voluntary organisations, to certain patients who have been detained in hospital under the MHA. Section 117 applies to a person who has been detained under section 3 or a hospital order with or without restrictions, but not to a person who has been detained for assessment under section 2 of the MHA.

No definition of aftercare is provided in the MHA, but in 1998 the Court of Appeal stated that it would normally include social work support, accommodation, the provision of domiciliary services and the use of a day centre and residential facilities. The House of Lords has since accepted this as a 'correct description'.

Although people who have been detained in hospital under section 2 of the MHA or received in-patient care as an informal patient will not receive aftercare services under section 117, their needs for other community care services should be assessed.

12.9   REVIEW OF THE MENTAL HEALTH ACT 1983

In June 2002 the Department of Health published a draft Mental Health Bill for England and Wales and sought comments by September 2002. The Bill is based upon the White Paper *Reforming the Mental Health Act* that was published in December 2000.

The proposals for reform, which include the introduction of powers to compulsorily treat people who are living in the community, have met with widespread opposition. Other areas of concern include the broad criteria for the use of compulsory powers, which are likely to lead to an increase in the number of individuals subject to compulsion and the lack of sufficient safeguards in relation to compulsory treatment. A coalition of over 60 organisations has formed 'The Mental Health Alliance' to campaign against these proposals.

In November 2003, the Secretary of State for Health announced that a revised Bill would be produced for pre-legislative scrutiny 'as soon as possible'.

12.10   FURTHER INFORMATION

Useful organisations

MENCAP
123 Golden Lane
London EC1Y ORT
Tel: 020 7454 0454
Fax: 020 7696 5540
Information@mencap.org.uk
<www.mencap.org.uk>

MIND
Granta House
15–19 Broadway
London E15 4BQ
Tel: 020 8519 2122
Infoline: 0845 766 0163
<www.mind.org.uk>

Mental Health Act Commission
Maid Marion House
56 Hounds Gate
Nottingham NG1 6BG
Tel: 0115 943 7100
Fax: 0115 943 7101
ChiefExec@mhac.trent.nhs.uk
<www.mhac.trent.nhs.uk>

Rethink
30 Tabernacle Street
London EC2A 4DD
Tel: 020 8974 6814
Info@rethink.org
Advice@rethink.org

Bibliography

Department of Health, *Code of Practice to the Mental Health Act 1983* (London: The Stationery Office, March 1999)

Department of Health, *Draft Mental Health Bill, Cm 5538 June 2002* (London: TSO) <www.doh.gov.uk/mentalhealth>

Hoggett, B., *Mental Health Law*, 4th edn (Sweet & Maxwell, 1996)

Jones, R., *Mental Health Act Manual*, 9th edn (Sweet & Maxwell, 2003)

Mental Health Act Commission Tenth Biennial Report 2001–2003, *Placed Amongst Strangers: Twenty Years of the Mental Health Act 1983 and Future Prospects for Psychiatric Compulsion* (London: TSO)

13   The Rights of Children and Young People

This chapter deals with:

- Introduction
- Parental responsibility
- Children involved in the separation or divorce of their parents
- Children involved with social services departments
- Adoption
- Young offenders
- Child witnesses
- Education
- Money, financial support and benefits
- Citizenship, nationality and refugees
- Travelling and leaving the country
- Further information

13.1   INTRODUCTION

Under both domestic and international law children's right to be protected from harm and to have their basic physical and social needs provided is uncontroversial. However, traditionally the rights of children have been limited by considerations about their inherent vulnerability. Central to this are concerns about their capacity to manage political and civil participatory rights. There has been a shift in attitude toward children's rights in the past decade. Whereas previously the approach was welfare oriented and sought only to provide for children's basic welfare needs, in recent years children have also come to be viewed as holders of a wider range of rights associated with the right to express their views and participate in the making of decisions that affect them directly. This shift in emphasis was reflected in the principles of the Children Act 1989 which was a consolidating legislative measure and is now the central pillar of law and policy relating to children. It provides for children's views to be heard and to be given due weight by courts and other bodies responsible for deciding on matters such as residence and contact between children and non-resident parents.

The legal definition of childhood remains quite fluid, and while children do not as such acquire full legal independence until they reach the age of 18 the law is somewhat inconsistent in that children can legally engage in certain random adult activities before that age. For example, children can buy cigarettes and join the armed forces at 16.

Similarly, it is accepted that children at the upper end of childhood can have the maturity and capacity to make important decisions about such matters as their own medical treatment. Nonetheless children's rights are restricted by two important considerations: firstly, their best interests and, secondly, the question of whether children have the mental capacity to exercise their rights responsibly. Striking a balance between these two principles is often a matter of substance and degree.

International law provides some guidance to law-makers and policy-makers in this jurisdiction. The United Nations Convention on the Rights of the Child 1989 (UNCRC), which is the most widely ratified international human rights treaty in existence, was ratified by the United Kingdom (UK) in 1991. It provides for a comprehensive catalogue of rights for children across the range and includes social, economic, cultural, civil and political rights. It also provides that children's best interests are to be a primary consideration for policy- and decision-makers and that the evolving capacity of children must also be factored into law and policy. Moreover, Article 12 of the UNCRC requires that children's views must be sought and given due weight in all matters affecting children. While the UNCRC has not been incorporated into English and Welsh law, and as a consequence is not directly applicable in this jurisdiction, it has both a persuasive value that impacts on policy-makers, and it is referred to with increasing frequency in judicial decisions at all levels. The Government is also required to report to its supervisory body – the United Nations Committee on the Rights of the Child (the UN Committee) – every five years, and the Committee can make comments on the level of Government compliance with the UNCRC and make recommendations for changes and improvement. The most recent report from the UN Committee was in October 2002, and it was highly critical of a range of domestic laws and practices.

A further layer of protection has been offered by the incorporation of the European Convention on Human Rights (the Convention) into English and Welsh law. The Convention includes a range of rights that are equally applicable to adults and children. It is clear from the case law of the European Court of Human Rights (ECHR) that the provisions of the Convention can be used effectively to uphold children's rights.

See also Chapter 1.

In addition, in June 2003 the Government appointed the first Minister for Children, Young People and Families, a move that was recommended in the report of the UN Committee in 2002. In September 2003 the Government published a Green Paper, 'Every Child Matters', which made provision for the creation of a new post of Children's Commissioner for England (the Children's Commissioner). The intention is that the Children's Commissioner will have a role in the development of all policies and programmes, but at present it is expected that this role will be largely symbolic.

13.2   PARENTAL RESPONSIBILITY

Parental responsibility is a term that was introduced by the Children Act 1989 to describe the legal relationship between parents and children. The definition of parental responsibility states that it governs all the rights, duties, powers and responsibility that by law a parent of a child has in relation to the child and his or her property. While the Children Act 1989 provides very little further guidance as to what is envisaged by the term, it has been interpreted by courts to describe a 'bundle of rights' associated with parental decision-making and control, and includes rights and duties with regard to education, choice of religion, administration of a child's property and choice of residence. It is important to note that all the provisions of the Children Act 1989 are subject to the guiding principle of the child's best interests, and consequently the exercise of parental responsibility to limitations where disputes arise either between holders of parental responsibility or between parents and children. Parental responsibility lasts until the child is 18, although at that upper end of childhood it should only be exercised in a way that is consistent with the child's evolving capacity and maturity.

Acquiring parental responsibility

Mothers always have parental responsibility for their child. Fathers can acquire parental responsibility in three ways:

- Where the parents are married the father automatically has parental responsibility.
- If the parents are unmarried and the father's name is on the birth certificate he has parental responsibility,
- If the parents are unmarried and the father is not named on the birth certificate he can acquire parental responsibility by entering into an agreement with the mother, by subsequent marriage to the mother, by order of the court or by obtaining a residence order (which governs where a child is to live) in relation to the child.

Other people can acquire parental responsibility for a child by way of a residence order. For example, when the mother's partner obtains a residence order to regularise their legal relationship with the child, he or she can obtain parental responsibility. Similarly, if the mother or parents are deceased a guardian appointed by the court for the child has parental responsibility. When a child is the subject of a care order in favour of a local authority, it shares parental responsibility with the mother or both parents. Where a child is in care voluntarily, parental responsibility remains with the parents.

It is important to note that persons who may have day-to-day responsibility for children such as teachers and childminders do not have parental responsibility but are under a duty of care to act as a reasonable parent would do to ensure the child's safety and in emergency circumstances may take reasonable steps to promote a child's welfare.

Sharing parental responsibility

All persons having parental responsibility can exercise it independently of each other by law, but in reality where there are significant differences of opinion between those holding parental responsibility such disagreements can often result in legal proceedings. The Children Act 1989 provides that a court can make a prohibited steps order or a specific issue order either to prevent certain action being taken or requiring a parent to do something. This may be something as significant as not changing schools or surrendering a child's passport to prevent removal from the jurisdiction.

Key areas of parental responsibility

Consultation with children

The Children Act 1989 does not as such require parents or persons holding parental responsibility either to involve children in the decision-making process or to take their views into account. However, the exercise of parental responsibility is limited when children are sufficiently mature and have the capacity to make decisions about their own future. This is as a consequence of the 1985 decision in *Gillick v Wisbech Health Authority* in which the House of Lords decided that a child under 16 could consent to medical treatment if he or she could understand what was involved in such treatment and was capable of expressing his or her views and wishes. This has come to be known as '*Gillick* competence', and while the House of Lords did not identify a specific age at which children were to be deemed to be sufficiently mature to have their views considered, it follows from *Gillick* that the older the child, the greater the weight that will be attached to their views. This approach is consistent with certain provisions of the UNCRC: Article 5, which requires that children's rights be exercised in accordance with their evolving capacities and Article 12, which requires that in all decisions affecting children due weight should be attached to their views.

Names

A child's parents have an unfettered right to name their child, and they are required by law to register the child's name within 42 days of the child's birth. Where only one person has parental responsibility that person can change the child's name without requiring the consent or permission of anyone else. But where, for example, a father has parental responsibility and does not agree to a change of name then it is considered good practice to ask the court to make a decision. In this situation the court will consider a range of factors, but the paramount consideration will be the welfare of the child. Other factors that will be considered by the court include the reasons for the change, any change in the child's circumstances that occurred since registration, such as separation of the parents, and, where relevant, the views of the child. Where a child becomes the subject of an adoption order, the adoptive parents acquire parental responsibility and have an absolute right to change a child's name.

With parental consent a child may use a different name from that on their birth certificate. If the child is *Gillick* competent and has sufficient maturity and understanding they may apply for a specific issue order to do this if their parents do not consent.

Religion

A child who is sufficiently mature in accordance with the *Gillick* principles is entitled to choose his or her own religion. Where a dispute arises either between parents or between parents and the child over the choice of religious upbringing, the paramountcy of the child's welfare will prevail in resolving the conflict. If a parent seeks to impose a particular religion on a child it will not be tolerated if it causes harm to the child. Article 9 of the Convention protects the right to freedom of thought, conscience and religion.

Medical treatment

A 16 year old has the right to consent to or refuse to consent to medical, surgical or dental treatment if the child is deemed *Gillick* competent, including contraceptive advice or treatment. A young person can give consent provided the person providing treatment is of the view that he or she understands the nature and consequences of the treatment.

Children under 18 may also refuse medical treatment, but under the wardship jurisdiction a court can order medical treatment, including termination of a pregnancy or sterilisation, if it is deemed necessary in the child's best interests. This power is most commonly used in cases where a young person refuses life-saving medical treatment as a consequence of an eating disorder or mental illness.

The ECHR has decided that compulsory medical treatment for the purposes of preventing death or serious injury does not amount to inhuman or degrading treatment contrary to Article 3. See also Chapter 1.

Consent to marriage

A marriage where one party is under 16 is void. Young people between 16 and 18 may marry with parental consent. If the parents are separated or divorced the consent of both parents is necessary, and if the child is in the care of the local authority it is necessary to obtain the consent of all persons having parental responsibility for the child.

Article 12 of the Convention protects the right of men and women of 'marriageable age' to marry. The prohibition on children under 16 years does not infringe the right to marry because Article 12 clearly permits states to regulate the age at which a person is able to marry.

Corporal punishment

A parent has the right to administer reasonable physical chastisement to a child. It is a defence to a charge of assault that the force used was no more than reasonable chastisement. The UN Committee indicated in 1996 and 2002 that it did not consider this to be compatible with the UNCRC, which prohibits physical punishment of children.

Following a recent decision of the ECHR the Government conducted a consultation exercise regarding the possible abolition of parental corporal punishment. It stopped short of abolition and instead issued guidelines to assist courts in defining the concept of reasonable chastisement, which requires such factors as age, sex, duration of the punishment and the manner and method of its execution to be taken into account.

Corporal punishment is prohibited as a form of punishment in all other circumstances including as a punishment following conviction for an offence, in education and in care or foster homes.

Leaving home

Young people under 16 cannot leave home unless their parents agree. Alternatively a court may make a residence order in favour of another adult if this is deemed to be in the child's best interests. This can be done on the adult's application or by the child if he or she is deemed to have sufficient understanding. The law relating to 16 to 17 year olds is not clear but it appears that they probably can leave home without parental consent. However, parents can apply to court for the return home of a child under 18 by seeking an injunction in wardship proceedings or a residence order. A court is unlikely to order the return of a child of 16 to 17 to return home against his or her wishes if the court can be satisfied that he or she is safe and that there is a clear breakdown of the family relationship.

Police will return a runaway child under 16 to his or her parents or to the local authority if he or she is in care unless they have reasonable cause to believe the child is in danger or at risk. In such circumstances the police may hold the child in police protection. The police then liaise with social services as to whether further action should be taken to protect the child. The police are unlikely to return a child over the age of 16 to his or her parents.

13.3   CHILDREN INVOLVED IN THE SEPARATION OR DIVORCE OF THEIR PARENTS

The Children Act 1989 aims to encourage parents to agree about the child's welfare in the event of separation or divorce by providing for the continuation of parental responsibility for divorced parents and by requiring the courts to refrain from making orders unless they are necessary in the child's best interests. This approach is reinforced by the development of conciliation and mediation processes to assist parents to reach agreement about the child's residence and issues of contact to the non-residential parent. In practice, however, family break-ups often end up in court where disputes between parents appear to be absent of considerations of the child's interest.

Where there is agreement between parents they are not required to attend court in divorce proceedings in relation to the children. The court must simply be satisfied that appropriate arrangements have been made for children, having received a written declaration to that effect and the divorce is granted. In cases where the court is concerned about the plans for the children it can order a welfare report, but this power is very rarely used. However, it is concerning that in an uncontested case there is no formal way in which children can express their views if they wish to do so.

In 2001 the Children and Family Court Advisory and Support Service (CAFCASS) was established with a number of functions. In this context the most important is the provision of a child and family reporter to carry out conciliation and reporting functions in disputes between parents over residence and contact.

Parents making applications for residence or contact with a child are normally required to attend a conciliation appointment with a child and family reporter. The purpose of the conciliation stage is to assist the parties to resolve their disputes. If this is not possible then the court may order a report to be prepared on the matter of residence or contact. A child and family reporter involved at the conciliation plays no further part in the process and does not participate in the preparation of any reports for the court.

In addition, the applications for residence and contact are made under section 8 of the Children Act 1989. Parents can also apply for a specific issue order requiring a particular action by another parent or for a prohibited steps order to prevent parents from taking certain steps, for example, removing a child from the other parent's care and control. Section 8 applications often involve the use of child and family reporters to provide the court with an objective assessment of what is in the child's best interests. Children and Young People may apply to court for section 8 orders provided they can demonstrate sufficient maturity and understanding as to the nature and consequences of any orders.

Paramountcy principle

When the court is considering any application relating to the upbringing of a child the welfare of the child is the paramount consideration. The concept of welfare is not defined in the Children Act 1989, but the following factors that constitute the 'welfare checklist' are used to assist the court in its determination:

- The ascertainable wishes and feelings of the child – in light of his or her age and understanding.
- The physical, emotional and educational needs of the child.
- The likely effect of any change on the child's circumstances.
- The age, sex, background and any other characteristics which the court considers to be relevant.
- Any harm that the child has suffered or is at risk of suffering.
- How capable the child's parents (and/or any other relevant person) are of meeting the child's needs; and
- The range of powers available to the court.

The child and family reporter is also required to take the welfare checklist into account in the preparation of his or her report.

Article 8 of the Convention – the right to respect for family life – impacts on this decision-making process in that a court must be aware of the parents' right to respect for their family life. The courts have taken the view that while a balance must be struck between the competing interests of parents and children, the welfare principle continues to predominate under the Children Act 1989. Any expectation that the Human Rights Act 1998 (HRA) would dilute the paramountcy of the welfare principle has not as yet been fulfilled. See also Chapter 1.

Representation of children

In disputes under section 8 of the Children Act 1989 children are not usually either represented or parties to the proceedings. Courts take the view that it is not in a child's best interests to be directly involved in disputes regarding their upbringing. Nonetheless provision is made for the wishes and views of children to be ascertained by the child and family reporter, and due weight is attached to those views depending on the child's age and maturity. It is highly unlikely, for example, that a court would order that a *Gillick* competent child should either reside with a parent or have direct contact with a parent if the child had expressed a wish not to do so. However, it is important to note that the views and wishes of the child are not determinative as the court will take other factors into account. It is arguable that this runs contrary to Article 12 of the UNCRC, which requires that due weight should be given to the views of children who are capable of expressing them in all decision-making processes affecting the child.

Contact disputes

The question of how much contact a child should have with a non-residential parent is a very difficult matter for the court to resolve to the satisfaction of the parents and the child. Under the Children Act 1989 contact is expressed as a right of the child, although the ECHR has recognised it as an element of a parent's family life. In striking a balance between the competing interests the courts are guided by considerations of the child's welfare as the paramount consideration, but the view in the vast majority of cases is that maintaining a relationship with both parents is in the child's best interests. Terminating direct contact between a child and a non-residential parent is a rare occurrence, and usually only happens where there has been violence or abuse of an extreme nature or where for other reasons the child does not wish to continue to have a relationship with his or her parents.

13.4   CHILDREN INVOLVED WITH SOCIAL SERVICES DEPARTMENTS

Children may become involved with social services departments in a range of circumstances including after a request has been made by parents for family support services, where concerns about child protection are raised, where children are taken into care and are being 'looked after' by the local authority, or where a child is placed for adoption.

Local authorities have primary responsibility for providing these services, but it is expected that there will be inter-agency co-operation between health services, the police and social services to protect the interest of children in need of support services. In recent years there has been a range of initiatives designed to improve children's services. In 2002 inspectorates carried out inspections of children's safeguards and released their findings in a document entitled *Safeguarding Children*, which was also a response to a Government White Paper released in 1998. In addition, the Victoria Climbie Inquiry Report also fed into this process, and in September 2003 the Government published *Keeping Children Safe*, which was a response to both reports. Coinciding with the publication of this report was the publication of a Green Paper, 'Every Child Matters', which provided for the establishment of a Children's Commissioner and proposed a range of other initiatives including the setting up of Local Safeguarding Children Boards and the establishment of a new post of Director of Children's Service who would be accountable for local authority education and social services. At the time of writing these proposals are being considered.

Local authority services

Family support
The local authority has a general duty to promote the welfare of children in need in its area and to enable children to be brought up by their families by providing a range of support services to the child and her family. This includes such services as advice, counselling, placement in family centres, day care provision, provision of holidays and recreational activities, and in exceptional circumstances, cash help. The concept of a 'child in need' is widely defined, and there is some considerable variation between one local authority and the next in terms of the practical assistance that is offered to families. The local authority can also ask for assistance from other departments and agencies, which must be given unless this would prejudice the normal provision of their services.

A local authority is not allowed to provide accommodation or assistance in relation to the essential living needs of a child or her family where the family are asylum seekers. This restriction does not apply to unaccompanied minors under the age of 17.

Accommodation

A local authority has the duty to provide accommodation to any child where the parents are unable to provide it for any reason. There is no distinction drawn between a child accommodated by the local authority to give brief period of respite to parents or a child accommodated for longer periods. However, there is a distinction between children who are voluntarily accommodated by the local authority and children who are the subject of care orders in that it is only in relation to the latter child that the local authority has parental responsibility.

The local authority has an obligation to provide accommodation to children over the age of 16 where it considers that not to do so would prejudice the welfare of the child. In practice local authorities are reluctant to provide accommodation to such children, and it can be equally difficult for them to obtain housing by seeking to rely on homelessness legislation. The law is unclear on whether a local authority has an obligation to accommodate children under 16 at their own request.

Child protection

Where a local authority has reasonable cause to suspect that a child in its areas is suffering or is likely to suffer significant harm it has a statutory duty to make enquiries. The purpose of such an enquiry is to decide what action if any is necessary to safeguard the child's welfare. It is usual to make an initial assessment, which involves inter-agency enquiries regarding the child's education, health, general welfare and any particular matters that may have acted as a catalyst for the child coming to the attention of the local authority in the first place. If necessary, a child protection conference can be convened to co-ordinate multidisciplinary responses to any perceived needs the child may have that require local authority input. At this point the decision is made as to whether or not the child should be put on the child protection register and what action if any is necessary. Most children on the child protection register remain living with their parents and it is viewed largely as a precautionary measure. However, in some cases the local authority may decide after conducting a core assessment that the child should be removed from parents or carers and that care proceedings need to be initiated.

It is a matter for concern that to a large degree the views and wishes of children themselves can be overlooked at this stage of the process. Children do not as a rule attend child protection conferences as their interests are usually represented by a children's guardian, appointed by CAFCASS to represent the child in care proceedings. However, older children who can demonstrate sufficient maturity and understanding can attend child protection conferences.

Emergency protection

Police protection

Where the police have reasonable cause to believe a child would otherwise suffer significant harm they can remove a child into police protection for a period of 72 hours. The police are required to ascertain the child's own views, to inform the parents at the earliest opportunity and to notify the local authority to ensure the child is accommodated. Where a senior officer is satisfied that the grounds for protection no longer exist the child must be released. In reality, however, police protection is very often followed by an application for an emergency protection order.

Emergency protection order

The local authority may apply for an Emergency Protection Order (EPO) for up to eight days. These applications are made in the family proceedings court before magistrates, and the court must be satisfied that such an order is required because there is reasonable cause to believe that a child is likely to suffer significant harm if he or she is not removed to local authority accommodation. The court is also required to consider whether the order is necessary in the best interests of the child. In so doing it must balance the need for protection of the child with the potential damage caused by the trauma of removal from parents or carers. An application for an EPO can be made without notice to the parents, but they do have a right to apply to court to have the order discharged. The EPO is usually the first step in the proceedings for a full care order in respect of a child. In order to address concerns that arose regarding the length of such proceedings from beginning to end, which in extreme cases could go on for a number of years, the Lord Chancellor's Department issued the 'Protocol for Judicial Management in Public Law Children Act Cases' in November 2003. This establishes a strict timetable that must be adhered to in such cases, and in particular requires local authorities to play an active role in managing the case to ensure that the matter can be resolved in ten months from the date of the application for the EPO to the final care order decision. At the time of writing the protocol has only just been introduced and it is hard to assess its impact.

Care and supervision proceedings

The local authority may apply for a care order, which allows the local authority to share parental responsibility with a parent and usually involves the removal of the child from the home and placement either within the family or with foster carers. A care order can only be made where the court is satisfied that the child is suffering, is at risk of suffering or is likely to suffer significant harm as a result of the way the parents are caring for the child or because the child is beyond parental control. Once these criteria are established the court must place the child's welfare first, and where appropriate take into account the views and feelings of the child.

There is a general obligation on the court to consider whether other orders or indeed no order is more appropriate than a care order, which is still viewed as quite a draconian measure. In particular the court should consider whether the child would be adequately protected by the making of a supervision order, which allows the local authority to monitor the child's needs and progress while the child lives at home or elsewhere. Similarly, the court should consider whether a residence order could be made to a relative, which allows the child to be brought up within the extended family. In any case the court is also required to consider what arrangements have been made for contact between the child and his or her family.

Following the introduction of the HRA the courts are required to ensure that decisions about care orders take into account the rights of parents under Article 6 of the Convention – the right to a fair hearing. Consequently, parents are entitled to be consulted at all stages of the decision-making process, and in general should be entitled to legal representation in proceedings unless they choose not to participate. ECHR decisions make it clear that parents and children continue to enjoy a family life together whether they are living together or separately, and also impose a general obligation on the State when it intervenes in the life of the family to have reunification as an urgent and consistent goal.

Care plans

When a local authority applies for a care or supervision order it is required to produce a 'care plan', which details the measures it intends to take in relation to the child's future such as placement, long-term proposals, contact with the family etc. A court has very limited powers in relation to the care plan in that it cannot impose conditions on the order or the plan. However, where a court disagrees with the care plan it can refuse to make the order and instead make an interim order until the plan is approved. A court should not make a care order if it does not approve the plan given the consequences that follow from the making of the order.

Where there has been a breach of the parent's or child's rights under the Convention, they can bring an action, and as part of that application a court can review the care plan. However, a court cannot substitute its own care plan for that of the local authority, but can only approve or refuse to approve it.

See also Chapter 2.

Representation of children

Children who are the subject of applications for care or supervision orders are parties to the proceedings, but in the vast majority of cases they are represented by a children's guardian appointed by CAFCASS. Most children's guardians have worked as social workers, but they are appointed to act independently and to represent the child's interests. A guardian works in partnership with the child's solicitor, and where it is considered appropriate they can instruct independent professional experts such as psychiatrists or psychologists to prepare assessments and reports to assist the court in deciding whether the local authority's application for a care order should be granted. The children's guardian, in addition, will present his or her own report for the court, which should include a clear account of the wishes and views of the child who is the subject of the proceedings. CAFCASS can appoint a solicitor to represent an older child separately, but this is only rarely used.

Looked-after children

Children who are the subjects of care proceedings and who are accommodated voluntarily are referred to as 'looked-after' children. The local authority has an obligation to safeguard the child's welfare and to provide accommodation and assistance while in addition giving due weight to the child's wishes and feelings. There is a distinction between children who are the subject of care orders in that the local authority acquires parental responsibility, which is shared with parents, whereas parents retain parental responsibility for children who are voluntarily accommodated.

The local authority has an obligation to make plans for the child as soon as possible on accommodation. In so doing it must take into account the child's welfare, health, education, contact with the family and eventual return home. The local authority is expected to find an education placement for a looked-after child within 20 days. Parents and the child must be consulted in relation to any decisions that are made about the child. Plans for children who are looked after must be recorded in writing and reviewed initially after four weeks, then after three months and thereafter every six months.

Where a child or parent is not happy with the care plan or with changes in the care plan they can make a formal complaint to social services. A looked-after child should also have a personal education plan, which is attached to the care plan.

Contact and reunification

The local authority has a general obligation to promote the reunification of children with their family as soon as is practicable. This principle has been reiterated in a series of cases before the ECHR, but English and Welsh courts take the view that reunification will only occur if it can be demonstrated to be appropriate and in the child's best interests. Where a child is the subject of a care order to the local authority the court's permission is required before the local authority can terminate contact between the child and its parents. In most cases such a proposal is only made where the local authority's plan is to have the child adopted. In considering the question of terminating contact between a child and its parents, courts are required to give consideration to the rights of both parents and children to have their family life respected under Article 8 of the Convention. It is not uncommon for adoption of older children to be open to allow for continued direct and indirect contact with parents and other family members. Where contact has been refused and a child has been freed for adoption a parent or family member may still apply to the court for contact but requires the leave of the court to do so.

Complaints

It is not possible to sue a local authority for negligence because of its decision whether or not to take a child into care. The law on this matter remains unclear and in a state of flux, but the ECHR has found that where a local authority failed to protect children from parental neglect Article 3 of the Convention was engaged. This does not translate into an actionable duty of care in respect of all stages of the decision-making processes, as local authorities continue to enjoy wide immunities for public policy reasons.

However, children do have a right to make formal complaints against the local authority. Complaints are investigated by the local authority itself, and in certain circumstances the local authority can appoint an independent representative. Matters can also be referred to a panel for consideration of the complaint. There are concerns that the complaints process is not particularly easy for children and young people to negotiate without assistance and, moreover, that it is not a transparent process.

Children leaving care

A child ceases to be in the care of the local authority when he or she is either returned to his or her parents after a period of voluntary accommodation or, where the child has been the subject of a care order, the order is either discharged or by reason of age. A care order automatically comes to an end when the child reaches 18 years. The Children (Leaving Care) Act 2000 expanded the local authority's obligations in this position. It requires the local authority to advise and assist the child, and it must carry out an assessment of the child's needs. It is also required to prepare a 'pathway plan' for the child and appoint a personal adviser to assist the child to move into an independent living situation. In addition, the local authority has an obligation to take reasonable steps to keep in touch with a child who was in care until he or she is aged 21.

Secure accommodation

This is accommodation provided for the purposes of restricting liberty. These orders may be made in criminal proceedings and by family proceedings courts. The County Courts and High Court can also make a secure accommodation order in the course of other proceedings. Children who are looked after by the local authority and are over 13 years of age may also be placed in secure accommodation for welfare reasons. The initial placement may be for 72 hours, after which an application must be made to court. The court needs to be satisfied that the child has a history of absconding and is likely to run away from any open placement, and in so doing is likely to suffer significant harm or to injure him or herself. If these criteria are established the court may make an initial order for up to three months and a subsequent order for up to six months. The court must not make an order if the child is not legally represented. The order can, however, be made if the child has been offered legal representation and refused it. In most cases it is considered appropriate for the child to be present in court when the order is made unless there are concerns that the child would be unruly or disruptive in court.

The local authority must review the criteria within one month of the order being made to consider whether it is still necessary. It must be reviewed every three months thereafter.

When the HRA was passed there were concerns that the use of secure accommodation orders would not be compatible with Article 5, which provides for the right of liberty and security of the person. Article 5(1)(e) provides an exception to the prohibition on deprivation of liberty to allow for children to be detained for educational supervision. In a recent decision the Court of Appeal found that secure accommodation orders were not incompatible with Article 5 because 'educational supervision' applied to much more than school attendance and included education in its broadest sense. In addition, the Court of Appeal decided that the rights of children and young people were safeguarded because all children who were the subject of such orders continued to enjoy the right to a fair hearing in Article 6(1) of the Convention.

13.5   ADOPTION

An adoption order extinguishes the legal relationship between a child and its biological family by transferring parental responsibility to the adoptive parents. Adoption is only an option where the child is under 18 and has never been married. A child can only be adopted with the consent of the birth parents, although this consent can be dispensed with if the parent either cannot be found or is deemed to be withholding consent unreasonably. The latter question is to be answered by applying an objective test in that a court must decide whether a reasonable parent in the position of the parent, taking into account all the circumstances of the case, would withhold consent. The circumstances of the case will often involve the parents having been responsible for exposing the child to a risk of significant harm through neglect or abuse as applications for adoption are often made at the end of care proceedings. When a local authority has obtained a full care order it is increasingly common for an application to be made for an order under section 18 of the Adoption Act 1976 to declare the child free for adoption. This allows a local authority or adoption agency to locate a suitable placement for a child. When a freeing order is made the parents of a child become former parents and are no longer deemed to have parental responsibility for the child. Where no placement is located for six months the adoption agency has an obligation to review the child's situation and determine what if any action should be taken in relation to the child.

The matter of post-adoption contact is a controversial one on which consistent practice has yet to emerge. The views of older children will be given due weight, but there can be a presumption that continued contact with the biological family can disrupt the new placement and thereby undermine the child's opportunity for stability in a new environment. A court will generally not make an order for post-adoption contact unless the new family are in agreement.

At 18 children can apply for a copy of their original birth certificate and for information about their birth family from the adoption agency that arranged the adoption. Adult adoptees and birth family members can also apply to the Registrar General for entry of their names on the Adoption Contact Register, which includes the names of adopted persons and the relatives of adopted persons.

13.6   YOUNG OFFENDERS

Under section 37 of the Crime and Disorder Act 1998 (CDA) the principal aim of the youth justice system is to prevent offending by children and young persons. The CDA seeks to achieve this aim by promoting a range of diversionary tactics that remove children from the criminal justice system and introducing a range of alternative sentences if children are thought to be acting in an anti-social manner. The use of such measures, however, is controversial because they effectively create status offences where behaviour that would not attract criminal sentences if it were committed by adults is criminalised in respect of children.

Criminal responsibility

Children below the age of ten cannot be charged with criminal offences as they are considered incapable of committing criminal offences. This is considerably lower than the age in most other countries, and in both 1995 and 2002 the UN Committee recommended that the age of criminal responsibility be raised. Under the CDA, children under the age of ten can be the subject of a Child Safety Order. The order has the effect of placing the child under the supervision of a social worker or the youth offending team, and it may require a child to comply with certain conditions such as curfews.

Another new measure made by the CDA is the introduction of Local Curfew Schemes, which allow the local authority, in consultation with the Home Office, to introduce a scheme whereby children are banned from being in a public place during certain hours unless they are accompanied by an adult. Police can take a child home and inform the local authority if they are of the view that the child breached the order. The local authority has an obligation to follow up on any breach by making its own enquiries. This scheme was originally intended to apply to children under ten but can now be used for older children as well.

A further initiative of the CDA is the anti-social behaviour order (ASBO), which can be used on any person over the age of ten years. The local authority or the police can make an application to a Magistrates' Court for an ASBO where it appears that a person or family is behaving in a manner that has caused or is likely to cause harassment, alarm or distress to a person or people not of the same household. This is a civil application, and the onus is on the defendant to disprove the allegations. ASBOs can last up to two years, and a breach of an ASBO is a criminal offence.

In 2002 the UN Committee recommended that the Government review the use of ASBOs because it considered that they were incompatible with the UNCRC. This is because they are 'status offences' and also because they can be imposed without compliance with the minimum fair trial guarantees in Article 6 of the Convention.

The CDA also removed the concept of 'doli incapax' under which children between the ages of ten and 13 were deemed incapable of knowing the difference between right and wrong. These children are now treated the same as other young people aged 14 to 17 years.

Police investigation, reprimands and warnings

The rules for police questioning, search and detention of young people are the same as for adults but young people have additional rights. Parents must be informed of the arrest and detention, and interviews should only take place in the presence of an appropriate adult. The appropriate adult can be a parent, guardian, social worker or other responsible adult aged at least 18. The role of the appropriate adult is unclear but they should be able to advise and assist the juvenile and to ensure the interview is conducted fairly.

When it is a first offence the police have the discretion to issue a reprimand instead of proceeding with prosecution. For a second offence a warning may be used. A second warning may only be issued if the latest offence is not serious and more than two years have elapsed since the making of the first warning. Reprimands and warnings can only be given if the young person admits the offence, has no previous convictions and it is considered contrary to the public interest for the offender to be prosecuted. Reprimands and warnings are made at the police station in the presence of the appropriate adult. Following a warning the young person is referred to the Youth Offending Team for an assessment to decide whether a rehabilitation programme is appropriate. Reprimands and warnings do not form part of a person's criminal record, although they may be brought if there are court proceedings in the future.

Criminal trials and sentencing

The majority of young people are tried in Youth Court. This is a specialist branch of the Magistrates' Court. Certain serious offences such as murder, manslaughter, rape, arson, aggravated burglary and robbery are heard in the Crown Court. In both courts there is a requirement that the welfare of the child is considered when sentencing, but this is a weaker requirement than in the family courts. Following a decision of the ECHR guidance was issued to remind judges of the importance of guaranteeing the fair trial rights of young people in accordance with Article 6. In particular they are required to ensure that children sit with their lawyers and understand the nature of the proceedings and the evidence that is being given against them. In addition, judges are required to provide regular breaks and to restrict reporting in the media where appropriate.

Sentencing

Community sentences
In common with adults, young people may be subject to a range of sentences including a fine, attendance order or supervision order. Supervision orders may include a range of conditions, such as participation in particular activities, night restrictions or a requirement that the child lives in social services accommodation for up to six months. New sentences under the CDA include reparation orders and action plan orders. These are intended to provide young people with the opportunity to avoid custodial sentences and to make amends to victims or to the community.

Referral orders are similar and were introduced by the Criminal Justice and Youth Evidence Act 1999. The process is aimed at the first-time offender who admits the offence and where the offence would only normally attract a fine. It allows the juvenile to be referred to the Youth Offending team and work is carried out to challenge their behaviour.

These measures were also of concern to the UN Committee because of the lack of clarity around the fair trial rights of young people.

Custodial sentence
The CDA introduced the detention and training order for young people between the ages of 12 and 17 years. The sentence is intended to be divided between a custodial stage and a training stage. It is available for 15 to 17 year olds if they are convicted of an offence that is so serious that only custody is appropriate and they are persistent offenders, or for 12 to 14 year olds who are convicted of a serious offence and the court is of the view that custody is appropriate and again they are persistent offenders. It can also be available for 11 to 12 year olds if made available by the Home Secretary where the child is found to be a persistent offender and custody is deemed necessary to protect the public. The training half of the sentence is supervised and it is intended to provide skills aimed at rehabilitation. This sentence can be made for 24 months provided that it does not exceed the adult sentence available for the offence.

Detention at Her Majesty's Pleasure
Young offenders convicted under the age of 18 of murder may be detained at Her Majesty's Pleasure, which is indefinite detention, firstly in social services secure accommodation transferring at 18 to a young offender institution and at 21 to prison. The length of detention, however, is set by the Lord Chief Justice and it is for the Parole Board to determine whether the young person should be released.

Detention under section 53 of the Children and Young Persons Act 1933
Young offenders under the age of 18 convicted of grave crimes that would attract a period of imprisonment of 14 years or more if committed by an adult may be convicted to a period of detention for periods in excess of 24 months provided that the sentence does not exceed the maximum term that would be imposed if an adult committed the offence. The court should determine the appropriate sentence for rehabilitation and deterrence, and for young people this is normally one half of the sentence before referral is made to the Parole Board. Young people are referred to the Parole Board for a determination as to whether it is safe to release the young person on licence once the tariff period has expired.

See also Chapters 5, 6 and 7.

13.7   CHILD WITNESSES

Children of any age can give evidence as a witness in a criminal trial if they can offer 'intelligible testimony', that is, they can understand the questions put to them and answer them in a way which can be understood by the court. Children under the age of 14 do not have to take the oath. For those over the age of 14 a court decides whether the evidence should be sworn or unsworn, on the basis of whether the child understands the solemnity of the occasion and the particular responsibility to tell the truth.

There is a presumption that unless the court considers it unjust, the evidence of children is given by way of a video recording, usually taken before the trial. Child witnesses can be cross-examined before the trial and that cross-examination can be shown to the court. Cross-examination can also take place on the day by way of a live video link-up.

13.8   EDUCATION

While education is recognised as a right of the child, international and domestic human rights law have tended to focus disproportionately on the rights of parents to control the content of their children's education. For example, Article 2, Protocol 1 of the Convention states that everyone has a right to education, and then goes on to say that the State has an obligation to respect the rights of parents to ensure that education and teaching of their children is in conformity with the parents' religious and philosophical convictions. The emphasis in education law and policy on the rights of parents as consumers is problematic because it dilutes the child's right to an education and it discourages acceptance of the importance of children's own views and wishes.

The law governing education in England and Wales is complex, not least because there is a range of different types of state maintained schools that have different forms of school governance. The majority of schools are fully funded by the local education authority (LEA). This section deals with the law relating to state schools only. With the exception of the ban on corporal punishment, independent schools fall outside the remit of the LEA, except if they are boarding schools in which case they must be regularly inspected by social services to monitor the welfare of the children.

Compulsory education
Children over the age of five and under the age of 16 are of compulsory education age and they must receive full-time education. Parents are required to ensure that a child receives efficient full-time education suitable to his or her age, ability and aptitude and to ensure that any special educational needs are met by attendance at school or otherwise. Parents may educate children at home or engage a private tutor, but the LEA must be satisfied that the education is of a sufficiently high standard. If the LEA thinks that a child is not attending school and is not receiving a suitable education elsewhere the LEA may serve on the parents a notice requiring them to satisfy the LEA that this is not the case. Where the parents fail to respond to this notice, the LEA can serve a school attendance order (SAO) requiring the parents

to register the child at a named school. Parents must be given notice of the LEA's intention to serve this order, and the named school must not be one from which the child has been excluded. Parents can try to have the child admitted to another school other than the one named in the order.

The SAO lasts while the child is of compulsory school age unless it is repealed by a court order. Where a parent fails to comply with the SAO he or she can be prosecuted before a Magistrates' Court and can be fined up to £1,000. In addition, the Magistrates' Court may also make a parenting order if it thinks that this would prevent further offences. This order can only last 12 months but may be quite expansive because it can require a parent to take measures specified in the order to avoid further truancy. The parent is also required to attend counselling for not more than three months. Breach of the parenting order is itself punishable by a fine of up to £1,000. Where a parent knows that a child is not attending school and fails to take steps to make the child attend, the parent can be fined up to £2,500 or imprisoned for not more than three months. A court that has convicted a parent for a failure to comply with a SAO can direct the LEA to apply for an education supervision order. The LEA does not have to do this but it must tell the court why it has chosen not to make an application.

The purpose of an education supervision order is to guide parents and children to ensure that the children receive a satisfactory education. The Department of Health has issued guidance on the use of education supervision orders, which last for up to one year initially, but may be extended for up to three years at a time. They cannot last beyond the point at which the child is no longer of compulsory school age.

Admissions

Parents have a right to state a preference for a school of choice for their child, unless that school is over-subscribed and it can be shown that admitting the child would prejudice the provision of efficient education or the use of the resources of the school. Children have no independent right to choose their school. In practice parents may not obtain a place for their child at the school of their choice. There is a right of appeal against a refusal of a school place, which is heard by an independent panel established by the LEA or the school governing body. Children, however, have no right to appeal.

Curriculum

Schools must ensure that there is a broadly balanced curriculum that 'promotes the spiritual, moral, cultural, mental and physical development of pupils at the schools and of society and prepares pupils for the opportunities, responsibilities and experience of adult life'. This must include religious education and sex education. Religious education must be included in the national curriculum but parents can request that the child be excused from religious worship or instruction. The ECHR has held that religious education should not proselytise or involve any kind of indoctrination. The LEA is responsible for taking steps to ensure that sex education is given in a way that has due regard to the value of family life and moral considerations. The Secretary of State must issue guidance to ensure that pupils are protected from teaching and materials that are inappropriate, having regard to the age and religious and cultural background of the pupils. In 2002 the UN Committee raised concerns about the high level of teenage pregnancies in the UK.

Until September 2003 schools were prohibited from 'promoting' homosexuality under section 28 of the Local Government Act 1986. As a result there was a general presumption that teachers were required to avoid any discussions of sexual orientation. In October 2002 the UN Committee indicated its concern about the discriminatory nature of this provision, and it was repealed in September 2003.

Special Educational Needs

LEAs must make special provision for children who have learning disabilities to ensure that they are provided with education that meets their needs. The general preference is that children with special educational needs (SEN) remain in mainstream schools.

Schools have an obligation to ensure that a child's special educational needs are identified and known to those involved in teaching the child. This process is done by way of assessment, and a child who has SEN is 'statemented' – a statement of the child's needs and measures that are to be taken to deal with those needs is provided. If parents are not satisfied with the eventual provisions or the nominated school, they may appeal to a Special Educational Needs Tribunal provided that they require the assessment of the child themselves. The question of whether a child requires assessment and statementing can often be contentious in that parents may wish to have a child statemented but can encounter considerable difficulties in convincing a school to undertake this process. Where the school refuses to statement a child the parents can appeal to the SEN Tribunal. Each school is required to have a Special Education Needs Co-ordinator (SENCO) who is responsible for overseeing the provision of SEN for a child within the school.

School discipline

School must have a disciplinary regime that promotes good behaviour and includes sanctions for breach of the school's own code. Schools have a right to set rules in relation to conduct both inside and outside the school. Guidance encourages schools to involve children and parents in the development of the school's disciplinary policies. Parents are required to enter into home–school agreements, which indicate their commitment to ensuring that children adhere to rules on matters such as attendance, discipline and homework. Children are directly involved in the drafting of such an agreement and are also required to sign it.

Following a series of cases before the ECHR in the early 1990s corporal punishment is now prohibited in all schools, including independent schools. However, teachers may use other forms of punishment to impose school discipline, including after-school detention.

Exclusions should only be used in the most extreme circumstances and as a measure of last resort. In 2002 detailed regulations were issued to LEAs on the circumstances in which children can be excluded and the procedural rights they have to appeal against their school's decision to permanently exclude them from school. Exclusions can be for one or more fixed periods but cannot exceed 45 days in one school year, unless it is a permanent exclusion. The head teacher must inform the child's parents of the exclusion, and must also inform the child and parents of the reason for the exclusion, whether he or she intends to apply for permanent exclusion and the right of appeal to the school governors or the LEA. Where a pupil is not informed of the right of appeal the decision to exclude could be the subject of judicial review. The school governors can order the headmaster to reinstate a child who has been excluded. The parents of a student who is not reinstated after an appeal can take an appeal to an education panel, which is required to act in accordance with Article 6 of the Convention (the right to a fair hearing). It is a matter of concern that children do not have a legal right to attend disciplinary hearings or appeal hearings in relation to their own exclusion. In 1995 and again in 2002 the UN Committee indicated that this was contrary to the spirit of Article 12 of the UNCRC.

See also Chapters 10 and 15.

13.9 MONEY, FINANCIAL SUPPORT AND BENEFITS

Child Support
Under the Child Support Acts of 1991 and 1995 and the Child Support, Pensions and Social Security Act 2000 parents have a duty to support their children financially until they are 18. This obligation continues after separation or divorce and is unaffected by whether the parent has parental responsibility or not. Child Support is administered by the Child Support Agency, which is a branch of the Benefits Agency. The amount of maintenance payable is calculated according to a standard formula, and although the welfare of the child can be taken into account in certain circumstances, the rules are complex and the outcome may not always appear to do so. Young people do not have a right to make their own applications for a maintenance assessment against their parents. However, people over 18 may apply to a court for maintenance if they are at school, in full-time or part-time education or in higher education or training.

Benefits
Children of 16 and 17 are not entitled to social security benefits as of right. They are expected to access work-based training through the Careers Service for which they are paid a training allowance. However, 16 to 17 year olds may apply for benefits in certain limited circumstances. They are entitled to income support if they are unable to work as a result of ill health or disability or pregnancy or the care of dependants. They may also be eligible to income-based job seeker's allowance (JSA) if they are available for work and training, and also qualify for income support, although in practice it may be difficult to satisfy the availability-for-work requirement. Children of 16 and 17 may be able to obtain JSA on a discretionary basis to avoid 'severe hardship'. This payment is made for 16 weeks but may be renewed. The Benefits Agency should take into account the young person's vulnerability to risk of any kind, including homelessness and whether there is anyone else to support them. Children under 18 may also be eligible for longer-term JSA hardship payments as they come within the definition of a vulnerable group. In these circumstances the Benefits Agency must look at whether there is a 'substantial risk' that the claimant will be without certain essential items such as food, clothes, heating and accommodation.

13.10   CITIZENSHIP, NATIONALITY AND REFUGEES

Citizenship and nationality

A child born in the UK before 1 January 1983 is automatically a British citizen irrespective of the nationality of his or her parents. Children born in the UK after that date are entitled to British citizenship only if one parent is a British citizen or is settled in the UK at the time of their birth. A child who is not a British citizen but is adopted by British citizens becomes entitled to citizenship from the time of the adoption order. See also Chapter 11.

Unaccompanied minors seeking refugee status

The same international obligations under the Convention on the Status of Refugees apply to children as to adults. However, in recognition of their particular vulnerability there are additional safeguards for children who apply for asylum in their own right. Children may have access to an adviser from the children's panel of the Refugee Council to assist and advise them in relation to their application and other matters such as claiming benefits and obtaining accommodation. Local immigration officers are obliged to notify the local authority of the arrival of an unaccompanied minor. A child's application for asylum should be given priority.

13.11   TRAVELLING AND LEAVING THE COUNTRY

Since October 1998 all children who were not on a valid ten-year passport need to have a passport of their own to travel abroad. A parent or other person with a residence order may take a child out of the country for a period of four weeks without the permission of non-residential parents or other holders of parental responsibility. This is to allow parents to take their children for holidays without requiring permission of the other parent. However, where a parent is concerned about the frequency of such trips or has fears that a parent may abduct a child he or she can apply to the court to impose restrictions on removal or require that a passport be surrendered.

Removal of a child from the jurisdiction on a more permanent basis is more complicated. Again the paramountcy of the child's welfare will prevail in considering whether such a move should be permitted. A court will also consider the impact of the removal on the child's relationship with his or her other parent and any siblings or extended family members who are to remain in the UK.

Where a child is removed from the jurisdiction without agreement it is possible to use the Hague Conventions on Child Abduction (the Hague Conventions), which provide a procedure for the summary return of abducted children. The aim is that the law of the country of habitual residence of the child should be enforced unless specific and somewhat restrictive grounds can be satisfied that the courts in the country of habitual residence should sort out any difficulties that need resolution. While courts must take into account the wishes and feelings of the child, children do not have a right to invoke the Hague Conventions in their own right.

13.12   FURTHER INFORMATION

Useful contacts

Adoption Contact Register
47 Hawthylands Road
Hailsham
East Sussex BN27 1EY
ukbirthhelp@lookupuk.com
<www.ukbirth-adoptionregister.com>

Advisory Centre for Education (ACE) Ltd
1c Aberdeen Studios
22 Highbury Grove
London N5 2DQ
Tel: 0808 800 5793
enquiries@ace.dialnet.com
<www.ace-ed.org.uk>

The After-Adoption Charity
Tel: 0161 839 4932
Actionline: 0800 056 8578 (10 a.m. – 9 p.m.)
information@afteradoption.org.uk
<www.afteradoption.org.uk>

British Youth Council
2 Plough Yard
Shoreditch High Street
London EC2A 3LP
Tel: 020 7422 8640
Fax: 020 7422 8646
mail@byc.org.uk
<www.byc.org.uk>

CAFCASS
2nd Floor, Newspaper House
8–16 Great New Street
London EC4A 3BN
Tel: 020 7210 4400
Fax: 020 7210 4422
webenquiries@cafcass.gov.uk
<www.cafcass.gov.uk>

Child Support Agency
PO Box 55
Brierley Hill
West Midlands DY5 1YL
Tel: 0845 713 3133
Fax: 0845 713 8924
<www.csa.gov.uk>

Children's Rights Alliance for England
94 White Lion Street
London N1 9PF
Tel: 020 7278 8222
Fax: 020 7278 9552
info@crae.org.uk
<www.crae.org.uk>

Childline
45 Folgate Street
London E1 6GL
Freephone: 0800 1111
<www.childline.org.uk>

The Children's Legal Centre
University of Essex
Wivenhoe Park
Colchester
Essex CO4 3SQ
Tel: 01206 873820
Fax: 01206 874026
<www.childrenslegalcentre.com>

National Youth Advocacy Service
99–105 Argyle Street
Birkenhead
Wirral CH41 6AD
Tel: 0151 649 8700
info@nyas.net
<www.nyas.net>

NSPCC
Weston House
42 Curtain Road
London EC2A 3NH
Tel: 0800 800 500
Fax: 020 7825 2525
help@nspcc.org
<www.nspcc.org.uk>

Voice for the Child in Care
Unit 4, Pride Court
80–82 White Lion Street
London N1 9PF
Tel: 020 7833 5792
Fax: 020 7713 1950
info@vcc-uk.org
<www.vcc-uk.org/vcc_public/default.asp>

United Kingdom Youth Parliament
7 Anstice Square
Madeley, Telford
Shropshire TF7 5BD
Tel: 01952 681994
mail@ukyouthparliament.org.uk

Tess Gill
Marcus Pilgerstorfer

14 The Rights of Workers

This chapter deals with:

- Contracts of employment
- Part time working and fixed term contracts
- Equal pay
- Rights arising on pregnancy
- Parental leave
- Time off to care for dependants
- Health, safety, sickness and disability
- Drug taking and drinking
- Claims
- Dismissal
- Redundancy
- Whistleblowers
- Unions
- Industrial action
- The European Convention on Human Rights
- Further information

14.1 CONTRACTS OF EMPLOYMENT

Employed or self-employed

Employment law has in the past generally only protected employees. Many new rights protect workers, including those working under a contract to provide services even though they are not employees; the category of 'worker' is therefore much wider than that of 'employee'. In discrimination cases and equal pay cases, workers under a personal contract to do work are also covered.

You will generally be an employee, and not self-employed, if the economic reality of the relationship is that you are not in business on your own account, or in ordinary language, 'Are you your own boss?' A crucial test is whether you and your employer owe each other certain obligations that include, on your part, the requirement to obey instructions and to do the work yourself; and on your employer's part to provide work – if available – and to pay you for the work done. Since there are tax advantages to the worker and tax and other advantages to the employer in establishing self-employed status, these are superficial temptations.

Self-employed workers are denied access to much employment protection legislation and are unprotected by the employer's compulsory insurance against industrial injuries. Unless you genuinely want to go into business on your own account, taking the risks inherent in such a practice, you should resist offers to become self-employed. Remember that even if your employer calls you self-employed and you are self-employed for tax and National Insurance purposes, you may be found to be an employee for the purposes of employment protection if you claim unfair dismissal or other statutory rights.

If you are supplied by an employment agency or business to do work for another company, you might still be an employee of that company rather than of the employment agency. Documents relating to your supply through the agency will be relevant to this question. Under the Conduct of Employment Agencies and Employment Businesses Regulations 2003, which came into force on 6 April 2004, the employment agency must specify your employment status, although this is not determinative should an Employment Tribunal later come to consider the issue.

Certain categories of worker are given employment protection rights although strictly they are not employees. For example:

- Apprentices enter into fixed-term contracts, which impose particular obligations upon the apprentice and the employer. There is a strict obligation to give and accept instruction in the trade, and termination generally requires the apprentice's parents' consent.
- Civil servants, including some National Health Service workers, work under terms of service with the Crown and do not have contracts of employment. Nevertheless, they have access to most of the employment legislation, and where they are excluded they have their own arrangements, for example, in relation to redundancy pay.
- People who hold office may or may not be employees, depending on the nature of the relationship with their 'employer'. Directors of companies, for example, may be office holders under company law and also be employees of their companies. Trade union officers hold office by virtue of their election in some cases, and are also employees of their union. Police officers hold office and are not employees, but they are covered by discrimination laws.
- Home workers may or may not be employees, depending on the nature of the relationship and upon whether they are engaged in business on their own account, applying the 'economic reality' and 'mutual obligation' tests.
- Casual workers may be self-employed or employees only for the time when they are engaged, even though they continue to work day after day for the same employer and take on all the appearances of a regular employee. If you can establish that all your contracts as a casual worker are linked under an 'umbrella' contract, or that you have worked continuously for the same employer, you may be successful in establishing that you are an employee and therefore have rights under the legislation on which you intend to rely.
- Trainees on government training schemes may or may not be employees, depending on the type of scheme and the arrangements for pay, but are covered by health and safety and discrimination legislation.
- Volunteers may be able to show that they are employees, particularly if they are claiming that they have been discriminated against. The definition of employment in discrimination legislation is wider than the definition for unfair dismissal situations. Volunteers should not be put off seeking employment law

advice in discrimination situations. Volunteers should gather all evidence of potential contractual obligations, including: their volunteer contract, any offer letter or other correspondence concerning their work, any expenses forms and any handbooks or policies covering their work. They should also inform their adviser of their working hours, their job description and any training that was required in order to volunteer with the organisation concerned.

Contents of a contract

Every employee has a contract of employment, which may or may not be in writing. It is important to remember that you may still be an employee working under a contract of employment even if nothing is written down. The fact that you have agreed to work and your employer has agreed to pay you is likely to constitute a contract of employment. If it is it not a contract of employment, it is likely to be a contract under which you have certain rights, for example, to be paid for the work you do, and not to be discriminated against on grounds of sex, race or disability. If a dispute arises as to the rate of pay or entitlement to bonus, it will be more difficult for you to prove that your version is correct, but that does not detract from the fact that you have contractual rights. A contract will generally consist of terms and conditions, which may be identified in any of the following forms:

Written statement

Within two months of your starting work, your employer must provide you with a statement, in writing, of the particulars of your terms of employment. This is not in itself a contract, but can be used as evidence of contractual terms before an Employment Tribunal. The terms included in the statement must include:

- The name of your employer.
- The date your employment started and whether any previous employment is regarded as continuous with it.
- The rate of pay or the method of calculating it and how often it is paid.
- Hours of work.
- Entitlement to holidays, holiday pay, sick pay, and whether or not a pension scheme exists.
- The length of notice to terminate the employment contract, which is required to be given by each side.
- Job title.
- If your employment is not intended to be continuous the period for which it is expected to continue, if it is for a fixed term, the date on which it is to end.
- Your place or places of work and whether you are required to work outside the UK.
- Whether any collective agreements directly affect your terms and conditions of work.

These particulars must be given in a single document unless they refer to another accessible document for particulars of incapacity, sick pay or pensions, or notice requirements. Any disciplinary rules that apply to you must be specified, as well as the name of any person to whom you can apply if you have a grievance or are dissatisfied with any disciplinary action, and the procedure that you must follow. Details of disciplinary rules need only be given if your employer employs at least 20 people. Another accessible document, such as a company handbook that contains this information, may be referred to.

When the relevant part of the Employment Act 2002 comes into force (which is expected to be October 2004), a letter of engagement or a written contract of employment will be able to form all or part of the written statement of the main terms and conditions, provided it includes some or all of the particulars referred to above and is given to you either before your employment begins or within the first two months.

If you are not given a written statement, you can make a claim to an Employment Tribunal, and if successful the Employment Tribunal will determine what particulars should have been given to you and what they should have said. When the Employment Act 2002 comes into force, it will also be possible in certain circumstances to get compensation where your employer has failed to provide you with a written statement of particulars, or has provided you with an inaccurate or incomplete one. The circumstances in which you will be able to get such compensation are when you make another sort of complaint to an Employment Tribunal, for example, a complaint of unfair dismissal, a claim for redundancy pay or a complaint of discrimination, and the Employment Tribunal finds in your favour. The Employment Tribunal can then award either two or four weeks' pay in addition to any other award you are given because of your employer's failure to provide you with a written statement of particulars. This is subject to a maximum of £270 per week for dismissals that occur after 1 February 2004.

As previously mentioned, the written statement provides strong evidence of what the agreed terms are, but does not in itself constitute the contract of employment – unless the necessary particulars are given in your contract of employment under the Employment Act 2002. As the written statement is just your employer's account of what are the terms of your contract, you can challenge the terms in it if they are not those to which you agreed. Even if you have signed to acknowledge receipt of the statement, it is not itself a contract. However, it is best only to agree to sign that you have received the document and not that you accept its contents as being true, so that if you later want to challenge any of the contents you are free to do so. You must be notified of any changes to your terms and conditions not later than one month after such changes take effect. Again, you may be referred to an accessible document, which contains the information as to such changes. Only changes to which you, or your union on your behalf, have agreed are binding upon you. If your employer unilaterally attempts to impose a change on you, you are entitled to record that you do not agree to the change and hold your employer to the original agreement. Your employer may counter-attack by dismissing you and offering you a new contract with the new terms. If you claim unfair dismissal, the Employment Tribunal would have to decide whether the employer had good business reasons for the changes and whether in all the circumstances the dismissal was fair.

Collective agreements
Frequently, many of these terms and conditions will be determined by agreements negotiated by trade unions on your behalf. The fruits of the negotiations between unions and employers are usually incorporated into your contract of employment, since either your written statement or the custom and practice at your workplace (which is reasonable, certain and notorious) will generally say so. Collective

agreements generally set terms and conditions such as wages, hours, holidays and sick pay, and will also provide the machinery for the resolution of disputes, discipline and grievances.

Itemised pay statement
Every time you are paid, you are entitled to a written statement setting out the gross pay, any variable or fixed deductions, net pay and, if not all the pay is paid in the same way, the method of payment for each part, for example, where a bonus is paid less frequently than basic pay. If you have fixed deductions for each pay period, it is sufficient for your employer to give you a statement in advance of what the fixed deductions are, and they must reissue it at least annually. If you are not given an itemised pay slip, then you can make a claim to an Employment Tribunal.

Work rules
Your employer may publish on notice boards or in employee handbooks a set of work rules. These do not necessarily form part of your contract, so that if you break any of them you may not automatically be breaking your contract of employment. At most, they are your employer's instructions about how the job is to be done and are not to be treated as rules cast in stone. They can be challenged if you make a claim to an Employment Tribunal arising out of, for example, your dismissal for breaking one.

Wages council orders and Agricultural Wages Boards
The Agricultural Wages Board sets minimum rates and rest days for agricultural workers. If agricultural workers are not paid the minimum rate wages, inspectors employed by the Department of Trade and Industry can prosecute the employer. A court can order the employer to pay a fine and to make payments of arrears of wages or repayment of deductions unlawfully made – for example, for accommodation. In addition, proceedings can be brought either by you or the wages inspector in the County Courts.

Breach of contract
Since it takes two parties to make a contract, both parties must agree changes to it. Otherwise there is a breach of contract, which, if sufficiently serious, entitles you to say the contract is at an end and to walk out (a constructive dismissal). Alternatively, as explained above, you can refuse to accept that the serious action or omission by your employers has brought the contract to an end and you can continue to work, while reserving your rights to make a claim in the courts for breach of the original contract. If the variation has an immediate practical effect, you are expected to object straight away; if it does not, you can wait until you feel the effects of the variation before complaining. A breach occurs when either party fails to carry out the agreed terms, or terms that have been implied by the courts or by custom and practice, or when you are dismissed with no or insufficient notice, unless you have committed gross misconduct. A sufficiently serious breach of contract will also entitle you to bring a claim of unfair dismissal.

Contractual obligations
This section contains the main contractual obligations between you and your employer.

National minimum wage

Workers have the right to be paid the national minimum wage. This means that all workers aged 22 or over must be paid a specified minimum hourly rate. At present the minimum hourly rate is set at £4.50. Workers aged 18 or over but who have not reached 22 are entitled to a minimum hourly rate of £3.80. Workers who have not reached their eighteenth birthday do not qualify for the minimum wage at present. Additionally, apprentices aged between 18 and 26 are not entitled to the minimum wage during the first year of apprenticeship. Specific detailed provisions exist for workers taking accredited training, entitling them to an hourly rate of £3.80 for the first six months of their employment. New rates have been set and are effective from 1 October 2004: £4.85 per hour for workers aged 22 or over and £4.10 for 18 to 22 year olds. Further, a new rate has been set for 16 to 17 year olds: £3.00 per hour.

Payment of wages

Employers are under a duty to keep records of the wages paid to their workers. You can inspect your records by making a written request to your employer. Employers must produce these records within 14 days of the request. If you are not being paid the minimum wage, you can contact the Inland Revenue enforcement agency or bring a claim yourself in the Employment Tribunal. The Inland Revenue enforcement agency can only enforce the national minimum wage in respect of workers who are still in employment.

You are entitled to be paid the minimum wage both for time when you are actually working and for time when you are available for work at or near your place of work. If, for example, your job requires you to be at a certain place ready to perform tasks as and when required you are entitled to be paid the minimum wage for the whole of that time even if you are free to do as you please between tasks.

The method and frequency of wages or salary are as set out in your written statement. If deductions are made unlawfully from your pay you can make a claim to an Employment Tribunal. Deductions are lawful only if you have given your consent in writing or if this is provided for in your contract. However, there are exceptions allowing your employer to make deductions in respect of: overpayment of wages and expenses; payments by law to public authorities; payments to third parties, for example to trade unions, or deductions following a strike or other industrial action. The law as to unlawful deductions applies not just to employees but to all workers provided they have undertaken to do the work personally.

Hours of work

Hours of work are determined by agreement either with you or with trade unions. The Working Time Regulations 1998 impose restrictions on the hours worked. The Regulations provide for:

- An average 48-hour maximum working week measured over a 17-week reference period – six months for certain types of work, or 12 months where a workforce or collective agreement so provides. You can opt out of this average 48-hour maximum where you agree with your employer in writing. This opt-out can be terminated by giving a maximum of three months' notice or, where no period of notice is specified in the agreement, by giving your employer seven days' notice of your wish to opt into the 48-hour maximum.

- For night workers an average of eight hours in a 24-hour period over a period of three months.
- A minimum of four weeks' paid annual leave. This must be taken and cannot be rolled over to the next year. However, if you leave during the year without having taken all your leave, your employer must make some payment in respect of your accrued leave. Although your employer must pay you for the leave you take under the Regulations, if he or she can show that your normal pay includes an element of holiday pay that element will count towards payment for your annual leave. If you have left having taken more than your accrued holiday pay this can only be recouped by your employer if there is a relevant agreement to that effect.
- Eleven hours' daily rest for adult workers in each 24-hour period.
- An uninterrupted weekly rest break of not less than 24 hours in each seven-day period – subject to exceptions.
- An uninterrupted rest break of 20 minutes, which can be taken away from the workplace where a worker's daily working time is more than six hours – this may be modified by a collective or workforce agreement.

There are numerous exemptions to the new regulations for certain types of workers, such as workers on board a sea-going fishing vessel, and certain activities undertaken by the armed forces, police or civil protection services. Until 31 July 2004, doctors in training are not entitled to many of the rights under the Regulations. There are some restrictions on the hours of young people below the age of 18.

If your employer refuses to comply with any of your working time rights, the Employment Tribunal can award compensation.

Obligation to provide work
As long as your employer pays you, they have no obligation to provide you with work. The right to work may be enforced only by:

- Employees who are offered the opportunity to earn commission or a bonus.
- Artists, actors, singers and performers whose careers are advanced by exposure.
- Highly skilled craft workers.

Claims for lost belongings
Although your employer is under an obligation to provide adequate storage for your clothing if you work in a factory, they are not generally liable to recompense you for losses unless they are aware of a history of thefts and have done nothing, or they know you are required to bring tools or clothing to work in order to carry out your job. In that case, it is more likely that you can claim.

Right to search
Your employer does not have the right to search you or your bag, unless you have agreed this in your contract or accepted it by long-standing custom and practice. Security officers have no general powers to search or detain you.

Suspensions and lay-offs
Your employer cannot impose a suspension or lay-off without pay and without your agreement. Suspension with pay, pending the investigation of an allegation of

misconduct against you, is often provided for in agreements, but unilateral suspension without pay for economic or disciplinary reasons is unlawful. If you are dismissed because of your employer's need for work of the kind you are engaged to do has diminished, you can claim redundancy pay if you are suspended or reduced to less than half-pay for more than four weeks. If there is no work at all, you can also claim a guarantee payment of £17.80 per day for up to five days per quarter.

Disciplinary and grievance procedures
When the Employment Act 2002 comes into force, statutory disciplinary and grievance procedures will be implied into every contract of employment. The standard disciplinary procedure requires your employer to inform you of any allegations in writing prior to holding a disciplinary meeting. Your employer must hold such a meeting before any action is taken. It must be held at a reasonable place and time but you must take all reasonable steps to attend that meeting. At the meeting, your employer must give you a proper opportunity to explain your case. Your employer must then notify you of the outcome of the meeting and of your right to appeal. If you wish to appeal, you must inform your employer, who must then invite you to a further meeting. The appeal must be conducted by a more senior manager than the person who conducted the original hearing, as long as that is reasonably practicable. The appeal meeting must be held at a reasonable place and time, but again you must take all reasonable steps to attend. At the appeal meeting, your employer must give you a proper opportunity to explain your case. After the meeting, your employer must inform you of the final decision. All stages of the procedure must be carried out without unreasonable delay.

The fact that these statutory procedures are implied into every contract of employment does not mean that your employer may not operate more detailed procedures. But any other procedure used by your employer must not be inconsistent with any of the requirements of the statutory procedures.

Once the Employment Act 2002 comes into force, it will be very important that you make use of the grievance procedure whenever you have a grievance about which you might eventually want to make a complaint to an Employment Tribunal, for example, if you believe your employer has unlawfully discriminated against you or if you believe your employer is behaving in such a way as to undermine the trust and confidence in your relationship. If you do not make use of the grievance procedure before making a complaint to an Employment Tribunal, it may not be able to hear your complaint at all. However, if you have raised your grievance in writing but your employer has not dealt with it within 28 days, then you may make a complaint to the Employment Tribunal even though the grievance procedure has not been completed.

Similarly, once the Employment Act 2002 comes into force, you must take care to comply with the requirements of either the disciplinary procedure or the grievance procedure and to co-operate with your employer in making sure the procedures are followed. If you do not, and as a result the procedure is not completed before you make a complaint to an Employment Tribunal, any compensation you are given by the Employment Tribunal may be reduced by up to 50 per cent. You must also make use of your right to appeal under either the disciplinary procedure or the grievance procedure because if you do not, then any compensation you are given by an Employment Tribunal in subsequent proceedings may be reduced by up to 50 per cent.

Personal data

You are entitled to see personal data held by your employer on computer and any other form of readily accessible information, such as personnel files and other employee records under the Data Protection Act 1998 (DPA). If the data are inaccurate, you may issue a notice requiring your employer to cease processing personal data about you, and you may be entitled to demand that any inaccuracies be corrected or removed. You may also be entitled to apply to a court to seek damages for the distress or damage that this has caused you. Not all categories of data fall within the DPA, as it provides for a number of important exceptions.

In processing your data, your employer is under a duty to comply with certain principles of data protection set out in the DPA. Personal data must be processed fairly and lawfully; data should be adequate, relevant and not excessive in relation to its purposes. Such data must not be kept for longer than is necessary. Employers who keep records of irrelevant data, such as marital or partnership status or vastly outdated disciplinary records, may be subject to challenge. The DPA also sets out requirements as to the conditions on which such data may be processed, which include the requirement to obtain the employee's consent. This may be done by making it a term of your contract of employment that you consent to such data processing. The processing must also be necessary for a specified purpose such as performance of the contract, compliance with a legal obligation, or to protect the vital interests of the employee. Increased protection is afforded to sensitive personal data, which include more intimate private matters such as your political opinions, religious beliefs, trade union membership, health and sexual life. You must have given your explicit consent or processing is necessary for a number of specified reasons such as legal obligation.

The DPA gives you the right to be told which personal data your employer is processing and to obtain copies of personal information held about you. You have four main rights under the DPA activated by a request to your employer and the payment of a maximum fee of £10. These are:

- The right to be told whether personal information is being held or processed by your employer.
- The right to be given a description of such personal data, the purposes for which they are being held and also the persons to whom the employer may disclose the data.
- The right to have the personal data communicated to you in an understandable form, such as a photocopy or printout.
- In cases where a decision is made using an automated process, such as performance-related pay methods, you are entitled to know the basis of the decision-making process.

Not all data is 'personal data'. The Court of Appeal has decided that the mere mention of your name in a document or e-mail is not enough (on its own) to make the contents of the document or e-mail 'personal data'. The data must be biographical in a significant sense and you must be the focus.

The Information Commissioner has published a Code of Practice for Employment Data on the use of personal data in employer/employee relationships.

See also Chapter 4.

Trust and confidence
You and your employer owe each other a duty not to act in a way that is likely to destroy or seriously damage the relationship of trust and confidence between employer and employee. This is often called 'the implied term of mutual trust and confidence'. The term may be breached by a failure to act as well as a positive action, for example, where an employer gives a benefit to all its employees except one. Whether or not the term has been breached in any particular case will depend on all the circumstances, including the seriousness of the conduct and its effect on the parties' relationship and whether the party in question had reasonable and proper cause for his or her actions. If your employer breaches the implied term of trust and confidence, this may constitute a fundamental breach of contract entitling you to resign and treat yourself as constructively dismissed. The implied term of trust and confidence does not apply on termination. This means it cannot be breached in respect of the termination process and (in appropriate cases) in respect of a series of events prior to termination. There must be a close enough connection between the alleged wrongdoing and the dismissal. This is not just a question of timing, and the fact that a dismissal results from conduct is not conclusive.

Duties of fidelity and confidentiality
You owe a duty of fidelity to your employer while you work and some aspects of that survive your leaving. While you are employed, you must not disclose confidential information, but you can use information that you remember. Furthermore, you must not remove and use your former employer's documents after you leave. There may be clear written instructions in your contract – known as restrictive covenants – that require you to keep information confidential or prevent you from setting up a business in competition with your former employer or from recruiting your colleagues to work for competitors. Such restrictions will be upheld by a court, provided they do not stop you earning a living and they are reasonable for the protection of your former employer's interests. However, a covenant is unreasonable if it restricts you for too long or from too large a geographical area, or if it prevents you earning a living. Information relating to your employer's specific trade secrets must be kept confidential even after you leave. Covenants to protect confidential information in a contract of services may survive the termination of the contract, even if your employer has breached your employment contract.

While employed, you must work for the one employer only during your working hours, but in the absence of some implied restriction on your working for others, you can work in your own time as you wish. Any money you make arising out of your employment belongs to your employer and you must account for it. If you produce written material for publication, your employer has the copyright over it. If you make inventions or create patents, your employer gets the benefit provided your normal duties include the likelihood of your making inventions. If you invent something of outstanding benefit to your employer, you can claim a fair share of the profits.

Duty to obey instructions

You are under a duty to obey instructions, provided these are lawful, reasonable and within the scope of the contract you have agreed. Other instructions will constitute breaches of the contract, for example, if you are instructed to do something that is against the criminal law or that is unsafe, unreasonable or outside the scope of the duties you have agreed to perform. If your contract is in any way illegal, for example, because of your intention to avoid tax by being paid cash in hand, the likely consequence is that you will be unable to claim rights under it. This means that you may not be able to claim unfair dismissal or other employment rights, although illegality is less likely to affect your rights under the discrimination legislation.

Previous convictions

You are under no obligation to disclose previous convictions, unless you are applying for a job in certain professions or occupations where disclosure is obligatory. You are entitled to answer 'no' to questions aimed at probing convictions that have become 'spent' after periods of time under the Rehabilitation of Offenders Act 1974. Answering negatively is neither a lie nor grounds for dismissal.

See also Chapter 3.

References

On leaving, your employer is not obliged to give you a reference. However, if your employer provides a reference there is a duty to take reasonable care to see that any reference is fair and accurate. There is an implied term in a contract of employment requiring the exercise of due care and skill in the preparation of a reference. If, as a result of a reference in which the writer failed to take reasonable care, the employee suffers loss, he or she may claim damages in the County Court. To claim damages you must show that the reference actually was given rather than you feared that it might be. You also need to show that a prospective employer relied on it. Public funding is available. Further, if a post-employment reference is discriminatory, you might be able to claim in respect of that illegal discrimination.

Time off

You have a right to time off without pay to be a member of a local council, health authority, school or college governing body, water authority, police authority, board of prison visitors or magistrates' bench, or for jury service. The amount of time off is that which is reasonable taking into account the effect of your absence on your employer's business. If your employer refuses to let you have time off for these reasons, you can bring a claim to the Employment Tribunal.

Flexible working

Employees who have responsibility as parents for children under six years old (or if the child is disabled, under 18 years old) have the right to request flexible working. This includes biological parents, adoptive parents and new partners of parents where they share childcare responsibilities. It does not include others, such as grandparents, aunts and uncles, even if they also share a house with the child unless they have parental responsibility for that child. The right will extend to agency workers as well as ordinary employees, but it will not extend to employees or agency workers who have been working for the same employer for less than 26 weeks.

You have the right to apply to your employer for a change in your terms and conditions to enable you to care for your children. The changes you propose must relate to the number of hours you are required to work, the times you are required to work those hours, or to where you are required to work. The types of working patterns you might apply to introduce into your terms and conditions are compressed hours, flexitime, home working, job-sharing, teleworking, term-time working, shift working, staggered hours, annualised hours and self-rostering.

You must put your application in writing to your employer. Your application must state that it is an application under section 80F of the Employment Rights Act 1996. You must explain clearly in your application your relationship with the child for whom you have parental responsibility. The application must also specify what change you are applying for and when you propose the change should become effective. You must consider what effects the change will have on your employer's business and explain the likely effects in your application, together with how, in your opinion, those effects might be dealt with. It is recommended that you use the Best Practice forms provided by the DTI. Although the form does not ask you to state why you need to work flexibly, you should explain your reasons clearly.

When your employer receives your application, he or she must arrange a meeting with you within 28 days to discuss your proposals. You have the right to be accompanied by a representative at that meeting. You and your employer might be able to agree a compromise at the meeting. If you do, your employer must write to you within 14 days confirming the compromise and the start date for the agreed changes to your terms and conditions. Your employer must accept your proposals unless they consider that one of the reasons set out in the Act applies to them. The reasons are:

- The burden of additional costs.
- Detrimental effect on your employer's ability to meet customer demand.
- Inability to reorganise work among existing staff.
- Inability to recruit additional staff.
- Detrimental impact on quality.
- Detrimental impact on performance.
- Insufficiency of work during the periods the employee proposes to work.
- Planned structural changes.

Your employer must notify you within 14 days of the meeting whether he or she has accepted or rejected your proposals. If he or she has rejected them, the notification must set out the business reasons and an explanation of why your request cannot be met. You then have a right to appeal within 14 days.

If your employer fails either to accept your proposals or to establish a business case for rejecting them for one of the permitted reasons, then you may make a complaint to an Employment Tribunal. You may also make a complaint if your employer has made a decision about your application that is based on incorrect facts. The Employment Tribunal may either order your employer to reconsider your application or award you compensation or both. The maximum amount of compensation that may be awarded is two weeks' pay (subject to a maximum of £270 per week). If your employer refuses your application to work part time it may also be indirect sex discrimination contrary to the Sex Discrimination Act 1975.

Your employer must not victimise you on the ground that you have made or proposed to make an application for flexible working. You may complain to an Employment Tribunal and get compensation if your employer subjects you to any detriment on that ground. If you are dismissed because you have made or proposed to make an application for flexible working, your dismissal will be automatically unfair and you may make a complaint of unfair dismissal to an Employment Tribunal and get compensation.

See also Chapter 10.

14.2   PART TIME WORKING AND FIXED TERM CONTRACTS

Part time workers

Less favourable treatment

If you are a part time worker (defined as someone who does not, according to the practice of the employer in question, work full time), you have the right to be treated as favourably as comparable full time employees who are employed on the same type of contract. The less favourable treatment may relate to terms and conditions of your contract, or any other detriment to which you might be subjected to by any act or failure to act by your employer. A comparable full time worker is someone who is employed on the same type of contract, is engaged in the same or similar work and is usually based at the same establishment.

If you show less favourable treatment, your employer can argue that it was objectively justified. To be justifiable, the reason for the treatment must be aimed at achieving a legitimate objective, necessary to achieve that aim and an appropriate way to achieve it.

Written reasons for treatment

If you believe that you have been treated less favourably because you are a part time employee, you may ask your employer to supply you with a written statement giving particulars of the treatment and reasons within 21 days of your request.

Any complaint of less favourable treatment should be presented to an Employment Tribunal within three months.

Fixed Term Employees (Prevention of Less Favourable Treatment) Regulations 2002

A fixed term contract is one which, in the normal course of events, will terminate either on the:

- Expiry of a specific term.
- Completion of a particular act.
- Occurrence or non-occurrence of a specific event other than reaching retirement age.

Less favourable treatment

You have the right not to be treated less favourably than a comparable permanent employee in respect of terms and conditions of your contract, or to be subjected to any other detriment by virtue of your employer's acts or failure to act. You must be able to point to a comparable permanent employee, who is employed by the same employer as you are, and you must both be engaged in the same or broadly similar work having regard to your qualifications and skills. Where there is no actual comparator at your place of work you can point to someone at a different site, provided he or she is employed by your employer.

There is no right for permanent employees not to be treated less favourably than fixed term employees.

If you make out less favourable treatment, your employer can argue that it is justified. Your employer can do so by showing that:

- The treatment is necessary for a particular reason (which must be aimed at achieving a legitimate objective, necessary to achieve that objective and an appropriate way to achieve the objective).
- Other aspects of your terms and conditions are more favourable and so offset the less favourable treatment.

Right to be told about permanent vacancies
Fixed term employees have the right to be informed of any permanent vacancies with the employer. This will be satisfied where the employer publishes vacancies in a medium that the fixed term employee has a reasonable opportunity of reading, for example, an internal memo.

Limited renewal of fixed term contracts
If you have been continuously employed under fixed term contracts for four years or more (discounting any period before 10 July 2002), and if your fixed term contract has been renewed or a new fixed term contract has been entered into, and if at the time of the most recent renewal or granting of contract the employment was not justified on objective grounds, then you will be regarded as having obtained a permanent contract of employment. Renewal includes extension.

Written reasons for treatment
If you believe that you have been treated less favourably because you are a fixed term employee, you may request that your employer supplies you with a written statement giving particulars of the treatment along with reasons within 21 days of your request.

A complaint of less favourable treatment must be presented to an Employment Tribunal within three months.

14.3   EQUAL PAY

Equal pay for women and men remains elusive for many women. In December 2001 the *Kingsmill Report* found that on average women who work full time earned only 82 per cent of men's salaries and women who work part time earned only 61 per cent.

Under the Equal Pay Act 1970 women are entitled not to be discriminated against by having less favourable terms of employment, including pay, if they are doing work that is the same as, or broadly similar to, that of a man in the same employment or employed in the same service, or if they are covered by a job evaluation scheme that gives them similar scores to a man doing different work, or if they are doing work that is of equal value to a man's. Pay is widely defined and includes all aspects of remuneration, including pension contributions.

If your job and that of the man you are comparing yourself with have been job-evaluated and your job scores less than his, you will have to prove that the scheme discriminates by, for example, giving undue weight to characteristics and abilities commonly possessed by men, or undervalues those of women. You can also compare yourself with a man who is doing work that is of equal value to yours whether or not his job has been evaluated under a job evaluation scheme. In these circumstances you may have quite different jobs.

To claim equal pay you must make a claim to an Employment Tribunal at any time before your employment has ended or within six months after. There is a form of questionnaire that you can use to ask your employer questions relevant to your claim. You can download the questionnaire from: <www.womenandequalityunit. gov.uk>. Your employer does not have to answer it but the Employment Tribunal may take any failure to answer into account when reaching a decision. If your claim is that your work is of equal value, the Employment Tribunal will decide whether to refer your claim to an independent expert appointed under the Equal Pay Act or decide the issue themselves. Unless your employer can convince the Employment Tribunal that there are no reasonable grounds for making the comparison, your claim is then assessed. If an expert is appointed to carry out the assessment, the Employment Tribunal may accept or reject the expert's report.

Even if you succeed in showing that your work is equal, your employer may defend your claim by proving the differences in pay or conditions are genuinely due not to sex but to another material factor. If a predominantly female group is generally paid less than a predominantly male group for like work or work of equal value, the material factor has to be objectively justified by the employer. This means that the employer will have to prove that the reason for the higher male pay corresponds to a real need on the part of the employer and is appropriate and necessary. If your employer can show a good non-discriminatory reason for only part of the difference in pay, you should succeed in respect of the balance.

Reasons for the inequality of pay put forward as material factors may include additional responsibility, the pressure of market forces and seniority. However, if you can show that the reasons themselves are discriminatory, such as seniority favouring men because they have on average longer service records, the defence should fail.

If you win, the Employment Tribunal can award arrears of pay for up to six years prior to the making of the claim and can change the terms of your contract to give you equality.

See also Chapter 10.

14.4   RIGHTS ARISING ON PREGNANCY

Maternity leave
Under the Employment Rights Act 1996 all pregnant employees have the right to:

- Paid time off for antenatal leave, 18 weeks' ordinary maternity leave, and not to be dismissed on account of pregnancy.

- Employees with at least six months' employment are entitled to statutory maternity pay for up to 18 weeks.
- Employees who have been continuously employed for at least one year at 11 weeks before the expected week of childbirth are entitled to an additional unpaid period of maternity leave. This starts immediately after the end of the 18th week of ordinary maternity leave and lasts for up to 29 weeks following the birth of the baby.

If your employer suspends you from your work during your pregnancy on health and safety grounds you must be paid.

In order to be entitled to maternity leave, you must notify your employer in writing, at least 28 days before the start of your leave, of the expected week of childbirth and when you intend to go on maternity leave. If you are eligible for additional maternity leave rights, it is presumed that you will take this extended leave unless you notify your intention to return early to the employer. If you wish to return before the end of ordinary or additional maternity leave, you must give your employer 21 days' notice.

Your employer can seek medical confirmation of your pregnancy. After the birth of your baby your employer can ask you to confirm in writing your intention to return to work.

You may be entitled by your contract or collective agreement to be paid while you are on leave, and to be paid above the minimum statutory maternity pay (SMP) levels. You can take advantage of whichever is better. SMP is available if you have been employed for 26 weeks including the 15th week before the expected week of birth. SMP is available from the eleventh week before birth and lasts for 18 weeks.

You are entitled to SMP at 90 per cent of your average earnings for the first six weeks of absence and 12 weeks' pay at the lower rate of £102.80.

The Employment Act 2002 has introduced the following changes:

- A new right to 26 weeks' paid adoption leave of up to £102.80 per week, together with a right to a further 26 weeks' unpaid adoption leave.
- The extension of ordinary maternity leave to 26 weeks, followed by 26 weeks of additional maternity leave.
- The period of statutory maternity pay is increased from 18 to 26 weeks.

Pregnancy-related dismissal
It is automatically unfair to dismiss you for a pregnancy-related reason or to fail to offer you a suitable available vacancy. If a redundancy has occurred during your maternity leave and it is not reasonably practicable to give you your old job back, you must be offered suitable alternative employment on terms that are no less favourable to you than to other employees. It will also be discrimination on grounds of sex to dismiss a woman for pregnancy-related reasons.

Paternity leave
The Employment Act 2002 introduced a new right for the mother or adopter's partner to take up to two weeks' 'paternity' leave paid at up to £102.80 a week. The partner could be the father, or someone (either female or male) who lives in an 'enduring family relationship' with the mother or adopter. In order to be eligible for

the leave, the partner must have been employed for not less than 26 weeks prior to the 14th week before the birth or adoption.

See also Chapter 10.

14.5   PARENTAL LEAVE

All employees who have been employed continuously for one year have the right to take parental leave for the purpose of caring for a child. The right applies to all employees whose children are born or have been placed for adoption. In such cases each parent has the right to take up to 13 weeks' leave for the purpose of caring for each child until the child's fifth birthday or in cases of adoption, the fifth anniversary of adoption or until the adopted child's 18th birthday, whichever is sooner. A maximum of four weeks' parental leave may be taken in a year, and this leave can only be taken in minimum blocks of one week's duration. Any period requested less than one week counts as one whole week. The leave is unpaid unless the employer agrees otherwise. Parents of disabled children are able to use their leave over a longer period, until the child's 18th birthday. The maximum period of leave for parents of disabled children is 18 weeks. Whether a child is disabled is determined by whether he or she is entitled to disability living allowance. People who wish to take parental leave immediately after the birth of their child, or when the child is placed for adoption, can do so if they have given their employer at least 13 weeks' notice of this before the expected week of childbirth or adoption. This leave cannot be postponed by employers under any circumstances. Employees can complain to an Employment Tribunal if their employer infringes these rights, and dismissal for exercising or seeking to exercise these rights will be automatically unfair.

During the leave period, the contract of employment continues and you are entitled to carry out the same job and on the same terms and conditions when you return. The mechanics of taking leave will be contained in a relevant collective or workforce agreement, or, if none exists, then the default provisions contained in accompanying regulations apply, which provide for specified periods of notice for requesting leave to be given by the employee. Employers have a limited right to postpone the leave by up to six months in certain instances.

14.6   TIME OFF TO CARE FOR DEPENDANTS

All employees, regardless of length of service, have the right to take a reasonable amount of time off to deal with family emergencies. Such absences are unpaid unless the employer agrees otherwise. The rights apply only to those providing care to a dependant, which includes the employee's spouse, parents, children or another person living in the same household who is not a tenant, boarder or lodger. Additionally, the right extends to any person who reasonably relies upon the employee for the purpose of providing assistance or making arrangements. Family emergencies include instances connected with the death, illness or injury of a family member, or where a dependant gives birth. The right also exists where an unexpected disruption has arisen in relation to care arrangements for a dependant, or where an incident occurs involving the worker's child at school.

You must inform your employer of the reason for your absence as soon as is reasonably practicable, as well as when you expect to return to work, unless this is impossible. You can bring a claim against your employer for unreasonably refusing to allow you to take time off.

14.7   HEALTH, SAFETY, SICKNESS AND DISABILITY

Health and Safety at Work Act 1974

The Health and Safety at Work Act 1974 imposes duties on all employers to ensure so far as is reasonably practicable the health, safety and welfare of their employees. This includes the provision of safe plant and systems of work, and making arrangements for the safe handling, storage and transport of all articles used at work. Information, instruction, training and supervision should be provided so as to ensure employees' health and safety.

If your employer breaks these obligations, the Health and Safety Executive inspectors can issue prohibition or improvement notices requiring the work to be stopped or the machinery to be improved. They also have power to prosecute your employer for offences under the Health and Safety at Work Act 1974.

If your trade union is recognised for collective bargaining, you have the right to appoint union safety representatives who are given rights under the Act to time off with pay and to carry out inspection of the workplace and of relevant documents. Employers must consult safety representatives on health and safety arrangements. Claims for time off can be made to an Employment Tribunal or complaints about safety can be made to the Health and Safety Executive.

General health and safety

Employers must keep workplaces clean, at a reasonable temperature, a minimum of 16¼°C, or 13¼°C when the work requires severe physical effort, free from humidity, well ventilated, well lit and well provided with toilets and clean floors. Dangerous machinery must be guarded or, when this is not practicable, other suitable steps taken. Cranes must be kept in good mechanical order and be regularly inspected. If you are working on processes involving danger to your eyes, you must be provided with and wear eye protection. Adequate drinking water and washing facilities must be provided. The atmosphere must be kept free of harmful dust and fumes.

Some of these obligations apply in all circumstances – they are 'absolute' duties and any breach of them will be a breach of the law. Some depend on what is practicable, in which case a lesser standard will suffice. Many of these obligations arise from regulations implementing European Union (EU) directives, which came into force on 1 January 1993. They replace many of the previous Factories Act 1961 provisions.

Specific regulations cover, for example, working with nuclear radiation, asbestos, lead and wood, and working in foundries and civil engineering.

First aid

Employers are obliged to provide first-aid facilities, including first-aid boxes and a number of trained first-aiders, depending on the nature of the risks posed by the employer's business and the number of employees. In hazardous workplaces, there should be one qualified first-aider where more than 50 persons are employed and two where more than 150 are employed.

Accidents and industrial diseases causing the loss of more than three days' working time must be notified to the Health and Safety Executive.

Fire safety

The Fire Precautions Act 1971 requires a fire authority to give a certificate to the occupiers of any workplace other than low-risk premises where an exemption has been granted or when there are fewer than 20 employees. This imposes duties on employers to ensure that fire precautions and means of escape are provided and maintained.

Sanctions

For breach of any of the Health and Safety regulations, the Health and Safety Executive may bring proceedings in the criminal courts and may issue prohibition and improvement notices.

Injuries at work

If you are injured at work you can bring a claim for compensation against your employer for negligence or breach of statutory duty on the basis that your employer has not provided safe tools or equipment, a safe workplace, proper training, or a safe system of work including assessing risks to your health and taking preventative measures when necessary.

A civil claim is made in either the County Court or the High Court depending on the seriousness of the injury or the disease you have contracted. Community Legal Services funding is available. You must claim within three years of the injury or disease, although you can sometimes claim later if you did not know that you were suffering from an injury or disease that is attributable to your employer's negligence. If successful, you will be awarded damages to compensate you for your injury and for financial losses such as loss of wages and expenses.

Psychiatric illness

Psychiatric illness caused by stress at work forms a significant proportion of work-related injuries. However, claims for compensation based on such illnesses are among the most difficult claims to bring successfully. If you think your work is the cause of your psychiatric illness, there are a number of hurdles that you have to overcome if you are to succeed in a claim against your employer.

You will have to show that you are suffering from a recognised psychiatric illness. In general terms, this means you must have evidence from a consultant psychiatrist who has diagnosed you with a specific psychiatric illness recognised by the World Health Organisation. A general diagnosis of stress will not be enough. You will need to prove that your illness is directly attributable to your work.

You will have to prove that it was reasonably foreseeable that you would suffer from such an illness as a result of the pressures of work. It is at this stage that the vast majority of cases fail because you will need to show that there were very clear danger signals that would have been obvious to your employer. The courts have held that there is no job that should be regarded as inherently likely to cause psychiatric injury, and your employer will generally be entitled to assume that you can withstand the normal pressures of your job unless he or she knows of some particular problem or vulnerability. It will not be enough that you told your employer you were suffering from stress. You are only likely to succeed if you can point to something of which your employer was aware such as a previous breakdown, or long periods of absence owing to stress before your final breakdown, or a clear indication from you or your doctor that there was a real risk you would suffer a breakdown. For example, it has been held that where an employee returned to work after a four-month absence for depression (and the illness was known to the employer) it was reasonably foreseeable that psychiatric illness might result from stress caused by the employer breaching its duty of care by failing to implement measures to assist with the employee's return to work. Where there is no such reason to anticipate injury to health, no compensation will be awarded.

You will have to show that there was something that your employer should reasonably have done to alleviate the pressures on you, having regard to all the circumstances, including the severity of the risk to your health, the degree of harm that could result, the costs of taking any steps to alleviate the pressure and any justifications for running the risk that your health may be damaged.

Sick pay
Many contracts and collective agreements contain arrangements for payment during times of sickness. If these are better than the minimum statutory sick pay (SSP) you are entitled to them by your contract. If you have made sufficient social security contributions, you will be entitled to SSP, payable by your employer. Provided you earn more than the lower earnings level of £77 you qualify for SSP for the first 28 weeks of absence, excluding the first three days. You get SSP at one flat rate of £64.35. You are entitled to no more than 28 weeks' SSP in any three-year period.

14.8   DRUG TAKING AND DRINKING

Drug addiction, like alcoholism, should be treated as an illness. In its advice booklet *Discipline and Grievances at Work* the Advisory, Conciliation and Arbitration Service (ACAS) urges employers to have a policy covering drug and alcohol problems. However, employers usually treat drug taking as misconduct giving the reason that drug taking, unlike alcohol, can be a criminal offence and employers can commit an offence under the Misuse of Drugs Act 1971 if they know that illegal drugs are being used or distributed on their premises. Research suggests that one in four of workplace accidents involves workers who have been drinking. Some 14 million working days are lost through alcohol abuse each year.

In the past, Employment Tribunals have usually found that dismissal is a reasonable response to drug taking or being under the influence of drink or drugs at work. However, there is an increasing trend towards treating long-term alcohol and to a lesser extent drug taking as an illness. Many employers have adopted a specific policy for dealing with alcohol- and drug-related problems. These may include taking time off for medical treatment. ACAS encourages this approach in *Discipline and Grievances at Work*. However, where an employee recklessly comes to work having been drinking or under the influence of drugs, dismissal is likely and will be held to be fair, especially if the work in question gives rise to danger in these circumstances.

Factors that a Employment Tribunal are likely to take into account include: whether the conduct was on or off duty; safety at work; contact with children or young people; the effect on the employer's reputation and business, and the illegality of the employee's actions. Off-duty conduct will not usually merit dismissal in itself, although it may if it affects the employee's ability to do the job or the employer's reputation. Even if the employee has been convicted of a drug offence, the employer must conduct a proper investigation before dismissing, otherwise it will be unfair as there may be mitigating circumstances. In one case, for instance, the employee did not smoke the cannabis found in his garden.

Personal problems leading to temporary drug taking or drinking have sometimes been seen as a factor that employers should take into account and restrict themselves to a warning rather than dismissal. Employment Tribunals often accept that an employer is entitled to assume that there is a safety risk in drug taking or drinking without there being any evidence. A worker who faces disciplinary charges connected with drugs or alcohol would do well to provide evidence that there was no safety risk.

The Transport and Works Act 1992 creates a number of criminal offences aimed at workers controlling vehicles – trains, trams, and so on – while being unfit through drink or drugs. In some workplaces, for example, there may be an absolute prohibition on possession of alcohol or drugs.

Drug and alcohol screening
Testing may not be carried out without the employee's consent. Consent may be obtained by making it a standard term in the contract of employment that employees consent to such tests. Random drugs screening and subsequent dismissal for a positive result has been held to be fair and not a breach of the right to a private life; the full factual circumstances will be relevant when deciding whether such a programme is fair in any particular case. The Transport and Works Act 1992 led to employers such as British Rail and London Underground introducing drug and alcohol tests.

The employer may require employees not to have any trace of the prohibited substance in their bloodstream. This gives rise to particular problems when applied to drugs, as some soft drugs are detectable for more than a month after consumption. It is doubtful whether dismissal would be justified in circumstances where drugs have been consumed off duty and give rise to no impairment in performance, and where no breach of the criminal law is involved.

14.9   CLAIMS

Most claims are brought before Employment Tribunals. Public funding is not available except for initial advice under the Community Legal Service's scheme for preparation and/or counsel's advice. Appeals from Employment Tribunals go to the Employment Appeal Tribunal (EAT) in London for which public funding is available. Public funding is also available if you are taking a case to the High Court.

Time limit
The first point to check is whether you are in time to bring a claim. Deadlines are strict, usually three months from the act complained of. This means that you should

count forward three months from the act, and then subtract one day, and submit your claim on that day. You can fax your claim to the tribunal at any time until midnight on the last day, but it is safer to fax the claim during working hours and call the tribunal to check that it has arrived safely. In equal pay claims, the time limit is six months from the termination of employment. Employment Tribunals can extend time in limited circumstances if it was not reasonably practicable for you to make your claim in time. In discrimination cases, time may be extended if it is just and equitable to do so, which gives the Employment Tribunal a wider discretion. Make sure you fill in, or have filled in on your behalf, the Originating Application to an Employment Tribunal form (IT1) and that it reaches the Central Office of Employment Tribunals for England and Wales. If you are not sure whether to pursue a claim or not, it is best to send your claim form in well within the time limit. You can always withdraw your claim at a later date if you decide not to proceed with it, although if you have behaved unreasonably the Employment Tribunal might award costs against you.

Documents

The organisation against which you are claiming – usually an employer but sometimes a trade union – will reply, setting out the grounds on which they resist the claim (this document is often referred to as an IT3 form). You may ask for further particulars of any matter they raise, and you can also be asked to give more particulars of your claim. Before commencing proceedings in a discrimination or equal pay claim, you may issue a questionnaire seeking to obtain information from your employer about the actions and policies you are challenging. If you have been dismissed, write a letter seeking written particulars of the reasons for your dismissal and ask for your employer to reply to it within 14 days.

An important step in the proceedings is the discovery of documents. You are entitled to see all documents relevant to your claim, including internal notes and minutes, which are particularly important in respect of claims for discrimination. If the employers do not provide documents, you can seek an order from the Employment Tribunal to this effect.

Representation

You can be represented at an Employment Tribunal by anyone you like or you can represent yourself. If you are claiming unfair dismissal, the employers present their case first because they must prove the reason for the dismissal. Their witnesses give evidence first. In cases where it is for the employee to prove the case such as discrimination, you will start.

If you think the hearing is likely to last more than the time allotted for it you should tell the Employment Tribunal so that they can fix a block of time for it. Otherwise the case will be adjourned with an interval in between.

The case is generally conducted by the chairman, who is a lawyer, but the Employment Tribunal also consists of two other lay members who are appointed by the Secretary of State for Trade and Industry from persons with experience in dealing with work-related problems. They have an equal say in the decision.

Awards

Employment Tribunals can award compensation, make recommendations of reinstatement or re-engagement if there is a finding of unfair dismissal, and make recommendations to employers to rectify discriminatory acts and policies. If there is a finding of discrimination, compensation may include compensation for injury to feelings and for any personal injury the discrimination has caused, such as psychiatric harm (for which a medical report would be necessary).

Costs

There is no general rule in Employment Tribunals that the unsuccessful side has to pay the other side's costs, and in the vast majority of cases each side will pay their own costs. However, in certain circumstances, an Employment Tribunal may order one side to pay some or all of the other side's costs. Those circumstances include where one party has behaved unreasonably in the way it has brought or conducted its case or if a party's case had no reasonable prospects of success. The maximum amount of costs that may be awarded by an Employment Tribunal is £10,000 if it assesses the amount summarily but unlimited if they are subject to a detailed assessment. If an Employment Tribunal makes an order that you must pay the costs of the other side, it is not permitted to take into account your ability to pay those costs, even if they are very high. Therefore, it is important that you only make a complaint to an Employment Tribunal if you are confident that you have some reasonable grounds for your complaint. The Employment Act 2002 will potentially alter this position because it authorises the amendment of the Employment Tribunal rules of procedure so that the Employment Tribunal can consider ability to pay when awarding costs. No such amendments have been made, and as such the rule that ability to pay is not considered must be followed for now.

Sometimes an Employment Tribunal will hold a hearing called a 'pre-hearing review'. This is a meeting where the Employment Tribunal considers what you have said in your application and what your employer has said in response. If the Employment Tribunal thinks that either side has a very weak case, it may require that party to pay a deposit of up to £500 as a condition for continuing. If an Employment Tribunal requires you to pay a deposit, you should give serious consideration to whether or not you want to continue: if you do decide to continue and you lose, there is a real risk that the Employment Tribunal will order you to pay the other side's costs. The statistics show that about 85 per cent of cases that go on to be heard by an Employment Tribunal after a deposit has been paid fail at the hearing.

There is nothing in the rules requiring Employment Tribunals to have warned you about costs before making a costs order. Employment Tribunals sometimes make 'costs warnings', and you should consider your position carefully in such circumstances. Employment Tribunals must avoid putting unfair pressure on litigants by such warnings.

Appeals

Appeals on points of law are made to the EAT. The EAT consists of a judge and two lay members. You may be represented by anyone you like at the EAT, but legal representation is advisable as the appeal has to be on a legal, not factual issue.

You can appeal from the EAT's decision to the Court of Appeal and then the House of Lords, again only on a legal issue. You must have permission either from the EAT or the Court of Appeal to take the case further.

14.10   DISMISSAL

A dismissal is the termination of a contract of employment by your employer. It can take many practical forms:

- You may be dismissed with or without or with less than your contractual notice.
- You may be made redundant or offered early retirement.
- You may resign in protest at your employer's words or behaviour. This is called constructive dismissal if your employer's action is serious enough.
- You may be given an ultimatum in which you can either resign or be dismissed.
- You may be the victim of a process of squeezing out over a period of time.
- If you are on a fixed term contract, your employer may refuse to renew it on its expiry.
- Your employer may refuse to take you back after a strike, or to re-engage you after your dismissal during a strike.
- Your employer may refuse to offer you a job after you have been on maternity leave.

There are only two kinds of dismissal in law upon which you can take action:

- *Wrongful dismissal*: when you are given less than your contractual period of notice or denied access to agreed procedures prior to dismissal.
- *Unfair dismissal*: when your employer has dismissed you for an automatically unfair reason (for example, pregnancy – see below), or where the procedure of your dismissal has been unfair.

Note that discriminatory dismissals may give you rights under both the unfair dismissal legislation and the discrimination legislation.

Notice

You are entitled to periods of notice depending on your length of service, and the written statement must include a note of your contractual entitlement. After one month's service you are entitled to one week's notice and thereafter at the rate of one week for each year of service, up to a maximum of 12 weeks. Of course, your contract may provide for longer periods than this, but if nothing is said, you are entitled to a reasonable amount of notice, which may exceed the statutory minimum.

If you do not get your contractual or statutory notice, you can bring a claim in the Employment Tribunal or sue for breach of contract in the County Court. If your employer has failed to follow a contractual disciplinary procedure you will also be entitled to claim compensation for the time it would have taken for your employer to go through all the stages of the contractual procedure.

You lose your right to notice if you are dismissed for gross misconduct. This term has not been defined by statute, but employers often give examples of gross misconduct either in the contract itself or in the staff handbook.

Reasons for dismissal

Provided you have been employed for one year at the date of dismissal, you are entitled to written particulars of the reasons for your dismissal. Following a written request, your employer must provide those reasons within 14 days. If this is not forthcoming, you can make a claim to an Employment Tribunal, which has the power to declare the reason for dismissal and to award two weeks' pay. If you are pregnant at the time of dismissal you are entitled to written reasons for dismissal without asking for it. If you are claiming unfair dismissal, you should seek written particulars in any event and add this to your claim if your employer does not comply.

Unfair dismissal

In order to claim unfair dismissal, you must have been continuously employed for at least one year unless you are claiming on the basis of race, sex, trade union discrimination, dismissal related to pregnancy, national minimum wage, working time rights, health and safety activities, making a protected disclosure, making an application for flexible working or, where in good faith, you seek to exercise a statutory employment protection right.

You can claim at any stage up to the age of 65, unless there is a lower normal retirement age at your workplace. The EAT has recently held that this rule is not indirectly discriminatory against men (it does not have a disparate effect on men and, in any event, would be justified). You may not be able to claim unfair dismissal if your contract, or part of your contract, is illegal and the tribunal decides that you knew about this, or co-operated with it.

If you bring a claim to an Employment Tribunal, your employer must show what the reason was for your dismissal.

Some dismissals are automatically unfair, for example, a dismissal for a pregnancy-related reason, or because the employee was an employee representative, or the reason for the dismissal was because the employee had made a complaint against the employer that his or her statutory rights had been infringed.

If the dismissal does not fall into one of these categories, the reason for the dismissal must fit into one of the following categories: conduct, capacity, redundancy, a legal restriction (for example, not having proper working papers) or some other substantial reason that could justify the dismissal.

Few employers have difficulty putting forward a reason, so the main dispute focuses on the reasonableness of the employer in deciding to dismiss for that reason and whether the employer has followed fair procedures, such as consulting employees before making them redundant or warning them before dismissing them for capacity.

Remedies for unfair dismissal

If you win your case, the Employment Tribunal must first consider whether you wish to be reinstated and, if so, must decide whether it is just and equitable to order that. If not, compensation should be awarded to take account of the losses you have suffered up to the date of the hearing and the amount of time you are likely to be unemployed, or if you have a job, to compensate you for any loss in pay in the new job. If you have claimed unemployment benefit, the amount of benefit you have received is deducted from the award of compensation. In addition, you should also get a payment equivalent to a redundancy payment that is called a basic award. In some cases, you may be able to get compensation for distress, humiliation, damage to your reputation or to your family life or similar matters caused by your dismissal. Such compensation is unusual and is unlikely to be awarded unless your employer had behaved particularly badly in dismissing you, for example, if your employer dismissed you on the basis of unfounded and very serious allegations that have severely damaged your reputation, or if the way you were dismissed was particularly humiliating, or if you were subjected to particularly abusive harassment by your employer that caused you to resign and claim constructive unfair dismissal. In principle, however, such losses are recoverable.

The amount an Employment Tribunal can award as compensation for unfair dismissal is capped at £55,000 (for dismissals after 1 February 2004) plus the basic award. If you were employed at a rate of pay below the national minimum wage, you will be paid compensation at the appropriate minimum wage rate.

After dismissal, you must take steps to try and find alternative work and, if you do not, your compensation may be reduced by a percentage. The Employment Tribunal may refuse to order reinstatement if you have contributed to your dismissal by your own actions.

In 2002–3, of the 43,510 unfair dismissal cases dealt with, 46 per cent resulted in an ACAS-negotiated settlement, 27 per cent were withdrawn, and 10 per cent were successful at the hearing, with 18 per cent of cases being dismissed. Of those cases disposed of at a hearing, 56 per cent were unsuccessful and 44 per cent were successful. The median award of compensation in 2002–3 was £3,225. Reinstatement or reengagement was awarded in 16 of the 4,158 of successful cases (0.004 per cent).

Breach of procedure

The existence of a disciplinary procedure in your contract of employment or collective agreement is important for both unfair and wrongful dismissal.

In unfair dismissal proceedings before the Employment Act 2002 comes into force, failure to go through either the agreed procedure or to adopt the 'rules of natural justice' (giving notice of an allegation, an opportunity for you to present your version of events) may result in the dismissal being unfair. In other words, a potentially fair dismissal can be made unfair if proper and reasonable procedures are not followed. In determining what is a fair and proper procedure, Employment Tribunals will have regard to the *Code of Practice on Disciplinary and Grievance Procedures* 2000, published by ACAS.

When the Employment Act 2002 comes into force in October 2004, your dismissal will be automatically unfair if the statutory disciplinary procedure has not been completed because your employer has failed to comply with it. However, if your employer has breached its own more detailed procedure but not the statutory procedure, then your dismissal will not be unfair if your employer can show that you would have been dismissed even if the correct procedure had been followed.

Furthermore, when the Employment Act 2002 comes into force, if the statutory procedure has not been completed because you have failed to comply with its requirements, for example, if you have unreasonably failed to attend a disciplinary meeting, then the Employment Tribunal may reduce your award by between 10 and 50 per cent. Your award may also be reduced by such an amount if you have failed to exercise your right of appeal against your dismissal.

If you are denied your rights under a contractual procedure (including the statutory procedures once the Employment Act 2002 comes into force) you may seek an injunction in the High Court to prevent your employer acting upon your dismissal or taking other disciplinary action until the procedure has been exhausted. This means you are to be treated as still employed, although perhaps not being required to work, until the full trial of your case for wrongful dismissal. Public funding is available for this type of claim.

14.11   REDUNDANCY

Redundancy occurs where your dismissal is wholly or mainly attributable to the fact that your employer's requirements for work of the particular kind you are employed to do has ceased or diminished, either temporarily or permanently. If you are dismissed for this reason, or put on short-term working (receiving less than half-pay) or are laid off for four weeks or more, you can claim a redundancy payment.

The payment is based on your age, length of continuous service and weekly pay. You are entitled to one and a half week's pay for each year of continuous employment when you are aged between 41 and 63 inclusive, one week's pay between the ages of 21 and 40 inclusive, and half a week's pay for each other year.

Weekly pay does not include all your earnings. Voluntary overtime is excluded but regular commission and bonuses are included. The maximum weekly pay allowable for redundancy purposes is £270 (from 1 February 2004).

You lose your right to a redundancy payment if you turn down an offer made by your employer to re-engage you on a new contract if the offer is of suitable alternative employment (the kind of work that would be regarded as suitable for you) and you have unreasonably refused to take it. The unreasonableness is judged by what your own circumstances are and is a more generalised test of reasonableness.

Before you are made redundant, you have a right to claim a reasonable amount of time off with pay in order to look for work or to retrain. If you accept an offer of new employment with the same employer or one of its associates, you have the right to a four-week trial period during which time you can quit the job and be regarded as redundant so that you do not prejudice your rights by taking the job for a trial period.

You need two years' continuous employment to qualify for redundancy pay. Your entitlement to redundancy pay is reduced if you have reached the age of 64.

If your employer disputes that there is a redundancy situation, for example, by claiming that there has simply been a reorganisation of the business without any lessening of the requirements for employees, or if you dispute the amount of money paid to you, you can make a claim to an Employment Tribunal.

You can also make a claim if you feel that you have been unfairly selected for redundancy or if the redundancy process has discriminated against you on the ground of your race, sex, sexual orientation, religion and/or disability.

If your employer is insolvent, you can make a claim for redundancy pay and other outstanding debts including notice and holiday pay to the Secretary of State for Employment.

Consultation
If an employer is 'proposing' to make at least 20 employees redundant within a period of 90 days or less, there is an obligation to consult employee representatives about a proposal to make any dismissal. This duty to consult does not arise where

an employer is only 'contemplating' making redundancies. There is a minimum consultation period: 30 days if 20 or more employees are to be dismissed, 90 days for 100 or more. Employee representatives are either trade union representatives or representatives appointed or elected by the employees. If a trade union is recognised in respect of affected employees, then the employer must consult the trade union representatives even where elected employee representatives in the workplace already exist. If the union or any employee representative claims that there has been inadequate consultation or none at all, it can make a claim to an Employment Tribunal, which can then make a protective award of compensation in favour of the employees who have been dismissed without the necessary consultation having taken place. The normal award is for the period that your employer has failed to consult unless there is a good reason for the failure due to particular circumstances.

Even where an employer proposes to make fewer than 20 employees redundant, it is part of a fair redundancy procedure that they are consulted.

Takeovers, mergers and transfers
If the business in which you work is transferred as a going concern to another employer, the Transfer of Undertakings Regulations 1981 protect all your terms and conditions with the new employer, including recognition of your union and your continuity of employment. If you are dismissed as a result of the transfer, you can claim unfair dismissal, which will be automatically unfair unless your employer proves that the dismissal was on account of an organisational or technical reason associated with the transfer. The employer must provide information as to the transfer and consult as to any measures affecting the employees that either the present employer or the new employer envisages will be taken in connection with the transfer. The information and consultation must be with trade union representatives or, where there are no such representatives, either representatives elected for the purpose of the consultation or appointed or elected for general purposes.

14.12   WHISTLEBLOWERS

Employees are protected from detriment if the reason for the employee's action arises from certain cases of whistleblowing – informing on improper practices of employers – where this amounts to a protected disclosure. The whistleblowing legislation is complex. We have set out below the main principles, but if you are considering blowing the whistle you should obtain legal advice before taking any further steps. A dismissal is automatically unfair if the reason for it is that the employee made a protected disclosure. The Employment Rights Act 1996 sets the parameters of what constitutes a protected disclosure, as well as the manner of the permissible disclosure by the worker. Different degrees of protection apply depending upon whether the disclosure was made internally within the employer's organisation, or externally to a third party.

A protected disclosure includes the disclosure of any information by a worker that in their reasonable belief tends to show that:

- A criminal offence has been, is about to be, or is likely to be committed.

- A person has failed, or is about to fail, to comply with a legal obligation imposed upon them. This includes an obligation imposed upon them by a contract of employment.
- The health and safety of any person has been, or is being or is likely to be endangered.
- A miscarriage of justice has occurred, is occurring, or is likely to occur.
- The environment has been, or is being, or is likely to be damaged.
- Information tending to show that one of the above matters has been, or is likely to be, deliberately concealed.

It is not necessary for the worker to show that the act concerned has or will occur. A reasonable belief is sufficient. It is immaterial that the act has taken place in the UK or elsewhere. The court determines the state of the employee's disclosure by reference to the date of his or her dismissal or detriment, not the date on which the disclosure was made. A disclosure of information is not a 'qualifying disclosure' if the person making the disclosure commits an offence by so making it – e.g. the Official Secrets Act 1989 – and action taken against an individual who makes such a disclosure might not breach Article 10 of the European Convention on Human Rights (the Convention).

Internal disclosures
The legislation favours internal disclosures because it gives employers the opportunity to address the situation. Workers are protected from detriment where, acting in good faith, they make a disclosure internally to their employer, or where they consider that another person is responsible to that person. A worker who deliberately sets out to embarrass or humiliate the employer may be denied protection on the ground that they were not acting in good faith. As already mentioned, a disclosure is not protected if the worker commits a criminal offence in making it, such as a breach of the Official Secrets Act.

Disclosure to other persons
If the employer has a procedure whereby the worker may make a disclosure to another person, that disclosure is protected. Disclosure to a legal adviser is also protected. Workers who are engaged by government bodies may make a disclosure to a Minister of the Crown. A worker may also make a disclosure in good faith to a person prescribed by the Public Interest Disclosure (Prescribed Persons) Order 1999/1549. For example, if an employee complains about the proper administration of a charity the Charity Commissioners are prescribed for this purpose.

Different protections apply to cases where disclosures are made to other persons. Aside from the requirements as to reasonable belief and good faith, in order to be protected, the worker must not act for personal gain. The worker also has to show that they reasonably believed that their employer would have subjected them to detriment if a disclosure was made internally, or that the evidence relating to the alleged failure would either be concealed or destroyed, or that an internal disclosure has already been made. Additionally, the worker has to show that the external disclosure was reasonable in all of the circumstances. This depends upon a number of factors, including to whom the disclosure was made, the seriousness of the failure, whether it is continuing or likely to arise in the future and other similar factors. Where the disclosure concerns an exceptionally serious matter, the worker need not make an internal disclosure or show that they anticipated employer retaliation, or that the evidence would be concealed, provided that in all of the circumstances it is reasonable for the worker to make the disclosure. The protection afforded in these circumstances will depend upon the nature of the alleged failure and its likely consequences.

Where a worker is victimised by the employer as a result of making a protected disclosure, a claim can be brought to an Employment Tribunal. Dismissals or selection for redundancy for making a protected disclosure are automatically unfair. The worker does not have to have been employed for a minimum period of time to make a claim. There is no limit on the compensation that can be awarded. Employment Tribunals can award interim relief in unfair dismissal claims.

Where a whistleblower makes a disclosure that is not protected, they are at the mercy of their employer. It is likely that the disclosure will amount to a breach of the duty of confidentiality or fidelity, and the employer can institute disciplinary procedures against the worker. In such cases, however, a worker may be able to pursue a general claim for unfair dismissal against their employer.

An employer may sue workers who have disclosed confidential information. In no circumstances can a worker reveal the trade secrets of the employer, which may be widely defined to include simple processes. Ex-employees may also be prevented by their contract of employment from revealing other information confidential to the employer, but the clause must not prevent the worker from being able to work in the future and the information must be defined. Injunctions may be obtained where such contracts are broken, leading to lengthy 'gagging' of ex-employees in some cases.

There is a right not to be unfairly dismissed or victimised if a worker who is a Health and Safety representative takes action when he or she believes workers to be in serious and imminent danger.

See also Chapter 9.

14.13 UNIONS

Why join a union?

Your rights as an individual worker are largely determined by the negotiating position you have with your employer, and individuals have little opportunity to influence the specific terms and conditions of employment. Although just fewer than one in three people in employment are members of trade unions, two-thirds have their terms and conditions affected by collective bargaining between their employer, or a group of employers, and trade unions.

Rights against employers

You are protected by the Trade Union and Labour Relations (Consolidation) Act 1992 against refusal of employment, dismissal – including selection for redundancy – and victimisation short of dismissal on the grounds that you are or are not a trade union member. This includes seeking to become a member and taking part, at an appropriate time outside working hours but on your employer's premises, in the activities of the union. You are also protected if the grounds of your dismissal or victimisation are your trade union activities in the past, for example, when you were working for another employer, when the basis of the employer's action is fear that you will repeat those actions in your current employment.

The rights entitle you to recruit members, hand out literature, collect subscriptions and hold meetings during the times when you are not working. If your employer allows you to talk while you are at work, you are also allowed to talk about trade union membership and to encourage people to join.

Any action or omission by your employer that is to your detriment is unlawful if your employer's purpose is to prevent or deter you from union membership or activity or to penalise you. This includes the refusal to allow representation by a union official in accordance with agreed procedures. Generally any form of disadvantage is unlawful as long as the target of the employer's action is genuinely 'trade union activity', including the presentation of, for example, a complaint or grievance relating to health and safety, and does not include merely the activities of a group of individuals who happen to be union members. The union content of the issue must be clear, and your employer's action must be taken against you as an individual and not as a form of retaliation against the union that may be seeking to organise. However, it is not unlawful for an employer to pay employees who opt out of collectively agreed terms and conditions a higher salary increase provided that this reasonably relates to the services provided by the worker and that there is no inhibition in the contract of employment that prevents the worker from being a member of a union. Further, the employer may be able successfully to raise the defence that it sought to further a change in the relationship with all or any class of its employees where 'sweeteners' are offered to those who opt out of collectively agreed terms and conditions.

You can make a claim to an Employment Tribunal. Compensation is available for dismissal and victimisation of up to £58,900 for dismissal, with further compensation available if your employer refuses to comply in full with an order for reinstatement or re-engagement made by the Employment Tribunal. Compensation for action short of dismissal is in the discretion of the Employment Tribunal and may include a sum for injury to feelings and reputation.

The most important remedy for dismissal is an order for reinstatement. In order to make a claim, you should use the 'interim relief' procedure available while you are under notice or during the first seven days after dismissal. This requires a certificate from a union official confirming that in their opinion you were dismissed because of your trade union activities and are likely to win a claim for unfair dismissal on those grounds. A very quick hearing will then be arranged by the Employment Tribunal, which has the power to order your employer to continue your contract until the full hearing of the case.

With the exception of the requirement of a union official's certificate, all of the above rights and procedures apply to someone who has been dismissed on the grounds that they refused to join or take part in the activities of a trade union.

Right to representation at disciplinary or grievance hearings

A worker who is required or invited to attend a disciplinary or grievance hearing is entitled upon reasonable request to be accompanied by a representative. The representative can be a co-worker, or a trade union official or employee whom the union certifies in writing has experience or training in representation matters. The right to bring a union representative exists even where the union is not recognised by the employer. However, the rights of representation are limited in that the representative may address the hearing, but may not answer questions on the worker's behalf, or cross-examine witnesses. If the worker encounters difficulties in obtaining a representative, they have the right to ask the employer to postpone the hearing for a reasonable time. Where an employer unreasonably refuses to allow a worker's representative to attend the hearing, the worker may have recourse to an Employment Tribunal for compensation.

Union recognition
Recognition means that your employer is prepared to negotiate with an independent trade union or unions over terms and conditions of employment. Negotiation is stronger than consultation, which is essentially a one-way process. The employer must consider representations but there is no joint decision-making. The Employment Relations Act 1999 introduces statutory procedures for the recognition of independent trade unions in workplaces employing more than 20 workers. The complex details of these procedures are outside the scope of this section. Generally, the emphasis is on voluntary recognition and agreement where possible between employers and trade unions. Where agreement is not possible, then an employer may be compelled to recognise a trade union for collective bargaining purposes in respect of a specified bargaining unit in which the majority of the workers are members of the union or otherwise following a ballot where the majority of the workers, and at least 40 per cent of those entitled to vote within the bargaining unit, support recognition of the union to act on their behalf. Where a trade union is recognised, collective bargaining will cover issues of pay, including defined pension contributions and benefits, hours and holidays at the minimum, unless the parties agree to negotiate additional matters.

A number of other legal advantages flow from recognition:

- The duty to deal with and give facilities to safety representatives appointed by the union under the Health and Safety at Work Act 1974.
- Consultation on occupational pensions.
- Consultation on redundancies, on takeovers and mergers and the automatic transfer of collective agreements. Where a union is recognised for classes of workers affected by collective redundancies, takeovers or mergers, the employer must consult with the trade union even where other appropriate employee representatives exist in the workplace.
- Disclosure of information, for instance, financial information, for the purposes of collective bargaining, with a legally enforceable right to obtain better terms and conditions if information is denied.
- Time off with pay for union representatives carrying out duties or training connected with collective bargaining, or time off without pay for union members attending internal union activities.

The right to time off can be enforced by a claim to an Employment Tribunal. It is available to shop stewards, staff representatives and other elected representatives. It enables them to prepare for negotiations, draw up plans, consult other members and officers, and negotiate. The amount of time off is that which is 'reasonable' for carrying out duties and training in connection with their industrial relations functions.

Quite separately, union members have the right to take time off for union activities, such as voting, attending union conferences and other matters of internal organisation. This right does not attract pay.

Union membership agreements can be negotiated with your employer. Since the Employment Acts 1988 and 1990, refusal of employment on the ground of unwillingness to join the union or victimisation on such grounds is unlawful.

All companies with 250 employees must include in their annual report a statement of the measures taken to provide information to, and to consult with, employees on matters of concern to them.

Rights within the union

There is a right not to be unjustifiably excluded or expelled from a trade union. Exclusion or expulsion may be justified if you do not satisfy the union's rules, for example, by not being employed in a specified trade or profession, or owing to your conduct other than having been a member of another trade union or a member of a political party. You can complain to an Employment Tribunal if your rights are infringed.

The relationship between you and your union is governed both by the union rulebook and by statute. The rulebook, together with custom and practice, sets up contractual rights entitling you to the benefits and the procedures contained in it. In addition, the rules of natural justice will generally apply to any disciplinary hearing within the union. These are the right to be given notice of the allegation made against you, the opportunity to state your case and to be heard by an impartial body within the union.

You have the right under the Trade Union Reform and Employment Rights Act 1993 not to have unjustifiable disciplinary action taken against you. You can complain to an Employment Tribunal, which can set aside the decisions of the union and award compensation.

Disciplinary action means expulsion, fines, deprivation of benefits or any other detriment. Discipline is unjustifiable if it is on the grounds of failing to participate in or support industrial action, even if a majority of the members involved voted in favour. Similarly, disciplinary action for refusing to break your contract of employment, or for following calls for action in breach of the union's rules, is unjustifiable. You also have a right to terminate your union membership and not to have your union subscriptions deducted from your salary without your agreement, which must be obtained every three years. You may complain to an Employment Tribunal if your employer makes an unauthorised deduction of subscriptions.

Political activities

A union may resolve to have a political fund and to require its members to pay contributions, part of which go into the fund. Activities of a party political nature must be paid for out of the political fund and not out of the general fund of the union. You have an absolute right to refuse to contribute to the political fund, and must not be disadvantaged for so doing under the Trade Union Act 1913. Ballots were held in all unions that had political funds, pursuant to the Trade Union Act 1984 (now the Trade Union Reform and Employment Rights Act 1993), and all passed resolutions favouring the continuance of such funds. Such ballots must be conducted every ten years.

Election of officers

The Trade Union Reform and Employment Rights Act 1993 provides that all officials – except certain senior officials nearing retirement – who have voting rights, or who attend and speak at the governing bodies of trade unions, must be elected by secret postal ballot every five years.

14.14   INDUSTRIAL ACTION

A trade dispute is a dispute between workers and their own employer about terms, conditions, suspension, duties, engagement of workers, allocation of work, discipline, union membership, negotiating procedures and union facilities. In the course of such a dispute you can persuade people not to work. But if you do it on behalf of the union because you are a lay or full-time officer, or if the union adopts your actions, the union must conduct a ballot, and such calls for action will only be lawful if taken within four weeks of the result of a successful ballot or a further four weeks if agreed by the employer. The ballot must ask all those at work at the time of the ballot who are likely to be asked to breach their contracts whether they are in favour. Small accidental mistakes in the ballot will not invalidate it.

Restrictions on the freedom to strike are placed on police and prison officers, apprentices (who must make up the time) and merchant seafarers. Limited action by postal workers is also restricted by law.

It does not matter what form the industrial action takes. It can be a strike, work to rule, ban on overtime (voluntary or compulsory), withdrawal of co-operation or boycotts.

A trade union organises 'official' industrial action in circumstances where they have acted lawfully and are therefore immune from liability. This is significant as workers who participate in official industrial action are protected from dismissal by their employer. In such cases, it is automatically unfair for an employer to dismiss an employee for taking part in official industrial action within a period of eight weeks starting from the date the employee began to take industrial action, or at any time after the eight-week period if the employee stopped participating in industrial action before the end of the eight-week period. In some cases, it will be automatically unfair to dismiss an employee who continues to take industrial action after the end of the eight-week period where the employer has failed to take appropriate and reasonable procedural steps to resolve the dispute. Where a dismissal is automatically unfair, an employee may be entitled to be reinstated to their old job.

A union can be sued for damages if it organises industrial action that is unlawful. Much 'secondary action', that is, action taken against an employer who is not a party to the main trade dispute, is unlawful. If the union has organised this, an injunction can be granted to prevent it, and claims for damages of up to £250,000, depending on the size of the union, can be awarded.

If employees take unprotected industrial action and the employer dismisses all those taking the action at the same workplace and none is re-engaged within three months, none of them has any claim for unfair dismissal. After the three-month period, selective re-engagement is permissible. This means that if you take part in unofficial or unprotected industrial action, you are always at risk whatever the form of industrial action.

Employers sometimes withhold pay for all or part of the time that you have been engaged in limited industrial action. They are entitled only to deduct a proportion of pay representing the proportion of your time lost by your action.

Action in pursuit of union membership agreements – the closed shop – is always unlawful.

Picketing of your own workplace – but nowhere else – during the course of a dispute is lawful provided that your purpose is peacefully to communicate information or persuade people not to work. A Code of Practice and one court decision recommend that there be a limit of six pickets on each entrance, but different numbers may be appropriate in different circumstances. Offences under public order legislation are the most likely criminal charges to arise out of picketing.

14.15   THE EUROPEAN CONVENTION ON HUMAN RIGHTS

Public authorities

Under section 6 of the Human Rights Act 1998 (HRA) public authorities are obliged to act compatibly with the rights in the Convention. In the context of unfair dismissal, it has been held that a public authority employer will not act reasonably if it violates its employee's Convention rights. However, employers who are not 'public authorities' for the purposes of the HRA are not obliged to comply with the rights in the Convention with regard to their employees, and you cannot bring a claim directly against your employer under the HRA.

The Convention is still relevant when the employer cannot be regarded as a public authority. All statutes must be read 'so far as it is possible to do so' in a way that is compatible with Convention rights. The EAT has recognised this obligation when considering the test of whether a dismissal is unfair under the Employment Rights Act 1996.

Courts and tribunals are included within the definition of 'public authorities' under section 6(3)(a) of the HRA and so are obliged to comply with the Convention when deciding cases, including cases between private persons. If the court or tribunal fails to provide a remedy for breach of a litigant's Convention rights by a third party, the court or tribunal may itself act unlawfully by failing to protect the rights of the applicant under the Convention.

Remedies

Only the High Court can make declarations of incompatibility that a particular statute is in conflict with a Convention right. An application requiring such a declaration would therefore have to be made in the High Court and may be by way of judicial review where the act of a public authority is at issue.

Right to a fair trial

Where claims are brought by workers, Article 6(1) of the Convention provides that there must be procedural fairness in the conduct of the litigation. There is some scope in certain situations for extending this to internal disciplinary hearings. However, Article 6 will be relevant only where the result of the disciplinary hearing would affect the worker's ability to carry out his or her profession elsewhere, for example, disciplinary hearings by the General Medical Council or Law Society.

One area of controversy surrounds the extent to which the Government is obliged to provide public funding for cases brought before Employment Tribunals. At present, public funding is not available for Employment Tribunal claims. Although it is permissible for a state to restrict the provision of public funding on the bases of the prospects of success of a case and the limited nature of public funds, it is arguable that the blanket denial of public funding for Employment Tribunal cases infringes the right to a fair hearing in some instances. The European Court of Human Rights (ECHR) has held that the denial of public funding can undermine an individual's right of effective access to a court. Whether this is so will depend upon the facts of each case. In particular, this will depend upon the degree of complexity of the Employment Tribunal procedure relating to the claim, as well as whether the litigation is likely to involve complicated points of law or the use of expert witnesses.

Respect for private and family life, home and correspondence

Article 8 of the Convention provides that everybody has the right to respect for his or her private life and correspondence, except where restrictions are necessary, for example, in the interests of public safety or for the prevention of crime and disorder.

There are numerous devices enabling employers to intrude into the privacy of workers, including monitoring telephone conversations, e-mail communications, reading correspondence, video surveillance, intimate searches, drug and alcohol testing as well as through means of detailed questionnaires when applying for positions and psychometric testing.

The ECHR decided that police surveillance of Alison Halford's telephone calls while she was an employee breached Article 8. It stated that telephone calls from business premises might form part of the worker's right to privacy. As the police had not warned Ms Halford that calls made from her office phone would be liable to interception, and that she had not been told that she could not use the phone to make personal calls, she had a reasonable expectation of privacy for such calls. This was violated by the act of police surveillance. In contrast, the ECHR accepted in a Swedish case the assertion that the State needs to collect information and maintain secret dossiers on candidates for employment in sensitive jobs, where there might be threats to national security. The Government had to identify those exceptional conditions and special jobs. There also had to be measures to ensure that the Government was not abusing its powers.

In the light of the Halford decision, the Government passed the Regulation of Investigatory Powers Act 2000, which makes it unlawful to listen to calls without authority.

Oftel has produced guidance for companies who record telephone conversations for business purposes. This guidance focuses on the reasonable expectation of privacy to which employees are entitled in the workplace under Article 8. It is no longer sufficient merely to warn workers that their telephone conversations at work may be recorded or monitored in order to remove their expectation of privacy, as it is unreasonable to assume that workers will never make or receive calls touching on personal or intimate matters. One solution would be for employers to provide workers with access to a telephone where they could make or receive personal calls, which would not be recorded.

The Regulation of Investigatory Powers Act 2000 also applies to the use of e-mail at work as workers are entitled to have a reasonable expectation of privacy at work.

Merely informing workers that their e-mail system is being monitored is not enough as circumstances may arise where they may need to make or receive mail touching on personal matters.

The right to privacy does not mean that employers can no longer monitor what workers do at the workplace. There are acceptable limits of interference with workers' privacy. Employers are permitted to monitor workers insofar as this is necessary and proportionate to their reasons for so doing. It may be permissible for an employer to retain itemised call and e-mail records in order to detect misuse. This is less intrusive than monitoring such communications in their entirety. A large number of employers now employ video surveillance on their premises and require workers to wear name badges, particularly in the retail and banking industries. The former may be related to reasons of security and would, in most cases, be viewed as reasonable in the circumstances. Excessive surveillance, for example, in changing rooms, may be viewed as unreasonable. The Court of Appeal has refused permission to appeal where an employee was dismissed after being filmed on CCTV having sex with a co-worker in a back office. The cameras were set up as the employee was suspected of theft (wrongly as it turned out). This case was found to be different from that of Alison Halford and no potential breach of Article 8 was identified. The wearing of name badges has come to be perceived as a useful tool in customer relations, and, again, will usually be justified on these grounds, as well as security.

In addition to Convention rights, there is an implied term in the contract of employment that employers will not without reasonable and proper cause conduct themselves in a manner calculated or likely to destroy, or seriously damage, the relationship of confidence and trust between themselves and their employees. If an employer opens your personal mail or tapes your telephone calls, such conduct may be interpreted as breaching this term, entitling you to resign and claim unfair constructive dismissal.

Some employers have introduced alcohol and drug screening of workers, but as a matter of law an employer is unable to do so without your consent. The same requirement applies to searches for drugs and alcohol. If such searches are contracted out to a third party such as a security firm, then this should be the subject of a specific provision within your contract of employment. If you refuse to consent to a search, whether or not there is a specific provision within the employment contract, it would be an assault to proceed with the search, and you may be entitled to resign in protest, claiming constructive dismissal. For this reason, your contract of employment may provide that refusal to co-operate with a search is a disciplinary offence. The EAT has expressed the view that the policy of random testing and subsequent dismissal for a positive drugs test will not necessarily breach Article 8 and will depend on all the circumstances of the case.

The right to privacy also encompasses issues of sexual orientation. In the *Smith and Grady v United Kingdom* case, the ECHR regarded sexual orientation as a most intimate part of an individual's private life. It decided that the Ministry of Defence policy that prohibited homosexual people from serving in the Armed Forces, as well as the inquisition system specifically designed to ascertain the sexual orientation of the suspect, infringed the claimants' right to respect for their private lives. This decision equally affects all employers. Unless particularly strong justification exists, employers cannot subject workers to detrimental treatment on the grounds of their sexual orientation.

Article 8 rights often conflict with other rights. For example, the EAT has had to decide whether a video taken by a nanny at her employer's home was admissible as evidence in her Employment Tribunal claim. The EAT concluded that it was appropriate for it to view the video in private, although this restricted the nanny's right to a public trial under Article 6, because it had to balance her right to a fair trial against the employer's concerns about their privacy under Article 8.

See also Chapter 3.

Freedom of thought, conscience or religion

Article 9 provides an absolute right to *hold* beliefs, but the right to *manifest* those beliefs may be subject to restrictions in the interests of matters such as safety and public morals and protection of the rights and freedoms of others. This right overlaps to a large extent with the right to freedom of expression, which is covered in greater detail below. It is clear that workers receive greater protection in relation to holding beliefs rather than when expressing them at the workplace.

Previously, there was no protection from discrimination on grounds of religion if a worker is required by his or her employer to take action contrary to his or her religious belief, unless the employee could show that the discrimination was on grounds of race. For example, a Rastafarian was dismissed for having dreadlocks, but his claim under the Race Relations Act was unsuccessful because the court decided that Rastafarians are not an ethnic group for the purposes of the Act. He would now be able to rely on Article 9 directly against his employer if it was a public authority.

New Regulations are now in force that prohibit discrimination on the grounds of religion or belief.

See also Chapter 10.

Freedom of religion has not been afforded such extensive protection as might be expected in the employment context under the Convention. One way of manifesting beliefs is to ask for time off to pray or attend religious ceremonies. In one case a Muslim teacher employed by a local education authority (LEA) asked for time off to attend prayers every Friday. He was offered variation in his working week but he refused the offer. His application was held to be inadmissible because the ILEA had given due regard to Article 9 in offering to reduce his hours and he was not entitled to absent himself from work in breach of his contract of employment. Similarly, a woman who objected to Sunday working had her claim declared inadmissible as she had been dismissed for refusing to work her contractual hours and she had the option of resigning.

The unsatisfactory justification for this approach is that when a worker appreciates that their contract conflicts with their religious beliefs, the freedom of religion is guaranteed in that they are free to resign. It is perhaps surprising therefore that a worker is capable of bargaining away their rights to religion with such ease. It remains to be seen whether domestic courts and Employment Tribunals will choose to follow such a restrictive interpretation of freedom of religion.

Freedom of expression

Freedom of expression includes the worker's right to communicate their beliefs, opinions or other information by words, images, pictures or actions intending to communicate an idea. It also covers issues such as dress codes and appearance at work. The ECHR has not given clear guidance on the scope of this right because each case is decided on its own facts. What is clear is that this right is severely limited. This is because of the competing rights between a worker's freedom of expression and the employer's right to manage the workplace. It is also clear that under the Convention, your freedom of expression may be restricted by your contract of employment to an extent, provided that you have freely agreed to this. To this extent, the rights to expression can be bargained away by the worker upon agreeing contractual terms.

The scope of the freedom of expression depends upon a number of factors, including the method and manner in which you express opinion or criticism, as well as the nature of the opinion. In one case, the dismissal of a teacher for criticising her employer on television for refusing to promote her on grounds of her sexual orientation was held not to violate her freedom of expression under Article 10. It was considered that the scope of her freedom of expression was partly determined by reference to her contractual duties and responsibilities. Therefore, it was relevant that she had accepted a responsible post in the education sector and had accepted certain restrictions on the right to freedom of expression by virtue of her professional responsibilities. Her suspension without pay was capable of being reasonably justified for the protection of the reputation of the teaching institution where she worked and also of her superiors. However, the extent of your contractual duties does not mean that your freedom of expression is always limited. Courts are likely to consider whether the allegations are supported by evidence, and also whether the matters have been raised and addressed internally.

The manner in which the freedom of expression is exercised is also relevant in deciding whether there has been a breach of Article 10. It has been stated on numerous occasions that where a worker is openly abusive and offensive in criticising superiors, sanctions can be imposed not because of the fact of the criticism levelled, but on grounds of the way in which this was raised. Other considerations include the need to protect the reputation of those criticised as well as whether the worker has disclosed information of a confidential nature.

Freedom of expression was also a factor in *Smith and O'Grady* v *United Kingdom*. Although the ECHR did not consider the issue fully, it was not prepared to discount the possibility that the Ministry of Defence's policy violated military personnel's freedom of expression. The ECHR considered that the homophobic policy effectively silenced personnel in relation to their sexual orientation and also created a constant need for vigilance and secrecy. To this extent, the policy clearly amounted to an unacceptable restriction of their freedom of expression.

Where an employer operates a homophobic policy, or dismisses employees on the basis of their sexual orientation, the dismissal may amount to a violation of the worker's freedom of expression. However, the ECHR indicated that if the sole reason for the detrimental treatment is the sexual orientation of the worker, then this is more appropriately to be dealt with as a violation of the right to privacy. This of course will not prevent workers from claiming that both of their rights to privacy and expression have been violated.

Freedom of expression covers the appearance and manner in which a worker chooses to dress because these matters represent an outward expression of one's personality. However, it is unlikely that the application of the Convention will have a significant impact upon an employer's discretion to stipulate modes of appearance and dress in the workplace. This is mainly because freedom of expression in this regard is likely to be limited by the express terms of your contract, or terms implied through dress codes or staff handbooks. Additionally, it is also arguable that the worker has given up their freedom of expression by acknowledging the employer's general power to give instructions as to how the work is performed, which includes matters of dress and appearance.

Freedom of assembly and association

Article 11 gives everyone the right to freedom of assembly and to freedom of association with others, including the right to form and join trade unions. The usual limitations are placed on these rights, such as permitting restrictions, which are necessary in a democratic society in the interests of national security, or public safety, or prevention of disorder or crime, or for the protection of the rights and freedom of others. In particular, Article 11 permits the impositions of lawful restrictions on the exercise of these rights by members of the armed forces, of the police or of the administration of the state. The cases taken to the ECHR have not been in favour of upholding collective rights in respect of trade organisation and activities. For example, in 1976 the ECHR decided in a Swedish case that there was no obligation on a state to conclude a collective agreement with a trade union on behalf of its members, though it did find that under Article 11 a trade union could present claims for its members, make representations on their behalf, and to negotiate.

The ECHR has held that the right to join a trade union includes the right not to be forced to join a trade union on the basis that the freedom to associate also includes the freedom not to associate.

In 2002, the ECHR rejected the trade union Unison's application to challenge the Court of Appeal's decision that a proposed strike, in opposition to the contracting out of the construction and operation of a new hospital to the private sector, was unlawful because the decision did not breach Article 11. The court held that the injunction upheld by the Court of Appeal constituted a restriction upon Unison's ability to protect the occupational interests of its members, and was contrary to Article 11(1). However, when considering whether such a restriction was permitted under the exceptions in Article 11(2), it found that the injunction pursued the legitimate objective of the right of the employer to conduct its business unhindered by industrial action. It held that despite the injunction, Unison retained the ability to take effective action if there was a threat to its members' terms and conditions of employment.

More recently, the ECHR decided the case of *Wilson and Palmer v United Kingdom*. The House of Lords had decided that the right to join a union involves no more than the right to hold a membership card and to use the services of the union so far as they do not impinge on the member's employer. Before the ECHR it was argued that two consequential rights necessarily flowed from the express right to union membership contained in Article 11: the right to be represented in negotiations with employers and the right not to be discriminated against for choosing to be so represented. The ECHR held that if employees are restrained from having trade unions make representations on their behalf, the protection afforded by Article 11 to their freedom of expression is 'illusory'. Further, English and Welsh law had not stopped the employers in that case from treating those employees who had refused to relinquish their right to representation by a trade union less favourably because there was a 'disincentive or restraint on the use by employees of union membership to protect their interests'. The ECHR decided that the UK had breached Article 11. A change in the law to reflect this decision is anticipated.

Trade unions may also bring actions on behalf of members who they can identify as being directly affected by the alleged human rights violation, provided that the union can demonstrate that it has authority to act on behalf of its members.

14.16   FURTHER INFORMATION

Useful organisations

Advisory Conciliation and Arbitration Service (ACAS)
Head Office:
Brandon House
180 Borough High Street
London SE1 1LW
Tel: 020 7210 3613
<www.acas.org.uk>

Department for Trade and Industry
1 Victoria Street
London SW1H 0ET
Tel: 020 7215 5000
enquiries@dti.gsi.gov.uk
<www.dti.gov.uk>

Employment Appeal Tribunal
Audit House
58 Victoria Embankment
London EC4Y 0DS
Tel: 020 7273 1040
Fax: 020 7273 1045
<www.employmentappeals.gov.uk>

Employment Tribunals
<www.employmenttribunals.gov.uk>

Health and Safety Executive (HSE)
HSE Infoline
Caerphilly Business Park
Caerphilly CF83 3GG
Tel: 0870 154 5500
<www.hse.gov.uk>

Trade Union Congress (TUC)
Congress House
Great Russell Street
London WC1B 3LS
Tel: 020 7636 4030

Chris Johnson, Angus Murdoch and Marc Willers,
with a conclusion by Andrew Ryder

15   The Rights of Gypsies and Travellers

This chapter deals with:

- Introduction
- Definitions of 'Gypsy' and 'Traveller'
- Planning permission for caravan sites
- Eviction
- Homelessness
- Racism and discrimination
- The right to healthcare
- The right to education
- Gypsies and Travellers and the media
- Future developments
- Further information

15.1   INTRODUCTION

Gypsies and Travellers first arrived in England and Wales in about 1500. Over the centuries they have been subjected to prejudice and discrimination. By the beginning of the twentieth century, while remaining effectively excluded from education and proper healthcare, they had at least arrived at a position where they were able to find places to stop for reasonable periods of time. For example, they were allowed to stop on the enormous areas of common land across England and Wales.

In *R v Lincolnshire CC ex parte Atkinson, Wealden DC ex parte Wales & Stratford* Justice Sedley gave a useful potted history of the last century as it related to Gypsies and Travellers:

> For centuries the commons of England provided lawful stopping places for people whose way of life was or had become nomadic. Enough common land survived the centuries of enclosure to make this way of life sustainable, but by section 23 of the Caravan Sites and Control of Development Act 1960 local authorities were given power to close the commons to Travellers. This they proceeded to do with great energy, but made no use of the concomitant power given to them by section 24 of the same Act to open caravan sites to compensate for the closure of the commons. By the Caravan Sites Act 1968, therefore, Parliament legislated to make the section 24 power a duty... for the next quarter of a century there followed a history of non-compliance with the duties imposed by the Act of 1968, marked by a series of decisions of this court holding local authorities to be in breach of

their statutory duty; but to apparently little practical effect. The default powers vested in central government, to which the court was required to defer, were rarely if ever used.

15.2   DEFINITIONS OF 'GYPSY' AND 'TRAVELLER'

The term 'travelling people' is one often used in both the United Kingdom and the Republic of Ireland. It can include:

- 'Gypsies' who may be of English, Welsh or Scottish descent, and who have Romany ancestry. 'Gypsies' have a specific meaning for the purposes of planning and local authority law, which is considered below.
- 'Irish Travellers' who are a nomadic Irish ethnic group with a separate identity, culture, language and history. There are many Irish Travellers resident in Britain for all or part of the year.
- 'Scottish Travellers' who, like Irish Travellers, have musical traditions, language and other histories that date back at least to the twelfth century.
- The Roma people who have moved to Britain from Central and Eastern Europe (of which Britain's Romany Gypsies are members).
- People with a long family history of travelling because they work with fairgrounds and circuses (also known as 'Travelling Show people').
- So-called 'New Travellers', some of whom may be second- or third-generation Travellers and/or may have Gypsy ancestry.

15.3   PLANNING PERMISSION FOR CARAVAN SITES

Before the enactment of the Criminal Justice and Public Order Act 1994 (CJPOA), local authorities had a statutory duty to provide caravan sites for Gypsies and Travellers under the Caravan Sites Act 1968. However, the CJPOA removed that duty and gave local authorities and the police draconian powers to evict Gypsies and Travellers from unauthorised sites.

The current policy towards Gypsies' and Travellers' caravan sites is found in the Circular 1/94, *Gypsy Sites and Planning* (Circular 1/94), which favours private over public site provision. Gypsies and Travellers should be 'encouraged' to purchase land themselves and apply to legitimise their own sites through the planning system.

In theory, requiring Gypsies and Travellers to use the planning system would seem an equitable approach, but for this policy to be credible there has to be some real prospect of obtaining planning consent for private sites. The House of Lords cast doubt on the effectiveness of this policy in *South Bucks v Porter*, *Wrexham CBC v Berry*, and *Chichester DC v Keet and Searle*. The judges observed that Gypsies' and Travellers' attempts to obtain planning permission almost always met with failure: statistics given to the court found that 90 per cent of applications made by Gypsies and Travellers had been refused and that the capacity of sites that had been authorised had fallen far short of what was needed.

Circular 1/94 suggests that local planning authorities should assess the need for Gypsies' and Travellers' caravan sites in their administrative areas and identify locations where the land use requirements of Gypsies and Travellers can be met. If suitable locations cannot be found, then the local authority should set clear and realistic criteria for establishing caravan sites. However, the use of development policies has been ineffective in providing more Gypsies' and Travellers' caravan sites because very few local authorities have identified suitable locations for such sites, and many of those that have adopted criteria-based policies rely upon unrealistic and unclear criteria. For example, some local authorities' policies exclude the creation of sites in the Green Belt when most of the available land in their area is Green Belt.

Recently, the House of Commons' Select Committee on the Housing Bill 2004 recommended to the Government that only the reintroduction of the statutory duty on local authorities to provide authorised camping sites would remedy the situation.

Gypsy status

Before planning permission for a caravan site can be obtained, the applicant must establish that he or she falls within the statutory definition of Gypsy, that is, has Gypsy status.

The leading case on Gypsy status before the Human Rights Act 1998 (HRA) came into force was *R v South Hams District Council ex parte Gibb*. The Court of Appeal considered whether the applicants were Gypsies for the purposes of the former duty to provide caravan sites in the Caravan Sites Act 1968, which defined Gypsies as 'persons of a nomadic habit of life, whatever their race or origin'. The Court of Appeal found the following matters were relevant in deciding whether the applicants in question were statutory Gypsies:

- A tradition of travelling.
- Travelling in a group.
- Travelling with an economic purpose.

The Court of Appeal decided that the definition of 'Gypsy' required a recognisable connection between the wandering or travelling and the way in which the persons concerned make or seek their livelihood. Persons, or individuals, who move from place to place merely as the fancy may take them and without any connection between the movement and their means of livelihood fall outside the statutory definition of 'Gypsy'.

Unfortunately, this judgment has often led to local planning authorities trying to 'prove' that the Gypsies and Travellers who live in their area are not statutory 'Gypsies' for the purpose of Circular 1/94.

The courts have also considered whether an individual can lose his or her Gypsy status, particularly in relation to cases where ill health has led to Gypsies or Travellers being unable to travel.

In *R v Shropshire CC ex parte Bungay* an aggrieved local resident who lived near a recently approved Gypsy site challenged the local authority's decision that a Gypsy family who had not travelled for 15 years because they were caring for their elderly and infirm parents were Gypsies. The judge held that a person could remain a Gypsy even if he or she did not travel, provided that his or her nomadism was held in abeyance and not abandoned.

In *O'Connor v the First Secretary of State and Bath & NE Somerset* a planning inspector had decided that the Traveller concerned was not a statutory Gypsy because she had become too ill to travel. The High Court decided that it was not enough to focus on the travelling currently being undertaken or likely to be undertaken in the future, but instead the following circumstances should be also considered:

- The person's history.
- The reasons for ceasing to travel.
- The person's future wishes and intentions to resume travelling when the reasons for settling have ceased to apply.
- The person's attitude to living in a caravan rather than a conventional house.

In *Wrexham CBC v the National Assembly for Wales and Berry* a planning inspector had allowed a planning enforcement appeal for a Gypsy family. However, his decision was challenged in the High Court on the ground that the elder breadwinner in the family, Mr Berry, was no longer a Gypsy because he had become too ill to continue to travel for work.

The High Court judge decided that he could not see anything in *Gibb* to suggest that, had the Court of Appeal been confronted with what might be described as a 'retired' Gypsy, it would have said that he or she was no longer a Gypsy because he or she had become too ill or too old to travel in order to search for work.

The Court of Appeal overturned the High Court decision because it found that there was no prospect of Mr Berry resuming a travelling life owing to his chronic ill health. The judges did accept, however, that a person may continue to have a 'nomadic habit of life' even though he or she is not travelling for the time being and may not do so for some considerable time, perhaps because of illness or the educational needs of his or her children, provided he or she has not abandoned a 'nomadic habit of life'.

Mr Berry appealed unsuccessfully to the House of Lords.

This decision seems to be unworkable in practice and in breach of the right to respect for private and family life, home and correspondence under Article 8 of the European Convention on Human Rights (the Convention). It also raises the question of whether other family members lose their Gypsy status when the 'breadwinner' becomes ill and is unable to travel. The effect of the Court of Appeal's decision is that Mrs Berry and her children lose their Gypsy status solely because their husband or father has become seriously ill and is unable to travel.

Personal circumstances

If a Gypsy or Traveller can establish 'Gypsy status' then he or she will have to produce some evidence to show that planning permission for a caravan site ought to be granted. In particular, it will be important to produce evidence of personal circumstances (for example, relating to the health of the family) and evidence of the need for a site.

Gypsies and Travellers living on unauthorised encampments find it particularly difficult to educate their children. The need to consider the educational needs of children when deciding whether to grant planning permission for a site was recognised in *Basildon DC v SSETR*, where the court stressed that the education needs of children are an important aspect of wider land use considerations in the provision of sites for Gypsies and Travellers and that there is considerable public interest in providing stable educational opportunities for Gypsy and Traveller children.

Need

In coming to a decision that balances the protection of the planning system alongside nomadic people's rights, account must be taken of 'need'. 'Need' in this context relates to two competing interests: the need for accommodation consistent with a nomadic lifestyle; and the need for the local authority to protect the environment.

The courts have held that the need for sites is an independent material consideration to be taken into account in arriving at decisions concerning sites for nomadic people. The issue of need has proved determinative in planning appeals before the Planning Inspectorate, as well as in the High Court when challenging or defending the Planning Inspectorate's decisions.

Conventional housing

In *Clarke* v *The Secretary of State for the Environment, Transport and the Regions and Tunbridge Wells Borough Council* a planning inspector had taken into account the previous offer of conventional housing to a Gypsy or Traveller family when he made his planning decision. The family had found the offer unacceptable, having never lived in a house in their lives. The High Court found that the decision breached the claimants' right to private and family life, home and correspondence under Article 8 of the Convention and stated:

> If [an immutable antipathy to conventional housing] be established then, in my judgment, bricks and mortar, if offered, are unsuitable, just as would be the offer of a rat infested barn. It would be contrary to Articles 8 and 14 to expect such a person to accept conventional housing and to hold it against him or her that he has not accepted it, or is not prepared to accept it, even as a last resort factor.

The Court of Appeal upheld this decision.

The European Convention on Human Rights

In *South Buckinghamshire District Council* v *Porter* the claimants had been living in mobile homes on land that they occupied in breach of planning control. The courts had granted an injunction requiring them to move off site, with the threat of imprisonment for failure to comply.

At the heart of the appeal lay Article 8 of the Convention and the question of whether in these cases the interference was 'necessary in a democratic society', that is, whether the injunction answers a 'pressing social need' and, in particular, whether it was proportionate to the legitimate aim pursued.

In earlier cases it had been held that the court had no role to play in deciding whether an injunction was appropriate, nor could the court consider matters of hardship that would occur once the injunction was granted, nor the availability of suitable alternative sites, health issues or educational requirements of the Gypsies' and Travellers' children. In effect, the court's role was reduced to one of a 'rubber-stamp' as those matters were taken as previously considered and given effect by the local authority.

In allowing the appeal, the Court of Appeal held that considerations of hardship and availability of alternative sites was not 'entirely foreclosed' at the injunction stage and to ignore these issues would not be consistent with the court's duty to act compatibly with the Convention.

The House of Lords dismissed the councils' appeal and recognised that the previous approach, even under domestic law, was 'too austere', and a more balanced approach was necessary (whether it pre-dated the HRA or not), as the previous approach seemed to suggest that even great hardship was irrelevant. Perhaps most significantly, the House of Lords held that the vulnerable position of Gypsies and Travellers as a minority group deserves more sympathetic attention than had previously been the case.

See also Chapter 1.

15.4   EVICTION

Local authority evictions

The CJPOA gives local authorities the power to direct persons who are unlawfully residing in vehicles on land in their area to leave. These powers extend to privately owned land. It is an offence to fail to comply with such a direction or to return within three months. A Magistrates' Court can make a removal order authorising the local authority to enter the land and remove the persons and vehicles.

It would usually be legitimate for a local authority to exercise its powers whenever Gypsies and Travellers who are camped unlawfully refuse to move on to an authorised local authority site where there are vacancies. However, where there are no such sites and the authority reaches the view that an unauthorised encampment is not causing a level of nuisance that cannot be effectively controlled, Circular 18/94 states that the authority should consider providing basic services such as toilets, a refuse skip and a supply of drinking water.

Circular 18/94 outlines how local authorities should exercise their powers, stating that they should be used in a humane and compassionate way, taking account of the rights and needs of the Gypsies and Travellers concerned, the owners of the land in question and the wider community whose lives may be affected by the situation. Authorities are reminded of their obligations under the Children Act 1989 (regarding the welfare of 'children in need'), the Housing Act 1985 (now the Housing Act 1996, regarding duties to homeless people) and also responsibilities regarding the provision of education for school-age children. It also states that local authorities should bear in mind possible assistance from local health and/or welfare services.

The courts have examined the scope of the Department of the Environment Circular 18/94 (Circular 18/94) in relation to local authorities' duties when considering evicting Gypsies and Travellers under the CJPOA, and in R v *Lincolnshire CC ex parte Atkinson* the judge decided that in addition to these statutory considerations, there were 'considerations of common humanity, none of which can be properly ignored when dealing with one of the most fundamental of human needs, the need for shelter with at least a modicum of security'.

In a planning enforcement case that was heard soon afterwards, the court held that in deciding whether or not to take enforcement action, local authorities should have regard to the personal circumstances of the Gypsies or Travellers and that such considerations should hold equal weight when considering breaches of planning controls.

In order to ensure that local authorities reach a balanced decision when deciding whether to evict Gypsies and Travellers from an unauthorised encampment, they should have in place some form of inquiry process and some method of evaluating and considering the relative merits of the information gleaned.

The courts have decided that local authorities should comply with this circular before deciding whether or not to evict Gypsies and Travellers from unauthorised sites. Where Gypsies and Travellers are unlawfully encamped on government-owned land, it is for the local authority, with the agreement of the land-owning department, to take any necessary steps to ensure that the encampment does not constitute a hazard to public health. It also sets out that government departments, including the National Assembly for Wales, should act in conformity with the advice that unauthorised encampments should not normally be allowed to continue where they are causing a level of nuisance that cannot be effectively controlled, particularly where local authority authorised sites are available. The converse of this, of course, is that 'toleration' should be considered if nuisance or annoyance is not being caused.

Police evictions

The CJPOA gives the police the power to remove Gypsies and Travellers where the landowner or occupier has taken reasonable steps to ask them to leave if the senior police officer present at the scene reasonably believes that they are trespassing on land with the common purpose of residing there and:

- They have caused damage to the land or to property or used threatening, abusive or insulting words or behaviour towards the occupier.
- Those persons have between them six or more vehicles on the land.

Failure to obey such a direction or returning to the land in question within three months is not only an offence but can result in arrest and impoundment of vehicles (the Travellers' homes), even before a Magistrates' Court order has been obtained.

In *R v The Chief Constable of the Dorset Constabulary ex parte Fuller* the court decided that the landowner must give Gypsies and Travellers a deadline before the police can use their powers under the CJPOA. In this case, the local authority and the police had given the Gypsies and Travellers notice to leave the land at the same time and with the same termination date, and the removal direction was quashed. However, the court also decided that the CJPOA powers were not in themselves incompatible with Article 8 of the Convention.

The Anti-Social Behaviour Act 2003, which came into force on 27 February 2004, gives further powers to the police to evict Gypsies and Travellers. A senior police officer now has the power to direct people to leave the land and to remove any vehicle or property that they have with them if he or she reasonably believes that:

- The person and one or more others (the trespassers) are trespassing on land.
- The trespassers have between them at least one vehicle on the land.
- The trespassers are present on the land with the common purpose of residing there for any period.
- If it appears to the officer that the person has one or more caravans in his or her possession, and that there is a suitable pitch on a relevant caravan site for that caravan.

Under these changes it appears that a single Gypsy or Traveller, travelling on his or her own, would not be caught by the new section. The pitch must be 'suitable', though there is no further definition of that term. The occupier no longer has to take reasonable steps to ask the Gypsies and Travellers to leave and there is no need for written notice to be served.

A person will commit an offence if he or she knows that a direction has been given and fails to leave the land as soon as reasonably practicable, or enters any land in the area of the relevant local authority as a trespasser within three months with the intention of residing there. This offence can be punished by imprisonment for a term not exceeding three months or a fine or both. A police constable may arrest a person committing this offence and may also seize and remove any vehicles. It is a defence if the person can show that he or she was not trespassing, had a reasonable excuse for failing to leave the land or entering other land, or was under the age of 18 years.

The giving of a direction will normally be effective without the need to take the matter to court, since the threat of arrest and impoundment of Gypsies' and Travellers' homes will usually be sufficient to persuade them to move. Any unlawful use of these powers may be challenged by way of judicial review, and an injunction to prevent the three-month ban being put into effect could be sought.

See also Chapter 2.

Guidance on Managing Unauthorised Camping

The Office of the Deputy Prime Minister and the Home Office issued the *Guidance on Managing Unauthorised Camping* (the ODPM Guidance) in February 2004. It replaces previous good practice guidance issued in 1998 and 2000.

The ODPM Guidance states that local authorities should consider welfare issues when deciding whether to proceed with eviction action *whatever* the method of eviction that is contemplated. All public authorities (including bodies such as the Forestry Commission, the Highways Agency, the Ministry of Defence and potentially even organisations such as Network Rail) must make some welfare inquiries or, if they decide to rely upon inquiries made by the local authority, take some account of the humanitarian considerations that are identified by those inquiries.

The ODPM Guidance also contains important guidance for the police when considering whether to use their powers under the CJPOA. Even without the ODPM Guidance, several High Court cases had indicated that the police must have regard to 'considerations of common humanity'.

The ODPM Guidance suggests that local authorities and the police draw up joint policies towards unauthorised encampments and highlights that, while the CJPOA powers can be used legitimately against encampments, it would not be appropriate for them to be the first response in every case. The decision to use the CJPOA must be an operational one, taken by the senior police officer at the scene, on the basis of whether 'appropriate triggers' are evident. Appropriate triggers might include:

- Individual criminal activity.
- Serious breaches of the peace.
- Disorder or significant disruption to the life of the local community.

The police should not adopt 'blanket policies' either for or against the use of their powers under the CJPOA.

The Home Office Circular 45/94 (Circular 45/94) reinforces that due consideration should be given to welfare needs and personal circumstances when the police are deciding whether or not to evict. Circular 45/94 indicates that the senior officer at the scene may wish to take account of the personal circumstances of the trespassers, 'for example, the presence of elderly persons, invalids, pregnant women, children and other persons whose well-being may be jeopardised by a precipitate move'. According to the Guidance, other personal circumstances that may be considered are ill health and the educational needs of any children (particularly those needs of children in school if eviction is contemplated within four weeks of the end of term or if the children have special education needs).

Even if the most pressing welfare concerns do not exist in the circumstances, any group of Gypsies and Travellers requires some consideration owing to the lack of suitable sites and the lack of any duty to provide suitable sites. Although the OPDM Guidance no longer uses the word 'toleration', if there is no significant nuisance or disruption caused by the encampment it effectively calls for toleration.

There are no obligations on private landowners to take account of humanitarian considerations when deciding whether to evict Gypsies and Travellers from an unauthorised encampment. However, if the landowner is using common law powers to evict, the ODPM Guidance suggests that police should always be notified of an eviction and called in to stand by to prevent a breach of the peace. If the police advise that it is inappropriate to carry out an eviction, it should always be delayed until an agreed time.

If the landowner exceeds the use of 'reasonable force', he or she may face an action for criminal damage, trespass to person or property or assault. If such an action were taken, the failure of the landowner to have regard to the ODPM Guidance may be relevant. If the landowner asks the local authority to evict Gypsies and Travellers under the CJPOA, they must have regard to the ODPM Guidance and carry out inquiries into the welfare of the Gypsies or Travellers.

It was for many years the practice of many landowners, such as the Forestry Commission, to obtain possession orders against Gypsies and Travellers not only covering the specific bit of land they were on but also all other land in their ownership in a large radius around the site in question. In *Drury* v *The Secretary of State for the Environment, Food and Rural Affairs*, the Court of Appeal made it clear that strong and clear evidence of the likelihood of trespass on the other areas of land is required and that such wide orders will only be made in 'exceptional circumstances'.

European Convention on Human Rights

The most relevant Articles of the Convention for the purposes of unauthorised encampments are 6, 8, 14 and Articles 1 and 2 of Protocol 1.

In *Chapman* v *United Kingdom* the European Court of Human Rights (ECHR) indicated that a home set up without lawful authority could still be a 'home' for the purposes of Article 8. This is further confirmed in the ODPM Guidance. When a public authority is considering whether interference with respect for home and family life is 'necessary in a democratic society', they will have to ask themselves whether there is a pressing social need for it; and it is proportionate to the aim of responding to that need.

'Proportionality' brings into play other matters with regard to unauthorised encampments beyond the (sometimes formulaic) undertaking of welfare inquiries. Is the land that the Gypsies and Travellers are on 'inappropriate'? If they are moved on, where will they go and where are the alternative temporary or transit sites? What provision of sites has the local authority in question made? These are now among the questions that must also be asked by public authorities when considering eviction action, and the HRA has had the effect of broadening the scope of what matters the local authority ought to take into account when deciding whether to evict Gypsies and Travellers from unauthorised encampments.

15.5   HOMELESSNESS

Under the Housing Act 1996, local authorities have a duty to provide accommodation to people who are judged to be 'homeless' and have a 'priority need' for accommodation (if they have children living with them, or elderly or disabled people). If a person is homeless and has a priority need, then the local authority can avoid its duty to provide accommodation only by showing either that he or she has a 'local connection' with another local authority's area that is stronger than the connection with theirs, or that the person is 'intentionally homeless' (for example, he or she was in housing or on a legal site, perhaps even some time ago, but left this legal accommodation for no good reason, or for a reason that was the fault of that person or a family member).

Housing departments should consider the needs of applicants for housing and, as far as is possible, provide them with 'suitable' accommodation. Providing 'suitable' accommodation may include providing a pitch on a public site; however, this is discretionary, and in areas where there are no pitches available Gypsies and Travellers will be offered conventional housing.

In *R* v *Carmarthenshire County Council ex parte Price* Mrs Price had made an application for housing to the local authority because she had no lawful place where she could pitch her caravans. After considering the matter, the local authority offered a house and sought to evict Mrs Price and her family from the local authority land that had previously been an encampment that the local authority had tolerated. The High Court quashed the local authority's decision to evict her.

Central to Mrs Price's case was the question of her 'cultural aversion to conventional housing'. The judge decided that when it tried to respect Mrs Price's Irish Traveller lifestyle the local authority had given too much weight to the fact that she had been prepared to live in conventional housing in 2001 and then had used this to justify disregarding her traditional lifestyle when it considered her wishes. The judge also decided that if the local authority had decided that Mrs Price's commitment to her traditional lifestyle was so powerful as to present great difficulty in her living in conventional housing, the authority had no duty to find her an authorised pitch or site; her commitment to her lifestyle was a significant factor in considering the extent to which the authority had to facilitate her traditional way of life.

On receiving a homeless application from a Gypsy or Traveller, the local authority must assess the Gypsy's or Traveller's aversion to conventional housing and then must see whether it can 'facilitate the Gypsy way of life'. Facilitating a Gypsy or Traveller lifestyle should involve a serious and extensive consideration of sites in the area (not just land owned by the local authority in question). This assessment should occur already as part of the homelessness strategies and reviews that each local authority is now obliged to produce every five years.

Mrs Price's homelessness application raises a number of other issues, which have not been resolved. What is the position for 'New Travellers'? What about the question of intentional homelessness decisions where the Gypsy or Traveller left conventional housing in the past owing to their inability to reside in such accommodation? What about the question of 'local connection' in cases concerning nomadic people, that is, if an applicant does not have a local connection with the local authority they apply to, they may be referred to another local authority where they do have such a connection?

One issue has recently been resolved. In *Myhill* v *Wealden District Council* two single, homeless Travellers argued that because of the greater likelihood of homelessness among Gypsies and Travellers as a result of the lack of authorised sites, difficulty in finding 'accommodation' and the possibility of criminal prosecution for staying at unauthorised encampments, they should be seen as being 'vulnerable' and thus 'in priority need'. Both the County Court and the High Court rejected this argument. The High Court stated that 'vulnerability' clearly related to the ability of the individual to deal with the condition of homelessness, rather than to the question of the difficulties that homeless Gypsies and Travellers would face.

In terms of interim accommodation, it is often argued that if Gypsies and Travellers are on land owned by the same local authority to whom the homelessness application has been made, and, if that land is not 'inappropriate', that they should be allowed to remain there in the meantime (perhaps in fulfilment of the interim accommodation duty).

Security of tenure

Gypsies and Travellers living on local authority Gypsy sites have no security of tenure. The Caravan Sites Act 1968 simply provides that possession can be obtained by a local authority if it gives a resident four weeks' notice to quit and then obtains a possession order from a court. There is no requirement that the local authority proves that it would be reasonable for possession to be granted, and the courts have no power to suspend the operation of such a possession order. The lack of security of tenure is in stark contrast to that enjoyed by council tenants living in conventional housing.

Two cases have challenged the lack of security of tenure for official site occupation under Articles 8 and 14 of the Convention. In each case the courts accepted the government's position that the introduction of security would undermine the need to maintain the possibility of nomadism of the residents – if they were secure, there might be less scope for Gypsies and Travellers to keep up a nomadic lifestyle and non-nomadic people might take up pitches on sites. This is a matter that may return to the higher courts in the future.

Problems of disrepair on sites might be susceptible to action as a statutory nuisance under the Environmental Protection Act 1990. Alternatively, although they have less obvious protection than council tenants in conventional housing, it may be possible for Gypsies and Travellers to rely on the express or implied terms of any licence agreement. Unfortunately, many residents are put off from taking action by their lack of security of tenure and their fear that they may be evicted.

15.6   RACISM AND DISCRIMINATION

In *Commission for Racial Equality* v *Dutton* the Court of Appeal held that Romany Gypsies were an ethnic group within the meaning of the Race Relations Act 1976

(RRA), having regard to the evidence of their shared history, geographical origin, distinct customs and language.

More recently in *O'Leary* v *Allied Domecq*, a case brought on behalf of Irish Travellers, the County Court accepted that Irish Travellers are also a distinct ethnic group for the purposes of the RRA. There are currently no reported cases relating to Gypsies or Travellers of other ethnic origins, but there seems to be no reason why Scottish or Welsh Travellers could not argue that they are members of separate ethnic groups. Whether such an argument is accepted is likely to depend upon the assessment of expert evidence.

Gypsies and Travellers who can show that they are members of a distinct ethnic group can use the RRA, supplemented by the Race Relations (Amendment) Act 2000 (RRA 2000), to combat the racism. Travellers that are not members of a distinct ethnic group cannot claim the protection of the RRA and RRA 2000, but they may be able to use Article 14 of the Convention to tackle discrimination by public bodies when their acts impinge upon other rights protected by the Convention.

If a Gypsy's or Traveller's race discrimination claim is to succeed then he or she must also show that he or she has been discriminated against in one or more ways that are unlawful under the RRA or the RRA 2000. For example, a pub or restaurant that refuses to serve 'travellers' would commit indirect discrimination because fewer Romany Gypsies and Irish Travellers could comply with the requirement than people of other racial groups and the requirement cannot be justified on non-racial grounds.

Racism and the police

The RRA imposes the general duty on police forces to carry out their functions with regard to the need to eliminate unlawful discrimination and to promote equality of opportunity and good relations between persons of different racial groups. In addition, the RRA makes chief constables liable for acts of racial discrimination by police officers under their direction and control.

In *Smith* v *Cheltenham Borough Council* (decided before the RRA 2000 was in force) a Gypsy woman and her daughter brought a claim against a local authority for breach of contract and against both the local authority and the police for breaching the RRA. The claimants had hired the Pittville Pump Rooms for the daughter's wedding reception and paid a deposit. Based on allegations of disorder in recent years, and rumours about the upcoming wedding, the police became concerned that the wedding celebrations might involve public disorder and informed the local authority of their concerns. The local authority attached conditions to the claimants' hire of the venue, including the payment of a large deposit and entry tickets, so the claimants booked an alternative venue (where the event took place without incident).

The judge decided that the local authority had breached the RRA. He decided that the police had no basis for their belief that the earlier disorder was linked with the claimants stating: 'the truth is that as soon as the word "Gypsy" appears assumptions are made that large numbers will descend and cause trouble'. The judge held that the local authority treated the claimants in an unfair and highhanded manner, in contrast with the way in which the organisers of the Hunt Ball, an event known to pose serious risks of disorder, were treated.

With regard to the claim against the individual police officers, the judge found that although 'the police had not acted well they had not knowingly aided the local authority to do an act made unlawful, as no officer was made party to the decision taken by the local authority'.

The Court of Appeal upheld the judgment.

Other examples of policing situations that may be unlawful under the RRA and RRA 2000 are:

- Raids on sites in pursuit of crime and disorder considerations, in which all vehicles are searched (unless there is a reasonable suspicion that all of the vehicles may be implicated in the ends the raid seeks to achieve). Police operations concerning a suspect or suspects in a house would not usually involve all other houses in the vicinity, so it is possible that such 'blanket' raids could be shown to be discriminatory.
- Excluding Gypsies and Travellers from the ethnicity monitoring of the use of discretionary powers (such as 'stop and search').
- Escorting recently evicted Gypsies and Travellers to county boundaries.
- Evicting all Gypsies and Travellers from an unauthorised encampment on the grounds of criminal or anti-social behaviour, when prosecution of a few members of a group would be appropriate on those grounds.
- Failure to properly investigate an alleged racist attack on a member of the Gypsy or Traveller communities.

European Convention on Human Rights

A victim of discrimination can bring a claim under the HRA, if the act of discrimination has some impact upon the enjoyment of the other rights and freedoms set out in the Convention.

The protection afforded by Article 14 is not limited to members of distinct ethnic groups and can be used by both traditional Gypsies and Travellers and New Travellers who consider themselves to be subject to discrimination in the enjoyment of their rights protected by the Convention. For example, a school's refusal to admit a Gypsy or Traveller child to a school on discriminatory grounds would have an impact upon the right to education protected by Article 2 of Protocol 1 of the Convention.

See also Chapter 10.

15.7   THE RIGHT TO HEALTHCARE

The health of Gypsies and Travellers

In 1995 the Minority Rights Group identified the following particular concerns about the health of the Gypsy population in the UK:

- Life expectancy of Gypsies and Travellers is poor and significantly less than that of the sedentary population.
- The Gypsy and Traveller birth rate is high and prenatal mortality, stillbirth mortality and infant mortality are significantly higher than the national average.
- There are numerous chronic illnesses suffered by Gypsies and Travellers (e.g. respiratory and digestive diseases, rheumatism).
- Many Gypsies and Travellers have an unbalanced diet, leading to deficiencies.

- Smoking is very common among Gypsies and Travellers.
- Gypsies have little, if any, dental care with access to such care being more difficult as a result of many dental practices opting out of the NHS.

In 2001 the Sheffield Adult Mental Health Collaborative Research Group Project began a two-year study of the health of Gypsies and Travellers. Preliminary research has already shown that:

- The health status of Gypsies and Travellers is poorer than matched urban deprived residents in terms of perceived overall health.
- Gypsies and Travellers suffer significantly higher levels of anxiety and depression than those from comparison groups.
- Both statutory health service providers and members of the Gypsy and Traveller community reported difficulties in access to appropriate services.

Access to healthcare

There are a number of reasons why Gypsies and Travellers have difficulty gaining access to healthcare. First, many Gypsies and Travellers are subject to a life of continual eviction in circumstances where there are not enough suitable places for them to camp. The bureaucracy associated with the National Health Service (NHS) also causes problems; for example, the completion of forms and the provision of information, such as dates of birth and history of previous healthcare, cause difficulties for illiterate Gypsies and Travellers.

In addition, some Gypsies and Travellers still experience discrimination at the hands of healthcare professionals. It seems that there is a general lack of cultural awareness on the part of service providers that can lead to discrimination and prejudice. For example, there are some GP surgeries that are still reluctant to register Gypsies and Travellers without a permanent address.

Under the National Health Service Act 1977 everyone has a right to healthcare provided by the NHS. What this means in practice is that no hospital should ever turn away someone who is the victim of an accident or illness, whoever that person may be and whether or not they have paid any national insurance contributions. However, only certain dental treatment and prescriptions are free or available at a reduced price if you are a child, someone who suffers from a long-term illness or disability (such as diabetes), or if you receive income support, a pension or family credit.

Although many Gypsies and Travellers go to casualty departments when they have an accident or illness, if Gypsies and Travellers can expect to be able to stay in an area for more than a few weeks, they can try to register with a local GP if they have any health problems that need attention.

Lists of doctors are available at main post offices. Some doctors are prevented from taking extra people on to their register if it is already too long, and you may have to go to several doctors before you find one that will allow you to register with him or her. If you are turned down by all doctors, whether or not it is because you are a Gypsy or Traveller, contact the local Primary Care Trust and tell them you have been rejected by all doctors, the reasons you have been given and any other reasons you consider relevant.

European Convention on Human Rights

The Convention does not include an express right to medical treatment. However, there could be circumstances where the failure to provide such treatment or the withdrawal of services could amount to a breach of the right to life (Article 2) and/or the prohibition on inhuman and degrading treatment (Article 3) of the Convention.

Health authorities, special health authorities, NHS Trusts, regulatory bodies and local authorities all have a duty as public bodies to comply with the provisions of the Convention. It also seems arguable that GPs should be considered to be public bodies when treating NHS patients.

Environmental health

Another area of concern to Gypsies and Travellers and healthcare practitioners alike is the link between the poor living environment and poor health of many Gypsies and Travellers.

While there is no statutory duty on local authorities to enable the provision of water to unauthorised encampments, Circular 18/94 advises local authorities to consider tolerating the presence of Gypsies and Travellers on temporary or unofficial sites and to examine ways of minimising the level of nuisance on such sites. Local authorities should be encouraged to comply with the advice in Circular 18/94 by providing basic services such as toilets, a refuse skip and a supply of drinking water.

Alternatively, it may be possible to persuade a local authority to provide water under the Children Act 1989 in circumstances where there are children 'in need' living on the site, that is, children who are unlikely to achieve or maintain, or to have the opportunity of achieving or maintaining, a reasonable standard of health or development without the provision of services by a local authority, or their health is likely to be significantly impaired or further impaired without the provision of such services.

15.8   THE RIGHT TO EDUCATION

Everyone has the right to education and local education authorities (LEAs) have a statutory duty to ensure that education is available for all children of compulsory school age (five to 16 year olds) in their area, appropriate to their age, abilities, aptitudes and any special educational needs that they might have. LEAs also have a duty to give parents in the area the opportunity to express a preference as to which school they wish their child to attend.

These duties apply to all children residing in the LEA's area, whether permanently or temporarily and, therefore, Gypsy and Traveller children residing with their families on temporary or unauthorised sites are included within this duty.

Most LEAs provide specialist Traveller Education Support Services who help Gypsy and Travelling pupils and parents to access education and provide practical advice and support to schools taking in Gypsy and Travelling pupils.

Although Gypsy and Travelling children of school age have the same legal right to education as anyone else, it is obviously practically difficult to claim or seek these rights without a permanent or legal place to stop. When a Gypsy or Traveller family with children of school age moves into an area they should contact the local Traveller Education Support Service for assistance.

The National Association of Teachers of Travellers produces an annual booklet listing the local Traveller Education Support Services, and can also provide information about books and other education resources just for Gypsy and Travelling children.

Children should be educated in accordance with their parents' wishes so far as that is compatible with the provision of efficient instruction and training and the avoidance of unreasonable public expenditure. LEAs have a duty to respect parents' religious and philosophical convictions. 'Respect' means more than simply 'acknowledge' or 'take into account' such views, but does not require the LEAs to cater for all parents' convictions, and there is no absolute right to choice of school or language of teaching.

Admissions to school

Gypsy and Traveller children should be admitted to schools on the same basis as any other children. However, Gypsy and Traveller parents should be aware that some schools may still rely upon admissions policies that disadvantage their children; for instance, an admissions policy that gives preference to children whose older brothers and sisters have already attended the school could be argued to unfairly disadvantage and unlawfully discriminate against Gypsy and Traveller families who have recently moved into the area.

Attendance at school

Parents have a duty to ensure that their children of compulsory school age receive efficient full-time education suitable to their age, ability, aptitude and any special educational needs that they may have either by regular attendance at school or otherwise. Failure to do so is an offence and can lead to prosecution. Schools must report unauthorised absences, and LEAs have a responsibility to prosecute parents in appropriate cases.

Gypsy and Traveller parents are protected from conviction for the non-attendance of their children at school where they can demonstrate that:

- They are engaged in a trade or business of such a nature that requires them to travel from place to place.
- The child has attended at a school as a registered pupil as regularly as the nature of that trade permits; and
- Where the child has attained the age of six years, they have attended school for at least 200 half-day sessions during the preceding school year (September to July).

However, there is some concern that this exception may in practice deny Gypsy and Traveller children equality of access in education, and the Department for Education and Skills (DfES) has recently emphasised the fact that Gypsy and Traveller parents should not regard the 200 half-day sessions as the norm but should continue to comply with their legal duty to ensure their children are receiving efficient suitable full-time education even when not at school.

To protect the continuity of learning for Gypsy and Traveller children, the DfES introduced the concept of 'dual registration'. If parents inform their 'base' school or the Traveller Education Support Service that the family will be travelling and intend to return by a given time, the school may keep the child's place for them and record their absence as authorised. The child can then register at other schools while the family is travelling.

Gypsy and Traveller parents can also take advantage of school-based distance learning whereby school teachers and the Traveller Education Support Service work together to provide pupils with a package of curriculum-based material to be taken away and studied by them while the family is travelling away from the area.

Special educational needs

A child with special educational needs will have a learning difficulty that requires special educational provision to be made. A child will have a learning difficulty if:

- He or she has a significantly greater difficulty in learning than the majority of children of the same age.
- He or she has a disability that either prevents or hinders him or her from making use of educational facilities of a kind generally provided for children of the same age in schools within the area of the LEA.
- The child is under the age of five years and is, or would be if special educational provision was not made, likely to fall within the categories when over that age.

If your children have started school late or attended school irregularly, they may be judged to have special needs, which may include remedial help with reading or even the necessity for them to go to a special school. There are rules about the way in which this decision on special needs is made, and if your children cannot read well you and your children will need someone who can help you through this process.

Transport to school

LEAs have to make appropriate arrangements to provide free transport for children to attend school unless the school is within walking distance, which is two miles (or three miles if the child is over eight years old). Alternatively, LEAs may 'as they think fit' provide funding for 'reasonable travelling expenses' for children for whom they have not made arrangements to provide free transport.

Exclusion from school

In 1996 Ofsted found that Gypsy and Traveller children suffer a disproportionately high level of school exclusion. If your child is threatened with exclusion then you should contact your local Traveller Education Support Service or the National Association of Teachers of Travellers for initial assistance, but you may need to seek legal advice as well. When a school contemplates excluding a child, it must follow the guidance published by the DfES in January 2002. Failure to do so could result in a successful legal challenge. Parents are entitled to make representations before any decision is taken, and there is provision for an appeal to be made against the decision to exclude a child from school.

If a child is excluded from a school the LEA will still have a duty to make arrangements for the provision of suitable education for that child.

Bullying at school

In 1996 Ofsted also found that Gypsy and Traveller children are often subject to bullying of a racist nature. Schools should have clear policies and strategies to deal with the prevention of bullying and the punishment of such behaviour. A school that fails to investigate and take action where bullying is alleged to have occurred may find itself subject to a claim for judicial review to force the school to act. Alternatively, a parent may bring a claim for negligence and/or possibly make an allegation that the school has subjected the child to degrading treatment by failing to prevent bullying behaviour by other pupils.

Discrimination and education
The RRA 2000 imposes a statutory duty on public bodies including LEAs and schools to promote race equality. Schools are required to:

- Prepare a written statement of their policies for promoting race equality and act upon them.
- Assess the impact of their policies on pupils, staff and parents from different racial groups, in particular the impact on attainment levels of these pupils.
- Monitor the operation of all the school's policies, in particular their impact on the attainment levels of pupils from different racial groups.

As part of complying with these duties, schools should have policies to help address bullying and racist behaviour. Ofsted will inspect schools' compliance with the RRA 2000 as part of their regular inspections.

Schools also have a general duty to promote race equality. Once again that duty is reinforced by specific duties designed to help schools meet the general duty. Each school must:

- Prepare a written statement of its policy for promoting race equality – a 'race equality policy'.
- Assess the impact of the school's policies, including its race equality policy, on pupils, staff and parents of different racial groups including, in particular, the impact on attainment levels of such pupils.

The fulfilment of these duties should be monitored by inspection bodies – including the Commission for Racial Equality (CRE), Ofsted and the Audit Commission. The CRE is able to issue a compliance notice to a public authority that it believes to be failing to fulfil any specific duty laid down and, if necessary, to seek a court order to enforce the notice. The CRE will also be empowered to issue Codes of Practice to provide guidance to public authorities on how to fulfil their general and specific duties.

See also Chapter 10.

Education other than at school
Parents have the option of educating their children at home. However, the education a child receives must be 'suitable education', that is, efficient education suitable to the child's age, ability, aptitude and any special educational needs he or she may have.

If a LEA considers that a child of school age is not receiving suitable education at home, it may serve the parents with a notice requiring them to satisfy the LEA that the child is receiving a satisfactory education.

If the LEA is not satisfied by the parents that the child is receiving a suitable education then it can serve the parents with a school attendance order requiring the parents to register a child at a named school. It is a criminal offence to fail to comply with a school attendance order, and conviction in the Magistrates' Court is punishable by a fine.

Before deciding to prosecute the parents, the LEA should consider whether it would be appropriate to take the alternative route of making an application in the family proceedings court for an education supervision order, which would last one year and would enable a supervisor or education social worker to advise, assist, befriend and give directions to both the child and the parents.

Pre-school children

LEAs also have a duty to secure sufficient provision in their area for nursery education. Children that have not had the benefit of any form of pre-school learning experience are at risk of underachievement. Traveller parents with children aged three and four should contact their LEA or Traveller Education Support Service for details of the facilities and programmes available in their area. Traveller parents should ask about local Sure Start programmes, which are designed to help transform the life chances of disadvantaged children under four years of age.

15.9   GYPSIES AND TRAVELLERS AND THE MEDIA

Gypsies and Travellers often suffer from negative and stereotyped articles about them in the press. Despite guidance to editors from bodies such as the CRE and the National Union of Journalists, the press at national and local levels consistently portray Gypsies and Travellers in an inflammatory, prejudicial, distorted and misleading fashion.

The press are subject to a self-regulation system by which they undertake to comply with a Code of Practice that is enforced by the Press Complaints Commission (PCC) from whom a copy of the code can be obtained. If you have a complaint about an item in a newspaper or a magazine that you believe breaks a clause of the Code of Practice, first write a letter of complaint to the editor. This is usually the quickest way of obtaining a correction or apology for inaccuracies. Give the editor at least seven days to reply, but do not wait longer than a month. If you are unhappy with the editor's response to your letter, then write a letter of complaint to the PCC.

If you wish to complain about a television programme you find offensive contact the Office of Communications (Ofcom) and use the standard complaints procedure.

15.10   FUTURE DEVELOPMENTS

The Institute for Public Policy Research (an influential and government-favoured think-tank) has released a report on Gypsies' and Travellers' accommodation entitled *Moving Forward*. The report states that there is an urgent need for the Government to address the shortage of authorised sites and to shift the issue away from criminalisation of Gypsies and Travellers through the use of public order and anti-social behaviour law towards provision, equality and the enforcement of rights. Combined with new interest and support from the Commission for Racial Equality, this report demonstrates that the difficulties facing Gypsies and Travellers are being 'mainstreamed' into civil liberties debates. The Government has also indicated that the Planning and Compulsory Purchase Bill 2004 together with a new circular 1/94 might require local authorities to identify specific pieces of land for site development.

The rights of Gypsies and Travellers are an important issue for a Government that has claimed to have a long tradition of championing minorities and the excluded. That reputation will be tarnished if it fails to deliver a fair and effective mechanism to provide more sites for Gypsies and Travellers at a time when it is trumpeting policy initiatives such as 'Decent Homes For All' and 'Cohesive and Sustainable Communities', which to date appear to have ignored the needs of the Gypsy and Traveller communities.

15.11   FURTHER INFORMATION

Useful organisations

Advisory Committee for the Education of Romany and Other Travellers (ACERT)
Moot House
The Stow
Harlow
Essex CM20 3AG
Tel: 01279 418 666

Commission for Racial Equality
St Dunstan's House
201–211 Borough High Street
London SE1 1GZ
Tel: 020 7939 0000
Fax: 020 7939 0001
info@cre.gov.uk
<www.cre.org.uk>

Community Law Partnership
Travellers' Advice Team
4th Floor
191 Corporation Street
Birmingham
B4 6RP
Tel: 0845 120 2980
office@communitylawpartnership.co.uk

Department for Education and Skills
Traveller Education team
4e Sanctuary Buildings
Great Smith Street
London SW1P 3BT
Tel: 0870 000 2288
info@dfes.gsi.gov.uk
<www.dfes.gov.uk>

Friends, Families and Travellers
Community Base
113 Queen's Road
Brighton BN1 3XG
Tel: 01273 234 777
Fax: 01273 234 778
fft@communitybase.org
<www.gypsy-traveller.org>

The Gypsy Council for Education, Culture, Welfare and Civil Rights
8 Hall Road
Aveley
Essex RM15 4HD
Tel/Fax: 01708 868 986
<thegypsycouncil@btinternet.com>

Minority Rights Group International
54 Commercial Street
London E1 6LT
Tel: 020 7422 4201
Fax: 020 7422 4200
minority.rights@mrgmail.org
<www.minorityrights.org>

National Association of Health Workers with Travellers
Balsall Heath Health Centre
43 Edward Road
Birmingham B12 9LB
Tel: 0121 446 4845
Fax: 0121 446 5936

National Association for Special Educational Needs
Nasen House
4/5 Amber Business Village
Amber Close
Amington
Tamworth B77 4RP
Tel: 01827 311 500
Fax: 01827 313 005
welcome@nasen.org

National Association of Teachers of Travellers
c/o Essex Traveller Education Service
Alec Hunter High School
Stubbs Lane
Braintree
Essex CM7 3NT
Tel/Fax: 01376 340 360
<www.essexcc.gov.uk>

National Gypsy Council
Greenacres Caravan Site
Hapsford, Helsby
Warrington
Cheshire WA6 OSS
Tel: 01928 723 130

National Health Service, Department of Health
Richmond House
79 Whitehall
London SW1A 2NS
Tel: 020 7210 4850
dhmail@doh.gsi.gov.uk
<www.doh.gsi.gov.uk>

National Romany Rights Association
The Bungalow
Roman Bank
Walpole St Andrews
Wisbech
Cambridgeshire PE14 7HP
Tel: 01945 780 326

Office of the Deputy Prime Minister
26 Whitehall
London
SW1A 2WH
Tel: 020 7944 4400
Fax: 020 7944 6589
<www.odpm.gov.uk>

Ofcom
Riverside House
2a Southwark Bridge Road
London SE1 9HA
Tel: 0845 436 3000
020 7981 3040
Fax: 0845 456 3333
contact@ofcom.org.uk
<www.ofcom.org.uk>

Ofsted
Alexandra House
32 Kingsway
London WC2B 6SE
Tel: 020 7421 6800
<www.ofsted.gov.uk>

Press Complaints Commission
1 Salisbury Square
London EC4Y 8AE
Tel: 020 7353 1248
Fax: 020 7353 8355
Textphone: 020 7583 2264 (for deaf and hard of hearing)
enquiries@pcc.org.com
<www.pcc.org.uk>

The Romany Guild
c/o Blenheim Crescent
London W11 2EG
Tel: 020 7727 2916

Traveller Law Reform Coalition
The Old Library Building
Willesden Green Library Centre
95 High Street
Willesden
London NW10 2ST
Tel: 07985 684 921
romanistan@yahoo.com/info@travellers-law.org
<www.travellers-law.org.uk>

Bibliography

Crawley, H., *Moving Forward: The Provision of Accommodation for Gypsies and Travellers* (London: Institute for Public Policy Research, 2004)

Department for Education and Skills, *Aiming High: Raising the Achievement of Gypsy Traveller Pupils, Guide to Good Practice on the Education of Traveller Children*, ref.: DfES/0443/2003

Department of the Environment, Circulars 1/94, 18/94

Fraser, A., *The Gypsies* (Oxford: Blackwell Publications, 1992)

Johnson, C. and Willers, M., *Gypsy and Traveller Law* (Legal Action Group 2004)

Kenny, P. and Thorpe, H., *Mobile Homes – an Occupier's Guide* (London: Shelter, 1997)

Morris, R. and Clements, L., *Gaining Ground: Law Reform for Gypsies and Travellers* (Hatfield: University of Hertfordshire Press, 1999)

Office of the Deputy Prime Minister, *Count of Caravans and Gypsy Families*, July 2003

Office of the Deputy Prime Minister, *Recommendation of Select Committee on the Housing Bill 2003*

Office of the Deputy Prime Minister and the Home Office, *Guidance on the Management of Unauthorised Camping*, 2004

Williams, T., *Private Gypsy Site Provision*, ACERT report, DETR

16   The Rights of the Bereaved

This chapter deals with:

- The rights over a dead body
- Formalities after death
- State investigations into a death
- Remedies
- Further information

This chapter does not deal with issues surrounding rights to the deceased's property, including wills and intestacy.

16.1   THE RIGHTS OVER A DEAD BODY

Possession of a dead body

It is a well-established principle of law that 'there is no property in a corpse'. This means that the law does not regard a corpse as property protected by rights. This means that there can be no 'ownership' of a dead body. The only exception is where a body or body parts acquire different attributes by virtue of the application of skill, for example, dissection or preservation techniques.

The questions that can arise after a death include:

- Who is entitled to bury the body or authorise a post mortem?
- Can relatives object to a post mortem and in what circumstances?
- Are those entitled to conduct post mortems permitted to retain organs or other tissues obtained during the procedure, and for what purpose can these body parts be used?

In order to answer these questions it is necessary to understand who has the right to possess a dead body. In the first place, anyone who has a duty to bury the deceased has the right to possess the body in order to bury it. In many cases the duty will fall upon the administrator or executor of the deceased's estate (that is, the deceased's property). An executor is a person appointed by the deceased's will to deal with the deceased's estate. An administrator is a person appointed by a court for the same purpose. If there is no executor, it is arguable that the person first entitled to a grant of administration of the estate should be also entitled to possession of the body in order to determine how to dispose of it. This is usually the spouse, nearest relative or next of kin or, in the case of a child, the parents. When the Civil Partnership Bill comes into force, it will award surviving civil partners the same rights with respect to administration of the estate as surviving spouses. This suggests that surviving civil partners will have the same duty to dispose of their partner's body as surviving spouses.

There are other people who might also be entitled to lawful possession of the body as a result of their duty to dispose of the body. If the body is lying on hospital premises, the hospital authorities will be in lawful possession of the body. If the Coroner has jurisdiction (the power to hold an inquest) (see below, p. 405, 'Inquests') he or she has the right to possession of the body for the purposes of his or her inquiries. This same authority is sufficient to permit the pathologist, as the Coroner's agent, to have the legal right of possession until the Coroner's inquiry has stopped.

Hospital post mortems and removal of organs and tissues

The Human Tissues Act 1961 (HTA) provides the legal authority for the use of a body, including removal of organs and tissues for therapeutic purposes, medical education or research and for the performance of a (non-coronial) post mortem.

Section 1 of the HTA concerns the use of the body for therapeutic purposes, medical education or research. It provides that the person in lawful possession of the body (assumed to be a hospital) may authorise the removal of any part from the body for these purposes if the deceased had requested in writing at any time (or orally in the presence of two or more witnesses during his or her last illness) that his or her body or part of it be used for these purposes after his or her death.

The hospital may also authorise the removal of any part of the body for these purposes if, having made reasonable enquiries, there is no reason to believe that the deceased had expressed an objection to his or her body being dealt with in this way after death or that a surviving spouse or a surviving relative of the deceased objects.

Section 2 of the HTA concerns post mortems for the purpose of confirming the causes of death or investigating the existence or nature of abnormal conditions. The hospital often arranges post mortem examinations to provide more information about the disease process or to confirm the cause of death. This may be especially important where there is the suspicion of a hereditary condition about which relatives need to be informed. The hospital may only arrange a post mortem if, after making 'such reasonable enquiries as may be practicable', there is no reason to believe that the deceased expressed an objection prior to his or her death, or that any spouse or surviving relative objects.

It is important that relatives realise that the hospital authority may lawfully undertake a post mortem, which may include removal of organs or tissue, including removal of organs for therapeutic, medical or research purposes, as long as the requirements of the HTA are satisfied. If relatives of the deceased object to the proposed course, they should make this known at the earliest opportunity. The HTA does not specifically require the hospital authority to obtain the consent of the deceased's personal representatives or relatives, but only requires them to take reasonable steps to ascertain if any relatives of the deceased object.

As long as reasonable steps are taken to ensure that no relatives of the deceased object to a post mortem, if the post mortem examination properly requires organs to be removed and retained for examination, no further consent is required. The position may be different if the post mortem examination, in addition, contemplated use of parts of a body for therapeutic, educational or research purposes: *AB* v *Leeds Teaching Hospital NHS Trust & Cardiff & Vale NHS Trust*.

If there is evidence to suggest that the deceased would have objected to a post mortem or if there is reason to believe that a surviving relative objects, the hospital should not proceed.

If a relative stipulates that consent to a hospital post mortem is conditional upon all organs being returned to the body, this gives rise to a duty of care at common law for medical staff to pass that information to the pathologist. Failure to do so would amount to a breach of that duty, and may be actionable. Similarly, although not a requirement of the HTA, the courts have held that medical staff owe relatives a duty of care when seeking consent for post mortem. This must involve some explanation of the procedures of a post mortem, including alerting them to the fact that organs might be retained. If this does not occur, and it is reasonably foreseeable in the individual circumstances that a relative would suffer a psychiatric injury if later told that their relative's organs had been retained, there may be an actionable claim in negligence.

The practice of removing and retaining organs from a dead person without the consent of the deceased's next-of-kin came under scrutiny recently, following inquiries into practices at hospitals throughout the UK. The *Royal Liverpool Children's Inquiry* 2001, for example, examined complaints that parents had been misled into believing that they were burying their deceased children intact, when in fact organs had been removed, which in many cases remained in storage. The inquiry recommended that the HTA should be amended to provide a test of 'fully informed consent' for the post mortem examination and retention of organs or tissues. This proposal reflects complaints that relatives are not always properly informed about the nature and extent of proposed retention of tissues and the fact that it can include removal of significant organs.

The Government has responded to such concerns with the introduction of the Human Tissue Bill (the Bill). The Bill proposes that the storage and use of a dead body for certain purposes shall be lawful only if done with 'appropriate consent'. Those purposes are:

- Determining the cause of death.
- Education, training or research (other than incidental to medical diagnosis or treatment).
- Establishing after a person's death the efficacy of any drug or other treatment administered to him or her; and/or
- Obtaining scientific or medical information and transplantation.

Under the proposed regime, 'appropriate consent' means, in relation to a child, either consent obtained from the child while alive or in the event that the child is not competent to deal with the issue of consent or has died, the person with parental responsibility for the child (see section 13.2, 'Parental responsibility', p. 311). In relation to an adult, an individual will have a right to give or withhold their consent to such activities while alive. Alternatively, an individual may appoint an adult to deal with the issue of consent after his or her death.

There are different ways of appointing a nominated representative:

- You can appoint one orally in the presence of at least two witnesses present at the same time.

- You can appoint one in writing if the document is signed by you or at your direction in the presence of at least one witness who witnesses the signature.
- You can appoint a representative in your will.

If neither the deceased nor a nominated representative has given or withheld consent, this should be obtained from the person who stood in a qualifying relationship to him or her immediately before he or she died. The qualifying relationships proposed are (ranked in the following order): (a) spouse or partner; (b) parent or child; (c) brother or sister; (d) grandparent or grandchild; (e) child of a person falling within paragraph (c); (f) stepfather or stepmother; (g) half-brother or half-sister; friend of longstanding. If activities are carried out without the appropriate consent this may, in appropriate circumstances, constitute an offence.

The Anatomy Act 1984 and the Anatomy Regulations 1988 set out the conditions that must be satisfied for anatomical examination of dead bodies for educational or research purposes. Similar provisions apply as for the removal of organs. The Bill contains proposed changes in the law relating to the storage and use of bodies for anatomical examination. These activities would require the appropriate consent. The Bill also creates offences in the commercial dealings in human material and imposes restrictions on transplants involving live donors (which are outside the scope of this chapter).

Under neither the current regime, nor under the Bill, should the hospital arrange a post mortem examination if the Coroner may have jurisdiction. If the death has been reported to the Coroner (see below, p. 405, 'Inquests'), organs should not be removed unless the Coroner has stated that he or she does not propose to carry out a post mortem examination or hold an inquest. Pressure should not, however, be brought to bear upon relatives to agree to a hospital post mortem because of the threat that otherwise the death will be reported to the Coroner.

The HTA does not apply to stillborn children. There are no specific legal provisions for the examination of a foetus under 24 weeks or the use of foetal tissues. Retention of foetal material for research or treatment purposes is governed by the *Code of Practice on the Use of Foetuses and Foetal Material in Research and Treatment*. This code provides guidance for good practice, including that the written consent of the mother should be obtained before any research involving the foetus or foetal tissue takes place. There is also guidance to professionals relating to the examination of all foetuses, contained within *The Foetal and Infant Post-Mortem: Brief Notes for the Professional (Confidential Enquiry into Stillbirths and Death in Infancy 1998)*, which also recommends that consent be obtained for examination of foetuses.

Coroner's post mortem examinations

The Coroner's office will usually carry out preliminary inquiries to ascertain whether the Coroner is likely to have jurisdiction (see below, p. 405, 'Inquests'). The ultimate decision is a judicial one that should be made by the Coroner, rather than the Coroner's officer. If the Coroner is satisfied that neither a post mortem nor an inquest is necessary, he or she will issue a form setting out the cause of death as certified by the attending doctor. The death can then be registered.

If the Coroner decides to hold an inquest, usually there will be a post mortem examination of the body. The post mortem is performed by a pathologist acting as the Coroner's agent and should be carried out as soon as reasonably possible after the death because the body cannot be released for burial until the Coroner is satisfied as to the cause of death. If, following a post mortem examination, the Coroner decides that it is unnecessary to hold an inquest (if the post mortem satisfactorily determines the cause of death), the Coroner will issue a different form from above certifying the cause of death for the Registrar.

Where a Coroner directs that a post mortem examination should take place, any relative who has notified the Coroner of his or her desire to attend has a right to be notified by the Coroner of the time and place of the examination, unless to do so would cause the examination to be unduly delayed. Any relative who has notified the Coroner is entitled to be represented at the post mortem by a legally qualified medical practitioner. If the relative has not been notified or has been notified too late to arrange representation, he or she may be entitled to a second post mortem by a pathologist of his or her own choice. While the Coroner remains in lawful possession of the body until his or her functions are complete, he or she has discretion to permit interference with the body for relatives to obtain a second post mortem opinion. Once the pathology report is available the Coroner must if requested supply a copy to any interested persons.

If a person swears on oath before the Coroner that he or she believes that the death was caused partly or entirely by the improper or negligent treatment of a doctor or other person, that doctor shall not be allowed to perform the post mortem, but may be represented at it. If the deceased died in hospital, the Coroner should not request a pathologist on the staff of, or associated with, the hospital to carry out a post mortem examination if the conduct of any member of staff is likely to be called into question or a relative of the deceased objects, unless obtaining another pathologist with suitable qualifications would unduly delay the examination. This rule is intended to ease any concerns that relatives may have about the independence of the examination. For similar reasons, it is undesirable for a prison doctor who may be a witness to perform a post mortem examination on a prisoner.

If for religious or other reasons there is an objection to a post mortem examination, the Coroner should be made aware of any objections as soon as possible. The Coroner may be able to satisfy him or herself by other inquiries (including non-invasive investigations) that the death is natural. If, however, the Coroner is of the opinion that the circumstances of the death require a post mortem examination, he or she must proceed with the examination, regardless of any objections from family members or others. If there are reasonable grounds for considering that the legal requirements for an investigation are not met, it may be possible to challenge the Coroner's decision by way of judicial review.

If the Coroner decides that a post mortem examination is not required or having undertaken a post mortem examination he or she is satisfied that the death was natural and there is no suggestion of violence or other unnatural circumstances, he or she should release the body for disposal to the person entitled to take possession of it. The Coroner will send a notice of the decision to the Registrar so that the death can be registered.

As for hospital post mortems, an issue has arisen about the extent to which the pathologist can make use of human material retained after a post mortem. The Coroners' Rules 1984 provide that the Coroner has authority to remove from the body and preserve material – which may include organs and tissues – that has a bearing on the cause of death for such period as the Coroner thinks fit. It was suggested that once the Coroner has discharged his or her duty to inquire into the cause of death, the right to possession of the body or parts should revert back to the executor or next of kin to exercise their duty to dispose of the body. However, as for hospital post mortem examinations, the position is that if, after the post mortem, organs or tissues are retained upon which work and skill have been applied, this material acquires the character of property and remains lawfully in the possession of the Coroner, who may then dispose of it: *AB* v *Leeds Teaching Hospital NHS Trust & Cardiff & Vale NHS Trust*.

If, during the course of a post mortem, organs or tissues are retained and the deceased is buried before the coronial use for the retained organ comes to an end, using the retained material for research without obtaining the consent of the relative will be contrary to the HTA. The HTA provides no remedy for such a breach, although relatives may have a cause of action under the European Convention for Human Rights (the Convention) as the court may take the view that such interference is a breach of Article 8(1) protecting the right to family life.

16.2   FORMALITIES AFTER DEATH

Reporting and registering a death

The failure of the registration, cremation certification and coronial investigation systems to detect the crimes of Dr Harold Shipman prompted Parliament to set up the Shipman Inquiry. The Shipman Inquiry found that families of a deceased person had little involvement in the processes of certification and investigation of a death. It also found that where a death occurs at home, the relatives, friends or carers of the deceased often do not know what is expected of them as their legal duty.

Before a body can be buried, cremated or otherwise disposed of, the cause of death must be certified by a doctor who has attended the deceased during his or her last illness or by a Coroner if he or she has assumed jurisdiction. The death can then be registered.

Under the Births and Deaths Registration Act 1953 there is a general requirement to notify the Registrar of Births and Deaths that a person has died. If the death occurred in England or Wales, you need to notify the Registrar of Births and Deaths for the district in which the person died. This notification enables registration of the death to take place. Details of the Registrar can be found in the local telephone directory.

If a person dies at home or in another house, there is a duty to attend the Registrar personally within five days of the death and to give the particulars that are required for registration. If a written notice of the death is sent to the Registrar within five days together with confirmation that a doctor has certified the cause of death, the period in which the informant must personally attend the Registrar is extended to 14 days.

The person who has this duty is the 'qualified informant'. A qualified informant is a relative present at the death or during the deceased's last illness, any other relative living in the district where the death occurred, anyone present at the death, the occupier or inmate of the house if he or she knew about the death or the person responsible for disposing of the body.

If the deceased did not die in a house the particulars for registration must be reported within five days of the death by the 'qualified informant' who, in this case, is either any relative with knowledge of any of the particulars for registration, any person present at the death, any person finding or taking charge of the body and any person responsible for disposing of the body, which can include any surviving spouse, next of kin, and which will include surviving civil partners (see above, p. 394, 'Possession of a dead body').

The birth and death of an infant who is stillborn must be registered within 42 days of the death. The following may register a stillbirth: the mother, father (if the child would have been legitimate if born alive), the occupier of the premises where the stillbirth occurred or a person present at the stillbirth or who found the infant. If the infant died before 24 weeks of pregnancy, the loss of the foetus is considered a miscarriage and there is no need to register the death.

If the deceased was attended by a doctor in the last illness before his or her death, that doctor must sign a medical certificate informing the Registrar of Birth and Deaths of his or her belief as to the cause of death. The doctor is not certifying the fact that a death has occurred, only his or her belief as to the cause of death, and there is no specific obligation upon the doctor to examine the body. It is only a doctor who attended the deceased during his or her last illness who can be required to sign a medical certificate as to the cause of death. If there is doubt about the cause of death, the doctor should report the death to the Coroner. Otherwise, the medical certificate is provided to the Registrar in order for the death to be registered. In practice the medical certificate is sent directly to the Registrar of Births and Deaths or provided to the next of kin for this purpose.

After a death occurs, the deceased's general practitioner will usually attend and will indicate if he or she is in a position to certify the cause of death. If no doctor is in a position to certify the cause of death, it will be reported to the Coroner.

As the onus is on the doctor in these circumstances both to certify the cause of death (if he or she is able) and decide whether there should be further inquiry by the Coroner, a great amount of trust is invested in a single medical practitioner. The Shipman Inquiry highlighted the danger that a doctor who attended the deceased in his or her last illness could falsely certify the cause of death, in order to avoid a report to the Coroner and an official inquiry into the death. This could occur not only in the extreme circumstances investigated by the Shipman Inquiry, but also in circumstances where a doctor knows that a death may have been caused or contributed to by lack of care or medical error and feels under pressure to certify the cause of death.

Once the medical certificate has been provided to the Registrar and the death has been registered, a copy of the death certificate will be issued upon payment. The Registrar will also issue a certificate of disposal, without which the body cannot be cremated or buried.

Reporting a death to the coroner

The Coroner is an independent judicial officer, who has a duty in particular circumstances to inquire into a death, for the purposes of finding out who the deceased was, and how, when and where he or she died. When a death occurs and a person is aware that there are circumstances that would require an inquest to be held, that person has a legal duty to notify the Coroner. The right to dispose of a body is subject to this duty to report the death in these circumstances to the Coroner, and it is an offence to bury or dispose of a body in order to prevent the Coroner making inquiries or holding an inquest. It is also an offence to obstruct a Coroner in the exercise of his or her duty, for example, by concealing a body or denying access to it.

The Coroner should be notified if, for example, the death was sudden and the cause is unknown, or if there is any suggestion of medical error or that some accident or industrial disease occurring before the death was a causative factor. Even if there is only a suspicion that any of these factors exist or contributed to the death, the matter should be reported to the Coroner before the body is buried or cremated. Any relatives or anyone close to the deceased who is concerned about the circumstances of a death and suspects foul play, medical error, accident or neglect should contact the local Coroner, whose details can be obtained from the local police station.

There is also a specific legal duty on authorities to report to the Coroner certain deaths, for example, if the deceased person died in a prison or young offender's institution. There is, however, no duty to report to a Coroner the death of a patient compulsorily detained in a mental hospital. See also Chapter 12.

The Registrar of Deaths is obliged to report deaths to the Coroner in circumstances where it appears that the Coroner may have jurisdiction – where the cause of death is unknown; where there is reason to believe the death was contributed to by abortion, or by violence, neglect, or other suspicious circumstances; where the death occurred during or within 24 hours of an operation or recovery from anaesthetic where there is reason to believe that the cause of death is related to the operation or anaesthesia or is due to industrial disease or poisoning; or where the deceased was not seen by a doctor during his or her last illness. The Registrar must also report to the Coroner an apparent stillbirth where there is reason to believe that the child was born alive.

If the death has been reported to the Coroner, the Registrar will be unable to register the death until he or she is informed by the Coroner either that he or she does not intend to hold an inquest, or, after a post mortem examination, the Coroner informs him or her of the cause of death. If the Coroner decides to hold an inquest, he or she must at the conclusion of the inquiry provide the necessary registration details to the Registrar to enable registration of the death to take place.

There may be religious or other reasons why relatives wish to avoid delay before disposal of the body, and in some areas religious groups have sought to make special arrangements with the Registrars and Coroners in their districts for occasions when a death occurs outside normal working hours. In some districts the Registrar will provide an out-of-hours service and the Coroner will arrange for post mortem examinations to take place at the weekend in order to facilitate early burial. In some districts the Coroner may permit an alternative to an invasive post mortem examination where this is possible to ascertain cause of death in this way. These arrangements are not, however, uniform throughout the country, and the Chair of the Shipman Inquiry suggested that the reasonable expectations of all sections of the community should be met and systems developed to facilitate speed in completing post-death formalities and to take into consideration objections to a post mortem examination.

Disposal of the body

If there is an executor or administrator, he or she is entitled to determine where and how the body is disposed, although he or she must not spend more than a reasonable amount on funeral expenses without specific authority or consent from the beneficiaries of the deceased's estate.

The executor has a duty to dispose of the deceased's body, and in the absence of an executor this duty falls on several other people: the parents of a deceased child with sufficient means, any householder upon whose premises the body lies, or the local authority in default of any of the above.

It is an offence for any such person, having sufficient means, to fail to discharge this duty. Other offences arising out of the use of a dead body include refusing to deliver it to the executors for burial, conspiring to prevent a lawful and decent burial, selling the body for dissection (except as is authorised under the HTA or the Anatomy Act 1984) and exposing a dead body in a public place if to do so would shock public decency.

A dead body can be kept in a house or other dwelling for a period of time before disposal, although this is subject to certain public health provisions relating to circumstances where the retention of a body in a building would endanger the health of others in that or neighbouring buildings. There are other strict regulations that apply where the deceased was suffering from a 'notifiable' disease, including cholera, plague, relapsing fever, smallpox, typhus or an infectious disease to which a local authority has applied the provisions of the Public Health Act 1968.

Burial

There is no requirement that a body should be buried in an authorised place, and burials do not have to take place in a traditional cemetery. A place of burial may be established on private ground, provided no statutory or other nuisance is caused. There may, however, be a restrictive covenant on the ground preventing the creation of graves, and an application would have to be made for the removal of the covenant if it was considered that the covenant no longer serves its original purpose. Burial in a woodland or nature-reserve burial ground has grown in popularity among those concerned with ecological burial. Usually a tree will be planted, instead of the usual headstone. The site must, however, have planning permission for such use.

Before a burial can take place, the executor or next of kin must obtain a certificate of disposal from the Registrar of Births and Deaths or a burial order issued by the Coroner. If the Coroner has jurisdiction and decides to hold an inquest, burial will usually be delayed until a post mortem or other examination has taken place, or where other interested parties indicate that such examinations may be required.

Cremation

Unlike burials, cremations may only occur in an authorised crematorium. When a person is cremated there is no opportunity for further examination of the body following exhumation, therefore additional safeguards are imposed to ensure that there are no suspicious circumstances necessitating further inquiry before a body is cremated. The regulations require an application (Form A) to be made for cremation. This is usually made by the executor or nearest relative of the deceased and must be supported by certificates from two medical practitioners certifying the cause of death and that there are no known circumstances justifying an inquest. The first doctor will usually be the attending doctor (who completes Form B); a second doctor will carry out his or her own inquiries and complete a confirmatory certificate (Form C).

The Coroner may issue a certificate (Form D) after a post mortem examination or a different certificate (Form E) at the conclusion of the inquest. If the body is being cremated following anatomical examination, a different certificate again is issued.

A cremation cannot take place until after the death has been registered, unless the Coroner has opened an inquest or directed a post mortem examination and he or she has given a certificate for cremation, or the Registrar has certified that the death is not one that must be registered because it took place outside England or Wales. Where a death has been reported to the Coroner, but the Coroner considers that he or she does not have jurisdiction and decides not to order a post mortem examination or an inquest, the death is registered by the Registrar for Births and Deaths.

After a certificate (or certificates if certified by two medical practitioners) has been issued, the authority of the Medical Referee of the Cremation Authority must be obtained. The Medical Referee must certify that the cause of death has been ascertained and there is no reason for any further inquiry or examination. The Medical Referee should not allow a cremation to take place where it appears that there are suspicious circumstances, unless an inquest has been opened and the Coroner has issued a certificate pursuant to that inquest.

In the case of a stillborn infant, the Medical Referee of the Cremation Authority must *also* be satisfied that the infant was stillborn, and the cremation may only take place if a registered medical practitioner, who has examined the infant, certifies that the infant was stillborn.

Exhumation

Once a person has been buried it is unlawful to disturb or remove a body without lawful authority. However, once a Coroner assumes jurisdiction over a body, he or she has the right to possession of the body and may order exhumation where it appears either that it is necessary for the purpose of his or her inquiry or for any criminal proceedings relating to the death or any other death in connected circumstances. The power to order an exhumation of the body is limited to these two purposes. If the Coroner decides that an exhumation is necessary for one of these purposes he or she will issue a warrant to the persons in charge of the burial ground or cemetery.

16.3   STATE INVESTIGATIONS INTO A DEATH

European Convention on Human Rights

In certain circumstances the State has a duty to carry out an official inquiry to investigate an individual's death. This duty arises from the obligations of the State under the Convention. One of the fundamental rights protected by the Convention is the right to life under Article 2.

The European Court of Human Rights (ECHR) has ruled that Article 2 of the Convention imposes upon the State a duty to carry out an effective investigation into a death where there is reason to believe that the deceased died in contravention of Article 2.

The ECHR only came into force in England and Wales on 2 October 2000, and the duty to investigate a death under Article 2 does not arise in respect of deaths occurring before this date: *Re McKerr*.

Individuals killed as a result of lethal force by state agents
In *McCann* v *United Kingdom* the ECHR held that the State has a duty to carry
out an official investigation into a death of a person killed by use of force by state
agents. If the State fails to carry out an effective investigation into a death in these
circumstances it will be in breach of the Convention whether or not the State is
found to be liable for the person's death. *Salman* v *Turkey* concerned the death in
custody of an individual, which was seemingly caused by ill treatment by police
officers. The ECHR held that the State was in breach of Article 2 both in relation to
its responsibility for the death *and* for failing to carry out an effective investigation
into the circumstances of the death.

The English and Welsh courts have confirmed that the duty to investigate an
individual's death is not confined solely to allegations of unlawful killing by state
agents.

Individuals who die while under the care and protection of the State
The requirement for an effective investigation also arises where a state authority
has failed to protect the individual's life where they had assumed liability for his or
her welfare. This includes situations in which people take their own lives (*Keenan* v
UK) or are killed by non-state actors while in custody. In *Edwards* v *United Kingdom*
the applicants were parents of the deceased, Christopher Edwards, who was killed
by his cellmate while detained in custody. Both the deceased and his cellmate had
a history of mental illness, and a private non-statutory inquiry commissioned by
three state agencies with statutory responsibilities towards Mr Edwards concluded
that both inmates should not have been in prison or sharing a cell. Relying upon
the fact that Mr Edwards had been wholly under the protection of and dependent
upon the state authorities at the time of his death, the ECHR held that the State had
a duty to conduct an effective official investigation into his death.

The ECHR has also held that the duty to investigate arises where it is complained
that the State knew or ought to have known that the deceased's life was at real and
immediate risk and failed to take adequate steps to protect him or her: *Osman* v *United
Kingdom*. This includes situations where the authorities know that an individual
presents a level of risk to him or herself.

Individuals dying from life-threatening injuries in suspicious circumstances
In *Menson* v *United Kingdom* the ECHR extended the duty yet further to circumstances
where there is no direct state responsibility for the individual, but the death occurred
in suspicious circumstances suggestive of unlawful killing. Mr Menson died of severe
burns after having informed the police that four white men had attacked him and
set fire to him. The police failed to take a statement from him. The applicants (Mr
Menson's family) were unsuccessful in proceedings before the ECHR. However, the
court held that the basic procedural requirements apply 'with equal force to the
conduct of an investigation into a life-threatening attack on an individual'. The court
considered that the obligation to safeguard the lives of those within its jurisdiction
imposed a duty upon the State to secure the right to life by putting in place an effective
official investigation where there is reason to suspect that a person has sustained
life-threatening injuries in suspicious circumstances. It was also observed that where
an attack upon an individual was racially motivated it was particularly important
that the investigation should be pursued with vigour and impartiality.

The nature of the investigation

The ECHR has held that an official state investigation into a death should be independent, effective, and reasonably prompt, involve a sufficient element of public scrutiny, and involve the next of kin to the extent necessary.

The involvement of the family in the inquiry process

An important feature of an investigation is the ability of the deceased's family to participate in the proceedings. If the relatives of the deceased are not able to participate effectively in any inquiry into the death, the investigation may be rendered insufficient for the purposes of Article 2. For example, in *Edwards v United Kingdom*, the ECHR held that the private inquiry had been insufficient for the State to discharge its duty where there was no power to compel witnesses and the family were unable to attend for all the proceedings or to ask questions.

In order to ensure that the family is able to participate effectively, it will sometimes be necessary for relatives to have legal representation. The State should have a system of funding this representation, and in exceptional circumstances, public funding should be made available regardless of the applicant's means.

Public scrutiny – the requirement for a formal finding of any failures

To be effective, it is important that any inquiry should have the ability formally and publicly to record any findings of failure on the part of the responsible state agencies that caused or contributed to the death.

An effective remedy

There is also authority to suggest that where the State has violated Article 2, it should also provide an effective remedy. In certain situations, however, in the absence of a claim for dependency or bereavement damages (see below, section 16.4, 'Remedies', p. 415), there will be no legal entitlement for relatives of an individual who has died to obtain compensation in respect of his or her death. In these circumstances it may be possible to bring a claim under the Human Rights Act 1998 (HRA) for compensation in respect of the death, even though there is otherwise no entitlement under English and Welsh law to damages.

Relatives have the right to expect that an investigation into an individual's death has the features identified. This has implications for police investigations, inquests and other inquiries that may be the means by which the State investigates a death. Thus, in cases of suspected homicide, relatives have the right to expect a prompt, effective police investigation. Where there are concerns that state authorities have failed in their duty towards the deceased, any subsequent inquiry should have the minimum features identified, including the involvement of the family to the necessary extent. Otherwise there will be a risk that the inquiry falls short of the requirements of a sufficient investigation.

Inquests

In many cases the inquest will be the means by which the State discharges its obligation to inquire into a death where there is an element of state responsibility, either for the death itself or the investigation of it or both. This was confirmed by ECHR in *McCann v United Kingdom*, which concerned the State's responsibility for and investigation of the shooting of members of the Provisional IRA who it was alleged were planning to plant a bomb in Gibraltar. The ECHR was satisfied that the obligation to hold an effective official investigation had been satisfied by the inquest. It concluded that the inquest had been lengthy, thorough, had included numerous witnesses and all parties had been represented.

An inquest will only satisfy the State's responsibility to investigate the death where its scope is sufficiently wide and it complies with the minimum features identified above. The ECHR observed in *McCann* v *United Kingdom* that the investigation should focus not only upon those who were allegedly directly responsible for the death, but also the planning and organisation of the operation that provided the context in which the death took place, including in this case whether the state agents had been properly instructed and trained.

Where an inquest is held that does not have these identified features it may not satisfy the obligation to investigate. *Wright* v *Secretary of State for the Home Department* concerned the death of a prisoner following negligent medical care. The judge decided that the inquest did not comply with the requirements of the Convention as an important witness had not been called to give evidence, it did not address the shortcomings in medical treatment and the family of the deceased had not been represented. The judge concluded that there had not been an effective official investigation and therefore the State had not discharged its obligation under Article 2.

The right to an inquest

An inquest must be held in circumstances where a Coroner is informed that the body of a person is lying within his or her district and there is *reasonable cause to suspect* that the individual died:

- A violent or unnatural death.
- A sudden death of which the cause is unknown.
- In prison or in such circumstances as to require an inquest under any other Act.

The Coroner only has a right to hold an inquest if one of these conditions is satisfied. Conversely, the Coroner cannot decide *not* to hold an inquest if one of the conditions is satisfied.

A 'body' does not include a non-viable foetus or a stillborn child, which did not breathe or show any other sign of life. If, however, the infant lived, even shortly, there is a right to an inquest in relation to his or her death. If there is any question about whether the infant was ever alive, the Coroner should treat this as a preliminary issue. If the Coroner concludes that the infant died before life independent of its mother, the death will be registered as a stillbirth in a similar way to that had there been a live birth.

In some cases only parts of a body are discovered within the Coroner's district. In these circumstances the Coroner should consider whether it is reasonable to assume that the tissue or body parts came from a dead body. The mere fact that parts of the body have been found does not necessarily mean that a death can be assumed.

If human remains do not constitute 'a body' or if no body exists but the Coroner has reason to believe that a death occurred in or near his or her district and the circumstances are such that an inquest would be held if there was a body, he or she should report the matter to the Secretary of State who may consider directing an inquest into the death.

An unnatural death

An 'unnatural' death has been defined as one where there is suspicion of foul play, wrongdoing such as negligence, or some peculiarity other than natural illness. Recently the Court of Appeal has held that a woman's death could be regarded as unnatural after her blood pressure was left unmonitored following a caesarean section delivery: *R v HM Coroner for Inner London North ex parte Touche*. The court held that where a person is suffering from a condition that if not monitored and treated in a routine way will result in death and that treatment or monitoring is omitted, the Coroner must hold an inquest unless he or she can say that there are no grounds for suspecting that the omission was an effective cause of death.

A violent death

A death may be considered 'violent' where a person is injured, intentionally or accidentally. This includes deaths where there is reasonable cause to suspect that the deceased took his or her own life.

A sudden death with the cause unknown

If the death is unexpected and either the terminal cause of death or the underlying condition is unknown an inquest will be held. In these circumstances the Coroner has the right to order a post mortem examination, and if this reveals conclusively that the death was natural, the Coroner need not hold an inquest, so long as none of the other statutory requirements to hold an inquest applies.

A death in custody

If the death occurred while the deceased was detained in prison the Coroner must hold an inquest. The term 'prison' is not defined, and it is arguable that it extends to other situations where the deceased person is restrained or deprived of his or her liberty, for example, if the deceased person died while detained at a police station or under the provisions of the Mental Health Act 1983 (MHA). The *Home Office Circular 35/69* recommends that Coroners should hold an inquest into the death of a person in any kind of legal custody.

Deaths outside England and Wales

Where a person dies outside England and Wales, the Coroner must still hold an inquest if the dead body comes to lie within his or her jurisdiction and if the circumstances of the death require it. The Coroner with jurisdiction is usually the Coroner for the district of the intended burial or cremation of the deceased. If the death has been the subject of an inquiry outside England and Wales the Coroner may be assisted by documents or reports that were available for those proceedings.

Adjournment for criminal trial

If a person has been charged with murder, manslaughter or infanticide of the deceased; dangerous driving or careless driving under the influence of drink or drugs causing the death of the deceased; or aiding, abetting, counselling or procuring the suicide of the deceased, the Coroner will adjourn the inquest until after the criminal proceedings have ended unless the Director of Public Prosecutions informs the Coroner that it is unnecessary.

After the conclusion of the criminal proceedings the Coroner may resume the inquest if there is sufficient cause. If the Coroner does not resume the adjourned inquest, he or she will send a certificate to the Registrar of Deaths stating the results of the criminal proceedings. If the Coroner does resume the inquest, the findings of the inquest are not permitted to be inconsistent with the outcome of the criminal proceedings.

The purpose and scope of inquests

An inquest is inquisitorial, rather than adversarial. This means that there are no opposing parties each trying to prove their case. The purpose of the inquest is to determine as far as the Coroner is able the identity of the deceased and where, when and how he or she came to die. These findings are then recorded on the inquisition form at the conclusion of the inquest. The inquest is not a mechanism for apportioning blame for the death. Indeed, the verdict at an inquest must not be expressed in such a way as to appear to determine criminal liability on the part of a named person or civil liability. For example, in the case of road traffic accidents, the Coroner will inquire into whether the death was accidental but will not seek to determine who, if anyone, bears responsibility for the accident.

The Coroner has a duty, however, to hold a sufficiently wide inquiry to determine how the deceased died. The question of 'how' a person died is not limited to establishing merely the medical cause of death and may require a critical examination of the circumstances in which the death occurred. If the inquest is the means by which the State will discharge its obligation to investigate breaches of the Convention contributing to the death, the Coroner should properly inquire into these aspects.

Inquest procedure

The requirement for a Coroner to sit with a jury

In certain circumstances the Coroner must sit with a jury to inquire into the relevant matters and decide the verdict. The Coroner must summon a jury if before he or she proceeds to hold an inquest, or in the course of an inquest begun without a jury, it appears that there is *reason to suspect* that one of the following criteria is satisfied, that:

- The death occurred in prison or in such a place or in such circumstances as to require an inquest under any other Act.
- The death occurred while the deceased was in police custody, or resulted from an injury caused by a police officer in the purported execution of his or her duty.
- The death was caused by an accident, poisoning or disease, notice of which is required to be given under any Act to a government department, any inspector or other officer of a government department or to an inspector appointed under the Health and Safety at Work Act 1974. The kind of cases in which there is a duty to report a death to a Government minister (and therefore call for a jury) includes deaths on railways, accidents on board British ships or involving civil or military aircrafts.

- The death occurred in circumstances the continuance or possible recurrence of which is prejudicial to the health or safety of the public or any section of the public. The Coroner will generally find that this section is satisfied where there is some evidence that the deceased's death was not a 'one-off' incident, but occurred because of system failures, inadequate safety measures or where steps could be taken to avoid similar fatalities in the future.

The right to participate at an inquest

The Coroner has a duty to notify (among others) the spouse, near relative or personal representative of the deceased where their names and addresses are known to him or her and any other interested persons who ask to be notified of the time and place of the inquest.

The Coroner also has discretion to permit other people to participate as interested persons. It is often the case that the Coroner will permit other close family members to participate as interested parties under these discretionary powers. Where close personal ties existed between the deceased and the bereaved, such as to constitute a family relationship for the purpose of Article 8 of the Convention (the right to private and family life), it is arguable that this discretion should be exercised to ensure that the right to family life is respected. Relationships that are likely to constitute a 'family relationship' for the purposes of Article 8 include cohabiting adults where there is sufficient commitment and stability in the relationship, including same-sex relationships, step-parents and dependent stepchildren, grandparents and grandchildren and other close relatives provided that there are sufficiently close links.

Funding and representation at the inquest

There is limited public funding available for preparatory work, which a lawyer may have to carry out to properly prepare for the inquest. There is also limited provision for public funding through the Lord Chancellor's Department, for legal representation at the inquest. The availability of this funding is restricted to cases that fulfil the 'exceptional cases' criteria set out in the *Funding Code* that accompanies the Access to Justice Act 2000.

The Lord Chancellor's Department has issued *Guidance on Applications for Exceptional Funding*. This guidance states that the applicant must be within the financial eligibility levels for public funding and must satisfy the Lord Chancellor that there is a significant wider public interest in having legal representation at the inquest, the client is a member of the deceased's immediate family and the circumstances of the death appear to be such that publicly funded representation is necessary to assist the Coroner to investigate the case effectively and establish the facts.

The Legal Services Commission (LSC) may ask the Secretary of State to waive the eligibility limit to enable the funding of legal representation at an inquest into the death of a member of the immediate family of the client. In considering whether to make such a request, the LSC will consider in particular whether Article 2 of the Convention is engaged. If there is evidence of state responsibility in respect of a death, immediate family members may be granted public funding for advocacy at the inquest into his or her death, even if they would otherwise fall outside the eligibility limits for such funding. Whether it is granted in these circumstances will be dependent upon the facts of each individual case.

Disclosure by the Coroner
There is no right for an interested person to receive all documents, including witness statements, that the Coroner has in his or her possession. However, the Coroner must supply interested persons with a copy of the post mortem report and any documents or notes put in evidence at the inquest. This obligation does not necessarily mean that the documents will be disclosed before the inquest, but as a matter of good practice the Coroner should be prepared to supply a copy of these documents in advance.

If a person dies in prison, in police custody, while detained under the MHA or where the Coroners Act 1988 is engaged, the Coroner should as a matter of good practice consider any application for advance disclosure very carefully, and agree to a request for disclosure if possible.

Although there is no right to the disclosure of witness statements and other documents before the inquest, interested persons will often require these to properly prepare for the inquest. In these circumstances the courts have decided that the Coroner must show that he or she has exercised fairly his or her discretion whether to release such documents: *R v HM Coroner for District of Avon ex parte Bentley*.

If the Coroner refuses to disclose documents, which had they been available to an interested person might have shifted the focus to a critical area of investigation, there may be a remedy to a higher court by way of judicial review. Where the death occurred in circumstances when Article 2 might be engaged, there are likely to be strong grounds for asking the Coroner to disclose documents to ensure that there is an adequate and sufficient investigation and to ensure that interested parties are able to participate in the inquest process.

Where the Coroner has refused to disclose statements and other documents, which he or she has received from other authorities, an application may be made to the holder of those documents for disclosure before the inquest. For example, an application for medical records may be made to the relevant healthcare trust. If the death occurred in police or prison custody, prison and custody records should be obtained and, as a matter of good practice, where the death occurred in custody, documents applied for should be provided before the inquest. The right to disclosure of information about the deceased is contained in the Data Protection Act 1998 and Access to Health Records Act 1990.

See also Chapter 4.

Evidence at the inquest
The Coroner has the right to summon witnesses to attend the inquest and has a wide discretion about who should be required to give evidence. Any interested person is entitled to make representations if it is considered that vital witnesses have not been called, and the Coroner should consider these requests carefully and give reasons for his or her decision if the application is refused.

If the Coroner wants to admit a witness statement, rather than call a witness, he or she can do so only if the evidence is unlikely to be disputed and there is no objection from an interested party. If the Coroner intends to read a witness statement from a witness whom he or she does not intend to call, an interested party has the right to object to this. Before introducing documentary evidence, the Coroner should inform interested persons at the inquest that they are entitled to see a copy of the documentary evidence and have a right to object to the admission of it. The only exception is if the maker of the document is unable to give oral evidence within a reasonable period.

The family of an individual who has died in suspicious circumstances should be aware that witnesses who may be implicated in the death are not required to give evidence that may incriminate them in criminal proceedings. If a witness in giving evidence is likely to incriminate him or herself in criminal proceedings, the Coroner will warn the witness that he or she may refuse to answer such a question. If this happens, interested parties still have the right to ask the witness questions, but the witness will be informed that he or she may choose not to answer the question.

Verdicts

Although there are suggested forms of words for the verdict on the back of the inquisition form, there is no requirement that the verdict should be in any particular form. In certain circumstances some form of words other than those suggested on the inquisition form may be regarded as more appropriately reflecting how the deceased died. All that is necessary is that the verdict is expressed in concise and ordinary language. The only requirement is that the verdict must not appear to determine any question of criminal or civil liability on the part of a named person.

The following verdicts are those suggested on the back of the inquisition form:

- *Natural causes*: This is appropriate where the evidence suggests that the deceased probably died as a result of some naturally occurring illness or disease process.
- *Died from industrial disease*: Where the deceased died from an illness or disease, caused by chemicals or other agents to which they were exposed through their occupation, this verdict is appropriate. For example, this verdict has been returned where it has been proven that an individual's death has resulted from asbestosis contracted through exposure to asbestos. In these circumstances the verdict may properly be recorded that the deceased died from industrial disease, rather than natural causes, which would otherwise be the appropriate verdict.
- *Died from dependence on drugs / non-dependent abuse of drugs*: Where an individual's death was a consequence of the use of drugs, this verdict is appropriate. It is usually returned in relation to illicit rather than prescription drugs. The verdicts distinguish between individuals who had a dependency upon the drugs they were abusing and those who did not.
- *Died from want of attention at birth*: This verdict is appropriate where the deceased died as a result of a lack of attention at birth. It may be relevant to the death of a mother or an infant at birth.
- *Killed himself or herself / whilst the balance of his mind was disturbed*: Before this verdict is returned the Coroner or jury should be satisfied beyond reasonable doubt that the deceased killed him or herself, and intended to do so. This is a high threshold, and usually there should be some positive evidence of the deceased's intention to kill him or herself, for example, a suicide note (this is not usually read in open court). A finding that an individual intended to take his or her own life should only be inferred from the evidence in the clearest circumstances where there can be no other explanation: *Re Davies (deceased)*. The Coroner should be satisfied that the deceased was capable of forming the

intention to take his or her own life and was not, for example, acting under a delusion as part of a mental illness or while under the influence of alcohol or drugs. If the deceased was suffering from a psychiatric condition when he or she died, the Coroner may record that the deceased killed him or herself while the balance of his mind was disturbed. Some Coroners now tend to use more medical terminology, such as that 'the deceased killed him or herself whilst suffering from a psychiatric illness'.

- *Died as the result of an attempted / self induced abortion*: This verdict is probably less relevant now than it was when medical termination of pregnancy was illegal and there was more recourse to self-termination of pregnancy.
- *Died as the result of an accident / misadventure*: For statistical purposes the verdicts of accident and misadventure are treated as the same, although in reality the verdicts have slightly different meanings. An accident connotes something over which there is no human control (e.g a tree falling onto the road causing fatalities), whereas misadventure suggests a lawful human act, which takes an unexpected turn and leads to death. There is some authority suggesting that the term 'misadventure' is without purpose or effect, nonetheless it continues to be a verdict returned by Coroners in appropriate circumstances. For example, if the deceased died as a consequence of some medical intervention (e.g. a surgical accident causing a fatal injury or a death resulting from side effects of prescription drugs), a verdict of misadventure will reflect that the deceased died as a result of a lawful human act that had unintended consequences. To return a verdict of accident or misadventure the Coroner or jury must be satisfied on the balance of probabilities that this is how the death occurred.
- *Was killed lawfully*: A person may be lawfully killed only in limited prescribed circumstances, for example, where the perpetrator inflicted a fatal injury while acting in self-defence.
- *Was killed unlawfully – murder, manslaughter, infanticide*: A verdict of unlawful killing encompasses findings of murder, infanticide or manslaughter (voluntary or involuntary). To return a verdict of unlawful killing the Coroner or jury needs to be satisfied beyond reasonable doubt that this is how the deceased came to his death. A Coroner cannot find any person guilty of any of these offences. In some circumstances it may be obvious that a particular person was involved. In other cases, it will be impossible to infer from the verdict who was responsible for the death, and it is not for the court to inquire into this. If, however, the Coroner or jury returns a verdict of 'unlawful killing', although there is no sanction as a result of the verdict in itself the expectation would be that the Director of Public Prosecution would institute proceedings.
- *Stillborn*: A stillborn infant is an infant born after 24 weeks, who did not breathe or show any other sign of life. If the Coroner finds that the infant was stillborn, he or she will indicate this on the inquisition form, but the remainder of the form will not be completed, as he or she cannot properly inquire into the death of a stillborn infant.
- *Open verdict*: An open verdict is appropriate where there is insufficient evidence to record any of the other verdicts, that is, the evidence fails to meet the required proof.
- *Neglect*: In the appropriate circumstances the Coroner or jury may add to the verdict a finding that the deceased's death was contributed to by neglect.

Neglect has a different meaning from the term 'negligence.' The definition of the term 'neglect' in a Coroner's court is set out in a case called *R* v *North Humberside Coroner ex parte Jamieson*. It was held that:

> Neglect in this context means a gross failure to provide adequate nourishment or liquid, or provide or procure basic medical attention or shelter or warmth for someone in a dependent position (because of youth, age, illness or incarceration) who cannot provide it for himself.

The first element of neglect is the proof of a gross failure to provide care to a person in obvious need. The failure must be more than transitory or a 'mere' error of judgement. The following are examples of situations upheld by the court as capable of constituting 'gross' failures: a police surgeon's failure properly to search the deceased and thereby discover a bottle of pills, the failure to procure for the deceased effective medical treatment, and failure to monitor blood pressure of a mother following birth. The Coroner or jury must also be satisfied that the deceased was a dependant person. This requirement will usually be satisfied if the deceased was known to be at risk of self-harm, had been diagnosed as suffering from a mental illness, or was detained in prison or under the care of medical practitioners. The neglect must be directly connected with the deceased's death and must be at least a contributory cause.

- *Self neglect*: This verdict is appropriate where a person dies due to his or her own self neglect, for example, an elderly person dying of hypothermia at home.
- *Narrative verdicts*: The Coroner is not required to return a verdict in one of the set formats set out above. It is sufficient to produce a short, factual statement setting out the circumstances of the death if this more fairly and accurately reflects how the deceased came to his or her death. The House of Lords has recently endorsed the use of the narrative form verdict as a mechanism of recording by what means and in what circumstances the deceased met his or her death: *R* v *Her Majesty's Coroner for the Western District of Somerset ex parte Middleton*. This may include where and when the death took place, the cause or causes of such death, the defects in the system that contributed to the death and any other factors that are relevant to the circumstances of the death.

Prevention of similar fatalities

The Coroner has power to report to a person or authority any action that he or she believes should be taken to prevent the recurrence of similar fatalities in the expectation that steps will be taken to prevent similar fatalities in the future.

Challenging a Coroner's decision

There is no right of appeal from an inquest. However, the Coroner's decision and/or the Inquisition may be challenged using (a) judicial review, (b) an application to the Divisional Court under section 13 of the Coroners Act 1988; or (c) an application to the High Court under the HRA.

Judicial review

The High Court may review the Coroner's decision and decide whether the inquisition should be quashed and a new inquest ordered. Some examples of circumstances where the court may be prepared to order a new inquest include where there has been insufficiency of inquiry, rejection of relevant evidence, refusal to allow representatives to make submissions on law, improper pressure on a jury to return a particular verdict or misdirecting the jury on the law. Judicial review is a discretionary remedy. One of the relevant aspects that the court will consider is whether it is possible that a new inquest would furnish a different verdict. See also Chapter 2.

Section 13 applications
Section 13 of the Coroners Act 1988 provides a further mechanism of challenge to the Divisional Court. An application can be made by or on the authority of the Attorney General to the High Court on grounds that the Coroner refuses or neglects to hold an inquest that ought to be held or, where an inquest has been held, that whether by reason of fraud, rejection of evidence, irregularity of proceedings, insufficiency of inquiry, the discovery of new facts or evidence or otherwise, it is necessary in the interests of justice that another inquest be held. If it is satisfied the High Court may order an inquest to be held into the death. An application must first be made to the Attorney General for his or her permission to make an application to the Divisional Court. If permission has been granted, the application proceeds to a full hearing by a Divisional Court. The procedure may be used in conjunction with judicial review proceedings.

Human Rights Act 1998
If the Coroner makes a decision that is inconsistent with the Convention then any individual affected by that decision may seek a remedy before the High Court. See also Chapter 2.

Complaints
The Home Office has administrative responsibility for Coroners, and any complaint about the administration of the Coroner service or the conduct of individual Coroners or their staff should be made first to the Coroner and if still unsatisfied to the Home Office, Coroners Section. The Home Office may refer the complaint to the Lord Chancellor, who is responsible for the discipline of Coroners.

Other inquiries into a death
The Coroner's inquest is not the only inquiry that looks into a death. There may be an internal investigation by the relevant authority or other statutory agencies may inquire into the death.

Deaths of patients under care of NHS healthcare providers
If a person dies in hospital and there are reasons to suspect the death may have occurred due to a medical accident or other untoward event, the hospital may hold an internal inquiry or an inquiry may be initiated by a complaint.

Deaths in police custody
After a person has died in police custody, the Association of Chief Police Officers' guidelines recommends that a senior police officer should secure the scene, contact the scenes of crime officers and contact the Coroner. A senior investigating officer

should be appointed to initiate an investigation. The Independent Police Complaints Commission (IPCC) may supervise the investigation. See also Chapter 2.

Deaths in prison
When a person dies while detained in a prison, an internal investigation will take place led by a senior investigating officer from the Prison Service, but at a prison other than the one in which the death took place. There is a requirement that the death is reported to the Coroner. Where the Coroner decides to hold an inquest, he or she is required to sit with a jury.

Deaths of patients detained under the Mental Health Act 1983
If a patient is compulsorily detained under the MHA there will be an internal investigation into the death, and if it is believed that the patient was the victim of a homicide the police must be informed. It is not a necessary requirement for the death of patients detained under the MHA to be reported to the Coroner, but the death should be reported to the Mental Health Act Commission.

Public inquiries
The Home Secretary may set up a public inquiry, usually if the circumstances surrounding the death are of significant public importance.

Discretionary inquiries
There is statutory provision for discretionary inquiries, including into railway accidents, road traffic accidents, accidents in railway construction, and deaths on ships registered in the United Kingdom.

16.4   REMEDIES

Criminal prosecutions
Murder is the unlawful killing of one human by another with intent to kill or cause grievous bodily harm. This is distinguished from the lesser offence of *voluntary manslaughter*, which may arise in the circumstances as for murder, but where the perpetrator has either diminished responsibility or there is provocation.

Involuntary manslaughter includes the offences of unlawful act manslaughter (an unlawful killing but where there is an absence of intent to kill or cause grievous bodily harm) and manslaughter by gross negligence (for which there may be corporate, rather than individual responsibility), which must be carefully distinguished from negligence and neglect.

The Crown Prosecution Service (CPS) decides whether there should be a criminal prosecution. Its decision-making process is governed by the Code for Crown Prosecutors. It states that there are two stages in the decision to prosecute. The first is the evidential test. If the case passes this test, the next step is to consider whether a public prosecution is required in the public interest. Unless there are compelling reasons not to do so, the CPS should give detailed reasons to the family of a deceased relative for any decision not to prosecute where there is suspicion that he or she was the subject of an unlawful homicide by an agent of the State.

If a decision is made not to prosecute, which is in breach of the Code of Practice or is so perverse that no reasonable prosecutor could have made it, the decision can be subject to judicial review in the High Court. However, in practice this is a step rarely taken and it is likely to be difficult to persuade a court to compel the CPS to prosecute.

Compensation for a criminal injury

If the deceased was the victim of a criminal injury, his or her relatives may be entitled to compensation under the state criminal compensation scheme, administered by the Criminal Injuries Compensation Authority (CICA). A claim should be made as soon as possible after the incident and in any event within two years of the date of the incident. A claim for compensation, including loss of dependency upon the deceased, may also be made by certain categories of relatives: a spouse, including a cohabitee who had lived with the deceased for two years before his or her death, a former spouse who was supported financially, a parent or child – whether or not a natural child – of the deceased. The scheme permits the payment of funeral expenses, subject to eligibility.

Internal complaints and disciplinary procedures

If there are concerns about the care that an individual received prior to his or her death, a complaint may be made to the relevant organisation.

If a complaint is made about a police officer, this will be recorded and investigated. At the conclusion of the investigation a report will be made to the IPCC to consider any proposals for disciplinary action. If a disciplinary hearing takes place, the complainant has a right to attend. Although the complainant may be supported by a friend or relative, there is no provision to allow legal representation. The hearing will also be held in private.

Where a person dies under NHS care, the National Health Service Complaints procedure applies. This is independent of any disciplinary action that may or may not follow from a successful complaint. The relatives of an individual who has died while under the care of the NHS do not have the right to be involved in the disciplinary process or to be informed of the outcome of such procedures. The complaints procedure requires a complainant to make a complaint within six months of the event or within six months of that there is something to complain about as long as that is not more than 12 months after the event itself. The time limits may be waived if there is a good reason why the complainant was not able to complain sooner. A complaint should first be made to the local organisation (e.g hospital, GP or dentist). If still dissatisfied, the complainant has the right to an independent review, which should be requested within 28 days of the outcome of the local resolution. A convener will consider the complaint and decide whether an independent review panel should be convened. If this takes place, the complainant will receive a copy of the panel's report. If the complainant is still dissatisfied he or she can ask the Health Service Commissioner to investigate the complaint.

There are no corresponding provisions for patients who die while under the care of private healthcare providers, who may be subject to their own internal complaints procedures.

A further complaint may be made to the Mental Health Act Commission if there is concern that a healthcare provider has failed to comply with the MHA and Code of Practice 1993.

Civil proceedings

If the deceased's death has resulted from some negligent act or omission, it may be possible to bring civil proceedings against the 'responsible' person or body. The courts have held that a duty to take reasonable care may exist where there is a close and proximate relationship between the person causing the injury and the deceased, the injury was reasonably foreseeable, and there are no public policy reasons why it should not be imposed. The type of relationships where a duty has been found to exist include those between a doctor and patient, the police and a suspect, a car driver and road user and an employer and employee. This list is not exhaustive.

If there was a breach of that duty of care that caused a fatal injury (in other words, if the care fell below a reasonable standard), the deceased's estate *may* be entitled to compensation. However, not all bereaved persons have a right to claim damages arising from a death.

There is a three-year time limit for the commencement of legal proceedings for personal injury caused by negligence. The time starts to run from the date of death, or earlier if the deceased was already involved in litigation arising from the injury that caused his or her death. There are certain exceptions to this strict time limit, and the court has a residual discretion to permit a claim brought out of time.

The Fatal Accidents Act 1976

The Fatal Accidents Act 1976 (FAA) provides financial compensation for the bereavement arising from the death of an individual. The people who are entitled to compensation for bereavement are: husbands, wives, and the parents of a child, or mother of an illegitimate child, who was under 18 years of age and who was never married. When the Civil Partnership Bill comes into force, surviving civil partners will also be entitled to compensation. The statutory sum recoverable is a fixed amount of £10,000. If the claim is on behalf of both parents of a child, the amount is divided equally between them. The parents of a child over 18, children of a deceased parent, parents of a stillborn infant and other relatives are not entitled to recover damages for bereavement no matter how closely associated with the deceased.

A problem often encountered is in relation to the death of an unmarried person over the age of 18 years whose parents seek to bring a claim arising out of the death, as there is no provision for an award in respect of bereavement damages under the FAA. In the absence of any claim for future financial dependency, it is unlikely that any action can be pursued, as the claim for damages will be extremely modest and unlikely to justify the cost of expensive legal action. Even where a parent may have a strong claim in negligence for the death of their adult child it is very often not worthwhile pursuing, unless there is a claim for dependency.

A person who was financially dependent upon (or dependent upon the services of) the deceased may be entitled to recover damages for the loss of that dependency. A wider category of persons than the class of relatives who are entitled to claim for bereavement damages are entitled to recover damages for their loss of dependency, including the costs they have incurred of any funeral expenses. In all cases it is necessary to prove that there was a reasonable expectation of financial benefit from the deceased. Those coming under the category of dependants for the purpose of the FAA are:

- A husband or wife, or former husband or wife of the deceased.
- When the Civil Partnership Bill comes into force, a civil partner or former civil partner of the deceased.
- A person who was living with the deceased as husband or wife for at least two years prior to the death.
- A parent or other dependant of the deceased.
- A person who was treated by the deceased as his or her parent.
- A child or other dependant of the deceased.
- A person who, in the case of a marriage to which the deceased was at any time a party, was treated by the deceased as a child of the family in relation to that marriage.
- A person who is a brother, sister, uncle, aunt, niece, nephew or cousin of the deceased.

The FAA provides that relationships of half blood are treated as relationships of whole blood, stepchildren are treated as children and illegitimate children are treated as legitimate children of their mother and the putative father. Relationships arising out of adoption are also included.

The FAA does not allow other persons who may have been financially dependent upon the deceased prior to his or her death to recover damages. Among those relationships currently not covered by the provisions of the FFA include those where the bereaved person was living with the deceased as husband or wife for a period of less than two years and, at the time of writing, couples in a same-sex relationship. It is arguable, however, that the FAA should now be interpreted in light of the Convention (Article 8) to extend the rights to couples in same-sex relationships that have been cohabiting for over two years in a stable relationship, whether or not they have entered into a civil partnership.

Damages for loss of dependency are calculated by working out the value of the contribution to the dependant that the deceased would have made over the years if it had not been for his or her death. This can include any non-financial contributions, such as the value of the services provided by a parent, who, for example, provided household housework and/or childcare services to the family. The value of such services must be quantified and in most cases, a report will be obtained from an expert in the provision of care services, who will help estimate the financial value of services that would otherwise have been provided freely by the deceased.

Additionally, or alternatively, damages may be claimed for the loss of the financial contribution the deceased would have made to the bereaved. An award is made in these circumstances where the deceased was spending a proportion of his or her income on the dependant person. In many instances this will be relevant where the 'breadwinner' in the family dies and other members of the family lose the financial contribution the deceased would have made to the family upkeep. However, a claim can be made where the deceased was making a relatively modest contribution, for example, to the upkeep of a teenage child from a previous marriage or to another person qualifying as a dependant for the purposes of the FAA.

The total value of the dependency is calculated by working out the annual value of the financial loss to the dependants. The figure reached is termed a 'multiplicand',

and it is multiplied by a figure that represents the number of years over which that loss will be suffered. This figure is termed a multiplier. In many cases the dependants will have had an expectation of dependency for many years into the future. A spouse may have had an expectation of dependency for the whole of the deceased's lifetime, although the value of that dependency may have changed as the deceased's earning capacity altered with promotion, retirement and other variables. A child of the deceased may only have been supported significantly until aged 16 or 18, after which time the dependency may have significantly reduced. In calculating the multiplier, lawyers use actuarial tables (called Ogden Tables), which set out the statistical life expectancies of the general population. These tables also allow the lawyer to work out the discount that should be applied for accelerated receipt of the damages, which are paid at the time of compensation, rather than over the course of the deceased's lifetime.

If the deceased is an infant child, it is necessary to prove a real likelihood that the child would have financially supported his or her parent or other relative. In some cases, particularly where there is a cultural tradition of the child supporting the elderly parents, this may be established, but in many cases the loss is regarded as too speculative if the infant was very young at the date of his or her death. In practice, this means that many claims in respect of the loss of an infant child only have a modest financial value, usually limited to the bereavement award and any funeral expenses.

The Law Reform (Miscellaneous Provisions) Act 1934

A claim may be made on behalf of the deceased's estate under the Law Reform (Miscellaneous Provisions) Act 1934 (LRA) for any pain and suffering the deceased suffered prior to and relating to his or her death. The LRA provides that any legal actions that the deceased might have had, or was pursuing at the time of his or her death – except for defamation – survive for the benefit of his or her estate. This means that the administrator or executor of the estate will be entitled to claim damages on the deceased's behalf where the deceased, had he or she lived, could have brought an action in respect of the matter that resulted in his or her death. Such awards will usually be made where the deceased survived for a period of time between the injury that resulted in his or her death and his or her eventual death. The value of these awards is usually modest, unless the deceased survived for a significant period between the injury and his or her death.

Compensation for nervous shock

If the bereaved witnessed the death or came across the immediate aftermath of an injury or death causing them to suffer shock leading to a psychiatric illness, they may have a claim for compensation for this injury. The legal test is very strict and requires the bereaved person to show a close tie of love and affection with the deceased. The law has in the past recognised that a parent, child, husband or wife will have such close ties of love and affection, and in these circumstances there is a rebuttable presumption that there is such a close tie. In relation to other relatives, it is necessary to prove that their relationship is so close as to be comparable to that of a parental or spousal relationship.

On this basis, in the past, the law has denied recovery to siblings and in one case a grandfather of the deceased. This does not mean that such relatives can never recover damages in the future, but it does mean that there is a significant onus to prove that their relationship was especially close. There is also a requirement to prove that the psychiatric injury resulted from shock, rather than witnessing a relative's demise over a long period, or simply witnessing their actual death in circumstances that are not sudden or shocking.

Stillborn infants

A claim for compensation arising from the death of a stillbirth infant is problematic. Any claim for loss of future financial dependency will be inevitably extremely speculative, and it is unlikely that damages will be awarded in these circumstances. The fact that the infant was not born alive means that there is no entitlement to a bereavement award under the FAA or on behalf of the estate of the infant under the LRA. The court may award damages for loss of expectation of a successful pregnancy and frustration of family plans, which result from the stillbirth of an infant due to negligence. A legitimate claim may also be made for any expenses associated with the stillbirth such as the purchase of items in preparation for the birth, such as baby clothing and furniture – generally referred to as the layette. In some circumstances, the parents of the deceased may fall within the category of persons entitled to compensation for psychiatric injury due to shock. Also, where the infant's death was due to alleged medical mismanagement of the labour, it is usually the case that the mother of the infant was owed a direct duty of care by the hospital, who will in those circumstances also be liable for any psychiatric injury that she suffered in consequence of a mismanaged labour, even if otherwise she would not satisfy the strict legal test for psychiatric injury due to shock.

If contemplating legal action, it is important to obtain specialist advice and assistance. Details of specialist solicitors can be obtained from the Law Society and, in the case of deaths arising from medical accidents, the charity Action for Victims of Medical Accidents may assist with advice and details of specialist lawyers.

16.5   FURTHER INFORMATION

Useful organisations

Action for Victims of Medical Accidents
Help line: 0845 123 2352
<www.avma.org.uk>

Association of Chief Police Officers
25 Victoria Street
London SW1H 0ET
Tel: 020 7227 3434
Fax: 020 7227 3400
info@acpo.police.uk
<www.acpo.police.uk>

Association of Nature Reserve Burial Grounds
6 Blackstone Mews
Blackstock Road
London N4 2BT

Tel: 0871 288 2098
Fax: 020 7354 831
ndc@alberyfoundation.org
<www.naturaldeath.org.uk>

Compassionate Friends
53 North Street
Bristol BS3 1EN
Tel: 0117 966 5202
Fax: 0117 914 4368
Help line: 0845 123 2304
info@tcf.org.uk
<www.tcf.org.uk>

Criminal Injuries Compensation Authority
Advice line: 0800 358 3601

Crown Prosecution Service
50 Ludgate Hill
London EC4M 7EX
Tel: 020 7796 8000
enquiries@cps.gsi.gov.uk
<www.cps.gov.uk>

Cruse Bereavement Care
126 Sheen Road
Richmond TW9 1UR
Tel: 020 8939 9530
Help line: 0870 167 1677
Fax: 020 8940 7638
info@crusebereavementcare.org.uk
<www.crusebereavementcare.org.uk>

General Medical Council
Regent's Place
350 Euston Road
London NW1 3JN
Tel: 0845 357 3456
gmc@gmc-uk.org
<www.gmc-uk.org>

**Independent Police Complaints
Commission (IPCC)**
90 High Holborn
London WC1V 6BH
Tel: 0845 300 2002
Fax: 020 7404 0430
<www.ipcc.gov.uk>

Mental Health Act Commission
Maid Marian House
56 Hounds Gate
Nottingham NG1 6BG
Tel: 0115 943 7100
Fax: 0115 943 7101
ChiefExec@mhac.trent.nhs.uk
<www.mhac.trent.nhs.uk>

**SAMM (Support after Murder and
Manslaughter)**
Cranmer House
39 Brixton Road
London SW9 6DZ
Tel: 020 7735 3838
enquiries@samm.org.uk
<www.samm.org.uk>

**SANDS (Stillbirth and Neonatal Death
Society)**
28 Portland Place
London W1N 4DE
Tel: 020 7436 5881
Help line: 020 7436 7940
Fax: 020 7436 3715
support@uk-sands.org
<www.uk-sands.org>

Bibliography

Albery, N. and Weinrich, S. (eds), *The New Natural Death Handbook* (London: Rider Books, 2002)
Code of Practice on the Use of Foetuses and Foetal Material in Research and Treatment
Dorries, C., *Coroner's Court* (Oxford: Blackstone Press, 2002)
The Foetal and Infant Post-Mortem: Brief Notes for the Professional (Confidential enquiry into)
Harris, P., *What to do when Somebody Dies* (London: Which? Books, 2002)
Home Office Circular 35/69
Matthews, P. and Foreman, J., *Jervis on Coroners* (London: Sweet & Maxwell, 2002)

Accessing UK Legal Resources

Books like *Your Rights* provide you with a useful overview of the general principles that apply in particular areas of law. If, however, you are keen to develop a more in-depth understanding on a particular topic, you will need to broaden the scope of your research by looking at primary sources, such as legislation and case law as well as other secondary sources, such as legal texts and journal articles.

Finding legal resources that are both accessible to the public and free or low-cost can be a challenge. We provide a list of such resources below. You will find many online resources as well details of libraries with particularly useful collections. Unfortunately, you will find that the majority of libraries in our list are located in London. If you live outside of London, it may be worth visiting your local library for suggestions on legal collections located in or near to your local area.

ONLINE RESOURCES

Legal portals and gateways

- **BAILII <www.bailii.org>**
  Developed by the British and Irish Legal Information Institute, this is a useful gateway to legal materials, including case law, legislation and journal articles.
- **Courtservice <www.courtservice.gov.uk>**
  Maintained by the Court Service, this website contains information about the court system, including forms and useful guidance as well as practice directions and some judgments.
- **Delia Venables <www.venables.co.uk/>**
  Maintained by Delia Venables, this very comprehensive site has a section on legal information for individuals and includes many links to free legal information.
- **EAGLE- I <www.ials.sas.ac.uk/links/eiuk.htm>**
  Maintained by the Institute of Advanced Legal Studies, this is a legal gateway to global legal information.
- **European Court of Human Rights <www.echr.coe.int>**
  Official website of the ECHR, this website contains useful information about the composition and operation of the ECHR as well as guidance for applicants, practice rules and the full text of the European Convention on Human Rights. You can also access HUDOC, the ECHR's searchable database of decisions.
- **HMSO <www.hmso.gov.uk>**
  Her Majesty's Stationery Office is a gateway to official information, including legislation.
- **Infolaw <www.infolaw.co.uk>**
  Aimed primarily at legal professionals, this website does provide free access to general legal resources.
- **Lawlinks <library.kent.ac.uk/library/lawlinks/resources.htm>**
  Maintained by the University of Kent, Lawlinks provides access to online legal information networks, a guide to the UK legal system and all aspects of legal research.
- **SOSIG <www.sosig.ac.uk/law/>**
  Maintained by the Institute of Advanced Legal Studies and the Bristol University Law Library, this is a legal gateway providing guidance and access to global legal information resources on the internet.

Primary sources of law: Acts and Bills of Parliament

- **BAILII <www.bailii.org>**
  Developed by the British and Irish Legal Information Institute, the site contains a database of UK legislation (2000 onwards), UK Statutory Instruments (2002 onwards) and Welsh Statutory Instruments (1999 onwards).
- **HMSO Legislation <www.legislation.hmso.gov.uk/legislation/uk.htm>**
  Managed by Her Majesty's Stationery Office, this site contains the full text of all Public and Local Acts of the UK Parliament (1988 onwards), the Explanatory Notes to Public Acts (1999 onwards) and Statutory Instruments (1987 onwards). Be aware that the Acts do not include subsequent amendments.
- **UK Parliament: Bills before Parliament <www.parliament.the-stationery-office. co.uk/pa/pabills.htm>**
  Provides a full list of Bills currently before Parliament with links to the full text of each Bill and subsequent amendments.

Primary sources of law: Case law

- **BAILII <www.bailii.org>**
  Developed by the British and Irish Legal Information Institute, the site contains a database of House of Lords decisions (1996 onwards), Court of Appeal decisions (1996 onwards), High Court decisions (1996 onwards), Employment Appeals Tribunal decisions (1999 onwards) and Immigration Appeals Tribunal decisions (1996 onwards).
- **Courtservice <www.courtservice.gov.uk>**
  Maintained by the Court Service, this website contains selected Court of Appeal judgments, with a searchable database.
- **Employment Appeals Tribunal <www.employmentappeals.gov.uk/>**
  Contains a fully searchable database of EAT decisions.
- **European Court of Human Rights <www.echr.coe.int/Eng/Judgments.htm>**
  Contains information about decisions of the European Court of Human Rights as well as a fully searchable database of judgments.
- **Lands Tribunal <www.landstribunal.gov.uk>**
  Contains a search facility of final decisions made by the Lands Tribunal (2000 onwards).
- **UK Parliament: House of Lords judgments <www.parliament.uk/about_lords/ about_lords>**
  Contains House of Lords judgments (1996 onwards). New judgments are uploaded two hours after being handed down.

LIBRARIES WITH LEGAL RESOURCES

London-based public/reference libraries

British Library
96 Euston Road
London NW1 2DB
Social Policy Information Service
Access: Public access by reader's ticket, reference only
Tel: 020 7142 7536
Fax: 020 7412 7761
<www.bl.uk>

British Library of Political and Economic Science (the LSE)
10 Portugal Street
London WC2A 2HD
Useful collections: UK Law, including law reports, periodicals and texts. Official publications and statistics collection. International and Comparative Law collection.
Access: Multi-tiered paid membership
Tel: 020 7955 7229
Fax: 020 7955 7454
<www.blpes.lse.ac.uk>

City Business Library
1 Brewer's Hall Garden
London EC2V 5BX
Useful collections: Business orientated non-specialist legal materials for local needs.
Access: Public Library, reference only
Tel: 020 7332 1812
Fax: 020 7600 1147

Guildhall Library
Aldermanbury
London EC2P 2EJ
Useful collections: Comprehensive collections of English Statutes, parliamentary papers and law reports. Current editions of Halsburys Law Service and Current Law but almost no legal textbooks
Access: Public Library, reference only
Tel: 020 7332 1868
<www.ihr.sas.ac.uk/gh>

Hammersmith Library
Shepherd's Bush Road
London W6 7AT
Useful collections: Basic legal reference sources including Halsburys Law Service, Current Law, Atkins' Court forms, White & Green books, Encyclopaedia of forms and precedents, Civil Procedure Rules. Law reports, inc. Official Series. Reasonable collection of legal textbooks
Access: Public Library with lending facilities, but legal materials are reference only
Tel: 020 8753 3823
Fax: 020 8753 3815

Holborn Library
32–389 Theobolds Road
London WC1X 8PA
Useful collections: Substantial amount of legal resources
Access: Public Library with lending facilities, but legal materials are reference only
Tel: 020 7974 6343

Institute of Advanced Legal Studies (IALS)
17 Russell Square
London WC1B 5DR
Useful collections: Includes legal source materials for the USA, Commonwealth and Western Europe. FLAG, foreign law guide. Substantial holdings in the area of international public law. Extensive web links to foreign material
Access: Admission charge for entry
Tel: 020 7862 5790
Fax: 020 7862 5770
<www.ials.sas.ac.uk/library/library.htm>

Westminster Reference Library
35 St Martin's Street
London WC2H 7HP
Useful collections: Small collection of legal textbooks and some legal reference services. Westminster Union List of periodicals
Access: Public Library
Tel: 020 7641 4634
Fax: 020 7641 4606
<www.westminster.gov.uk/libraries/special/index.cfm>

Depositories for legal documents

Bodleian Law Library/ European Documentation Centre
Manor Road
Oxford OX1 3UR

Bodleian Library, Oxford
Broad Street
Oxford OX1 3BG
Tel: 01865 277 180
Fax: 01865 277 105
<www.bodley.ox.ac.uk>

Cambridge University Library
West Road
Cambridge CB3 9DR
Tel: 01223 333 000
Fax: 01223 333 160
Library@lib.cam.ac.uk
<www.lib.cam.ac.uk>

National Library of Wales
Aberystwyth
Ceredigion
Wales SY23 3BN
Tel: 01970 632 800
Fax: 01970 615 709
holi@llgc.org.uk

Index